Fodor's 21st Edition

Alaska

The complete guide, thoroughly up-to-date

Packed with details that will make your trip

The must-see sights, off and on the beaten path

What to see, what to skip

Vacation itineraries, walking tours, day trips

Smart lodging and dining options

Essential local dos and taboos

Transportation tips

Key contacts, savvy travel advice

When to go, what to pack

Clear, accurate, easy-to-use maps

W9-AAL-337

Fodor's Travel Publications • New York, Toronto, London, Sydney, Auckland
www.fodors.com

Fodor's Alaska

EDITOR: William Travis

Editorial Contributors: Stephanie Adler, Mary Engel, Robin Mackey Hill, Sue Kernaghan, Dr. Charles Lane, Mike Miller, Stanton H. Patty, Don Pitcher, Tom Reale, Melissa Rivers, Caragh Rockwood, Helayne Schiff, M. T. Schwartzman, Bill Sherwonit, Kent Sturgis, Eric Troyer, Peggy Wayburn, Howard C. Weaver

Editorial Production: Kristin Milavec

Maps: David Lindroth Inc., *cartographer;* Rebecca Baer and Bob Blake, *map editors*

Design: Fabrizio La Rocca, *creative director;* Guido Caroti, *art director;* Jolie Novak, *senior picture editor;* Melanie Marin, *photo editor*

Cover Design: Pentagram

Production/Manufacturing: Yexenia Markland

Cover Photograph: Larry Ulrich/Stone (Denali National Park)

Copyright

Twenty-first Edition

ISBN 0–679–00877–2

ISSN 0271–2776

Special Sales

Fodor's Travel Publications are available at special discounts for bulk purchases for sales promotions or premiums. Special editions, including personalized covers, excerpts of existing guides, and corporate imprints, can be created in large quantities for special needs. For more information, contact your local bookseller or write to Special Markets, Fodor's Travel Publications, 280 Park Avenue, 10th Floor, New York, NY 10017. Inquiries from Canada should be directed to your local Canadian bookseller or sent to Random House of Canada, Ltd., Marketing Department, 1265 Aerowood Drive, Mississauga, Ontario L4W 1B9. Inquiries from the United Kingdom should be sent to Fodor's Travel Publications, 20 Vauxhall Bridge Road, London SW1V 2SA, England.

PRINTED IN THE UNITED STATES OF AMERICA

10 9 8 7 6 5 4 3 2 1

Important Tip

Although all prices, opening times, and other details in this book are based on information supplied to us at press time, changes occur all the time in the travel world, and Fodor's cannot accept responsibility for facts that become outdated or for inadvertent errors or omissions. So **always confirm information when it matters,** especially if you're making a detour to visit a specific place.

III

CONTENTS

Maps

ON THE ROAD WITH FODOR'S

THE MORE YOU KNOW before you go, the better your trip will be. Alaska's most fascinating Native museum or nature trail could be just around the corner from your hotel, but if you don't know it's there, it might as well be on the other side of the globe. That's where this book comes in. It's a great step toward making sure your next trip lives up to your expectations. As you plan, check out the Web as well. Guidebooks have been helping smart travelers find the special places for years; the Web is one more tool. Whatever reference you consult, be savvy about what you read, and always consider the source. Images and language can be massaged to make places appear better than they are. And one traveler's quaint is another's grimy. Here at Fodor's, and at our on-line arm, Fodors.com, our focus is on providing you with information that's not only useful but accurate and on target. Every day Fodor's editors put enormous effort into getting things right, beginning with the search for the right contributors—people who have objective judgment, broad travel experience, and the writing ability to put their insights into words. There's no substitute for advice from a like-minded friend who has just come back from where you're going, but our writers, having seen all corners of Alaska, are the next best thing. They're the kind of people you'd poll for tips yourself if you knew them.

A Midwesterner who moved to Alaska in 1984, **Tom Reale** has traveled extensively throughout the state, writing about it and about wilderness adventures for a variety of publications. He and his wife hunt, fish, camp, backpack, ski, and hike at every opportunity.

Don Pitcher's knowledge of Alaska comes from a dozen seasons spent guiding visitors to brown-bear viewing areas, counting salmon at fish weirs, studying fires in Wrangell–St. Elias National Park, and building trails in rainy Southeast Alaska. He is the author of guidebooks on Alaska, Wyoming, Washington, and Berkeley, California, and today lives in Homer with his wife, Karen, and their daughter, Aziza Bali.

Vancouver-born freelance writer **Sue Kernaghan** is a fourth-generation British Columbian. "The family's been in B.C. so long we've had a swamp named after us," she says. Between Fodor's assignments, Sue writes management books.

An Anchorage resident since 1982, writer **Bill Sherwonit** has contributed stories about Alaska to a wide variety of newspapers, magazines, and books and is the author of four books on Alaska and, most recently, the pocket field guide *Alaska's Bears*. When not teaching a class on "wilderness writing" at the University of Alaska, Sherwonit lent his outdoors expertise to the Parks and Wilderness Adventures and Bush chapters; wrote Close-Up essays on Mt. McKinley, the trans-Alaska pipeline, and the northern lights; and enriched the Books and Videos primer.

Don't Forget to Write

Your experiences—positive and negative—matter to us. If we have missed or misstated something, we want to hear about it. We follow up on all suggestions. Contact the Alaska editor at editors@fodors.com or c/o Fodor's, 280 Park Avenue, New York, New York 10017. And have a fabulous trip!

Karen Cure
Editorial Director

Alaska

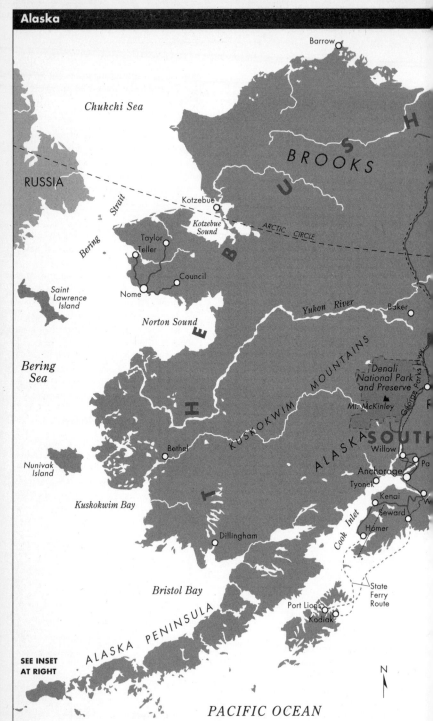

Chukchi Sea

RUSSIA

BROOKS

Kotzebue

Kotzebue Sound

ARCTIC CIRCLE

Taylor
Teller

Council

Nome

Bering Strait

Norton Sound

Saint Lawrence Island

Yukon River

Baker

Bering Sea

KUSKOKWIM MOUNTAINS

Denali National Park and Preserve

Mt. McKinley

George Parks Hwy

ALASKA SOUTH

Willow

Pa

Anchorage

Nunivak Island

Bethel

Tyonek

Kenai

We

Seward

Kuskokwim Bay

Cook Inlet

Homer

Dillingham

State Ferry Route

Bristol Bay

Port Lions

Kodiak

ALASKA PENINSULA

SEE INSET AT RIGHT

N

PACIFIC OCEAN

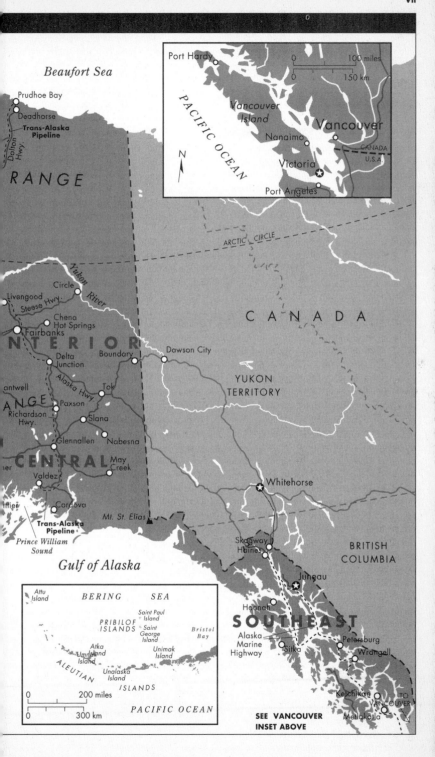

ESSENTIAL INFORMATION

AIR TRAVEL

Alaska Airlines is the flagship carrier to Alaska, with year-round service from Seattle to Anchorage, Juneau, Fairbanks, Ketchikan, and towns around the state. In addition, the airline has direct flights between Chicago and Anchorage. Its partner, Horizon Air, connects to many other western U.S. cities. American, Continental, Delta, and United all have year-round flights to Anchorage from Seattle; Northwest offers service from Minneapolis–St. Paul. Other airlines provide nonstop Anchorage flights in the summer from some Lower 48 cities: American from Dallas, America West from Phoenix, Delta from Salt Lake City and Atlanta, Northwest from Detroit, and United from Chicago and San Francisco. Delta also offers summertime service between Fairbanks and Anchorage. Hawaiian Vacations has charter flights two or three times a week aboard Hawaiian Airlines jets flying between Anchorage and Honolulu.

International travel connections to Alaska have improved in recent years, with nonstop flights to Anchorage from a number of cities in Asia and Europe. Year-round service is offered from Tokyo on Northwest and from Seoul on Korean Air. In summer, Canada 3000 has flights from Vancouver, China Airlines from Taipei, Condor Air from Frankfort, and LTU International Airways from Dusseldorf, Germany. Magadan Airlines flies to the Russian cities of Khabarovsk, Vladivostok, and Magadan. Balair flies into Anchorage from Zurich, with a stop in Whitehorse, Yukon.

If you are traveling from Britain, Continental Airlines flies from Gatwick, Birmingham, or Manchester via Newark and Seattle; Delta from Gatwick to Cincinnati or Salt Lake City; and United from Heathrow via San Francisco or Chicago. For travel between Alaska and Canada, contact Canada 3000 (from Vancouver) or Air North (from Whitehorse). Travelers from Australia and New Zealand can take Qantas into Los Angeles out of Sydney, Melbourne, or Auckland. Air New Zealand flies from Sydney and Auckland to Los Angeles. United flies from Sydney to Los Angeles and San Francisco, and to Los Angeles from Melbourne and Auckland.

Commercial air travel to major towns in Alaska is usually by jet or turboprop. Scheduled air-taxi and air-charter services provide access to smaller towns and remote locales, using propeller-driven Bush aircraft that land on wheels, on floats, or on skis. Helicopters are increasingly popular for flightseeing and fast transport.

Most of Alaska's wild places can be reached only by air, but don't consider that a drawback. Small planes have played a legendary part in the state's history: Bush pilots have helped explore Alaska and have been responsible for many dramatic rescue missions. But be aware that small planes cannot transport more than a limited amount of gear and cannot fly safely in poor weather. Your dropoff, as well as your pickup, flight is therefore subject to delays, which are sometimes counted in days, not hours. When traveling in remote areas away from any towns or villages, be sure to **carry extra food.** Although most villages have general stores, fresh produce tends to be expensive and sometimes unavailable. Note also that some items are not allowed on commercial aircraft. This includes campstove fuel and the so-called "bear mace" (pepper spray) sold in camping-goods stores.

Air North provides service from Fairbanks or Juneau to Dawson City and Whitehorse in the Yukon. Contact the following airlines for other flights within Alaska: Bering Air for flights from Nome or Kotzebue to smaller communities of the Far North; ERA Aviation for flights to Cordova, Homer, Iliamna, Kenai, Kodiak, Valdez, plus Whitehorse in the Yukon Territory and 17 western Alaska villages; Frontier Flying Service, Warbelow's Air Ventures, and Larry's Flying Service for flights out of Fairbanks to Interior destinations and between Anchorage and Fairbanks; and Peninsula Airways for flights to western Alaska, including Aniak, Dutch Harbor, McGrath, Dillingham, King Salmon, Sand Point, St. Paul, and St. George.

BOOKING

When you book **look for nonstop flights** and **remember that "direct" flights stop at least once.** Try to avoid connecting flights, which require a change of plane. For more booking tips and to check prices and make online flight reservations, log on to www.fodors.com

CARRIERS

➤ MAJOR AIRLINES: **Air New Zealand** (☎ 800/262–1234; 800/063–385 in Australia; 0800/737–000 in New Zealand, WEB www.airnz.com). **Alaska Airlines** (☎ 800/426–0333. **American** (☎ 800/433–7300, WEB www.aa.com). **America West** (☎ 800/235–9292, WEB www.americawest.com). **Canada 3000** (☎ 877/359–2263. **Continental** (☎ 800/525–0280; 0800/776–464; 01293/776–464 in the U.K., WEB www.continental.com). **Delta** (☎ 800/221–1212; 0800/414–767 in the U.K., WEB www.delta.com). **Korean Air** (☎ 800/438–5000, WEB www.koreanair.com). **Northwest** (☎ 800/225–2525, WEB www.nwa.com). **Qantas** (☎ 800/227–4500; 800/112–121 in Australia; 800/808–767 in New Zealand, WEB www.qantas.com). **United** (☎ 800/241–6522; 800/722–5243 in Canada; 0800/888–555 in the U.K.; 131-777 in Australia, WEB www.ual.com).

➤ SMALLER AIRLINES: **Air North** (☎ 867/668–228; 800/764–0407 in Alaska; 800/661–0407 in Canada, WEB www.airnorth.yk.net). **Bering Air** (☎ 907/443–5464 or 800/478–4111, WEB www.beringair.com). **ERA Avia-**tion (☎ 907/266–8394 or 800/866–8394, WEB www.eraaviation.com). **Frontier Flying Service** (☎ 907/474–0014 or 800/478–6779, WEB www.frontierflying.com). **Hawaiian Vacations** (☎ 907/243–2323 or 800/770–2700, WEB www.hawaiianvacations.com). **Larry's Flying Service** (☎ 907/474–9169, WEB www.larrysflying.com). **PenAir** (☎ 907/243–2323, or 800/448–4226, WEB www.penair.com). **Warbelow's Air Ventures** (☎ 907/474–0518 or 800/478–0812, WEB www.warbelows.com).

CHECK-IN & BOARDING

Assuming that not everyone with a ticket will show up, airlines routinely overbook planes. When everyone does, airlines ask for volunteers to give up their seats. In return, these volunteers usually get a certificate for a free flight and are rebooked on the next flight out. If there are not enough volunteers, the airline must choose who will be denied boarding. The first to get bumped are passengers who checked in late and those flying on discounted tickets, so **get to the gate and check in as early as possible,** especially during peak periods.

A $350-million redevelopment project at Ted Stevens Anchorage International Airport is under way, and work will not be completed until 2004. When it is finished, the project will include a direct rail link to downtown Anchorage. Check with your airline for any expected delays caused by the construction work, or visit the airport's Web site, www.aiaterminalproject.com.

Always **bring a government-issued photo I.D. to the airport;** a passport is best. You will be asked to show it before you are allowed to check in.

CUTTING COSTS

The least expensive airfares to Alaska must usually be purchased in advance and are nonrefundable. It's smart to **call a number of airlines, and when you are quoted a good price, book it on the spot**—the same fare may not be available the next day. Always **check different routings.** Travel agents, especially low-fare specialists (☞ Discounts & Deals), are helpful.

Consolidators are another good source. They buy tickets for scheduled international flights at reduced rates from the airlines, then sell them at prices that beat the best fare available directly from the airlines, usually without restrictions. Sometimes you can even get your money back if you need to return the ticket. Carefully read the fine print detailing penalties for changes and cancellations, and **confirm your consolidator reservation with the airline.**

The Internet is an increasingly important source for discount travel information. Two helpful sites are **Travelocity** (WEB www.travelocity. com) and **Expedia** (WEB www.expedia. com). If you have flexibility in your travel dates, **check airline Internet sites for special last-minute deals.** Alaska Airlines (www.alaskaair.com) and some other carriers have specials to and from Alaska. These generally allow only a maximum one-week stay, but can sometimes cost less than half the going rate.

➤ CONSOLIDATORS: **Cheap Tickets** (☎ 800/377–1000). **Discount Airline Ticket Service** (☎ 800/576–1600). **Unitravel** (☎ 800/325–2222). **Up & Away Travel** (☎ 212/889–2345). **World Travel Network** (☎ 800/409–6753).

Although there are no Alaska-based consolidators, Non Stop Air Service is a wholesaler that provides discounted tickets to travel agencies, including its sister company, **One Stop Travel** (☎ 800/770–4440, WEB www. onestoptravel.net).

ENJOYING THE FLIGHT

For more legroom, **request an emergency-aisle seat.** Don't sit in the row in front of the emergency aisle or in front of a bulkhead, where seats may not recline. If you have dietary concerns, **ask for special meals when booking.** These can be vegetarian, low-cholesterol, or kosher, for example. On long flights, try to maintain a normal routine, to help fight jet lag. At night, **get some sleep.** By day, **eat light meals, drink water** (not alcohol), and **move around the cabin** to stretch your legs. For additional jet-lag tips consult *Fodor's FYI: Travel Fit & Healthy* (available at bookstores everywhere).

All flights to and within Alaska are smoke free, including charter flights and flights into the Bush.

FLYING TIMES

Average travel time is 13 hours from New York to Anchorage, 8 hours from Chicago, 7 hours from Dallas, and 6 hours from Los Angeles. Travel times from other destinations depend on your connection, since you'll need to route through other cities to get to Anchorage.

HOW TO COMPLAIN

If your baggage goes astray or your flight goes awry, complain right away. Most carriers require that you **file a claim immediately.**

➤ AIRLINE COMPLAINTS: U.S. Department of Transportation **Aviation Consumer Protection Division** (✉ C-75, Room 4107, Washington, DC 20590, ☎ 202/366–2220, WEB www.dot.gov/ airconsumer). **Federal Aviation Administration Consumer Hotline** (☎ 800/322–7873).

AIRPORTS

➤ AIRPORT INFORMATION: **Ted Stevens Anchorage International Airport** (ANC; ☎ 907/266–2525). **Vancouver International Airport** (YVR; ☎ 604/ 303–3603).

BEARS

If you're lucky—and careful—the sight of one of these magnificent creatures in the wild can be a highlight of your visit. By respecting bears and exercising care in bear country, neither you nor the bear will suffer from the experience. Remember that bears don't like surprises. Make your presence known by talking, singing, rattling a can full of gravel, or tying a bell to your pack, especially when terrain or vegetation obscures views. Travel with a group, which is noisier and easier for bears to detect. If possible, walk with the wind at your back so your scent will warn bears of your presence. And avoid bushy, low-visibility areas whenever possible.

Give bears the right-of-way—lots of it—especially a sow with cubs. Don't camp on animal trails; they're likely to be used by bears. If you come across a carcass of an animal, or detect its odor, avoid the area entirely; it's likely a bear's food cache. Store all food and garbage away from your campsite in airtight or specially designed bearproof containers. The Park Service supplies these for hikers in Denali and Glacier Bay national parks, and requires that backcountry travelers use them.

If a bear approaches you while you are fishing, stop. If you have a fish on your line, cut your line. If you do encounter a bear at close range, don't panic, and, above all, don't run. You can't outrun a bear, and by fleeing you could trigger a chase response from the bear. Talk in a normal voice to help identify yourself as a human. If traveling with others, stand close together to "increase your size." If the bear charges, it could be a bluff; as terrifying as this may sound, the experts advise standing your ground. If a brown bear actually touches you, then drop to the ground and play dead, either flat on your stomach or curled in a ball with your hands behind your neck. If you don't move, a brown bear will typically break off its attack once it feels the threat is gone. If you are attacked by a black bear, you are probably better off fighting back with rocks, sticks, or anything else you find since black bears are more likely to attack a person intentionally. Polar bears can be found in remote parts of the Arctic, but tourists are highly unlikely to encounter them in the summer months.

For more information on bears, ask for the brochure "Bear Facts: The Essentials for Traveling in Bear Country" from any of the Alaska Public Lands offices.

ALASKA PUBLIC LANDS OFFICES

Get details on Alaska's vast public lands from Alaska Public Lands Information Centers in Ketchikan, Tok, Anchorage, and Fairbanks, or on the Internet at www.nps.gov/aplic/center. The information centers are listed below.

➤ INFORMATION CENTERS: **Alaska Public Lands Information Center** (✉ 605 W. 4th Ave., Anchorage, ☎ 907/271–2737; 250 Cushman St., Suite 1A, Fairbanks 99701, ☎ 907/456–0527, FAX 907/456–0154; 50 Main St., Ketchikan, ☎ 907/228–6214; Mile

1314, Alaska Hwy., Tok, ☎ 907/883–5667). **Southeast Alaska Discovery Center** (✉ 50 Main St., Ketchikan 99901, ☎ 907/228–6220, FAX 907/228–6234).

BIKE TRAVEL

Cyclists will find a wide variety of conditions in Alaska. The main highways are heavily trafficked in the summer, and the shoulders are often not particularly wide. Bikers traveling between such crowded routes as Anchorage to Seward are risking their lives. A better bet would probably be to choose less-traveled roads and trails. Mountain bikes are available for rent in the larger Alaskan towns, or you can bring your own. Ferry travelers pay a small extra charge to transport bikes. Pick up an Alaska cycling guidebook, including *Alaska Bicycle Touring Guide* by Pete Praetorius and Alys Culhane (Denali Press) and *Mountain Bike Alaska* by Richard Larson (Glacier House Publications), for further details.

➤ BIKE RENTALS: **Beaver Sports** (✉ 3480 College Rd., Fairbanks, ☎ 907/479–2494, WEB www.beaversports. net). **The Bicycle Shop** (✉ 1035 W. Northern Lights Blvd., Anchorage, ☎ 907/276–5219). **Downtown Bicycle Rental** (✉ 245 W. 5th Ave., Suite 212, Anchorage, ☎ 907/279–5293, WEB www.alaska-bike-rentals.com). **Mountain Gears** (✉ 210 N. Franklin St., Juneau, ☎ 907/586–4327).

BIKES IN FLIGHT

Most airlines accommodate bikes as luggage, provided they are dismantled and boxed. Airlines sell bike boxes, which are often free at bike shops, for about $5 (it's at least $100 for bike bags). International travelers can sometimes substitute a bike for a piece of checked luggage at no charge; otherwise, the cost is about $100. Domestic and Canadian airlines charge $25–$50.

BOAT & FERRY TRAVEL

If you are looking for a casual alternative to a luxury cruise, **travel as Alaskans do, aboard the ferries of the Alaska Marine Highway System.** When planning your trip, **ask about special onboard programming.** Forest Service naturalists ride the larger ferries in summer, providing a running commentary on sights. In addition, the Arts-on-Board Program presents educators and entertainers on selected summer sailings. The Alaska Marine Highway ferries travel within Alaska and between Bellingham, Washington, and the towns of the Inside Passage. The Marine Highway also links up with British Columbia Ferries in Prince Rupert.

CUTTING COSTS

The **AlaskaPass** allows unlimited travel on bus, ferry, and rail lines in Alaska, along with bus and ferry travel in British Columbia and the Yukon. Passes are available for 15 or 22 consecutive days of travel ($649 and $749 respectively), as well as for 8 days of travel in a 12-day period ($549) or 12 days of travel in a 21-day period ($699).

➤ DISCOUNT PASSES: **AlaskaPass** (✉ Box 351, Vashon, WA 98070-0351, ☎ 206/463–6550 or 800/248–7598, FAX 206/463–6777, WEB www.alaskapass.com).

FARES & SCHEDULES

Make reservations for ferry travel by calling the Alaska Marine Highway System, which will mail the tickets, or you can pick them up from the ferry office at your starting point. Request a copy of its printed schedule over the phone, or find it on the Internet at www.dot.state.ak.us/ferry.

PAYING

You can pay for ferry travel by credit card (American Express, Discover, MasterCard, or Visa), cashier's check, money order, certified check, or personal check from an Alaskan bank.

➤ BOAT & FERRY INFORMATION: **Alaska Marine Highway** (✉ Box 25535, Juneau 99802-5535, ☎ 907/465–3941 or 800/642–0066, FAX 907/277–4829, WEB www.dot.state.ak.us/ferry). **B.C. Ferries** (✉ 1112 Fort St., Victoria V8V 4V2, ☎ 250/386–3431 or 888/223–3779, FAX 250/381–5452, WEB www.bcferries.bc.ca).

BUS TRAVEL

A number of companies provide bus or van service connecting towns in South Central and Interior Alaska. Alaska Direct Bus Lines operates year-round intercity van service between points in

Alaska and the Canadian Yukon on most major highways. Alaskon Express, a subsidiary of Gray Line of Alaska, operates intercity service mid-May through mid-September, including stops in Skagway, Fairbanks, Anchorage, and Seward. The Parks Highway Express provides summertime van service between Seward and Anchorage, continuing north to Denali National Park. Seward Bus Lines has year-round service connecting Anchorage with Seward, and Homer Stage Lines provides year-round service between Anchorage and Homer and summertime service between Homer and Seward. Greyhound Lines serves Vancouver, with service as far north as Whitehorse in the Yukon. Quick Shuttle bus service runs between Vancouver and Seattle. Smoking is prohibited on all buses or vans. Contact the individual companies for their scheduled service.

➤ BUS INFORMATION: **Alaska Direct Bus Lines** (✉ Box 100501, Anchorage 99510, ☎ 907/277–6652 or 800/770–6652). **Alaskon Express** (✉ 300 Elliott Ave. W, Seattle, WA 98119, ☎ 206/281–3535 or 800/478–6388, FAX 206/301–5282, WEB www.graylineofalaska.com). **Greyhound Lines of Canada** (☎ 604/482–8747 or 800/661–8747, WEB www.greyhound.ca). **Homer Stage Line** (✉ 3339 Fairbanks St., Anchorage 99503, ☎ 907/883–3914, FAX 907/235–0565). **Parks Highway Express** (✉ Box 84278, Fairbanks 99708, ☎ 907/479–3065 or 888/600–6001, WEB www.alaskashuttle.com). **Quick Shuttle** (☎ 604/244–3744 or 800/665–2122, WEB www.quickcoach.com). **Seward Bus Line** (✉ 3339 Fairbanks St., Anchorage 99503, ☎ 907/224–3608, WEB www.sewardbusline.com).

CUTTING COSTS

The **AlaskaPass** allows unlimited travel on bus, ferry, and rail lines in Alaska (see Cutting Costs in Boat & Ferry Travel).

PAYING

Accepted forms of payment vary among the bus companies, but all accept MasterCard and Visa, along with traveler's checks.

BUSINESS HOURS

Most Alaskan stores are open weekdays from 9 AM to 5 PM, though many have longer hours and remain open on weekends. All the larger towns have at least one convenience store that stays open all the time. In small Bush villages the general store may be open just a few hours per day and closed on Sunday, whereas in larger cities the larger grocery stores remain open 24 hours a day, seven days a week.

BANKS & OFFICES

Banks and credit unions are typically open weekdays 10–5, and some have limited Saturday hours, particularly in Anchorage, Fairbanks, and Juneau. Most government and other offices are open weekdays 9–5, though some close at 4:30.

GAS STATIONS

Many Alaskan gas stations remain open until 10 PM, and in the larger towns and cities, some stay open 24 hours a day. Most are also open on weekends, particularly along the main highways. In the smallest villages gas may be available only on weekdays, but these settlements typically have only a few miles of roads.

MUSEUMS & SIGHTS

Hours of sights and attractions are denoted in the book by the clock icon, ☉. Museums in smaller Southeast Alaska towns typically open whenever a cruise ship or ferry is in port, even if it is late on a Sunday evening. See specific town descriptions for more information.

PHARMACIES

Pharmacy hours vary across Alaska, but most local hospitals have a pharmacy that provides service at any hour. The Carrs store at 1650 West Northern Lights Boulevard in Anchorage has a 24-hour pharmacy.

SHOPS

Alaskan gift shops are typically open weekdays, or whenever cruise ships are in port. Gift shops in Anchorage are generally open year-round, but in other towns many places close in October and reopen in May.

CAMERAS & PHOTOGRAPHY

Alaska is one of the world's premier spots for nature and wildlife photography. For most purposes, an ISO 200 speed film is sufficient, though ISO 400 is better for low-light situations. You'll need to take into account the extraordinary qualities of Alaska's slanting light (the sun is never directly overhead, and there are long shadows). Many professional photographers use Fuji's Sensia II or Velvia, along with Kodak's Ektachrome 100SW color slide films. For action shots and low light, you may want to choose a higher-speed film. Digital cameras have improved dramatically in the last few years, and are increasingly being used by both amateurs and professional photographers.

A zoom lens covering 28-105 mm is adequate for most Alaskan scenes, but longer telephoto lenses (200 mm and up) are useful for wildlife photos. A tripod is essential in dimly lighted situations and highly recommended for photographing wildlife with a telephoto lens.

Not everyone in Alaska appreciates being photographed, particularly in smaller Native villages where locals have sometimes been exploited by photographers. Ask for permission before taking a photograph of someone. Many museums do not allow flash or tripods, and photography is restricted or prohibited inside Russian Orthodox churches and certain Native cemeteries.

The Kodak Guide to Shooting Great Travel Pictures (available at bookstores everywhere) is loaded with tips.

➤ PHOTO HELP: Kodak Information Center (☎ 800/242–2424).

EQUIPMENT PRECAUTIONS

A plastic bag or umbrella will help keep your camera dry during wet weather. Winter travelers may need to contend with extremely cold conditions, which can greatly reduce battery life, fog lenses, and even cause complete mechanical failure. Be sure to **pack extra batteries for your camera,** especially when heading into remote areas. Lens fogging can be lessened by storing the camera and lenses in a cool place.

Don't pack film and equipment in checked luggage, where it is much more susceptible to damage. X-ray machines used to view checked luggage are becoming much more powerful and therefore are much more likely to ruin your film. Always **keep film and tape out of the sun.** Carry an extra supply of batteries, and **be prepared to turn on your camera or camcorder** to prove to security personnel that the device is real. Always **ask for hand inspection of film,** which becomes clouded after repeated exposure to airport X-ray machines, and **keep videotapes away from metal detectors.**

FILM & DEVELOPING

Print film is available almost everywhere in Alaska, but slide film is often not available outside the larger towns and cities. Both types tend to be expensive (up to $8 for a 24-exposure roll), so carry plenty. All the larger towns have film developing and printing available, and many also have one-hour photo labs.

CAR RENTAL

Rates in the larger towns begin around $45 a day and $280 a week for an economy car with air-conditioning (not needed in Alaska), an automatic transmission, and unlimited mileage. You're likely to pay at least $50 per day and $300 per week from the major companies; more for four-wheel drives. Reserve well ahead for the summer season, particularly for the popular minivans and sport utility vehicles. Be sure to ask in advance about discounts if you have an AAA or Costco card.

➤ MAJOR AGENCIES: **Alamo** (☎ 800/327–9633; 020/8759–6200 in the U.K.). **Avis** (☎ 800/331–1212; 800/879–2847 in Canada; 02/9353–9000 in Australia; 09/525–1982 in New Zealand; 0870/606–0100 in the U.K.). **Budget** (☎ 800/527–0700; 0144/227–6266 in the U.K., through affiliate Europcar). **Dollar** (☎ 800/800–4000; 0124/622–0111 in the U.K., where it is known as Sixt Kenning; 02/9223–1444 in Australia). **Hertz** (☎ 800/654–3131; 800/263–0600 in Canada; 020/8897–2072 in the U.K.; 02/9669–2444 in Australia; 09/256–8690 in New Zealand). **National Car Rental** (☎ 800/227–7368; 0845/722–2525 in the U.K., where it is known as National Europe).

➤ SMALLER AGENCIES: **Payless** (☎ 800/729–5377). **Thrifty** (☎ 907/276–2855 or 800/367–2277).

CUTTING COSTS

To get the best deal, **book through a travel agent who will shop around.** Also **price local car-rental companies,** although the service and maintenance may not be as good as those of a major player. Remember to ask about required deposits, cancellation penalties, and drop-off charges if you're planning to pick up the car in one city and leave it in another. If you're traveling during a holiday period, also make sure that a confirmed reservation guarantees you a car.

➤ LOCAL AGENCIES: Local companies are often a good source for low rates, especially on a weekly basis. **Affordable New Car Rentals** (☎ 907/243–3370 or 800/248–3765 in Anchorage; 907/452–7341 in Fairbanks). **Arctic Rent-A-Car** (☎ 907/561–2990 in Anchorage; 907/479–8044 in Fairbanks). **Denali Car Rental** (☎ 907/276–1230 or 800/757–1230 in Anchorage). **Kodiak Auto Rental** (☎ 907/486–4900 on Kodiak Island). **Rent-A-Wreck** (☎ 907/583–2558 in Anchorage). **U-Save Auto Rental** (☎ 907/272–8728 in Anchorage; 800/254–8728 in Anchorage).

INSURANCE

When driving a rented car you are generally responsible for any damage to or loss of the vehicle as well as for any property damage or personal injury that you may cause. Before you rent, see what coverage your personal auto-insurance policy and credit cards provide.

For about $15–$20 per day, rental companies sell protection, known as a collision- or loss-damage waiver (CDW or LDW), that eliminates your liability for damage to the car. In most states you don't need a CDW if you have personal auto insurance or other liability insurance. However, **make sure you have enough coverage to pay for the car.** If you do not have auto insurance or an umbrella policy that covers damage to third parties, purchasing liability insurance and a CDW or LDW is highly recommended.

REQUIREMENTS & RESTRICTIONS

In Alaska you must be 21 (and no older than 99) to rent a car, and rates may be higher if you're under 25. You'll pay extra for child seats (about $3–$5 per day), which are compulsory for children under five, and for additional drivers (about $2–$5 per day). Non-U.S. residents will need a reservation voucher, a passport, a driver's license (written in English), and a travel policy that covers each driver, when picking up a car.

SURCHARGES

Before you pick up a car in one city and leave it in another, **ask about drop-off charges or one-way service fees,** which can be substantial. Note, too, that some rental agencies charge extra if you return the car before the time specified in your contract. To avoid a hefty refueling fee, **fill the tank just before you turn in the car,** but be aware that gas stations near the rental outlet may overcharge.

CAR TRAVEL

Driving to Alaska is a popular alternative to flying or cruising, especially for RVers, but you'll need to **set aside plenty of time.** Though journeying through Canada on the Alaska Highway can be exciting, the trek from the Lower 48 states is a long one. It's a seven-day trip from Seattle to Anchorage or Fairbanks, covering close to 2,500 mi. From Bellingham, Washington, and the Canadian ports of Prince Rupert and Stewart, you can link up with ferry service along the Marine Highway to reach southeastern Alaska.

The Alaska Highway begins at Dawson Creek, British Columbia, and stretches 1,442 mi through Canada's Yukon to Delta Junction; it enters Alaska at Tok. The two-lane highway is paved for its entire length and is open year-round. Highway services are available about every 50 mi–100 mi (sometimes at shorter intervals).

The rest of the state's roads are found almost exclusively in the South Central and Interior regions. They lie mainly between Anchorage, Fairbanks, and the Canadian border. Only one highway extends north of Fairbanks, and a couple run south of Anchorage to the Kenai Peninsula. These roads vary from four-lane freeways to nameless two-lane gravel roads and are generally open and maintained year-round.

The Glenn Highway begins at Tok and travels south to Anchorage. The Richardson Highway parallels the Alaska pipeline from Fairbanks south to the port city of Valdez. The Seward Highway heads south from Anchorage through the Kenai Mountains to Seward, with the branch Sterling Highway heading southwest to Kenai and Homer. The George Parks Highway connects Anchorage and Fairbanks, passing Denali National Park en route. The Steese Highway runs northwest of Fairbanks to the gold-rush town of Circle. The Dalton Highway begins at the end of the Elliott Highway, 73 mi north of Fairbanks, and leads 414 mi to Deadhorse, the supply center for the Prudhoe Bay oil fields. This gravel truck route presents unique challenges; **contact the Alaska Public Lands Information centers in Fairbanks, Tok, or Anchorage if you plan to drive the Dalton Highway** or visit their Web site at aurora.ak.blm.gov/dalton.

If you plan extensive driving in Alaska, join an automobile club such as AAA that offers towing and other benefits. Because of the long distances involved, you should seriously consider a plan (such as AAA Plus) that extends towing benefits to 100 mi in any direction.

The Milepost, available in bookstores or from Morris Communications, is a mile-by-mile guide to sights and services along Alaska's highways.

➤ CONTACTS: **Alaska Public Lands Information Center** (✉ 605 W. 4th Ave., Anchorage, ☎ 907/271–2737; 250 Cushman St., Suite 1A, Fairbanks 99701, ☎ 907/456–0527, FAX 907/456–0154; 50 Main St., Ketchikan, ☎ 907/228–6214; Mile 1314, Alaska Hwy., Tok, ☎ 907/883–5667). *The Milepost* (Morris Communications, ✉ 735 Broad St., Augusta, GA 30901, ☎ 907/272–6070 or 800/726–4707, FAX 907/258–5360, WEB www.themilepost.com).

GASOLINE

Gas prices in the Anchorage area are comparable with those in the Lower 48, but expect to pay more elsewhere. You will probably pay around 30¢ per gallon more in towns such as Juneau or Ketchikan, and far more in remote areas, particularly small villages off the road network, where fuel must be flown in. Fuel prices in Canada along the Alaska Highway are also very high.

ROAD CONDITIONS

If you are planning to drive to Alaska, come armed with patience. Road construction sometimes creates long delays on the Canadian side of the border, so don't plan a tight schedule. Also, frost damage creates dips in the road that require slower driving.

Driving in Alaska is much less rigorous than it used to be, although it still presents some unusual obstacles. Moose often wander onto roads and highways. If you come across one while driving, it's best to **stop your car and wait for the moose to cross.** The moose will usually move on its own. Be especially vigilant when driving at dusk or night, since moose can be active at all hours.

Flying gravel is a hazard to watch for along the Alaska and Dalton highways, especially in summer. A bug screen will help keep gravel and kamikaze insects off the windshield, but few travelers use them. Some travelers use clear, hard plastic guards to cover their headlights. (These are inexpensive and are available from almost any garage or service station along the major access routes.) Don't cover headlights with cardboard or plywood because you'll need your lights often, even in daytime, as dust is thrown up by traffic passing in both directions. (Headlights must be used at all times on the Seward Highway south of Anchorage.)

Unless you plan to undertake one of the remote highways (especially the Dalton Highway to Prudhoe Bay), you won't need any special equipment. But **be sure that the equipment you do have is in working condition,** from tires and spare to brakes and engine. Carrying spare fuses, spark plugs, jumper cables, a flashlight with extra batteries, a tool kit, and an extra fan belt is recommended.

If you get stuck on any kind of road, be careful about pulling off; the shoulder can be soft. In summer it stays light late, and though traffic is also light, one of Alaska's many good Samaritans is likely to stop to help

and send for aid (which may be many miles away). In winter, pack emergency equipment—a shovel, tire chains, such high-energy food as nuts or chocolate, flasks of hot beverages, and extra-warm clothing and blankets to help you through the wait for aid, should you need it. Never head out onto unplowed roads unless you are prepared to walk back.

Cellular phones are an excellent idea for travel in Alaska, particularly on the main roads, but check with your service provider for coverage. AAA members may also want to upgrade to the "Plus" policy, which allows for towing of up to 100 mi if you break down. Road maps are available at gas stations and grocery stores throughout Alaska.

RULES OF THE ROAD

Alaska honors valid driver's licenses from any state or country, and the speed limit on most state highways is 55 mph, but much of the Parks Highway (between Wasilla and Fairbanks) and the Seward Highway (between Anchorage and Seward) is 65 mph. Unless otherwise posted, you may make a right turn on a red light after coming to a complete stop. Seat belts are required on all passengers in Alaska and children under age four must be in child safety seats. State troopers rigorously enforce speed limits along the main highways.

Headlights must be used at all times on the Seward Highway south of Anchorage. State law requires that slow-moving vehicles **pull off the road at the first opportunity if leading more than five cars.** This is particularly true on the highway between Anchorage and Seward, where RV drivers have a bad reputation for not pulling over. Alaskans don't take kindly to being held up en route to their favorite Kenai River fishing spot.

RVS

The secret to a successful RV trip to Alaska is preparation. Expect to drive on more gravel and rougher roads than you're accustomed to. Batten down everything; tighten every nut and bolt in and out of sight, and don't leave anything to bounce around inside. Travel light, and your tires and suspension system will take less of a beating. Protect your headlights and the grille area in front of the radiator. Make sure you **carry adequate insurance to cover the replacement of your windshield.**

Most of Alaska's public campgrounds accommodate trailers, but hookups are available only in private RV parks. Water can be found at most stopping points, but it may be limited for trailer use. Think twice before deciding to pull an RV during the spring thaw. The rough roadbed can be a trial.

CHILDREN IN ALASKA

Be sure to plan ahead and **involve your youngsters** as you outline your trip. When packing, include things to keep them busy en route. On sightseeing days try to schedule activities of special interest to your children. If you are renting a car, don't forget to **arrange for a car seat** when you reserve. For general advice about traveling with children, check out *Fodor's FYI: Travel with Your Baby* (available in bookstores everywhere).

FLYING

If your children are two or older, **ask about children's airfares.** As a general rule, infants under two not occupying a seat fly at greatly reduced fares or even for free.

Experts agree that it's a good idea to use safety seats aloft for children weighing less than 40 pounds. Airlines set their own policies: U.S. carriers usually require that the child be ticketed, even if he or she is young enough to ride free, since the seats must be strapped into regular seats. Do **check your airline's policy about using safety seats during takeoff and landing.** And since safety seats are not allowed everywhere in the plane, get your seat assignments early.

When reserving, **request children's meals or a freestanding bassinet** if you need them. But note that bulkhead seats, where you must sit to use the bassinet, may lack an overhead bin or storage space on the floor.

LODGING

Most hotels in Alaska allow children under a certain age to stay in their parents' room at no extra charge, but others charge for them as extra adults; be sure to **find out the cutoff age for children's discounts.**

➤ BEST CHOICES: **Comfort Inn Ship Creek** (⊠ 111 Ship Creek Ave., Anchorage 99501, ☎ 907/277–6887 or 800/228–5150, FAX 907/274–9830). **Frontier Suites Airport Hotel** (⊠ 9400 Glacier Hwy., Juneau 99801, ☎ 907/790–6600 or 800/544–2250, FAX 907/790–6612, WEB www.frontiersuites.com). **Snowshoe Inn** (⊠ 826 K St., Anchorage 99501, ☎ 907/258–7669, FAX 907/258–7463). **SpringHill Suites by Marriott** (⊠ 3401 A St., Anchorage 99503, ☎ 907/562–3247 or 888/287–9400, FAX 907/562–3250, WEB www.springhillsuites.com).

SIGHTS & ATTRACTIONS

Places that are especially appealing to children are indicated by a rubber-duckie icon (☺) in the margin.

CONSUMER PROTECTION

Whenever shopping or buying travel services in Alaska, **pay with a major credit card,** if possible, so you can cancel payment or get reimbursed if there's a problem. If you're doing business with a particular company for the first time, **contact your local Better Business Bureau and the attorney general's offices** in your state and (for U.S. businesses) the company's home state as well. Have any complaints been filed? Finally, if you're buying a package or tour, always **consider travel insurance** that includes default coverage (☞ Insurance).

➤ BBBs: **Council of Better Business Bureaus** (⊠ 4200 Wilson Blvd., Suite 800, Arlington, VA 22203, ☎ 703/276–0100, FAX 703/525–8277, WEB www.bbb.org).

CUSTOMS & DUTIES

When shopping, **keep receipts** for all purchases. Upon reentering the country, **be ready to show customs officials what you've bought.** If you feel a duty is incorrect or object to the way your clearance was handled, note the inspector's badge number and ask to see a supervisor. If the problem isn't resolved, write to the appropriate authorities, beginning with the port director at your point of entry.

IN AUSTRALIA

Australian residents who are 18 or older may bring home $A400 worth of souvenirs and gifts (including jewelry), 250 cigarettes or 250 grams of tobacco, and 1,125 ml of alcohol (including wine, beer, and spirits). Residents under 18 may bring back $A200 worth of goods. Prohibited items include meat products. Seeds, plants, and fruits need to be declared upon arrival.

➤ INFORMATION: **Australian Customs Service** (Regional Director, ✉ Box 8, Sydney, NSW 2001, Australia, ☎ 02/9213–2000, FAX 02/9213–4000, WEB www.customs.gov.au).

IN CANADA

Canadian residents who have been out of Canada for at least seven days may bring home C$500 worth of goods duty-free. If you've been away fewer than seven days but more than 48 hours, the duty-free allowance drops to C$200; if your trip lasts 24–48 hours, the allowance is C$50. You may not pool allowances with family members. Goods claimed under the C$500 exemption may follow you by mail; those claimed under the lesser exemptions must accompany you. Alcohol and tobacco products may be included in the seven-day and 48-hour exemptions but not in the 24-hour exemption. If you meet the age requirements of the province or territory through which you reenter Canada, you may bring in, duty-free, 1.14 liters (40 imperial ounces) of wine or liquor *or* 24 12-ounce cans or bottles of beer or ale. If you are 16 or older you may bring in, duty-free, 200 cigarettes and 50 cigars. Check ahead of time with Revenue Canada or the Department of Agriculture for policies regarding meat products, seeds, plants, and fruits.

You may send an unlimited number of gifts worth up to C$60 each duty-free to Canada. Label the package UNSOLICITED GIFT—VALUE UNDER $60. Alcohol and tobacco are excluded.

➤ INFORMATION: **Revenue Canada** (✉ 2265 St. Laurent Blvd. S, Ottawa, Ontario K1G 4K3, Canada, ☎ 613/993–0534; 800/461–9999 in Canada, FAX 613/991–4126, WEB www.ccra-adrc.gc.ca).

IN NEW ZEALAND

Homeward-bound residents 17 or older may bring back $700 worth of souvenirs and gifts. Your duty-free allowance also includes 4.5 liters of wine or beer; one 1,125-ml bottle of spirits; and either 200 cigarettes, 250 grams of tobacco, 50 cigars, or a combination of the three up to 250 grams. Prohibited items include meat products, seeds, plants, and fruits.

➤ INFORMATION: **New Zealand Customs** (Custom House, ✉ 50 Anzac Ave., Box 29, Auckland, New Zealand, ☎ 09/300–5399, FAX 09/359–6730, WEB www.customs.govt.nz).

IN THE U.K.

From countries outside the EU, including the U.S., you may bring home, duty-free, 200 cigarettes or 50 cigars; 1 liter of spirits or 2 liters of fortified or sparkling wine or liqueurs; 2 liters of still table wine; 60 ml of perfume; 250 ml of toilet water; plus £136 worth of other goods, including gifts and souvenirs. If returning from outside the EU, prohibited items include meat products, seeds, plants, and fruits.

➤ INFORMATION: **HM Customs and Excise** (✉ Dorset House, Stamford St., Bromley, Kent BR1 1XX, U.K., ☎ 020/7202–4227, WEB www.hmce.gov.uk).

IN THE U.S.

U.S. residents who have been out of the country for at least 48 hours (and who have not used the $400 allowance or any part of it in the past 30 days) may bring home $400 worth of foreign goods duty-free.

U.S. residents 21 and older may bring back 1 liter of alcohol duty-free. In addition, regardless of your age, you are allowed 200 cigarettes and 100 non-Cuban cigars. Antiques, which the U.S. Customs Service defines as objects more than 100 years old, enter duty-free, as do original works of art done entirely by hand, including paintings, drawings, and sculptures.

You may also mail or ship packages home duty-free: up to $200 worth of goods for personal use, with a limit of one parcel per addressee per day (except alcohol or tobacco products or perfume worth more than $5);

label the package PERSONAL USE and attach a list of its contents and their retail value. Do not label the package UNSOLICITED GIFT or your duty-free exemption will drop to $100. Mailed items do not affect your duty-free allowance on your return.

➤ INFORMATION: **U.S. Customs Service** (✉ 1300 Pennsylvania Ave. NW, Washington, DC 20229, WEB www. customs.gov; inquiries ☎ 202/354–1000; complaints c/o ✉ 1300 Pennsylvania Ave. NW, Room 5.4D, Washington, DC 20229; registration of equipment c/o ✉ Resource Management, ☎ 202/927–0540).

DINING

The restaurants we list are the cream of the crop in each price category. Restaurants are indicated in the text by a knife-and-fork icon, ✕ , and establishments denoted by ✕🔲 stand out equally for their restaurants and rooms.

For restaurants:

CATEGORY	ALASKA*	VANCOUVER AND VICTORIA*
$$$$	over $25	over C$30
$$$	$16–$25	C$23–C$30
$$	$9–$15	C$13–C$22
$	under $9	under C$13

per person for a main course at dinner

MEALTIMES

Alaskan restaurants typically serve breakfast until 10 or 11, lunch from 11 to 2, and dinner starting around 4. Unless otherwise noted, the restaurants listed in this guide are open daily for lunch and dinner.

RESERVATIONS & DRESS

Reservations are always a good idea: we mention them only when they're essential or not accepted. Book as far ahead as you can, and reconfirm as soon as you arrive. We mention dress only when men are required to wear a jacket or a jacket and tie.

SPECIALTIES

Alaska is best known for its seafood, particularly such stars as king salmon, halibut, king crab, and shrimp. Anchorage and Juneau have superb restaurants specializing in fresh seafood,

but you will also discover seafood on the menu in virtually any coastal Alaskan town. The open-air salmon bakes in Juneau, Tok, Denali National Park, and Fairbanks serve excellent, all-you-can-eat grilled salmon and halibut. Anchorage has the greatest diversity of restaurants, including classy steak houses, noisy brew pubs, authentic Thai eateries, and a wide variety of other ethnic places.

WINE, BEER & SPIRITS

Alcohol is sold at liquor stores in most Alaskan towns and cities along the road system, as well as in settlements along the Inside Passage. Alcoholism is a devastating problem in Native villages, and because of this many of these Bush communities are "dry" (no alcohol allowed) or "damp" (limited amounts allowed for personal use, but alcohol cannot be sold). Be sure to check the rules before flying into a Bush community with alcohol, or you might find yourself charged with illegally importing alcohol.

Alaska's best-known microbrew is made by Alaskan Brewing Company in Juneau. Its Alaskan Amber is available in six-packs or on draft throughout the Pacific Northwest. Anchorage is home to several popular brew pubs, and their beers are sold in local liquor stores. Homer Brewing Company in the town of Homer sells its beers in local bars or in take-away bottles. You'll also find brew pubs in Haines, Ketchikan, and Wasilla.

DISABILITIES & ACCESSIBILITY

Travelers with disabilities will find good facilities at the most popular tourist areas, particularly places that deal with large numbers of elderly cruise-ship passengers. Some Forest Service cabins are wheelchair accessible, and the state ferries and trains are well set up to accommodate passengers with disabilities. In general, Bush Alaskan villages are not at all wheelchair friendly, with rough gravel roads and minimal facilities. Travelers with disabilities may also have difficulties getting into and out of the small aircraft used to reach these villages.

Alaska Snail Trails has an eight-passenger minibus designed especially for travelers with disabilities on trips ranging from 1 to 10 days. The bus includes wheelchair lifts and tie-downs. They also provide tours for those without disabilities who prefer an easy pace.

Alaska Welcomes You! has a complete database of accessible accommodations, attractions, and tours. It also books tours, cruises, and other trips customized to personal abilities. Access Alaska is a nonprofit assisted-living center in Anchorage. It produces a helpful free listing of accessible hotels and restaurants, car and van rental info, tour companies, and other details for travelers with disabilities. Accessible Vans of Alaska in Anchorage rents wheelchair-accessible vehicles to disabled persons and their families.

➤ LOCAL RESOURCES: **Access Alaska** (✉ 3710 Woodland Dr., Suite 900, Anchorage 99517, ☎ 907/248–4777; 800/770–4488 in AK; 907/248–8799 TTY; FAX 907/248–0639, WEB www.alaska.net/~access). **Accessible Vans of Alaska** (✉ 2000 Dowling Rd. Suite 8, Anchorage 99507, ☎ 907/563–8267 or 877/563–8267, FAX 907/562–6117, WEB www.alaskavans.com). **Alaska Snail Trails** (✉ Box 210894, Anchorage 99521, ☎ 907/337–7517 or 800/348–4532, WEB www.alaskasnailtrails.com). **Alaska Welcomes You!** (✉ Box 91333, Anchorage 99509, ☎ 907/349–6301 or 800/349–6301, FAX 907/344–3259, WEB www.accessiblealaska.com).

LODGING

All larger hotels in Alaska have at least one handicapped-accessible room, and those built since the mid-1990s often have several such rooms. Most bed-and-breakfasts are not as wheelchair-friendly; contact B&B referral agencies for those with accessible facilities. Alaska Welcomes You! or Alaska Snail Trails can set up accessible lodging throughout the state.

RESERVATIONS

When discussing accessibility with an operator or reservations agent, **ask hard questions.** Are there any stairs, inside *or* out? Are there grab bars next to the toilet *and* in the shower/tub? How wide is the doorway to the room? To the bathroom? For the most extensive facilities meeting the latest legal specifications, **opt for newer accommodations.**

TRANSPORTATION

Alaska Direct Bus Lines offers a 10% discount to passengers with disabilities for intercity travel. AnchorRide provides transportation for senior citizens and those with disabilities within the Anchorage area. Hertz has hand-controlled rental cars in Anchorage. The Alaska Marine Highway System has elevators on eight of its nine vessels and accessible cabins on its six vessels equipped with staterooms. ERA Helicopters has wheelchair lifts at its Juneau and Denali National Park locations. Alaska Cab offers lift-equipped van service in Anchorage, or contact the city-run Anchor Ride service at least a day in advance. The Alaska Railroad has cars that are accessible for people who use wheelchairs; cars also have wheelchair locks and lifts. Seward, Portage, Whittier, Anchorage, Talkeetna, Denali National Park, and Fairbanks stations all have lifts, with at least one lock-down for service on all trains. The Whittier shuttle train offers free passage to cars with a plastic DISABLED PERSON'S PARKING IDENTIFICATION placard, but you will also need to have a completed application for disabled parking and a driver's license. Contact the Alaska Railroad for details.

➤ BUS TRAVEL: **Alaska Direct Bus Lines** (✉ Box 501, Anchorage 99501, ☎ 907/277–6652 or 800/770–6652). **Anchor Ride** (☎ 907/562–8444).

➤ CAR RENTAL: **Hertz** (☎ 800/654–3131; 800/654–2280 TTY).

➤ FERRY TRAVEL: **Alaska Marine Highway** (☎ 907/465–3941 or 800/642–0066, FAX 907/277–4829, WEB www.dot.state.ak.us/ferry).

➤ FLIGHTSEEING: **ERA Helicopters** (☎ 907/266–8351 or 800/843–1947, WEB www.eraaviation.com).

➤ TAXIS: **Alaska Cab** (☎ 907/563–5353).

➤ TRAIN TRAVEL: **Alaska Railroad** (☎ 907/265–2494 in Anchorage; 907/458–6025 in Fairbanks; 800/544–0552; FAX 907/265–2323, WEB www.akrr.com).

➤ COMPLAINTS: **Aviation Consumer Protection Division** (☞ Air Travel) for airline-related problems. **Civil Rights Office** (✉ U.S. Department of Transportation, Departmental Office of Civil Rights, S-30, 400 7th St. SW, Room 10215, Washington, DC 20590, ☎ 202/366–4648, FAX 202/366–9371, WEB www.dot.gov/ost/docr/index.htm) for problems with surface transportation. **Disability Rights Section** (✉ U.S. Department of Justice, Civil Rights Division, Box 66738, Washington, DC 20035-6738, ☎ 202/514–0301 or 800/514–0301; 202/514–0383 TTY; 800/514–0383 TTY, FAX 202/307–1198, WEB www.usdoj.gov/crt/ada/adahom1.htm) for general complaints.

TRAVEL AGENCIES

In the United States, the Americans with Disabilities Act requires that travel firms serve the needs of all travelers. Some agencies specialize in working with people with disabilities.

➤ TRAVELERS WITH MOBILITY PROBLEMS: **Access Adventures** (✉ 206 Chestnut Ridge Rd., Scottsville, NY 14624, ☎ 716/889–9096, dltravel@prodigy.net), run by a former physical-rehabilitation counselor. **Accessible Vans of America** (✉ 9 Spielman Rd., Fairfield, NJ 07004, ☎ 877/282–8267, FAX 973/808–9713, WEB www.accessiblevans.com). **CareVacations** (✉ 5-5110 50th Ave., Leduc, Alberta T9E 6V4, Canada, ☎ 780/986–6404 or 877/478–7827, FAX 780/986–8332, WEB www.carevacations.com), for group tours and cruise vacations. **Flying Wheels Travel** (✉ 143 W. Bridge St., Box 382, Owatonna, MN 55060, ☎ 507/451–5005 or 800/535–6790, FAX 507/451–1685, WEB www.flyingwheelstravel.com).

DISCOUNTS & DEALS

Be a smart shopper and **compare all your options** before making decisions. A plane ticket bought with a promotional coupon from travel clubs, coupon books, and direct-mail offers or on the Internet may not be cheaper than the least expensive fare from a discount ticket agency. And always keep in mind that what you get is just as important as what you save. The **AlaskaPass** allows unlimited travel on bus, ferry, and rail lines in Alaska (*see* Cutting Costs *in* Boat & Ferry Travel).

DISCOUNT RESERVATIONS

To save money, **look into discount reservations services** with toll-free numbers, which use their buying power to get a better price on hotels, airline tickets, even car rentals. When booking a room, always **call the hotel's local toll-free number** (if one is available) rather than the central reservations number—you'll often get a better price. Always ask about special packages or corporate rates.

➤ AIRLINE TICKETS: ☎ 800/FLY–ASAP.

➤ HOTEL ROOMS: **Players Express Vacations** (☎ 800/458–6161, WEB www.playersexpress.com). **RMC Travel** (☎ 800/245–5738, WEB www.rmcwebtravel.com). **Turbotrip.com** (☎ 800/473–7829, WEB www.turbotrip.com).

PACKAGE DEALS

Don't confuse packages and guided tours. When you buy a package, you travel on your own, just as though you had planned the trip yourself. Fly/drive packages, which combine airfare and car rental, are often a good deal.

ECOTOURISM

Concern for the environment has spawned a worldwide movement called ecotourism, or green tourism. Ecotourists aim to travel responsibly, taking care to conserve the environment and respect indigenous populations. For information about environmental concerns peculiar to Alaska as well as a list of resources and ecotour operators, *see* Planning a Wilderness Adventure *in* Chapter 2.

GAY & LESBIAN TRAVEL

Alaska is a politically conservative state, and openly gay and lesbian travelers may not be well accepted in some towns. Although Fairbanks and Juneau both have active gay and lesbian communities, Anchorage is the real center for Alaska, with two gay bars (Mad Myrna's and the Raven), along with gay-oriented travel agencies, stores, and a theater company (Out North Contemporary Art House) that sometimes presents related plays. For gay and lesbian information, **Identity** (☎ 907/258–4777, WEB www.alaska.net/~identity) produces a helpful business directory each year, along with a monthly newsletter. For details about the gay and lesbian scene, consult *Fodor's Gay Guide to the USA* (available in bookstores everywhere).

➤ GAY- & LESBIAN-FRIENDLY TRAVEL AGENCIES: **Different Roads Travel** (✉ 8383 Wilshire Blvd., Suite 902, Beverly Hills, CA 90211, ☎ 323/651–5557 or 800/429–8747, FAX 323/651–3678, lgernert@tzell.com). **Kennedy Travel** (✉ 314 Jericho Tpke., Floral Park, NY 11001, ☎ 516/352–4888 or 800/237–7433, FAX 516/354–8849, WEB www.kennedytravel.com). **Now Voyager** (✉ 4406 18th St., San Francisco, CA 94114, ☎ 415/626–1169 or 800/255–6951, FAX 415/626–8626, WEB www.nowvoyager.com). **Skylink Travel and Tour** (✉ 1006 Mendocino Ave., Santa Rosa, CA 95401, ☎ 707/546–9888 or 800/225–5759, FAX 707/546–9891, WEB www.skylinktravel.com), serving lesbian travelers.

HEALTH

PESTS & OTHER HAZARDS

During the summer months Alaska is infamous for its sometimes-dense clouds of mosquitoes and other biting insects. They are generally the worst in Interior Alaska but can be an annoyance throughout the state. Be sure to bring mosquito repellents containing DEET. Also popular (but less effective) is the Avon product Skin So Soft. Mosquito coils may be of some help if you are camping out or staying in remote cabins. Headnets are sold in local sporting-goods stores and are a wise purchase if you plan to spend extended time outdoors.

HOLIDAYS

Major national holidays include New Year's Day (Jan. 1); Martin Luther King, Jr., Day (3rd Mon. in Jan.); President's Day (3rd Mon. in Feb.); Memorial Day (last Mon. in May); Independence Day (July 4); Labor Day (1st Mon. in Sept.); Thanksgiving Day (4th Thurs. in Nov.); Christmas Day (Dec. 25); and New Year's Eve (Dec. 31).

INSURANCE

The most useful travel-insurance plan is a comprehensive policy that includes coverage for trip cancellation and interruption, default, trip delay, and medical expenses (with a waiver for pre-existing conditions).

Without insurance you will lose all or most of your money if you cancel your trip, regardless of the reason. Default insurance covers you if your tour operator, airline, or cruise line goes out of business. Trip-delay covers expenses that arise because of bad weather or mechanical delays. Study the fine print when comparing policies.

Always **buy travel policies directly from the insurance company**; if you buy them from a cruise line, airline, or tour operator that goes out of business you probably will not be covered for the agency or operator's default, a major risk. Before making any purchase, **review your existing health and home-owner's policies** to find what they cover away from home.

➤ TRAVEL INSURERS: In the U.S.: **Access America** (✉ 6600 W. Broad St., Richmond, VA 23230, ☎ 804/285–3300 or 800/284–8300, FAX 804/673–1586, WEB www.previewtravel.com), **Travel Guard International** (✉ 1145 Clark St., Stevens Point, WI 54481, ☎ 715/345–0505 or 800/826–1300, FAX 800/955–8785, WEB www.noelgroup.com).

FOR INTERNATIONAL TRAVELERS

For information on customs restrictions, *see* Customs & Duties.

CAR TRAVEL

Driving in the United States is on the right. Do **obey speed limits** posted along roads and highways. Watch for lower limits in small towns and on back roads. Always **strap children under age four into approved child-safety seats.**

CURRENCY

The dollar is the basic unit of U.S. currency. It has 100 cents. Coins include the copper penny (1¢); the silvery nickel (5¢), dime (10¢), quarter (25¢), and half-dollar (50¢); and the golden $1 coin, replacing a now-rare silver dollar. Bills are denominated $1, $5, $10, $20, $50, and $100, all green and identical in size; designs vary.

ELECTRICITY

The U.S. standard is AC, 110 volts/60 cycles. Plugs have two flat pins set parallel to each other.

EMERGENCIES

For police, fire, or ambulance, **dial 911** (0 in rural areas).

INSURANCE

Britons and Australians need extra medical coverage when traveling overseas.

➤ INSURANCE INFORMATION: In the U.K.: **Association of British Insurers** (✉ 51–55 Gresham St., London EC2V 7HQ, U.K., ☎ 020/7600–3333, FAX 020/7696–8999, WEB www.abi.org.uk). In Australia: **Insurance Council of Australia** (✉ Level 3, 56 Pitt St., Sydney, NSW 2000, Australia, ☎ 03/9614–1077, FAX 03/9614–7924). In Canada: **RBC Insurance** (✉ 6880 Financial Dr., Mississauga, Ontario L5N 7Y5, Canada, ☎ 905/816–2400; 800/668–4342 in Canada, FAX 905/816–2498, WEB www.royalbank.com). In New Zealand: **Insurance Council of New Zealand** (✉ Box 474, Wellington, New Zealand, ☎ 04/472–5230, FAX 04/473–3011, WEB www.icnz.org.nz).

MAIL & SHIPPING

You can buy stamps and aerograms and send letters and parcels in post offices. Stamp-dispensing machines can occasionally be found in airports, bus and train stations, office buildings, drugstores, and the like. You can also deposit mail in the stout, dark blue, steel bins at strategic locations everywhere and in the mail chutes of large buildings; pickup schedules are posted.

For mail sent within the United States, you need a 34¢ stamp for first-class letters weighing up to 1 ounce (23¢ for each additional ounce) and 21¢ for domestic postcards. For overseas mail, you pay 80¢ for 1-ounce airmail letters, 70¢ for airmail postcards, and 35¢ for surface-rate postcards. For Canada and Mexico you need a 60¢ stamp for a 1-ounce letter and 50¢ for a postcard. For 70¢ you can buy an aerogram—a single sheet of lightweight blue paper that folds into its own envelope, stamped for overseas airmail.

To receive mail on the road, have it sent c/o General Delivery at your destination's main post office (use the correct five-digit zip code). You must pick up mail in person within 30 days and show a driver's license or passport.

PASSPORTS & VISAS

When traveling internationally, **carry your passport** even if you don't need one (it's always the best form of I.D.) and **make two photocopies of the data page** (one for someone at home and another for you, carried separately from your passport). If you lose your passport, promptly call the nearest embassy or consulate and the local police.

Visitor visas are not necessary for Canadian citizens, or for citizens of Australia and the United Kingdom who are staying fewer than 90 days.

➤ AUSTRALIAN CITIZENS: **Australian Passport Office** (☎ 131–232). **U.S. Office of Australia Affairs** (✉ MLC Centre, 19-29 Martin Pl., 59th floor, Sydney, NSW 2000, Australia).

➤ CANADIAN CITIZENS: **Passport Office** (☎ 819/994–3500; 800/567–6868 in Canada).

➤ NEW ZEALAND CITIZENS: **New Zealand Passport Office** (☎ 04/494–0700 for application procedures; 0800/225–050 in New Zealand for application-status updates). **U.S. Office of New Zealand Affairs** (✉ 29 Fitzherbert Terr., Thorndon, Wellington, New Zealand).

➤ U.K. CITIZENS: **London Passport Office** (☎ 0870/521–0410) for application procedures and emergency passports. **U.S. Embassy Visa Information Line** (☎ 01891/200–290). **U.S. Embassy Visa Branch** (✉ 5 Upper Grosvenor Sq., London W1A 1AE, U.K.); send a self-addressed, stamped envelope. **U.S. Consulate General** (✉ Queen's House, Queen St., Belfast BTI 6EO, Northern Ireland).

TELEPHONES

All U.S. telephone numbers consist of a three-digit area code and a seven-digit local number. Within most local calling areas, dial only the seven-digit number. Within the same area code, dial "1" first. To call between area-code regions, dial "1" then all 10 digits; the same goes for calls to numbers prefixed by "800," "888," and "877"—all toll-free. For calls to numbers preceded by "900" you must pay—usually dearly.

For international calls, dial "011" followed by the country code and the local number. For help, dial "0" and ask for an overseas operator. The country code is 61 for Australia, 64 for New Zealand, 44 for the United Kingdom. Calling Canada is the same as calling within the United States. Most local phone books list country codes and U.S. area codes. The country code for the United States is 1.

For operator assistance, dial "0." To obtain someone's phone number, call directory assistance, 555–1212 or occasionally 411 (free at public phones). To have the person you're calling foot the bill, phone collect; dial "0" instead of "1" before the 10-digit number.

At pay phones, instructions are usually posted. Usually you insert coins in a slot (25¢–35¢ for local calls) and wait for a steady tone before dialing. When you call long-distance, the operator will tell you how much to insert; prepaid phone cards, widely available in various denominations, are easier. Call the number on the back, punch in the card's personal identification number when prompted, then dial your number.

LODGING

The lodgings we list are the cream of the crop in each price category. We always list the facilities that are available—but we don't specify whether they cost extra: when pricing accommodations, always ask what's included and what costs extra.

For hotels:

CATEGORY	ANCHORAGE*	ELSEWHERE IN ALASKA*
$$$$	over $210	over $150
$$$	$140–$210	$110–$150
$$	$85–$140	$75–$110
$	under $85	under $75

CATEGORY	VANCOUVER AND VICTORIA*
$$$$	over C$200
$$$	C$150–C$200
$$	C$100–C$150
$	under C$100

All prices are for a standard double room in high season, excluding tax and service.

Assume that hotels operate on the **European Plan** (EP, with no meals) unless we specify that they use the **Continental Plan** (CP, with a Continental breakfast), **Modified American Plan** (MAP, with breakfast and dinner), or the **Full American Plan** (FAP, with all meals).

APARTMENT RENTALS

If you want a home base that's roomy enough for a family and comes with cooking facilities, **consider a furnished rental.** These can save you money, especially if you're traveling with a group. Home-exchange directories sometimes list rentals as well as exchanges.

➤ INTERNATIONAL AGENTS: **Hideaways International** (✉ 767 Islington St., Portsmouth, NH 03801, ☎ 603/430–4433 or 800/843–4433, FAX 603/430–4444, WEB www.hideaways.com; membership $129).

B&BS

➤ RESERVATION SERVICES: **Alaska Adventures & Accommodations** (✉ 507 E. St., Anchorage 99501, ☎ 907/344–4676 or 888/655–4723, FAX 907/349–4676, WEB www.see-alaska.com). **Alaska Available Reservations & Travel Service** (✉ 3213 Minnesota Dr., Suite B, Anchorage 99503, ☎ 907/277–9900, FAX 907/272–1899, WEB www.alaskaavailable.com). **Alaska Bed & Breakfast Association Innside Passage Chapter** (✉ Box 22800, Juneau 99802, ☎ 907/789–8822, FAX 907/780–4673, WEB www.accommodations-alaska.com). **Alaska Private Lodgings/Stay With a Friend** (✉ Box 200047, Anchorage 99520, ☎ 907/258–1717, FAX 907/258–6613, WEB www.alaskabandb.com). **Alaska Sourdough Bed & Breakfast Association** (✉ 889 Cardigan Circle, Anchorage 99503, ☎ 907/563–6244). **Mat-Su Chapter, Bed-&-Breakfast Association of Alaska** (✉ Box 873507, Wasilla 99687, ☎ 907/376–4461 or 800/401–7444, FAX 907/376–4461, WEB www.alaskabnbhosts.com).

CAMPING

Camping in Alaska needn't be a daunting experience: think of it as camping elsewhere in the Lower 48, except that the mosquitoes are worse and there's a greater likelihood of a nighttime bear visit. Some newcomers to bear country are uneasy sleeping in a tent, but encounters are rare. The midnight sun can also keep tent campers awake. Whether you're in a tent or an RV, you'll need warm bedding, insect repellent, rain protection, and tight containers in which to **store food inside your vehicle,** where it's less likely to tempt bears.

Public campgrounds in Alaska are operated by the U.S. Forest Service, State Division of Parks and Outdoor Recreation, National Park Service, and Bureau of Land Management. Of the national parks, only Denali has developed car camping facilities, and these campsites fill quickly. Several other Alaskan national parks have walk-in campgrounds, and all parks allow backcountry camping. In addition to the public campgrounds, private RV parks can be found in Alaska's larger towns.

➤ INFORMATION: **Alaska Public Lands Information Centers** (⌧ 605 W. 4th Ave., Suite 105, Anchorage 99501, ☎ 907/271–2737, FAX 907/277–2744; 250 Cushman St., Suite 1A, Fairbanks 99701, ☎ 907/456–0527, FAX 907/456–0154). **Southeast Alaska Discovery Center** (⌧ 50 Main St., Ketchikan 99901, ☎ 907/228–6220).

HOME EXCHANGES

If you would like to exchange your home for someone else's, **join a home-exchange organization,** which will send you its updated listings of available exchanges for a year and will include your own listing in at least one of them. It's up to you to make specific arrangements.

➤ EXCHANGE CLUBS: **HomeLink International** (⌧ Box 47747, Tampa, FL 33647, ☎ 813/975–9825 or 800/638–3841, FAX 813/910–8144, WEB www.homelink.org; $98 per year). **Intervac U.S.** (⌧ Box 590504, San Francisco, CA 94159, ☎ 800/756–4663, FAX 415/435–7440, WEB www.intervacus.com; $93 yearly fee includes one catalogue and on-line access).

HOSTELS

No matter what your age, you can **save on lodging costs by staying at hostels.** In some 5,000 locations in more than 70 countries around the world, Hostelling International (HI), the umbrella group for a number of national youth-hostel associations, offers single-sex, dorm-style beds and, at many hostels, rooms for couples and family accommodations. Membership in any HI national hostel association, open to travelers of all ages, allows you to stay in HI-affiliated hostels at member rates; one-year membership is about $25 for adults (C$26.75 in Canada, £9.30 in the U.K., $30 in Australia, and $30 in New Zealand); hostels run about $10–$25 per night. Members have priority booking for any available bunks; they're also eligible for discounts around the world, even on rail and bus travel in some countries.

➤ ORGANIZATIONS: **Hostelling International—American Youth Hostels** (⌧ 733 15th St. NW, Suite 840, Washington, DC 20005, ☎ 202/783–6161, FAX 202/783–6171, WEB www.hiayh.org). **Hostelling International—Canada** (⌧ 400–205 Catherine St., Ottawa, Ontario K2P 1C3, Canada, ☎ 613/237–7884, FAX 613/237–7868, WEB www.hostellingintl.ca). **Youth Hostel Association of England and Wales** (⌧ Trevelyan House, 8 St. Stephen's Hill, St. Albans, Hertfordshire AL1 2DY, U.K., ☎ 0870/870–8808, FAX 01727/844–126, WEB www.yha.org.uk). **Australian Youth Hostel Association** (⌧ 10 Mallett St., Camperdown, NSW 2050, Australia, ☎ 02/9565–1699, FAX 02/9565–1325, WEB www.yha.com.au). **Youth Hostels Association of New Zealand** (⌧ Box 436, Christchurch, New Zealand, ☎ 03/379–9970, FAX 03/365–4476, WEB www.yha.org.nz).

HOTELS

Alaskan motels and hotels are similar in quality to those in the Lower 48 states. Most Alaskan motels are independent, but you'll find the familiar chains (including Best Western, Comfort Inn, Days Inn, Hampton Inn, Hilton, Holiday Inn, Marriott, Super 8, and Sheraton) in Anchorage. Westmark Hotels is a regional chain, owned by cruise-tour operator Holland America Westours, with 15 locations, including hotels in Anchorage, Fairbanks, Kenai, Kodiak, Sitka, and Valdez in Alaska, plus Beaver Creek and Whitehorse in Canada's

Yukon Territory. Princess Tours owns a luxury hotel in Fairbanks and lodges outside Denali National Park, near Denali State Park, and on the Kenai Peninsula. All hotels listed have private bath unless otherwise noted.

➤ TOLL-FREE NUMBERS: **Best Western** (☎ 800/528–1234, WEB www.bestwestern.com). **Choice** (☎ 800/221–2222, WEB www.hotelchoice.com). **Clarion** (☎ 800/252–7466, WEB www.hotelchoice.com). **Comfort** (☎ 800/228–5150, WEB www.comfortinn.com). **Days Inn** (☎ 800/325–2525, WEB www.daysinn.com). **Fairfield Inn** (☎ 800/228–2800, WEB www.marriott.com). **Hilton** (☎ 800/445–8667, WEB www.hilton.com). **Holiday Inn** (☎ 800/465–4329, WEB www.basshotels.com). **Hyatt Hotels & Resorts** (☎ 800/233–1234, WEB www.hyatt.com). **Marriott** (☎ 800/228–9290, WEB www.marriott.com). **Ramada** (☎ 800/228–2828, WEB www.ramada.com). **Sheraton** (☎ 800/325–3535, WEB www.starwood.com).

WILDERNESS LODGES

To really get away from it all, **book a remote lodge** with rustic accommodations in the middle of breathtaking Alaskan wilderness. Some of the most popular are in the river drainages of Bristol Bay, in Southeast Alaska, and along the Susitna River north of Anchorage. Most of these lodges place a heavy emphasis on fishing; a stay generally includes daily guided fishing trips, as well as all meals. They can be astronomically expensive (daily rates of $250–$600 per person), so if you're not interested in fishing, you won't want to seek these out. Lodges in and near Denali National Park emphasize the great outdoors, and some even include wintertime dogsledding. Activities focus on hiking, rafting, flightseeing, horseback riding, and natural-history walks. For getting deep into the wilderness, these lodges are an excellent alternative to the hotels and cabins outside the park entrance.

MEDIA

NEWSPAPERS & MAGAZINES

Alaska's primary statewide newspaper is the *Anchorage Daily News*. Other papers with substantial regional coverage are the *Fairbanks Daily News-Miner* and the *Juneau Empire*. *Alaska Magazine* covers the state on a monthly basis and is distributed nationally.

RADIO & TELEVISION

Most larger Alaskan communities have their own commercial AM or FM radio stations. Alaska also has an extensive network of public stations, with National Public Radio/Alaska Public Radio affiliates based in 20 different towns. The flagship station is KSKA 91.1 FM in Anchorage, but public radio can also be heard in many of the smallest villages around the state. Native-owned KNBA 90.3 FM, in Anchorage, broadcasts a mix of music and programming (without ads) aimed at the state's large Native community.

Most Alaskan hotels and motels have cable or satellite television reception, providing a wide selection of channels. The primary Anchorage TV stations are KIMO channel 13 (ABC), KTVA channel 11 (CBS), KTUU channel 2 (NBC), KTBY channel 4 (Fox), and KAKM channel 7 (PBS). In Fairbanks they are KATN channel 2 (ABC), KTVF channel 11 (CBS and NBC), K07UU channel 7 (Fox), and KUAC channel 9 (PBS). In Juneau they are KJUD channel 8 (ABC) and KTOO channel 3 (PBS).

MONEY MATTERS

Prices throughout this guide are given for adults. Substantially reduced fees are almost always available for children, students, and senior citizens. For information on taxes, *see* Taxes.

ATMS

All the larger towns (and most places with a bank) in Alaska now have ATMs, but don't expect to find one in the remote Bush villages. Nearly all ATMs in Alaska charge a fee (typically $1.50) if you don't have an account.

CREDIT CARDS

Throughout this guide, the following abbreviations are used: AE, American Express; D, Discover; DC, Diners Club; MC, MasterCard; and V, Visa.

➤ REPORTING LOST CARDS: **American Express** (☎ 800/441–0519). **Diners Club** (☎ 800/234–6377). **Discover** (☎ 800/347–2683). **MasterCard**

(☎ 800/307–7309). **Visa** (☎ 800/
847–2911).

NATIONAL PARKS

Look into discount passes to save
money on park entrance fees. The
National Parks Pass ($50) gets you
and your companions free admission
to all parks for one year. (Camping
and parking are extra.) A percentage
of the proceeds from sales of the pass
will fund National Parks projects.
Both the Golden Age Passport ($10),
for those 62 and older, and the Golden
Access Passport (free), for travelers
with disabilities, entitle holders to free
entry to all national parks, plus 50%
off fees for the use of many park
facilities and services. You must show
proof of age and of U.S. citizenship or
permanent residency (such as a U.S.
passport, driver's license, or birth
certificate) and, if requesting Golden
Access, proof of disability. The Golden
Age and Golden Access passes are
available at all national parks wherever entrance fees are charged. The
National Parks Pass is available by
mail or through the Internet.

➤ PASSES BY MAIL: **National Park
Service** (✉ National Park Service/De-
partment of Interior, 1849 C St. NW,
Washington, DC 20240, ☎ 202/208–
4747, WEB www.nps.gov). **National
Parks Pass** (✉ 27540 Mentry Ave.,
Valencia, CA 91355, ☎ 888/467–
2757, WEB www.nationalparks.org).

OUTDOORS & SPORTS

FISHING

License fees for nonresidents are $10
for a 1-day permit, $20 for 3 days,
$30 for 7 days, $50 for 14 days, and
$100 for an annual license. If you're
going to be fishing for king salmon,
an additional stamp that doubles
these costs is required. Licenses are
also available in-state from sporting-
goods stores, charter-boat operators,
and fishing lodges.

➤ INFORMATION AND LICENSES: **Alaska
Department of Fish and Game** (✉ Box
25525, Juneau 99802-5525, ☎ 907/
465–4180 for seasons and regulations; 907/465–2376 for licenses,
WEB www.state.ak.us/local/akpages/
fish.game).

PACKING

Wherever you go in Alaska (and
especially in the Southeast), **be prepared for rain.** To keep yourself dry,
pack a collapsible umbrella or **bring a
rain slicker.** Not all of Alaska has the
fierce winters that are usually associated with the state. Winter in the
Southeast and South Central coastal
regions is relatively mild—Chicago
and Minneapolis experience harsher
weather than Juneau. It's a different
story in the Interior, where temperatures in the subzero range and biting
winds keep most visitors indoors.

The best way to keep warm under
colder conditions is to **wear layers of
clothing, starting with thermal underwear and socks.** The outermost layer
should be lightweight, windproof,
rainproof, and hooded. Down jackets
(and sleeping bags) have the disadvantage of becoming soggy when wet; the
newer synthetics (particularly wind-
block fabrics) are the materials of
choice, though wool is still used.
Footgear needs to be sturdy, and if
you're going into the backcountry,
be sure it's waterproof. Rubber boots
are often a necessity in coastal areas.
When wearing snow boots, be certain
they are not too tight. Restricting your
circulation will only make you colder.

Although Alaskan summers are mild,
it's a good idea to **bring along rain
gear, as sudden storms are common.**
An extra sweater or jacket for cool
evenings will come in handy.

Befitting the frontier image, dress is
mostly casual day and night. Bring
along one outfit that is appropriate
for "dress up," if you enjoy doing so,
though it's not necessary.

UVA/UVB **sunscreen, insect repellent,
and sunglasses are necessities.** A pair
of binoculars will help you track any
wildlife you encounter.

In your carry-on luggage, **pack an
extra pair of eyeglasses or contact
lenses** and **enough of any medication
you take** to last the entire trip. You
may also ask your doctor to write a
spare prescription using the drug's
generic name, since brand names may
vary from country to country. In
luggage to be checked, **never pack
prescription drugs or valuables.** To

avoid customs delays, carry medications in their original packaging. And don't forget to carry with you the addresses of offices that handle refunds of lost traveler's checks. Check *Fodor's How to Pack* (available in bookstores everywhere) for more tips.

CHECKING LUGGAGE

How many carry-on bags you can bring with you is up to the airline. Most allow two, but not always, so make sure that everything you carry aboard will fit under your seat or in the overhead bin, and get to the gate early. Note that if you have a seat at the back of the plane, you'll probably board first, while the overhead bins are still empty.

If you are flying internationally, note that baggage allowances may be determined not by piece but by weight—generally 88 pounds (40 kilograms) in first class, 66 pounds (30 kilograms) in business class, and 44 pounds (20 kilograms) in economy.

Airline liability for baggage is limited to $1,250 per person on flights within the United States. On international flights it amounts to $9.07 per pound or $20 per kilogram for checked baggage (roughly $640 per 70-pound bag) and $400 per passenger for unchecked baggage. You can buy additional coverage at check-in for about $10 per $1,000 of coverage, but it excludes a rather extensive list of items, shown on your airline ticket.

Before departure, **itemize your bags' contents** and their worth, and label the bags with your name, address, and phone number. (If you use your home address, cover it so potential thieves can't see it readily.) Inside each bag, **pack a copy of your itinerary.** At check-in, **make sure that each bag is correctly tagged** with the destination airport's three-letter code. If your bags arrive damaged or fail to arrive at all, file a written report with the airline before leaving the airport.

SAFETY

Alaska is big, wild, and not particularly forgiving, so travelers lacking outdoor experience need to take precautions when venturing away from the beaten path. If you lack backcountry skills or feel uncomfortable

handling yourself if a bear should approach (☞ Bears), take a guided trip instead or join a class at the National Outdoor Leadership School (☎ 907/745–4047, WEB www.nols.edu), which is based in Palmer (an hour north of Anchorage).

SENIOR-CITIZEN TRAVEL

The Alaska Railroad offers senior citizens a 50% discount during off-peak months (late September–early May). The Alaska Marine Highway offers discounted fares year-round. Alaska Direct Bus Lines offers a 10% discount for intercity travel.

To qualify for age-related discounts, **mention your senior-citizen status up front** when booking hotel reservations (not when checking out) and before you're seated in restaurants (not when paying the bill). When renting a car, ask about promotional car-rental discounts, which can be cheaper than senior-citizen rates.

➤ EDUCATIONAL PROGRAMS: **Elderhostel** (✉ 11 Ave. de Lafayette, Boston, MA 02111–1746, ☎ 877/426–8056, FAX 877/426–2166, WEB www.elderhostel.org). **Interhostel** (✉ University of New Hampshire, 6 Garrison Ave., Durham, NH 03824, ☎ 603/862–1147 or 800/733–9753, FAX 603/862–1113, WEB www.learn.unh.edu).

SHOPPING

The best buys in Alaska are products of native materials made by Native peoples and other artists and craftspeople living in the state. Before you buy, **make sure the local crafts are genuine.** The state has adopted two symbols that guarantee the authenticity of crafts made by Alaskans. A hand symbol indicates the item was made by one of Alaska's Native peoples. A polar bear verifies that the item was made in Alaska. If some items with these tags seem more expensive than you expected, examine them closely and you'll probably find that they are handmade, one-of-a-kind pieces.

Although these symbols are designed to ensure authentic Alaska and Native-made products, **it doesn't mean that items lacking them are not authentic.** This applies in particular to Native artists who may or may not go through the necessary paperwork to obtain the silver hand labels. They often come to town and sell items directly to shop owners for cash. It pays to shop around, ask questions, and learn about the different types of Native crafts from around the state.

SIGHTSEEING GUIDES

A couple of companies operate sightseeing tours statewide. For local sightseeing outfits in individual cities and towns, *see* Tours *in* the chapter A to Z sections.

➤ SIGHTSEEING-TOUR COMPANIES: **Alaska Sightseeing/Cruise West** (☎ 206/441–8687 or 800/426–7702, WEB www.cruisewest.com). **Glacier Bay Tours and Cruises** (☎ 907/697–2226 in summer; 800/451–5952 year-round, WEB www.glacierbaytours.com. **Gray Line of Alaska** (☎ 907/277–5581 or 800/544–2206, FAX 907/225–9386, WEB www.graylineofalaska.com).

STUDENTS IN ALASKA

Student discounts are available at many Alaskan museums and other attractions.

➤ I.D.s & SERVICES: **Council Travel** (CIEE; ✉ 205 E. 42nd St., 15th floor, New York, NY 10017, ☎ 212/822–2700 or 888/268–6245, FAX 212/822–2699, WEB www.councilexchanges.org) for mail orders only, in the United States. **Travel Cuts** (✉ 187 College St., Toronto, Ontario M5T 1P7, Canada, ☎ 416/979–2406; 800/667–2887 in Canada, FAX 416/979–8167, WEB www.travelcuts.com).

TAXES

SALES TAX

Alaska does not impose a state sales tax, but individual cities and boroughs have their own. Anchorage has no sales tax.

TIME

Nearly all of Alaska lies within the Alaska time zone, 20 hours behind Sydney, 9 hours behind London, 4 hours behind New York City, 3 hours behind Chicago, and 1 hour behind Los Angeles. The nearly unpopulated Aleutian Islands are in the same time zone as Hawaii, 5 hours behind the East Coast.

TIPPING

In addition to tipping waiters and waitresses, taxi drivers, and baggage handlers, it is common in Alaska to tip others who provide personalized services. Tour bus drivers who offer a particularly informative trip generally receive a tip from passengers at the end of the tour. A small amount left in your hotel room is also much appreciated by the cleaning staff. Fishing guides are commonly tipped around 10% by their clients, particularly if the guide helped them land a big one. In addition, gratuities may also be given to pilots following a particularly good flightseeing or bear-viewing trip, but the amount is up to your own discretion.

TOURS & PACKAGES

Because everything is prearranged on a prepackaged tour or independent vacation, you'll spend less time planning—and often get it all at a good price.

BOOKING WITH AN AGENT

Travel agents are excellent resources. However, it's a good idea to collect brochures from several agencies, as some agents' suggestions may be influenced by relationships with tour and package firms that reward them for volume sales. If you have a special interest, **find an agent with expertise in that area**; ASTA (☞ Travel Agencies) has a database of specialists worldwide.

Make sure your travel agent knows the accommodations and other services of the place they're recommending. Ask about the hotel's location; room size; beds; and whether it has a pool, room service, or programs for children, if you care about these. Has your agent been there in person or sent others whom you can contact?

Do some homework on your own, too: local tourism boards can provide information about lesser-known and small-niche operators, some of which may sell only direct.

BUYER BEWARE

Each year consumers are stranded or lose their money when tour operators—even large ones with excellent reputations—go out of business. So

check out the operator. Ask several travel agents about its reputation, and try to **book with a company that has a consumer-protection program.** (Look for information in the company's brochure.) In the United States, members of the National Tour Association and the United States Tour Operators Association are required to set aside funds to cover your payments and travel arrangements in the event that the company defaults. It's also a good idea to choose a company that participates in the American Society of Travel Agents' Tour Operator Program (TOP); ASTA will act as mediator in any disputes between you and your tour operator.

Remember that the more your package or tour includes the better you can predict the ultimate cost of your vacation. Make sure you know exactly what is covered, and **beware of hidden costs.** Are taxes, tips, and transfers included? Entertainment and excursions? These can add up.

➤ TOUR-OPERATOR RECOMMENDATIONS: **American Society of Travel Agents** (☞ Travel Agencies). **National Tour Association** (NTA; ✉ 546 E. Main St., Lexington, KY 40508, ☎ 859/226–4444 or 800/682–8886, WEB www.ntaonline.com). **United States Tour Operators Association** (USTOA; ✉ 342 Madison Ave., Suite 1522, New York, NY 10173, ☎ 212/599–6599 or 800/468–7862, FAX 212/599–6744, WEB www.ustoa.com).

FLIGHTSEEING

Although flightseeing is expensive, it's not only the best way to grasp the expansiveness and grandeur of the land but also the only way to reach remote parts of Alaska. However, it can be dangerous. Before your flight, contact the air tour operator to check how long the company has been in service, its accident/incident statistics, and its safety procedures. If possible, try to meet with and talk to your pilot before the trip. Know where you're going and how long the trip will take. Avoid trips with long stopovers in remote areas—drastic weather changes can result in the cancellation or complication of your return flight. Pay attention to the safety message at the start of the flight, especially noting

the location of emergency survival gear. The long distances, mountainous terrain, and challenging weather conditions are all hazardous factors, but pilot error, due sometimes to passenger interference, is often involved. Never push a pilot to do something he or she is reluctant to do, such as circle low over a bear, and never pressure the pilot to hurry up. It is much better to miss your scheduled landing or departure of your ship than to push a pilot to fly in unsafe weather conditions.

For flightseeing operators, *see* regional A to Z sections.

GROUP TOURS

Among companies that sell tours to Alaska, the following are nationally known, have a proven reputation, and offer plenty of options. The classifications used below represent different price categories, and you'll probably encounter these terms when talking to a travel agent or tour operator. The key difference is usually in accommodations, which run from budget to better, and better-yet to best.

➤ SUPER-DELUXE: **Abercrombie & Kent** (✉ 1520 Kensington Rd., Suite 212, Oak Brook, IL 60521-2141, ☎ 630/954–2944 or 800/323–7308, FAX 630/954–3324).

➤ DELUXE: **Maupintour** (✉ 1421 Research Park Dr., Suite 300, Lawrence, KS 66049-3858, ☎ 785/843–1211 or 800/255–4266, FAX 785/331–1057). **Tauck Tours** (✉ Box 5027, 276 Post Rd. W, Westport, CT 06881-5027, ☎ 203/226–6911 or 800/468–2825, FAX 203/222–7702, WEB www.tauck.com).

➤ DELUXE/FIRST-CLASS: **Globus** (✉ 5301 S. Federal Circle, Littleton, CO 80123-2980, ☎ 303/797–2800 or 800/221–0090, FAX 303/347–2080).

➤ FIRST-CLASS AND TOURIST-RANGE: **Brendan Tours** (✉ 15137 Califa St., Van Nuys, CA 91411, ☎ 818/785–9696 or 800/421–8446, FAX 818/902–9876). **Collette Tours** (✉ 162 Middle St., Pawtucket, RI 02860, ☎ 401/728–3805 or 800/340–5158, FAX 401/728–4745). **Gadabout Tours** (✉ 700 E. Tahquitz Canyon Way, Palm Springs, CA 92262-6767, ☎ 760/325–5556 or 800/952–5068, FAX 760/325–5127).

Mayflower Tours (✉ Box 490, 1225 Warren Ave., Downers Grove, IL 60515, ☎ 630/435–8235 or 800/ 323–7604, FAX 630/960–3575). **Trafalgar Tours** (✉ 11 E. 26th St., Suite 1300, New York, NY 10010, ☎ 212/ 689–8977 or 800/854–0103, FAX 800/ 457–6644).

➤ BUDGET: **Cosmos** (☞ Globus).

PACKAGES

Like group tours, independent vacation packages are available from major tour operators and airlines. Packages may include fly-drive itineraries with bed-and-breakfast accommodations or ferry-liner tours. The companies listed below offer vacation packages in a broad price range.

➤ INDEPENDENT VACATION PACKAGES: **Alaska Airlines Vacations** (✉ Box 69677, Seattle, WA 98168, ☎ 800/ 468–2248, WEB www.alaskaair.com). **Alaska Bound** (✉ 321 E. Lake St., Petoskey, MI 49770, ☎ 616/439– 3000 or 888/252–7527, FAX 616/439– 3004, WEB www.alaskabound.com). **Alaska Rainforest Tours** (✉ 1873 Shell Simmons Dr., Juneau, AK 99801-9398, ☎ 907/463–3466, FAX 907/463–4453 or 800/463–4453, WEB www.alaskarainforesttours.com). **Gorp Travel** (✉ 10055 Westmoor Dr., Suite 215, Westminster, CO 80021, ☎ 720/877–8500 or 877/440– 4677, FAX 303/635–0658, WEB www. gorp.com). **Gray Line of Alaska** (☎ 907/277–5581 or 800/544–2206, WEB www.graylineofalaska.com). **Knightly Tours** (✉ Box 16366, Seattle, WA 98116, ☎ 206/938–8567 or 800/426–2123, FAX 206/938–8498). **Viking Travel** (✉ Box 787, Petersburg 99833, ☎ 907/772–3818 or 800/327–2571, FAX 907/772–3940, WEB www.alaska-ala-carte.com).

➤ FROM THE U.K.: **Arctic Experience Ltd.** (✉ 29 Nork Way, Banstead, SM7 1PB, ☎ 01737/218–800). **Kuoni Travel** (✉ Kuoni House, Dorking, RH5 4AZ, ☎ 01306/742–222). **Vacation Canada** (✉ Cambridge House, 8 Cambridge St., Glasgow G2 3DZ, ☎ 0141/332–1511 or 0345/090–905).

THEME TRIPS

➤ BICYCLING: **Alaska Bicycle Adventures** (✉ 907 E. Dowling Rd., Suite 29, Anchorage 99518, ☎ 907/243–

2329 or 800/770–7242, FAX 907/243– 4985, WEB www.alaskabike.com). **Backroads** (✉ 801 Cedar St., Berkeley, CA 94710-1800, ☎ 510/527– 1555 or 800/462–2848, FAX 510/527– 1444, WEB www.backroads.com). **Timberline** (✉ 7975 E. Harvard, No. J, Denver, CO 80231, ☎ 303/759– 3804 or 800/417–2453, FAX 303/368– 1651, WEB www.timbertours.com).

➤ BIRD-WATCHING: **Victor Emanuel Nature Tours** (✉ Box 33008, Austin, TX 78764, ☎ 512/328–5221 or 800/ 328–8368, FAX 512/328–2919, WEB www. ventbird.com). **Wilderness Birding Adventures** (✉ 5515 Wild Mountain Rd., Eagle River 99577, ☎ FAX 907/694– 7442, WEB www.wildernessbirding. com). **Wings** (✉ 1643 N. Alvernon Way, Suite 105, Tucson, AZ 85712, ☎ 520/320–9868 or 888/293–6443, FAX 520/320–9373, WEB www. wingsbirds.com).

➤ CAMPING: **Alaska Wildland Adventures** (✉ Box 389, Girdwood 99587, ☎ 907/783–2928 or 800/334–8730, FAX 907/783–2130, WEB www. alaskarivertrips.com). **CampAlaska Tours** (✉ Box 872247, Wasilla, AK 99687, ☎ 907/376–9438 or 800/ 376–9438, FAX 907/376–2353, WEB www.campalaska.com).

➤ CANOEING, KAYAKING, AND RAFTING: **Alaska Discovery** (✉ 5449 Shaune Dr., Suite 4, Juneau 99801, ☎ 907/ 780–6226 or 800/586–1911, FAX 907/ 780–4220, WEB www.akdiscovery. com). **Alaska River Adventures** (✉ Box 725, Cooper Landing 99572, ☎ 907/595–2000 or 888/836–9027, FAX 907/595–1533, WEB www. alaskariveradventures.com). **Alaska Wildland Adventures** (☞ Camping). **Alaska Worldwide Adventures** (✉ Box 220204, Anchorage 99522, ☎ 907/349–2964 or 888/842–2964, FAX 907/344–6877). **CampAlaska Tours** (☞ Camping). **James Henry River Journeys** (✉ Box 807, Bolinas, CA 94924, ☎ 415/868–1836 or 800/ 786–1830, FAX 415/868–9033). **OARS** (✉ Box 67, Angels Camp, CA 95222, ☎ 209/736–4677 or 800/346–6277, FAX 209/736–2902, WEB www.oars. com). **REI Adventures** (✉ Box 1938, Sumner, WA 98390-0800, ☎ 800/622– 2236, FAX 253/395–8160, WEB www. rei.com). **TrekAmerica** (✉ Box 189, Rockaway, NJ 07866, ☎ 973/983–

1144 or 800/221–0596, FAX 973/983–8551).

➤ DOGSLEDDING/IDITAROD: **Birch Trails Sled Dog Tours** (✉ 22719 Robinson Rd., Chugiak 99567, ☎ FAX 907/688–5713). **Chugach Express Dog Sled Tours** (✉ Box 261, Girdwood 99587, ☎ 907/783–2266, FAX 907/783–2625). **Godwin Glacier Dog Sled Tours** (✉ Box 2711, Seward 99664, ☎ 907/224–8239 or 888/989–8239, WEB www.alaskadogsled.com). **Hush Puppy Kennel** (✉ Box 8621, Indian 99540, ☎ 907/566–5767). **Mush a Dog Team** (✉ 20644 Birchwood Loop Rd., Chugiak 99567, ☎ 907/688–1391, FAX 907/688–7731). **Sky Trekking Alaska** (✉ Box 871370, Wasilla 99687, ☎ FAX 907/373–4966, ☎ 800/525–3153, WEB www.skytrekkingalaska.com). **Sourdough Outfitters** (✉ Box 90, Bettles 99726, ☎ 907/692–5252, FAX 907/692–5557, WEB www.sourdoughoutfitters.com).

➤ FERRY TOURS: **Knightly Tours** (☞ Packages). **Viking Travel** (☞ Packages).

➤ HIKING: **Alaska Wilderness Experience** (☞ Canoeing, Kayaking, and Rafting). **Backroads** (☞ Bicycling). **Mountain Travel-Sobek** (✉ 6420 Fairmount Ave., El Cerrito, CA 94530, ☎ 510/527–8100 or 800/227–2384, FAX 510/525–7710, WEB www.mtsobek.com). **Timberline** (☞ Bicycling).

➤ LEARNING VACATIONS: **Earthwatch Institute** (✉ Box 9104, 680 Mt. Auburn St., Watertown, MA 02272, ☎ 617/926–8200 or 800/776–0188, FAX 617/926–8532). **National Audubon Society** (✉ 700 Broadway, New York, NY 10003, ☎ 212/979–3066, FAX 212/353–0190). **Natural Habitat Adventures** (✉ 2945 Center Green Ct., Boulder, CO 80301, ☎ 303/449–3711 or 800/543–8917, FAX 303/449–3712). **Nature Expeditions International** (✉ 6400 E. El Dorado Circle, Suite 210, Tucson, AZ 85715, ☎ 520/721–6712 or 800/869–0639, FAX 520/721–6719). **Naturequest** (✉ 30872 South Coast Hwy., Suite 185, Laguna Beach, CA 92651, ☎ 949/499–9561 or 800/369–3033, FAX 949/499–0812). **Oceanic Society Expeditions** (✉ Fort Mason Center, Bldg. E, San Francisco, CA 94123-1394, ☎ 415/441–1106 or 800/326–7491, FAX 415/474–3395). **Questers** (✉ 381 Park Ave. S,

New York, NY 10016, ☎ 212/251–0444 or 800/468–8668, FAX 212/251–0890). **Sierra Club** (✉ 85 2nd St., 2nd floor, San Francisco, CA 94105, ☎ 415/977–5522, FAX 415/977–5795). **Smithsonian Study Tours and Seminars** (✉ 1100 Jefferson Dr. SW, Room 3045, MRC 702, Washington, DC 20560, ☎ 202/357–4700, FAX 202/633–9250).

➤ NATIVE TOURS: **A.L.E.U.T. Tours** (✉ Unalaska, ☎ 907/581–6001). **Alexander's Overnight River Adventure** (✉ Box 62, Nenana 99760, ☎ 907/474–3924). **Athabasca Cultural Journeys** (☎ 907/829–2261 or 800/423–0094). **Cape Fox Tours** (✉ Box 6656, Ketchikan 99901, ☎ 907/225–4846, WEB www.capefoxtours.com). **Dig Afognak** (✉ Afognak Native Corporation, 215 Mission Rd., Suite 212, Kodiak 99615, ☎ 907/486–6014 or 800/770–6014, WEB www.afognak.com/dig). **Kiana Lodge** (✉ Box 210269, Anchorage 99521, ☎ 907/333–5866, FAX 907/338–8447). **Northern Alaska Tour Company** (✉ Box 82991, Fairbanks 99708, ☎ 907/474–8600 or 800/474–1986, FAX 907/474–4767, WEB www.northernalaska.com). **Tour Arctic** (✉ 1001 E. Benson Blvd., Anchorage 99508, ☎ 907/265–4157 or 800/478–2000, FAX 907/265–4123). **Tundra Tours** (✉ Box 189, Barrow 99723, ☎ 907/852–3900 or 800/478–8520, WEB www.topoftheworldhotel.com).

➤ NATURAL HISTORY: **Alaska Up Close** (✉ Box 32666, Juneau 99803, ☎ 907/789–9544, FAX 907/789–3205). **Alaska Wildland Adventures** (☞ Camping). **Great Alaska Adventure Lodge** (✉ 33881 Sterling Hwy., Sterling 99672, ☎ 907/262–4515 or 800/544–2261, FAX 907/262–8797 in summer, WEB www.greatalaska.com). **Wilderness Birding Adventures** (☞ Bird-Watching).

➤ PHOTOGRAPHY: **Joseph Van Os Photo Safaris** (☎ 206/463–5383, WEB www.photosafaris.com). **Steve Gilroy's Alaska Photo Tours** (✉ Box 141, Talkeetna 99676, ☎ 907/733–3051 or 800/799–3051, FAX 907/733–3052, WEB www.alaska.net/~photoak).

➤ RV TOURS: **Alaska Highway Cruises** (✉ 18384 Redmond Way, Redmond, WA 98052, ☎ 425/497–

1212 or 800/323–5757, FAX 425/882–2479, WEB www.alaskarv.com).

➤ SPORTFISHING: **Alaska River Adventures** (☞ Canoeing, Kayaking, and Rafting). **Alaska Wildland Adventures** (☞ Camping). **Cutting Loose Fishing Expeditions** (✉ Box 447, Winter Park, FL 32790-0447, ☎ 407/629–4700 or 800/533–4746, FAX 407/740–7816). **Fishing International** (✉ Box 2132, Santa Rosa, CA 95405, ☎ 707/542–4242 or 800/950–4242, FAX 707/526–3474, WEB www.fishinginternational.com). **Great Alaska Adventure Lodge** (☞ Natural History). **Rod & Reel Adventures** (✉ 566 Thomson La., Copperopolis, CA 95228, ☎ 209/785–0444, FAX 209/785–0447, WEB www.rodreeladventures.com). **Sport Fishing Alaska** (✉ 9310 Shorecrest Dr., Anchorage 99515, ☎ 907/344–8674 or 888/552–8674, FAX 907/243–9447, WEB www.alaskatripplanners.com).

➤ WILDERNESS HIGH ADVENTURES: **Alaska-Denali Guiding** (✉ Box 566, Talkeetna 99676, ☎ 907/733–2649, FAX 907/733–1362, WEB www.denaliexpeditions.com). **Brooks Range Aviation** (✉ Box 10, Bettles 99726, ☎ 907/692–5444 or 800/692–5443, FAX 907/692–2185, WEB www.brooksrange.com). **Ketchum Air Service** (✉ Box 190588, Anchorage 99519, ☎ 907/243–5525 or 800/433–9114, FAX 907/243–8311, WEB www.ketchumair.com). **Sourdough Outfitters** (☞ Dogsledding).

TRAIN TRAVEL

The state-owned Alaska Railroad has service connecting Seward, Anchorage, Denali National Park, and Fairbanks. Amtrak serves Seattle and Vancouver; VIA Rail Canada serves Vancouver and Prince Rupert, British Columbia.

Travel aboard the Alaska Railroad is leisurely (Anchorage to Fairbanks is an all-day trip), so you can enjoy spectacular scenery along the way. Some cars have narration, and food is available onboard in the dining car and at the café. And unlike bus travel, train travel allows you to get up and stretch your legs. Some private tour companies that offer a more glitzy trip between Anchorage and Fairbanks hook their luxury railcars to the train. For a less expensive alterna-

tive, **ride one of the public dome cars,** owned and operated by the railroad. Seating in the public cars is unassigned, and passengers take turns under the observation dome. The railroad's public cars are a great place to meet resident Alaskans.

Except for the Seward–Anchorage leg, all service operates year-round. Trains run daily in summer; service is reduced from September to late May. Dining cars are available on all trains.

For a scenic and historic trip between Skagway and Fraser, British Columbia, take the White Pass & Yukon Route, which follows the treacherous path taken by prospectors during the Klondike gold rush of 1897–98. A bus links the terminal at Fraser with Whitehorse, capital of the Yukon Territory.

CUTTING COSTS

The **AlaskaPass** allows unlimited travel on bus, ferry, and rail lines in Alaska; *see* Cutting Costs *in* Boat & Ferry Travel.

FARES & SCHEDULES

Tickets can be purchased in advance over the phone using a credit card. If your reservation is a month or more ahead of time the company will mail you the ticket, otherwise travelers can pick them up at the departure station. Travel agents also sell tickets for travel aboard the Alaska Railroad.

➤ TRAIN INFORMATION: **Alaska Railroad** (✉ Box 107500, Anchorage 99510, ☎ 907/265–2494 in Anchorage; 907/458–6025 in Fairbanks; 800/544–0552, FAX 907/265–2323, WEB www.akrr.com). **Amtrak** (☎ 800/872–7245). **VIA Rail Canada** (☎ 800/561–3949). **White Pass & Yukon Route** (✉ Box 435, Skagway 99840, ☎ 907/983–2217; 800/343–7373 in the U.S. and Canada, WEB www.whitepassrailroad.com).

PAYING

Cash, Discover, Visa, and MasterCard are accepted.

RESERVATIONS

Advance reservations are highly recommended for midsummer train travel, particularly between Seward and Anchorage and between Anchorage and Denali National Park.

TRANSPORTATION AROUND ALASKA

Visitors to Alaska arrive by air, highway, and aboard ships and ferries. Cruise ships are a particularly popular way to travel, especially in Southeast Alaska, where many towns (including the state capital of Juneau) are not accessible by road. The Alaska Marine Highway ferry system provides car and passenger service throughout Southeast Alaska, as well as a number of towns in South Central Alaska and out to the Aleutian Islands.

The famous Alaska Highway is the primary road access into the state, starting in Dawson Creek, British Columbia, and continuing 1,390 mi to Delta Junction, Alaska. A network of two-lane highways connects the main towns and cities in South Central and Interior Alaska, including Anchorage and Fairbanks. Jet service is available to Alaska's cities and larger towns. Smaller Bush planes (sometimes on floats) are the lifeblood of more remote parts of Alaska.

TRAVEL AGENCIES

A good travel agent puts your needs first. Look for an agency that has been in business at least five years, emphasizes customer service, and has someone on staff who specializes in your destination. In addition, **make sure the agency belongs to a professional trade organization.** The American Society of Travel Agents (ASTA), with more than 26,000 members in some 170 countries, is the largest and most influential in the field. Operating under the motto "Without a travel agent, you're on your own," it maintains and enforces a strict code of ethics and will step in to help mediate any agent-client disputes if necessary. ASTA also maintains a Web site that includes a directory of agents. (If a travel agency is also acting as your tour operator, *see* Buyer Beware *in* Tours & Packages.)

➤ LOCAL AGENT REFERRALS: American Society of Travel Agents (ASTA; ☎ 800/965-2782 24-hr hot line, FAX 703/739-7642, WEB www.astanet. com). Association of British Travel Agents (✉ 68–71 Newman St., London W1T 3AH, U.K., ☎ 020/7637–2444, FAX 020/7637–0713, WEB www. abtanet.com). Association of Canadian Travel Agents (✉ 130 Albert St., Suite 1705, Ottawa, Ontario K1P 5G4, Canada, ☎ 613/237–3657, FAX 613/ 237–7502, WEB www.acta.net). Australian Federation of Travel Agents (✉ Level 3, 309 Pitt St., Sydney NSW 2000, Australia, ☎ 02/9264–3299, FAX 02/9264–1085, WEB www.afta.com. au). Travel Agents' Association of New Zealand (✉ Box 1888, Wellington 10033, New Zealand, ☎ 04/499–0104, FAX 04/499–0827, WEB www. taanz.org.nz).

VISITOR INFORMATION

The Alaska Travel Industry Association (a partnership between the state and private businesses) publishes the *Alaska Vacation Planner,* a free comprehensive information source for statewide travel year-round. Alaska's regional tourism councils distribute vacation planners highlighting their local attractions. The official State of Alaska Web site contains additional information and links.

➤ STATEWIDE INFORMATION: **Alaska Travel Industry Association** (✉ Box 143361, Anchorage 99514–3361, ☎ 907/929–2200 or 800/862–5275, WEB www.travelalaska.com). **Alaska Internet Travel Guide** (✉ WEB www. alaskaone.com). **AlaskaGuidebook. com** (✉ WEB www.alaskaguidebook. com). **Alaska Public Lands Information Center** (✉ WEB www.nps.gov/ aplic). **Alaska Marine Highway System** (✉ ☎ 800/642-0066, WEB www. dot.state.ak.us/ferry).

State of Alaska (✉ Box 110809, Juneau 99811-0809, ☎ 907/465–2012, FAX 907/465–3767, WEB www. state.ak.us).

➤ REGIONAL INFORMATION: **Kenai Peninsula Tourism Marketing Council** (✉ 150 N. Willow, Kenai 99611, ☎ 907/283–3850 or 800/535–3624, FAX 907/283–2838, WEB www. kenaipeninsula.org). **Southwest Alaska Municipal Conference** (✉ 3300 Arctic Blvd., Suite 203, Anchorage 99503, ☎ 907/562–7380, FAX 907/ 562–0438, WEB www.swamc.org). **Southeast Alaska Tourism Council** (✉ Box 20710, Juneau 99802-0710, ☎ 907/586–4777 or 800/423–0568,

FAX 907/463–4961, WEB www.
alaskainfo.org).

➤ CITY INFORMATION: **Juneau Web**
(WEB www.juneau.com). **Alaska Anchorage** (WEB www.anchorage.net). **Fairbanks** (WEB www.explorefairbanks.com).

➤ BRITISH COLUMBIA AND YUKON:
Tourism British Columbia (✉ Box
9830, Victoria, British Columbia
V8W 9W5, ☎ 800/435–5622, WEB
www.hellobc.com). **Tourism Yukon**
(✉ Box 2745, Whitehorse, Yukon
Territory Y1A 5B9, ☎ 867/667–
5340, FAX 867/667–3546). **Tourism
Victoria** (✉ 1175 Douglas St., Suite
710, V8W 2E1, ☎ 250/953–2033,
FAX 250/361–9733). **Vancouver Tourist InfoCentre** (✉ 200 Burrard St.,
☎ 604/683–2000).

➤ IN THE U.K.: **Alaskan Tourist Information Board** (✉ 2 The Billings, Wal-
nut Tree Close, Guildford, AK GU1
4YD, ☎ 0891/100–727, FAX 01483/
451–361). Calls are charged at 50p
per minute at all times.

WEB SITES

Do check out the World Wide Web
when you're planning your trip.
You'll find everything from weather
forecasts to virtual tours of famous
cities. Be sure to **visit Fodors.com**
(www.fodors.com), a complete travel-
planning site. You can research prices
and book plane tickets, hotel rooms,
rental cars, vacation packages, and
more. In addition, you can post your
pressing questions in the Travel Talk
section. Other planning tools include
a currency converter and weather
reports, and there are loads of links to
other travel resources.

WHEN TO GO

Because Alaska is so big, each region
experiences a different climate, and
seasons come and go at different
times of the year.

Most visitors choose summer because
of the warmer temperatures and long
evenings with midnight sun. From
June through August, you can expect
pleasantly warm, long days—Fairbanks shines under a staggering 22
hours of daylight in late June—and
cool, comfortable nights. In summer,

the sun does not set for more than
2½ months in Barrow, north of the
Arctic Circle (approximately a third
of Alaska lies north of this invisible
line). Even as far south as Juneau, you
can see a glow of twilight in the sky
at midnight. In winter, of course, the
situation is reversed, and the sun does
not rise for more than two months in
Alaska's northernmost regions. South
Central Alaska, including the Anchorage area, gets about 5½–6 hours of
daylight in mid-December.

Adapting to this Arctic pattern of
light, all life in Alaska crowds everything it can into the long period of
sunlight—plants grow profusely (cabbages sometimes top 100 pounds and
delphiniums can reach 12 ft tall) and
bloom furiously. If you're camping
during these midsummer months, a
sleep shade may be more valuable
than a flashlight.

Keep in mind that Alaska is not a
land of perpetual ice and snow—97%
of the state is snow-free during those
long summer days. In fact, in parts of
the Interior, temperatures can reach
into the 90s, and thunderstorms are
frequent.

Of course, with fair weather comes
an onslaught of tourists and generally higher prices for rooms, tours,
and transportation. Summer, particularly late June through July, also
brings on plagues of mosquitoes,
thanks to breakup (when frozen
ground thaws), which creates the
soggy little bogs these nuisances
just love. The peak summer travel
months, July and August, are also
the rainiest throughout South Central and Interior Alaska. Fortunately,
in perpetually wet Southeast Alaska,
these months are the driest portion
of the year.

The weather can change in dramatic
and unpredictable fashion. Storms
brewed in the Gulf of Alaska, for
instance, can arise in the blink of an
eye. The frigid air of the polar regions
can mean snowstorms on the 4th of
July—and a hot summer day on the
5th. Southwest Alaska and the Aleutian chain are rained and fogged in all
too frequently, but just when you've

given up on the weather, the clouds will miraculously vanish. Throughout the state, winds are apt to race from the mountains with no warning. These winds are so strong they can wrestle a freestanding tent from your hands and send it tumbling over the tundra.

To avoid the summer crowds and peak season prices, go during spring or fall. May and June are the driest months in Southeast Alaska. Late August through early September (depending on the latitude) brings special autumn bonuses: above the brilliant foliage, skies may be unbelievably blue, and the mountains and glaciers are often enhanced by fresh dustings of snow. Daytime temperatures should still be quite pleasant, though evenings get progressively nippier.

Contrary to popular belief, Alaska does not close down for winter. Yes, it gets cold, and the nights grow long,

but Alaskans have come up with some rousing means of taking their minds off the weather. Winter is the season for skiing, sledding, ice-skating, dog mushing, ice fishing, and other sports. Major events such as the Iditarod Trail Sled Dog Race, held in March, help both residents and visitors shrug off the cold. The annual Fur Rendezvous, in Anchorage each February, is a raucous, action-packed celebration, highlighted by the traditional Miners' and Trappers' Costume Ball. The long nights are also ideal for viewing the northern lights, particularly in the Fairbanks area.

CLIMATE

The following are the average daily maximum and minimum temperatures for several Alaskan cities.

► FORECASTS: **Weather Channel Connection** (☎ 900/932–8437), 95¢ per minute from a Touch-Tone phone.

ANCHORAGE

Jan.	22F	– 6C	May	55F	13C	Sept.	55F	13C
	7	–14		38	3		40	4
Feb.	25F	4C	June	62F	17C	Oct.	41F	5C
	9	13		47	8		27	– 3
Mar.	31F	– 1C	July	65F	18C	Nov.	27F	– 3C
	14	–10		50	10		14	–10
Apr.	43F	6C	Aug.	63F	17C	Dec.	20F	– 7C
	27	– 3		49	9		6	–14

BARROW

Jan.	– 9F	–23C	May	24F	– 4C	Sept.	34F	1C
	–22	–30		13	–11		27	– 3
Feb.	–12F	–24C	June	39F	4C	Oct.	22F	– 6C
	25	–32		29	– 2		12	–11
Mar.	– 8F	–22C	July	46F	8C	Nov.	7F	–14C
	22	–30		33	1		– 5	–21
Apr.	7F	–14C	Aug.	44F	7C	Dec.	– 4F	–20C
	8	–22		33	1		–17	–27

FAIRBANKS

Jan.	– 2F	–19C	May	59F	15C	Sept.	54F	12C
	–20	–29		35	2		33	1
Feb.	11F	–12C	June	71F	22C	Oct.	35F	2C
	10	–23		46	8		18	– 8
Mar.	23F	– 5C	July	72F	22C	Nov.	12F	–11C
	4	–20		48	9		– 5	–21
Apr.	42F	6C	Aug.	66F	19C	Dec.	1F	–17C
	17	– 8		44	7		–16	–27

FESTIVALS AND SEASONAL EVENTS

Top seasonal events include the Anchorage Fur Rendezvous in February, the Iditarod Trail Sled Dog Race in March, Juneau's Alaska Folk Festival in April, Sitka's Alaska Day Celebration in October, and Fairbanks's Oktoberfest in the fall. For exact dates, request a copy of the state "Vacation Planner" from the Alaska Division of Tourism (☞ Visitor Information *in* Smart Travel Tips A to Z).

➤ JAN.: Bethel's **Kuskokwim 300** (☎ 907/543–3300) is one of the state's premier sled-dog races. At Seward's **Polar Bear Jump Off,** (☎ 907/224–5230) bare skin meets barely above-freezing water. **Anchorage Folk Festival,** at the University of Alaska Anchorage, features hundreds of performers and musical workshops over two busy weekends. ☎ *907/566–2334,* WEB www.folkmusic.org.

➤ MID-JAN.–FEB.: **Sled-Dog Racing** (☎ 907/562–2235) season in Anchorage begins with sprints every weekend.

➤ EARLY FEB.: **Tent City Winter Festival** (☎ 800/367–9745) in Wrangell captures the flavor of Alaska's early days. At the **Cordova Iceworm Festival,** (☎ 907/424–7260) a 140-ft ice worm parades through city streets. Other events include a talent show and fun fair.

➤ MID-FEB.: Participants in the **Yukon Quest International Sled Dog Race** (☎ 907/452–7954, WEB www.yukonquest.com) mush their way between Whitehorse, the Yukon Territory, and Fairbanks. Anchorage's **Fur Rendezvous** (☎ 907/277–8615, WEB www.furrondy.net) delivers more than 150 events—from snowshoe softball to the Open World Championship Sled Dog Races.

➤ EARLY MAR.: The **World Ice Art Championships and Winter Carnival** (☎ 907/452–1105) brings the finest ice artists to downtown Fairbanks.

➤ EARLY–MID-MAR.: The **Iditarod Trail Sled Dog Race** (☎ 907/376–5155 or 800/545–6874, WEB www.iditarod.com) stretches 1,049 mi from Anchorage to Nome. More than 70 dog teams compete in the world's premier sled-dog race.

➤ MID-MAR.: The **Bering Sea Ice Golf Classic** (☎ 907/443–5535) is played with orange golf balls on the pack ice of the Bering Sea near Nome during the Iditarod. The seasonal "Nome National Forest" (150 or so abandoned Christmas trees) provide forest cover.

➤ LATE MAR.: The three-day **Camai Dance Festival** (☎ 907/543–1977, WEB www.bethelarts.com) in Bethel attracts dance groups from throughout Alaska and also from outside the state.

➤ EARLY APR.: The **World Extreme Skiing Championships** (☎ 907/835–2108, WEB www.wesc.com) lures the world's best daredevil skiers to Valdez. The **Alaska Folk Festival** (☎ 907/463–3316, WEB www.juneau.com/aff) in Juneau is a mix of music, handmade crafts, and foods.

➤ MID-APR.: The **Alyeska Spring Carnival** (☎ 907/754–2259 or 800/880–3880) holds court at the Alyeska Resort & Ski Area, 40 mi southeast of Anchorage. The featured event is the Slush Cup in which skiers and snowboarders attempt to ski across a slushy pond at the base of the mountain.

➤ LATE APR.–EARLY MAY: During the **Copper River Delta Shorebird Festival** (☎ 907/424–7260) in Cordova, there are tours to beaches to witness the migration of millions of shorebirds.

➤ MID-MAY: The **Little Norway Festival** (☎ 907/772–4636) in picturesque Petersburg salutes the town's Scandinavian heritage.

➤ LATE MAY: The **Kodiak Crab Festival** (☎ 907/486–5557) brings good food, a parade, footrace, survival suit race, and the blessing of the fleet. **Juneau Jazz 'n Classics** (☎ 907/463–3378, WEB www.juneau.com/music) features performances by regionally and nationally known classical and jazz musicians over a 10-day period.

➤ JUNE: The **Sitka Summer Music Festival** (☎ 907/747–6774, WEB www.sitkamusicfestival.org) is a monthlong series of chamber music performances.

➤ LATE JUNE: The **Midnight Sun Baseball Game** (☎ 907/451–0095) celebrates the longest day of the year in Fairbanks. The game begins at 10:30 PM with no need for stadium lights.

➤ JULY 4: The **Mt. Marathon Race** (☎ 907/224–8051) in Seward is a rugged race up the 3,000-ft mountain. The best vantage point is right below the trail's starting line.

➤ MID-JULY: The **World Eskimo–Indian Olympics** (☎ 907/452–6646) in Fairbanks tests participants in such skills as ear pulling, the knuckle hop, and the blanket toss.

➤ MID-AUG.: **Southeast Alaska State Fair**(☎ 907/766–2476) brings exhibits, music, and other fun-filled activities to the Haines Fairgrounds.

➤ LATE AUG.–EARLY SEPT.: The **Alaska State Fair** (☎ 907/745–4827 or 800/850–3247, WEB www.alaskastatefair.org) in Palmer is the state's big end-of-summer blowout. Don't miss the famous 90-pound cabbages and other gargantuan vegetables.

➤ MID-OCT.: The **Alaska Day Celebration** (☎ 907/747–5940) brings out the whole town of Sitka to celebrate October 18, the day the United States acquired Alaska from Russia. The weeklong festival includes a period costume ball and a parade. The **Quyana Alaska Native Dance Festival** (☎ 907/274–3611) in Anchorage provides a taste of Alaska's Native culture.

➤ MID-NOV.: The **Athabascan Old Time Fiddling Festival** (☎ 907/452–1825) enlivens Fairbanks with traditional Native music.

➤ LATE NOV.: The **Carrs Great Alaska Shoot-out** (☎ 907/786–1230, WEB www.shootout.net) takes place at Sullivan Arena in Anchorage, where some of the best college basketball teams in the country compete.

➤ EARLY DEC.: The offbeat **Talkeetna Winterfest** (☎ 907/733–2330) combines competitive athletic events for women in the Wilderness Women Contest with competitive bidding for eligible mountain man bachelors at the Bachelor Society Ball.

DESTINATION: ALASKA

THE MANY ALASKAS

ALASKA HAS ALWAYS HELD a special place in the public imagination. Early explorers wrote of an otherworldly landscape populated by hardy Native peoples, of a place where gold filled the hills, where salmon were so abundant that you could walk across streams on their backs, and where wild animals roamed the seemingly infinite forests. Today's travelers come for different reasons, but they still discover a vibrant cultural heritage, a stunning landscape, great fishing, and abundant wildlife in one of the world's most magnificent wild places.

Alaska is a place where northern lights color the cold winter sky, where the summer sun circles the horizon, where Native people still hunt whale and walrus, where brown bears catch salmon in wide rivers, where mountaineers work their way across glaciers, where bush pilots land floatplanes on remote backcountry lakes, where crab boats toss in the wild stormy waves of the Bering Sea, and where vast stretches of land lie undeveloped and unpeopled. If one word could be applied to Alaska, it would be "wilderness." If you enjoy the outdoors and wild places, you will fall head over heels in love with this vast and extraordinarily beautiful state.

Alaska occupies the westernmost edge of the North American continent. Canada's Yukon Territory lies to the east. Mother Russia is westward just across the Bering Strait. It is a massive place: a map of Alaska superimposed on the continental United States would stretch from the Atlantic to the Pacific and from Canada to Mexico. Alaskans enjoy telling how they could cut Alaska in half and still make Texas the third-largest state. Then they brag about having the highest mountain in North America (Mt. McKinley), the nation's biggest oil field (Prudhoe Bay), and a glacier larger than Rhode Island (Matanuska Glacier). Some of its citizens live closer to Japan than to their own state capital, Juneau.

But it is more than scale and geography—and more than a tired list of superlatives—that sets Alaska apart from the rest of the country. For the visitor, Alaska is youth, energy, space, wildness. A traveler to Alaska senses excitement, a feeling of adventure, the moment he or she steps ashore from a cruise ship in a misty port or arrives by jetliner in a northern city where the architecture is a haphazard blend of back-home modern and frontier shabby.

There is something different about Alaska. For many visitors, it is almost like a first trip to a foreign land. Yes, the language is the same. There are Big Macs and Wal-Mart stores. Summertime temperatures are comfortable, a bit cooler than in Seattle or Vancouver, British Columbia, along the coast; it's even warmer in the Interior, where welcome hotel air conditioners hum. Alaska is not the stuff of icy legends in all seasons. But there is also something almost unsettling about Alaska for the first-time visitor. It seems to be a land of many places, many kinds of experiences—too big to comprehend.

That is the key—the many Alaskas.

A grandmother rides a tourist helicopter to walk on a glacier. A few yards from the safe zone selected by the pilot there are deep crevasses that could gulp down a house. "Scary," she says, "but exhilarating." Sea kayakers near Ketchikan paddle past verdant islands, mist rising from the forest after last night's rain. Hundreds of anglers line the banks of the Kenai River on a warm summer weekend, all hoping to pull in a monster king salmon. Far to the west in the village of Kwethluk, a Yup'ik woman prepares for winter, hanging strips of smoked salmon up to dry. A youngster panning for gold in Nome yells out when he finds a shiny flake among the swirling sands, never dreaming that the pan was "salted" by a kindly miner. Late on a June night in Barrow, visitors watch the midnight sun dip almost to the horizon and then bounce upward again like a fiery ball. Boaters on the fabled Yukon River drift with the current, spellbound, watching the high-speed dives of peregrine falcons above rocky cliffs.

Deep in Denali National Park and Preserve, visitors see grizzly bears bounding across the tundra and moose munching on willows by the road. Near Fairbanks, other visitors reach out to touch a silvery tube—the trans-Alaska oil pipeline, which transports crude from Prudhoe Bay 800 mi across Alaska to Valdez, zigzagging through the wilderness like a giant snake. In Glacier Bay National Park, a small cruise ship is anchored for the night across from the face of a booming glacier. There are volleys of sound, like gunshots; then huge slabs of ice break away and tumble into the bay. Harbor seals ride the ice rafts like stowaways; bald eagles ride the air currents above. In the ship's lounge, passengers are cooling their cocktails with slivers of slow-to-melt glacier ice that is millions of years old.

Near the town of Cordova in Prince William Sound, another realm of glaciers, a lone birder on the delta of the Copper River trains binoculars on a trio of trumpeter swans. Nowhere else in the world can a visitor see such a concentration of trumpeters—as many as 1,000 nest here from late spring into fall. And out in the Pribilof Islands, which seem like dots in the Bering Sea between Alaska and Siberia, the surf crashes on rookeries swarming with thousands of northern fur seals. A cacophony of sound comes from the cliffs above as thousands of seabirds swirl around nest sites.

This is the real Alaska—the many Alaskas—a destination for personal discoveries. But there is more to Alaska for the traveler than spectacular scenery and wilderness experiences. One of Alaska's best attractions is its warm, welcoming hosts—the people. The friendliness is easy to understand when one realizes that Alaska, in many ways, still is a frontier. Communities are widely scattered, linked mostly by airplanes instead of roads. Residents still depend on one another as in pioneer times. There still are gentle places where doors are never locked and car keys are left in ignitions. Alaska's population of about 621,000 spreads across 586,400 square mi.

Because there are so few Alaskans, they band together for common causes—but they also scrap like family. Anchorage and Fairbanks (the two largest cities) thrive on feuding. Hometowners in Fair-

banks think Anchorage is too glitzy for Alaska. They joke that "the real Alaska begins about 10 miles outside Anchorage." Partly true: the city does have high-rise hotels, posh restaurants, and Alaska-size Wal-Marts, but it also has a delightful waterfront trail, world-class cross-country skiing right in town, and magnificent Chugach State Park—second largest in America—just a 15-minute drive away. Anchorage residents fire back, calling the much smaller Fairbanks "a hick town, the ice-fog capital of the world." Partly true: Fairbanks does suffer through winters when the thermometer seems perpetually stuck at 30 below zero, but it also experiences delightfully warm summers, and the University of Alaska brings an unexpected level of culture. Residents of both Anchorage and Fairbanks complain about Juneau's rainy weather and high prices, but they miss the quaint downtown, the drive-up glacier, and the verdant forested beauty that surrounds the city.

The squabbling is all in fun—most of the time.

There have been three ballot measures in the past two decades to move the state capital from Juneau, in Southeast Alaska, to Willow and Wasilla, 70 mi and 40 mi, respectively, north of Anchorage. In 1974 voters approved moving their capital but were deterred eight years later by the cost of constructing a new capitol building.

The scars haven't healed yet from that fray. If Alaska in general has a malady, it would be called regionalism. That's pretty easy to understand, too. Alaska is so big that it has conflicting resource interests. The commercial fishermen of coastal Alaska don't want oil tankers endangering their salmon, halibut, and crab harvests. Business leaders in Anchorage and Fairbanks are unabashed boosters of the petroleum industry that fuels their economies.

Despite kind words for public consumption, there still is residual racism in Alaska. The Native peoples—Eskimo, Indian, and Aleut—continue a long struggle to gain equal footing with Caucasian Alaskans. Old-timers remember not-so-long-ago signs in shop windows that read NO DOGS OR NATIVES ALLOWED. They also remember how Native children were punished in schools for daring to speak their traditional languages. Those days of overt discrimination are over, but tensions still remain just below the surface. Natives complain that their views and cultural traditions are ignored, especially by the Republican-dominated state legislature. Whites often think all Natives are alcoholics on the government dole.

There is one thing that unites—not divides—Alaskans: their shared memories of being held back as a territory, until statehood in 1959. Those were the days when Alaskans couldn't vote for a U.S. president. In territorial times, their governors were appointed by the president without a vote of the people. When prestatehood Alaskans traveled by air between Alaska and Seattle, they were subjected to customs and immigration inspections. From the time the first statehood bill was introduced in Congress, it took Alaskans 40 years to pin a star to the U.S. flag.

The hard feelings from the statehood fight may help explain some of the headlines outsiders read during the oil-pipeline debate. Environmental leaders and outside editorial writers were about as welcome as influenza when they organized a well-orchestrated (but unsuccessful) battle against construction of the pipeline. Most Alaskans wanted the line, viewing it as a source of revenue for their money-short state—money for schools and social programs. Well, the pipeline was built (completed in 1977), and the Prudhoe Bay oil still flows, supplying America with about one-fourth of its crude oil. Oil taxes also provide much of the funding for state government.

While the pipeline was under construction, environmentalists were winning a bigger battle: getting more of Alaska set aside by the federal government for national parks, wildlife refuges, wild rivers, and other wilderness areas. Today, Alaska's national parklands stretch from the jade fjords of Southeast Alaska to the tundra of the lonely Arctic—51 million acres covering about 13% of the state. Alaska holds 70% of all parklands in the nation and 90% of all wildlife refuges.

That federal action didn't win enthusiastic support from most Alaskans, who believe Uncle Sam, now controlling 60% of Alaska's land area, still has too much say over the affairs of a sovereign state. For visitors and the tourist industry, however, the parks, refuges, and wild rivers that make up half these federal lands are treasures. They belong to the nation, not just to Alaska.

The Alaska you see today is young, high-spirited, and mostly untrampled. There was another kind of Alaska back in the mists of time.

Perhaps 20,000 years ago came the forebears of today's Native peoples. The first travelers to Alaska trekked from Asia to the North American continent across land bridges that long ago disappeared under the choppy waters of the Bering Sea. They migrated in small waves, following fish and game for food. Some of the nomads continued across the Arctic to Canada and Greenland. Some stayed in what today is Alaska. Others moved on, all the way to the southern tip of South America. You'll find a vibrant culture in the Native villages, where traditions such as ivory and totem carving still are living arts.

The peaceful life of the Native peoples ended in 1741, when the Russians "discovered" Alaska (the Natives, naturally, knew it was there all the time). Alaska became Russian America for 126 years. The Russians, spreading out as far as northern California, came to gather the hides of sea otters and fur seals. At first the Natives fought back—the Tlingits drove them from outposts at Sitka and Yakutat. But it was a battle that the Russians would eventually win.

Russia sold Alaska to the United States in 1867—for $7.2 million, or about 2¢ an acre. (Ironically, $7.2 million was the value of the first shipment of crude oil moved by tanker after the trans-Alaska pipeline was completed.) Alaska's biggest holiday, Alaska Day, on October 18, celebrates this remarkable real estate transaction. Alaska's Russian heritage remains a vivid thread in Alaskan life. You can find it in the family names of the Native peoples who were crushed by their Russian rulers. Left behind, in addition to mixed-blood offspring, were onion-dome Russian Orthodox churches all across Alaska.

Things moved quickly, almost in a blur, soon after Alaska became American territory: gold stampedes through Alaska to the Klondike in Canada's Yukon Territory, followed by gold rushes down the Yukon River and to the beaches of Nome on the

Bering Sea and into the hills and valleys around Fairbanks in the heart of Alaska.

During World War II, Japanese planes bombed the U.S. Navy base at Dutch Harbor in the Aleutians in 1942, and a few days later enemy troops occupied two of the Aleutian Islands, Attu and Kiska. A terrible battle was fought at Attu the next year to win back the island. Military records say the percentage of American casualties was second only to the fight for Iwo Jima in the Pacific combat theater. Some of the GIs stayed in Alaska after the war, rearing families and homesteading. They opened small businesses, put down roots, and joined the pioneers in building a new kind of Alaska. And then came the final momentum that led to statehood in January 1959.

But some people still aren't convinced that Alaska is in the United States. Not long ago, a Fairbanks man received a letter from an aviation school in Miami, where he had applied for entrance. It said: "We are enclosing proper forms for clearance with the American consulate and for obtaining your visa." And then there was the traveler from California who wrote the Alaska Division of Tourism to ask if American currency could be used in Alaska.

Oh, well. You're going to love Alaska, USA.

You have to applaud a place where the first session of the first territorial legislature (in 1913) approved voting rights for women as one of the first orders of business. It would be another seven years before the amendment granting suffrage to women was added to the U.S. Constitution. In this colorful land called Alaska, where it sometimes is difficult to distinguish tall tales from true stories, this one is on the record.

— Don Pitcher

WHAT'S WHERE

In a place as big as Alaska, it's no surprise to find incredible variations of geography, topography, and climate. Of the 20 highest mountains in the United States, 17 are in Alaska: the state boasts 19 peaks higher than 14,000 ft. And nearly all of the Southeast lies in a rain forest, the Tongass National Forest, while the northernmost part of the state is a precipitation desert.

Anchorage
Alaska's biggest city (population more than 261,000) is the state's only true metropolis. You'll find a varied selection of ethnic restaurants and a performing arts center, home to theater groups, an opera company, and an orchestra. The Anchorage Museum of History and Art houses an outstanding collection of historic and contemporary Alaskan art. The Alaska Native Heritage Center celebrates the rich diversity of the state's original inhabitants. At nearby Lake Hood—the largest and busiest seaplane base in the world—the Alaska Aviation Heritage Museum preserves rare examples of the planes that helped tame the wilderness.

Southeast Alaska
The Southeast encompasses the Inside Passage—more than a century ago the traditional route to the Klondike goldfields and today the centerpiece of Alaska cruises. Here are glacier-filled fjords and the justly famous Glacier Bay National Park. Juneau, the state's waterlocked capital, is also in the Southeast, as are fishing villages such as Petersburg and Ketchikan, which is known for its totem-pole carving. An onion-dome cathedral accents Sitka, the onetime capital of Russian America. Each fall, up to 4,000 eagles gather just outside Haines. Nearby Skagway is filled with historic buildings from the heyday of the Klondike Gold Rush, and is a favorite stop for cruise ship passengers.

South Central Alaska
Beyond Anchorage, South Central is an outdoor playground for fishing, hiking, wildlife-watching, and rafting. Especially well-visited are the towns of Seward and Homer on the Kenai Peninsula. The truly adventurous can ski in Valdez; more sedate downhill runs can be found at Mt. Alyeska Ski Resort, 40 mi south of Anchorage. Kodiak, 100 mi offshore in the Gulf of Alaska, is the second-largest island in the United States. Known as the Emerald Island for its green-carpeted mountains, this is the home of the famous Kodiak brown bear, which can weigh up to 1,500 pounds and is the biggest terrestrial carnivore on earth.

The Interior

Bounded by the Brooks Range to the north and the Alaskan Range to the south, the Interior is home to Mt. McKinley, the highest peak in North America, and to Denali National Park. Fairbanks, founded in 1901 by a merchant and a prospector who together struck it rich in their respective endeavors, is today Alaska's second-largest city. Fairbanks is the gateway to the Far North—the towns of the Arctic and the Bering Coast that are connected mainly by air—and to Canada's Yukon Territory, whose Gold Rush history is preserved in towns such as Dawson City and Whitehorse.

The Bush

The Bush, more a spirit than a place, is the last frontier of the Last Frontier. From Nome to Barrow, much of the ground is permanently frozen, and for months at a time the sun never sets—or never rises. In the Arctic are the hardy Eskimo people and the Prudhoe Bay oil fields, near Barrow, America's northernmost community. Prospectors still pan for gold on the beach in Nome, where they are occasionally joined by a wandering polar bear. Only one road leads up to the Arctic, the Dalton Highway. Otherwise, the only link between these outposts of civilization is by air or sea—unless you happen to have a sled-dog team, a snowmobile, or a Rollagon (a vehicle specially designed for crossing tundra).

The Alaska Peninsula and Aleutian Islands have steaming volcanoes and fast-changing weather. Katmai National Park's Novarupta and Mt. Katmai have kept things steamy through the years, and the park is also a prime brown bear viewing ground. The Bering seacoast, a watery wilderness of more than 100,000 square miles, arcs from Bristol Bay to the Arctic Circle.

PLEASURES AND PASTIMES

Bicycling

Biking can be a rewarding adventure in accessible parts of the state. The paved-road system is straightforward, and automobile traffic is usually light on most Alaska roads. However, the road shoulders can be narrow, and people tend to drive fast in rural areas. Unpaved highways are bikeable but are tougher going; expect dust, ruts, and flying gravel.

Anchorage has an excellent bike-trail system—one along the coast and several others inland. You can take your bike on the Alaska Railroad and bike in Denali National Park. Although the park road is largely unpaved, it has a good dirt surface and only light traffic. You can also bring your bike on Alaska's ferry system for an extra charge. Use it to explore the Southeast's charming communities and surrounding forests, but come prepared for heavy rain. Companies that rent bicycles in the Southeast seem to cycle in and out of business faster than you can shift gears. Your best bet, if you don't bring your own, is to call local bike shops, parks and recreation departments, or visitor information centers for rental information.

Many Interior residents are avid bikers, and mountain biking has become a hot sport here. Fairbanks has miles of scenic bike paths along the Chena River and into the city's outskirts. Most roads have wide shoulders and, of course, those incredible Alaska views. Trails used in winter by mushers, snowmobilers, and cross-country skiers are taken over by mountain bikers when the snow melts.

Boating

With its numerous streams and rivers, Alaska is a natural for waterborne exploration. In the Southeast, the busiest river for running is the Mendenhall; in South Central, it's the Kenai. White-water boaters often spend their weekends playing in the whitecaps of the Nenana River, near Denali National Park in the Interior. Remember that Alaska has some serious white water: unless you are experienced, do not undertake a boating expedition without a professional guide. Numerous operators run river trips throughout the state (☞ Tours & Packages *in* Smart Travel Tips A to Z).

CANOEING➤Canoes are generally safe and comfortable, and they're suitable for many of Alaska's protected waterways, particularly those around the Kenai Peninsula and Southeast's Admiralty Island. It's likely that you'll have one or more portages on a canoe trip, and carrying a canoe over demanding terrain is not easy. Canoes can be transported outside via floatplane, but passengers are not allowed on such trips, requiring a separate (and expensive) flight. You can, however, carry a canoe on a car to your river put-in; excellent Alaskan rivers accessible by car include the Delta, the Gulkana, the Fortymile, and Beaver Creek.

KAYAKING➤Sea kayaking is big among Alaskans. It was the Aleuts who invented the kayak (or *bidarka*) in order to fish and hunt sea mammals. When early explorers encountered the Aleuts, they compared them to sea creatures, so at home did they appear on their small ocean crafts. Kayaks have the great advantage of portability, and some models can be broken down and carried on a ferry or small aircraft. Less practical but perhaps more important advantages are that they give the boater a feel for the water and a view from water level. They are also more stable than canoes. Oceangoing kayakers will find offshore adventures, especially in the protected waters of the Southeast, Prince William Sound, or out of Kenai Fjords National Park.

RAFTING➤Rafts take multiple passengers, are reasonably comfortable, and can be broken down and readily packed for transportation on a human back or via small plane. White water is almost as thrilling on a raft as in a kayak, although a raft is more cumbersome to handle.

SAILING➤The beautiful Prince William Sound, with tidewater glaciers and forested islands, has good winds in late summer. Whittier is the usual port of entry, and numerous charter boats dock here. Other South Central sailing towns are Seward, Valdez, and Cordova. The protected waters of Southeast Alaska have fickle winds, but you'll discover quite a few sailboats in Juneau, Ketchikan, and Sitka.

Dining
Alaska's primary claim to gastronomic fame is seafood. The rich coastal waters produce prodigious quantities of halibut, salmon, crab, and shrimp, along with such specialties as abalone, sea urchin, herring roe, and sea cucumbers (a favorite in Japan). If you haven't yet tasted fresh Alaskan salmon, do so here—there's nothing quite like a barbecued Copper River

king salmon. Alaska, unlike Norway, Chile, or British Columbia, does not allow salmon farming, so you can be guaranteed of having wild fish from the ocean. Be sure, however, to ask if the seafood is fresh or frozen, particularly during the off-season.

In general, the quality of Alaskan restaurants is directly proportional to the population. In the smallest villages you may be hard pressed to even find a shop selling greasy burgers and fries. Most larger towns have the requisite McDonald's, Burger Kings, and Subways, along with standard all-American restaurants serving bacon-and-egg breakfasts, iceberg lettuce salads, and fresh-from-the-freezer pizza dough. Fortunately, not everything is this bad. In towns with a significant tourist presence—such as Haines, Homer, Ketchikan, Petersburg, Seward, Sitka, or Skagway—you'll always find cafés serving espresso and baked goods, plus at least one restaurant where the food is fresh and delicious. Anchorage, Juneau, and Fairbanks all have a wide range of eateries, with something to please everybody. Not surprisingly, Anchorage—with almost half the state's population—has the best selection, including ethnic food from all corners of the globe, creative seafood restaurants, half a dozen brew pubs, vegetarian cafés, European-style bakeries and delis, and gourmet restaurants.

Alaskan dining is an informal affair: it is virtually impossible to find a restaurant here where formal attire is required. In even the fanciest restaurants, appropriate attire simply means a spiffy shirt and pants for men, and a pair of pants or a comfortable skirt or dress for women.

Dogsledding
Alaskans are dog crazy. With more and more mushers offering wintertime tours, you can try anything from a half-hour jaunt outside Anchorage to a two-week outing in the Brooks Range or an expedition along the Iditarod Trail. You can participate as much or as little as you like, riding in the basket and being pampered at an overnight lodge or helping harness the dogs and taking a turn on the back of the sled. When choosing a tour, make sure your musher has the experience to handle the unpredictable blizzard, moose encounter, or runaway team. In the summer, some mushers put wheels on their sleds,

giving you a taste of dogsledding without the snow and cold.

Fishing

With more than 3 million lakes and more coastline than the rest of the United States combined, Alaska has no shortage of fishing spots. People from all over the world come to Alaska for a chance to land a trophy salmon (the record is 97 pounds) or a 200-pound-plus halibut. If you're driving through Alaska, you can fish from the roadside in the Interior and on the Kenai Peninsula. In the Southeast you can sink a line right off the docks. If you're a truly serious fisherman, though, a guided boat charter or a stay at a fly-in fishing lodge is the ultimate Alaska fishing adventure. Many companies assemble sportfishing packages that include everything you'll need, from transportation to tackle. Bag limits and special provisions vary throughout the state's 12 sportfishing-management areas.

Flightseeing

The magnitude of Alaska can perhaps best be comprehended from the air. Every major destination from the Southeast to the Arctic has flightseeing services that will show you Alaska from a bird's-eye view. It's an experience not to be missed.

Gardens and Giant Vegetables

Alaska has a short growing season, but the days of midnight sun produce some of the biggest blooms you'll ever see. Anchorage beautifies its downtown parks each summer with spectacular plantings, and every August the Alaska State Fair (☞ Festivals and Seasonal Events) in Palmer is a showcase for 90-pound cabbages and other oversize vegetables.

National Parks and Forests

Alaska has 15 national parks, preserves, and monuments; two national forests; and 16 national wildlife refuges. The most visited of all is Denali National Park, site of Mt. McKinley, at 20,320 ft the tallest peak in North America. Wrangell–St. Elias National Park, east of Anchorage, is the largest national park in the United States— six times the size of Yellowstone.

Shopping

Alaska, believe it or not, is a big shopping state. In most respects, shopping in Alaska is not unlike shopping in the contiguous United States. Most of the larger cities have department stores and malls, and they accept the same credit cards you use at home.

NATIVE CRAFTS➤Among the most prized items sought by souvenir hunters are Native crafts. In particular, look for carvings of walrus ivory, soapstone, jade, and wood, and for items made of fur. You'll find a wide choice of jewelry, mukluks (seal- or reindeer-skin Eskimo boots), masks, totem poles, paintings, and baskets. The state has adopted two symbols that guarantee the authenticity of crafts made by Alaskans: a hand symbol indicates the item was made by one of Alaska's Native peoples; a polar bear marks an item as made in Alaska. Better prices are found in the more remote villages where you buy directly from the artisan, or at crafts fairs such as Anchorage's downtown Saturday Market.

Each of the Native groups is noted for particular skills; their wares are sold throughout the state. Eskimo art, native to the Arctic and other areas of the Bush, includes animal carvings of walrus ivory, spirit masks, dance fans, baskets made of baleen (a fibrous material found in the mouths of bowhead whales), and jewelry fashioned from walrus ivory, jade, baleen, or a combination of the three.

The Tlingit of Southeast Alaska are known for their totems and other wood carvings, as well as for baskets and hats woven from spruce root and cedar bark. Tsimshian Indians also work with spruce root and cedar bark, and Haida Indians are noted basket makers and totem and slate carvers.

Athabascans specialize in skin sewing, fur garments, and beadwork. The Aleuts' grass basketry is considered among the best in the world.

LOCAL BOUNTY➤Bringing home smoked and canned salmon allows you to transport a taste of Alaska even if you aren't an angler. Also look for birch syrup, a distinctively flavorful Alaska-only product found in local shops and at crafts fairs. In communities with a Russian past, such as Kodiak and Sitka, Russian nesting dolls are easily found in local shops.

Skiing and Snowboarding

Although it has no lack of snow or mountains, Alaska is not a big ski destination. Numerous opportunities, however, exist for both downhill and cross-country adventures. You can charter a helicopter to go backcountry skiing in the Valdez area, or visit one of the downhill areas near Anchorage, Fairbanks, or Juneau. Ski in the summer by chartering a plane to a glacier in Denali National Park. At Juneau, Eaglecrest is across from the city on the slopes of Douglas Island. Skiing is also done on the glaciers of the Juneau Ice Field, reached by helicopter. Turnagain Pass, 59 mi from Anchorage on the Seward Highway, is often trafficked with backcountry skiers and snowmobilers. Mt. Alyeska, 40 mi south of Anchorage, is where 1994 Olympic gold-medal champion Tommy Moe perfected his form. Hilltop Ski Area and Alpenglow are small alpine ski areas within 10 mi of downtown Anchorage. Valdez is home to the World Extreme Skiing Championships every April. Cross-country skiers will find many miles of world-class groomed trails in Anchorage. Additional cross-country ski trails can be found around Fairbanks, Homer, and Palmer. Snowboarding has more than caught on in South Central Alaska—particulary with the high-school and college set—and boarders are welcome at all three Anchorage ski areas. Rentals are available at the various ski areas and outdoor equipment shops.

GREAT ITINERARIES

Planning a trip to Alaska requires a careful look at both your interests and finances. Those who prefer luxury travel in organized groups will probably choose a cruise ship vacation. For independent travelers visiting Alaska, an endless array of options appear. The state is far too big and undeveloped to see it all in a short period, so unless you have all summer—and are able to print your own money—you'll need to be very selective.

Highlights of Alaska

10 to 14 days

Sprawling national parks of unspoiled wilderness, wildlife viewing in Kenai Peninsula, breathtaking views from the overlooks of Chugach Mountains outside Anchor-

age: Alaska begs to be experienced. Besides seeing many natural wonders, you can gain a sense of the state's culture from the communities that dot its limited highway system. Start or end this survey with two or three days in Anchorage.

SEWARD➤ **2 to 3 Days.** Surrounded by lush mountains at the head of Resurrection Bay, Seward is the primary gateway to Kenai Fjords National Park. Here you can spot whales, sea otters, and puffins on coastal wildlife tours, walk to the icy snout of Exit Glacier, or explore the massive cold-water tanks at Alaska SeaLife Center, a research and visitor facility with examples of many of Alaska's marine mammals and seabirds. *See* Kenai Peninsula *in* Chapter 6.

KENAI AND SOLDOTNA➤ **1 to 2 days.** The sportfishing hubs of South Central Alaska, these sister cities lie along the world-famous Kenai River, a clear-flowing, aqua-color stream. Five species of Pacific salmon spawn here each summer, including the mighty king, which may weigh 80 to 90 pounds or more. When not watching the salmon runs, you can take a stroll through Kenai's old town, which includes the Holy Assumption Russian Orthodox Church, or dig some clams at Clam Gulch, 24 mi south of Soldotna. *See* Kenai Peninsula *in* Chapter 6.

HOMER➤ **2 to 3 days.** This end-of-the-road coastal town proclaims itself the halibut capital of the world, but it also has a thriving community of artists and writers. Take a water taxi to nearby Kachemak Bay State and Wilderness Park, a rugged coastal wilderness of rain forest, jagged mountains, sheltered bays, pale blue glaciers, and abundant wildlife. A fishing charter includes an opportunity to view whales, seals, and porpoises close up. Before or after a wilderness excursion, visit the Pratt Museum, which has a saltwater aquarium, wildflower garden, and cultural and natural history displays. The Bunnell Street Gallery showcases work by local artists. *See* Kenai Peninsula *in* Chapter 6.

TALKEETNA➤ **1 day.** This small, rural community is the gateway to Denali. Mountaineers congregate here before flying into the Alaska Range; flightseers fly above it—sometimes even landing on glaciers. Denali National Park's entrance area is another 140 mi up the highway. You can also take sportfishing charters or join locals for libations and a game of pool in the historic Fairview Inn. *See* Matanuska-Susitna Valley and Beyond *in* Chapter 6.

FAIRBANKS➤ **2 days.** Born as a gold-mining camp at the start of the 20th century, the Golden Heart of Alaska's Interior is the starting point for trips into much of northern Bush Alaska, including several remote wilderness parks accessible only by air. Near town, you can hike the nature trails in Creamer's Field Migratory Waterfowl Refuge, where you might spot waterfowl, cranes, songbirds, or even a moose or bear. Or visit Alaskaland, a pioneer theme park with museums, an art gallery, Native displays, and a gold rush exhibit. *See* Fairbanks *in* Chapter 7.

Wilderness Alaska

10-16 days

Grizzly bears and herds of caribou, placid bays and white-water rapids, the colorful dance of the northern lights: Alaska's wildlands are an outdoor playground for nature lovers. Though some areas are remote and expensive to visit, you can access several of the state's premier parks, refuges, and other public lands from the highway system and nearby gateway communities.

DENALI NATIONAL PARK AND PRESERVE➤ **3 to 4 days.** Larger than the state of Massachusetts, Alaska's oldest and most famous parkland is a wilderness of high mountains, glacial rivers, northern forest, and expansive tundra plains. Mt. McKinley, also popularly known as Denali (the High One), rises 20,320 ft into the heavens, while grizzly bears roam alpine meadows and lowland valleys and wolves hunt caribou, moose, and Dall sheep. Opportunities are plentiful for camping, hiking, and river rafting in one of the country's most beautiful landscapes. *See* Denali National Park *in* Chapter 7.

DENALI STATE PARK➤ **1 to 2 days.** Little Denali, as it is sometimes called, has some of South Central Alaska's best tundra hikes, along the Curry-Kesugi Ridge. The park's spectacular views of Mt. McKinley, North America's highest peak, are among the finest anywhere. At Byers Lake, just off the busy George Parks Highway, you can camp or stay in public-use cab-

ins. Popular activities are picnicking, boating, fishing, and watching for moose, loons, beavers, or the black bears that fish for spawning salmon. *See* Matanuska-Susitna Valley and Beyond *in* Chapter 6.

CHUGACH STATE PARK➤ **2 to 3 days.** Anchorage's half-million-acre backyard wilderness includes 3,350-ft Flattop Mountain, Alaska's most-climbed peak. Dozens of glaciers, jagged spires, tundra meadows, forested valleys, grizzlies, moose, and a couple of wolf packs populate this natural expanse. You can camp, picnic, view wildlife, or pick berries. The more active can hike, climb mountains, ride horses, and fish. The park's major access points are all within a short drive of Alaska's largest city. *See* Prince William Sound *in* Chapter 6.

CHUGACH NATIONAL FOREST➤ **1 to 2 days.** Sprawling across much of the Kenai Peninsula and Prince William Sound, this 6-million-acre national forest has vast wooded lowlands, glacially carved mountains, and pristine coastal areas. While visiting, you can stay in campgrounds or the public-use cabins that dot the trails, saltwater beaches, and alpine lakes. *See* Prince William Sound *in* Chapter 6.

KENAI NATIONAL WILDLIFE REFUGE➤ **1 to 2 days.** Covering nearly 2 million acres, the Kenai refuge encompasses part of the vast Harding Icefield as well as rugged peaks and forested lowlands inhabited by moose, black bears, and grizzlies. You can set up camp in one of its 14 road-accessible campgrounds and spend your time canoeing or kayaking its myriad rivers and lakes. *See* Kenai Peninsula *in* Chapter 6.

KENAI FJORDS NATIONAL PARK➤ **2 to 3 days.** Tidewater glaciers, rugged fjords, and a wide variety of ocean life are highlights of this spectacular coastal parkland. Explore the park's perimeters on coastal wildlife tours based in Seward. Sea otters, sea lions, porpoises, and tens of thousands of seabirds-maybe even a whale or two-can be spotted from a tour boat. You can also fly in, stay in public-use cabins, and travel by kayaks in bays devoid of other humans. After a short hike on a trail at the end of the park road, you'll be face to face with the heavily crevassed Exit Glacier. *See* Kenai Peninsula *in* Chapter 6.

1 CRUISING IN ALASKA

Alaskan cruises are hot. Many cruise lines
are putting their newest and biggest ships
here, but if you want to sail with only
12 other people instead of 2,000, you'll
find a cruise to suit you, too. Hundreds of
thousands of people cruise Alaska's Inside
Passage every year, watching in awe
as glaciers and mountains glide by and
sprinting from port to starboard at reports
of whale sightings. Cruising in Alaska is
an easy, leisurely, and practical way
to cover great distances.

By M. T.
Schwartzman

Updated by
Sue Kernaghan

ALASKA, IT WOULD SEEM, was made for cruising. The traditional route to the state is by sea, through a 1,000-mi-long protected waterway known as the Inside Passage. From Vancouver in the south to Skagway in the north, it winds around islands large and small, past glacier-carved fjords, and along hemlock-blanketed mountains. This great land is home to breaching whales, nesting eagles, spawning salmon, and calving glaciers. Most of the towns here can be reached only by air or sea. Juneau, in fact, is the only water-locked state capital in the United States. Beyond the Inside Passage, the Gulf of Alaska leads to Prince William Sound—famous for its marine life and more fjords and glaciers—and Anchorage, Alaska's largest city.

An Alaska cruise is no longer the exclusive domain of retirees. Following the latest trend in cruising, more and more families are setting sail for Alaska. The peak season falls during summer school vacation, so children are now a common sight aboard ship. Cruise lines have responded with programs designed specifically for children and with some discount shore excursions for youngsters under 12. Shore excursions have become more active, often incorporating activities families can enjoy together, such as bicycling, kayaking, and hiking. For adults, too, the cruise lines now offer more than ever before. Alaska is one of cruising's showcase destinations, so the lines are putting their grandest ships up here.

Itineraries give passengers endless choices—from Bering Strait cruises, which include a crossing to the Russian Far East, to more traditional loop cruises of the Inside Passage, round-trip from Vancouver. A few smaller boats sail only in Prince William Sound, away from big-ship traffic. Bingo and bridge tournaments, deck games, contests, demonstrations, and lectures are offered daily. You'll also find trendier pursuits: computer classes, stress-management seminars, and talks on financial planning. Enrichment programs, such as art demonstrations and local history lectures, are becoming increasingly popular. Some lines hire celebrity or Native speakers, naturalists, or local personalities.

On the big ocean liners, you can eat practically all day and night. There's often a selection of healthy choices for nutrition-conscious eaters. Some ships coordinate your dining-room meals with your exercise program in the health club.

Nearly every day, your ship will make a port call. Alaska port cities are small and easily explored by foot, but if you prefer to be shown the sights, ship-organized shore excursions are available. These range from touring by typical city bus to flightseeing with a landing on a glacier, charter fishing, river rafting, and visiting Native American communities. The programs change annually as the lines search for just the right mix of leisure and learning.

Luxury ships are not your only option for traveling to Alaska. Small ships trace the coastline for close-up landscapes and more contact with wildlife, and a rugged expedition vessel is a good choice for adventurers. And for more independent types, there's no better way to see Alaska than aboard the ferries of the Alaska Marine Highway System.

CHOOSING YOUR CRUISE

Every ship has its own personality, depending on its size, the year it was built, and its intended purpose. Big ships are more stable and offer a huge variety of activities and facilities. Smaller ships feel intimate, like private clubs. For every big-ship fan there is somebody who would never set foot aboard one of these "floating resorts."

The type of ship you choose is the most important factor in your Alaska cruise vacation, since it will determine how you see Alaska. Big ships sail farther from land and visit major ports of call such as Juneau, Skagway, and Ketchikan. Small ships spend much of their time hugging the coastline, looking for wildlife, waterfalls, and other natural and scenic attractions.

Types of Ships

Ocean Liners

Alaska's ocean liner fleet represents the very best that today's cruise industry has to offer. Virtually all ships are newly built, with atrium lobbies, state-of-the-art health spas, high-tech lounges, and elaborate dining rooms. They are a comfortable, and sometimes even luxurious, way to tour Alaska's major ports of call and scenic attractions. By night they come alive with Vegas-style revues, pulsating discos, cabaret, and comedy acts. Some of the latest liners have cabins with verandas—a great bonus in Alaska for watching the scenery go by from the privacy of your own stateroom. The newest cruise liners are lined with glass throughout their corridors and public rooms, so you're never far from the sea—or from a great view of "The Great Land."

Expedition Ships

Vessels of this type are designed to reach into the most remote corners of the world. Shallow drafts allow them to navigate up rivers, close to coastlines, and into shallow coves. Hulls may be hardened for sailing in Arctic ice. Motorized rubber landing craft, known as Zodiacs, are kept onboard, making it possible for passengers to put ashore almost anywhere. However, because the emphasis during cruises aboard expedition ships tends to be on learning and exploring, the ships don't have casinos, shows, multiple bars and lounges, and other typical diversions. Instead, for entertainment they have theaters for lectures, well-stocked libraries, and enrichment programs led by experts.

Coastal Cruisers

Designed more for exploring than entertaining, these are smaller than the expedition ships. They, too, are able to sail to remote waterways and ports, but unlike the expedition ships, they do not have ice-hardened hulls. Some have forward gangways for bow landings or carry a fleet of Zodiac landing craft. Coastal cruisers offer few onboard facilities and public spaces—perhaps just a dining room and a lounge.

Ferry Liners

The state ferry system is known as the Alaska Marine Highway because its vessels carry vehicles as well as passengers. Each ferry has a car deck that can accommodate every size vehicle, from the family car to a Winnebago motor home. This capability presents an opportunity for independent travelers with wanderlust: you can take your vehicle ashore, drive around, even live in it, and then transport it with you to the next port of call. Once the ferry reaches Skagway or Haines, the only Inside Passage towns connected to a road system, you can drive farther north to Fairbanks and Anchorage on the Alaska Highway.

Itineraries

Ocean liner sailings come chiefly in two varieties: round-trip Inside Passage loops and one-way Inside Passage–Gulf of Alaska cruises. Both itineraries are typically seven days. However, if you want to combine a land tour with your Inside Passage loop, you will spend only three or four days aboard ship. On the other hand, Inside Passage–Gulf of Alaska cruises allow you to spend a full week aboard ship and still take a pre- or post-cruise land tour. A few lines schedule longer one-way or round-trip sailings from Vancouver, San Francisco, Seattle, or Los Angeles. Coastal cruisers and expedition ships typically sail within Alaska, setting out from Juneau, Sitka, or other Alaskan ports.

The routes and views will also vary by the size of vessel. Smaller ships can navigate narrow channels, straits, and fjords. Larger vessels must sail farther from land, so don't expect to see much wildlife from the deck of a megaship.

Cruise Tours

Most cruise lines give you the option of an independent, hosted, or fully escorted land tour before or after your cruise. Independent tours allow maximum flexibility. You have a preplanned itinerary with confirmed hotel reservations and transportation arrangements, but you're free to follow your interests and whims in each town. A hosted tour is similar, but tour company representatives are available along the route to help out should you need assistance.

On fully escorted tours, you travel with a group, led by a tour director. Activities are preplanned (and typically prepaid), so you have a good idea of how much your trip will cost (not counting incidentals) before you depart.

Modes of tour transportation range from plane to bus, rail to ferry. Most cruise-tour itineraries include a ride aboard the Alaska Railroad in a private, glass-dome railcar. Running between Anchorage, Denali National Park, and Fairbanks, Holland America Tours' and Carnival's *McKinley Explorer,* Princess Tours' *Midnight Sun Express Ultra Dome,* and Royal Celebrity Tours' *Wilderness Express* railcars offer unobstructed views of the passing land and wildlife.

Of the ocean liner fleet, only the *Vision of the Seas, Radiance of the Seas, Universe Explorer, Norwegian Sky,* and *Norwegian Wind* are not currently offering cruise-tour packages with land segments in Alaska. They may, however, have tours in the Canadian Rockies. In addition to full-length cruise tours, many cruise lines have pre- or post-cruise hotel and sightseeing packages in Vancouver or Anchorage lasting one to three days.

Cruise Costs

Per diems are an average daily price for Alaska itineraries during peak season, based on published brochure rates: if you shop around and/or book early you will undoubtedly pay less. In addition to your cruise per diem are extra costs, such as **airfare** to the port city. Only the most expensive Alaska cruises include airfare. Virtually all cruise lines offer air add-ons, which may or may not be less expensive than the latest discounted fare from the airlines. **Shore excursions** can be a substantial expense; the best in Alaska are not cheap. But, skimp too much on your excursion budget, and you'll deprive yourself of an important part of the Alaska experience.

Shipboard accounts enable passengers to charge onboard purchases and settle their accounts at the end of the cruise with a credit card, traveler's checks, or cash. Virtually all cruise ships operate as cashless societies. You can sign for wine at dinner, drinks at the bar, shore excursions, gifts in the shop—virtually any expense you may incur aboard ship. On some lines, an imprint from a major credit card is necessary to open an account. Otherwise, a cash deposit may be required and a positive balance maintained to keep the shipboard account open. Either way, you will want to open a line of credit soon after settling in if an account was not opened for you at embarkation. This can easily be arranged by visiting the purser's office in the central atrium or main lobby.

Tipping is another extra. At the end of the cruise, it's customary to tip your room steward, server, and the person who buses your table. Expect to pay an average of $7.50 to $10 per day per passenger in tips. Some lines are moving away from the traditional method of tipping. Norwegian Cruise Lines, for example, gives you the option of adding a flat $10 per day to your onboard account to cover tips; Radisson Seven Seas and Holland America have tipping-optional policies, though many passengers tip anyway. Each ship offers guidelines.

Single travelers should be aware that there are few single cabins on most ships. Taking a double cabin for yourself can cost as much as twice the advertised per-person rates (which are based on two people sharing a room). Some cruise lines will find roommates of the same sex for singles so that each can travel at the regular per-person, double-occupancy rate.

When to Go

Cruise season runs from mid-May to late September. The most popular sailing dates are from late June through August. Although Alaskan weather never carries any guarantees, sunshine and warm days are apt to be most plentiful from mid-June through August. June and July are the driest months to cruise. For shoppers, bargains can be found both early and late in the season.

Cruising in the low seasons provides plenty of advantages besides discounted fares. Availability of ships and particular cabins is greater in the low and shoulder seasons, and fewer tourists are in the ports. In spring, wildflowers are abundant, and you're apt to see more wildlife along the shore, because the animals have not yet gone up to higher elevations. Alaska's early fall brings the splendor of autumn hues and the first snowfalls in the mountains. The animals have returned to low ground, and shorter days bring the possibility of seeing the northern lights. Daytime temperatures along the cruise routes in May, June, and September are in the 50s and 60s. July and August averages are in the 60s and 70s, with occasional days in the 80s.

November is the best month for off-season ferry travel, after the stormy month of October and while it's still pretty warm in the Inside Passage (temperatures will average around 40°F). It's a good month for wildlife-watching as well. Some animals show themselves in greater numbers during November. In particular, humpback whales are abundant off Sitka and bald eagles congregate by the thousands near Haines.

BEFORE YOU GO

Tickets and Vouchers

After you make the final payment for your cruise, the cruise line will issue your cruise tickets and vouchers for airport–ship transfers. Depending on the airline, and whether you have purchased an air-sea package, you may receive your plane tickets or charter-flight vouchers at the same time; you may also receive vouchers for any shore excursions, although most cruise lines issue these aboard ship. Should your travel documents not arrive when promised, contact your travel agent or call the cruise line directly. If you book late, tickets may be delivered directly to the ship.

What to Pack

Certain packing rules apply to all cruises: always take along a sweater to counter cool evening ocean breezes or overactive air-conditioning. A rain slicker is essential—many travelers who plan on indulging in some of the more active shore excursions pack a complete rain suit. Be prepared to dress in layers, since temperatures can vary considerably during the day. Make sure you take at least one pair of comfortable walking shoes for exploring port towns. Waterproof footwear will be useful as well. Ankle-high rubber boots are ideal for many shore trips. No two cruises have quite the same dress policy, but evening dress on Alaskan cruises tends to fall into two categories: semiformal on the ocean liners and casual on the smaller ships. On semiformal cruises men generally wear a jacket and tie to dinner. Women should pack one long gown or cocktail dress for every two or three formal evenings onboard. On smaller cruises, shipboard dress is usually informal.

Generally speaking, plan on one outfit for every two days of cruising, especially if your wardrobe contains many interchangeable pieces. Ships often have convenient laundry facilities as well. Don't overload your luggage with extra toiletries and sundry items; they are easily available in port and in the ship's gift shop (though usually at a premium price). Soaps, and sometimes shampoos and body lotion, are often placed in your cabin compliments of the cruise line.

Take an extra pair of eyeglasses or contact lenses in your carry-on luggage. If you have a health problem that requires a prescription drug, pack enough to last the duration of the trip or have your doctor write a prescription using the drug's generic name, because brand names vary from country to country. Always carry prescription drugs in their original packaging to avoid problems with customs officials. Don't pack them in luggage that you plan to check, in case your bags go astray. Pack a list of the offices that supply refunds for lost or stolen traveler's checks.

ARRIVING AND DEPARTING

If you have purchased an air-sea package, you will be met by a cruise-company representative when your plane lands at the port city and then shuttled directly to the ship in a bus or minivan. Some cruise lines arrange to transport your luggage between airport and ship—you don't have to hassle with baggage claim at the start of your cruise or with baggage check-in at the end. If you decide not to buy the air-sea package but still plan to fly, ask your travel agent if you can use the ship's transfer bus anyway; if you do, you may be required to purchase a round-trip transfer voucher (about $40). Otherwise, you will have to arrange for your own transportation to the ship.

Embarkation

Check-In

On arrival at the dock, you must check in before boarding your ship. A cruise-line official will collect or stamp your ticket, inspect or even retain your passport or other official identification, and give you the keys to your cabin. Seating assignments for the dining room are often handed out at this time, too.

After this you may be required to go through a security check and to pass your hand baggage through an X-ray inspection. These are the same machines in use at airports, so ask to have your photographic film inspected by hand.

Although it takes only 5 or 10 minutes per family to check in, lines are often long, so aim for off-peak hours. The worst time tends to be immediately after the ship begins boarding; the later it is, the less crowded. For example, if boarding begins at 2 PM and continues until 4:30, try to arrive after 3:30.

Boarding the Ship

You will be escorted to your cabin by a steward, who will carry your hand luggage. The rest of your bags will be inside your cabin when you arrive or will come shortly thereafter. If your bags don't arrive within a half hour before sailing, contact the purser. If you are among the unlucky few whose luggage doesn't make it to the ship in time, the purser will trace it and arrange to have it flown to the next port of call.

Disembarkation

The last night of your cruise is full of business. On most ships you must place everything except your hand luggage outside your cabin door, ready to be picked up by midnight. Color-coded tags, distributed to your cabin in a debarkation packet, should be placed on your luggage before the crew collects it. Your designated color will later determine when you leave the ship and will also help you retrieve your luggage on the pier.

Your shipboard bill is left in your room during the last day. To pay the bill (if you haven't already put it on your credit card) or to settle any questions, you must stand in line at the purser's office. Tips to the cabin steward and dining staff are distributed on the last night.

The next morning, in-room breakfast service is usually not available because stewards are too busy. Most passengers clear out of their cabins as soon as possible, gather their hand luggage, and stake out a chair in one of the public lounges to await the ship's clearance through customs. Be patient—it takes a long time to unload and sort thousands of pieces of luggage. Passengers are disembarked by groups according to the color-coded tags placed on luggage the night before; those with the earliest flights get off first. If you have a tight connection, notify the purser before the last day, and he or she may be able to arrange faster preclearing and debarkation for you.

SHORE EXCURSIONS

Shore excursions arranged by the cruise line are a convenient way to see the sights, although you pay extra for this convenience. Before your cruise, you'll receive a booklet describing the shore excursions your cruise line offers. A few lines let you book excursions in advance; all sell them onboard during the cruise. If you cancel your excursion, you may incur penalties, the amount varying with the number of days remaining until the tour. Because these trips are specialized, many have limited capacity and are sold on a first-come, first-served basis.

Among the many options available, some are "musts." At least once during your cruise, try flightseeing—it's the only way you'll grasp the expansiveness and grandeur of the land. Go to an evening salmon feast, where you'll savor freshly caught fish cooked over an open fire in a natural setting. And experience an outdoor adventure—you don't have to be athletically inclined to raft down a river or paddle a sea kayak along the coastline.

SAFETY AT SEA

Fire Safety

The greatest danger facing cruise-ship passengers is fire. All the ships reviewed in this book must meet certain international standards for fire safety. The latest rules require that ships have sprinkler systems, smoke detectors, and other safety features. However, these rules are designed to protect against loss of life. They do not guarantee that a fire will not happen; in fact, fire is a relatively common occurrence on cruise ships. The point here is not to create alarm but to emphasize the importance of taking fire safety seriously.

Fire safety begins with you, the passenger. Once settled into your cabin, find the location of your life vests and review the emergency instructions inside the cabin door or near the life vests. Make sure your vests are in good condition and learn how to secure the vest properly. Make certain the ship's purser knows if you or your companion has some physical infirmity that may hamper a speedy exit from your cabin. In case of a real emergency, the purser can quickly dispatch a crew member to assist you. If you are traveling with children, be sure that child-size life jackets are placed in your cabin.

Within 24 hours of embarkation, you will be asked to attend a mandatory lifeboat drill. Do so and listen carefully. If you have any questions, ask them. If you are unsure of how to use your vest, now is the time to ask. Only in the most extreme circumstances will you need to abandon ship—but it has happened. The few minutes you spend learning the right procedure may serve you well in a mishap.

Health Care

Quality medical care at sea is another important safety issue. All big ships are equipped with medical infirmaries to handle minor emergencies. However, these should not be confused with hospitals. No international standards governing medical facilities or personnel aboard cruise ships exist, although the American Medical Association has recommended that such standards be adopted. If you have a preexisting medical condition, discuss your upcoming cruise with your doctor. Pack an extra supply of any medicines you might need. Once aboard, see the ship's doctor and alert him or her to your condition, and discuss treatments or emergency procedures before any problem arises. Passengers with potentially life-threatening conditions should seriously consider signing up with a medical evacuation service. You should review your health insurance to make sure you are covered while on a cruise.

The most common minor medical problems confronting cruise passengers are seasickness and gastrointestinal distress. Modern cruise ships, unlike their transatlantic predecessors, are relatively motion-free vessels with computer-controlled stabilizers, and they usually sail in relatively calm waters. If, however, you do feel queasy, you can always get seasickness pills aboard ship. (Many ships give them out for free at the front desk.)

Outbreaks of food poisoning happen from time to time aboard cruise ships. Episodes are random; they can occur on ships old and new, big and small, budget and luxury. The Centers for Disease Control and Prevention (CDC) monitors cruise-ship hygiene and sanitation procedures, conducting voluntary inspections twice a year of all ships that sail regularly from U.S. ports (this program does not include ships that never visit the United States). For a free listing of the latest ship scores, visit the centers' Web site at www.cdc.gov.

A high score on the CDC report doesn't mean you won't get sick. Outbreaks have taken place on ships that consistently score very highly; conversely, some ships score very poorly yet passengers never get sick. So use these scores as a guideline and factor them in with other considerations when choosing your ship.

Crime on Ships

Crime aboard cruise ships has become headline news, thanks in large part to a few well-publicized cases. Most people never have any type of problem, but you should exercise the same precautions aboard ship that you would at home. Keep your valuables out of sight—on big ships virtually every cabin has a small safe in the closet. Don't carry too much cash ashore, use your credit card whenever possible, and keep your money in a secure place, such as a front pocket that's harder to pick. Single women traveling with friends should stick together, especially when returning to their cabins late at night. And be careful about whom you befriend, as you would anywhere, whether it's a fellow passenger or a member of the crew. You may be on vacation, but criminals rarely take a holiday. Don't be paranoid, but do be prudent.

THE CRUISE FLEET

The Alaska cruise fleet is diverse: passenger capacities range from more than 2,000 people to only a dozen. Lifestyle aboard these ships also runs the gamut, from elegant to coastal cruisers, depending upon the type of ship and its onboard facilities. Bigger ships tend to be more formal, especially when it comes to evening dress. Smaller ships are more casual, and the dress code for dinner is usually "come as you are."

Ocean Liners

Carnival Spirit. On the *Carnival Spirit,* Carnival brings the "Fun Ship" experience to Alaska, with such family-friendly amenities as four pools, including one with a retractable roof for all-weather swimming, a children's wading pool and giant water slide, and a Camp Carnival program for children ages 2 through 15. Public-room decor is brightly colored and energetic, and the glass-enclosed portions of the promenade create a protected viewing perch. For additional glacier gazing, 80% of all cabins have ocean views, while 80% of those also have private balconies. ⊠ *Carnival Cruise Lines, Carnival Pl., 3655 N.W. 87th Ave., Miami, FL 33178-2428,* ☎ *800/327–9501,* WEB *www.carnival.com. 3 restaurants, 12 bars, pizzeria, in-room safes, room service, 5 pools, hair salon, outdoor hot tubs, sauna, spa, steam room, aerobics, gym, jogging, shops, casino, dance club, video games, children's programs, library, laundry services, chapel, business services, meeting rooms. Average per diem: $270–$400.*

Crystal Harmony. The only Alaska-bound liner offering 12-day round-trip sailings from San Francisco, the *Crystal Harmony* is exceptionally sleek and sophisticated. Spacious and well equipped—including Internet access and computer training facilities—the ship has plenty of open deck space for watching the scenery, plus a forward observation lounge with oversize windows, set high above the bridge. Overall, this is one of Alaska's most elegant vessels. Cabins are especially roomy; more than half have a private veranda. ⊠ *Crystal Cruises, 2049 Century Park E, Los Angeles, CA 90067,* ☎ *310/785–9300 or 800/*

446–6620, WEB *www.crystalcruises.com. 4 restaurants, 13 bars, café, grill, outdoor café, in-room data ports, in-room safes, in-room VCRs, minibars, room service, 2 pools, hair salon, outdoor hot tubs, sauna, spa, steam room, driving range, putting green, aerobics, gym, paddle tennis, shops, casino, cinema, nightclub, video games, library, laundry services, business services. Average per diem: $400–$500.*

Infinity and Summit. Dramatic exterior glass elevators, a glass-dome pool area, and a window-wrapped ship-top observation lounge keep the magnificence of Alaska well within passengers' view on *Infinity,* and her newly launched sister ship, *Summit.* These ships are among the largest in Celebrity Cruises' fleet and each stocks plenty of premium amenities including a flower-filled conservatory, music library, expansive spa, Internet café, a golf simulator, and name-brand boutiques. Cabins are bright and spacious; 80% have ocean views, and 74% of those include private verandas. With a staff member for every two passengers, and 24-hour butler service in the suites; service is especially attentive. ⊠ *Celebrity Cruises, 1050 Caribbean Way, Miami, FL 33132-2096,* ☎ *800/437–3111,* WEB *www.celebritycruises.com. 3 restaurants, 6 bars, café, coffee shop, tea shop, in-room data ports, in-room safes, in-room VCRs, minibars, room service, indoor pool, hair salon, hot tubs, outdoor hot tubs, sauna, spa, steam room, aerobics, basketball, gym, jogging, paddle tennis, shops, casino, cinema, video games, library, children's programs, laundry services, business services, meeting rooms. Average per diem: $250–$500.*

Legend of the Seas. At 24 knots, the *Legend of the Seas* is one of the fastest cruise ships on the Alaska run. Large windows throughout the public areas provide great views of the passing landscape. Onboard amenities include an 18-hole minigolf course, Internet access, and a pool with a sliding glass roof. The bright, spacious cabins include family suites, which can accommodate up to eight people, connecting staterooms, and cabins with private balconies. ⊠ *Royal Caribbean International, 1050 Caribbean Way, Miami, FL 33132,* ☎ *800/327–6700 or 800/255–4373,* WEB *www.royalcaribbean.com. 2 restaurants, 8 bars, room service, 2 pools, hair salon, hot tubs, sauna, spa, steam room, aerobics, gym, jogging, paddle tennis, ping-pong, shuffleboard, shops, casino, nightclub, video games, library, children's programs, laundry services, business services, meeting rooms. Average per diem: $150–$250.*

Norwegian Sky. Alaska's only ocean liner to operate its cruises out of Seattle, the *Norwegian Sky* comes with all the bells and whistles of Alaska's biggest ships, including a variety of dining options and an Internet café. Cabins have Internet access as well, so you can bring your laptop (the cost of e-mailing from the ship is much lower than the cost of calling). Other public rooms include a wine bar, a sports bar, and a cigar club. Spinning, aerobics, and yoga classes; a 24-hour health club with expansive ocean views; and the full-service Balinese-theme Mandara Spa mean you can (if you choose) turn your cruise into a spa vacation. But what makes Norwegian Cruise Line's ship different from other large ships is its relaxed onboard atmosphere. Passengers have neither assigned dining room tables or meal times, nor do they have to follow dress codes at night thanks to Norwegian's "Freestyle Cruising" policy. Freestyle Cruising also enables passengers to add their tips to their shipboard bill, and to relax in their staterooms while waiting to disembark. ⊠ *Norwegian Cruise Line, 7665 Corporate Center Dr., Miami, FL 33126,* ☎ *305/436–4000 or 800/327–7030,* WEB *www.ncl. com. 5 restaurants, 8 bars, coffee shop, outdoor café, pizzeria, tapas bar, in-room safes, refrigerators, room service, 2 pools, hair salon, outdoor hot tubs, sauna, spa, steam room, aerobics, basketball, gym, jog-*

ging, shuffleboard, volleyball, shops, cabaret, casino, nightclub, show-room, video games, library, children's programs, laundry services, business services, meeting rooms. Average per diem: $300–$400.

Norwegian Wind. The most distinctive design features aboard the *Norwegian Wind* are its extensive terracing and abundant use of picture windows. Instead of one big dining room, four smaller restaurants, a sports bar, an outdoor cafe, and a pizzeria create a more intimate ambience. Thanks to Norwegian Cruise Line's "Freestyle Cruising" policy, passengers don't have seating assignments but can instead eat where they want, when they want, and with whom they want. Freestyle Cruising also gives passengers the option to add their tips to their shipboard bill, and to relax in their staterooms while waiting to disembark on the last morning of the cruise. Extensive use of floor-to-ceiling windows, terraced decks, a wraparound promenade, and picture windows in the cabins make this an ideal ship for taking in the gorgeous views. Convertible sofas in the cabins, connecting staterooms, and activity-filled children's and teens' programs make this a good choice for family cruising. ⊠ *Norwegian Cruise Line, 7665 Corporate Center Dr., Miami, FL 33126,* ☎ *305/436–4000 or 800/327–7030,* WEB *www.ncl. com. 4 restaurants, 6 bars, coffee shop, outdoor café, pizzeria, sports bar, in-room safes, room service, pool, hair salon, hot tubs, steam room, sauna, spa, aerobics, basketball, gym, jogging, paddle tennis, volleyball, shops, casino, nightclub, showroom, video games, library, children's programs, laundry services, business services, meeting rooms. Average per diem: $300–$400.*

Radiance of the Seas. Introduced in 2001, *Radiance of the Seas* is larger than Royal Caribbean's other Alaska vessels, and incorporates innovative stylings such as 12-deck-high glass elevators that face the sea. Amenities include an Internet center, rock-climbing wall, a billiards room with self-levelling pool tables, and a mini-golf course. The African-theme solarium, with its retractable glass roof, pool, hot tubs, palm trees, and waterfalls, provides a pleasant escape from inclement Alaskan weather. More than 80% of all cabins have ocean views, and more than 70% of those include private verandas. ⊠ *Royal Caribbean International, 1050 Caribbean Way, Miami, FL 33132,* ☎ *800/327–6700 or 800/ 255–4373,* WEB *www.royalcaribbean.com. 3 restaurants, 8 bars, outdoor café, minibars, room service, 3 pools, hair salon, hot tub, outdoor hot tub, sauna, spa, steam room, putting green, aerobics, basketball, jogging, gym, shuffleboard, shops, casino, cinema, nightclub, showroom, video games, library, children's programs, laundry services, business services, meeting rooms. Average per diem: $200–$400.*

Ryndam, Statendam, and Veendam. The style of these ships can best be described as classic revival, combining the old and new in one neat package. From the outside, they look bigger than they really are, thanks to their megaship profile. Inside, they dramatically express Holland America's past in a two-tier dining room, replete with dual grand staircases framing an orchestra balcony. Although the ships are structurally identical, Holland America has given each its own distinct personality in the layout and decor of the public rooms. An abundance of glass, outdoor deck space, and a retractable roof over the main pool make these good ships for Alaska cruising. Great views can be found along the wraparound promenade, on the top-deck observation lounge, and in the glass-lined dining room. All standard outside cabins come with a small sitting area and a real tub; suites have private verandas, in-room VCRs, and minibars. Tipping is optional, but passengers tend to tip anyway. A naturalist and a Native artist-in-residence sail aboard each Alaska cruise, and the Passport to Fitness Program encourages a healthy diet and exercise. ⊠ *Holland America Line Westours, 300 Elliott Ave. W, Seattle, WA 98119,* ☎ *206/281–3535 or 877/724–5425,* WEB *www.hollandamerica.com. 2 restaurants, 5 bars, outdoor café, ice cream parlor, room service, 2 pools, hair salon, outdoor hot tubs, sauna, spa, steam room, aerobics, gym, shops, casino, cinema, showroom, video games, library, children's programs, laundry services, business services. Average per diem: $300–$700.*

Seven Seas Navigator. With just 490 guests and pampering service standards, the *Seven Seas Navigator* feels spacious and luxurious. Every stateroom aboard is an ocean view suite, ranging from 300 to more than 1,000 square ft, and 90% of them have private, teak-deck balconies. Other high-end hallmarks include one crew member for every 1.5 passengers; single, open seating in the two dining rooms; and free wine with dinner. Tips are also included in the cruise fare. ⊠ *Radisson Seven Seas Cruises, 600 Corporate Dr., Suite 410, Fort Lauderdale, FL 33334,* ☎ *800/477–7500 or 800/285–1835,* WEB *www.rssc.com. 2 restaurants, 4 bars, outdoor café, in-room safes, minibars, room service, pool, hair salon, spa, aerobics, gym, shops, casino, dance club, laundry services, business services. Average per diem: $400–$700.*

Star Princess. One of the newest and, with capacity for 2,600 passengers, one of the largest ships in the Alaskan fleet, the *Star Princess* includes such modern amenities as a pool where you can swim against the current, a pool with a retractable roof, an Internet café, and a 9-hole putting green. There's also a wedding chapel where you can be officially married at sea by the ship's captain. ⊠ *Princess Cruises, 24305 Town Center Dr., Santa Clarita, CA 91355,* ☎ *661/753–0000 or 800/568–3262,* WEB *www.princess.com. 6 restaurants, 12 bars, in-room safes, refrigerators, room service, 4 pools, hair salon, outdoor hot tubs, sauna, spa, steam room, aerobics, basketball, gym, jogging, paddle tennis, shuffleboard, shops, casino, cinema, nightclub, showroom, library, children's programs, laundry services, business services. Average per diem: $200–$400.*

Sun Princess, Dawn Princess, Sea Princess, and Ocean Princess. The sister ships *Sun Princess, Dawn Princess, Sea Princess,* and *Ocean Princess* offer an abundance of private balconies (more than 70% of outside cabins have them). Each subtly decorated vessel has two main showrooms and two main passenger dining rooms, an international food court with a 270-degree view over the bow of the ship, an Italian-style pizzeria, a wine and caviar bar, a steak house, and a patisserie for coffee and drinks. ⊠ *Princess Cruises, 24305 Town Center Dr., Santa Clarita, CA 91355,* ☎ *661/753–0000 or 800/568–3262,* WEB *www.princess.com. 4 restaurants, 9 bars, food court, outdoor café, patisserie, pizzeria, refrigerators, room service, 3 pools, hair salon, outdoor hot tubs, sauna, spa, steam room, aerobics, basketball, gym, jogging, paddle tennis, shuffleboard, volleyball, shops, casino, cinema, library, children's programs, coin laundry services, business services. Average per diem: $142–$370.*

Universe Explorer. World Explorer Cruises' strong suit is education, and passengers should not expect the glitz and glamour of some newer ships. The line's vessel (formerly the *Enchanted Seas* of Commodore Cruise Line) was built in 1958 as a transatlantic liner, but World Explorer has modified it to serve as a floating classroom. Rather than the disco and casino typically found on cruise ships, the *Universe Explorer* has a computer learning center and a 15,000-volume library—the largest at sea. Several other public rooms include a forward observation lounge. The ship's itinerary incorporates more ports of call than other lines, long port stays, and an excellent array of shore excursions.

On any given sailing, you may travel in the company of four or five experts in history, art, geology, marine life, music, or geography. Cabins and public rooms are simple, spacious, and comfortable. ✉ *World Explorer Cruises, 555 Montgomery St., San Francisco, CA 94111,* ☎ *415/820–9200 or 800/854–3835,* WEB *www.wecruise.com. 2 restaurants, 3 bars, lounge, massage, basketball, gym, shop, cinema, library, laundry services, meeting room. Average per diem: $150–$170.*

Vision of the Seas. The *Vision of the Seas* has dramatic balconied dining rooms and tiered showrooms. For great views, the ship has a Viking Crown Lounge on the uppermost deck with wraparound glass. The indoor-outdoor deck area of the Solarium Spa is especially well suited to cruising in often rainy Alaska. The *Vision* has relatively large cabins and more balconies than Royal Caribbean's previous megaships. About one quarter of the cabins have private verandas. The ships also have specially designed family suites with separate bedrooms for parents and children. ✉ *Royal Caribbean International, 1050 Caribbean Way, Miami, FL 33132,* ☎ *800/327–6700 reservations; 800/255–4373 brochures,* WEB *www.royalcaribbean.com. 2 restaurants, 6 bars, room service, 2 pools, hair salon, outdoor hot tubs, sauna, spa, steam room, aerobics, jogging, gym, shuffleboard, shops, casino, showrooom, video games, library, children's programs, laundry services, business services, meeting rooms. Average per diem: $250–$450.*

Volendam and Zaandam. These two new ships are structurally similar to Holland America's other vessels, with the signature two-tier dining room and retractable roof over the main pool, but they are newer and slightly larger, with such features as Internet centers and practice-size tennis courts. All standard outside cabins come with a bathtub and all suites and mini-suites have private verandahs. As with other Holland America Lines, tipping is optional, but passengers tend to tip anyway. A naturalist and a Native American artist-in-residence sail aboard each Alaska cruise, and the Passport to Fitness Program encourages a healthy diet and exercise. ✉ *Holland America Line Westours, 300 Elliott Ave. W, Seattle, WA 98119,* ☎ *206/281–3535 or 877/724–5425,* WEB *www.hollandamerica.com. 3 restaurants, 6 bars, outdoor café, ice cream parlor, room service, 2 pools, hair salon, outdoor hot tubs, sauna, spa, steam room, 2 tennis courts, aerobics, gym, shops, casino, cinema, video games, library, children's programs, laundry services. Average per diem: $230–$530.*

Expedition Ships

Clipper Odyssey. Clipper Cruise Line's newest member of its fleet, the *Clipper Odyssey,* brings elements of a luxury yacht experience to small-ship cruising in Alaska. The ship carries a fleet of Zodiac landing craft to take passengers ashore in remote locations. On every voyage, onboard experts share their knowledge of the region's cultures, wildlife, history, or geography. The dining room is well appointed, yet casual attire is the norm: men tend to bring out a sports coat only for the Captain's Farewell party. Each cabin has an ocean view, and each bathroom contains a shower and full tub. Other onboard amenities include beauticians and Internet access. ✉ *Clipper Cruise Line, 7711 Bonhomme Ave., St. Louis, MO 63105,* ☎ *314/727–2929 or 800/325–0010,* WEB *www.clippercruise.com. 2 bars, dining room, minibars, outdoor hot tub, gym, library. Average per diem: $400–$600.*

Wilderness Adventurer. This is a friendly ship with the casual comforts of home. The coffee's always on and you'll never need a jacket and tie for dinner. Alaskan art enhances the otherwise simple surroundings, and varnished wood imbues a nautical feel. A library of books and videos has a nice selection of Alaska titles. There are no TVs, but you can watch these tapes—or your own wildlife footage—on the community VCR in the main lounge. The most important asset of this ship is its naturalists, who put their hearts into their work. They lead kayak excursions and shore walks and get as much of a thrill as the passengers do whenever wildlife is sighted. Cabins and public areas were completely upgraded in 2000. ⊠ *Glacier Bay Cruiseline, 226 2nd Ave. W, Seattle, WA 98119,* ☎ *800/451–5952 U.S. and Canada,* WEB *www.glacierbaytours.com. Dining room, lounge. Average per diem: $400–$500.*

Wilderness Discoverer. This addition to the Glacier Bay fleet was formerly American Canadian Caribbean Line's *Mayan Prince.* You can expect the same general ambience and genuine enthusiasm from the crew that you would find aboard the *Wilderness Adventurer,* as well as brand new fixtures and furnishings following a 2001 refurbishment. ⊠ *Glacier Bay Cruiseline, 226 2nd Ave. W, Seattle, WA 98119,* ☎ *800/451–5952,* WEB *www.glacierbaytours.com. Dining room, lounge. Average per diem: $300–$500.*

Wilderness Explorer. The Wilderness Explorer is billed as a "floating base camp" for "active adventure," and that's no exaggeration. Sea-kayak outings may last more than three hours (a 5-mi paddle). Discovery hikes cross dense thickets and climb rocky creek beds. You'll spend most of your time off the ship—a good thing, since you wouldn't want to spend much time on it. The ship is pleasant enough—mostly late-1960s mod with a dash of old-world leather and even Greek Revival accents. But the public spaces are very limited and the cabins are positively tiny. This ship should be considered only by the serious outdoor enthusiast. ⊠ *Glacier Bay Cruiseline, 226 2nd Ave. W, Seattle, WA 98119,* ☎ *800/451–5952,* WEB *www.glacierbaytours.com. Dining room, lounge. Average per diem: $300–$350.*

Coastal Cruisers

Executive Explorer. As the name suggests, the *Executive Explorer* is a plush ship. Its appointments include rich wood paneling throughout; deep, padded armchairs in the main lounge; and a gallery like display of nearly 100 Alaskan prints. The main lounge has forward-facing observation windows; the dining room has color TV monitors. Even the stairwells have picture windows for views of the passing scenery. Outside observation areas include a partially covered sundeck, which gives a lofty perspective four decks above the water—an unusually high perch for such a small ship. Cabins have more artwork, two more big picture windows (unusually large for a ship this size), roomy closets, and other cabin amenities not often found in small-ship cabins. ⊠ *Glacier Bay Cruiseline, 226 2nd Ave. W, Seattle, WA 98119,* ☎ *800/451–5952 U.S. and Canada,* WEB *www.glacierbaytours.com. Dining room, lounge, in-room VCRs, minibars. Average per diem: $400–$500.*

Safari Escape, Safari Quest, and Safari Spirit. Alaska's smallest cruise ships are tiny even by small-ship standards, carrying just 12 to 21 passengers. Yet they come with all kinds of creature comforts usually associated with bigger ships—some staterooms have private hot tubs, balconies, and king-size beds, and all three yachts have an "under the stars" outdoor hot tub. All drinks are included in the fare, including beer, wine, and liquor, as are all shore excursions, including flightseeing. A professional naturalist provides informal lectures and accompanies passengers on kayaking and fishing expeditions. ⊠ *American Safari Cruises, 19101 36th Ave. W, Suite 201, Lynnwood, WA 98036,* ☎ *425/776–4700 or 888/862–8881,* WEB *www.amsafari.com. Bar, din-*

ing room, lounge, in-room VCRs, outdoor hot tub, boating, library. Average per diem: $800–$1,000.

Sea Bird and Sea Lion. These small, shallow-draft ships have the freedom to sail through narrow straits and visit out-of-the-way areas that are inaccessible to big ships. The boats forgo port calls at larger, busier towns and instead spend time making Zodiac raft landings, conducting wildlife searches, and stopping for beachcombing and barbecuing in Tracy Arm. These ships are not for claustrophobics, as the ship's storage capacity, the size of the crew, and the number of public areas have been cut back to carry 70 passengers. All cabins are technically outside staterooms, but Category 1 rooms have only a high port light (a very small porthole). Both ships are equipped with underwater microphones and videos, allowing passengers to hear and see what's going on beneath the waves. ⊠ *Lindblad Expeditions, 720 5th Ave., New York, NY 10019,* ☎ *212/765–7740 or 800/527–6298,* WEB *www. expeditions.com. Lounge, dining room, boating, library. Average per diem: $500–$600.*

Spirit of Alaska. Cruise West's original overnight vessel is still its coziest. Cabins are cheerfully decorated, with warm peach walls and brightly colored bedspreads. You are never by yourself in the lounge, and meals in the homey dining room resemble a family affair soon after the cruise has begun. Sleek and small, the *Spirit of Alaska* feels like a real yacht. Toilets and showers are a combined unit (the toilet is inside the shower). Suites and some outside cabins have TVs for watching videos. As with other Cruise West ships, the ambience is casual, and a naturalist sails with every voyage. ⊠ *Cruise West, 4th & Battery Bldg., Suite 700, Seattle, WA 98121,* ☎ *206/441–8687 or 800/ 888–9378,* WEB *www.cruisewest.com. Dining room, lounge. Average per diem: $350–$500.*

Spirit of Columbia. Structurally similar to Cruise West's *Spirit of Alaska,* the *Spirit of Columbia* has an interior design inspired by the national-park lodges of the American West, with a color scheme based on muted shades of evergreen, rust, and sand. All suites and deluxe cabins have a mini-refrigerator, an armchair, and a small desk. The Columbia deluxe cabin stretches the width of the vessel; just under the bridge, its row of forward-facing windows gives a captain's-eye view of the ship's progress. Suites and deluxe cabins have TVs, but only for watching videos. As with other Cruise West vessels, the focus here is on Alaskan scenery, wildlife, and culture, rather than shipboard diversions; a naturalist is onboard for every cruise. ⊠ *Cruise West, 4th & Battery Bldg., Suite 700, Seattle, WA 98121,* ☎ *206/441–8687 or 800/888–9378,* WEB *www.cruisewest.com. Dining room, lounge. Average per diem: $450–$600.*

Spirit of Discovery. Floor-to-ceiling windows in the main lounge provide stunning views aboard this snazzy cruiser. Blue-suede chairs, a wraparound bench sofa at the bow, and a mirrored ceiling make the chrome-filled lounge look especially swanky. From here, passengers have direct access to a large outdoor viewing deck, one of two aboard. This is great for those who don't want to trudge upstairs every time a whale is spotted. Deluxe cabins have mini-refrigerators, and many cabins have extra-large picture windows; two cabins are reserved for single travelers. Toilets and showers are a combined unit. Suites and some outside cabins have TVs for watching videos. ⊠ *Cruise West, 4th & Battery Bldg., Suite 700, Seattle, WA 98121,* ☎ *206/441–8687 or 800/ 888–9378. Dining room, lounge. Average per diem: $400–$500.*

Spirit of Endeavour. One of Cruise West's largest and fastest ships, the *Spirit of Endeavour* provides ample deck space and a lounge with large picture windows for superb views. Most of the cabins have picture windows, all are outside, and some cabins have connecting doors, which make them convenient for families traveling together. All cabins have TVs and VCRs, but only for watching videos; some have refrigerators. ⊠ *Cruise West, 4th & Battery Bldg., Suite 700, Seattle, WA 98121,* ☎ *206/441–8687 or 800/888–9378,* WEB *www.cruisewest.com. Dining room, lounge, library. Average per diem: $450–$500.*

Spirit of '98. With its rounded stern and wheelhouse, old-fashioned smokestack, and Victorian decor, the *Spirit of '98* evokes a turn-of-the-20th-century steamer. Inside and out, mahogany adorns this elegant ship. Overstuffed chairs upholstered in crushed velvet complete the gold rush–era motif. For private moments, you'll find plenty of nooks and crannies aboard the ship, along with the cozy Soapy's Parlor at the stern, with a small bar and a few tables and chairs. All cabins are outside with picture windows, and all have TVs, but only for watching videos. ⊠ *Cruise West, 4th & Battery Bldg., Suite 700, Seattle, WA 98121,* ☎ *206/441–8687 or 800/888–9378,* WEB *www.cruisewest.com. Bar, dining room, lounge, in-room VCRs. Average per diem: $450–$500.*

Spirit of Oceanus. Cruise West's flagship vessel, launched in 2001, is its most luxurious. Marble and polished hardwood enrich the public areas, and cabins, which range from 215 to 353 square ft. All the staterooms are outside, and 12 of them have a teak-floor private balcony. A naturalist travels on every cruise, and the ship carries a fleet of Zodiacs for close-up visits to glaciers, waterfalls, and icebergs. Breakfast and lunch are served on deck when the weather permits. ⊠ *Cruise West, 4th & Battery Bldg., Suite 700, Seattle, WA 98121,* ☎ *206/441–8687 or 800/888–9378,* WEB *www.cruisewest.com. Dining room, 2 lounges, in-room safes, in-room VCRs, refrigerators, outdoor hot tub, gym, library. Average per diem: $500–$800.*

Yorktown Clipper. The *Yorktown Clipper* is a stylish coastal cruiser with a casual sophistication. There are only a few public rooms—which are bright and comfortable—and deck space is limited. Onboard naturalists and Zodiac landing craft enhance the emphasis on destination. Floor-to-ceiling windows in the lounge and large windows in the dining room allow sightseeing in all weather. Cabins are all outside, and most have large windows. The crew is young and enthusiastic. ⊠ *Clipper Cruise Line, 7711 Bonhomme Ave., St. Louis, MO 63105,* ☎ *314/727–2929 or 800/325–0010,* WEB *www.clippercruise.com. Bar, dining room, lounge. Average per diem: $300–$400.*

Ferry Liners

Alaska Marine Highway System. Serving 32 ports of call in Alaska as well as Bellingham, Washington, and Prince Rupert, British Columbia, Alaskan ferries are a scenic option for getting to and around Alaska. Ferry travel is rather slow: maximum speed is 16.5 knots, compared with 21 knots or better for the typical ocean liner. But it's a great way to take in the landscape, collect your thoughts, jot down some notes in a journal—and maybe see a whale or two. The ferry also affords freedom of movement. Unlike the big cruise ships, which follow a set itinerary, ferries come and go daily; you can get on and off whenever you wish, and stay as long as you want. In between ports of call, you get to see places that few other tourists visit. Stops are often made at smaller communities, such as Angoon and Tenakee Springs—just a strip of houses on stilts huddled along the shoreline. Another advantage of ferry travel is cost: fares are affordable, and the food, served cafeteria style, is hearty and cheap. The ferries are less than luxurious, but they are certainly comfortable enough. Each has a glass-lined observation lounge, and the larger ferries have a bar. Cabins on the Alaskan ferries are simple but serviceable. They book up almost instantly for cruises during the summer season, but a number of tour operators sell packages that include shipboard accommodations. It's essential to book in advance if you're traveling with a vehicle. One of the most established is **Knightly Tours** (⊠ Box 16366, Seattle, WA 98116, ☎ 206/938–8567 or 800/426–2123, ℻ 206/938–8498). ⊠ *Alaska Marine Highway System, 6858 Glacier Hwy., Juneau 99801–7909,* ☎ *800/642–0066,* ℻ *907/277–4829,* WEB *www.state.ak.us/ferry.*

2 PARKS AND WILDERNESS ADVENTURES

Fly over a thundering herd of caribou above the Arctic Circle, watch bears on Kodiak and Admiralty islands, drift past bellowing sea lions on the Kenai Peninsula, wander by volcanoes in Katmai National Park, kayak through icebergs in Glacier Bay, bike up to the Chugach Mountains for a stupendous view of the Cook Inlet and Anchorage, or have a floatplane drop you by a secluded Forest Service cabin and cast your fishing line in complete solitude. Alaska has more than 100 million protected acres to explore.

By Peggy
Wayburn and
Mary Engel

Updated by
Bill Sherwonit

I N THE ALEUT LANGUAGE, the word *Alaska* means "the Great Land"—
an appropriate name for the 49th of the United States, the one with
more land in parks, wilderness areas, and wildlife refuges than all
the other states combined. In fact, about one-third of Alaska's 375 million acres is set aside in protected public lands.

These are lands not only of prodigious scale but of prodigious beauty.
Four great mountain ranges—St. Elias, Alaska, Brooks, and Chugach—
sweep through Alaska: one is the highest coastal range in the world;
another includes the highest point of the North American continent (Mt.
McKinley, 20,320 ft); the third lies north of and roughly defines the Arctic Circle; and the fourth arcs through Alaska's most populous region.
In between the mountains are rugged canyons, treeless valleys, softly
rolling hills, flower-filled meadows, limpid lakes, blue-iced glaciers,
waterfalls, deep-shadowed rain forests, and spacious tundras. Adding
to this wealth are some 47,000 mi of spectacular tidal coastline.

Because of its relative inaccessibility and frequently demanding climate,
most of this extraordinary area has remained largely undeveloped
since it was acquired by the United States in 1867. (The United States
paid Russia all of $7.2 million for this treasure.) First called Indian Coun-
try and then made a district, Alaska became a proper territory in 1912.
However, except for military and federal reservations and a handful
of homesites, the first extensive subdivision of Alaska did not occur
until 1959, when the territory achieved statehood.

At that time Congress granted the new state 104 million acres to be
selected out of more than 300 million acres of "vacant, unappropriated public land," which up to that time had been administered in Alaska
by the Bureau of Land Management (or BLM, the federal agency that
is charged with caring for the country's uncommitted public lands). In
1970 another congressional act—the Alaska Native Claims Settlement
Act (ANCSA)—gave to Alaska's Native people an additional 44 million acres to be chosen from the remaining unappropriated lands. And
in 1980, the Alaska National Interest Lands Conservation Act (ANILCA)
established federal protection for about 104 million acres of outstanding Alaska land for the use and enjoyment of all the American
people—and indeed of people throughout the world. Gaining passage
of this legislation is considered by many to be the most extraordinary
environmental achievement in the country's history.

Alaska's protected federal lands now include nearly 55 million acres
of national parks (administered by the National Park Service), 77 million acres of national wildlife refuges (administered by the United
States Fish and Wildlife Service), 26 wild and scenic rivers totaling nearly
2 million acres (administered by federal agencies), and 5.7 million
acres of land administered by the United States Forest Service as wilderness areas. (Forest Service "multiple use" lands total more than 23 million acres.) Alaska's remaining vacant and unappropriated public land
still administered by the BLM now totals somewhere around 84.7
million acres and will continue to decline as land is allotted. Along with
the federally protected lands established in Alaska by the passage of
ANILCA in 1980, approximately 3.2 million acres of superb lands are
set aside as state parks.

Because Alaska's public lands are as varied as they are magnificent,
recreational opportunities within them are likewise varied. They range
from such spectator sports as wildlife viewing to rigorous participa-
tory sports such as mountaineering (there are still many unclimbed peaks
for intrepid climbers to scale). Many of these lands are only partially

Parks and Wildlife Refuges

Barrow

Chukchi Sea

Colville River

B R O O K S

Noatak National Preserve

Noatak River

Cape Krusenstern National Monument

IGICHUK HILLS

Kotzebue

Kiana

Gates of the Arctic National Park and Preserve

ENDICOTT MO

RUSSIA

Bering Strait

Bering Land Bridge National Preserve

Kotzebue Sound

Kobuk Valley National Park

SCHWATKA MOUNTAINS

Kobuk River

Selawik National Wildlife Refuge

Kobuk

Bettles

ARCTIC CIRCLE

Teller

Council

Koyukuk National Wildlife Refuge

Kanuti National Wildlife Refuge

Nome

Saint Lawrence Island

Yukon River

Livengo

Norton Sound

Nowitna National Wildlife Refuge

Fair

I N T E

Bering Sea

Innoko National Wildlife Refuge

KUSKOKWIM MOUNTAINS

Denali National Park and Preserve

Mt. McKinley ▲

Cantwell

Den Stat

Yukon Delta National Wildlife Refuge

Kuskokwim River

ALASKA

S O U T H

Bethel

Wasilia

Nunivak Island

Anchorage

Tyonek

Lake Clark National Park and Preserve

Kenai

Palm

Whit

Kuskokwim Bay

Togiak National Wildlife Refuge

Wood-Tikchik State Park

Cook Inlet

KENAI PEN.

Sew

Homer

Kenai Fjords National Park

McNeil River State Game Sanctuary ■

Dillingham

Round Island

King Salmon

Katmai National Park and Preserve

Kenai National Wildlife Refuge

Kachem State

Bristol Bay

Becharof National Wildlife Refuge

Port Lions

Shuyak Island State Park

Chugach National Forest

Kodiak

Kodiak National Wildlife Refuge

ALASKA PENINSULA

Aniakchak National Monument and Preserve

Izembek National Wildlife Refuge

Alaska Peninsula National Wildlife Refuge

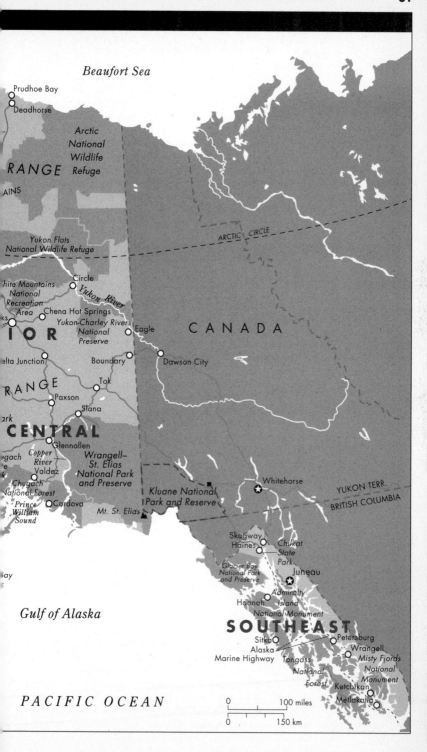

Beaufort Sea

Prudhoe Bay
Deadhorse

Arctic
National
Wildlife
Refuge

RANGE

AINS

ARCTIC CIRCLE

Yukon Flats
National Wildlife Refuge

hite Mountains
National
Recreation
Area

Circle
Yukon River

Chena Hot Springs

Yukon-Charley Rivers
National
Preserve

Eagle

CANADA

ks

IOR

elta Junction

Boundary

Dawson City

RANGE

Tok

Paxson

Stana

ark

CENTRAL

Glennallen

gach
e

Copper
River

Valdez

Wrangell–
St. Elias
National Park
and Preserve

Whitehorse

YUKON TERR.

Kluane National
Park and Reserve

BRITISH COLUMBIA

Chugach
National Forest

Cordova

Prince
William
Sound

Mt. St. Elias

Skagway
Haines

Chilkat
State
Park

ay

Glacier Bay
National Park
and Preserve

Juneau

Gulf of Alaska

Hoonah

Admiralty
Island
National Monument

SOUTHEAST

Sitka
Alaska
Marine Highway

Petersburg

Wrangell

Misty Fjords
National
Monument

Tongass
National
Forest

Ketchikan

Metlakatla

PACIFIC OCEAN

0   100 miles

0   150 km

accessible: although you can drive to some, you will more often have to go by air—usually air taxi—or boat to the area of your choice.

Thousands of mountains in this state not only haven't been climbed but also haven't been named. The state's most visited parks are Denali National Park and Preserve, Glacier Bay National Park and Preserve, Kenai Fjords National Park, and Chugach State Park; however, this doesn't mean a backpacker or kayaker can't have a remote wilderness experience there. Parks closer to roads, and closer to Anchorage and Fairbanks, are likely to have more visitors, but that doesn't necessarily translate into the numbers encountered in parks in the Lower 48. On the other hand, if you're after a truly remote and out-of-the-way experience, you may want to try some of the least-visited places in the state, such as Wood-Tikchik State Park, where one lonely ranger patrols 1.55 million acres, or Aniakchak National Monument and Preserve, south of Katmai, where a ranger can go days or sometimes weeks without seeing a visitor.

PLANNING A WILDERNESS ADVENTURE

Camping

Hundreds of campgrounds—both public and private—exist along Alaska's road system. But if you wish to explore Alaska's vast backcountry, you will almost certainly have to establish your own campsites (though some park units do have remote tent sites). Before heading into the backcountry, contact the appropriate management agency for any advice or restrictions. Several variables must be considered whenever camping in the backcountry, including water sources, good drainage (you don't want to end up swamped in heavy rains), protection from high winds, and the presence of any game trails (which should be avoided, particularly if bears are known to inhabit the area). Campers are also advised to practice "low-impact" camping techniques to minimize damage to the environment. For example: carry out *all* garbage; avoid camping on fragile vegetation, which can be easily trampled; if possible, camp on already established sites; never cut standing trees; wash yourself, your clothes, and your dishes at least 100 ft from water sources; bring a trowel and dig "cat-hole" latrines for human waste at least 100 ft from your camp, water sources, and trails; burn or carry out toilet paper. When traveling in trail-less areas (particularly tundra), fan out instead of walking single file, again to avoid trampling vegetation. Alaska's weather is unpredictable: anticipate delays, especially when traveling to backcountry areas by plane, and bring more food and fuel than you think you'll need.

Ecotourism

Concern for the environment has spawned a worldwide movement called ecotourism, or green tourism. Ecotourists aim to travel responsibly, taking care to conserve natural environments and show respect for local, indigenous populations. Ecotourism typically is smaller scale and involves more visitor education than traditional tourism; often, visitors are led by guides who know the local natural history of plants, animals, and landscape and are familiar with local cultures. It is also slower paced, and therefore allows visitors to have a closer connection to the areas that they explore. Ecotourists are encouraged to experience the landscape and its wildlife on their own terms, instead of rushing from one destination to another. As one Alaskan guide says, "Slow down, take a deep breath, feel where you are." For a state publication on ecotourism, contact the **Alaska Travel Industry Association** (✉ 2600 Cordova St., Suite 201, Anchorage 99501, ☎ 907/929–2200). **Recreational Equipment Inc.** (✉ 1200 W. Northern Lights Blvd., Anchorage 99503, ☎ 907/272–4565) has a helpful brochure titled "Minimum Impact Camping" as well as a useful handout on backpacking equipment needs.

If you want to enjoy the wilderness while limiting your impact on it, the Ecotourism Society, a nonprofit research and advocacy group based in Alexandria, Virginia, gives these tips: know what type of adventure you want (for example, remote wilderness backpacking or wilderness lodge with heated cabins and gourmet meals); choose a local guide or a well-trained naturalist as your guided-tour operator; learn about local customs and pertinent facts about the nature of your destination before starting your trip; get clear instructions on how to approach wildlife and how to dispose of wastes; choose low-impact transportation and guided outfits that place limits on group size.

A large and still-growing number of ecotour companies operate in all regions of the state.

Equipment

Get the best equipment you can afford; it's a must in Alaska.

Backpacking

First decide whether to get a pack with an internal or external frame. If you choose the latter, pick one that balances the pack upright when you set it on the ground; this is a great help in the many areas of Alaska that don't have trees. Internal frames are an advantage when going through brush, which is common in Alaska. A rainproof cover for your pack is a good idea, even if it's just a heavy plastic garbage bag (bring along extras).

Camping

Because winterlike storms can occur at almost any time of year, a four-season tent is highly recommended—one that can withstand strong winds and persistent rainfall. There are few things worse than being stuck in a battered, leaky tent with a storm raging outside. Tie-down ropes and tent flies are essential items, and mosquito netting is another must. For sleeping comfort, bring a sleeping pad to add cushioning and insulation beneath your sleeping bag. Be sure your bag is warm enough for the expected range of conditions; even in midsummer, nighttime temperatures may fall to the freezing mark, especially in the mountains. You should also carry a lightweight stove with fuel; if nothing else, you'll need to boil your water to protect against *Giardia* (an intestinal parasite). Firewood is often a scarce item in Alaska, and what there is may be wet. The burning of wood in many parklands is now frowned upon or prohibited in order to protect the habitat.

Day Pack

When setting out for a day hike from a base camp, it's wise to carry a pack stocked with a few essentials. These include a knife, preferably a multifunction pocketknife; a first-aid kit, including bandages and moleskin; a cup and spoon, on which you may wish to bang to alert bears; a bottle of drinking water; extra candy bars or gorp (nuts, chocolate, and raisins); a warm sweater or jacket and windproof rain gear, in case the weather suddenly changes (be sure to avoid cotton clothing; cotton does not retain body warmth when wet); waterproof matches (you can make these by coating kitchen matches with wax) and other fire starters, such as a candle or heat tab; a flare or flashlight; a topographical map; toilet paper; sunglasses; bug repellent; duct tape, for all kinds of emergencies; and a compass.

A note about compasses: the farther north you travel, the more the compass needle will be skewed upward and to the east of north by several degrees. U.S. Geological Survey maps show this difference between magnetic and true north—called magnetic declination—at the bottom; with these maps, you can use your compass accordingly—otherwise, allow for this deviation as you do your compass reading.

Terrain

Forests

Forest trails are often wet, especially in coastal lowlands, and they may be soggy or potholed—sometimes they're even blocked with beaver dams. Trails through forested lands are difficult to maintain. The ground stays wet much of the time, and brush grows back quickly after it is cut. Especially nasty is devil's club, a large, attractive plant that is armored thickly with stinging needles. Virtually all hiking country in the Southeast is part of the 17-million-acre Tongass National Forest, administered by the U.S. Forest Service. Several popular trails have also been built within Chugach National Forest and Chugach State Park in South Central Alaska. Although the Forest Service does not consider trail maintenance a top priority, it is a good source for checking the latest condition of backcountry roads and paths.

Rivers

Crossing Alaska's rivers requires care. Many are swift, glacial, silty streams that are harder to read than clear-water streams. Many flow over impermeable bottoms (either rock or permafrost), which means a good rain can raise water levels a matter of feet, not inches, in just a short time. Warm days can also dramatically increase the meltwater from glaciers. Be aware of weather changes that might affect the ease of river crossings. Look for the widest, most shallow place you can find, with many channels. This may entail traveling up- or downstream. A guide who knows the region is invaluable at such times.

A sturdy staff—your own or made from a handy branch—is useful to help you keep your balance and measure the depths of silty water. You may find it easier to uncinch your pack when crossing a swift stream; you can then shed it if you need to. Avoid wearing a long rain poncho; it can catch the water like a sail catches wind and tip you off your feet. For added stability it may help for two or more people to link arms when crossing. Hikers debate the best footwear for crossing Alaskan rivers. Some take along sneakers and wear them through the water; others take off their socks so they will remain dry and can comfort cold feet on the opposite shore. But bear in mind that Alaskan waters are probably frigid, and the bottom is usually rough; bare feet are not advised. One school even advocates wearing your boots—socks and all—and continuing your hike with wet feet.

Tundra

Tundra hiking—especially in higher alpine country—can be a great pleasure. In places, the ground is so springy you feel like you're walking on a trampoline. In the Arctic, however, where the ground is underlaid with permafrost, you will probably find the going as wet as it is in the Southeast, particularly at lower elevations. The summer sun melts the top, often a thin layer above the permafrost, leaving puddles, small lakes, and marshy spots behind. Comfortable waterproof footgear can help when traversing such wet landscapes. Tundra travel can require the skill of a ballet dancer if the ground is tufted with tussocks (mushroom-shape clumps of grass making slippery, unstable hummocks). This can quickly tire those not used to it.

Wilderness Safety

Alaska's terrain is rugged, demanding care and strength. Its weather is often wet and cold, even in summer. Always be prepared for storms and winterlike conditions, particularly when traveling through the state's mountain ranges or along its jagged coastline, where the weather can change dramatically with little warning.

Be sure you're in good shape before venturing into backcountry—or travel with an experienced guide. Do your homework and prepare yourself for the type of landscape you'll be visiting. If you are traveling by boat along the coast, bring a tide book; some of Alaska's coastal areas have tidal swings of 30 ft–40 ft. If hiking or backpacking overland, know in advance whether you'll have to cross large glacial rivers. Pay attention to the weather, which can greatly influence the ease or difficulty of crossing those streams.

Bring the essentials you'll need to follow your chosen route and keep track of your location. Use maps (preferably 1 inch:1 mi maps published by the U.S. Geological Survey) and a compass at the very minimum. Some adventurers now carry cell phones, though they might not always be useful in remote wilderness areas. Other options for emergency use are electronic locator devices and handheld aviation radios.

When you're hiking in a national park, national forest, wildlife refuge, state park, or any other kind of protected, administered land, plan to check in and out with a ranger or person staffing the reserve. Be sure to leave plans and an itinerary with at least one trustworthy person before you go. Be as specific as you can about your destination and estimated date of return, and leave the names of people to call in case of an emergency. Be prepared for unexpected delays; Alaska's weather can play havoc with air and water transportation. One of the most common phrases used by wilderness explorers in Alaska is "weather permitting."

Hypothermia—the lowering of the body's core temperature—is an ever-present threat in Alaska's wilderness. To help avoid it, be sure to wear warm clothing (in layers) when the weather is cool and/or wet; this includes a good wind- and waterproof parka or shell, warm head- and hand gear, and waterproof or water-resistant boots. Be sure to eat regularly and drink enough liquids to stay properly hydrated.

The onset of hypothermia can be recognized by the following symptoms: shivering, accelerated heartbeat, and goose bumps; this may be followed by loss of judgment, clumsiness, loss of control over bodily functions, slurred speech, disorientation, and unconsciousness and, in the extreme, can result in death. If you notice any of these symptoms in yourself—whether from overexertion, sweating (which can act as a refrigerating agent), or improper clothing—stop, light a fire, and warm yourself, using your sleeping bag if necessary; a cup of hot tea or another warm drink also helps. If your clothes are wet, change immediately. And be sure to put on a warm hat (most of the body's heat is lost through the head). If the weather is wet and/or windy, it may be necessary to set up a tent and curl up in a sleeping bag to get out of the weather. If you notice these symptoms in a traveling companion, follow the same procedure. The most important thing is to stop heat loss. If there are only two of you, stay together: a person with hypothermia should never be left alone.

Finally, Alaska's waters, even its wild rivers, often carry *Giardia,* which can cause diarrhea and sap your strength. Boil your drinking water in the Bush.

Wildlife Viewing

Alaska is one of the few places in the country where you can easily view wildlife in its natural state. It's unique among the 50 United States for its vast resource of protected wilderness, and is rich in birds, animals, and fish. Alaska's wild beauty adds a powerful dimension to any wildlife-viewing experience.

Alaska's 375 million acres support nearly 1,000 species of animals—mammals, birds, and fish. The 105 different mammals range from whales to shrews (Alaska's shrews are the smallest of North America's land mammals, weighing ¹⁄₁₀ ounce). The more than 400 species of birds range from hummingbirds to bald eagles, including species found nowhere else in North America. Migrant birds come here annually from every continent and many islands to take advantage of Alaska's rich breeding and rearing grounds: its wetlands, its rivers, its shores, and its tundras. Among the 430 different kinds of fish—including five different kinds of salmon—some weigh more than 300 pounds (halibut) and others weigh often less than a pound (arctic grayling).

The most prodigious numbers of animals can be seen during periods of migration. The state is strategically positioned for creatures that migrate vast distances. Some birds, for instance, fly from the southern tip of South America to nest and rear their young on sandbars in Alaska's wild rivers. Others travel from parts of Asia to enjoy an Alaskan summer. The arctic tern is the greatest of these long-distance voyagers, coming here all the way from Antarctica. Sea mammals congregate in great numbers in the waters of Prince William Sound, the Panhandle, the Gulf of Alaska, and the Bering, Beaufort, and Chukchi seas. Tens of thousands of caribou move between Canada and Alaska across the Arctic slope. Anadromous fish by the millions swim up Alaska's rivers, returning unerringly to the place where they were born.

Bears live in virtually every part of the state, and though they are often solitary, it is not unusual to see a mother bear with cubs. In some areas the bears gather in large numbers to feed upon rich runs of salmon. Several world-class bear-viewing areas attract visitors, from Southeast to Southwest Alaska. Moose abound in the wetter country of the Southeast, as well as in South Central and Interior Alaska. Caribou wander over the tundra country of the Arctic, sub-Arctic, and even South Central, although there are fewer in this part of the state. The coastal mountains of the Southeast and South Central harbor wild goats, and the mountains of the South Central, Interior, and Arctic regions are home to snow-white Dall sheep, which sometimes come down to the streams in the summer. Wolves and lynx, though not so easily seen, live in many parts of the Southeast, South Central, Interior, and Arctic regions, and if you're lucky, a wolf may dash across the road in front of you, or a smaller mammal, such as the arctic fox, may watch you when you're rafting or even when you're traveling on wheels.

Strategies for Spotting Wildlife

Know what you're looking for. Have some idea of the habitat the wildlife you seek thrives in. Season and time of day are critical. You may want to view during twilight, which during summer in certain parts of Alaska can last all night. Interestingly, winter may be the best time to look for wolves because they stand out against the snow (not true for the arctic fox, which turns white in winter). You may have only a few hours out of the day during which you can look, and in northern Alaska, there won't be any daylight at all during the winter months.

Be careful. Keep a good distance, especially with animals that can be dangerous (☞ The Bear Facts box, *below*). Whether you're on foot or in a vehicle, don't get too close. A pair of good binoculars or a scope is well worth the extra weight. Don't get too close to or touch a fox (if you're traveling with pets, keep them leashed). The fox you admire may be carrying rabies. **Move slowly,** stop often, look, and listen. The exception is when you see a bear; you may want to let the animal know you're there. Avoid startling an animal and risking a dangerous confrontation, especially with a mother bear with cubs or a mother moose with calf. **Keep your hat on** if you are in territory where arctic terns or pomarine jaegers nest. Both species are highly protective of their nests and young, and they are skillful dive-bombers. Occasionally, they connect with human heads, and the results can be painful.

Be prepared to wait; patience often pays off. And if you're an enthusiastic birder or animal watcher, **be prepared to hike over some rough terrain**—Alaska is full of it—to reach the best viewing vantage. **Respect and protect** both the animal you're watching and its habitat. Don't chase or harass the animals. The willful act of harassing an animal is punishable in Alaska by a $1,000 fine. This includes flushing birds from their nests and purposely frightening animals with loud noises.

Don't disturb or surprise the animals, which also applies to birds' eggs, the young, the nests, and such habitats as beaver dams. It's best to let the animal discover your presence quietly, if at all, by keeping still or moving slowly (except when viewing bears or moose). If the animal should be disturbed, limit your viewing time and leave as quietly as possible. **Don't use a tape recorder** to call a bird or to attract other animals if you're in bear country, as you might call an angry bear. And **don't feed the animals,** as any creature that comes to depend on humans for food almost always comes to a sorry end.

Best Viewing

Even those traveling by car in Alaska have abundant opportunity to spot wildlife. For those traveling by boat, the **Alaska Marine Highway**—the route plied by Alaska's state ferries—passes through waters rich with fish, sea mammals, and birds. Throughout the Southeast, ferries often provide sightings of whales and virtually always of bald eagles. **Kenai Fjords National Park,** a mecca for those interested in sea mammals and seabirds, provides excellent tour-boat opportunities. Smaller boats and touring vessels are found in such places as **Glacier Bay National Park and Preserve,** an especially good place to spot humpback whales, puffins, seals, shorebirds, and perhaps a black or brown bear. **Denali National Park and Preserve** is known worldwide for its wildlife; you are likely to see grizzlies, moose, Dall sheep, caribou, foxes, golden eagles, and perhaps even wolves. The **Alaska Chilkat Bald Eagle Preserve** hosts the world's largest gathering of bald eagles each fall and winter.

BEARS

You can't be absolutely sure you'll spot a grizzly bear in **Denali National Park** (✉ Box 9, Denali National Park 99755, ☎ 907/683–2294) but your chances are better than 50-50. Talk with the staff at the visitor center near the park entrance when you arrive.

Katmai National Park (✉ Box 7, King Salmon 99613, ☎ 907/246–3305), on the Alaska Peninsula, has an abundance of bears—on average more than one brown bear per square mile, among the highest densities of any region in North America. In July, when the salmon are running up Brooks River, bears concentrate around Brooks River Falls, resulting in a great view of these animals as they fish, and the spectacle of hundreds of salmon leaping the falls.

THE BEAR FACTS

ALASKA IS SOMETIMES called "bear country," and for good reason. It is the only one of our nation's 50 states to be inhabited by all three North American ursine species: the polar bear, black bear, and brown bear (also known as grizzly). The statewide population of each species thrives, thanks largely to Alaska's abundance of wild, remote, and undeveloped regions.

You'll find few places in Alaska where bears don't share the landscape. Even Anchorage, with its urban developments and large human population, is visited by black and brown bears. Wherever you venture in Alaska, keep in mind these tips for travel in bear country:

Avoid sudden encounters. Whenever possible, travel in open country, during daylight hours, and in groups. Make noise—talking or singing is preferable to "bear bells"—and leave your dog at home. Most attacks occur when a bear is surprised at close quarters or feels threatened.

Stay alert. Look for signs of bear, such as fresh tracks, scat, matted vegetation, or partially consumed salmon.

Choose your tent site carefully. Pitch the tent away from trails, streams with spawning salmon, and berry patches. Avoid areas that have a rotten smell or where scavengers have gathered; these may indicate the presence of a nearby bear cache, and bears aggressively defend their food supplies.

Keep your food away from campsites. Cook meals at least 100 feet from tents and store food and other odorous items away from campsites. Hang them in trees where possible or store your food in bear-resistant food containers. Avoid strong-smelling foods and clean up after cooking and eating. Store garbage in airtight containers or burn it, and pack up the remains.

If you encounter a bear:

Identify yourself. Talk to the bear, to identify yourself as a human. Don't yell. And don't run. Running from a bear usually will trigger a bear's predatory instincts, and a bear can easily outrun you. Back away slowly, and give the bear an escape route. Don't ever get between a mother and her cubs.

Bigger is better. Bears are less likely to attack a larger target. Therefore, increase your apparent size. Raise your arms above your head to appear larger and wave them slowly, to better identify yourself as a human. With two or more people, it helps to stand side by side. In a forested area it may be appropriate to climb a tree, but remember that black bears and young grizzlies are agile tree climbers.

Play dead. If a bear charges and makes contact with you, fall to the ground, lie flat on your stomach or curl into a ball, hands behind your neck, and remain passive. If you are wearing a pack, leave it on. Once a bear no longer feels threatened it will usually end its attack. Wait for the bear to leave before you move. The exception to this rule is when a bear displays predatory behavior. Instead of simply charging, a bear hunting for prey will show intense interest while approaching at a walk or run and it may circle, as if stalking you. But remember that such circumstances are exceedingly rare and most often involve black bears, which are much smaller and less aggressive than grizzlies.

Kodiak National Wildlife Refuge, on Kodiak Island, is an excellent place to see brown bears. Contact the refuge headquarters (⊠ 1390 Buskin Rd., Kodiak 99615, ☎ 907/487–2600).

The **McNeil River State Game Sanctuary,** on the Alaska Peninsula, hosts the world's largest gathering of brown bears—as many as 70 have been counted at one time at McNeil Falls—and thus affords unsurpassed photographic opportunities. Peak season, when the local salmon are running, is early June through mid-August. Much-sought-after reservations are available by a lottery conducted in March by the Alaska Department of Fish and Game (⊠ 333 Raspberry Rd., Anchorage 99518, ☎ 907/267–2182).

At **Pack Creek,** on Admiralty Island, you'll see brown bears (the coastal equivalents of grizzlies) fishing for spawning salmon—pink, chum, and silver. To get here, you can fly (air charter) or take a boat from Juneau. If you time your visit to coincide with the salmon runs in July and August, you will almost surely see bald eagles and flocks of gulls, too. Permits are required to visit during the peak bear-viewing period; contact **Admiralty Island National Monument** (⊠ 8461 Old Dairy Rd., Juneau 99801, ☎ 907/586–8795).

The **Silver Salmon Creek Lodge** (⊠ Box 3234, Soldotna 99669, ☎ 888/872–5666) conducts a bear-viewing program along the shores of western Cook Inlet, near Lake Clark National Park, with lodging, meals, and guide services for both bear-viewing and sportfishing.

BIRDS

If you come on your own, try the following sure and easily accessed bets. In **Anchorage,** walk around Potters Marsh or Westchester Lagoon or along the Coastal Trail for shorebirds, waterfowl, and the occasional bald eagle. Songbird enthusiasts are likely to see many species in town or neighboring Chugach State Park. The **Anchorage Audubon Society** has a bird-report recording (☎ 907/338–2473). In **Juneau,** visit the Mendenhall Wetlands State Game Refuge, next to the airport, for ducks, geese, and swans (there are trails and interpretive signs). In **Fairbanks,** head for the Creamer's Field Migratory Waterfowl Refuge on College Road. Here, if you're lucky, you might see sandhill cranes in summer and spectacular shows of ducks and geese in spring.

Great crowds of bald eagles visit the Chilkat River, near **Haines** in Southeast Alaska, each November and December. In the summer, rafting on almost any Alaskan river brings the near certainty of sighting nesting shorebirds, arctic terns, and merganser mothers trailed by chicks. Approximately 200 species of birds have been sighted on the **Pribilof Islands,** but you will almost certainly need to be part of a guided tour to get there.

CARIBOU

The migrations of caribou across Alaska's Arctic regions are wonderful to watch, but they are not always easy to time because of annual variations in weather and routes that the herds follow. The U.S. Fish and Wildlife Service and Alaska Department of Fish and Game will have the best guess as to where you should be and when. Or you can settle for seeing a few caribou in places such as Denali National Park.

MARINE ANIMALS

At **Round Island,** outside Dillingham in the Southwest, bull walruses by the thousands haul out during the summer. Part of the Walrus Islands State Game Sanctuary, Round Island can be visited by permit only. For details, contact the **Alaska Department of Fish and Game** (⊠ Box 1030, Dillingham 99576, ☎ 907/842–2334). Access is by floatplane or, more commonly, by boat. Expect rain, winds, and the possibility of being weathered in. Rubber boots are essential, as are a four-season tent, high-quality rain gear, and plenty of food.

It's easier, but still expensive, to visit the remote **Pribilof Islands**—where about 80% of the world's northern fur seals and 200 species of birds can be seen—but you may also encounter fog and Bering Sea storms. Tours to the Pribilofs leave from Anchorage. Contact the **Alaska Maritime National Wildlife Refuge** (⊠ 2355 Kachemak Bay Dr., Suite 101, Homer 99603-8021, ☎ 907/235–6546 or 907/235–6961) for information about wildlife-viewing opportunities.

WILDERNESS ADVENTURES

Vacationing in Alaska can be a lot more than viewing glaciers. Visitors are taking advantage of the increasing number of trips and tours that make it possible for them to spend a week or two (or more) learning—and performing—feats they've only fantasized about, from horsepacking within sight of Mt. McKinley to mushing through some of the state's most challenging landscapes, including Gates of the Arctic National Park. Below you'll find some recommended trips, questions to consider, and suggestions to help you choose the right program. When comparing offerings, be sure to consider the following.

To reserve a spot, most operators require you to put down a deposit by a particular day and then pay the rest sometime before the starting date. In most cases, if you cancel your reservation, you get at least a partial refund, but policies vary widely. **Find out how far in advance you must cancel to get a full refund,** and ask whether any allowances are made for cancellations due to medical emergencies. If cancellation insurance is available, you may want to take it. You'll receive a full refund regardless of why you don't show up as planned.

Taxes are generally not included in the quoted price and they can add substantially to the cost of your trip. Depending on the program, you should also **ask about gratuities**—inquire about which members of the tour personnel customarily get tipped and what the average rate is.

Dogsledding

"Hike!" commands a musher as he releases a brake. They don't call it "mushing" for nothing. The word is from the French *moucher,* which means "to go fast." And the dogs do. On command, a team of surprisingly small but amazingly strong huskies charges off, howling and yowling excitedly. Of all the wild sporting adventures out there, dogsledding may be the wildest—not only because it's exotic but also because you're literally out in the wilds with pack animals, just like a polar explorer.

Dogsledding is not for everyone. For one thing, you have to like the cold. You also have to like roughing it. Even the nicest accommodations are only a step or two removed from camping, and with camping out comes cooking out. Most important, you have to like dogs—a lot. Contrary to the romantic image you may have of sled dogs, they're not all cuddly, clean Siberian huskies. They're often mutts—that is, mixed-breed Alaskan huskies—and often not particularly well groomed.

Here are some facts to consider when choosing your trip: on some mushing trips, participants travel by cross-country skiing or snowshoeing, rather than actually mushing, for at least part of the trip; some introduction to these sports is usually included in your orientation. If you're not interested in skiing or snowshoeing, make sure you'll be given a sled. It's always smart to **get a good idea of how strenuous the outfitter's pace is.** If you're expecting a relaxing vacation, make sure you **don't pick an outfitter who'll have you doing everything** from hitching up the dogs to pitching tents.

Outfitters

Chugach Express Sled Dog Tours. Visitors can go mushing for one-half, one, or two hours, in a valley surrounded by the Chugach Mountains, about an hour's drive south of Anchorage. The longer tour includes a kennel visit and "everything you wanted to know about sled dogs," including dog care, feeding, breeding, and equipment. Participants also have the chance to drive the team on the two-hour tour. ⊠ *Box 143, Girdwood 99587,* ☎ *907/783–2262,* ℻ *907/783–2262.*

Redington Sled Dog Rides. Raymie Redington, son of the Iditarod Trail Sled Dog Race's founding father, Joe Redington Sr., leads half-hour to overnight mushing trips along the historic Iditarod Trail. ⊠ *Mile 12.5 Knik Rd., HC30, Box 5420, Wasilla 99654,* ☎ ℻ *907/376–6730.*

Sourdough Outfitters. This company offers 6- to 11-day sledding expeditions from January through April within the Gates of the Arctic National Park, one of the last great wilderness areas in the world. It also leads one-day trips in and around the community of Bettles, where the outfit is based. The owners provide all camping gear plus special boots, heavy-hooded parkas, insulated windproof mittens, and snowshoes. ⊠ *Box 66, Bettles 99726,* ☎ *907/692–5252,* ℻ *907/692–5557,* ꞃ *www.sourdoughoutfitters.com.*

Glacier Trekking

An estimated 100,000 glaciers flow out of Alaska's mountains, covering 29,000 square mi—or 5% of the state. These slow-moving "rivers of ice" concentrate in the Alaska Range, Wrangell Mountains, and the state's major coastal mountain chains: the Chugach, St. Elias, Coast, and Kenai ranges. Alaska's largest glacier, the Bering, covers 2,250 square mi—twice the size of Rhode Island.

Glaciers are formed where annual snowfall exceeds melting. As it accumulates, snow is buried and recrystallized. Eventually it becomes compacted into dense, airless ice, sometimes thousands of feet thick. Where glaciers reach tidewater, as at Glacier Bay and Kenai Fjords National Parks, they may calve immense icebergs.

Many glaciers can be approached from Alaska's road system or coastal waters—but don't try to walk on them, or even get too close, without the proper gear and training. Large chunks of ice sometimes fall from a glacier's snout with no forewarning; unwitting sightseers have been killed by such ice blocks when standing too close. Unprepared visitors have also slipped and fallen to their deaths in the glacier's crevasses. If you're an adventurous backcountry traveler, glaciers present icy avenues into the remote corners of several premier mountain wilderness areas, including Denali, Wrangell–St. Elias, and Kenai Fjords national parks and Chugach and Kachemak Bay state parks.

Glacier travel, however, should be attempted only after you've been properly trained. Glacier terrain includes a mix of ice, rock debris, and often-deep surface snow; sometimes frigid pools of meltwater collect on the surface or icy rivulets flow across the glacier. Most dangerous are glacier crevasses. Sometimes hidden by snow, these cracks in the ice may be hundreds of feet deep and several feet wide, presenting life-threatening traps for unwary travelers. Though some are only inches wide, others may be several yards across and hundreds of feet deep.

In spring and early summer (a popular time for glacier trekking), these crevasses may be hidden by snow. If you haven't been taught proper glacial travel and crevasse-rescue techniques, **hire a backcountry guide** to provide the necessary gear and expertise.

The staffs of parks and other public lands can provide a list of guides who operate on their lands. When contacting guides, **determine how well they know the mountains and glaciers you wish to explore.** Explain your own goals and abilities and be sure to **ask what sort of training you'll receive** as well as the length of trips and the amount of gear you'll be required to carry, especially for longer treks. Guides normally provide group gear, such as tents and tarps, and specialized glacier-travel equipment, such as ice axes, helmets, ropes, and crampons. However, they will expect you to **provide your own personal equipment.** In some cases, guides will rent gear (such as sleeping bags or packs) to clients. On day hikes, a guide may bring along a gourmet lunch or snack food. On longer expeditions, because of weight considerations, the food is more likely to be lightweight, such as freeze-dried meals.

Because you'll be in the mountains, always be prepared for cool, wet weather, even in summer. April through June are considered the prime months for glacial travel; but even then, conditions can be wintry in the mountains, with subfreezing temperatures. Beyond June, glacial crevasses tend to "open up" as snow melts, making travel more difficult and dangerous; plus the weather is often stormier in July and August. Most guides plan their trips so that hikers and backpackers will have time to relax and enjoy the landscape, but as with hiking and ski trips, it's a good idea to **ask about the travel schedule and number of miles to be covered daily.**

Outfitters

Alaska-Denali Guiding. Whether it's on mountaineering expeditions to Mt. McKinley or less extreme treks into the Alaska Range, this company takes wilderness explorers on glacier treks through Denali National Park's pristine backcountry. Clients have a chance to learn the area's natural and human history while exploring Denali's rugged mountain landscape. ⊠ *Box 566, Talkeetna 99676,* ☎ *907/733–2649,* FAX *907/733–1362,* WEB *www.denaliexpeditions.com.*

St. Elias Alpine Guides. Based in the town of McCarthy, within Wrangell–St. Elias National Park, St. Elias Alpine Guides conducts day hikes to nearby glaciers and also leads extended glacier treks into the wild backcountry of this "mountain kingdom." ⊠ *Box 111241, Anchorage 99511,* ☎ *907/345–9048 or 888/933–5427 year-round; 907/554–4445 summer only;* FAX *907/345–9049,* WEB *www.steliasguides.com.*

Ultima Thule Outfitters. Based at a fly-in-only lodge on the Chitina River within Wrangell–St. Elias National Park, Ultima Thule leads a variety of guided activities in the surrounding mountains, including glacier treks, mountaineering, and Nordic and telemark skiing. Other adventures include mushing, wildlife viewing, and rafting. A longtime presence in the St. Elias Mountains, Ultima Thule is known as much for its family-style hospitality as its scenic backcountry adventures. ⊠ *Box 109, Chitina 99566,* ☎ FAX *907/258–0636,* WEB *www.ultimathulelodge.com.*

Hiking and Backpacking

From Southeast coastal rain forest to Interior mountain meadows with spectacular views of Mt. McKinley and alpine tundra in the high Arctic, Alaska presents some of the continent's finest opportunities for wilderness hiking and backpacking. Or, if remote backcountry is not your preference, it's possible to travel well-maintained and well-marked trails on the edges of Alaska's largest city and still get a taste of the wild.

Chugach State Park, along Anchorage's eastern edge, has dozens of trails, many of them suited for "frontcountry" explorers. And though it is best known for its "trail-less wilderness," Denali National Park has several easy-to-hike trails near the park entrance. These, however, are exceptions to the rule. Most of Alaska remains pristine wilderness, with few or no trails. In such areas it's best to **be an experienced backcountry traveler** who understands the dangers and challenges of trail-less wilderness terrain, how to behave in bear country, how to navigate using map and compass techniques, and how to cross glacial streams.

For those without such experience, **hire a backcountry guide** to provide the necessary expertise. The staffs of refuges, forests, and parks can provide a list of outfitters and guides who operate on their lands. When contacting guides, determine how well they know the place you wish to explore. Explain your own goals and abilities and be sure to **ask about the difficulty of the terrain** you'll be traveling as well as the amount of gear you'll be required to carry. Guides normally provide group gear, such as tents and tarps, and expect you to **provide your own personal equipment.** In some cases, guides will rent gear (such as sleeping bags or packs) to clients. On day hikes, a guide may bring along a gourmet lunch or snack food. On longer expeditions, because of weight considerations, the food is more likely to be lightweight, such as freeze-dried meals. It's best to **go with small groups** to minimize the impact on the landscape and wildlife. It's best to go with fewer than 10 people, and 6 or fewer is ideal. The weather varies greatly throughout the state, but hikers and backpackers should always be prepared for cool, wet weather, even in midsummer. The best time to visit also varies greatly. In most parts of the state, June through August are considered the prime months for summer backcountry trips. July is usually the warmest month, but also the buggiest. Most guides plan their trips so that hikers and backpackers will have time to relax and enjoy the landscape or look for wildlife, but it's a good idea to **ask about the travel schedule and number of miles to be covered daily.**

Outfitters

Alaska-Denali Guiding. Though perhaps best known for its mountaineering expeditions on Mt. McKinley, this company leads a variety of hiking and backpacking expeditions in Denali national and state parks. The company emphasizes a "holistic" approach to its trips. You have a chance to learn the area's natural and human history while exploring the Denali landscape and watching wildlife. ⊠ *Box 566, Talkeetna 99676,* ☎ *907/733–2649,* FAX *907/733–1362,* WEB *www. denaliexpeditions.com.*

Alaska Nature Tours and Backcountry Outfitters. This company in Southeast Alaska leads hiking trips into the Alaska Chilkat Bald Eagle Preserve near Haines from May through September, with an emphasis on the area's natural history. ⊠ *Box 491, Haines 99827,* ☎ *907/ 766–2876,* FAX *907/766–2844,* WEB *www.kcd.com/aknature.*

Arctic Treks. Wilderness hiking and backpacking trips explore areas throughout the Arctic region's Brooks Range, including two of North America's most remote and ruggedly beautiful wildlands: Gates of the Arctic National Park and the Arctic National Wildlife Refuge. ⊠ *Box 73452, Fairbanks 99707,* ☎ *907/455–6502,* FAX *907/455–6522,* WEB *www.arctictreksadventures.com.*

St. Elias Alpine Guides. For more than two decades, this outfitter has been taking people into a part of Alaska that some people call North

America's mountain kingdom: the St. Elias and Wrangell mountain ranges. Based in the town of McCarthy, within Wrangell–St. Elias National Park, St. Elias Alpine Guides leads a full spectrum of day activities, including ghost-town tours of the Kennicott Mine, glacier walks, mountain hikes, and nature tours. The company also guides mountain ascents and extended backpacking expeditions. ⊠ *Box 111241, Anchorage 99511,* ☎ *907/345–9048 or 888/933–5427 year-round; 907/554–4445 summer only;* 𝖥𝖠𝖷 *907/345–9049,* 𝖶𝖤𝖡 *www.steliasguides.com.*

Horsepacking

There are no traffic jams and no overcrowded campgrounds on horse-packing vacations. The farther into the wilderness you go, the more untouched and spectacular the landscape. You can also cover a lot more ground with less effort than you can while backpacking. All outfitters who operate on federal lands are required to have a permit.

To minimize a horsepacking group's impact on the environment, most are limited to 12 riders. Some go down to just three or four. Most outfits post at least two wranglers for 12 guests, and some bring along another person who serves as cook and/or assistant wrangler.

It's a good idea to **find out how much time is spent in the saddle** each day and how difficult the riding is. Six hours is a long day in the saddle, and although some outfitters schedule that much, most keep the riding time to about four hours. Most trips move at a walk, and there may be varying opportunities to trot, lope, and even gallop.

On trips into the wilderness, expect the food to be generally straightforward cowboy fare, cooked over a campfire or cookstove. Although a cook goes along on some trips, guides often pull double duty in the kitchen, and often a little help from group members is willingly accepted. If you have any dietary restrictions, make arrangements beforehand. For lodging, don't allow yourself to be surprised: **find out what the rooms are like** if you're going to be staying in motels or cabins, and if the trip involves camping, **ask about the campsites** and about shower and latrine arrangements.

Outfitters

Castle Mountain Outfitters. Based in the Matanuska Valley between the Talkeetna and Chugach mountains, this outfitter conducts a variety of trips, from guided hour-long horseback rides to two-week horsepacking expeditions into the mountain wilderness. ⊠ *Box 115, Chickaloon 99674,* ☎ *907/745–6427,* 𝖥𝖠𝖷 *907/745–6428.*

North Country Outfitters. This Tok-based concern organizes horsepacking trips in parts of South Central and Interior Alaska. ⊠ *Box 453, Tok 99780,* ☎ *907/883–5506,* 𝖥𝖠𝖷 *907/883–5500.*

River Rafting

From the Southeast Panhandle to the far reaches of the Arctic, Alaska is blessed with an abundance of wild, pristine rivers. The federal government has officially designated more than two dozen of Alaskan streams as "Wild and Scenic Rivers," but hundreds more would easily qualify for that description. Some meander gently through forests or tundra. Others, fed by glacier runoff, rush wildly through mountains and canyons.

Because so much of Alaska is roadless wilderness, rivers often serve as the best avenues to explore the landscape and view wildlife. This is especially true in several of Alaska's premier parklands and refuges. Here, as elsewhere, rivers are ranked according to their degrees of difficulty.

Class I rivers are considered to be "easy" floats with minimal rapids; at the other extreme, Class VI rivers are extremely dangerous to nearly impossible to navigate. Generally only very experienced river runners should attempt anything above Class II on their own. Rafters and other river travelers should also be aware that river conditions change considerably from season to season and sometimes day to day. Always check ahead to determine a river's current condition. Do-it-yourselfers would be wise to consult two books on Alaska's rivers: *Fast & Cold: A Guide to Alaska Whitewater* (Skyhouse) by Andrew Embick (though intended primarily for white-water kayakers, it has good information for rafters as well) and *The Alaska River Guide: Canoeing, Kayaking, and Rafting in the Last Frontier* (Alaska Northwest Books) by Karen Jettmar.

Fortunately you don't have to be an expert river runner to explore many of Alaska's premier waterways. Experienced rafting companies operate throughout the state. Some outfits emphasize extended wilderness trips and natural-history observations, whereas others specialize in thrilling one-day (or shorter) floats through Class III and IV white water that will get your adrenaline pumping. And some combine a little of both.

As with other guided activities, it always pays to **do your homework.** If you'll be traveling in a park or refuge, request a list of commercial operators from park staff. It is always essential to **find out how long a guide has been operating** on the river of your choice. Ask about the dangers, and the river's degree of difficulty. Be certain that the guide gives you a safety talk before going on the water. Find out what gear and clothing are required. Ask if you'll be paddling or simply riding as a passenger. Be sure you know how to react if you do get flipped out of the raft or if the boat overturns. Reputable rafting companies will discuss all of this, but it never hurts to ask.

Outfitters

Alaska Discovery. Guests take 10-day trips down two of North America's wildest rivers, the Tatshenshini and Alsek. The river trips begin in Canada and end in one of Alaska's premier parklands, Glacier Bay, as rafters float between peaks nearly 3 mi high and through valleys inhabited by grizzlies, moose, and sometimes wolves. The company also does combined rafting and hiking trips in the Arctic National Wildlife Refuge. ⊠ *5310 Glacier Hwy., Juneau 99801,* ☎ *907/780–6226 or 800/586–1911,* ℻ *907/780–4220,* WEB *www.akdiscovery.com.*

Denali Raft Adventures. A variety of river trips are conducted on the glacially fed, white-water Nenana River, which skirts the eastern boundary of Denali National Park. Trips vary from two-hour Class I–II scenic floats or white-water canyon trips with big rapids to all-day floats and overnight outings. The two-hour scenic and canyon trips can also be combined. ⊠ *Box 190, Denali Park 99755,* ☎ *907/683–2234 or 888/683–2234,* ℻ *907/683–1281,* WEB *www.denaliraft.com.*

Nova. This outfitter has been rafting Alaska's rivers since 1975. For most of that time, the company has specialized in full-, part-, or multiday white-water trips down the Matanuska, Chickaloon, and Talkeetna rivers in South Central Alaska. Over the past decade, Nova has expanded its reach and now also leads float trips in Wrangell–St. Elias and Gates of the Arctic national parks. White-water ratings on their rivers range from Class I to Class V. ⊠ *Mile 76, Glenn Hwy., Box 1129, Chickaloon 99674,* ☎ *907/745–5753 or 800/746–5753,* ℻ *907/745–5754,* WEB *www.novalaska.com.*

Wilderness Birding Adventures. The owners are both experienced river runners and expert birders. Among their trips is a rafting, hiking, and birding expedition through one of the world's last great wilderness areas, the Arctic National Wildlife Refuge. ⊠ *Box 103747, Anchorage 99510,* ☏ FAX *907/694–7442.*

Sea Kayaking

One of the country's fastest-growing sports, sea kayaking can be as thrilling or as peaceful as you make it. More stable than a white-water kayak and more comfortable than a canoe, a sea kayak—even one loaded with a week's worth of gear—is maneuverable enough to poke into hidden crevices, explore side bays, and beach on deserted spits of sand.

Anyone who doesn't mind getting a little wet and has an average degree of fitness can be a sea kayaker. The basic stroke is performed in a circular motion with a double-bladed paddle; you pull one blade through the water while pushing forward with the other through the air. Most people pick it up with a minimal amount of instruction. Don't assume, though, that if you've done 10 minutes without tipping over you'll be adequately prepared to circumnavigate Glacier Bay National Park. There's a lot to learn, and until you know your way around tides, currents, and nautical charts, you should go with an experienced guide who also knows what and how to pack and where to pitch a tent. A reputable outfitter can supply such a guide.

In choosing an outfitter, your primary concern should be safety. An outfitter should be equipped with both the proper technical and first-aid gear and should know what to do with them. Question every outfitter carefully so that you know what you're getting into.

It is essential to **find out how long the guides have been leading trips** and how long they have been leading in the area where you want to go. Generally it is best to have a guide who knows an area very well. A qualified guide's first visit to an area can also be exciting, but *only if* that guide has had extensive experience elsewhere.

It is important for you to **honestly evaluate your own tolerance for cold, dampness, and high winds.** Nothing can ruin a trip faster than pervasive discomfort.

Always **ask whether the outfitter stocks a variety of boats,** so you can experiment until you find the kayak that best fits your weight, strength, ability, and paddling style.

Outfitters

Alaska Discovery. One of Alaska's oldest outfitters, this company has been running low-impact, nature-oriented adventure tourism since 1972. Experienced guides know Southeast Alaska intimately, and they emphasize both sea-kayaking skills and safety in their instruction. Destinations include Glacier Bay, Icy Bay, Russell Fjord, and Granite Fjord. ⊠ *5310 Glacier Hwy., Juneau 99801,* ☏ *907/780–6226 or 800/ 586–1911,* FAX *907/780–4220,* WEB *www.akdiscovery.com.*

Spirit Walker Expeditions, Inc. This veteran Southeast company offers guided wilderness sea kayaking trips that combine a mix of scenery, wildlife, solitude, and paddling within the Inside Passage. Guides prepare meals, offer instruction, and provide all needed paddling gear. Beginners are welcome. ⊠ *Box 240, Gustavus 99826,* ☏ *907/697–2266 or 800/529–2537,* FAX *907/697–2701,* WEB *www.seakayakalaska.com.*

Sunny Cove Sea Kayaking Company. Weeklong trips in and around Kenai Fjords National Park in South Central Alaska include five nights of camping at Northwestern Fjord, where kayakers can paddle among icebergs, seals, and seabirds as tidewater glaciers calve in the distance. Day trips navigate within Resurrection Bay, near Seward. Tours include kayaking equipment and instruction, meals, and lots of chances to see wildlife. Combination tours with Kenai Fjords Cruises are also offered. ✉ *Box 3332, Seward 99664,* ☎ *907/224–8810; 800/770–9119 for reservations;* ℻ *907/224–8811,* WEB *www.sunnycove.com.*

Skiing

It may not have the reputation of several other western states, but Alaska offers plenty of skiing terrain for both Nordic skiers and downhill racers. Three of Alaska's largest cities—Anchorage, Fairbanks, and Juneau—have nearby alpine ski areas, complete with equipment rentals, ski schools, and other amenities. Many of Alaska's towns, both large and small, have regularly maintained trails for cross-country skiers. Anchorage's trail system is considered among the nation's finest and has hosted world-class races.

For those who are more ambitious, Alaska's wilderness areas present unlimited opportunities—and lots of challenges. Unless you are knowledgable in winter backcountry travel, camping techniques, and avalanche dangers, the best strategy is to **hire a guide when exploring Alaska's backcountry on skis.** Given the extremes of Alaska's winters, your primary concern should be safety: **be sure your guide has had avalanche-awareness and winter-survival training.** Conditions can change quickly, especially in mountainous areas, and what began as an easy cross-country ski trip can suddenly become a survival saga if you're not prepared for the challenges of an Alaska winter.

As with other backcountry activities, **verify that your guide is familiar with the region you'll be visiting.** Know what specialized equipment is necessary for the conditions you'll face and be clear about your own limitations. If you're a novice, you don't want to start out on difficult terrain or travel long distances without proper preparation. When you are prepared, the rewards of backcountry skiing are well worth the hardships and challenges: immense solitude and quiet, sparkling skies; fantastic landscapes; and, if you're lucky, a display of northern lights or perhaps the distant howling of wolves.

Outfitters

Alaska-Denali Guiding. Cross-country ski trips of varying lengths and degrees of difficulty wind through Denali national and state parks, with an emphasis on natural history as well as backcountry exploration and the challenges of winter travel. ✉ *Box 566, Talkeetna 99676,* ☎ *907/ 733–2649,* ℻ *907/733–1362,* WEB *www.denaliexpeditions.com.*

Alaska Nature Tours and Backcountry Outfitters. This company in Southeast Alaska rents ski gear and, from December through March, leads Nordic ski trips into the Alaska Chilkat Bald Eagle Preserve near Haines. Visitors who come in early winter are likely to see many of the bald eagles that visit the preserve annually. ✉ *Box 491, Haines 99827,* ☎ *907/766–2876,* ℻ *907/766–2844,* WEB *www.kcd.com/aknature.*

Ultima Thule Outfitters. Based at a fly-in-only lodge on the Chitina River within Wrangell–St. Elias National Park, Ultima Thule leads a variety of guided activities in the surrounding mountains, including alpine treks and Nordic and telemark skiing. Other adventures include mushing, wildlife viewing, rafting, and mountain climbing. A longtime presence in the St. Elias Mountains, Ultima Thule is known as much for its family-style hospitality as its scenic backcountry adventures. ✉ *Box 109, Chitina 99566,* ☎ ℻ *907/258–0636,* WEB *www.ultimathulelodge.com.*

Sportfishing

Home to hundreds of species of fish, including many highly prized catches, Alaska's more than 3 million lakes and thousands of miles of coastal waters are an angler's paradise. All five species of Pacific salmon (king, silver, sockeye, pink, and chum) spawn in Alaska's waters, alongside ample quantities of rainbow trout, steelhead, arctic char, Dolly Varden char, arctic grayling, northern pike, and halibut.

A few fish reach huge proportions: for example, a world-record king salmon weighing 97¼ pounds was caught in Alaska's Kenai River, and halibut exceeding 300—and occasionally 400—pounds are annually caught in Pacific Ocean waters. But some anglers will tell you that bigger isn't necessarily better. Sockeye, among the smallest salmon, are considered by many to be both the best tasting and best fighting, pound for pound, of any fish. And though the arctic grayling commonly weighs a pound or less, it is a favorite among fly fishermen.

Roadside fishing for salmon, trout, char, and grayling is possible in South Central and Interior Alaska. In fact Alaska's best-known salmon stream, the Kenai River, is road accessible. But in most of the state, prime fishing waters can be reached only by boat or air. Not surprisingly, hundreds of fishing charters and dozens of sportfishing lodges operate statewide, attracting anglers from around the world. Southwest Alaska, in particular, is known as a fisherman's heaven, but many of its prime spots are remote and expensive to reach.

You should be aware that sportfishing regulations vary widely from area to area. Licenses are required for both fresh- and saltwater fishing. To learn more about regulations, contact the **Alaska Department of Fish and Game** (✉ Box 25526, Juneau 99802-5526, ☎ 907/465–4180 for sportfishing seasons and regulations; 907/465–2376 for licenses). Information on local fishing guides and/or sportfishing lodges can be obtained from parks and refuges around the state as well as the chamber of commerce offices in many communities.

When hiring a guide, **find out how long a company has worked in the area.** The guide can also tell you what species are likely to be caught, catch limits, and any equipment or special clothing needs. Normally, all necessary fishing gear is provided and the guides will teach you the appropriate fishing techniques. In some cases, catch-and-release ethics may be emphasized.

Outfitters and Charters

Alaskan Fishing Adventures. Anglers are guided in several areas of the Kenai Peninsula south of Anchorage, including Resurrection Bay, Cook Inlet, and the Kenai River, home of the famous "Kenai Kings," salmon that may reach 90 pounds or more. Among the other species they catch are halibut, sockeye and silver salmon, and rainbow trout. Boats have a four–person limit on rivers, six–person limit on saltwater. ✉ *Box 2457, Soldotna 99669,* ☎ *800/548–3474,* FAX *707/251–9687,* WEB *www.alaskanfishing.com.*

Central Charter Booking Agency. In Homer, this company can arrange fishing trips in outer Kachemak Bay and Lower Cook Inlet, areas known for excellent halibut fishing. Though most charters focus on halibut, some also fish for salmon. Boat sizes vary considerably; some have a 6-person limit, whereas others can take up to 25 passengers. ✉ *4241 Homer Spit, Homer 99603,* ☎ *907/235–7847; 800/478–7847 in Alaska;* FAX *907/235–2895,* WEB *www.centralcharter.com.*

Great Alaska Adventure Lodge. Among other adventure trips, this Kenai River lodge offers a variety of fishing packages including three fly-in camps and three saltwater locations. Boats have a four–person limit on rivers, six–person limit on saltwater. Expert guides can get you into king, silver, and pink salmon; halibut; rainbow trout; and grayling. Stories are traded at happy hour and during dinner in the lodge. ⊠ *33881 Sterling Hwy., Sterling 99672,* ☎ *907/262–4515 or 800/544–2261,* FAX *907/262–8797,* WEB *www.greatalaska.com.*

King Salmon Guides. Guides operate throughout the Bristol Bay region, in world-class fishing destinations from Katmai National Park to Lake Iliamna. Species include salmon, rainbow trout, char, and grayling. Anglers, up to six per boat, can go out for one or several days. Packages range from lodge-based trips to tent camping and "x-stream" trips that combine hiking and fishing. ⊠ *Box 602, King Salmon 99613,* ☎ *800/976–2202,* FAX *907/246–7645.*

Alaska's Top Fish and Their Sources

Species	Common Name	Where Found
Arctic Char (F, S)	Char	SC, SW, NW, I, A
Arctic Grayling (F)	Grayling	SE, SC, SW, NW, I, A
Brook Trout (F)	Brookie	SE
Burbot (F)	Lingcod	SC, SW, NW, A
Chinook (F, S)	King Salmon	SE, SC, SW, I
Chum Salmon (F, S)	Dog Salmon	SE, SC, SW, NW, I
Coho Salmon (F, S)	Silver Salmon	SE, SC, SW, NW, I
Cutthroat Trout (F, S)	Cutthroat	SE, SC
Dolly Varden (F, S)	Dolly	SE, SC, SW, NW, I, A
Lake Trout (F)	Laker	SC, SW, NW, I, A
Northern Pike (F)	Northern	SC, SW, NW, I
Hammerhandle Pacific Halibut (S)	Halibut	SE, SC, SW, NW
Pink Salmon (F, S)	Humpie	SE, SC, SW, NW, I
Smelt (F, S)	Smelt	SE, SC, SW, NW, I, A
Rainbow Trout (F)	Rainbow	SE, SC, SW, I
Sheefish (F)	Shee, Inconnu	NW, I
Sockeye Salmon (F, S)	Red Salmon	SE, SC, SW, NW, I
Steelhead (F, S)	Steelie	SE, SC, SW

(F) = *Freshwater*	A = *Arctic*	SC = *South Central*
(S) = *Saltwater*	I = *Interior*	SE = *Southeast*
(F, S) = *Freshwater*	NW = *Northwest*	SW = *Southwest*
and Saltwater		

Whale-Watching Cruises

A close encounter with whales in their natural environment can be a thrilling experience. Hearing the resonant whoosh of a cetacean exhaling and witnessing such acrobatics as "spy-hopping" (a whale poking its head straight out of the water for a look around), breaching, and skimming, you can't help but feel their awesome presence.

It's possible to see migrating whales along much of Alaska's coast from June through August: from the Southeast region's Inside Passage to South Central's Prince William Sound, Kodiak Archipelago, and Kenai Fjords National Park, and then north through the Bering, Chukchi, and Beaufort seas in Arctic waters. A wide variety of whales can be observed, though those most commonly seen on whale-watching trips are killer whales, or orcas, and humpbacks.

Whale-watching is not the average spectator sport. It's more like a seagoing game of hide-and-seek. Whales are unpredictable, so be prepared to wait and watch patiently, scanning the water for signs. Sometimes it seems that the whales don't want to be watched; other times they might rub up against the boat. Also unpredictable are the weather and sea conditions. You can get wet and chilled, and possibly seasick.

Most cruises travel in or through waters that attract several species, although some focus on a particular type of whale. If you **ask when the best time to take a specific trip is,** you may find out that the sighting record is better during some months than others. You have to **weigh the pros and cons of traveling on small versus large boats.** Make sure you know what kind of boat is used for the trip you are considering. A trip with 15 people is certain to be quite different from one with 150.

Tour Companies

Kenai Fjords Tours. A wide variety of tours are offered, including exploring Resurrection Bay and Kenai Fjords National Park in South Central Alaska. They range from three-hour natural-history tours to five-hour gray whale–watching tours (April 1–mid-May only) and full-day cruises to Aialik Bay or Northwestern Fjord. Prime-time whale-watching for orcas and humpbacks is June through August. Most of the company's boats are 75 ft–95 ft long, with room for 90–149 passengers, but it also has a smaller vessel with a 22-passenger limit. ⊠ *Box 1889, Seward 99664,* ☎ *907/224–8068 or 800/478–8068,* ℻ *907/ 224–8934,* ⟨WEB⟩ *www.kenaifjords.com.*

Mariah Tours. This outfit offers the "small-boat alternative" for whale-watching and glacier tours of Kenai Fjords National Park. Its two boats carry no more than 22 people (including crew) each. Mariah runs 8- to 9½-hour tours to Aialik Bay and Northwestern Fjord, respectively, from May 1 through September 15. Besides killer and humpback whales, wildlife watchers are likely to see bald eagles, sea otters, sea lions, seals, and thousands of seabirds. ⊠ *Box 1889, Seward 99664,* ☎ *907/224–4560 in summer; 800/270–1238;* ℻ *907/224–8934,* ⟨WEB⟩ *www.kenaifjords.com.*

Spirit of Adventure. Daily trips into Glacier Bay National Park run from the dock at Bartlett Cove, near Glacier Bay Lodge. Watching for whales, as well as calving glaciers, is part of the daily routine. Uniformed Park Service naturalists provide local expertise. ⊠ *Bartlett Cove, Box 199, Gustavus 99826 (⊠ 226 2nd Ave., Seattle, WA 98119),* ☎ *907/ 697–2226 in summer; 800/451–5952;* ℻ *206/623–7809,* ⟨WEB⟩ *www. glacierbaytours.com.*

3 ANCHORAGE

Alaska's biggest city is the state's only true metropolis and an excellent base from which to explore Alaska. You'll find a varied selection of ethnic restaurants and a performing arts center that hosts theater groups, an opera company, and an orchestra. The Anchorage Museum of History and Art houses an outstanding collection of historic and contemporary Alaskan art, and the Alaska Native Heritage Center celebrates the diversity of the state's original inhabitants.

By Robin
Mackey Hill
and Howard
C. Weaver

Updated by
Don Pitcher

A MID THE WILD COUNTRYSIDE that crowds around it on all sides, Anchorage has grown into a vigorous, spirited, cosmopolitan city—by far Alaska's largest and most sophisticated. The relative affluence of this white-collar city—with a sprinkling of olive drab from nearby military bases—attracts fine restaurants and pricey shops, first-rate entertainment, and world-class sporting events. Flashy modern towers stab the skyline, and colorful flowers spill from hundreds of baskets on downtown lampposts. Traffic from the city's busy international airport, served by more than 15 international and domestic airlines, lends Anchorage a more cosmopolitan air than you might expect from a city with a population of more than 261,000, nearly half the people in the state. You'll also discover some development you may not have come to Alaska to see—14 McDonald's, 2 Wal-Marts, a 16-plex movie theater, and dozens of espresso bars. Those who live in the Bush joke about "being able to see Alaska from Anchorage," but the city has not entirely lost touch with its frontier spirit. Sled-dog races are still among the most revered events held here, moose often roam along city bike trails, and spectacular country is just a short drive away.

First incorporated in 1920, Anchorage is still a young city. The median age of 30 years and an aggressive style make it—not the capital city of Juneau—the state's power center. Nearly everything was built in the last few decades. An Anchorage home dating from the 1950s almost merits historic status. In addition to acting as the center for oil development in the state, Anchorage hustles its living as a government, banking, transportation, and communications hub.

Anchorage residents are primarily from elsewhere in America—including oil workers from such conservative oil-patch states as Oklahoma and Texas—and the attitudes they bring have added fuel to the fire of the conservative, pro-development mentality that characterizes the city, and Alaska, as a whole. Although representing less than 8% of the population, Alaskan Native peoples add an important cultural dimension. A growing Asian population is also having an impact, with well-stocked Asian food stores and restaurants an increasingly familiar sight.

Anchorage got its start with the construction of the federally built Alaska Railroad, completed in 1917, and traces of the city's railroad heritage remain today. Once the tracks were laid, the town grew because its pioneer forerunners actively sought growth by hook and—not infrequently—by crook. City officials used to delight in telling how they tricked a visiting member of Congress into dedicating a site for a not-yet-approved federal hospital.

Boom and bust periods followed major events: an influx of military bases during World War II; a massive buildup of Arctic missile-warning stations during the Cold War; reconstruction following the devastating Good Friday earthquake of 1964; and in the late 1960s the biggest bonanza of all—the discovery of oil at Prudhoe Bay and the construction of the trans-Alaska pipeline. Not surprisingly, Anchorage positioned itself as the perfect home for the new pipeline administrators and support industries, and it attracts a large share of the state's oil-tax dollars.

In the last decade, Anchorage has become an increasingly important focus of travelers to Alaska. The central location, relatively mild climate, and excellent transportation system make it a natural place to begin or end a trip.

Pleasures and Pastimes

Hiking and Walking

Anchorage is a hiker's paradise, with everything from paved, in-town trails to rugged dirt paths through the Chugach Mountains. The city is laced with more than 120 mi of paved urban trails that meander through wooded greenbelts and quiet neighborhoods. Easiest of these is the Tony Knowles Coastal Trail, an 11-mi ribbon of asphalt beginning downtown and stretching west to Kincaid Park. Pick up a guide to local hiking trails at the Alaska Public Lands Information Center (☞ Sights to See *in* Exploring Anchorage) or at area bookstores. A note of caution: when hiking in the hills, be sure to wear hiking boots and to take plenty of water, rain gear, and a light jacket—the weather can change with little warning. And although bear encounters are rare, be alert and make noise when walking in thick brush.

Shopping

Anchorage offers shopping to match any taste and price range. Souvenir shops selling everything from painted gold pans to plastic totem poles can be found on nearly every downtown block. Native Alaskan handicrafts of all kinds are sold at many of the gift shops downtown. Check for the official polar bear symbol, which means the item was made in Alaska. A hand symbol indicates an article was made locally by Native artisans. Tlingit and Haida Indian traditional arts and crafts include button blankets, wood carvings, and silver jewelry. Athabascan Indian craftspeople are known for their beadwork, which adorns slippers, headbands, and jewelry. Eskimo handicrafts include ivory and soapstone carvings and baleen baskets. Aleut grass baskets are so fine and tightly woven that some can hold water.

EXPLORING ANCHORAGE

With the exception of downtown, Anchorage's widely scattered neighborhoods make for a city that is not particularly pedestrian friendly. Most shops and services are clustered along busy thoroughfares, so visiting them on foot is not only unpleasant but dangerous. Fortunately, the city has a decent local bus system. Downtown, however, invites walking. The grid plan was laid out with military precision by the Army Corps of Engineers, and streets and avenues run exactly east–west and north–south, with numbers in the first direction and letters of the alphabet or Alaska place-names (Barrow, Cordova, Denali, etc.) in the other. The only aberration is the absence of a J Street—a concession, some say, to the city's early Swedish settlers, who had difficulty pronouncing the letter.

You'll find plenty to do year-round in Anchorage, though most visitors, particularly first-timers, might be happiest in June, July, or August, when the days are longer and the temperatures warmer. Locals embrace the 18-plus hours of daylight. Dog walkers, bikers, golfers, and softball players are out until it gets dark, which in late June can be nearly midnight. Spring comes late and fall early to Anchorage. These are less desirable times to visit because weather can be cool and rainy and some attractions might be closed.

Numbers in the text correspond to numbers in the margin and on the Anchorage map.

Great Itineraries

Anchorage presents a wide variety of things to see and do, so before you put on your comfortable shoes and grab your camera, take a few minutes to figure out what you're most interested in—seeing wildlife, shopping, taking a hike in the surrounding Chugach Mountains, or soaking up some of Alaska's rich Native culture.

IF YOU HAVE 1 DAY

Take a stroll through downtown Anchorage to acquaint yourself with the fine shops and galleries, historic sites, museums, and parks. Take a walk along the Tony Knowles Coastal Trail if the weather's cooperating. If you have a car, explore the city highlights, including the Alaska Aviation Heritage Museum and the new Alaska Native Heritage Center. End the day with some window-shopping downtown or dinner and a walk along the Delany Park Strip. Several places are open late if coffee and dessert—or beer and nachos, for that matter—sound like the perfect nightcap.

IF YOU HAVE 3 DAYS

Follow the one-day itinerary; then head south along the Seward Highway for views of Potter Marsh and Turnagain Arm. Drive 40 mi to the community of Girdwood, with its several good restaurants, scenic hiking trails, and inviting shops. Continue farther down the highway to Alyeska Resort at Girdwood, where you can ride the tram to the 2,300-ft level for lunch with a view. Head south of Girdwood to Portage Glacier and the Begich-Boggs Visitor Center, all the while looking for Dall sheep and beluga whales. Back in Anchorage on day three, consider visiting some of the special-interest museums or, if it's the season, taking in a baseball game at Mulcahy Stadium. A hike along one of the city's many bike trails or in the neighboring Chugach Mountains will give you an appreciation of the role nature plays in the lives of those who make Anchorage their home. Bears and moose roam the park, which has trails from 2 mi to 30 mi in length.

Fodor's Choice

No two people will agree on what makes a perfect vacation, but here are some of our Anchorage favorites for starters. Each of these is detailed later in this chapter.

Taste Treats

★ **Microbrews.** Brew pubs are the latest trend in Anchorage, with several to choose from, including Glacier BrewHouse, Moose's Tooth Pub & Pizzeria, and the Snowgoose Restaurant.

Dining

★ **Marx Brothers' Cafe.** From the made-at-your-table Caesar salad to the homemade butter-pecan ice cream, the food is always memorable at this romantic little Anchorage restaurant. $$$–$$$$

★ **Seven Glaciers.** This fine-dining spot perched halfway up Mt. Alyeska in Girdwood offers fabulous views of Turnagain Arm alongside carefully prepared and artfully presented entrées. $$$–$$$$

★ **Sacks Café.** Consistently fine and innovative food, a big-city feel, and unhurried service make this perhaps the best place in Anchorage for lunch or dinner before the theater. $$$

After Hours

★ **Midnight sunset.** To have a window seat on a clear summer's eve at Anchorage's Simon and Seafort's is nothing to take for granted. The restaurant's spacious bar is a haunt of locals and visitors alike.

Lodging

★ **Alyeska Prince Hotel.** Alaska's first all-season resort is a full-service hotel in Girdwood with world-class downhill skiing in winter and hiking in summer. $$$$

New and Noteworthy

Several new restaurants arrived on the scene recently, including **Ristorante Orso,** a delightful Italian place in the heart of downtown. In 2000, Anchorage International Airport was renamed **Ted Stevens Anchorage International Airport** in honor of the state's senior U.S. senator who is known for his ability to win funding for major Alaska projects. One of these projects is the airport itself, which is currently being renovated. The construction will continue until 2004, and by 2002 there will be a direct Alaska Railroad link between the airport and downtown Anchorage.

Downtown Anchorage

A Good Walk

Start at the **Log Cabin Visitor Information Center** ①, where friendly volunteers answer questions and racks of brochures line the walls. The marble statue in front of **Old City Hall** ② next door honors William Seward. Along 4th Avenue are some of Anchorage's original buildings. They date from 1920, when Anchorage was incorporated. Catercorner from the Old City Hall is the **Alaska Public Lands Information Center** ③, one of four in the state that provide information on all of Alaska's public lands.

Take F Street north downhill to 2nd Avenue, the site of original townsite homes built by the Alaska Engineering Commission, which also built the Alaska Railroad in the early 1900s. A neighborhood marker at the intersection of F Street and 2nd Avenue tells of Anchorage's first mayor, Leopold David, and the start of the Anchorage Women's Club. Photographs from the city's early days line the banks of Ship Creek.

Walk east along 2nd Avenue past the Eisenhower Memorial to a set of stairs leading down to the **Alaska Railroad depot** ④. Salmon run up the creek all summer. It's easy to watch them from the banks of **Ship Creek** ⑤, north of the depot.

Ask Anchorage residents what the best thing about living in the city is, and many will say that it's the **Tony Knowles Coastal Trail** ⑥, a recreational trail that begins west of 2nd Avenue and curls along Cook Inlet. Follow 2nd Avenue to K Street, go south a block to 3rd Avenue, and follow 3rd Avenue westward to **Resolution Park** ⑦, with its statue of Captain Cook. From here you can admire the grand vistas over Cook Inlet to Mt. McKinley and other peaks in the Alaska Range. The **Oscar Anderson House Museum** ⑧, off the coastal trail at the north end of Elderberry Park, was Anchorage's first permanent frame house, built in 1915 by city butcher Oscar Anderson. Elderberry Park, just in front of the house, is a good place for children to run off steam, watch passing trains, and look for whales off the coastline. If young travelers are getting restless, head back up the 5th Avenue hill to the **Imaginarium** ⑨, an experiential science museum with a great gift shop.

Walk down 5th Avenue past the Egan Convention Center (✉ 555 W. 5th Ave., ☎ 907/263–2800), whose lobby has several modern Native Alaskan sculptures and a beaded curtain that evokes the northern lights. Across the street is a park (Town Square) that's packed with flowers in the summer, and just southwest of it is the **Alaska Center for the Performing Arts** ⑩. Continue on to A Street and 7th Avenue for the entrance to the **Anchorage Museum of History and Art** ⑪, which occupies the whole block between 6th and 7th avenues. The red metal sculpture out front is a favorite hide-and-seek site for children.

56

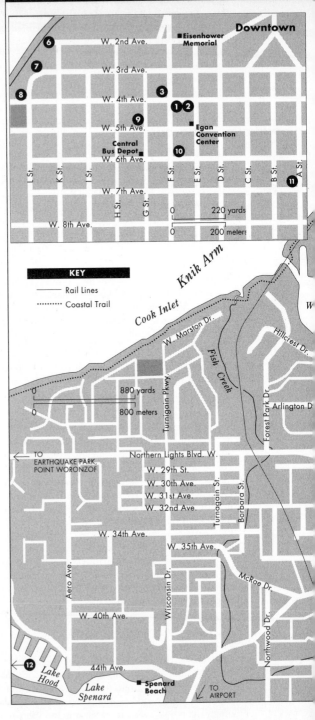

Anchorage

Downtown

W. 2nd Ave.
Eisenhower Memorial
W. 3rd Ave.
W. 4th Ave.
Egan Convention Center
W. 5th Ave.
Central Bus Depot
W. 6th Ave.
L St.
K St.
I St.
F St.
E St.
D St.
C St.
B St.
A St.
W. 7th Ave.
H St.
G St.
0   220 yards
0   200 meters
W. 8th Ave.

KEY

—— Rail Lines
.... Coastal Trail

Knik Arm
Cook Inlet
W. Marston Dr.
Fish Creek
Hillcrest Dr.
Forest Park Dr.
Arlington D
Turnagain Pkwy.
0   880 yards
0   800 meters
TO EARTHQUAKE PARK, POINT WORONZOF
Northern Lights Blvd. W.
W. 29th St.
W. 30th Ave.
W. 31st Ave.
W. 32nd Ave.
Turnagain St.
Barbara St.
W. 34th Ave.
W. 35th Ave.
Aero Ave.
Wisconsin Dr.
McRae Dr.
Northwood Dr.
W. 40th Ave.
44th Ave.
Lake Hood
Lake Spenard
Spenard Beach
TO AIRPORT

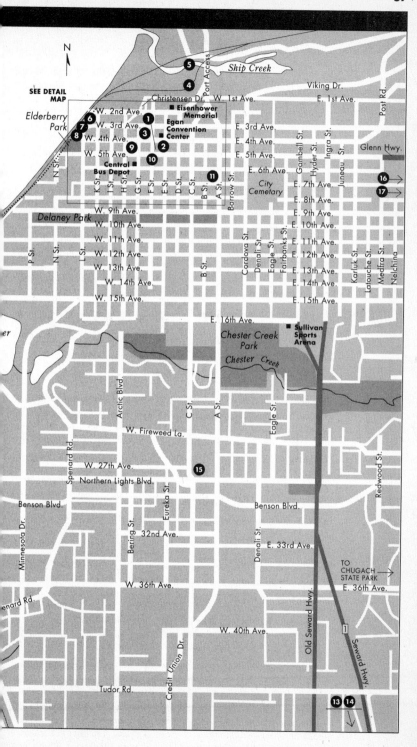

N

SEE DETAIL MAP

Elderberry Park

Ship Creek

Port Access

Viking Dr.

E. 1st Ave.

Post Rd.

Christensen Dr. W. 1st Ave.

W. 2nd Ave.

■ Eisenhower Memorial

W. 3rd Ave.

Egan Convention Center

E. 3rd Ave.

E. 4th Ave.

W. 4th Ave.

Glenn Hwy.

W. 5th Ave.

E. 5th Ave.

Central Bus Depot ■

E. 6th Ave.

City Cemetary

E. 7th Ave.

W. 9th Ave.

E. 8th Ave.

Delaney Park

W. 10th Ave.

E. 9th Ave.

W. 11th Ave.

E. 10th Ave.

W. 12th Ave.

E. 11th Ave.

W. 13th Ave.

E. 12th Ave.

W. 14th Ave.

E. 13th Ave.

W. 15th Ave.

E. 14th Ave.

E. 15th Ave.

E. 16th Ave.

Chester Creek Park

■ Sullivan Sports Arena

Chester Creek

Arctic Blvd.

W. Fireweed La.

C St.

A St.

Eagle St.

Redwood St.

W. 27th Ave.

Spenard Rd.

Northern Lights Blvd.

Eureka St.

Benson Blvd.

Benson Blvd.

Minnesota Dr.

Bering St.

32nd Ave.

Denali St.

E. 33rd Ave.

TO CHUGACH STATE PARK

...enard Rd.

W. 36th Ave.

E. 36th Ave.

Old Seward Hwy.

Seward Hwy.

Credit Union Dr.

W. 40th Ave.

Tudor Rd.

K St.   I St.   H St.   G St.   F St.   E St.   D St.   C St.   B St.   A St.   Barrow St.

Gambell St.   Hyder St.   Ingra St.   Juneau

P St.   N St.   L St.

Cordova St.   Denali St.   Eagle St.   Fairbanks St.

Karluk St.   Latouche St.   Medfra St.   Nelchina

B St.

TIMING

This walking tour should take two to three hours, or longer if you get caught up in shopping and museum-hopping.

Sights to See

⑩ **Alaska Center for the Performing Arts.** This distinctive stone-and-glass building fronts on an expansive park filled with brilliant flowers all summer. Take a look inside for upcoming events, or just relax amid the blossoms on a sunny afternoon. You can watch IMAX films or slide shows on the northern lights. Hour-long tours are available. ⊠ *621 W. 6th Ave., at G St.,* ☎ *907/263–2900; 907/263–2787 for tickets,* WEB *www.alaskapac.org.* ☉ *Daily 8–5; free tours May–Sept., Wed. and Fri. 1 PM; Oct.–Apr., Wed. 1 PM.*

☙ ❸ **Alaska Public Lands Information Center.** This is a great one-stop source of information on all of Alaska's public lands, including national and state parks, national forests, and wildlife refuges. Make reservations for a state ferry, watch nature videos, learn about plants and animals, or head to the theater for films highlighting different parts of the state. There's a trip-planning computer for public use, plus maps and guidebooks for sale. ⊠ *605 W. 4th Ave., at F St.,* ☎ *907/271–2737.* ☉ *Memorial Day–Labor Day, daily 9–5:30; Labor Day–Memorial Day, weekdays 10–5:30.*

❹ **Alaska Railroad depot.** Outside this historic station are totem poles and a locomotive built in 1907. A monument in front of the depot relates the history of the railroad, which played an important role in the city's growth. During February's Fur Rendezvous festival, model-train buffs set up their displays here. ⊠ *411 W. 1st Ave.,* ☎ *907/265–2494.* ☉ *Daily, depending on train schedules.*

☙ ⑪ **Anchorage Museum of History and Art.** A fine collection of historic and contemporary Alaskan art is exhibited along with wonderful dioramas and displays on Alaskan history and village life. The first-floor atrium is often the site of free daily presentations, which occur June through August, by local artists and authors. Visitors can join an informative 45-minute tour or step into the theater to watch a film on Alaska. A café spills out into the atrium, serving delicious lunches from the Marx Brothers' Cafe, and the gift shop sells classy souvenirs. ⊠ *121 W. 7th Ave.,* ☎ *907/343–4326; 907/343–6173 for recorded information,* WEB *www.anchoragemuseum.org.* ⬛ *$6.50.* ☉ *Mid-May–mid-Sept., Fri.–Mon. 9–6, Tues.–Thurs. 9–9; mid-Sept.–mid-May, Tues.–Sat. 10–6, Sun. 1–5.*

☙ ❾ **Imaginarium.** Children can stand inside a giant soap bubble at the bubble lab, hold a starfish in the marine exhibit, learn about the northern lights, or take a galaxy tour in the planetarium at this experiential science museum. Other attractions include such "radical reptiles" as an iguana, an alligator, and even a 19-ft python. It's a fun house for children and adults alike. ⊠ *737 W. 5th Ave.,* ☎ *907/276–3179.* ⬛ *$5.* ☉ *Mon.–Sat. 10–6, Sun. noon–5.*

❶ **Log Cabin Visitor Information Center.** A giant jade boulder stands outside this Bush-style log cabin, whose sod roof is festooned with huge hanging baskets of flowers. Anchorage calls itself "Air Crossroads of the World" (it's a major stopping point for cargo jets en route to Asia), and a signpost out front marks the mileage to many international destinations. After a stop in the visitor center cabin, step out the back door to a more spacious visitor center stacked with brochures. ⊠ *4th Ave. and F St.,* ☎ *907/274–3531,* WEB *www.anchorage.net.* ☉ *June–Aug., daily 7:30–7; May and Sept., daily 8–6; Oct.–Apr., daily 9–4.*

② Old City Hall. This 1936 building now houses offices of the Anchorage Convention and Visitors Bureau. A few exhibits and historic photos are right inside the lobby. Out front, take a look at the marble sculpture of William Seward, the secretary of state who engineered the purchase of Alaska from Russia. ⊠ *524 W. 4th Ave.*

③ Oscar Anderson House Museum. City butcher Oscar Anderson built Anchorage's first permanent frame house in 1915 at a time when most of Anchorage consisted of tents. A Swedish Christmas open house is held the first two weekends of December. Guided half-hour tours are available whenever the museum is open. ⊠ *420 M St.,* ☎ *907/274–2336.* ≦ *$3.* ⊙ *June–mid-Sept., Tues.–Sat. 11–4; mid-Sept.–May, by appointment.*

⑦ Resolution Park. A cantilevered viewing platform dominated by a monument to Captain Cook is found in this tiny park. Mt. Susitna, known as the Sleeping Lady, is the prominent low mountain to the northwest. Mt. McKinley—referred to by most Alaskans by its traditional name, Denali—is often visible 125 mi away. ⊠ *3rd Ave. at L St.*

⑤ Ship Creek. The creek is dammed here, with a footbridge across the dam. You'll see a waterfall; salmon running upstream; anglers; and, above it all, the tall buildings of downtown. ⊠ *Whitney Rd.*

⑥ Tony Knowles Coastal Trail. This recreational trail can be crowded with strollers, runners, bikers, dog walkers, and in-line skaters on sunny summer evenings, particularly around Westchester Lagoon. In winter, cross-country skiers take to it by storm. The trail begins off 2nd Avenue, west of Christensen Drive, and curls along Cook Inlet for approximately 11 mi to Kincaid Park, beyond the airport. In summer, you might spot beluga whales offshore in Cook Inlet. Access points are on the waterfront at the ends of 2nd, 5th, and 9th avenues and at Westchester Lagoon.

Midtown and Beyond

A Good Drive

Head west on Northern Lights Boulevard past Earthquake Park, 2 mi after Minnesota Drive. Signs describe the devastating power of the 1964 earthquake, the largest ever recorded in Alaska, with a magnitude of 8.5 on the Richter scale. Another 1¾ mi west on Northern Lights Boulevard is Point Woronzof, great for scenic views of Cook Inlet, Mt. Susitna (Sleeping Lady), the Alaska Range, and Mt. McKinley.

Turn left out of the parking lot at Point Woronzof and go back east along Northern Lights Boulevard 1½ mi to Aircraft Drive. Turn right and continue south and east along roads skirting the edge of two large lakes, Lakes Spenard and Hood. Lake Spenard has a beach where hardy souls may take a dip. Along Lake Hood—the world's largest and busiest seaplane base—you'll see planes (and geese) take off and land. The **Alaska Aviation Heritage Museum** ⑫, overlooking the south end of the lake and 1½ mi from the intersection with Aircraft Drive, has more than 30 vintage aircraft.

Take the first left out of the parking lot at the aviation museum and head 2 mi east on International Airport Boulevard to Minnesota Drive. Take Minnesota south about 9 mi (it becomes O'Malley Road and crosses Seward Highway) to the **Alaska Zoo** ⑬, set in wilderness with shaded trails. From the zoo, take a right on O'Malley and head back 2 mi to Seward Highway. Three miles south on the highway is the turnoff to **Potter Marsh** ⑭, where Canada geese, arctic terns, and other migratory birds make their home in summer.

From Potter Marsh, head north on Old Seward Highway for 8 mi and turn left (west) on Northern Lights Boulevard to C Street, where you will find the **Alaska Heritage Library and Museum** ⑮. This outstanding small museum displays Native artifacts and photos. From here, take Benson Boulevard (a one-way street just south of Northern Lights) back to Old Seward Highway. Go left (north) and make a right (east) on 15th Avenue, which becomes DeBarr Road, and a left (north) on Muldoon Road to the Glenn Highway. The entrance to the **Alaska Native Heritage Center** ⑯ is on the north side of this intersection. The center is a must-see for anyone interested in Native peoples. End your Anchorage tour at the **Elmendorf Air Force Base Wildlife Museum** ⑰, which displays mounted grizzlies, polar bears, birds, moose, and more. Get there by heading west from the Alaska Native Heritage Center on Glenn Highway to Boniface Parkway. Turn right (north) and follow it to the base entrance.

TIMING

Driving the route without stopping will take about two hours. You should allow from a half day to a full day, depending on the amount of time you'd like to spend at the sights.

Sights to See

🖐 ⑫ **Alaska Aviation Heritage Museum.** This cramped facility presents the state's unique aviation history with 25 vintage aircraft, a theater, an observation deck along **Lake Hood,** and a gift shop. Highlights include a historic Fairchild American Pilgrim and a Stearman C2B, the first plane to land on Mt. McKinley back in the early 1930s. Volunteers are working to restore many of the planes and are eager to talk shop. ⊠ *4721 Aircraft Dr.,* ☏ *907/248–5325.* 🌂 *$8.* ⊙ *Mid-May–Sept., daily 9–6; Oct.–mid-May, by appointment.*

★ ⑮ **Alaska Heritage Library and Museum.** This peaceful, well-organized museum in the lobby of a large midtown bank displays a variety of Alaskan Native artifacts, including baskets, dolls, paintings, and rare books. ⊠ *National Bank of Alaska, 301 W. Northern Lights Blvd., at C St.,* ☏ *907/265–2834,* WEB *www.nationalbankofalaska.com/heritage.htm.* 🌂 *Free.* ⊙ *Late May–early Sept., weekdays noon–5; early Sept.–late May, weekdays noon–4.*

🖐 ⑯ **Alaska Native Heritage Center.** Situated on a 26-acre site facing the Chugach Mountains, this extraordinary facility opened in 1999. Inside, a spacious Welcome House introduces you to Alaska's Native peoples through interpretive displays, artifacts, photographs, demonstrations, performances, and films. Also here is a café and gift shop. Next to the lake outside, five village exhibits representing Alaska's varied Native heritage acquaint you with the traditional structures and culture of Native peoples. The easiest way to reach the Heritage Center is via the **4th Ave. Trolley** (☏ 907/257–5635). A $22 ticket includes round-trip transportation from downtown plus access to the center. ⊠ *8800 Heritage Center Dr. (Glenn Hwy. at Muldoon Rd.),* ☏ *907/330–8000,* WEB *www.alaskanative.net.* 🌂 *$20 in summer; $7 in winter.* ⊙ *Mid-May–Sept., daily 9–6; Oct.–mid-May, weekends noon–5.*

🖐 ⑬ **Alaska Zoo.** Siberian tigers, musk ox, seals, moose, and a variety of Alaskan birds call this home—you'll even find the state's only elephant. The star attractions are Oreo, a brown bear, and Ahpun, a polar bear. You can hop a city bus here from downtown. ⊠ *4731 O'Malley Rd., 2 mi east of New Seward Hwy.,* ☏ *907/346–3242,* WEB *www.alaskazoo.com.* 🌂 *$7.* ⊙ *May–Labor Day, daily 9–6; Labor Day–Apr., Wed.–Mon. 10–5.*

⊙ ⑰ **Elmendorf Air Force Base Wildlife Museum.** Mounted grizzlies, polar bears, birds, moose, and more live at this self-guided museum. Look for the 10½-ft brown bear, which misses the world record by only ⅛ inch. There are also hands-on displays. ⊠ *8481 19th St., Bldg. 4-803, ask for directions at the Boniface Rd. gate,* ☏ *907/552–2282 for recorded information,* WEB *www.elmendorf.af.mil.* ☒ *Free.* ⊙ *Tues.–Thurs. and Sat. 3–4:45, Fri. noon–5.*

⑭ **Potter Marsh.** Canada geese and other migratory birds as well as the occasional moose or beaver frequent this marsh about 10 mi south of downtown on the Seward Highway. An elevated boardwalk makes viewing easy. The **Potter Point Section House,** an old railroad service building just south of the marsh, operates as a state park office. Out front is an old engine with a rotary snowplow that was used to clear avalanches. ⊠ *Seward Hwy.,* ☏ *907/345–5014.* ⊙ *Weekdays 8–4:30.*

OFF THE
BEATEN PATH

EKLUTNA NATIVE VILLAGE – This tiny cluster of homes, a small indigenous community 26 mi north of Anchorage on the Glenn Highway, is the oldest continually inhabited Athabascan Indian site in the area. At the village cemetery, note the hand-built Siberian-style prayer chapel, traditional Russian Orthodox crosses, and 80 colorful Native spirit houses. Admission includes an informative 30-minute tour. A gift shop sells Native crafts. ☏ *907/688–6026,* WEB *www.eklutna.com.* ☒ *Tours $6.* ⊙ *Mid-May–mid-Sept., daily 8–6.*

GIRDWOOD – Forty miles southeast of Anchorage near the head of Turnagain Arm, the town of Girdwood is a ski resort, summer vacation spot, and home to an eclectic collection of locals. It sits in the trees within a deep valley and is backdropped by tall mountains on three sides. The main attraction is the Mt. Alyeska Ski Resort, the largest ski area in Alaska and home to the Alyeska Prince Hotel. Besides offering the obvious winter attractions, the town draws visitors with its mountain hiking, several restaurants, and gift shops open all year. Girdwood is wetter than Anchorage; it is often raining (or snowing) here when the sun is shining 40 mi to the north.

DINING

When it comes to eating out, many visitors to Alaska naturally think seafood. After all, fishing in Alaska is a multimillion-dollar industry employing thousands of people. For those eager to sample the fruits of those labors, dining out in Anchorage is a pleasure. Several restaurants—from formal dining rooms to casual pubs—serve such favorites as halibut, salmon, Alaskan king crab legs, scallops, oysters, and mussels.

Ethnic restaurants, especially Thai and other Asian styles, and a growing number of places with extensive vegetarian menus offer variety. In the last few years half a dozen microbreweries with adjoining restaurants have opened, two of them downtown, giving the area a convivial spirit. Espresso bars have also taken root all over town. For a quick lunch downtown, track down one of the 4th Avenue vendors for a reindeer sausage with grilled onions.

A city ordinance in 2000 banned all smoking in Anchorage restaurants, except for bars that also serve meals. Most Anchorage restaurants are open daily in summer, with reduced hours in winter. Only a few places require reservations, but it's always best to call ahead, especially for dinner. For price ranges, *see* the dining price chart *in* Smart Travel Tips A to Z.

62

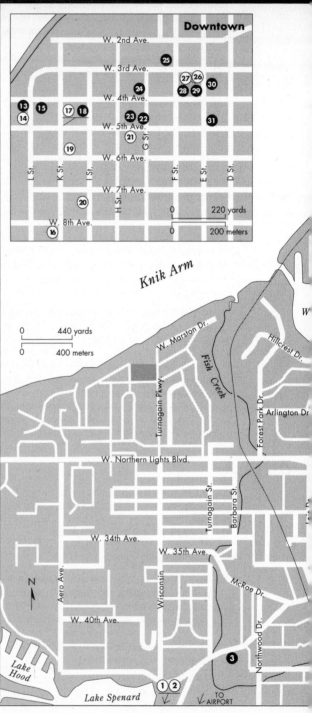

Anchorage Dining and Lodging

63

Downtown

American/Casual

\$\$–\$\$\$ ✕ **Glacier BrewHouse.** Always packed with locals, the cavernous, wood-beam BrewHouse serves ales, stouts, lagers, and pilsners. Dinner selections range from thin-crusted, 10-inch pizzas to barbecued salmon, New York pepper steak, and jambalaya fettuccine. The atmosphere is loud and jovial, and you can watch the hardworking chefs in the open kitchen. The brewery sits behind a glass wall, and the same owners operate Ristorante Orso, next door. ⊠ *737 W. 5th Ave.,* ☎ *907/274–2739,* ᴡᴇʙ *www.glacierbrewhouse.com. AE, D, DC, MC, V. No lunch Sun.*

\$–\$\$ ✕ **Sweet Basil Cafe.** This small, friendly café serves delectable lunchtime sandwiches, such as the spicy andouille sausage, on freshly baked bread. Pastas, salads, wraps, tacos, pastries, and light breakfasts fill out the menu. The juice bar is one of a handful in Anchorage, and the lattes may be the best in downtown. ⊠ *335 E St.,* ☎ *907/274–0070,* ꜰᴀx *907/274–2434. AE, D, DC, MC, V. Closed Sun. No dinner.*

\$ ✕ **Downtown Deli.** Owned by Alaska's governor, Tony Knowles, this deli serves a variety of favorites, from pastrami sandwiches to chopped chicken liver. Lunch and dinner include Alaska touches such as grilled halibut or salmon and reindeer stew. The dark, rich chicken soup comes with either noodles or homemade matzo balls, and breakfasts range from omelets to cheese blintzes. Wooden booths offer privacy, or sit out front at the sidewalk tables for some people-watching. Service is efficient and cheery. ⊠ *525 W. 4th Ave.,* ☎ *907/276–7116. Reservations not accepted. AE, D, DC, MC, V.*

Contemporary

\$\$\$\$ ✕ **Crow's Nest.** Elegant cuisine is the order of the day, along with the best view in Anchorage—the Chugach Mountains to the east, the Alaska Range to the north, and the sprawling city of Anchorage below. It's best known for an extraordinary six-course set menu: \$80 per person, or \$115 per person with wine pairings. The wine cellar is equally impressive. Everything is presented in an elegant atmosphere, with plenty of starched linen, brass, and teak. The menu always includes seafood, along with game and other meats. ⊠ *On top of the Hotel Captain Cook, 5th Ave. and K St.,* ☎ *907/343–2217,* ᴡᴇʙ *www.captaincook.com. Reservations essential. AE, D, DC, MC, V. Closed Sun. No lunch.*

\$\$\$–\$\$\$\$ ✕ **Marx Brothers' Cafe.** The little frame house on the bluff that houses
★ this place, a local favorite for more than 20 years, was built in 1916 and refurbished by the three "Marx Brothers"—Jack Amon, Van Hale, and Ken Brown. Chef Jack's *melitzanosalata* (eggplant spread) appetizer is an Anchorage institution, and the outstanding made-at-your-table Caesar salad is a superb opener for the baked halibut with a macadamia crust served with coconut curry and mango chutney. For dessert, try the warm wild-berry crisp with Alaskan birch syrup and butter-pecan ice cream. The wine list includes more than 400 international choices, and the restaurant has received the *Wine Spectator* Award of Excellence. A second Marx Brothers' Cafe is housed within the Anchorage Museum of History and Arts. ⊠ *627 W. 3rd Ave.,* ☎ *907/278–2133,* ᴡᴇʙ *www.marxcafe.com. Reservations essential. AE, DC, MC, V. Closed Sun. Sept.–May. No lunch.*

\$\$\$–\$\$\$\$ ✕ **Simon and Seafort's Saloon & Grill.** The high ceilings and big windows here overlook Cook Inlet and light up the brass-and-wood interior. The diverse menu includes prime rib (aged 28 days) and pasta, but the main attraction here is seafood—fish is blackened, grilled, fried, or prepared any other way you like it. Try the crab legs or grilled Alaskan salmon with toasted hazelnut butter. The brandy ice—vanilla ice cream whipped with brandy, Kahlúa, and crème de cacao—is always a deliciously decadent affair here. The bar is a great spot for microbrews and appetizers. ⌧ *420 L St.,* ☎ *907/274–3502. Reservations essential. AE, DC, MC, V. No lunch Sun.*

$$$ ✕ **Sacks Café.** Another longtime Anchorage favorite, this bright, post-
★ modern restaurant serves light American and ethnic cuisine such as grilled lamb with sun-dried tomato curry sauce, roasted Portobello mushrooms with udon noodles, or spicy pan-seared scallops. For lunch, try the New York steak sandwich or a vegetarian panini. Fresh flowers adorn all tables, and a separate bar area provides a friendly atmosphere for singles. The café is especially crowded during lunch. Brunch is served 11–2:30. ⌧ *328 G St.,* ☎ *907/276–3546 or 907/274–4022,* ⊞ *www. sackscafe.com. Reservations essential. AE, MC, V.*

Eclectic

$$–$$$ ✕ **Snow City Cafe.** At this unassuming cafe along "lawyer row," you'll find dependably good and reasonably priced meals. Formica tables, mismatched chairs, and fluorescent lights fill its interior, and the young staff comes from the anything-goes school of facial jewelry. The menu lists vegetarian specials, pastas, Alaskan seafood, and such hometown favorites as meat loaf or roasted chicken and mashed potatoes. Arrive early for the popular weekend breakfasts or be prepared to wait. There's live music some evenings, including an open mike session on Sunday night. ⌧ *4th Ave. at L St.,* ☎ *907/272–2489,* ⊠ *907/272–6338. No dinner Mon.–Tues. AE, D, DC, MC, V.*

Italian

$$–$$$$ ✕ **Ristorante Orso.** This attractive eatery opened in 2000, and has quickly
★ established itself as a star on the city's culinary scene. Peach-red walls and earthy photos from Tuscany accent the interior. Alaskan touches flavor rustic Italian dishes, including traditional pastas, fresh seafood, wood-grilled meats, and locally famous desserts—most notably a decadent molten chocolate cake served with vanilla ice cream and Sambuca syrup. Be sure to ask about the day's specials, or try the lamb osso buco with sweet and sour pearl onions, roma tomatoes, kalamata olives, and polenta. The large and airy bar serves the same menu, and a cozy upstairs room offers a quieter, more romantic setting. Ristorante Orso ("bear" in Italian) is owned by the same folks who operate the adjacent and equally popular Glacier BrewHouse. ⌧ *737 W. 5th Ave.,* ☎ *907/222–3232,* ⊠ *907/277–1033. AE, D, DC, MC, V.*

Japanese

$$–$$$$ ✕ **Kumagoro.** A favorite of the suit-and-tie lunch crowd, Kumagoro also has Japanese-style breakfasts, a take-out deli with such specialties as herring roe on kelp, and a sleek sushi bar (open evenings only). The best items on the dinner menu are the sizzling salmon or beef teriyaki, both served with miso (soybean) soup and salad. With the *shabu-shabu* dinner ($26 per person), you cook your own meats and vegetables in a stockpot of boiling broth. Inexpensive homemade *ramen* (deep-fried Japanese-style noodles) soups are also available. All entrée prices include a 10% gratuity. ⌧ *533 W. 4th Ave.,* ☎ *907/272–9905. AE, D, DC, MC, V.*

Steak

$$–$$$$ ✕ **Club Paris.** If you haven't visited Anchorage in a decade or so, you'll find Alaska's oldest steak house has barely changed since it opened in 1957. In fact, many of the friendly staff—from the chef to the waitresses—have been here since the 1980s. The restaurant is filled with dark woods and an old-fashioned feel, and serves tender, flavorful steaks of all kinds, including a 4-inch-thick filet mignon. Also on the menu are sandwiches (lunch only), freshly ground hamburgers, salads, and Alaskan seafood. If you have to wait for a table, have a martini at the

bar and order the hors d'oeuvres tray ($26)—a sampler of top sirloin steak, cheese, and prawns that could be a meal for two. For dessert, try their key lime pie or New York–style cheesecake. ☒ *417 W. 5th Ave.,* ☏ *907/277–6332. AE, D, DC, MC, V. No lunch Sun.*

Greater Anchorage

American

$–$$$ ✕ **Gwennie's Old Alaskan Restaurant.** Historic Alaskan photos, stuffed animals, and memorabilia adorn this old family favorite, just south of city center toward the airport. Lunch and dinners are available—including an all-you-can-eat beef barbecue for just $12—but the restaurant is best known for its old-fashioned breakfasts, available all day. Try the sourdough pancakes, reindeer sausage and eggs, or crab omelets. ☒ *4333 Spenard Rd.,* ☏ *907/243–2090. AE, D, DC, MC, V.*

Cajun/Creole

$$–$$$$ ✕ **Double Musky Inn.** Anchorage residents say eating here is worth the one-hour drive south to Girdwood and the inevitable wait for dinner. It's quite noisy, and the decor consists of tacky art and Mardi Gras souvenirs, but huge Sitka spruce trees frame the windows for a scenic setting. The diverse menu mixes Cajun-style meals with such favorites as garlic seafood pasta, rack of lamb, French pepper steak, and lobster kebabs. For dessert lovers, the biggest attraction here is the gooey, chocolate-rich Double Musky pie. The restaurant is smoke free except for the lounge. ☒ *Crow Creek Rd., Girdwood,* ☏ *907/783–2822,* WEB *www. doublemuskyinn.com. Reservations not accepted. AE, D, DC, MC, V. Closed Mon. and Nov. No lunch.*

Contemporary

$$$–$$$$ ✕ **Jens'.** This dining spot may be in a midtown strip mall, but it's tastefully decorated with Alaskan art and serves fine food. The dinner menu changes daily and almost always includes Alaskan salmon, halibut, and rockfish. Other specialties are rack of lamb, tenderloin of veal, and their justly famous pepper steak. Head chef Jens Hansen's heritage shows through at lunch when the Danish specials appear, along with soups, salads, pastas, and vegetarian meals. For a lighter evening meal, sample the appetizers in the wine bar. ☒ *701 W. 36th Ave.,* ☏ *907/ 561–5367. AE, D, DC, MC, V. Closed Sun. and Jan. No lunch Sat., no dinner Mon.*

$$$–$$$$ ✕ **Seven Glaciers.** A 60-passenger aerial tram—free with dinner reser-
   ★   vations, otherwise $19 round-trip—carries you to this refined yet relaxing mountainside restaurant, perched at the 2,300-ft level of Mt. Alyeska in the ski resort town of Girdwood, 40 minutes south of Anchorage. In the comfortable dining room, overlooking seven glaciers, you'll enjoy artfully presented dinner entrées such as smoked and grilled salmon with spicy green chili dumplings and grilled Portobello mushrooms on angel-hair pasta. Appetizers—particularly the peppered Dungeness crab cakes—are extraordinary, but prices reach lofty heights. A special four-course menu ($70 including a matched wine) is available nightly. Lunchtime visitors should ask about the tram-and-lunch special for $19, the same price as the tram ride alone. Both tram and restaurant are wheelchair-accessible. ☒ *Alyeska Prince Hotel, 1000 Arlberg Rd., Girdwood,* ☏ *907/754–2237. Reservations essential. AE, D, DC, MC, V. Closed Mon.–Thurs. Nov.–mid-Apr. No lunch.*

Eclectic

$–$$$ ✕ **New Sagaya's City Market.** This international deli and grocery is an excellent spot for quick sit-down lunches, baked goods, and coffee at the Kaladi Brothers espresso bar. The in-house bakery (L'Aroma) cranks out specialty breads and pastries of all types, and you can make your own picnic by piling on imported olives, cheeses, and cured meats. Nine-inch California-style pizzas are baked in a wood-fired oven and feature toppings of pesto, fresh herbs, Italian meats, seafood, and goat cheese. Chinese food, sandwich wraps, chicken teriyaki, home-made soups, salads, and even stuffed cabbage fill out the deli menu. You can eat inside on the sheltered patio or grab an outside table on a summer afternoon. The grocery store sells gourmet foods, and has one of the best seafood counters in town. Their staff will even box and ship your fish via Federal Express. A second New Sagaya's is across from the University Center Mall. ⊠ *900 W. 13th Ave.,* ☎ *907/274–6173,* FAX *907/274–2042;* ⊠ *3700 Old Seward Hwy.,* ☎ *907/562–9797,* FAX *907/274–2042,* WEB *www.newsagaya.com. AE, D, DC, MC, V.*

Italian

$$–$$$ ✕ **CampoBello Bistro.** Tucked into a midtown mall, CampoBello has surprisingly sophisticated Italian entrées and sinful desserts. Step inside for a romantic lunch or dinner surrounded by splashes of modern art on the walls and candles on the tables. Specialties include seafood crepes, veal marsala, and scampi Mediterranean—a rich blend of shrimp, sun-dried tomatoes, capers, spinach, and feta cheese over fettuccine. Highlights include ample servings, attentive service, and an impressive wine list, particularly the range of Italian choices. ⊠ *601 W. 36th Ave.,* ☎ *907/563–2040. AE, DC, MC, V. No lunch weekends. No dinner Sun.–Mon.*

Mexican

$$–$$$ ✕ **Mexico in Alaska.** Since 1972 the most authentic Mexican food in town, and maybe even in Alaska, has been served here. Owner Maria Elena Ball befriends everyone, particularly young children. Favorite dishes—all are subtle and not greasy—include lime-marinated fried chicken, *chilaquiles* (tortilla casserole with mole sauce), and *entremesa de queso* (melted cheese, jalapeños, and onions with homemade tortillas). Lunch buffets are served on weekdays and Sunday, and a vegetarian menu is available. The restaurant is several miles south of downtown, so you'll need to drive or catch the city bus. ⊠ *7305 Old Seward Hwy.,* ☎ *907/349–1528. AE, D, MC, V. No lunch Sun.*

Pizza

$$–$$$ ✕ **Moose's Tooth Pub & Pizzeria.** This down-home brew pub and pizze-★ ria in midtown, just off the Seward Highway north of 36th Avenue, seems perpetually packed with jovial locals. Pizzas and handcrafted beers, including more than a dozen ales, ambers, porters, and stouts, are the order of the day, and the homemade root beers, cream sodas, and ginger ales are also delicious. You can match these unique brews with one of the 40 different pizzas with such varied toppings as roasted red peppers, jalapeños, cream cheese, halibut, and capers. Weekday lunches are a real bargain, starting at just $5 for a slice of pizza and a salad. ⊠ *3300 Old Seward Hwy.,* ☎ *907/258–2537,* WEB *www.moosestooth.net. D, DC, MC, V.*

Thai

$–$$$ ✕ **Thai House Restaurant.** Among the Thai restaurants scattered around Anchorage, this is one of the best, with authentic Thai cooking, quick and friendly service, and an unpretentious setting; it's housed in an old Dairy Queen on a busy street corner. You will find all the standard offerings, such as fresh rolls, *pad Thai* (spicy cooked noodles with shrimp, chicken, and eggs), and *tom khar gai* (a flavorful soup of coconut milk, chicken, lemongrass, and ginger), along with something you aren't likely to find in Thailand: stir-fried curry Dungeness crab. Vegetarians can choose from a dozen nonmeat choices. ⊠ *830 E. 36th Ave.,* ☎ *907/563–8616,* FAX *907/562–9490. AE, MC, V.*

Vegetarian

$ ✕ **Middle Way Cafe & Coffee House.** This cramped little lunchtime niche serves a wide variety of vegetarian and nonvegetarian dishes, including gussied-up grain-and-soy burgers, turkey cranberry sandwiches, and jumbo whole-grain tortillas wrapped around combinations of organic veggies, falafel, brown rice, and beans. You can get a fruit smoothie at the juice bar, choose from 35 different teas, or enjoy an espresso. Be sure to check out the daily specials. ⊠ *1200 W. Northern Lights Blvd.,* ☎ *907/272–6433. Reservations not accepted. No credit cards. Closed Sun.*

LODGING

Several hotels in Anchorage offer top-drawer amenities, with summertime rates to match. Smaller inns and 175 or so bed-and-breakfasts offer character and quaint amenities at more modest prices. Within the last several years a dozen new hotels have added 1,400 rooms; the largest is a 20-story downtown Marriott Hotel that opened in 2000. Most hotels in Anchorage are downtown, in midtown, or along Spenard Avenue. Girdwood, 40 mi south of downtown along the Seward and Alyeska highways, has ski-resort amenities. For a listing of hotels, inns, and B&Bs, contact the Anchorage Convention and Visitors Bureau. For campgrounds in and around town, contact the Alaska Public Lands Information Center (☞ Sights to See *in* Exploring Anchorage). In summer, reservations are a must for the major hotels; many places fill up months in advance. For price ranges, *see* the Anchorage lodging price chart *in* Smart Travel Tips A to Z.

Downtown

$$$$ 🏨 **Anchorage Marriott Downtown.** The largest of a dozen Anchorage lodging places completed in the last several years, the Marriott is a full-service hotel that appeals to business travelers, tourists, and corporate clients. The hotel's **Cafe Promenade** serves American cuisine with an Alaskan flair. All guest rooms have huge windows; views are breathtaking from the top floors. A bright decor predominates throughout, with well-designed furnishings that include workstation desks with two-line phones, data ports, and voice mail. Guests staying on the top three levels of this 20-story hotel have access to a concierge lounge and are served a light breakfast, along with evening hors d'oeuvres and desserts. Other amenities include complete business and fitness centers. ⊠ *820 W. 7th Ave., 99501,* ☎ *907/279–8000 or 800/228–9290,* ℻ *907/ 279–8005,* 🕸 *www.marriott.com. 393 rooms, 3 suites. Restaurant, bar, room service, indoor pool, hot tub, gym, shops, concierge, business services, meeting rooms. AE, D, DC, MC, V.*

$$$$ 🏨 **Hotel Captain Cook.** The three towers of this hotel take up a full city block; one rises 20 floors above Anchorage and is capped by the Crow's Nest Restaurant. The dark decor, with teak paneling lining the interior walls, recalls Captain Cook's voyages in the South Pacific. The nautical theme is carried out in the guest rooms as well, which have prints of the areas explored by Cook. A 24-hour business center houses computers with Internet access, copy and fax machines, plus secretarial services (for a fee). The most luxurious accommodation is found on the 19th floor of Tower III—a sprawling, 1,600-square-ft two-bedroom suite, which costs a mere $1,500 per night. ⊠ *5th Ave. and K St., 99501,* ☎ *907/ 276–6000 or 800/843–1950,* ℻ *907/343–2298,* 🕸 *www.captaincook. com. 451 rooms, 96 suites. 3 restaurants, in-room data ports, room service, pool, hair salon, hot tub, sauna, health club, racquetball, shop, concierge, business services, meeting room. AE, D, DC, MC, V.*

$$$$ ⊡ **Sheraton Anchorage.** A half mile east of downtown and bordering
on a run-down part of town, the 16-story Sheraton has 32 rooms specially set up for business travelers. The glass-canopy lobby has a jade-
tile staircase, acres of cream-color marble, and a modern and airy lobby.
Guest rooms all include voice mail, an iron and ironing board, hair dryer,
coffeemaker, and air conditioning. Get a room high up on the north side
to watch F-16s and other jets flying tight patterns over nearby Elmendorf Air Force Base. A downstairs restaurant (Ptarmigan Bar and Grill)
serves three meals a day, and a 15th-floor restaurant (Josephine's) is open
for Sunday brunch with a view. ⊠ *401 E. 6th Ave., 99501,* ☎ *907/276–
8700 or 800/325–3535,* FAX *907/276–7561,* WEB *www.sheraton.com. 375
rooms, 5 suites. Restaurant, bar, room service, hot tub, sauna, health
club, meeting room. AE, D, DC, MC, V.*

$$$–$$$$ ⊡ **Anchorage Hilton.** Alaska's largest hotel, the Hilton is just a block
from city center. Native Alaskan designs, along with glass cases con-
taining menacingly posed grizzly and polar bears adorn the ample
lobby. Well-maintained rooms, decorated in a contemporary style with
oak and maple furnishings, have data ports and voice mail. You'll also
find two restaurants and lounges, plus a large conference center. Re-
quest a north-facing room on the upper levels for Mt. McKinley vis-
tas. ⊠ *500 W. 3rd Ave., 99501,* ☎ *907/272–7411 or 800/245–2527,*
FAX *907/265–7142,* WEB *www.anchoragehilton.com. 572 rooms, 23
suites. 2 restaurants, 2 lounges, in-room data ports, pool, health club,
airport shuttle. AE, D, DC, MC, V.*

$$$–$$$$ ⊡ **Anchorage Hotel.** The little Anchorage Hotel building has been
   ★   around since 1916, and was one of the few buildings to survive the
1964 earthquake with relatively minor damage. Experienced travelers
call it the only hotel in Anchorage with charm: the original sinks and
tubs have been restored and upstairs hallways are lined with old An-
chorage photos. Each room includes a fully stocked minibar, plus
phone data ports, irons, and hair dryers. The lobby, its fireplace crack-
ling in chilly weather, has a quaint European feel, and the staff is adept
at meeting your needs. A Continental breakfast is served each morn-
ing in the lobby. Request a corner room if possible; rooms facing the
street may have some traffic noise. The junior suites include comfort-
able sitting areas and kitchenettes. ⊠ *330 E St., 99501,* ☎ *907/272–
4553 or 800/544–0988,* FAX *907/277–4483. 16 rooms, 10 junior suites.
Minibars, meeting room. AE, D, DC, MC, V.*

$$$$ ⊡ **Anchorage Westmark Hotel.** This 13-story hotel has comfortable
rooms with dark teak furnishings and small private balconies. Reserve
a room or suite on the higher floors for the best mountain views. (Do
not confuse the Westmark Hotel with the reasonably priced but far more
basic Westmark Inn.) ⊠ *720 W. 5th Ave., 99501,* ☎ *907/276–7676
or 800/544–0970,* FAX *907/276–3615,* WEB *www.westmarkhotels.com.
182 rooms, 18 suites. Restaurant, coffee shop, room service, meeting
room. AE, D, DC, MC, V.*

$$$–$$$$ ⊡ **Comfort Inn Ship Creek.** On the banks of Ship Creek, this popular
family hotel is a short walk northeast of the Alaska Railroad depot.
Rooms, which can be a bit noisy at times, come in a variety of config-
urations; some are executive suites, some have kitchens, and some have
jetted tubs. All guests receive a substantial Continental breakfast each
morning. The hotel stocks a limited number of fishing poles for guests
who want to try their luck catching salmon in Ship Creek. Bikes are
also available. ⊠ *111 Ship Creek Ave., 99501,* ☎ *907/277–6887 or 800/
362–6887,* FAX *907/274–9830,* WEB *www.comfortinn.com. 88 rooms, 12
suites. Pool, hot tub, gym, business services. AE, D, DC, MC, V.*

$$$–$$$$ ⊡ **Inlet Tower Suites.** Built in 1953, this 14-story building in a resi-
dential area south of downtown offers spacious rooms and suites. All
include microwaves and small refrigerators, and the suites contain

separate kitchenettes. Corner rooms, particularly those on the northeast side, provide expansive views. ⊠ *1200 L St., 99501, ☎ 907/276–0110 or 800/544–0786, ℻ 907/258–4914. 153 rooms, 26 suites. Restaurant, no-smoking room, hair salon, sauna, gym, laundry facilities, airport shuttle, free parking. AE, D, DC, MC, V.*

$$$ 🏠 **Sleeping Lady Bed & Breakfast.** This attractive B&B is just steps away from the Tony Knowles Coastal Trail and easy walking distance from downtown restaurants and shopping. Unwind on the large back deck and take in the lengthy summer sunsets over Cook Inlet. Four spacious and private guest rooms are attractively furnished, with three facing the water. The largest contains high arched windows and a fireplace. Guests have access to a kitchenette, and are served a delicious breakfast each morning. No children allowed. ⊠ *545 M St., 99501, ☎ 907/258–4455, ℻ 907/258–4955, 🌐 www.anchsleepingladybnb.com. 4 rooms. MC, V.*

$$$ 🏠 **Voyager Hotel.** This four-story hotel caters to both business and leisure
 ★   travelers. Attention to detail shows in the complete kitchens, sofa beds, coffeemakers, irons and ironing boards, quality linens, voice mail, and data ports in the rooms. Upstairs, west-side rooms have views of the inlet. Smoking is not permitted in the hotel. ⊠ *501 K St., 99501, ☎ 907/277–9501 or 800/247–9070, ℻ 907/274–0333. 38 rooms. In-room data ports, no-smoking rooms. AE, D, DC, MC, V.*

$$–$$$ 🏠 **Copper Whale Inn.** This small inn is on the edge of downtown with a view across Cook Inlet to Sleeping Lady and other mountains. All rooms are furnished with cherrywood beds, and most have private baths. A light breakfast is served each morning. At other times, great food is available just a few steps away at Simon and Seafort's. Owner Tony Carter, a marine biologist, leads an excellent all-day wildlife ecotour for $65. ⊠ *440 L St., 99501, ☎ 907/258–7999, ℻ 907/258–6213 or 888/942–5346, 🌐 www.copperwhale.com. 15 rooms. Dining room. AE, D, DC, MC, V.*

$$–$$$ 🏠 **Snowshoe Inn.** This small and friendly no-smoking inn is opposite the downtown corporate towers. Comfortable rooms contain refrigerators, microwaves, and VCRs, and two of the suites have Jacuzzi tubs and king-size beds. A big Continental breakfast is served each morning in the lobby. ⊠ *826 K St., 99501, ☎ 907/258–7669, ℻ 907/258–7463. 13 rooms, 3 suites. Refrigerators, laundry service. D, MC, V.*

$$ 🏠 **Merrill Field Inn.** A mile east of downtown and across from Anchorage's small-plane airfield, this well-maintained family motel has reasonable prices and clean rooms, each with a microwave oven, refrigerator, and hair dryer. Rooms are a bit small, but kitchenettes are also available. ⊠ *420 Sitka St., 99501, ☎ 907/276–4547 or 800/898–4547, ℻ 907/276–5064, 🌐 www.merrillfieldinn.com. 39 rooms. AE, D, DC, MC, V. CP.*

$$ 🏠 **Oscar Gill House.** This historic home in a quiet neighborhood along Delaney Park Strip was originally built in the settlement of Knik (north of Anchorage) in 1913. Three years later, Gill floated it by boat to Anchorage, where he later served as the mayor for three terms and then Speaker of the Territorial House. Lovingly renovated in 1993, it has been transformed into a comfortable B&B, with downtown attractions a short walk away. Two rooms share a bath, and the third contains a private bath and Jacuzzi tub. Little touches include down comforters, bicycles, and a delicious breakfast. ⊠ *1344 W. 10th Ave., 99501, ☎ ℻ 907/279–1344, 🌐 www.oscargill.com. 3 rooms. AE, MC, V.*

Greater Anchorage

$$$$ 🏠 **Alyeska Prince Hotel.** This large and luxurious hotel sits at the base
 ★   of Mt. Alyeska Ski Resort, an hour south of Anchorage in Girdwood.

The hotel is surrounded by lush forests, and some rooms offer views of the Chugach Mountains. Rooms are on the small side, but all have heated towel racks, ski-boot storage, bathrobes, and slippers, plus phones are in both the bathrooms and bedrooms. A spectacular aerial tram (free if you have dinner reservations) transports diners to the Seven Glaciers restaurant at the 2,300-ft level of the mountain. ⊠ *1000 Arlberg Rd., Box 249, Girdwood 99587,* ☎ *907/754–1111 or 800/880–3880,* FAX *907/754–2200,* WEB *www.alyeskaresort.com. 296 rooms, 11 junior suites. 2 restaurants, bar, sushi bar, in-room safes, refrigerators, room service, indoor pool, hot tub, massage, sauna, gym, ice-skating, cross-country and downhill skiing, shop, meeting room. AE, D, DC, MC, V.*

$$$$ ⊞ **Millennium Anchorage Hotel.** Perched on the shore of Lake Hood,
★ the Millennium (formerly called the Regal Alaskan) is a great place from which to watch planes come and go. The lobby resembles a hunting lodge with its stone fireplace and trophy heads and mounted fish on every wall. The luxuriously appointed guest rooms continue the inviting Alaskan theme. Most have colorful Native Alaskan–style bedding and moose-shape cast-iron lamps. All rooms have small refrigerators, coffeemakers, and hair dryers. Most rooms are no-smoking. The restaurant here is locally famous for its enormous Sunday brunch buffets ($27). ⊠ *4800 Spenard Rd., 99517,* ☎ *907/243–2300 or 800/544–0553,* FAX *907/243–8815,* WEB *www.millennium-hotels.com. 243 rooms, 5 suites. Restaurant, lobby lounge, no-smoking rooms, refrigerators, room service, hot tub, sauna, steam room, gym, laundry service, airport shuttle. AE, D, DC, MC, V.*

$$$–$$$$ ⊞ **Courtyard by Marriott.** Near the airport, this modern hotel is abuzz with business travelers. The restaurant serves breakfast and dinner, but only limited room service in the evening. Most rooms are designated no-smoking. Some rooms have a whirlpool bath and king-size bed; all have two phones, coffeemakers, and hair dryers. ⊠ *4901 Spenard Rd., 99517,* ☎ *907/245–0322 or 800/321–2211,* FAX *907/248–1886,* WEB *www.marriott.com. 148 rooms, 6 suites. Restaurant, no-smoking rooms, room service, pool, hot tub, sauna, gym, laundry service, meeting room, airport shuttle. AE, D, DC, MC, V.*

$$$–$$$$ ⊞ **Mahogany Manor.** Hidden behind a tall fence along busy 15th Avenue, this rambling B&B with Native Alaskan art throughout provides a quick escape from city life. Unwind with the expansive decks, large picture windows, indoor waterfall, fireplaces, and big-screen television. An unusual 19-ft hot tub and jetted lap pool occupies a lower deck. The spacious three-room suite is good for families and small groups. A generous Continental breakfast is served, and you have access to a separate kitchen. ⊠ *204 E. 15th Ave., 99501,* ☎ *907/278–1111,* FAX *907/258–7877,* WEB *www.mahoganymanor.com. 4 rooms. Dining room, pool, hot tub. AE, MC, V.*

$$$ ⊞ **Hampton Inn.** Midway between the airport and downtown, the Hampton has all the now-standard room features: designer furnishings, refrigerators, microwaves, coffeemakers, hair dryers, data ports, and voice mail. Guests are treated to a Continental breakfast buffet. Business travelers will appreciate Internet access and fax services, and families will enjoy the indoor pool and hot tub. ⊠ *4301 Credit Union Dr., 99503,* ☎ *907/550–7000 or 800/426–7866,* FAX *907/561–7330,* WEB *www.stonebridgecompanies.com. 101 rooms. Breakfast room, in-room data ports, refrigerators, indoor pool, hot tub, gym, laundry service, business services, meeting room. AE, D, DC, MC, V.*

$$$ ⊞ **SpringHill Suites by Marriott.** This midtown Anchorage hotel, near the city's main public library and a new 16-plex movie theater, offers spacious suites with separate living and sleeping areas. Each has either a king bed or two double beds with a pull-out sofa, plus a microwave, refrigerator, data port, coffeemaker, and two TVs. A light Continen-

tal breakfast buffet is served. Up to six people can stay in these suites for the same price. ✉ *3401 A St., 99503,* ☎ *907/562–3247 or 888/ 287–9400,* FAX *907/562–3250,* WEB *www.springhillsuites.com. 102 suites. Breakfast room, refrigerators, indoor pool, gym, laundry facilities, airport shuttle. AE, D, DC, MC, V.*

$ 🏠 **Qupqugiaq Inn.** Hidden behind a bland, boxy exterior, this inexpensive inn with the unpronounceable name is a cross between a motel and a hostel. The interior architecture of "Q Inn" is distinctive, with curved walls and bright pine accents. This is a good option for budget travelers who tolerate the lack of in-room phones and small quarters while appreciating the clean and well-maintained facilities. Guests have access to a communal kitchen and sitting room. CampoBello Bistro, the downstairs café, is right across the street. ✉ *640 W. 36th Ave., 99503,* ☎ *907/562–5681,* WEB *www.qupq.com. 16 rooms, 4 with shared bath. Café. AE, MC, V.*

NIGHTLIFE AND THE ARTS

The Arts

Visitors and those new to Anchorage are often surprised by the variety—and high quality—of cultural activities in this town of a quarter-million people. In addition to top-name touring groups and performers, a sampling of local productions, including provocative theater, children's shows, improvisational troupes, Buddhist lectures, photography exhibits, poetry readings, and Native Alaskan dance performances, are always going on around town. The Friday entertainment section of the *Anchorage Daily News* is packed with events and activities. Tickets for many cultural events can be purchased at any Carrs grocery store. **Carrs Tix** (☎ 907/263–2787 or 800/478–7328, WEB www.tickets.com) has recorded information on cultural events of the week and the option to buy tickets by phone or from their Web site.

The **Alaska Center for the Performing Arts** (✉ 621 W. 6th Ave., ☎ 907/ 263–2787 or 907/263–2900) has three theaters and hosts local performing groups as well as traveling production companies that in the last few years have brought *Cats, Les Misérables,* and *Phantom of the Opera* to the Anchorage stage. The lobby box office, open from Monday to Saturday 10–6, sells tickets to a variety of productions and is a good all-around source of cultural information. During the summer, you can watch IMAX movies at the Center for the Performing Arts, along with a special northern lights show.

Opera and Classical Music

The **Anchorage Opera** (☎ 907/279–2557, WEB www.anchorageopera.org) produces two or three operas during its November–March season. The **Anchorage Symphony Orchestra** (☎ 907/274–8668, WEB www.anchoragesymphony.org) performs classical concerts October through April. The box office of the Alaska Center for the Performing Arts sells tickets for both.

Theater

The **Alaska Center for the Performing Arts** hosts the Anchorage Opera and the Anchorage Symphony Orchestra among other major performances. **Cyrano's Off-Center Playhouse** (✉ 4th Ave. and D St., ☎ 907/ 274–2599) mounts innovative productions in a cozy theater connected to a namesake café and bookstore. **Out North Contemporary Art House** (✉ 1325 Primrose St., just west of Bragaw Rd. off DeBarr Rd., ☎ 907/ 279–8200, WEB www.outnorth.org), whose productions are thought-provoking and, at times, controversial, often earns critical acclaim from local reviewers. Student productions from the **University of Alaska Anchorage Theater** (✉ 3211 Providence Dr., ☎ 907/786–4721) are timely and well done. The theater is intimate, with seating on three sides.

Nightlife

Anchorage does not shut down when it gets dark. Bars here—and throughout Alaska—open early (in the morning) and close as late as 3 AM on weekends. The *Anchorage Daily News* entertainment section, published on Friday, has a complete listing of entertainment options, ranging from concerts and theater to movie listings and a roundup of nightspots featuring live music.

Bars and Nightclubs

Chilkoot Charlie's (✉ 2435 Spenard Rd., ☎ 907/272–1010, WEB www. koots.com), a rambling timber building with sawdust floors, two stages and three dance floors, loud music (rock or swing bands) nightly, and rowdy customers, is where young Alaskans go to get crazy. Choose from 75 different beers on draught, plus another 35 in bottles. Lots of old-timers favor the dark bar of **Club Paris** (✉ 417 W. 5th Ave., ☎ 907/277–6332). Once the classiest place in downtown Anchorage, with its Paris mural and French street lamps hanging behind the bar, it has lost the glamour but not the faithful clientele. There's mostly swing on the jukebox.

Snowgoose Restaurant (✉ W. 3rd Ave. and G St., ☎ 907/277–7727) is a good place to unwind with beer inside or on the outside deck overlooking Cook Inlet. **F Street Station** (✉ 325 F St., ☎ 907/272–5196), a crowded little downtown bar, is a delightful spot for a perfectly prepared and reasonable lunch or dinner. Check the board for the day's specials, or just enjoy a beer and appetizers with the suit-and-tie crowd. A half-dozen small tables are available, or you can eat at the bar and chat with the chefs as they work. A trendy place for the dressy "in" crowd, the bar at **Simon and Seafort's Saloon and Grill** (✉ 420 L St., ☎ 907/274–3502) has stunning views of Cook Inlet, a special single malt Scotch menu, and a wide selection of imported beers.

Anchorage's gay nightlife centers on a pair of bars, both of which attract a mixed crowd that includes straight folks, gays, and lesbians. **Mad Myrna's** (✉ 530 E. 5th Ave., ☎ 907/276–9762) spins country sounds most nights, karaoke on Wednesday, and drag shows every Friday. The **Raven** (✉ 708 E. 4th Ave., ☎ 907/276–9672) is a smoky neighborhood hangout where you'll meet regulars over a game of billiards.

Comedy

Mr. Whitekeys is the proprietor of **Fly by Night Club** (✉ 3300 Spenard Rd., ☎ 907/279–7726), a self-proclaimed "sleazy Spenard nightclub." Every summer, the "Whale Fat Follies" revue features tacky Alaska jokes, accomplished singing, and the boogie-woogie piano of Mr. Whitekeys himself. To really appreciate all the inside jokes, it helps to attend with a local. Shows start at 8; it's a good idea to reserve several days in advance. The club is smoke free Tuesday, Wednesday, and Thursday night; it's closed Sunday–Monday and January–March.

Live Music

See Friday editions of the *Anchorage Daily News* for complete listings of upcoming concerts and other musical performances. On most summertime Fridays, open-air concerts are performed at noon on the stage in front of the **Old City Hall** (✉ 524 W. 4th Ave.). A wide range of performers play at the **Saturday Market** (✉ 3rd Ave. and E St., ☎ 907/272–5634) every Saturday from late May to mid-September.

Chilkoot Charlie's is another exceptionally popular party place, with live music every night of the week. Anchorage's favorite singles bar, **Humpy's Great Alaskan Alehouse** (✉ 610 W. 6th Ave., ☎ 907/276–2337) serves up rock, blues, and folk, along with dozens of microbrews (including more than 40 beers on tap) and surprisingly tasty pub grub. It's noisy, smoky, and always packed.

Blues Central/Chef's Inn (✉ 825 W. Northern Lights Blvd., ☎ 907/272–1341), a modest and smoky eatery, is also a blues mecca that features live bands on weekend nights. Tony Lamas and Wranglers are the uniform of choice at South Anchorage's country venue, **Long Branch Saloon** (✉ 1737 E. Dimond Blvd., ☎ 907/349–4142).

Latin music fans crowd the dance floor at the downtown **Club Soraya** (✉ 333 W. 4th Ave., ☎ 907/563–5940), open Friday–Sunday nights. Mexican food is also served here. Anchorage's jazz joint is **Jass Alley** (✉ 900 W. 5th Ave., ☎ 907/279–5277), with Continental cuisine nightly and live music on weekends. DJs spin reggae at **The Moment** (✉ 3230 Old Seward Hwy., ☎ 907/274–7242) on Saturday and Sunday nights. Downtown's **Snow City Cafe** (✉ 4th Ave. at L St., ☎ 907/272–2489) serves up open-mike sessions on Sunday evening.

OUTDOOR ACTIVITIES AND SPORTS

Participant Sports

Bicycling, Running, and Walking

Anchorage has more than 120 mi of paved bicycle trails, and many streets have marked bike lanes. Although busy during the day, downtown streets are uncrowded and safe for cyclists in the evening. The **Tony Knowles Coastal Trail** and other bike trails in Anchorage are used by runners, cyclists, in-line skaters, and walkers. The trail from Westchester Lagoon at the end of 15th Avenue runs 3 mi to Earthquake Park and then continues an additional 8 mi to Kincaid Park. A number of running events are held annually in Anchorage: the largest are the late-April **Heart Run**, the **Alaska Run for Women** in early June, and the **Mayor's Midnight Sun Marathon** in late June.

Bike rentals are available in midtown from the **Bicycle Shop** (✉ 1035 W. Northern Lights Blvd., ☎ 907/276–5219). **Downtown Bicycle Rental** (✉ 245 W. 5th Ave., ☎ 907/279–5293, WEB www.alaska-bike-rentals.com) rents mountain bikes and offers trail recommendations.

Bird-Watching

Popular bird-watching places include the Tony Knowles Coastal Trail, which provides access to Westchester Lagoon and nearby tide flats, along with Potter Marsh on the south end of Anchorage. The local chapter of the **Audubon Society** (☎ 907/278–3007) refers local birders who will advise you on the best bird-watching spots. You can also sign up for bird-watching classes and field trips. **Wilderness Birding Adventures** (☎ 907/694–7442, WEB www.wildernessbirding.com) guides bird-watching trips both in the Anchorage area and throughout Alaska. A **bird hot line** (☎ 907/338–2473) tracks the latest sightings in town.

Canoeing and Kayaking

Local lakes and lagoons, such as Westchester Lagoon, Goose Lake, and Jewel Lake, have favorable conditions for boating. More adventurous paddlers will want to head to Whittier or Seward for sea kayaking. Rent sea kayaks from **Kayak and Custom Adventures Worldwide** (✉ 19042 Baidarka St., Chugiak 99567, ☎ 907/258–3866 or 800/288–3134, WEB www.kayakak.com), which also leads day trips in the Seward area. Better known as REI, **Recreational Equipment Inc.** (✉ 1200 W. Northern Lights Blvd., ☎ 907/272–4565, WEB www.rei.com) sells and rents all sorts of outdoor gear, including canoes and sea kayaks.

Fishing

Nearly 30 local lakes are stocked with trout. You must have a valid Alaska sportfishing license. Jewel Lake in south Anchorage and Mirror and Fire lakes near Eagle River all hold fish. Coho salmon return to Ship Creek (downtown) in August, and king salmon are caught between late May and early July. Campbell Creek and Bird Creek just south of town are also good spots. Fishing licenses may be purchased at any Carrs grocery or local sporting goods store. Call the **Alaska Department of Fish and Game** (☎ 907/267–2218) for licensing information.

Golf

Anchorage Golf Course (☎ 907/522–3363) on O'Malley Road has 18 holes with greens. Golf carts and clubs are available for rent. **Russian Jack Springs** (☎ 907/333–8338) is run by the city and generally open May–September. It has 9 holes, synthetic greens, and clubs for rent. **Tanglewood Lakes Golf Club** (☎ 907/345–4600) is a relatively new, 9-hole course in south Anchorage.

Ice-Skating

Ben Boeke (✉ 334 E. 16th Ave., ☎ 907/274–5715) is a city-run indoor ice arena that has open skating and skate rentals year-round. The **Dimond Ice Chalet** (✉ 800 E. Dimond Blvd., ☎ 907/344–1212) has an indoor ice rink at Dimond Mall that is open to the public daily, with lessons and skate rentals.

Racquet Sports and Fitness Club

The park strip at 9th Avenue and C Street has several tennis courts. On the south side of Anchorage, the **Dimond Athletic Club** (✉ Box 771343, Eagle River 99577, ☎ 907/344–7788) has a lap pool, Nautilus equipment, free weights, saunas, hot tubs, steam rooms, and racquetball courts, plus a variety of exercise classes. You can buy a daily guest pass for $15.

Rafting

Eagle River Rafting (✉ Box 771343, Eagle River 99577, ☎ 907/689–7238 or 800/375–7395, FAX 907/689–7238, WEB www.eaglerafting.com) leads six-hour float trips on the Eagle River just north of Anchorage. **Nova** (✉ Box 1129, Chickaloon 99674, ☎ 907/745–5753 or 800/746–5753, FAX 907/745–5754, WEB www.novalaska.com) organizes white-water and float trips in the Anchorage area. Check with the Log Cabin Visitor Information Center or the Anchorage Yellow Pages for additional listings.

Skiing

Cross-country skiing is extremely popular in Anchorage. Locals ski on trails in town at Kincaid Park or Hillside, and farther away at Girdwood Valley, Turnagain Pass, and Chugach State Park. Downhill skiing is convenient to downtown.

Mt. Alyeska Ski Resort (☎ 907/754–1111; 800/880–3880; 907/754–7669 for recorded information, WEB www.alyeskaresort.com), at Girdwood, 40 mi south of the city, is a full-service resort with a day lodge, hotel, restaurants, six chairlifts, a tram, a vertical drop of 2,500 ft, and runs for all abilities. The tram ($19) is open during the summer, providing access to the Seven Glaciers restaurant and hiking trails. **Alyeska Accommodations** (☎ 907/783–2000, FAX 907/783–2425) can set you up in a privately owned cabin or condo. **Alpenglow at Arctic Valley** (☎ 907/428–1208; 907/249–9292 for recorded information, WEB www.skialpenglow.com) is a small ski area just north of Anchorage.

On the edge of town, **Hilltop Ski Area** (☎ 907/346–1446, WEB www. hilltopskiarea.org) is a favorite ski area with families.

Ski sales and rentals are available from **Recreational Equipment Inc.** (✉ 1200 W. Northern Lights Blvd., ☎ 907/272–4565, WEB www.rei.com). The locally owned **Alaska Mountaineering and Hiking** (✉ 2633 Spenard Rd., ☎ 907/272–1811, WEB www.alaskan.com/amh) outdoors shop has a highly experienced staff and plenty of cross-country skis for sale or rent.

Spectator Sports

Baseball

Anchorage is home to two semiprofessional baseball teams made up of college players. Many players have gone on to star in the major leagues. Both teams play at Mulcahy Stadium next to the Sullivan Arena. The **Anchorage Bucs** (☎ 907/561–2827, WEB www.anchoragebucs.com) have a dozen or so former players currently in the majors, including such standouts as Wally Joyner, Jeff Kent, and Bobby Jones. The **Glacier Pilots'** (☎ 907/274–3627, WEB www.glacierpilots.com) most famous player was Mark McGwire, but many other future major leaguers played for them over the years.

Basketball

The University of Alaska Anchorage hosts the **Great Alaska Shootout** at the Sullivan Arena over Thanksgiving weekend. In addition, the UAA Seawolves men's and women's basketball teams play on campus during the winter months.

Dogsled Races

World Championship races are run in mid-February, with three consecutive 25-mi heats through downtown Anchorage, out into the foothills, and back. People line the route with cups of coffee in hand to cheer on their favorite mushers. The three-day races are part of the annual **Fur Rendezvous,** one of the largest winter festivals in the United States. Other attractions include a snow sculpture competition, car races, the Miners and Trappers Ball, a carnival, and even snowshoe softball. The festival office (✉ 400 D St., No. 200, 99501, ☎ 907/277–8615, WEB www.furrondy.net) has a guide to the events.

In March, mushers and their dogs compete in the 1,049-mi **Iditarod Trail Sled Dog Race** (Iditarod Trail Headquarters, ☎ 907/376–5155 or 800/545–6874, WEB www.iditarod.com). The race commemorates the delivery of serum to Nome by dog mushers during the diphtheria epidemic of 1925. The serum run was the inspiration for the animated family film *Balto.* Dog teams leave downtown Anchorage and wind through the Alaska range, across the Interior, out to the Bering Sea coast, and on to Nome. Depending on weather and trail conditions, winners can complete the race in nine days. (☞ The Last Great Race on Earth box, *below.*)

Hockey

The **University of Alaska Anchorage** has a Division I NCAA hockey team that draws several thousand loyal fans to home games at the Sullivan Arena. The West Coast Hockey League's **Anchorage Aces** (☎ 907/258–2237, WEB www.anchorageaces.com) play minor-league professional hockey in the arena.

SHOPPING

Mall and Department Store

Anchorage's **5th Avenue Mall** occupies a city block at 5th Avenue and A Street and contains dozens of stores spread over several levels, including

THE LAST GREAT RACE ON EARTH

SINCE 1973, mushers and their sled-dog teams have raced more than 1,100 mi across Alaska in a marathon vision quest unlike any other: the Iditarod Trail Sled Dog Race, the longest sled-dog race in the world. After a ceremonial start in downtown Anchorage on the first Saturday in March, dog teams wind through Alaska, battling almost every imaginable winter challenge. In any given year, Iditarod mushers may have to endure extreme cold, deep snow, gale-force winds, whiteouts, river overflow, moose attacks, and dog fights. Racers contending for the challenge also face exhaustion and hallucinations that result from their sleep deprivation. Ten days later, the "Last Great Race on Earth" ends with spectacular fanfare in Nome, on the Bering Sea coast.

The Iditarod's origins can be traced to two events: an early 1900s long-distance race called the All-Alaska Sweepstakes and the delivery of a lifesaving serum to Nome by dog mushers during a diphtheria outbreak in 1925. Fascinated with the trail's history, Alaskan sled-dog enthusiasts Dorothy Page and Joe Redington Sr. staged the first race in 1967 to celebrate the role of mushing in Alaska's history. Only 50 mi long and with a purse of $25,000—no small amount at that time—it attracted the best of Alaska's competitive mushers. Enthusiasm waned in 1969, however, when the available winnings fell to $1,000. Instead of giving up, Redington enlarged it.

In 1973, after three years without a race, he organized a 1,000-mi race from Anchorage to Nome, with a then-outrageous purse of $50,000. Critics scoffed, but 34 racers entered. First place went to a little-known musher named Dick Wilmarth, who finished in 20 days. Redington then billed the Iditarod as a 1,049-mi race (still the official distance). There was no question it was at least 1,000 mi long and the 49 was intended to symbolize Alaska, the 49th state.

The race actually begins in Wasilla, home of the Iditarod headquarters, a few miles from Anchorage. The first few hundred miles take mushers and dogs through wooded lowlands and flat hills, including a stretch known as "moose alley." Teams then cross the Alaska Range, where they face extreme cold, fierce blizzards, and a narrow, boulder-filled canyon known as the Dalzell Gorge. Beyond the Alaska Range, they enter Interior Alaska, with Athabascan villages and gold-rush ghost towns, including Iditarod. Only a few abandoned and weather-beaten buildings now mark the site of the race's namesake.

Next, the trail follows the frozen Yukon River, then cuts over to the Bering Sea coast for the final 270-mi "sprint" to Nome. It was here, in 1985, that Libby Riddles drove her team into a blinding blizzard, en route to a victory that made her the first woman to win the race. Since then, Susan Butcher (now retired) has won the race four times. But the all-time record holder is Rick Swenson, with five victories.

Nearly 30 years later, Redington's long-distance dream has gained international acclaim. The race purse for the 2000 Iditarod topped $500,000, with $60,000 to the champion. Dozens of journalists from around the world report from the trail, and entrants have represented 14 countries. Though racers such as Butcher; Swenson; and three-time winners Martin Buser, Doug Swingley, and Jeff King draw the biggest crowds and the most media attention, all mushers—and dogs—that reach Nome are appropriately treated like champions after surviving their 1,100-mi run across Alaska's wilderness.

a JCPenney. The top level houses a food court for quick, inexpensive meals. Just across 6th Avenue, and connected by a skywalk to the 5th Avenue Mall, is Alaska's only **Nordstrom.** The city's largest shopping mall, **Dimond Center,** is on the south end of town at Dimond Boulevard and Old Seward Highway. In addition to dozens of shops, Dimond Center houses a movie theater. Nearby are several large big-box discount stores.

Market

During the summer, Anchorage's **Saturday Market** (☎ 907/272–5634) is open in the parking lot at 3rd Avenue and E Street. Browse here for Alaska-made crafts, fresh produce, and ethnic food. It's open from mid-May to mid-September, Saturday 10–6.

Specialty Shops

Art

Alaska's oldest gallery, **Artique** (✉ 314 G St., ☎ 907/277–1663, WEB www.artiqueltd.com) sells paintings, prints, and jewelry by prominent Alaskan artists. **Decker/Morris Gallery** (✉ 621 W. 6th Ave., south side of Alaska Center for the Performing Arts, ☎ 907/272–1489) carries works by better-known Alaskan artists—both Native and non-Native—contemporary originals and prints, jewelry, and sculpture. **Tundra Arts** (✉ 425 D St., ☎ 907/276–0190) displays the works of 40 different Alaskan artists and crafts workers.

Books

Barnes & Noble Booksellers (✉ 200 E. Northern Lights Blvd., at A St., ☎ 907/279–7323) has an enormous variety of books and magazines, plus a café serving Starbucks coffees. **Borders Books & Music** (✉ 1100 E. Dimond Blvd., west of Seward Hwy., ☎ 907/344–4099) stocks a diverse selection of titles and has a café. **Cook Inlet Book Company** (✉ 415 W. 5th Ave., ☎ 907/258–4544 or 800/240–4148, WEB www.alaskasbooks.com) has the largest collection of Alaskan titles in the state and a substantial newspaper and magazine section. **Metro Music & Book Store** (✉ 530 E. Benson Blvd., ☎ 907/279–8622) is great for browsing and carries a well-thought-out inventory of fiction and non-fiction. The collection of CDs is easily the best in Alaska, and you're welcome to listen to any of them before buying.

Gift Ideas

Alaska Native Heritage Center (✉ 8800 Heritage Center Dr., Glenn Hwy. at Muldoon Rd., ☎ 907/330–8000 or 800/315–6608, WEB www.alaskanative.net) houses a gift shop selling a range of Native crafts. Several downtown shops sell quality Native Alaskan artwork, but the best buys can be found in the gift shop at the **Alaska Native Medical Center** (✉ 4315 Diplomacy Dr., at Tudor and Bragaw Rds., ☎ 907/729–1122), which is open weekdays 10–2 and from 11 to 2 on the first and third Saturday of the month.

Laura Wright Alaskan Parkys (✉ 343 W. 5th Ave., ☎ 907/274–4215) sells distinctive Eskimo-style "parkys" (parkas) and will custom-sew one for you. **Oomingmak** (✉ 6th Ave. and H St., ☎ 907/272–9225, WEB www.qiviut.com), a 30-year-old Native-owned cooperative, sells items made of qiviut, the warm undercoat of the musk ox. Scarves, shawls, and tunics are knitted in traditional patterns.

Frozen seafood and smoked fish are available from **10th and M Seafoods** (✉ 1020 M St., ☎ 907/272–3474; 301 Muldoon Rd., ☎ 907/337–8831). **New Sagaya's City Market** is a gourmet market with an excellent selection of fresh seafood. If you don't want to carry the fish with you, the market will pack and ship it home.

Although furs may not be to everyone's taste or ethics, a number of Alaska fur companies have stores and factories in Anchorage. One of the city's largest and best-known furriers is **David Green Master Furrier**(⊠ 130 W. 4th Ave., ☎ 907/277–9595, WEB www.davidgreenfurs.com). **Alaska Fur Exchange** (⊠ 4417 Old Seward Hwy., ☎ 907/563–3877, WEB alaskaguide.com) has a large midtown store that sells both furs and Native artwork.

Jewelry
The **Kobuk Valley Jade Co.** (⊠ Olympic Circle, Girdwood, ☎ 907/783–2764), at the base of Mt. Alyeska, sells a wide variety of hand-polished jade pieces as well as Native masks, baskets, and jewelry.

ANCHORAGE A TO Z

To research prices, get advice from other travelers, and book travel arrangements, visit www.fodors.com.

AIRPORTS AND TRANSFERS
Ted Stevens Anchorage International Airport is 6 mi from downtown Anchorage on International Airport Road. It is served by Alaska, America West, American, Continental, Delta, Northwest, and United airlines, along with a number of international carriers. Several carriers, including ERA and PenAir, connect Anchorage with smaller Alaskan communities. Floatplane operators and helicopters serve the area from Lake Hood, which is adjacent to and part of Anchorage International Airport. There are also a number of smaller air taxis and air-charter operations at Merrill Field, 2 mi east of downtown on 5th Avenue.

Ted Stevens Anchorage International Airport is in the midst of a $350-million redevelopment that will be completed in 2004. When finished, the project will include a direct rail connection from the airport to downtown Anchorage. Check with your airline for any expected delays caused by the construction, or contact the airport.
➤ AIRPORT INFORMATION: **Ted Stevens Anchorage International Airport** (☎ 907/266–2529, WEB www.aiaterminalproject.com).

AIRPORT TRANSFERS
Taxis queue up at the lower level of the airport terminal outside the baggage-claim area. Alaska Cab, Borealis Shuttle, Checker Cab, Yellow Cab, and Anchorage Taxi Cab (☞ Taxis) all operate here; you'll get whichever cab is next in line. Most charge about $17, not including tip, for the ride to downtown hotels.

BOAT AND FERRY TRAVEL
Cruise ships sailing the Gulf of Alaska and the Alaska Marine ferries call in Seward, several hours by train or bus south of Anchorage. The South Central route of the Alaska Marine Highway connects Kodiak, Port Lions, Homer, Seldovia, Seward, Valdez, Cordova, and Whittier.
➤ BOAT AND FERRY INFORMATION: **Alaska Marine Highway System** (⊠ 6858 Glacier Hwy., Juneau 99801-7909, ☎ 907/465–3941 or 800/642–0066, FAX 907/277–4829, WEB www.dot.state.ak.us/ferry).

BUS TRAVEL
The municipal People Mover covers the whole Anchorage bowl. Get schedules and information from the central bus depot at 6th Avenue and G Street. The one-way fare is $1 for rides outside the downtown area; rides within downtown are free.
➤ BUS INFORMATION: **People Mover** (☎ 907/343–6543, WEB www.peoplemover.org).

CAR TRAVEL

Only one road leads to Anchorage from the north and only one road out to the south. The Glenn Highway enters Anchorage from the north and becomes 5th Avenue near Merrill Field; this route will lead you directly into downtown. Gambell Street leads out of town to the south, becoming New Seward Highway at about 20th Avenue. South of town, it becomes the Seward Highway.

EMERGENCIES

➤ DOCTORS AND DENTISTS: **Physician-referral service** (☎ 907/261–4900 at Providence; 907/264–1722 or 800/265–8624 at Alaska Regional).

➤ EMERGENCY SERVICES: **Police, fire, and ambulance** (☎ 911). **Poison Control Center** (☎ 907/261–3193).

➤ HOSPITALS: **Alaska Regional Hospital** (✉ 2801 DeBarr Rd., ☎ 907/276–1131, WEB www.alaskaregional.com). **First Care** (✉ 3710 Woodland Dr., ☎ 907/248–1122; 1301 Huffman Rd., ☎ 907/345–1199). **Providence Alaska Medical Center** (✉ 3200 Providence Dr., ☎ 907/562–2211, WEB www.providence.org).

➤ 24-HOUR PHARMACY: **Carrs** (✉ 1650 W. Northern Lights Blvd., at Minnesota Dr., ☎ 907/297–0560).

LODGING

B&BS

➤ LOCAL AGENTS: **Alaska Adventures & Accommodations** (✉ 507 E St., No. 206, 99501, ☎ 907/344–4676 or 888/655–4723, FAX 907/349–4676, WEB www.see-alaska.com). **Alaska Available Reservation Service** (✉ 3213 Minnesota Dr., Suite B, 99503, ☎ 907/277–9900, FAX 907/272–1889, WEB www.alaskaavailable.com). **Alaska Private Lodgings/Stay With a Friend** (✉ Box 200047, 99520, ☎ 907/258–1717, FAX 907/258–6613, WEB www.alaskabandb.com). **Alaska Sourdough Bed & Breakfast Association** (✉ 889 Cardigan Circle, 99503, ☎ 907/563–6244, WEB www.travelalaska.net).

TAXIS

Prices for taxis are $2 for pickup, plus an additional $2 for each mile. Most people in Anchorage telephone for a cab; it is not common to hail one. Allow 20 minutes for arrival of the cab during morning and evening rush hours. Alaska Cab has taxis with wheelchair lifts. Borealis Shuttle has lower rates if you are willing to share the ride.

➤ TAXI COMPANIES: **Alaska Cab** (☎ 907/563–5353). **Anchorage Taxi Cab** (☎ 907/245–2207). **Borealis Shuttle** (☎ 907/276–3600 or 888/436–3600, WEB www.borealisshuttle.com). **Checker Cab** (☎ 907/276–1234). **Yellow Cab** (☎ 907/272–2422).

TOURS

FLIGHTSEEING

Any air-taxi company (check the Anchorage Yellow Pages) can arrange for a flightseeing trip over Anchorage and environs. The fee will be determined by the length of time you are airborne and the size of the plane. Tours of about an hour and a half generally cost around $150–$200 per person. Three-hour flights over Mt. McKinley, including a landing on a remote backcountry lake, run about $200 per person.

ERA Helicopters offers a 50-minute trip over Anchorage and the Chugach Mountains, or a two-hour glacier expedition that includes a landing on the ice. ERA Classic Airlines offers travelers a nostalgic air cruise aboard elegantly restored DC-3s from the 1940s. These 90-minute flights vary in destination depending upon the weather, flying over Mt. McKinley or the mountains of South Central Alaska. Ketchum Air Service on Lake

Hood has a number of flightseeing tours, including one to Mt. McKinley, as well as fly-in service to remote lake cabins for hunting and fishing, and houseboat rentals. Also at Lake Hood, Rust's Flying Service flies ski-planes over Mt. McKinley that include a landing on Ruth Glacier—a spectacular alpine amphitheater high on the mountain.

► CONTACTS: **ERA Classic Airlines** (☎ 907/266–8394 or 800/866–8394, FAX 907/266–8483). **ERA Helicopters** (☎ 907/266–8351 or 800/843–1947, FAX 907/266–8349, WEB www.eraaviation.com). **Ketchum Air Service** (☎ 907/243–5525 or 800/433–9114, WEB www.ketchumair.com). **Rust's Flying Service** (☎ 907/243–1595 or 800/544–2299, WEB www.flyrusts.com).

ORIENTATION TOURS

► CONTACTS: **Alaska Sightseeing/Cruise West** (✉ 349 Wrangell St., Anchorage 99501, ☎ 907/276–1305 or 800/666–7375, FAX 907/272–5617, WEB www.cruisewest.com). **Fourth Ave. Theatre Trolley Tours** (✉ 612 W. 4th Ave., Anchorage 99501, ☎ 907/276–5603). **Gray Line of Alaska** (✉ 745 W. 4th Ave., No. 200, Anchorage 99501, ☎ 907/277–5581 or 800/478–6388, WEB www.graylineofalaska.com).

WILDLIFE VIEWING

Kenai Fjords Tours offers day packages to Kenai Fjords National Park April through November.

► CONTACTS: **Kenai Fjords Tours** (✉ 513 W. 4th Ave., ☎ 907/276–6249 or 800/468–8068, FAX 907/276–1064, WEB www.kenaifjords.com).

TRAIN TRAVEL

The Alaska Railroad runs between Anchorage and Fairbanks via Denali National Park and Preserve daily, mid-May–September, and also south between Anchorage and Seward during the same period. Year-round passenger service is available from Anchorage north to Talkeetna. Call for schedule and fare information.

► TRAIN INFORMATION: **Alaska Railroad** (☎ 907/265–2494 or 800/544–0552, WEB www.akrr.com).

TRANSPORTATION AROUND ANCHORAGE

If, like many visitors to Alaska, you bring your RV or rent one on arrival, you should note that parking downtown on weekdays is challenging for an RV. The big parking lot on 3rd Avenue between C and E streets is a good place to park and walk. Parking usually is not a problem in other parts of town, and most of the big discount stores allow free parking in their lots.

VISITOR INFORMATION

► CONTACTS: **Alaska Public Lands Information Center** (✉ 4th Ave. and F St., ☎ 907/271–2737, WEB www.nps.gov/aplic/center). **Anchorage Convention and Visitors Bureau** (ACVB; ✉ 524 W. 4th Ave., 99501-2212, ☎ 907/276–4118, FAX 907/278–5559, WEB www.anchorage.net). **Daily events** recording (☎ 907/276–3200). **Log Cabin Visitor Information Center** (✉ 4th Ave. and F St., ☎ 907/274–3531).

4 VANCOUVER AND VICTORIA

Cosmopolitan Vancouver enjoys a spectacular setting. Tall fir trees stand practically downtown, rock spires tower close by, the ocean laps at the doorstep, and people from every corner of the earth create a vibrant atmosphere. On Vancouver Island just west of Vancouver, the capital of British Columbia, Victoria, clings to its British past, but you'll still see many signs of the distinctive heritage of the Pacific Northwest.

V ANCOUVER AND VICTORIA AREN'T IN ALASKA, but so many
Alaska cruises originate or make a stop here that the cities are
essential to the Alaska experience. Rich cultural sights and excellent restaurants fill each city, making for a welcome stop to complement your Alaskan adventure.

By Melissa
Rivers

Updated by
Sue Kernaghan

Pleasures and Pastimes

Dining

A diverse gastronomic experience awaits the visitor in cosmopolitan
Vancouver and, to a lesser extent, Victoria. A wave of Asian immigration
and tourism has brought a proliferation of upscale Asian eateries.
Cutting-edge restaurants currently perfecting and defining Pacific
Northwest fare—including such homegrown regional favorites as
salmon and oysters, accompanied by British Columbia wines—have
become some of the city's leading attractions. A bylaw bans smoking
in all Vancouver and Victoria restaurants. For approximate costs, *see*
the dining price chart *in* Smart Travel Tips A to Z.

Lodging

The hotel industry is a major business for Vancouver, which hosts large
numbers of conventioneers, businesspeople, and others used to an above-
average level of service. Although by some standards pricey, properties
here are highly competitive, and you can expect the service to reflect this.
In Victoria as in Vancouver, you'll find a wide range of accommodations,
from luxury hotels and chains to bed-and-breakfast inns. Most small inns
and B&Bs in Vancouver and Victoria ban smoking indoors, and all hotels in the area offer nonsmoking rooms. For approximate costs, *see* the
lodging price chart *in* Smart Travel Tips A to Z.

VANCOUVER

Vancouver is a young city, even by North American standards. Just over
100 years old, it was not yet a town in 1871, when British Columbia
became part of the Canadian confederation. Still, Vancouver's history,
such as it is, remains visible to the naked eye: eras are stacked east to
west along the waterfront like some century-old archaeological dig—
from cobblestone, late-Victorian Gastown to shiny postmodern glass
cathedrals of commerce.

Exploring Vancouver

There is much to see and do in Vancouver, but when time is limited
(as it usually is for cruise-ship passengers), the most popular options
are a walking tour of Gastown and Chinatown and a driving or biking tour of Stanley Park, one of two 1,000-acre wilderness parks
within the city limits (the other, Pacific Spirit Park, lies near the University of British Columbia). The heart of Vancouver—which includes
the downtown area, Stanley Park, and the West End high-rise residential
neighborhood—sits on this peninsula hemmed in by English Bay and
the Pacific Ocean to the west; by False Creek, the inlet home to
Granville Island, to the south; and by Burrard Inlet, the working port
of the city, to the north, past which loom the North Shore mountains.

*Numbers in the text correspond to numbers in the margin and on the
Downtown Vancouver and Stanley Park maps.*

A Good Walk: Downtown Vancouver

Most cruise ships visiting Vancouver dock at **Canada Place** ①, where
you can stroll around the cruise-ship–style decks for great ocean and

Downtown Vancouver

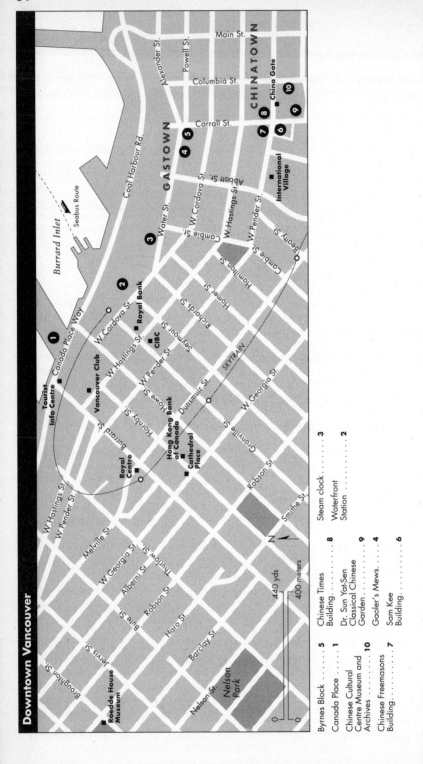

Burrard Inlet

Seabus Route

GASTOWN

CHINATOWN

China Gate

International Village

Main St.
Powell St.
Alexander St.
Columbia St.
Carrall St.
Water St.
W. Cordova St.
Abbott St.
W. Hastings St.
W. Pender St.
Cambie St.
Hamilton St.
Homer St.
Richards St.
Seymour St.
SKYTRAIN
W. Georgia St.
Granville St.
Dunsmuir St.
Beatty St.

Coal Harbour Rd.

Canada Place Way

Tourist Info Centre
Vancouver Club
Royal Bank
CIBC
Royal Centre
Hong Kong Bank of Canada
Cathedral Place
Reedde House Museum

W. Hastings St.
W. Pender St.
W. Cordova St.
W. Hastings St.
W. Pender St.
Howe St.
Hornby St.
Burrard St.
Melville St.
W. Georgia St.
Alberni St.
Robson St.
Haro St.
Barclay St.
Nelson St.
Smithe St.

Thurlow St.
Bute St.
Jervis St.
Broughton St.

Nelson Park

N

440 yds
400 meters
0

Byrnes Block **5**	Chinese Times Building **8**	Steam clock **3**
Canada Place **1**	Dr. Sun Yat-Sen Classical Chinese Garden **9**	Waterfront Station **2**
Chinese Cultural Centre Museum and Archives **10**	Gaoler's Mews . . **4**	
Chinese Freemasons Building **7**	Sam Kee Building **6**	

mountain views or catch a film at the IMAX theater. Across Canada Place Way (next door to the Waterfront Centre Hotel) you'll find the Vancouver Tourist Info Centre. The colonnaded building to the east of Canada Place, on West Cordova Street, is **Waterfront Station** ②, Vancouver's original train terminal. Take a peek at the murals inside, then continue east along Water Street into Gastown. Named for saloon keeper "Gassy" Jack Deighton, this is Vancouver's oldest neighborhood. The first stop, at the corner of Water and Richards streets, is **The Landing,** a 1905 warehouse that now houses upscale shops, a brew pub, and a restaurant. At the window at the rear of the lobby, you can take in scenic views of Burrard Inlet and the North Shore mountains. A block east, at the corner of Water and Cambie streets, you can see and hear the world's first **steam clock** ③ (it chimes on the quarter hour). About two blocks east, you'll pass **Gaoler's Mews** ④, a courtyard tucked behind 12 Water Street. Two buildings of historical and architectural note are the **Byrnes Block** ⑤ on the corner of Water and Carrall streets and the Hotel Europe (1908–09) at Powell and Alexander streets, Vancouver's first reinforced concrete structure. A statue of Gassy Jack stands on the west side of Maple Tree Square, at the intersection of Water, Powell, Alexander, and Carrall streets, where he built his first saloon.

To reach Chinatown while avoiding Vancouver's rough Skid Row area, backtrack two blocks on Water Street through Gastown to Cambie Street, and then head south to Pender Street and east to Carrall Street. The corner of Carrall and Pender streets, now the western boundary of Chinatown, is one of the neighborhood's most historic spots. It's here that you'll find the **Sam Kee Building** ⑥; the **Chinese Freemasons Building** ⑦; and, directly across Carrall Street, the **Chinese Times Building** ⑧. It's best to view the buildings from the south side of Pender Street, where the Chinese Cultural Centre stands. From here you'll see important details that adorn the upper stories. The style of architecture in Vancouver's Chinatown is patterned after that of Canton and won't be seen in any other Canadian cities.

Also on the south side of Pender Street, just east of Carrall Street, is the brightly painted, four-column China Gate. Built by a group of Beijing artisans for the Chinese Pavilion at Expo '86, the gate (and some dragons) now guards the entrance to the Chinese Cultural Centre complex. Step through the gate and into the courtyard behind. To your right is the entrance to the **Dr. Sun Yat-Sen Classical Chinese Garden** ⑨, the first authentic classical Chinese garden built outside China. Straight ahead is the entrance to Dr. Sun Yat-Sen Park, a free public park also built in a classical Chinese style. A short path through the park will take you out to Columbia Street, where, to your left, you'll find the entrance to the **Chinese Cultural Centre Museum and Archives** ⑩, a museum and art gallery celebrating Chinese-Canadian culture. Finish up by poking around in the open-front markets and import shops that line several blocks of Pender and Keefer streets (one block south of Pender Street), running east.

TIMING

The walk itself will take about an hour, depending on your pace. Allow extra time for shops, for the museum, and for the guided tour of the Sun Yat-Sen Garden in Chinatown.

Sights to See

⑤ **Byrnes Block.** Vancouver's oldest brick building was constructed on the site of Gassy Jack Deighton's second saloon after the 1886 Great Fire, which wiped out most of the fledgling settlement of Vancouver. The two-story building houses offices on the upper floor and retail shops, including a Native art gallery, a cigar shop, and a coffee bar on the ground floor. The entrance to Gaoler's Mews is immediately next to the Byrnes Block. ⊠ *2 Water St.*

❶ Canada Place. When Vancouver hosted the Expo '86 world's fair, this former cargo pier was transformed into the Canadian pavilion. The complex, which now encompasses the luxurious **Pan Pacific Hotel**, the **Vancouver Convention and Exhibition Centre**, the **World Trade Centre**, and the city's main cruise-ship terminal, mimics the style and size of a luxury ocean liner. You can stroll its exterior promenade and admire views of Burrard Inlet, Stanley Park, and the North Shore mountains. At the prow (the north end) the **CN IMAX Theatre** (☎ 604/682–4629; ▣ IMAX $10.50) shows films on a five-story-high screen. The roof, shaped like five sails, has become a Vancouver skyline landmark. ⊠ *999 Canada Place Way,* ☎ *604/775–8687,* ₩ₑ₈ *www.canadaplace.ca.*

❿ Chinese Cultural Centre Museum and Archives. This Ming dynasty–style facility is dedicated to promoting an understanding of Chinese-Canadian history and culture. The art gallery on the first floor hosts traveling exhibits by Chinese and Canadian artists. A compelling permanent exhibit on the second floor traces British Columbia history from a Chinese point of view. ⊠ *555 Columbia St.,* ☎ *604/658–8880,* ₩ₑ₈ *www. cccvan.com.* ▣ *C$4.* ☉ *Tues.–Fri. 1–5; weekends 11–5.*

❼ Chinese Freemasons Building. Two completely different facades distinguish this fascinating structure, dating from about 1901, on the northwest corner of Pender and Carrall streets: Cantonese-imported recessed balconies adorn the side facing Pender Street; the Carrall Street side displays the Victorian-Italianate style common throughout the British Empire. It was in this building that Dr. Sun Yat-Sen hid for months from the agents of the Manchu dynasty while he raised funds for its overthrow, which he accomplished in 1911. ⊠ *3 W. Pender St.*

❽ Chinese Times Building. Around the turn of the 20th century, police officers could hear the clicking sounds of clandestine mah-jongg games played after sunset on the building's hidden mezzanine floor. Attempts by vice squads to enforce restrictive policies against the Chinese gamblers proved fruitless, because police were unable to find the players. This building on the north side of Pender Street just east of Carrall Street dates to 1902. The *Chinese Times* newspaper was published in this building from 1939 to 1994. ⊠ *1 E. Pender St.*

★ ❾ Dr. Sun Yat-Sen Classical Chinese Garden. The first authentic Ming dynasty–style garden constructed outside of China, this garden was built in 1986 by 52 artisans from Suzhou, the Garden City of the People's Republic. It incorporates design elements and traditional materials from several of that city's centuries-old private gardens. As you walk along the paths, remember that no power tools, screws, or nails were used in the construction. Guided tours, included in the price of admission, are conducted throughout the day; call for times. The free public **Dr. Sun Yat-Sen Park,** next door, is also in the style of a traditional Chinese garden. Plans are currently in place to build a seven-story pagoda with cultural displays and a tearoom in the park's southeast corner. ⊠ *578 Carrall St.,* ☎ *604/689–7133 or 604/662–3207.* ▣ *C$7.50.* ☉ *May–June 14 and Sept., daily 10–6; June 15–Aug., daily 9:30–7; Oct.–Apr., daily 10–4:30.*

❹ Gaoler's Mews. The cobblestone courtyard and the mews leading off it resemble a hidden slice of Victorian England. Once the site of the city's first civic buildings—the constable's cabin, customshouse and a two-cell log jail—the mews today are home to architectural offices, a courtyard café, and an Irish pub. ⊠ *Behind 12 Water St.*

6 Sam Kee Building. *Ripley's Believe It or Not!* recognizes this structure, dating from about 1913, as the narrowest office building in the world. In 1913, when the city confiscated most of merchant Chang Toy's land to widen Pender Street, he built in protest on what he had left—just 6 ft. These days the building houses an insurance agency whose employees make do with the 4-ft-10-inch-wide interior. ⊠ *8 W. Pender St.*

3 Steam clock. The world's first steam clock, built by Ray Saunders of **Landmark Clocks** (⊠ 123 Cambie St., ☎ 604/669–3525), is powered by the same underground steam system that heats many Vancouver buildings. On the quarter hour a whistle blows; on the hour a huge cloud of steam spews from the clock. ⊠ *Corner of Cambie and Water Sts.*

2 Waterfront Station. This former Canadian Pacific Railway passenger terminal was built between 1912 and 1914 as the western terminus for Canada's transcontinental railway. After Canada's railways merged, the station became obsolete, but a 1978 renovation transformed it into an office–retail complex and depot for SkyTrain, SeaBus, and West Coast Express passengers. In the main concourse, panels near the ceiling depict the scenery travelers once saw on journeys across Canada. Here you can catch a 13-minute SeaBus trip across the harbor to the waterfront public market at Lonsdale Quay in North Vancouver. ⊠ *601 W. Cordova St.,* ☎ *604/521–0400 for SeaBus and SkyTrain; 604/683–7245 for West Coast Express.*

A Good Biking or Driving Tour: Stanley Park

A morning or afternoon in Stanley Park gives you a capsule tour of Vancouver that includes beaches, the ocean, the harbor, Douglas fir and cedar forests, and a look at the North Shore mountains. One of the most popular ways to see the park is to walk, rollerblade, or cycle along Vancouver's famous Seawall Walk, a 9-km (5½-mi) seaside pathway around the park's circumference. The seawall now extends an additional mile to just west of the cruise-ship terminal at **Canada Place,** so you can start your ride from there. Alternatively, rent a bike on Denman Street near the park entrance and start your ride at the foot of Alberni Street next to Lost Lagoon. Go through the underpass, veer right, and follow the cycle path markings to the seawall. Cyclists must ride in a counterclockwise direction, wear a helmet, and stay on their side of the path.

It's also possible to see the park by car, entering at the foot of Georgia Street and driving counterclockwise around the one-way Stanley Park Drive. An even better option is to take the free **Stanley Park Shuttle,** which provides frequent transportation between the park entrance and all the major sights daily from mid-June to mid-September.

Whether you're driving, cycling, or rollerblading, the first sight you'll pass on your right is the Tudor-style Vancouver Rowing Club, a private athletic club established in 1903. Watch for the information booth on the left, and the turnoff to the renowned **Vancouver Aquarium Marine Science Centre** ⑪, the **Miniature Railway and Children's Farmyard** ⑫ and Painters' Corner, where artists sell their work. Also near the information booth, Salmon Demonstration Stream has information about the life cycle of this important resource. As you continue along the main road or the seawall, the next thing you'll pass is the Royal Vancouver Yacht Club. About ½ km (⅓ mi) farther is the causeway to Deadman's Island, a former burial ground for the local Salish people and now a small naval training base that is not open to the public. The site of the **totem poles** ⑬, a bit farther down the road and slightly inland on your left, is a popular photo stop. Ahead at the water's edge, just past the sign for Hallelujah Point, is the **Nine O'Clock Gun** ⑭. To

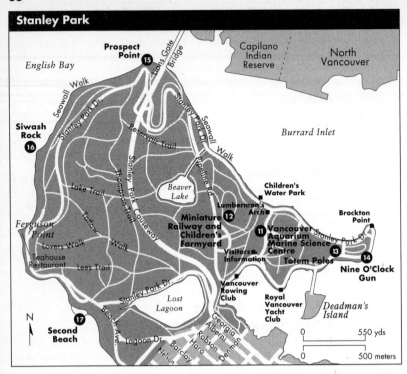

the north is Brockton Point and its small but functional lighthouse and foghorn.

Inland on your left is Brockton Oval, where you can catch a rugby game in winter or a cricket match in summer. Next, on the water side, watch for the *Girl in a Wetsuit,* a sculpture on a rock just offshore that resembles Copenhagen's Little Mermaid. A little farther along the seashore, you'll see a replica of the dragon-shape figurehead from the S.S. *Empress of Japan,* which plied these waters between 1891 and 1922.

At Km 3 (Mi 2) is Lumberman's Arch, a log archway dedicated to workers in Vancouver's first industry. The Children's Water Park across the road is also popular throughout the summer. About 2 km (1¼ mi) farther is the Lions Gate Bridge—the halfway point of the seawall. Just past the bridge is **Prospect Point** ⑮. From the seawall you can see where cormorants nest. The drive climbs high to a viewing point, snack bar, and restaurant at the top of Prospect Point. Continuing around the seawall or the drive, you'll come to the English Bay side and the beginning of sandy beaches. The imposing rock just offshore is **Siwash Rock** ⑯, the focus of a Native legend. The road and the seawall pass the large heated pool at **Second Beach** ⑰ and emerge from the park into a high-rise residential neighborhood, the West End. Here you'll find plenty of places to stop for coffee, ice cream, or a drink along Denman, Davie, or Robson streets.

TIMING

A driving tour, with time out for stops and photos, will take about an hour. You'll find pay parking lots near most of the sights in the park; a C$5 ticket (C$3 between October and March) allows you to park all day and to move between lots. A biking tour will take several hours. Add at least two hours to tour the aquarium thoroughly, and you've filled a half- to full-day tour.

Sights to See

☝ ⑫ **Miniature Railway and Children's Farmyard.** A child-size steam train takes youngsters and adults on a ride through the woods of Stanley Park. Just next door is a farmyard full of tame, pettable critters, including goats, rabbits, and guinea pigs. ⊠ *Off Pipeline Rd., in Stanley Park,* ☎ *604/257–8530.* 💲 *Each site C$2.50.* ☉ *June–Sept., daily 11–4; Oct.–May, weekends and school holidays 11–4 (weather permitting).*

⑭ **Nine O'Clock Gun.** At this cannonlike apparatus by the water, a stick of dynamite was detonated each night at 9 o'clock alerting ships in port to correctly set their chronometers to the local time. The cannon is still fired electrically each evening.

⑮ **Prospect Point.** Here cormorants build their seaweed nests along the cliff's ledges. The large black diving birds are distinguished by their long necks and beaks; when not nesting, they often perch atop floating logs or boulders. Another remarkable bird found along the park's shore is the beautiful great blue heron, which reaches up to 4 ft tall and has a wingspan of 6 ft. The oldest heron rookery in British Columbia is in the trees near the aquarium. The top of Prospect Point, at 211 ft the highest point in the park, has breathtaking views of the North Shore and Burrard Inlet.

☝ ⑰ **Second Beach.** In summer the main draw is the 50-meter pool with water slides and lifeguards. The shallow end fills up on hot days, but the lap-swimming section is usually deserted. Nearby you'll also find a sandy beach, a playground, and covered picnic sites. ⊠ *Stanley Park,* WEB *www.city.vancouver.bc.ca/parks/2.htm.* 💲 *Beach free, pool C$4.* ☉ *Late-May–Labor Day, daily 10–8.*

⑯ **Siwash Rock.** Legend tells of a Native American who, about to become a father, bathed persistently to wash his sins away so that his son could be born pure. For his devotion he was blessed by the gods and immortalized in the shape of Siwash Rock, just offshore. Two small rocks, said to be his wife and child, are up on the cliff just above the site. The rock is visible from the seawall; however, if you're driving you'll need to park and take a short path through the woods. A sign marks the trail.

⑬ **Totem poles.** Totem poles were not made in the Vancouver area but were an important art form among native peoples along British Columbia's coast. These eight poles include replicas of poles originally brought to the park from the north coast in the 1920s, as well as poles carved specifically for the park by First Nations artists. The several styles of poles represent a cross-section of B.C. native groups, including the Kwakiutl, Haida, and Nishga. The combination of carved animals, fish, birds, and mythological creatures represents clan history. An information center near the site has a snack bar and interpretive information about the poles.

☝ ★ ⑪ **Vancouver Aquarium Marine Science Centre.** This research and educational facility is a delight for children and natural-history buffs. In the Amazon rain-forest gallery you can walk through a jungle setting populated with piranhas, caimans, and tropical birds and vegetation. Other displays, many with hands-on features for children, show the underwater life of coastal British Columbia, the Canadian Arctic, and the tropics. Huge tanks have large windows for underwater viewing of beluga whales and playful sea otters. Whale shows are held several times a day. Be prepared for lines on weekends and school holidays. ⊠ *Stanley Park,* ☎ *604/659–3474,* WEB *www.vanaqua.org.* 💲 *C$12.95.* ☉ *July–Labor Day, daily 9:30–7; Labor Day–June, daily 10–5:30.*

Dining

Chinese

$$-$$$$ ✕ **Imperial Chinese Seafood.** This elegant Cantonese restaurant in the art deco Marine Building, two blocks west of the Canada Place cruise-ship terminal, has two-story, floor-to-ceiling windows with spectacular views of Stanley Park and the North Shore mountains across Burrard Inlet. Lobster, crab, or shrimp from the live tanks is recommended, as is the dim sum, served every day from 11 to 2:30. ⊠ *355 Burrard St.,* ☎ *604/688–8191. Reservations essential. DC, MC, V.*

$ ✕ **Hon's Wun-Tun House.** Mr. Hon has been keeping Vancouverites in Chinese comfort food since the 1970s. The best bets on the 300-item menu (nothing is more than C$11) are the pot stickers (dumplings that come fried, steamed, or in soup), the wonton and noodle dishes, and anything with barbecued meat. The shiny Robson Street location has a separate kitchen for vegetarians and an army of fast-moving waitresses keeping your tea topped up. The older Chinatown outlet is atmospherically steamy and crowded. ⊠ *1339 Robson St.,* ☎ *604/685–0871; 268 Keefer St.,* ☎ *604/688–0871. Reservations not accepted. MC, V at Robson St.; no credit cards at Keefer St.*

Contemporary

$$$–$$$$ ✕ **Five Sails.** A special-occasion restaurant at the Pan Pacific Hotel, Five Sails has a stunning panoramic view of Canada Place, Lions Gate Bridge, and the lights of the North Shore across the inlet. The simple white-tablecloth and candlelight decor doesn't attempt to compete with the view. The broad-reaching, seasonally changing menu takes its inspiration from both Europe and the Pacific Rim. Highlights have included slow-roasted translucent B.C. salmon, and roasted duck with foie gras and pear mille-feuille. ⊠ *Pan Pacific Hotel, 300–999 Canada Pl.,* ☎ *604/891–2892. AE, DC, MC, V. No lunch.*

$$–$$$$ ✕ **Aqua Riva.** This lofty, lively modern room just yards from the Canada Place cruise-ship terminal affords striking views over the harbor and the North Shore mountains. Food from the wood-fired oven, rotisserie, and grill includes thin-crust pizzas with innovative toppings, grilled salmon, spit-roasted chicken, and a selection of pastas, salads, and sandwiches. There's a long microbrewery beer and martini list, too. ⊠ *200 Granville St.,* ☎ *604/683–5599. Reservations essential. AE, DC, MC, V.*

$$–$$$ ✕ **Raintree at the Landing.** In a beautifully renovated historic building in Gastown, this spacious restaurant has waterfront views, cozy fireplaces, and a wine list with Pacific Northwest vintages. The seasonal menu and daily specials focus on healthy cuisine using regional ingredients in innovative seafood dishes, luxurious soups, bread baked in-house, and several vegetarian options. ⊠ *375 Water St.,* ☎ *604/688–5570. AE, DC, MC, V.*

$$–$$$ ✕ **Teahouse Restaurant.** This former officers' mess in Stanley Park is perfectly poised for watching sunsets over the water. The seasonally changing West Coast Continental menu includes such specialties as roasted pear salad, seafood risotto, and rack of lamb. In summer you can dine on the patio, or, year-round, treat yourself to a traditional English afternoon tea. ⊠ *7501 Stanley Park Dr., at Ferguson Point, Stanley Park,* ☎ *604/669–3281. Reservations essential. AE, MC, V. No afternoon tea Sun.*

$$–$$$ ✕ **Water Street Café.** The tables at this popular Gastown café spill out onto the sidewalk for front-row views of the steam clock across the street. Inside, the slate-blue-and-white decor with tall windows overlooking bustling Water Street creates a cheerful, casual lunch or dinner atmosphere. It's tempting to pick one of the dozen or so varieties of pasta, but the crab chowder and the Fanny Bay oysters also are good choices. The breads are baked fresh daily. ⊠ *300 Water St.,* ☎ *604/689–2832. AE, MC, V.*

Pacific Northwest

$$–$$$$ ✕ **Liliget Feast House.** This intimate downstairs room resembles the interior of a longhouse, with wooden walkways across pebble floors, contemporary First Nations art on the walls, and cedar-plank tables with tatami-style benches. It's one of the few places in the world serving the original Northwest Coast First Nations cuisine. A feast platter lets you try most of the offerings, which include bannock bread, baked sweet potato with hazelnuts, alder-grilled salmon, rabbit with wild berry sauce, venison strips, oysters, mussels, and steamed fern shoots. ⊠ *1724 Davie St.,* ☎ *604/681–7044. Reservations essential. AE, DC, MC, V. No lunch. Closed Tues. and Wed. in Feb. and Mar.*

Seafood

$$$–$$$$ ✕ **C.** With dishes such as rare grilled ahi tuna served with potato and pea samosa; roasted sablefish with Israeli couscous; and octopus-bacon wrapped scallops, C has established itself as Vancouver's most innovative seafood restaurant. In addition to the lunch and dinner menus, C has a raw bar offering sashimi, shellfish, and caviar; an elaborate Sunday brunch; and, at weekday lunch, a West Coast seafood dim sum. The ultramodern interior is done in cool grays (described by some as Captain Nemo meets Zen). The patio, overlooking a marina and well away from traffic, is a pleasant place to while away a summer afternoon. ⊠ *2–1600 Howe St.,* ☎ *604/681–1164. Reservations essential. AE, DC, MC, V. No lunch Sat.*

Lodging

$$$$ 🏨 **Pan Pacific Hotel.** Most cruise ships calling at Vancouver arrive at
★ Canada Place, a striking waterfront facility shaped like an ocean liner. Besides the cruise-ship terminal and the Vancouver Convention and Exhibition Centre, Canada Place is also home to this luxurious 23-story hotel. Among the dramatic features of the three-story atrium lobby are a totem pole and waterfall. Modern rooms overlook the Burrard Inlet, the mountains beyond, or the city skyline. The restaurants and health club facilities are among the city's finest. ⊠ *300–999 Canada Pl., V6C 3B5,* ☎ *604/662–8111; 800/663–1515 in Canada; 800/937–1515 in the U.S.;* FAX *604/685–8690,* WEB *www.panpac.com. 504 rooms, 39 suites. 3 restaurants, coffee shop, minibars, no-smoking floor, room service, pool, hair salon, outdoor hot tub, sauna, spa, steam room, health club, indoor track, dry cleaning, laundry service, concierge, business services, travel services, parking (fee). AE, DC, MC, V.*

$$$$ 🏨 **Sutton Place.** The feel here is more of an exclusive European guest
★ house than a large modern hotel. Guest rooms are furnished with rich, dark woods, and the service is gracious and attentive. The hotel's Fleuri restaurant is known for its French Continental cuisine, Sunday brunch, and weekend evening chocoholic bar. A full European health spa (also open to nonguests) offers Le Stone therapy—a massage using river stones—as well as wraps, facials, manicures, reflexology, and massage therapy. La Grande Residence (part of Sutton Place), an apartment hotel suitable for stays of at least a week, is next door at 855 Burrard. ⊠ *845 Burrard St., V6Z 2K6,* ☎ *604/682–5511 or 800/961–7555,* FAX *604/682–5513,* WEB *www.suttonplace.com. 350 rooms, 47 suites. Restaurant, bar, indoor lap pool, hot tub, sauna (women only), spa, steam room (men only), health club. AE, D, DC, MC, V.*

$$$–$$$$ 🏨 **O Canada House.** Designated as a Heritage Site by the city of Vancouver, this beautifully restored 1897 Victorian within walking distance from downtown is where the first version of "O Canada," the national anthem, was written in 1909. Each spacious bedroom is appointed in late-Victorian antiques; modern comforts, such as in-room TVs, VCRs, phones, and bathrobes, help make things homey. The top-floor room is enormous, with two double beds and a private sitting area. A separate one-room coach house in the garden is the most romantic option. Guests also have the use of a guest pantry and a parlor with a fireplace. Breakfast, served in the dining room or on the wraparound porch, is a lavish affair. ⌧ *1114 Barclay St., V6E 1H1,* ☎ *604/688–0555 or 877/688–1114,* ℻ *604/488–0556,* WEB *www.ocanadahouse.com. 7 rooms. Free parking. MC, V.*

$–$$ 🛏 **Sylvia Hotel.** To stay here from June through August you'll need to book six months to a year ahead. This ivy-covered 1912 building is so popular because of its low rates and near-perfect location, about 25 ft from the beach on scenic English Bay, 200 ft from Stanley Park, and a 20-minute walk from Robson Street. The unadorned rooms all have private baths, phones, and TVs, and the suites all have kitchens. ⌧ *1154 Gilford St., V6G 2P6,* ☎ *604/681–9321,* ℻ *604/682–3551,* WEB *www. sylviahotel.com. 97 rooms, 22 suites. Restaurant, lobby lounge, room service, dry cleaning, laundry service, parking (fee). AE, DC, MC, V.*

Nightlife and the Arts

For information on events, pick up a free copy of the *Georgia Straight,* available at cafés and bookstores around town, or look in the entertainment section of the *Vancouver Sun* (Thursday's paper has listings in the "Queue" section). The **Arts Hotline** (☎ 604/684–2787, WEB www.allianceforarts.com) has the latest lineups in a wide range of entertainment. For tickets, book through **Ticketmaster** (☎ 604/280–4444, WEB www.ticketmaster.ca).

Nightlife

BARS, PUBS, AND LOUNGES

A massive deck with expansive False Creek views is the big draw at **Bridges** (⌧ 1696 Duranleau St., ☎ 604/687–4400), near the Public Market. There's a cozy pub and a fine dining restaurant at the same site. Near Stanley Park and attached to the seaside restaurant of the same name, **Cardero's Pub** (⌧ 1583 Coal Harbour Quay, ☎ 604/669–7666) has deep leather couches, marina views, and recycled ship timbers as well as other nautical touches; the pub grub is top-notch. **The Creek** (⌧ Granville Island Hotel, 1253 Johnston St., ☎ 604/685–7070) is a popular microbrewery lounge with lush velour booths and leather chairs, a fireplace, a pool table, and a seaside patio. The in-house vats brew eight varieties of German-style lagers and ales. **Dix Brew Pub** (⌧ 871 Beatty St., ☎ 604/682–2739) complements its selection of in-house brewed lagers with zesty Southern-style barbecue.

For a pint of properly poured Guinness and live traditional Irish music, try the **Irish Heather** (⌧ 217 Carrall St., ☎ 604/688–9779) in Gastown. Both the pub and the restaurant upstairs serve traditional Irish food. The **900 West** (⌧ 900 W. Georgia St., ☎ 604/669–9378) wine bar at the Fairmont Hotel Vancouver has 75 wines available by the glass. You could spend a whole evening at the **Sand Bar** (⌧ 1535 Johnson St., ☎ 604/669–9030) on Granville Island. It's part seafood restaurant—offering, among other things, an oyster bar and crab and lobster from live tanks—and it's also a pub, with an all-day tapas menu, deep leather chairs, and a rooftop patio with striking views over False Creek. On weekend evenings it morphs into a nightclub as patrons hit the dance floor. At **Steamworks** (⌧ 375 Water St., ☎ 604/689–2739), on the edge of Gastown, the brew master uses an age-old steam process and large copper kettles to create six to nine beers. The **Yaletown Brewing Company** (⌧ 1111 Mainland St., ☎ 604/681–2739) is based in a renovated warehouse with a glassed-in brewery, turning out eight tasty beers. It also has a lively singles-scene pub and a restaurant with an open-grill kitchen.

The **Gastown Comedy Store** (✉ 19 Water St., ☎ 604/682–1727) has stand-up and other comedy acts. The **TheatreSports League** (☎ 604/738–7013), a hilarious improv troupe, performs at the New Review Stage on Granville Island. The **Vancouver International Comedy Festival** (☎ 604/683–0883), held in late July and early August, brings an international collection of improv, stand-up, circus, and other acts to Granville Island. **Yuk Yuks Comedy Club** (✉ 750 Pacific Blvd. S, in the Plaza of Nations Expo site, ☎ 604/687–5233) is a popular stand-up venue.

DANCE CLUBS

The Commodore Ballroom (✉ 868 Granville St., ☎ 604/739–7469), a 1929 dance hall rich with memories for generations of Vancouverites, reopened in late 1999 after years of closure. Restored to its earlier Art Deco glory, complete with its massive sprung dance floor, the Commodore has done a lot to revitalize the city's live music scene. Live bands, which have so far included such major Canadian names as Bryan Adams and Blue Rodeo, play six nights a week; Tuesday is DJ night.

The fashionable **Voda** (✉ 783 Homer St., ☎ 604/684–3003), in the Westin Grand Hotel, is one of the few places for which Vancouverites dress up. The intimate club is popular with thirtysomething professionals who come for the live salsa on Tuesday, and the Motown, underground house, and soul selections the rest of the week.

The Arts

THEATRE

The **Arts Club Theatre** (✉ 1585 Johnston St., ☎ 604/687–1644) operates two stages on Granville Island and the **Stanley Theatre**, a former movie palace at 2750 Granville Street. All three theaters present performances year-round. **Bard on the Beach** (☎ 604/739–0559) is a summer series of Shakespeare's plays performed in tents on the beach at Vanier Park. The **Queen Elizabeth Theatre** (✉ 600 Hamilton St., ☎ 604/665–3050) is a major venue for ballet, opera, and other events. **Theatre Under the Stars** (☎ 604/687–0174) performs musicals at Malkin Bowl, an outdoor amphitheater in Stanley Park, during July and August. **The Vancouver Fringe Festival** (☎ 604/257–0350, WEB www.vancouverfringe.com), Vancouver's annual theater festival, is staged in September at various venues in Yaletown and on Granville Island. The **Vancouver Playhouse** (✉ 649 Cambie St., ☎ 604/665–3050), in the same complex as the Queen Elizabeth Theatre, is the leading venue in Vancouver for mainstream theatrical shows.

MUSIC

The hot line of the **Coastal Jazz and Blues Society** (☎ 604/872–5200) has information about concerts and clubs. The society also runs the **Vancouver International Jazz Festival**, which lights up 40 venues around town every June. **Festival Vancouver** (☎ 604/221–0080, WEB www.festivalvancouver.bc.ca) is Vancouver's biggest music event, with up to 60 performances of orchestral, chamber, choral, world music, early music, opera, and jazz in venues around the city during late July and early August. The **Vancouver Symphony Orchestra** (☎ 604/876–3434) is the resident company at the Orpheum Theatre (✉ 601 Smithe St.).

Shopping

Unlike many cities where suburban malls have taken over, Vancouver is full of individual boutiques and specialty shops. Antiques stores, ethnic markets, art galleries, and high-fashion outlets abound. Store hours are generally 9:30–6 Monday, Tuesday, Wednesday, and Saturday; 9:30–9 Thursday and Friday; and 10–5 Sunday.

Shopping Districts and Malls

About two dozen high-end art galleries, antiques shops, and Oriental-rug emporiums are packed end to end between 5th and 15th avenues on Granville Street, in an area known as **Gallery Row. Oakridge Shopping Centre** (⊠ 650 W. 41st Ave., at Cambie St., ☎ 604/261–2511) has chic, expensive stores that are fun to browse through. The **Pacific Centre Mall** (⊠ 700 W. Georgia St., ☎ 604/688–7236), on two levels and mostly underground, takes up three city blocks in the heart of downtown. **Robson Street** stretching from Burrard to Bute streets is full of boutiques and cafés. A commercial mecca has developed around **Sinclair Centre** (⊠ 757 W. Hastings St.), catering to sophisticated and pricey tastes.

Bustling **Chinatown**—centered on Pender and Main streets—is full of restaurants and markets. **Commercial Drive,** north of East 1st Avenue, is the heart of Vancouver's Italian and Latin American communities. You can sip cappuccino in coffee bars, or buy sun-dried tomatoes or an espresso machine. Craftspeople and market gardeners sell their wares at the **Granville Island Public Market** (☎ 604/666–6477) on Granville Island in False Creek. The island is also home to galleries, craft shops, and a wealth of artisans' studios. In **Little India,** on Main Street around 50th Avenue, curry houses, sweets shops, grocery stores, discount jewelers, and silk shops abound. Treasure hunters enjoy the 300 block of **West Cordova Street,** near Gastown, where offbeat shops sell curios, vintage clothing, and locally designed fashions.

Department Stores

The Bay (⊠ 674 Granville St., at Georgia St., ☎ 604/681–6211), founded as part of the fur trade in the 17th century, is now a midprice department store downtown. Modelled on the Paris's Colette store, **Bruce** (⊠ 1038 Alberni St., ☎ 604/688–8802) is Vancouver's first "lifestyle" department store, offering the latest in designer fashion, home decor, and eyewear. **Eaton's** (⊠ 701 Granville St., ☎ 604/685–7112) is a midprice, fashion-oriented department store. **Holt Renfrew** (⊠ 633 Granville St., ☎ 604/681–3121) focuses on high fashion for men and women.

Specialty Stores

ANTIQUES

Three key antiques hunting grounds are Gallery Row on Granville Street; the stretch of antiques stores along Main Street from 16th to 30th Avenues; and along Front Street, between 6th and Begbie Streets near New Westminster Quay in New Westminster.

Love's Auctioneers (⊠ 1635 W. Broadway, ☎ 604/733–1157) auction antiques on the last Wednesday and Thursday of each month at 6 PM. **The Vancouver Antique Centre** (⊠ 422 Richards St., ☎ 604/669–7444) has 15 antiques and collectibles dealers under one roof.

ART GALLERIES

Gallery Row along Granville Street between 5th and 15th avenues is home to about a dozen high-end contemporary art galleries. You'll also find a number of notable galleries on the downtown peninsula.

Buschlen Mowatt (⊠ 1445 W. Georgia St., ☎ 604/682–1234) exhibits the works of contemporary Canadian and international artists. The **Diane Farris Gallery** (⊠ 1565 W. 7th Ave., ☎ 604/737–2629) often showcases hot new artists. The **Douglas Reynolds Gallery** (⊠ 2335 Granville St., ☎ 604/731–9292) has one of the city's finest collections of Northwest Coast First Nations art. The **Inuit Gallery of Vancouver** (⊠ 206 Cambie St., Gastown, ☎ 604/688–7323 or 888/615–8399) exhibits Northwest Coast and Inuit art. The **Marion Scott Gallery** (⊠ 481 Howe St., ☎ 604/685–1934) specializes in Inuit art.

BOOKS

Vancouver's two **Chapters** stores (✉ 788 Robson St., ☎ 604/682–4066; 2505 Granville St., at Broadway, ☎ 604/731–7822) are enormous, with a café in each location and a series of author readings and other performances. **Duthie Books** (✉ 2239 W. 4th Ave., ☎ 604/732–5344) is a long-established homegrown favorite for literary titles. **MacLeod's Books** (✉ 455 W. Pender St., ☎ 604/681–7654) is one of the city's best antiquarian and used bookstores. **Wanderlust** (✉ 1929 W. 4th Ave., ☎ 604/739–2182) carries thousands of travel books and maps, as well as luggage and travel accessories.

CLOTHES

For unique men's and women's clothing, try **Dorothy Grant** (✉ 757 W. Hastings St., ☎ 604/681–0201) in Sinclair Centre, where traditional Haida designs meld with modern fashion. **Dream** (✉ 311 W. Cordova St., ☎ 604/683–7326) is where up-and-coming local designers sell their wares. Men's and women's fashions by Versace, Dolce Gabbana, Prada, and others are available at **Leone** (✉ 757 W. Hastings St., ☎ 604/683–1133) in Sinclair Centre. You'll find handmade Italian suits, knitwear, accessories, and other upscale menswear at stylish **Madison Men's Wear** (✉ 1050 W. Pender St., ☎ 604/683–2122).

If your tastes are traditional, don't miss **Straiths** (✉ 900 W. Georgia St., ☎ 604/685–3301) in the Fairmont Hotel Vancouver, where you'll find tailored designer fashions for men and women. **Wear Else?** (✉ 2372 W. 4th Ave., ☎ 604/732–3521; ✉ 4401 W. 10th Ave., ☎ 604/221–7755; ✉ Oakridge Shopping Centre, 650 W. 41st Ave., at Cambie St., ☎ 604/266–3613) is a popular women's wear shop with attentive service; the chain offers both business and casual clothes, including shoes and accessories.

GIFTS

Museum and gallery gift shops are among the best places to buy high-quality souvenirs—West Coast Native art, books, music, jewelry, and other items.

The **Clamshell Gift Shop** (✉ Vancouver Aquarium Marine Science Centre, ☎ 604/659–3413 or 800/663–0562) in Stanley Park sells souvenir clothing, and aquatic-theme toys and gifts. The **Gallery Shop** (✉ 750 Hornby St., ☎ 604/662–4706) in the Vancouver Art Gallery sells a good selection of prints and cards. **Hill's Native Art** (✉ 165 Water St., ☎ 604/685–4249), in Gastown, has Vancouver's largest selection of First Nations art. **Lattimer Gallery** (✉ 1590 W. 2nd Ave., ☎ 604/732–4556), near Granville Island, is full of Native arts and crafts in all price ranges.

The **Museum of Anthropology Gift Shop** (✉ 6393 N.W. Marine Dr., ☎ 604/822–3825) on the University of British Columbia campus stocks Northwest Coast jewelry, carvings, and prints, as well as a good collection of books on First Nations history and culture. The **Museum Shop** (✉ 639 Hornby St., ☎ 604/687–8266) in the Canadian Museum of Craft and Design has a delightful collection of one-of-a-kind handmade items. At the **Salmon Shop** (✉ 1689 Johnston St., ☎ 604/669–3474), in the Granville Island Public Market, you can pick up fresh or smoked salmon wrapped for travel. One of Vancouver's most extensive, but least known, Native art collections is hidden in the back room at the **The Three Vets** (✉ 2200 Yukon St., ☎ 604/872–5475), a camping equipment store. Ask any staff member to show you.

JEWELRY

Birks (✉ 698 W. Hastings St., ☎ 604/669–3333) takes up the grand lower floor of a neoclassical building that was the former headquarters of the Canadian Imperial Bank of Commerce. **Cartier Jewellers** (⊠ 408 Howe St., ☎ 604/683–6878) is the Vancouver outlet of the famous jewelry chain. **Palladio** (⊠ 855 W. Hastings St., ☎ 604/685–3885) carries modern, high-fashion jewelry in gold and platinum.

VICTORIA

The capital of British Columbia, Victoria is the oldest city (founded 1843) on Canada's west coast and the first European settlement on Vancouver Island. Today Victoria is a compact seaside town laced with tea shops and gardens. Though it's quite touristy during the high summer season, it's also when the city is at its prettiest, with flowers hanging from 19th-century lampposts and strollers enjoying the beauty of Victoria's natural harbor.

Exploring Victoria

Great views, lush gardens, and fine museums are the highlights of a visit to Victoria's walkable downtown. For the visitor on a short stop in Victoria, a trip to popular Butchart Gardens is worthwhile if you've got the time.

Numbers in the text correspond to numbers in the margin and on the Downtown Victoria map.

A Good Walk and Tour

For some wonderful views, begin your tour of Victoria on the waterfront at the Tourism Victoria Visitor Information Centre. Just across the way is the **Empress Hotel** ⑱, a majestic railway hotel that originally opened in 1908. A short walk around the harbor along the Inner Harbour Walk (take any of the staircases from Government Street down to the water level) will take you to the **Royal London Wax Museum.** Originally Victoria's steamship terminal, this colonnaded building is now home to more than 300 wax figures. Across Belleville Street is the **Parliament Buildings** ⑲ complex, where British Columbia's provincial legislature sits. Cross Government Street to reach the **Royal British Columbia Museum** ⑳, where you can explore thousands of years of history. Just behind the museum and bordering Douglas Street are the totem poles and ceremonial longhouse of Thunderbird Park; **Helmcken House** ㉑, the oldest house in Victoria; and the tiny 19th-century **St. Ann's Schoolhouse.** A few blocks south on Douglas Street will take you to beautiful seaside Beacon Hill Park. A few blocks west of the park on Government Street is **Emily Carr House,** the birthplace of one of British Columbia's best-known artists. From the park, go north on Blanshard Street to see the grounds and chapel of **St. Ann's Academy** ㉒. Then take Belleville Street west to Douglas Street and stop off at the glass-roof **Crystal Garden Conservation Centre** ㉓, where you can see a menagerie of endangered tropical birds and animals and hundreds of flowers.

From Crystal Garden, continue on Belleville Street to Government Street, Victoria's main shopping thoroughfare. Head north about five blocks to Government and View streets, where you'll find the entrance to the cobblestone **Bastion Square,** the original site of Fort Victoria and the Hudson's Bay Company trading post, which now has restaurants and small shops. Just north of Government and View, on the right-hand side of Government Street, is the entrance to Trounce Alley, a pretty pedestrian-only shopping arcade. Back at Bastion Square, you can stop in at the **Maritime Museum of British Columbia** ㉔ and learn about an important part of the province's history.

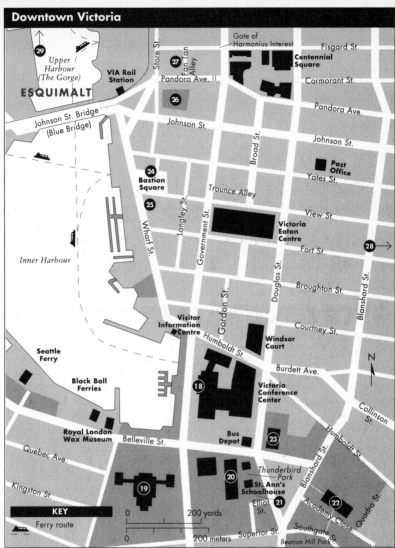

Downtown Victoria

Upper / Harbour (The Gorge)

ESQUIMALT

VIA Rail Station

Store St.

Fan Tan Alley

Pandora Ave. II

Gate of Harmonius Interest

Fisgard St.

Centennial Square

Cormorant St.

Pandora Ave.

Johnson St. Bridge (Blue Bridge)

Johnson St.

Broad St.

Johnson St.

Post Office

Yates St.

Bastion Square

Trounce Alley

View St.

Langley St.

Wharf St.

Inner Harbour

Government St.

Victoria Eaton Centre

Fort St.

Douglas St.

Broughton St.

Gordon St.

Courtney St.

Visitor Information Centre

Humboldt St.

Windsor Court

Burdett Ave.

Blanshard St.

Collinson St.

Seattle Ferry

Victoria Conference Center

Black Ball Ferries

Royal London Wax Museum

Belleville St.

Bus Depot

Humboldt St.

Quebec Ave.

Kingston St.

Thunderbird Park

St. Ann's Schoolhouse

Blanshard St.

Academy Close

Quadra St.

Elliot St.

Southgate St.

Superior St.

Beacon Hill Park

KEY

Ferry route

0   200 yards

0   200 meters

N

Chinatown **27**	
Craigdarroch Castle **28**	
Crystal Garden Conservation Centre **23**	
Fairmont Empress Hotel **18**	
Helmcken House . . **21**	

Maritime Museum of British Columbia **24**	
Market Square . . **26**	
Parliament Buildings **19**	
Point Ellice House **29**	

Royal British Columbia Museum **20**	
St. Ann's Academy **22**	
Victoria Bug Zoo **25**	

Around the corner, to the south of Bastion Square on Wharf Street, is the **Victoria Bug Zoo** ㉕, a creepy-crawly attraction popular with children. North of Bastion Square a few blocks, on Store Street between Johnson Street and Pandora Avenue is **Market Square** ㉖, one of the most picturesque shopping districts in the city. Across Pandora Avenue is the entrance to the narrow, shop-lined Fan Tan Alley, which leads to Fisgard Street, the heart of **Chinatown** ㉗. A 15-minute walk or a short drive east on Fort Street will take you to Joan Crescent and lavish **Craigdarroch Castle** ㉘ and the nearby Art Gallery of Greater Victoria. In summer, a ride on Harbour Ferries from the Inner Harbour will take you to **Point Ellice House** ㉙, a historic 19th-century waterside home and garden.

TIMING

Many of the sights are within easy walking distance of one another and the tour could be covered in half a day. However, allot a full day if you plan on visiting the Royal British Columbia Museum and the other museums.

Sights to See

㉗ **Chinatown.** The Chinese were responsible for building much of the Canadian Pacific Railway in the 19th century, and their influences still mark the region. If you enter Chinatown from Government Street, you'll walk under the elaborate **Gate of Harmonious Interest,** made from Taiwanese ceramic tiles and decorative panels. Along the street, merchants display fragile paper lanterns, embroidered silks, and imported fruits and vegetables. **Fan Tan Alley,** just off Fisgard Street, holds claim not only to being the narrowest street in Canada but also to having been the gambling and opium center of Chinatown, where games of mah-jongg, fan-tan, and dominoes were played. It's now lined with tiny shops.

㉘ **Craigdarroch Castle.** This lavish mansion was built as the home of British Columbia's first millionaire, Robert Dunsmuir, who oversaw coal mining for the Hudson's Bay Company. He died in 1889, just a few months before the castle's completion. Converted into a museum depicting turn-of-the-20th-century life, the castle has elaborately framed landscape paintings, stained-glass windows, carved woodwork—precut in Chicago for Dunsmuir and sent by rail—and a beautifully restored painted ceiling in the drawing room. ✉ *1050 Joan Crescent,* ☎ *250/592–5323,* WEB *www.craigdarrochcastle.com.* ✑ *C$8.* ☽ *Mid-June–Labor Day, daily 9–7; early-Sept.–mid-June, daily 10–4:30.*

♨ ㉓ **Crystal Garden Conservation Centre.** Opened in 1925 as the largest saltwater swimming pool in the British Empire, this glass-roof building is now filled with exotic flora and home to a variety of endangered tropical birds and animals, including flamingos, tortoises, macaws, lemurs, bats, and butterflies. ✉ *713 Douglas St.,* ☎ *250/381–1213,* WEB *www. bcpcc.com/crystal.* ✑ *C$7.50.* ☽ *July–Aug., daily 8:30–8; Sept.–Oct. and Apr.–June, daily 9–6; Nov.–Mar., daily 10–4:30.*

♨ ⑱ **The Fairmont Empress Hotel.** Opened in 1908 by the Canadian Pacific Railway, the Empress is one of the grand château-style hotels you'll find in many Canadian cities. Designed by Francis Rattenbury, who also designed the Parliament Buildings, the Empress, with its solid Edwardian grandeur, has become a symbol of the city. The ingredients that made the 472-room hotel a tourist attraction in the past—old-world architecture and ornate decor, a commanding view of the Inner Harbour—are still here. The archives, a historical photo display, are open to the public. Nonguests can also stop by the Empress for a traditional afternoon tea (reservations recommended), meet for a curry under the tiger skin in the Bengal Room, or enjoy the superb regional cuisine in the Empress Room restaurant. **Miniature World** (☎ 250/385–9731), a display of doll-size dioramas, including one of the world's longest model railways, is on the Humboldt Street side of the complex. ✉ *721 Government St.,* ☎ *250/384–8111,* WEB *www.fairmont.com.* 🖃 *Afternoon tea C$46 in summer, C$24 in winter, Miniature World C$8.*

㉑ Helmcken House. The oldest house in Victoria was erected in 1852 for pioneer doctor and statesman John Sebastian Helmcken. It is a treasure trove of history, from the family's Victorian furnishings to the doctor's intriguing collection of 19th-century medical tools. Audio tours last 20 minutes. Behind Helmcken House is **Thunderbird Park,** with totem poles and a ceremonial longhouse constructed by Kwakiutl Chief Mungo Martin. Next door is **St. Ann's Schoolhouse,** one of British Columbia's oldest schools (you can view the interior through the door). ✉ *10 Elliot St.,* ☎ *250/361–0021,* WEB *www.heritage.gov. bc.ca/helm/helm.htm.* 🖃 *C$5.* ☉ *May–Oct., daily 10–5; Nov.–Apr., Thurs.–Mon. noon–4; some Christmas programs.*

㉔ Maritime Museum of British Columbia. In Victoria's original courthouse, hand-built boats, model ships, Royal Navy charts, photographs, uniforms, and ship's bells chronicle British Columbia's seafaring history. An 1899 hand-operated cage lift, believed to be the oldest continuously operating elevator in North America, ascends to the third floor, where an 1888 Vice-Admiralty courtroom looks set for a court-martial. ✉ *28 Bastion Sq.,* ☎ *250/385–4222,* WEB *mmbc.bc.ca.* 🖃 *C$6.* ☉ *Daily 9:30–4:30; call for extended summer hours.*

㉖ Market Square. During Victoria's late-19th-century heyday, this three-level square, originally the courtyard of an old inn, provided everything a sailor, miner, or up-country lumberjack could want. Now, beautifully restored to its original architectural, if not commercial, character, it's a traffic-free, café- and boutique-lined hangout. ✉ *560 Johnson St.,* ☎ *250/386–2441.*

★ **⑲ Parliament Buildings.** Designed by Francis Rattenbury, who also designed the Fairmont Empress Hotel, these massive stone structures, completed in 1898, dominate the Inner Harbour. Two statues flank the main doors: one of Sir James Douglas (1803–77), who chose the site where Victoria was built, and another of Sir Matthew Baille Begbie (1819–94), the man in charge of law and order during the gold rush. Atop the central dome is a gilded statue of Captain George Vancouver (1757–98), the first European to sail around Vancouver Island. A statue of Queen Victoria (1819–1901) stands in front of the complex. More than 3,000 lights outline the buildings at night. The interior is lavishly appointed with marble floors, stained-glass windows, and murals depicting scenes from the province's history. From the public gallery, when the legislature is in session (usually during the spring and early summer), you can watch British Columbian democracy at work; tradition has the opposing parties sitting 2½ sword lengths apart. Informative half-hour tours are free. ✉ *501 Belleville St.,* ☎ *250/387–3046,* WEB *www.BC2000. gov.bc.ca.* 🖃 *Free.* ☉ *June–Labor Day, daily 8:30–5 (up to 23 tours a day); Sept.–May, weekdays 8:30–5; last tour 4 PM.*

㉙ Point Ellice House. This restored 1860s Italianate villa overlooking the Upper Harbour has the largest collection of Victorian furnishings in western Canada. Tea with home-baked goodies is served on the lawn. You can also take an audio tour of the house, stroll in the gardens, or try your hand at croquet. To get here, take a Harbour Ferries boat from the dock in front of the Empress Hotel. Reservations are recommended for tea. ✉ *2616 Pleasant St.,* ☎ *250/380–6506,* WEB *www.heritage.gov.bc.*

ca/point/point.htm. ⊠ *C$5, $17 with tea.* ☉ *Mid-May–mid-Sept., daily noon–5. Tea daily noon–4.*

★ ⓒ ⑳ **Royal British Columbia Museum.** Easily the best attraction in Victoria, this museum is as much a research and educational center as a diversion for tourists, and its exhibits, gripping with their visual and sound effects, are all informed by historical context. The definitive First Peoples exhibit includes a genuine Kwakwaka'wakw longhouse (the builders retain rights to its ceremonial use) and provides insights into the daily life, art, and mythology of both coastal and interior peoples, before and after the arrival of Europeans. The Modern History Gallery re-creates most of a frontier town, complete with cobblestone streets, silent movies, and rumbling train sounds. The Natural History Gallery re-creates the sights, sounds, and smells of many B.C. natural habitats, and the Open Ocean exhibit mimics a submarine journey. Century Hall, opened in 1999, reviews British Columbia's most recent 100 years. An on-site IMAX theater shows *National Geographic* films on a six-story-high screen. ⊠ *675 Belleville St.,* ☎ *250/387–3701 or 800/661–5411,* WEB *www.royalbcmuseum.bc.ca.* ⊠ *C$10.65, IMAX theater C$9.50, combination ticket C$18.15.* ☉ *Sat.–Wed. 9–5, Thurs. and Fri. 9–7:45; theater daily 10–8; call for show times.*

㉒ **St. Ann's Academy.** This former convent and school, founded in 1858, played a central role in British Columbia's pioneer life. Closed in 1974, it was carefully restored and reopened as a historic site in 1997. The academy's little chapel, the first Roman Catholic cathedral in Victoria, now looks just as it did in the 1920s. The 6-acre grounds, with fruit trees and herb and flower gardens, are also being restored as historic landscapes in their own right. ⊠ *835 Humboldt St.,* ☎ *250/953–8828,* WEB *www.bcpcc.com/stanns.* ⊠ *Free.* ☉ *Mid-May–mid-Oct., daily 10–4; mid-Oct.–mid-May, daily noon–4 (closed statutory holidays).*

ⓒ ㉕ **Victoria Bug Zoo.** Kids of all ages are drawn to this offbeat, two-room minizoo. Many of the bugs—mostly large tropical varieties, such as stick insects, scorpions, and centipedes—can be held; staff members are on hand to dispense scientific information. ⊠ *1107 Wharf St.,* ☎ *250/384–2847,* WEB *www.bugzoo.bc.ca.* ⊠ *C$6.* ☉ *July–Aug., daily 9–9; Sept.–June, daily 9:30–5:30.*

OFF THE
BEATEN PATH

BUTCHART GARDENS – This impressive 50-acre garden, 21 km (13 mi) north of downtown Victoria, on the way to the Swartz Bay ferry terminal, grows more than 700 varieties of flowers in its sunken, Italian, Japanese, and rose gardens. In summer, many of the exhibits are illuminated at night, and fireworks light the sky over the gardens every Saturday night. Also on the premises are a seed and gift shop, two restaurants, and a café. ⊠ *800 Benvenuto Ave., Brentwood Bay,* ☎ *250/652–5256 or 250/652–4422,* WEB *www.butchartgardens. com.* ⊠ *Mid-June–Sept., C$19.25; discounted rates in winter.* ☉ *June 15–Sept. 1, daily 9 am–10:30 pm; Sept. 2–15, daily 9–9; pt. 16–June 14, daily 9 am–dusk.*

Dining

Italian

$$–$$$$ ✕ **Il Terrazzo.** A charming redbrick terrace edged by potted greenery, lighted by flickering candles, and warmed by fireplaces and overhead heaters makes Il Terrazzo, tucked away off Waddington Alley and not visible from the street, the locals' choice for romantic alfresco dining in Victoria. Scallops dipped in roasted pistachios and garnished with arugula, Belgian endive, and mango salsa; grilled lamb chops on angel-

hair pasta with tomatoes, garlic, mint, and black pepper; and other hearty northern Italian dishes come piping hot from the restaurant's authentic wood oven. ⊠ *555 Johnson St., off Waddington Alley (call for directions),* ☏ *250/361–0028. Reservations essential. AE, MC, V. No lunch Sun. Oct.–Apr., no lunch Sat.*

Pacific Northwest

$$–$$$$ ✕ **Cafe Brio.** One of Victoria's most enjoyable restaurants is set in an
★ Italian villa–style building, a little north of the Inner Harbour. Candlelight, hardwood floors, lush Modigliani nudes, and rich gold walls create a warm glow. The daily menu depends on what's fresh that day (very fresh—the café works in partnership with local organic farms and serves the produce the same day it's harvested). Specialties have included confit of duck with potato gnocchi and truffle oil, a melt-in-the-mouth red wine–braised lamb shank, and seared jumbo Alaskan scallops served with preserved lemon and sorrel butter. Good vegetarian options are always available, and an extensive wine list goes easy on the markups. ⊠ *944 Fort St.,* ☏ *250/383–0009. AE, MC, V. No lunch weekends. No lunch Nov. and Jan.–Apr.*

$$–$$$$ ✕ **The Victorian Restaurant.** Intimate dining with striking views over
★ the Inner Harbour highlight this 45-seat restaurant in the Ocean Pointe Resort Hotel. The chef prepares such elegantly presented regional dishes as wild mushroom and truffle soup, roast rack of lamb with maple and juniper glaze, and pheasant breast with goat cheese and sun-dried cranberry mousse. The wine list won the *Wine Spectator*'s Award of Excellence in 1999. ⊠ *Ocean Pointe Resort Hotel and Spa, 45 Songhees Rd. (across the Johnson Street Bridge from downtown Victoria),* ☏ *250/360–5800. Reservations essential. DC, MC, V. Closed Jan. and Mon.–Tues. in Nov.–Apr. No lunch.*

$$–$$$ ✕ **Camille's.** Quiet and intimate, Camille's is tucked away in a heritage building off Bastion Square. The menu concentrates on fresh local products, and such regional exotica as ostrich, quail, and emu often appear, too. These, and favorites such as roast venison with wild mushroom polenta and grainy Dijon-and-mint-crusted lamb, are served in generous portions. An extensive 300-item wine list is one of the best on the island. ⊠ *45 Bastion Sq.,* ☏ *250/381–3433. AE, MC, V. No lunch; no dinner Mon. in winter.*

$$–$$$ ✕ **Herald Street Caffe.** This art-filled bistro in Victoria's warehouse dis-
★ trict is an established favorite among Victorians and visitors alike. The menu changes seasonally but always features fresh local cuisine, daily fish grills, great pastas made in-house, and good vegetarian selections, many prepared with intriguing Asian accents. If available, try the East Coast mussels steamed in a lemon Szechuan peppercorn sauce, followed by calamari in a tomato-dill ratatouille with crumbled feta, or free-range beef tenderloin stuffed with a wild mushroom chestnut pâté. ⊠ *546 Herald St.,* ☏ *250/381–1441. Reservations essential. AE, DC, MC, V. No lunch Mon.–Tues.*

Seafood

$$–$$$ ✕ **The Blue Crab Bar and Grill.** Fresh daily seafood and expansive harbor views make this modern and airy restaurant a popular lunch and dinner spot. Signature dishes include roasted spring salmon with sweet and sour fennel, Dungeness crab and shrimp cakes, and a scallop and jumbo prawn sautée, though the long list of daily specials is always tempting. The attached lounge area, open nightly until 1 AM, has more casual, lower-priced fare and equally impressive views. ⊠ *146 Kingston St., in the Coast Harbourside Hotel and Marina,* ☏ *250/480–1999. AE, D, DC, MC, V.*

$ ✕ **Barb's Place.** This funky, blue-painted take-out shack floats on the quay where the fishing boats dock, west of the Inner Harbour off Erie Street. Cod, lingcod, halibut, oysters, seafood burgers, chowder, and carrot cake are all prepared fresh on the premises. If you eat on the picnic tables on the wharf, you'll have a front row view of the vessels such as paddle wheelers, houseboats, and vintage fishing boats that moor in the harbor. Ferries sail to Fisherman's Wharf from the Inner Harbor. ✉ *Fisherman's Wharf, Erie St.,* ☎ *250/384–6515. MC, V. Closed late Oct.–early Mar.*

Vegetarian

$–$$ ✕ **Re-Bar Modern Foods.** This bright and cheery café in Bastion Square is *the* place for vegetarians in Victoria, though the almond burgers, veggie enchiladas, decadent home-baked goodies, and big breakfasts will keep omnivores happy. An extensive tea and fresh-juice selection shares space with espresso, microbrews, and local wines on the drinks list. ✉ *50 Bastion Sq.,* ☎ *250/361–9223. AE, MC, V. No dinner Sun. No dinner Mon., Oct.–Mar.*

Lodging

$$$$ 🏨 **Abigail's Hotel.** A Tudor-style inn built in 1930, Abigail's is within
★   walking distance of downtown. The guest rooms are attractively furnished in an English arts-and-crafts style, and down comforters, together with whirlpool tubs and fireplaces in many rooms, add to the pampering atmosphere. Six large, luxurious rooms in the Coach House have whirlpool tubs, king-size four-poster beds, and wood-burning fireplaces. All of Abigail's rooms have phones but no TVs. A lavish hot breakfast is included in the rate. ✉ *906 McClure St., V8V 3E7,* ☎ *250/388–5363 or 800/561–6565,* FAX *250/388–7787,* WEB *www.abigailshotel.com. 22 rooms. Breakfast room, library, dry cleaning, laundry service, free parking. AE, MC, V.*

$$$$ 🏨 **Beaconsfield Inn.** This 1905 registered heritage building just four blocks from the Inner Harbour is one of Victoria's most faithfully restored Edwardian mansions. Antique furniture, mahogany floors, fireplaces, stained-glass windows, Ralph Lauren fabrics, and such period details as the Edwardian wooden canopied tub in one room render each room and suite unique. Lavish breakfasts, afternoon tea in the conservatory, and evening sherry around the library fire complete the prewar country house ambience. ✉ *998 Humboldt St., V8V 2Z8,* ☎ *250/ 384–4044,* FAX *250/384–4052,* WEB *www.beaconsfieldinn.com. 7 rooms, 2 suites. Breakfast room, library, free parking. MC, V.*

$$$$ 🏨 **The Fairmont Empress.** As far as movie stars and minor nobles are concerned, the Empress is the only place to stay in Victoria. Opened in 1908, this harborside château has aged gracefully. Its sympathetically restored Edwardian decor and top-notch service recall a more gracious age. A concierge floor, called Entrée Gold, provides boutique-hotel intimacy within the larger hotel. ✉ *721 Government St., V8W 1W5,* ☎ *250/384– 8111 or 800/441–1414,* FAX *250/381–4334,* WEB *www.fairmont.com. 457 rooms, 19 suites. 2 restaurants, lounge, fans, in-room data ports, minibars, no-smoking floors, room service, pool, hot tub, sauna, spa, gym, shops, dry cleaning, laundry service, concierge, business services, convention center, parking (fee). AE, D, DC, MC, V.*

$$$$ 🏨 **Ocean Pointe Resort Hotel and Spa.** Across the "blue bridge" (John-
★   son Street Bridge) from downtown Victoria, the waterfront Ocean Pointe has a resort's worth of facilities, including a full spa. You'll find expansive views of the Inner Harbour and the Parliament Buildings across the water from the hotel's striking two-story-high lobby windows and half of the guest rooms. Standard rooms are spacious, and the apartment-size suites have kitchenettes and separate living and dining areas.

✉ *45 Songhees Rd., V9A 6T3,* ☎ *250/360–2999 or 800/667–4677,* FAX *250/360–5856,* WEB *www.oprhotel.com. 212 rooms, 34 suites. 2 restaurants, bar, wine shop, air-conditioning, in-room data ports, mini-bars, room service, indoor pool, hair salon, hot tub, sauna, 2 tennis courts, health club, jogging, racquetball, squash, shop, baby-sitting, laundry service, concierge, business services, meeting room, travel services, parking (fee). AE, DC, MC, V.*

$$$ 🖼 **Swans.** Across the road from the waterfront in Victoria's old town, and walking distance from most of the city sights, this 1913 former warehouse is one of the city's most attractive boutique hotels. There's a brewery, restaurant, and pub on the first floor and a nightclub in the cellar. High-ceiling, apartmentlike suites, all with kitchens and decorated with the owner's extensive Pacific Northwest art collection, fill the upper floors. ✉ *506 Pandora Ave., V8W 1N6,* ☎ *250/361–3310 or 800/668–7926,* FAX *250/361–3491,* WEB *www.swanshotel.com. 30 suites. Restaurant, pub, wine shop, no-smoking floor, room service, nightclub, laundry services, meeting room, parking (fee). AE, DC, MC, V.*

Nightlife and the Arts

For entertainment listings, pick up a free copy of *Monday Magazine* (it comes out every Thursday) or call the Talking Telus Pages at 250/953–9000.

Nightlife

BARS AND CLUBS

High-energy dance music draws a young crowd to the **Boom Boom Room** (✉ 1208 Wharf St., ☎ 250/381–2331) on the waterfront. The DJs at **Liquid** (✉ 15 Bastion Sq., ☎ 250/385–2626) play Top 40, dance, R&B, and hip-hop tunes. The **Snug Pub,** about 10 minutes from downtown in the Oak Bay Beach Hotel (✉ 1175 Beach Dr., ☎ 250/598–4556) is the nearest thing to a traditional English pub in Victoria, with a cozy Tudor ambience and a waterside deck. The **Strathcona Hotel** (✉ 919 Douglas St., ☎ 250/383–7137) is something of an entertainment complex, with a pub and restaurant, a sports bar, a hillbilly-theme bar, and a nightclub—beach volleyball is played on the roof in the summertime. The DJs at the dance club **Sweetwater's** (✉ Market Square, 27-560 Johnson St., ☎ 250/383–7844) appeal to a wide age group with Top 40 dance and old-time rock and roll tunes.

BREW PUBS

Pub culture is an important part of life in Victoria, and many of the city's most atmospheric pubs brew their own beer. The **Ale Trail** (☎ 800/667–2291), a must for beer connoisseurs, hosts a tour with tastings of Victoria's microbreweries and brew pubs. The summertime deck over the gorge at the **Harbour Canoe Club** (✉ 450 Swift St., ☎ 250/361–1940) is a delightful place to while away a summer afternoon; you can even rent canoes and kayaks here. The former power station has been stylishly redone and has a wide range of in-house brews (including one made with maple syrup), top-notch bar snacks, and a restaurant.

Chic and arty **Hugo's** (✉ 625 Courtney St., ☎ 250/920–4844) serves lunch, dinner, and four of its own brews. This multipurpose night spot is a pub by day, a lounge in the early evening, and a dance club at night. Across the Johnson Street bridge, **Spinnakers Brew Pub** (✉ 308 Catherine St., ☎ 250/386–2739) pours Victoria's most extensive menu of microbrews in an atmospheric setting, with a waterfront patio, a double-sided fireplace, and a multitude of cozy rooms filled with pub paraphernalia. The excellent pub grub and in-house restaurant make this a popular eatery. **Swan's Pub** (✉ 1601 Store St., ☎ 250/361–3310), in a 1913 heritage building, serves its own microbrews in a room decorated with Pacific Northwest art and has live music Sunday through Thursday nights.

The Arts

MUSIC

Pacific Opera Victoria (☎ 250/385–0222) performs three productions a year in the Royal Theatre (✉ 805 Broughton St., ☎ 250/386–6121). The **Victoria Symphony** (☎ 250/385–6515) plays in the Royal Theatre (✉ 805 Broughton St., ☎ 250/386–6121) and at the University Centre Auditorium (✉ Finnerty Rd., ☎ 250/721–8480). The **TerriVic Jazz Party** (☎ 250/953–2011) showcases internationally acclaimed musicians every April at seven venues around Victoria. The **Victoria Jazz Society** (☎ 250/388–4423) organizes an annual JazzFest International in late June and the Vancouver Island Blues Bash in Victoria every Labour Day weekend.

THEATER

An old church houses the **Belfry Theatre** (✉ 1291 Gladstone Ave., ☎ 250/385–6815), whose resident company specializes in contemporary Canadian dramas. **Langham Court Theatre** (✉ 805 Langham Ct., ☎ 250/384–2142), a small theater in a residential neighborhood, is the home stage of the long-established Victoria Theatre Guild, which stages the work of well-known playwrights. **McPherson Playhouse** (✉ 3 Centennial Sq., ☎ 250/386–6121) hosts touring theater and dance companies.

Shopping

Shopping Districts and Malls

Victoria Eaton Centre (✉ 1 Victoria Eaton Centre, at Government and Fort Sts., ☎ 250/381–4012), a department store and mall, holds about 100 boutiques and restaurants. **Antique Row,** on Fort Street between Blanshard and Cook streets, is home to more than 60 antiques, curio, and collectibles shops. **Market Square** (✉ 560 Johnson St., ☎ 250/386–2441) has everything from fudge, music, and comic books to jewelry, local arts, and New Age accoutrements. High-end fashion boutiques, craft shops, and galleries line **Trounce Alley,** a pedestrian-only lane north of View Street between Broad and Government streets.

Specialty Stores

Most of Victoria's specialty shops can be found on or near Government Street stretching north from the Empress Hotel.

At **Artina's** (✉ 1002 Government St., ☎ 250/386–7000 or 877/386–7700) you can find unusual Canadian art jewelry—mostly handmade, one-of-a-kind pieces. The **Cowichan Trading Co., Ltd.** (✉ 1328 Government St., ☎ 250/383–0321) sells First Nations jewelry, art, moccasins, and Cowichan Indian sweaters. The **Fran Willis Gallery** (✉ 1619 Store St., upstairs, ☎ 250/381–3422) shows contemporary Canadian paintings and sculpture. **Hill's Native Art** (✉ 1008 Government St., ☎ 250/385–3911) sells souvenirs and original West Coast First Nations art. As the name would suggest, **Irish Linen Stores** (✉ 1019 Government St., ☎ 250/383–6812) stocks fine linen, lace and hand-embroidered items—handkerchiefs, napkins, tablecloths, and place mats. **Munro's Books** (✉ 1108 Government St., ☎ 250/382–2464), in a restored 1909 building, is one of Canada's prettiest bookstores. At **Starfish Glassworks** (✉ 630 Yates St., ☎ 250/388–7827) you can watch glassblowers create original works.

VANCOUVER AND VICTORIA A TO Z

To research prices, get advice from other travelers, and book travel arrangements, visit www.fodors.com.

AIRPORTS AND TRANSFERS

Vancouver International Airport is on an island about 23 km (14 mi) south of downtown. An airport improvement fee is assessed on all flight departures: C$5 for flights within British Columbia, C$10 for flights within North America, and C$15 for overseas flights. Air Canada, Alaska Airlines, American Airlines, Canadian Airlines, Continental Airlines, and United fly into the airport. Victoria International Airport is served by Air B.C., Canadian Airlines, Horizon Air, Pacific Coastal, and WestJet Airlines. Kenmore Air Harbour offers direct daily floatplane service from Seattle to Victoria's Inner Harbour.

West Coast Air offers floatplane service between downtown Vancouver and Victoria's Inner Harbour; the 35-minute flights leave several times a day. Harbour Air also provides frequent harbor-to-harbor floatplane service. Helijet International has helicopter service from downtown Vancouver and Vancouver International Airport to downtown Seattle and downtown Victoria. The Vancouver heliport is near Vancouver's Pan Pacific Hotel.

➤ AIRPORT INFORMATION: **Vancouver International Airport** (☎ 604/276–6101, WEB www.yvr.ca). **Victoria International Airport** (☎ 250/953–7500). **Kenmore Air Harbour** (☎ 425/486–1257 or 800/543–9595, WEB www. kenmoreair.com). **West Coast Air** (☎ 604/606–6888 or 800/347–2222, WEB www.westcoastair.com). **Harbour Air** (☎ 604/688–1277 or 800/ 665–0212, WEB www.harbour-air.com). **Helijet International** (☎ 604/ 273–1414, 250/382–6222, or 800/665–4354, WEB www.helijet.com).

AIRPORT TRANSFERS

The drive from the airport to downtown Vancouver takes 20–45 minutes, depending on the time of day. Vancouver airport hotels offer shuttle service to and from the airport. Victoria International Airport is about 30 minutes from downtown Victoria. The Vancouver Airporter Service provides service to major downtown hotels from 5:23 AM until midnight for C$12 one-way, C$18 round-trip. Yellow Cab serves the whole Vancouver area; Black Top is a reliable local company. Taxi fare to downtown is about C$23. Limousine service from LimoJet Gold costs about C$34 one-way.

In Victoria the Airporter bus service drops off passengers at most major hotels. The fare is $13 one-way, $23 round-trip. Taxis are available from Empress Taxi and Victoria Taxi. The fare to downtown is about C$38.
➤ TAXIS AND SHUTTLES: **Airporter** (☎ 250/386–2525, WEB www.air-porter.travel.bc.ca). **Black Top** (☎ 604/681–2181). **Empress Taxi** (☎ 250/381–2222). **LimoJet Gold** (☎ 604/273–1331). **Vancouver Airporter Service** (☎ 604/946–8866 or 800/668–3141). **Victoria Taxi** (☎ 250/ 383–7111). **Yellow Cab** (☎ 604/681–1111).

BOAT AND FERRY TRAVEL

B.C. Ferries operates daily service between Vancouver and Victoria (1 hour, 35 minutes sailing time). The Vancouver terminal is in Tsawwassen, 38 km (24 mi) southwest of downtown. In Victoria, ferries arrive at and depart from the Swartz Bay Terminal at the end of Highway 17, 32 km (20 mi) north of downtown Victoria. Vehicle reservations on Vancouver to Victoria and Nanaimo routes are optional and cost $15 in addition to the fare. Clipper Navigation operates year-round passenger-only service between Victoria and Seattle (two–three hours sailing time) on the *Victoria Clipper.* Washington State Ferries cross daily, year-round, between Sidney, just north of Victoria, and Anacortes, Washington (three hours; one sailing a day each way). Black Ball Transport operates car ferries between Victoria and Port Angeles, Washington (1 hour, 35 minutes).

In Vancouver, the SeaBus is a 400-passenger commuter ferry that crosses Burrard Inlet from the foot of Lonsdale (North Vancouver) to downtown. The ride takes 13 minutes and costs the same as the bus (and it's much faster). With a transfer, connection can be made with any Translink bus or SkyTrain.

Aquabus Ferries connect several stations on False Creek including Science World, Granville Island, Stamp's Landing, and the Hornby Street dock. Some of the boats can also take bicycles. The company also operates two historic wooden boats on some runs and offers 45-minute False Creek tours from its Granville Island dock. False Creek Ferries offers foot passenger service between the Aquatic Centre on Beach Avenue, Granville Island, Science World, Stamps Landing, and Vanier Park. They also offer 20- and 40-minute tours of False Creek.

In Victoria, Victoria Harbour Ferries operate daily between March and October and on sunny weekends the rest of the year, making eight stops around the Inner Harbour, including the Empress Hotel and Fisherman's Wharf.

➤ BOAT AND FERRY INFORMATION: **Aquabus Ferries** (☎ 604/689–5858, WEB www.aquabus.bc.ca). **B.C. Ferries** (☎ 250/386–3431; 888/223–3779 in British Columbia outside Victoria, WEB www.bcferries.com). **Black Ball Transport** (☎ 250/386–2202; 360/457–4491 in the U.S., WEB www.northolympic.com/coho). **Clipper Navigation** (☎ 250/382–8100 in Victoria; 206/448–5000 in Seattle; 800/888–2535 elsewhere, WEB www.victoriaclipper.com). **False Creek Ferries** (☎ 604/684–7781, WEB www.granvilleislandferries.bc.ca). **Victoria Harbour Ferries** (☎ 250/708–0201, WEB www.harbourferry.com). **Washington State Ferries** (☎ 250/381–1551; 206/464–6400 in the U.S.; 888/808–7977 in WA only, WEB www.wsdot.wa.gov/ferries).

BUS TRAVEL

Vancouver's Translink system comprising buses, the SeaBus, and the SkyTrain can get you just about anywhere you need to go. Exact change (C$1.75 in Vancouver, C$2.50 to C$3.50 to the suburbs) or a FareSaver ticket (available from convenience stores) is required. Day passes, good for unlimited travel all day, cost $7. For route details, pick up the free visitor's transit guide, called *Discover Vancouver on Transit,* at the Tourist InfoCentre. B.C. Transit runs a fairly extensive service in Victoria and the surrounding areas. An all-day pass costs C$5.50. Double decker buses run on some routes.

➤ BUS INFORMATION: **B.C. Transit** (☎ 250/382–6161, WEB www.bctransit.com). **Translink** (☎ 604/521–0400, WEB www.translink.bc.ca).

CAR TRAVEL

From the south, I–5 from Seattle becomes Highway 99 at the U.S.–Canada border. Vancouver is a three-hour drive (226 km/140 mi) from Seattle. It's best to avoid border crossings during peak times such as holidays and weekends. Highway 1, the Trans-Canada Highway, enters Vancouver from the east. To avoid traffic, arrive after rush hour (8:30 AM).

Vancouver's rush-hour traffic is horrendous and starts early—about 3 PM on weekdays. The worst bottlenecks outside the city center are the

North Shore bridges, the George Massey Tunnel on Highway 99 south of Vancouver, and Highway 1 through Coquitlam and Surrey. Parking downtown is both expensive and tricky to find.

EMERGENCIES

➤ DOCTORS: **Medicentre** (✉ 1055 Dunsmuir St., lower level, Vancouver, ☎ 604/683–8138).

➤ EMERGENCY SERVICES: **Police, fire, ambulance** (☎ 911).

➤ HOSPITALS: **St. Paul's Hospital** (✉ 1081 Burrard St., Vancouver, ☎ 604/682–2344). **Victoria General Hospital** (✉ 1 Hospital Way, off Helmcken Rd., Victoria, ☎ 250/727–4212).

➤ LATE-NIGHT PHARMACIES: **London Drugs** (✉ 911 Yates St., ☎ 250/381–1113). **Shopper's Drug Mart** (✉ 1125 Davie St., ☎ 604/669–2424).

LODGING

B&BS

Garden City B&B Reservation Service can make B&B reservations in Victoria and elsewhere on Vancouver Island. Super, Natural B.C., operated by the provincial Ministry of Tourism, can reserve accommodations anywhere in B.C. Town & Country Bed and Breakfast Reservations Service books B&Bs in Vancouver and Victoria.

➤ LOCAL AGENTS: **Garden City B&B Reservation Service** (✉ 660 Jones Terr., Victoria V8Z 2L7, ☎ 250/479–1986, FAX 250/479–9999, WEB www.bc-bed-breakfast.com). **Super, Natural B.C.** (☎ 800/435–5622, WEB www.hellobc.com). **Town & Country Bed and Breakfast Reservations Service** (✉ 2803 W. 4th Ave., Box 74542, Vancouver V6K 1K2, ☎ 604/731–5942, WEB www.townandcountrybedandbreakfast.com).

TOURS

Gray Line, the largest tour operator, leads orientation tours of both cities. The Vancouver Trolley Company runs turn-of-the-20th-century-style trolleys through Vancouver on a two-hour narrated tour of the major sights including Gastown, Chinatown, Granville Island, and Stanley Park. A day pass (C$24) allows you to complete one full circuit, getting off and on as often as you like. The Pacific Wilderness Railway Company runs a 2½-hour round-trip vintage train excursion from Victoria's Pandora Street station to the top of Malahat Mountain, north of Victoria. The trip is made twice a day, early June to late September. The regular fare is $32; a first class ticket, which includes lunch, is $69. Tally-Ho Horsedrawn Tours offers a get-acquainted session with downtown Victoria that includes Beacon Hill Park. Victoria Carriage Tours has horse-drawn tours of the city.

➤ CONTACTS: **Gray Line** (☎ 604/879–3363 in Vancouver; 250/388–5248 in Victoria, WEB www.grayline.ca). **Pacific Wilderness Railway Company** (☎ 800/267–0610; 250/381–8600, WEB www.pacificwilderness-railway.com). **Tally-Ho Horsedrawn Tours** (☎ 250/383–5067, WEB www.tallyhotours.com). **Vancouver Trolley Company** (☎ 604/801–5515 or 888/451–5581, WEB www.vancouvertrolley.com). **Victoria Carriage Tours** (☎ 877/663–2207; 250/383–2207, WEB victoriacarriage.com).

TRAIN TRAVEL

In Vancouver, the Pacific Central Station is the hub for rail and bus service. From here, VIA Rail provides transcontinental service through Jasper to Toronto three times a week. Amtrak has service between Seattle; Vancouver; and Eugene, Oregon. Passenger trains leave the B.C. Rail station for Whistler and the interior of British Columbia. In Victoria, the VIA Rail station on Pandora Street provides service between Victoria, Nanaimo, and Courtenay.

Part of an effort to revive streetcar service in Vancouver, the volunteer-run Downtown Historic Railway operates two restored electric trams (built in 1905 and 1913) along a 5-km (3-mi) track between Science World and Granville Island. The trams, which also stop at First Avenue and Ontario Street and at Leg-in-Boot Square, near Sixth Avenue and Moberly Street, operate 12:30 PM–5 PM weekends and holidays from late May to early October. The adult fare is $2.

➤ TRAIN INFORMATION: **Amtrak** (☎ 800/872–7245, WEB www.amtrak.com). **B.C. Rail** (✉ 1311 W. 1st St., North Vancouver, ☎ 604/631–3500 or 800/663–8238, WEB www.bcrail.com). **Downtown Historic Railway** (☎ 604/665–3903 or 604/325–9990, WEB www.city.vancouver.bc.ca/engsvcs/streetcar). **Pacific Central Station** (✉ Main St. and Terminal Ave., near the Main St. SkyTrain station, ☎ 604/662–7575). **VIA Rail** (☎ 800/561–8630 in Canada; 800/561–3949 in the U.S., WEB www.viarail.ca).

VISITOR INFORMATION

➤ TOURIST INFORMATION: **Super, Natural B.C.** (☎ 800/435–5622, WEB www.hellobc.com). **Tourism Victoria** (✉ 812 Wharf St., V8W 1T3, ☎ 250/953–2033, FAX 250/382–6539, WEB www.tourismvictoria.com). **Vancouver Tourist InfoCentre** (✉ 200 Burrard St., ☎ 604/683–2000, FAX 604/682–6839, WEB www.tourismvancouver.com).

5 SOUTHEAST ALASKA

INCLUDING KETCHIKAN, JUNEAU, HAINES, SITKA, AND SKAGWAY

Alaska's Southeast encompasses the Inside Passage—once the traditional route to the Klondike goldfields and today the centerpiece of many Alaskan cruises. Here are densely forested islands, cliff-rimmed fjords, and spectacular Glacier Bay National Park. Juneau—said to be the nation's most scenic capital—is also here, as are fishing towns such as Petersburg and Ketchikan, which is also known for its totem-pole carving. An onion-dome cathedral accents Sitka, the onetime capital of Russian America.

By Mike Miller

Updated by
Don Pitcher

S OUTHEAST ALASKA STRETCHES BELOW THE STATE like the tail of a kite. It is a world of massive glaciers, fjords, and snowcapped peaks. The largest concentration of coastal glaciers on earth can be viewed at Glacier Bay National Park and Preserve, one of the region's most prized attractions. Lush stands of spruce, hemlock, and cedar blanket thousands of islands. Bays, coves, lakes of all sizes, and swift, icy rivers provide some of the continent's best fishing grounds—and scenery as majestic and unspoiled as any in North America. Many of Southeast Alaska's wildest and most pristine landscapes are within Tongass National Forest, which encompasses nearly 17 million acres—or almost three-quarters of the Panhandle's land.

Like anywhere else, the Southeast has its drawbacks. For one thing, it rains a lot. If you plan to spend a week or more here, you can count on showers during at least a few of those days. Die-hard southeasterners simply throw on a slicker and rubber boots and shrug off the rain. Their attitude is philosophical: without the rain, there would be no forests; no lakes; no streams running with world-class salmon and trout; and no healthy populations of brown and black bears, moose, deer, mountain goats, and wolves. Locals also know that the rain keeps people from moving in; without it in such profusion Southeast Alaska would probably look more like Seattle.

Another disadvantage—or advantage, depending on your point of view—is an almost total lack of connecting roads between the area's communities. To fill this void, Alaskans created the Marine Highway System of passenger and vehicle ferries that have staterooms; observation decks; cafeterias; cocktail lounges; and heated, glass-enclosed solariums.

The Southeast's natural beauty and abundance of wildlife have made it one of the world's fastest-growing cruise destinations. About 20 big cruise ships ply the Inside Passage during the height of the summer. Regular air service to the Southeast is available from the Lower 48 states and other parts of Alaska.

The Native peoples you'll meet in the Southeast coastal region are Tlingit, Haida, and Tsimshian. These peoples, like their coastal neighbors in British Columbia, preserve a culture rich in totemic art forms, including deeply carved poles, masks, baskets, and ceremonial objects. Many live among non-Natives in modern towns and continue their own traditions.

A pioneer spirit dominates the towns of Southeast Alaska. Residents—some from other states, some with roots in the "old country," some who can trace their ancestors back to the gold-rush days, and some whose ancestors came over the Bering Land Bridge from Asia thousands of years ago—are an adventurous lot. The rough-and-tumble spirit of the Southeast often combines with a worldly sophistication: those who fish are also artists, Forest Service workers may run a bed-and-breakfast on the side, and homemakers may be Native dance performers.

Pleasures and Pastimes

Ferry-Hopping
The **Alaska Marine Highway** (☎ 907/465–3941 or 800/642–0066, FAX 907/277–4829, WEB www.dot.state.ak.us/ferry) is the primary means of transportation along the Inside Passage, with service to most towns on a daily basis. Most northbound travelers hop aboard the ferry in Bellingham, Washington, or Prince Rupert, British Columbia. Ferries

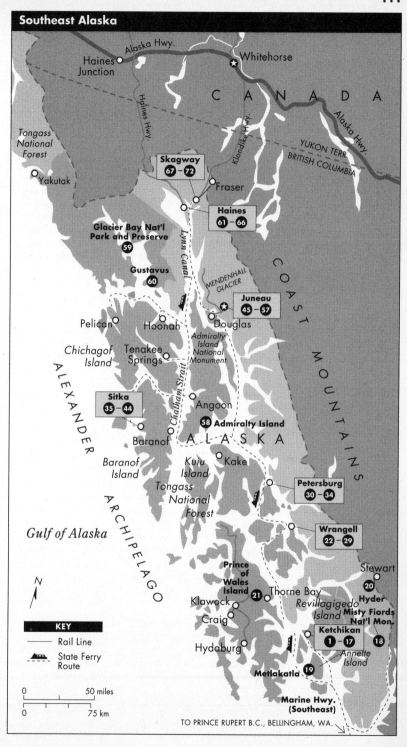

Southeast Alaska

can transport vehicles of all sizes, but reservations are necessary, especially out of Bellingham.

Fishing

Southeast Alaska is an angler's paradise. You'll find salmon and halibut charter boats, fishing lodges (some near the larger communities, others remote and accessible only by floatplane), fly-in mountain-lake lodges where the fishing is for trout and char, and—bargain hunters take special note—more than 150 remote but weather-tight cabins operated by the U.S. Forest Service.

Hiking and Backpacking

Trekking woods, mountains, and beaches is Southeast Alaska's unofficial regional sport. Some of the trails are abandoned mining and logging roads. Others are natural routes—in some sections, even game trails—meandering over ridges, through forests, and alongside streams and glaciers. A few—most notably the Chilkoot Trail out of Skagway—offer historical significance along with grand scenery. The Alaska Division of Parks Southeast regional office in Juneau will send you a list of state-maintained trails and parks in the Panhandle; local visitor bureaus and recreation departments can also help.

Shopping

Southeast Alaska has an abundance of fine artists and artisans, and most towns have galleries exhibiting their works. Tlingit and Haida handicrafts include totem poles of all sizes, wooden masks, paddles, bentwood boxes, and button blankets. You'll find these items at gift shops up and down the coast. If you want to be sure of authenticity, buy items tagged with the state-approved AUTHENTIC NATIVE HANDICRAFT FROM ALASKA label. Virtually every community has at least one canning and/or smoking operation that packs and ships local seafood, smoked and canned salmon included.

Tongass National Forest

The country's largest national forest, the Tongass, (✉ 50 Main St., Ketchikan 99901, ☎ 907/228–6220, WEB www.fs.fed.us/r10/tongass) stretches the length of Alaska's Panhandle and encompasses nearly 17 million acres, or three-fourths of the Southeast region. Old-growth, temperate rain forest covers much of the area, which includes rugged mountains, steep fjords, glaciers, and ice fields within its boundaries. Its lands and waters teem with a wide variety of animals: black and brown bears, bald eagles, Sitka black-tailed deer, mountain goats, wolves, marine mammals, and dozens of sea- and shorebird species. Two national monuments, Admiralty Island near Juneau and Misty Fiords near Ketchikan, are within its borders.

Exploring Southeast Alaska

The Southeast Panhandle stretches some 500 mi from Yakutat at its northernmost point to Ketchikan and Metlakatla at its southern end. At its widest the region measures only 140 mi, and in the upper Panhandle just south of Yakutat, it's a skinny 30 mi across. Most of the Panhandle consists of a sliver of mainland buffered by islands.

More than 1,000 islands line the Inside Passage—most of them mountainous with lush covers of timber (though large clear-cuts are also common). Collectively they constitute the Alexander Archipelago. Most communities are on islands rather than on the mainland. The principal exceptions are Juneau, Haines, and Skagway, plus the hamlets of Gustavus and Hyder. Island outposts include Ketchikan, Wrangell, Petersburg, Sitka, and the villages of Craig, Pelican, Metlakatla, Kake,

Angoon, and Hoonah. Bordering Alaska just east of the Panhandle lies the Canadian province of British Columbia.

You can get to and around Southeast Alaska by ship or by plane, but forget arriving by car or RV unless your destination is Haines, Skagway, or Hyder, which are connected by road to the Alaska Highway. Elsewhere in the Southeast, the roadways typically run just a few miles out from towns and villages; then they dead-end. (If you wish to drive up the Alaska Highway and then visit road-isolated communities, you can reserve vehicle space on Alaska's state ferries.)

Numbers in the text correspond to numbers in the margin and on the Ketchikan, Wrangell, Petersburg, Sitka, Juneau, Glacier Bay Park and Preserve, Haines, and Skagway maps.

Great Itineraries

Like all of Alaska's regions, the Southeast covers a vast area (even though it represents a thin slice of the state), and most of its communities, as well as its parks, national forest lands, and other wildlands, are accessible only by boat or plane. You should therefore allow yourself at least a week here. If you have only a few days, it might be best to fly into one of Southeast Alaska's larger communities—such as Juneau, Sitka, or Ketchikan—and then take a state ferry to one or two nearby Panhandle communities. Or fly to a remote destination. Most visitors explore the Inside Passage on cruise ships, which generate their own schedules. But plenty of adventures await ambitious independent travelers who plan ahead and ride state ferries instead of cruise ships.

IF YOU HAVE 5 DAYS

Spend two or three days in **Juneau** 45–57. Go south via the state ferry to **Sitka** 35–44, ancestral home of the Tlingit and once the capital of Russian America. Spend the next two days exploring this town and nearby sights, possibly taking in a performance by Russian-style dancers at Centennial Hall. Active travelers can go sea kayaking, hiking, fishing, and wildlife cruising. Instead of going south from Juneau, another option is to travel northwest to **Gustavus** 60 and nearby **Glacier Bay National Park and Preserve** 59, one of America's premier parklands, where tidewater glaciers, rugged mountain scenery, and abundant marine wildlife await.

IF YOU HAVE 7 DAYS

Many cruises to Southeast Alaska last seven days, and a week is also sufficient time for independent travelers to see at least a cross section of the region by traveling aboard state ferries and aircraft. Starting at **Ketchikan** 1–17, known for its totem poles, the Alaska Marine Highway regularly makes stops at all of the region's larger communities: **Wrangell** 22–29, with its ancient petroglyphs; **Petersburg** 30–34, which has a strong Norwegian influence; **Sitka** 35–44, former capital of Russian America; **Juneau** 45–57, the state capital; **Haines** 61–66, known for its bald eagles and Native dance troupe; and **Skagway** 67–71, a gold rush–era throwback. It also serves several smaller communities such as **Kake, Angoon, Tenakee Springs,** and **Hoonah.** Give yourself time to see local sights and visit one or more out-of-town destinations, such as **Admiralty Island** 58, **Glacier Bay National Park and Preserve** 59, **Misty Fiords National Monument** 18, **Hyder** 20, or **Prince of Wales Island** 21.

When to Tour Southeast Alaska

The best time to visit is from May through September, when the weather is mildest, rain is less frequent, daylight hours are longest, wildlife is most abundant, the fishing is best, and festivals and tourist-oriented activities are in full swing.

Fodor's Choice

No two people will agree on what makes a perfect vacation, but here are some of our Southeast favorites for starters. Each of these is detailed later in this chapter.

Uniquely Alaska

★ **Alaska Chilkat Bald Eagle Preserve.** Each fall and winter, several thousand bald eagles gather in Southeast Alaska's Chilkat Valley near Haines to feed on chum salmon, making this the largest gathering of eagles anywhere in the world.

★ **Ketchikan totem poles.** These enduring symbols of Native life are all over the Ketchikan area, from the 200-year-old collection at the Totem Heritage Center to dozens of more recently carved poles in Saxman and Totem Bight.

★ **Sitka National Historical Park.** This peaceful and scenic park celebrates Sitka's rich Russian and Native heritages, with a historic Russian building and colorful totem poles.

★ **White Pass & Yukon Route Railroad.** One of America's most famous historic rail routes departs from Skagway and parallels the White Pass Trail used by gold miners in 1898. Period railcars and old steam engines add to the charm.

Taste Treats

★ **Alaskan Amber.** Brewed in Juneau by the Alaskan Brewing and Bottling Company and served statewide, this beer deserves its widespread praise and numerous awards.

Dining

★ **Gustavus Inn.** The owners of this tranquil country inn just a few miles from Glacier Bay National Park pride themselves on artfully prepared seafood, salads from the organic garden, and homemade desserts. $$$$

★ **The Fiddlehead.** One of Juneau's favorite restaurants, this is a delightful place adorned with light woods, gently patterned wallpaper, stained glass, and historic photos. The food is healthy, generously served, and eclectic. $$–$$$$

★ **Salmon Bake.** In Juneau, the salmon bake—an Alaskan tradition—is perfected at Gold Creek Salmon Bake and Thane Ore House. $$

After Hours

★ **Red Dog Saloon.** Juneau's favorite watering hole brings back the raucous days of the gold rush—especially when cruise ships are in town.

★ **Red Onion Saloon.** In this 1898 Skagway landmark, bartenders dressed in period costume serve patrons at the original mahogany bar where "Soapy" Smith might have sat.

Lodging

★ **Thayer Lake Lodge.** One of the Southeast's pioneer lodges, Thayer Lake provides rustic comfort in the midst of coastal rain forest on private land within Admiralty Island National Monument. $$$$

★ **Waterfall Resort.** This upscale wilderness fishing lodge occupies an old salmon cannery on Prince of Wales Island. Bountiful meals, personal service, luxurious accommodations, and great fishing attract business executives. $$$$

★ **Golden North Hotel.** Built in 1898 in the heyday of Skagway's gold rush, this is Alaska's most historic hotel. The interior has been lovingly restored with Victorian-era furnishings, and a downstairs brew pub attracts a crowd most evenings. $$–$$$

New and Noteworthy
In Skagway, the historic City Hall has recently undergone a major face-lift, and a similarly styled building has been added behind—the **Trail of '98 Museum**. In Juneau, the opulent **Garside House B&B** opened in 2001, with a fine hilltop location and luxurious accommodations.

KETCHIKAN

Ketchikan, which has more totem poles than anywhere else in the world, is perched on a large island at the foot of Deer Mountain (3,000 ft). The site at the mouth of Ketchikan Creek was a summer fish camp of the Tlingit until white miners and fishermen came to settle the town in 1885. Gold discoveries just before the turn of the 20th century brought more immigrants, and valuable timber and commercial-fishing resources spurred new industries. By the 1930s the town bragged it was the "salmon-canning capital of the world." You will still find some of the Southeast's best salmon fishing here.

Exploring Ketchikan

You can see a lot on foot in Ketchikan's compact downtown. For many travelers, the town offers the first taste of Alaska. If this is true for you, you will not be disappointed. Ketchikan rises steeply from the busy fishing docks, with staircases climbing to hillside homes. Downtown's favorite stops include the Spruce Mill Development shops and Creek Street. A bit farther away you'll find the Totem Heritage Center and Deer Mountain Hatchery. Out of town (but included on most bus tours) are two longtime favorites: Totem Bight State Historical Park and Saxman Native Village.

On the highway in either direction, you won't go far before you run out of road. The North Tongass Highway ends about 18 mi from downtown, at Settler's Cove Campground. The South Tongass Highway terminates at a power plant about 8 mi from town. Side roads soon end at campgrounds and at trailheads, viewing points, lakes, boat-launching ramps, and private property.

A Good Walk
The best place to begin a walking tour of Ketchikan is from the helpful **Ketchikan Visitors Bureau** ①. Just a few steps up Mill Street is the **Spruce Mill Development** ②, filled with shops and restaurants. Next door, learn about Southeast Alaska's wild places at the **Southeast Alaska Discovery Center** ③. Continue up Mill Street past minuscule **Whale Park** ④, with its Chief Kyan totem pole, and turn right on Stedman Street. Cross the bridge to **Thomas Street** ⑤, overlooking a busy boat harbor. Continue walking along Stedman to the *Return of the Eagle* ⑥ mural before turning left on Deermont Street. Follow it uphill several blocks to the **Totem Heritage Center** ⑦ and its collection of ancient totem poles. Just across the footbridge are **Deer Mountain Hatchery** ⑧ and **City Park** ⑨. From here, Park Avenue runs parallel to Ketchikan Creek, heading downhill to the fish ladder and Salmon Carving next to **Salmon Falls** ⑩. Look uphill to see the historic **Grant Street Trestle** ⑪; it's about a 20-minute walk down Park Avenue, or you can call a cab from the hatchery.

From the fish ladder, a boardwalk path parallels Ketchikan Creek and leads to the infamous **Creek Street** ⑫. For a side trip, take the short funicular ($2) to **WestCoast Cape Fox Lodge** ⑬ and back before continuing down Creek Street boardwalk to **Dolly's House** ⑭. Retrace your steps up the boardwalk and cross the **Creek Street Footbridge** ⑮, where you can watch salmon heading upstream in the summer. In front of you is the Chief Johnson Totem Pole, carved in 1989, and just to

116

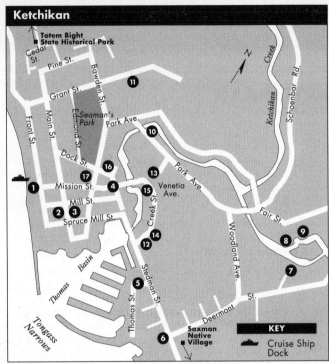

your right is the **Tongass Historical Museum** ⑯, with interesting relics from the early days of mining and fishing. Turn left on Bawden Street to pass historic **St. John's Church** ⑰.

TIMING

This walking tour should take around two or three hours, stops included. If you are looking for an easier and shorter version (approximately one hour), omit the leg of the walk that leads to Totem Heritage Center, Deer Mountain Hatchery, and City Park. (Local bus tours typically include these sights as well as Totem Bight State Historical Park and Saxman Native Village.)

Sights to See

⑨ City Park. The Deer Mountain Hatchery and Heritage Center lead into this small park, which has picnic tables and paved paths and is bisected by Ketchikan Creek. ✉ *Park and Fair Sts.*

⑫ Creek Street. Ketchikan's infamous red-light district once existed here. Today the small, colorful houses, built on stilts over the creek waters, have been restored as trendy shops.

⑮ Creek Street Footbridge. Stand over Ketchikan Creek for good salmon viewing when the fish are running in midsummer.

⑧ Deer Mountain Hatchery. Tens of thousands of salmon are annually dispersed into local waters at the hatchery on Park Avenue. The hatchery, owned by the Ketchikan Indian Corporation, has exhibits on traditional Native fishing and gives guided tours. The hatchery is also a good place to see and photograph bald eagles up close. ✉ *429 Deermount St.,* ☎ *907/225–5158.* ▭ *$6.* ☉ *Mid-May–Sept., daily 8:30–4:30.*

⑭ Dolly's House. Creek Street's most famous brothel has been preserved as a museum, complete with furnishings, beds, and a short history of the life and times of Ketchikan's best-known madam. ⊠ *Creek St.,* ☎ *907/225–6329.* 🎫 *$4.* ⊗ *Open daily whenever cruise ships are in port.*

⓫ Grant Street Trestle. At one time virtually all of Ketchikan's walkways and streets were made from wooden trestles, but now only one remains, constructed in 1908.

❶ Ketchikan Visitors Bureau. The helpful visitors bureau is right next to the cruise-ship docks. A third of its space is occupied by day-tour, flight-seeing, and boat-tour operators. ⊠ *131 Front St., 99901,* ☎ *907/225–6166 or 800/770–3300.* ⊗ *May–Sept., daily 7–5 ('til 6 PM when cruise ships are docked); Oct.–Apr., weekdays 8–5.*

❻ *Return of the Eagle.* Twenty-one Native students created this colorful mural on a wall of the Robertson Building on the Ketchikan campus of the University of Alaska–Southeast. ⊠ *Stedman St.*

⓱ St. John's Church. Built in 1903, this church is the oldest remaining house of worship in Ketchikan. Its interior is formed from red cedar cut in the Native-operated sawmill in nearby Saxman. ⊠ *Bawden St.*

❿ Salmon Falls. Get out your camera and set it for fast speed at the falls, fish ladder, and wooden Salmon Carving, just off Park Avenue on Married Man's Trail. When the salmon start running in midsummer, thousands leap the falls (or take the easier fish ladder route) to spawn in Ketchikan Creek's waters farther upstream. Many can also be seen in the creek below the falls. ⊠ *Married Man's Trail, off Park Ave.*

👋 **❸ Southeast Alaska Discovery Center.** Museum-quality exhibits, including one on the rain forest, focus on the resources, Native cultures, and ecosystems of Southeast Alaska at this impressive visitor center. The U.S. Forest Service and other federal agencies provide information on Alaska's public lands. Especially helpful for independent travelers is the inviting "trip-planning room," where you can relax on Mission-style furniture while consulting books, maps, and videos about the sights in Ketchikan and the Southeast. The multimedia show "Mystical Southeast Alaska" is shown every half hour during the summer in the center's theater. ⊠ *50 Main St.,* ☎ *907/228–6220.* 🎫 *$4 May–Sept., free Oct.–Apr.* ⊗ *May–Sept., daily 8:30–4:30; Oct.–Apr., Tues.–Sat. 8:30–4:30.*

❷ Spruce Mill Development. The attractive Mill Street complex is modeled after 1920s-style cannery architecture. Spread over 6½ acres along the waterfront, five buildings contain a mix of retail stores, souvenir shops, galleries, and restaurants. Cruise ships moor just a few steps away, filling the shops with tourists all summer long. ⊠ *Spruce Mill and Front Sts.*

❺ Thomas Street. From this street you can see Thomas Basin, one of four harbors in Ketchikan and home port to a variety of pleasure and commercial-fishing boats.

⓰ Tongass Historical Museum. Native artifacts and pioneer relics revisit the mining and fishing eras at this small museum in the same building as the library. Exhibits include a big and brilliantly polished lens from Tree Point Lighthouse and the bullet-riddled skull of a notorious brown bear called Old Groaner. Other exhibits change periodically, but always include Tlingit Native items. ⊠ *629 Dock St.,* ☎ *907/225–5600.* 🎫 *$2.* ⊗ *May 15–Sept., daily 8–5; Oct.–May 14, Wed.–Fri. 1–5, weekends 1–4.*

★ **❼ Totem Heritage Center.** You can get a close-up view at this rare collection of authentic Native totems dating from almost two centuries ago. You can also watch a video about the preservation efforts and take a guided tour. Outside are several more recently carved poles. ⊠ *Deermount St.*, ☎ *907/225–5900.* ☞ *$4.* ☉ *May–Sept., daily 8–5; Oct.–Apr., weekdays 1–5.*

⓭ **WestCoast Cape Fox Lodge.** For a stunning view of the harbor and fine dining, walk to the top of steep Venetia Avenue or take the funicular ($2) ride up from Creek Street. ⊠ *800 Venetia Way,* ☎ *907/225–8001 or 800/426–0670,* WEB *www.westcoasthotels.com.*

❹ **Whale Park.** This park, catercorner from St. John's Church, is the site of the **Chief Kyan Totem Pole.** Just up the street is the **Chief Johnson Totem Pole,** raised in 1989 and a replica of the 1901 totem on the same site.

OFF THE
BEATEN PATH

TOTEM BIGHT STATE HISTORICAL PARK – The poles at Ketchikan's two most famous totem pole parks (the other is at Saxman Native Village) are, for the most part, 60-year-old replicas of older totem poles brought in from outlying villages as part of a federal works–cultural project during the late 1930s. Totem Bight has many totem poles and a hand-hewn Native tribal house and sits on a scenic spit of land facing the waters of Tongass Narrows. The clan house here is open daily in the summer. Most bus tours of Ketchikan include Totem Bight in their itinerary, but there is no public transportation to the site. ⊠ *N. Tongass Hwy., 10 mi north of town,* ☎ *907/247–8574.*

SAXMAN NATIVE VILLAGE – A 2½-mi paved walking path–bike trail parallels the road from Ketchikan to the village of Saxman, named for a missionary who helped Native Alaskans settle here before 1900. A totem park dominates the center of Saxman, with poles moved here in the 1930s from abandoned village sites. Saxman's Beaver Clan tribal house is said to be the largest in the world. Carvers create totem poles and totemic art objects in the adjacent carver's shed (free and open whenever the carvers are working), and a theater hosts a multimedia presentation that tells the story of Southeast Alaska's Native peoples. You can see the totem park if you walk or drive out on your own, but to visit the tribal house and theater you must take a tour. ⊠ *S. Tongass Hwy., 2 mi south of town,* ☎ *907/225–4846,* WEB *www.capefoxtours.com.*

Dining and Lodging

$$$–$$$$ ✕ **Salmon Falls Resort.** This huge, octagonal restaurant is a half-hour drive from town, but the local seafood and steaks make the trip more than worthwhile. The restaurant is built of pine logs, and at the center of the dining room, a 40-ft section of 48-inch pipe manufactured to be part of the Alaska pipeline rises to support the roof. The dining area overlooks the waters of Clover Passage, where sunsets can be vivid red. Specialties include blackened salmon and prawns stuffed with crabmeat. ⊠ *Mile 17, N. Tongass Hwy., 99901,* ☎ *907/225–2752; 800/247–9059 outside Alaska,* WEB *www.salmonfallsresort.net. AE, MC, V. Closed Oct.–Apr.*

$$–$$$$ ✕ **Steamers.** Anchoring Ketchikan's Spruce Mill Mall, this lively and
★ spacious restaurant has an extensive menu of fresh seafood, pasta, and steaks. Vegetarian choices are also available, and the servings are certain to fill you up. Try the captain's platter: salmon, halibut, prawns, and scallops cooked any way you like. The back bar pours 19 draught beers (including a number of Alaskan brews), along with a substantial wine list and 300 different liquors. Tall windows face Ketchikan's busy waterfront, where cruise ships and floatplanes vie for your attention. Occasional live acts add to the fun at this noisy eatery. ⊠ *76 Front St.,* ☎ *907/225–1600,* FAX *907/225–9420. AE, D, DC, MC, V.*

$–$$$$ ✕ **Annabelle's Keg and Chowder House.** Inside the historic Gilmore Hotel, this Victorian-style restaurant serves a tempting choice of seafood and pastas including daily specials, five kinds of chowder, and steamer clams. Prime rib on Friday and Saturday evenings is a popular favorite, and an espresso bar and semiformal lounge with a jukebox add a friendly ambience. ✉ *326 Front St.,* ☎ *907/225–6009,* ℻ *907/225–7442. AE, D, MC, V.*

$$$$ ⌂ **The Landing.** This Best Western property is named for the state ferry landing directly across the road. Decor is modern, with standard motel furnishings. The small lobby has a fireplace and Mission-style furniture. All rooms have microwaves and refrigerators. The Landing Restaurant is always packed with a hungry breakfast clientele and with families. Upstairs, Jeremiah's Fine Food and Spirits offers fine dining in cozy digs and a relaxing no-smoking lounge built around a stone fireplace. ✉ *3434 Tongass Ave., 99901,* ☎ *907/225–5166 or 800/428–8304,* ℻ *907/225–6900,* 🌐 *www.bestwestern.com. 76 rooms. 2 restaurants, café, gym, airport shuttle. AE, D, DC, MC, V.*

$$$$ ⌂ **The Narrows Inn.** Four miles from town, the Narrows is a modern lodge with a delicious on-the-premises steak and seafood restaurant and a waterfront bar. The rustic, natural wood trim and themed prints on the walls brighten the small hotel rooms. Waterside rooms have balconies overlooking Tongass Narrows—a good place to watch seals, otters, and eagles. The inn added three larger executive rooms with king beds, honor bars, and microwaves in 2001. They also operate a van with scheduled runs into Ketchikan for dining and shopping. ✉ *Box 8296, 99901,* ☎ *907/247–2600 or 888/686–2600,* ℻ *907/247–2602,* 🌐 *www.narrowsinn.com. 47 rooms. AE, D, MC, V.*

$$$$ ⌂ **WestCoast Cape Fox Lodge.** One of Ketchikan's poshest properties offers scenic views of the town and harbor from 135 ft above the village. An open lobby with a roaring fire, Tlingit and Haida artifacts, and a grand piano make for a cozy, luxurious setting. Spacious rooms include Shaker-style furnishings, the traditional Tlingit tribal colors (red, black, and white), and watercolors of Native Alaskan birds. All rooms have views of either Tongass Narrows or Deer Mountain (and the parking lot). Heen Kahidi Restaurant at the Cape Fox serves seafood, pasta, chicken, steaks, and a big Sunday brunch buffet ($15). Be sure to reserve one of the window tables that overlook Ketchikan. ✉ *800 Venetia Way, 99901,* ☎ *907/225–8001; 866/225–8001 for reservations;* ℻ *907/225–8286,* 🌐 *www.westcoasthotels.com. 70 rooms, 2 suites. Restaurant, lobby lounge, no-smoking rooms, room service, meeting room. AE, D, DC, MC, V.*

$$$–$$$$ ⌂ **Cedars Lodge.** Nothing in the plain, square exterior of this hotel or in its spartan lobby hints at the deluxe accommodations within. Two of the guest rooms are split-level with circular stairways, and many rooms have a full kitchen and whirlpool bath. Windows are large and some open up with a view of the busy water and air traffic in Tongass Narrows. Simple American fare is served at a buffet dinner and breakfast (summers only, and open to the public). A wide variety of fishing and lodging packages are available. The most popular option includes four nights' lodging and three days of fishing for $1,508–$1,718 per person. These rates include airport shuttle, lodging, guided fishing and processing, and meals. Lodging-only rates are available if space is available. ✉ *1471 Tongass Ave., Box 8331, 99901,* ☎ *907/225–1900 or 800/813–4363,* ℻ *907/225–8604,* 🌐 *www.cedarslodge.com. 13 rooms. Restaurant, room service, fishing. AE, D, DC, MC, V.*

$$–$$$ ⌂ **Gilmore Hotel.** The Gilmore has a European feel, and because of such features as a 1930s-style lobby, it's on the National Register of Historic Places. Apart from some welcome modern touches, no elevator

exists in this three-story building, and the rooms are quite small. All the same, everything is well maintained, and courtesy van service is offered. Annabelle's Keg and Chowder House serves seafood, pasta, and prime rib. ⊠ *326 Front St., 99901,* ☎ *907/225–9423 or 800/275–9423,* FAX *907/225–7442,* WEB *www.gilmorehotel.com. 38 rooms, 2 suites. Restaurant, bar, café. AE, D, DC, MC, V.*

Guided Tours

Owned by Goldbelt Native corporation, **Alaska Cruises** (☎ 907/225–6044 or 800/228–1905, FAX 907/225–8636, WEB www.goldbelttours.com) runs harbor tours of the Ketchikan waterfront and also provides speedy catamaran excursions from downtown Ketchikan to Misty Fiords National Monument. A Native Alaskan company, **Cape Fox Tours** (☎ 907/225–4846, FAX 907/225–3137, WEB www.capefoxtours.com) leads tours of Saxman Native Village and the historic George Inlet Cannery. You can book most of these tours aboard the cruise ships or at Ketchikan Visitors Bureau.

Nightlife and the Arts

Bars

Ketchikan is a party town, so you won't have any trouble finding something going on at several downtown bars. Drop by **Ketchikan Brewing Company** (⊠ 607 Mission St., ☎ 907/247–5221) for free samples of its Gateway Golden, Deer Mountain Amber, Black Bear Porter, and Spruce Tip Ale (yes, it is flavored with spruce tips). Most Ketchikan bars offer them on draft. **First City Saloon** (⊠ 830 Water St., ☎ 907/225–1494) is the main dance spot, with live rock, blues, or jazz Wednesday–Saturday. **Pioneer Bar** (⊠ 122 Front St., ☎ 907/225–3210) delivers a countrified mix of rock and country and western on weekends.

Outdoor Activities and Sports

Fishing

Sportfishing for salmon and trout is excellent in the Ketchikan area, in either saltwater or freshwater lakes and streams. Contact the **Ketchikan Visitors Bureau** for information on guide services and locations.

Spectator Sports

The Great Alaskan Lumberjack Show. Begun in 2000, this 90-minute lumberjack contest provides a taste of old-time woodsman skills, including ax throwing, bucksawing, springboard chopping, logrolling duels, and a 50-ft tree climb that ends in a free fall. Shows take place in a covered grandstand directly behind the Spruce Mill Development and go on rain or shine all summer. ⊠ *50 Main St.,* ☎ *907/225–9050 or 800/320–9049,* WEB *www.lumberjackshow.com.* ⊡ *$29.* ☉ *May–Sept., 3 times daily; hrs vary.*

Hiking

If you're an avid hiker, the 3-mi trail from downtown to the top of **Deer Mountain** will repay your efforts with a spectacular panorama of the city below and the wilderness behind. The trail begins at the corner of Fair and Deermount streets. **Ward Cove Recreation Area,** about 6 mi north of town, provides easier hiking next to lakes and streams and beneath towering spruce and hemlock trees; it also has several designated picnic spots.

Scuba Diving

Alaska Diving Service (⊠ 4845 N. Tongass Ave., ☎ 907/225–4667) rents tanks and equipment and guides you to the best places to dive.

Sea Kayaking

Locals and visitors alike enjoy paddling around the nearby protected waters, especially those in Misty Fiords National Monument. **Southeast Exposure** (☎ 907/225–8829 in summer, WEB www.southeastexposure.com) rents canoes and kayaks, gives kayaking classes, and guides trips. **Southeast Sea Kayaks** (☎ 907/225–1258 or 800/287–1607) leads kayak tours of Ketchikan's historic waterfront and provides kayak lessons and rentals.

Shopping

Art Galleries

AlaskaMade Gallery (✉ 123 Stedman St., ☎ 907/225–5404, WEB www.alaskamade.com) is a small creekside gallery with art, ulus, cards, gifts, and even Alaskan-roasted coffees.

Scanlon Gallery (✉ 318 Mission St., ☎ 907/247–4730 or 800/690–4730) displays prints from a number of well-known Alaska artists, including Byron Birdsall, Rie Muñoz, John Fehringer, Barbara Lavalle, and Jon Van Zyle.

Design, art, and clothing converge in the stylish **Soho Coho Contemporary Art and Craft Gallery** (✉ 5 Creek St., ☎ 907/225–5954 or 800/888–4070, WEB www.trollart.com), where you'll find an eclectic collection of art and T-shirts featuring the work of owner Ray Troll—best known for his wacky fish art—as well as that of other Southeast Alaskan artists.

Books

Upstairs from the Soho Coho Gallery, **Parnassus** (✉ 5 Creek St., ☎ 907/225–7690) is a book lover's bookstore with many Alaskan titles and a knowledgeable staff.

Seafood

For some of the Southeast's best canned, smoked, or frozen salmon and halibut, along with crab, clams, and all kinds of other seafood, try either of the two locations of **Salmon Etc.** (✉ 10 Creek St., ☎ 907/225–6008; 800/354–7256 outside Alaska; ✉ 322 Mission St., ☎ 907/225–6008, WEB www.salmonetc.com).

AROUND KETCHIKAN

Misty Fiords National Monument

18 *40 mi east of Ketchikan by air.*

Misty Fiords National Monument is a wilderness of cliff-faced fjords (or fiords if you follow the monument's spelling), mountains, and islands with an abundance of spectacular coastal scenery, wildlife, and recreational opportunities. Small boats enable close-up views of breathtaking vistas. Travel on these waters can be an almost mystical experience, with the greens of the forest reflected in waters as still as black mirrors. You may find yourself in the company of a whale, see a bear fishing for salmon along the shore, or even pull in your own salmon for an evening meal. Note, however, that the name Misty refers to the weather you're likely to encounter in this rainy part of Alaska. ✉ *3031 Tongass Ave., Ketchikan 99901,* ☎ *907/225–2148.*

Metlakatla

19 *12 mi south of Ketchikan.*

The village of Metlakatla is on Annette Island, just a dozen miles from busy Ketchikan but a world away culturally. A visit to this quiet and conservative place offers the chance to learn about life in a small Inside Passage Native community. Local taxis can take visitors to other sights around the island, including Yellow Hill and the old Air Force Base.

In most Southeast Native villages, the people are Tlingit or Haida in heritage. Metlakatla is the exception; here most folks are Tsimshian. They moved to the island from British Columbia in 1887, led by William Duncan, an Anglican missionary from England. The new town grew rapidly and soon included dozens of buildings laid out on a grid of streets—a cannery, a sawmill, and a church that could seat a thousand people. Congress declared Annette Island a federal Indian reservation in 1891, and it remains the only reservation in Alaska today. Father Duncan continued to control life in Metlakatla for decades, until the government finally stepped in shortly before his death in 1918.

During World War II the U.S. Army built a major **Air Force Base** 7 mi from Metlakatla that included observation towers for Japanese subs, airplane hangars, gun emplacements, and housing for 10,000 soldiers. After the war, it served as Ketchikan's airport for many years, but today the long runways are virtually abandoned save for a few private flights.

Metlakatla's religious heritage still shows through today. The clapboard **William Duncan Memorial Church,** topped with two steeples, burned in 1948 but was rebuilt several years later. It is one of nine churches in tiny Metlakatla. **Father Duncan's Cottage** is maintained as it was when he was alive and includes numerous artifacts, personal items, and historic photographs. ⊠ *Corner of 4th Ave. and Church St.,* ☎ *907/886–4441 or 888/886–8687.* ⊘ *When cruise ships are in port or by appointment.*

Father Duncan worked hard to eliminate traditional Tsimshian beliefs and dances, so he would probably not approve of recent efforts to re-learn the old ways. Today the people of Metlakatla proudly perform these old dances and stories. The best place to see this is at the traditional **longhouse,** which faces Metlakatla's boat harbor. Three totem poles stand on the back side of the building, and the front is covered with a Tsimshian design. Inside are displays of Native crafts and a model of the fish traps that were once common throughout the Inside Passage. Native dance groups perform here on Wednesday and Friday in summer. Just down from the longhouse is an **Artists' Village** where booths display locally made arts and crafts. ☎ *907/886–8688.* ⊘ *May–mid-Sept., Wed. 7–noon, Fri. 3–7:30.*

Two miles from town is a boardwalk path that leads up the 540-ft **Yellow Hill.** Distinctive yellow sandstone rocks and panoramic vistas make this a worthwhile detour on clear days.

Dining and Lodging

$$–$$$$ ✕ **Uncle Fred's Cafe.** Across from the Tsimshian longhouse, Uncle Fred's serves the best meals in town. Its menu includes burgers, fresh fish, hand-cut fries, fresh-baked breads and pies, homemade soups, and daily specials. Be sure to save room for a slice of their homemade cheesecake. ⊠ *Across from Longhouse,* ☎ *907/886–5007. No credit cards. Closed Sun.–Mon. No breakfast.*

$$–$$$$ ⊞ **Metlakatla Hotel and Suites.** This two-story building offers both standard motel accommodations and three spacious apartments with full kitchens and one or two bedrooms. All rooms include private baths, TVs, and VCRs, and two have Internet hookups. Private decks have been added to the upstairs rooms. Reasonably priced and filling family-style breakfasts and dinners ($10) are served. ⊠ *3rd Ave. and Lower Milton St., 99926,* ☎ *907/886–3456,* FAX *907/886–3455. 8 rooms, 3 apartments. Dining room. AE, D, MC, V.*

Guided Tours

Run by the Metlakatla Indian community, **Metlakatla Tours** (☎ 907/886–4441 or 877/886–8687) leads a variety of local tours in the summer, including one with a dance performance, a visit to the cannery, and a salmon bake. **ProMech Air** (☎ 907/886–3845 or 907/225–3845) has scheduled floatplane flights between Ketchikan and Metlakatla. You can catch a ferry operated by the **Alaska Marine Highway System** to Metlakatla from Ketchikan.

Hyder

 90 mi northeast of Ketchikan.

The tiny town of Hyder sits at the head of narrow Portland Canal, a 70-mi-long fjord northeast of Ketchikan. The fjord marks the border between Canada and the United States, and Hyder sits just 2 mi from the larger town of Stewart, British Columbia. Highway 37A continues over spectacular Bear Pass from Stewart, connecting these towns with the rest of Canada.

The 1898 discovery of gold and silver in the surrounding mountains brought a flood of miners to the Hyder area, and the town eventually became a major shipping port. Mining remained important for decades, but a devastating 1948 fire destroyed much of the town, which had been built on pilings over the water. Mining still takes place here, but the beauty of the area now attracts increasing numbers of tourists. Today, quiet Hyder calls itself "the friendliest ghost town in Alaska."

The town of Hyder is small, and has only a handful of tourist-oriented businesses, a post office, and library. Nearby Stewart has more to offer, including a bank, museum, hotels, restaurants, and camping. You will need to check in at Canadian customs (open 24 hours) before crossing the border from Hyder into Stewart. Canadian money is primarily used in Hyder, but greenbacks are certainly accepted.

The **Stewart Historical Society Museum** contains wildlife displays and exhibits on the region's mining history. ⊠ *6th and Columbia Sts.,* ☎ *250/636–2568.* ⊡ *$2.* ☉ *June–Sept., weekdays 1–4.*

The **Toastworks Museum** in Stewart houses more than 600 antique kitchen appliances, some more than two centuries old. The same building houses a juice and coffee bar with smoothies, espresso, and Internet access. ⊠ *306 5th St.,* ☎ *250/636–2344.* ⊡ *$3.* ☉ *May–Sept., daily 10–6.*

An **old stone storehouse** stands along the road as you enter Hyder. Built in 1896, this is the oldest masonry building in Alaska.

Six miles north of Hyder on Salmon River Road is the **Fish Creek Wildlife Observation Site.** From late July to early September, the salmon attract black and brown bears here, which, in turn, attract more than a few photographers. The creek produces some of the largest chum salmon anywhere. Twenty-five mi east of Stewart on Highway 37A is the imposing **Bear Glacier.** The glacier sits across a small lake that is often crowded with icebergs. A dirt road from Hyder leads 17 mi to remote **Salmon Glacier,** one of few glaciers accessible by road in Southeast Alaska.

Getting "Hyderized" is a term that you will hear upon arrival in the area. The walls of Hyder's **Glacier Inn** (⊠ Main St., ☎ 250/636–9243) are papered with thousands of signed bills, including those of countless tourists. The tradition supposedly began when prospectors would tack a dollar bill on the wall in case they were broke when they returned.

Dining and Lodging

$$–$$$ ✕ **Bitter Creek Cafe.** This bustling Stewart café has a wide variety of food, including gourmet pizza, lasagna, burgers, seafood, and even Mexican. The quirky interior features a fun collection of antiques, including a 1930 Pontiac. The outside deck is a fine place to relax on a summer afternoon. ⊠ *5th Ave., Stewart,* ☎ *250/636–2166. AE, MC, V. Closed Nov.–Mar.*

$$ 🛏 **Grandview Inn.** This modern two-story hotel is Hyder's nicest place to stay. All rooms are pretty standard, with private baths and TVs but no phones. Six of the rooms have two double beds; the others all include one bed and a fully equipped kitchenette. ⊠ *Box 49, 99923,* ☎ *250/636–9174,* 🆉 *250/636–2673. 10 rooms. Kitchenettes (some). AE, DC, MC, V. Closed Nov.–Mar.*

Guided Tours

Seaport Limousine (☎ 250/636–2622) leads guided tours of the Hyder area, including Fish Creek and Salmon Glacier. **Taquan Air** (☎ 907/225–8800 or 250/636–9150) has year-round service between Ketchikan and Hyder every Monday and Thursday.

Prince of Wales Island

㉑   *15 mi east of Ketchikan.*

Prince of Wales Island stretches more than 130 mi from north to south, making it the largest island in Southeast Alaska. Only two American islands—Kodiak in Alaska and Hawaii in the Hawaiian chain—are larger. Prince of Wales (or "P.O.W." as locals call it) has a diversity of landforms, a plethora of wildlife, and world-class sportfishing. The island has long been a major source of timber, both on Tongass National Forest lands and those owned by Native corporations. Clear-cut logging activity has, however, slowed dramatically in recent years, and today the island's economy is diversifying somewhat into tourism and sportfishing.

Approximately 7,000 people live on Prince of Wales Island, scattered in small villages and towns around the island. A network of 1,500 mi of roads—nearly all built to access clear-cuts—crisscross the island, providing connections to even the smallest settlement. Most of these are gravel, but the main routes are asphalt, and additional sections are paved each year. With the prevalence of roads combined with easy ferry and air access from Ketchikan, you can easily explore this island.

The primary commercial center for Prince of Wales is **Craig,** on the island's western shore. This town of 2,000 retains a hard-edged aura fast disappearing in Inside Passage towns where tourism now holds sway. Commercial fishing (two canneries), sportfishing, and logging and government jobs support this community. Although sightseeing attractions are slim, the town exudes a frontier spirit, and its small boat harbors buzz with activity.

The **Alaska Marine Highway System** provides ferry service to Prince of Wales from Ketchikan most days in the summer. The ferry terminal is in the tiny settlement of Hollis, 31 mi from Craig on a paved road.

A half-dozen miles from Craig is the Tlingit village of **Klawock,** with a sawmill, cannery, hatchery, and the island's only airport. The town is best known for its striking display of 21 totem poles in **Totem Park.** Several of these colorful poles were moved here in the 1930s when an old village site was abandoned; others are more recent carvings. Klawock is also home to **Prince of Wales Hatchery** (☎ 907/755–2231), where salmon and steelhead are raised in a canal adjacent to Klawock

Lake. It's open for tours in the summer. Along the bay, you'll find **St. John's by the Sea Catholic Church,** with its stained-glass windows picturing Alaskan Natives.

The Haida village of **Hydaburg,** approximately 40 mi south of Klawock (via chip-sealed road), lies along scenic Sukkwan Strait. A small collection of **totem poles** occupies the center of this Haida settlement, the only one in Alaska. Originally from British Columbia's Queen Charlotte Islands, the Haida Natives settled here around 1700.

A number of large natural caverns pockmark northern Prince of Wales Island. The best-known of these, **El Capitan Cave,** has one of the deepest pits in the United States and is open to the public. The Forest Service leads free El Capitan tours during the summer, but reservations (☎ 907/828–3304) are required and no children under age seven are permitted.

Dining and Lodging

$$–$$$ ✕ **Shelter Cove Lodge.** Tall windows front the water at this modern restaurant and lodge along the South Boat Harbor in Craig. Fresh seafood tops the menu, along with steaks, a soup and salad bar, delectable desserts, and nightly specials. Prime rib attracts the locals on Friday and Saturday nights. The 10-room lodge offers all-inclusive three-day fishing packages ($2,800 per person double occupancy). ✉ *703 Hamilton Dr., Craig, 99921,* ☎ *907/826–2939 or 888/826–3474,* 📠 *907/826–2941,* 🖳 *www.sheltercovelodge.com. AE, MC, V. Restaurant closed Jan.–Mar.*

$$$ ✕🛏 **Ruth Ann's Motel.** Victorian-style furnishings and decor flavor this classy motel. The honeymoon suite includes a large hot tub and kitchenette. Across the street, the popular **Ruth Ann's Restaurant** serves a variety of homestyle food. Ask for a table in the back room, where picture windows face the harbor. ✉ *300 Water St., Craig 99921,* ☎ *907/ 826–3378,* 📠 *907/826–3293. 14 rooms, 1 suite. AE, D, DC, MC, V. Closed Jan.*

$$$$ 🛏 **McFarland's Floatel.** Across the bay from the logging town of Thorne Bay on the eastern side of Prince of Wales sits this quiet resort, accessible only by boat or floatplane. Each of the four beachfront log cabins sleeps up to six people, and includes a loft, woodstove, full kitchen, and private bath (but no televisions or phones). The owner will pick up guests from town or you can fly directly from Ketchikan to the lodge. A 200-ft walkway from shore leads you to the floating main lodge, which serves a hearty home-cooked seafood dinner ($25 per person). A gift shop sells co-owner Jeannie McFarland's pine-needle raffia baskets. She is also the author of two books on raffia baskets, and teaches basketry workshops. Charter fishing trips are available, or you can rent a skiff and fishing gear and head out on your own. ✉ *Box 19149, Thorne Bay 99919,* ☎ *907/828–3335 or 888/828–3335,* 🖳 *mcfarlandsfloatel. com. 4 cabins. MC, V.*

$$$$ 🛏 **Waterfall Resort.** At this upscale fishing lodge, you sleep in Cape
★ Cod–style cottages from the 1930s, eat bountiful meals with all the trimmings, and fish from custom-built cabin cruisers under the care of a fishing guide. You can also have the fish you caught processed, packaged, and shipped. A three-night minimum stay with all meals and floatplane fare from Ketchikan comes to around $3,000 per person. This former commercial salmon cannery is a popular retreat for business groups. ✉ *Box 6440, Ketchikan 99901,* ☎ *907/225–9461; 800/544– 5125 outside Alaska;* 📠 *907/225–8530,* 🖳 *www.waterfallresort.com. 10 lodge rooms, 4 suites, 26 cabins. Restaurant, boating, fishing. AE, D, MC, V. Closed early Sept.–mid-May.*

WRANGELL

Next up the line is the town of Wrangell, on an island near the mouth of the fast-flowing Stikine River. A small, unassuming timber and fishing community, Wrangell has existed under three flags. Known as Redoubt St. Dionysius when it was part of Russian America, the town was renamed Fort Stikine under the British.

Exploring Wrangell

The rough-around-the-edges town of Wrangell is off the track of the larger cruise ships, so it does not suffer from tourist invasions to the degree that Ketchikan and Juneau do. The town is fairly compact, and most sights are within walking distance of the city dock or ferry terminal.

A Good Walk

A good place to start your tour is at the stalls selling local goods and souvenirs outside the **Wrangell Visitor Center** ㉒, close to the city docks in the Stikine Inn. Head through town along Front Street, stopping at **Kiksetti Totem Park** ㉓ before turning onto Shakes Street to see Wrangell's most interesting sight, **Chief Shakes Island** ㉔. You will probably want to spend time here just soaking in the harbor view and examining the old totem poles. **Chief Shakes's grave site** ㉕ is on the hill overlooking Wrangell Harbor. Get there from Chief Shakes Island by turning right on Case Avenue. From the grave site, head up Church Street to the **Wrangell Museum** ㉖ for another taste of the past. Get to the **Irene Ingle Public Library** ㉗ by continuing up Church Street and turning right on 2nd Street. The next stop is the private little museum called **Our Collections** ㉘, on Evergreen Avenue approximately ⅓ mi north of the ferry terminal. Keep going another ⅓ mi out Evergreen Avenue to **Petroglyph Beach** ㉙, where ancient etchings are visible along the shore.

TIMING

It is a 1½-mi walk between Petroglyph Beach and Chief Shakes Island, so you should plan at least three hours to complete the walk and sightseeing around town.

Sights to See

㉔ **Chief Shakes Island.** Some of the finest totem poles in Alaska are preserved on the island, Wrangell's number one visitor attraction. Walk over the footbridge off the harbor dock to see a tribal house constructed in the 1930s as a replica of one that was home to many of the various Shakes and their peoples. ⊠ *Off Shakes St.,* ☎ *907/874–3747.* ☞ *$2 donation requested.* ☉ *Open when cruise ships are in port (ask at the Wrangell Visitor Center) or by appointment.*

㉕ **Chief Shakes's grave site.** Buried here is Shakes V, who led the local Tlingits during the first half of the 19th century. The site is on Case Avenue, marked by two killer-whale totem poles. ⊠ *Case Ave.*

㉗ **Irene Ingle Public Library.** The library, behind the post office, has two ancient petroglyphs out front. ⊠ *124 2nd St.,* ☎ *907/874–3535.*

㉓ **Kiksetti Totem Park.** You'll find impressive totem poles at this pocket-size park of Alaska greenery. ⊠ *Front St.*

㉘ **Our Collections.** This private museum displays thousands of items—clocks, animal traps, waffle irons, tools—the Bigelows have gathered and used themselves over the past 60 years of Alaska living. The collection, run by Elva Bigelow, is in a large metal building on the water side of Evergreen Avenue. ⊠ *Evergreen Ave.,* ☎ *907/874–3646.* ☞ *Donations accepted.* ☉ *Open for groups of cruise-ship and ferry passengers or by appointment.*

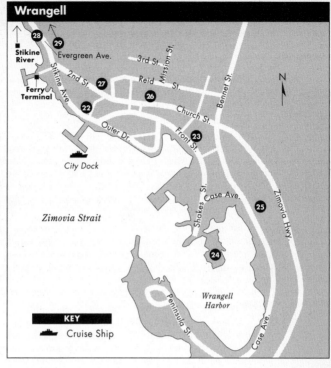

Wrangell

Zimovia Strait

City Dock

Wrangell Harbor

KEY
🚢 Cruise Ship

🟢**29** **Petroglyph Beach.** Scattered among other rocks at this public beach are three dozen or more large stones bearing designs and pictures chiseled by unknown, ancient artists. No one knows why the rocks at this curious site were etched the way they were; perhaps they were boundary markers or messages. You can access the beach via a boardwalk, where you'll find signs describing the site along with carved replicas of the petroglyphs. You are welcome to use these replicas to make a rubbing from rice paper and charcoal or crayons (available in local stores). Because the original petroglyphs can be damaged by physical contact, the state discourages visitors from creating a rubbing off the rocks. ⊠ ⅔ *mi north of ferry terminal off Evergreen Ave.*

🟢**26** **Wrangell Museum.** A bootlegger's still and aviation and communication memorabilia are some of the historical artifacts composing this collection. The decorative house posts from Chief Shakes's clan house (believed to have been carved in the late 1700s), petroglyphs, woven Native baskets from the turn of the 20th century, totem poles, and other local relics round it out. It's on the lower floor of the community center, between the Presbyterian church and the high school. ⊠ *318 Church St.,* ☎ *907/874–3770.* 🎫 *$3.* ☉ *May–late Sept., weekdays 10–5, Sat. 1–4, Sun. when ferry or cruise ships are in port; late Sept.–Apr., Tues.–Fri. 10–4 or by appointment.*

🟢**22** **Wrangell Visitor Center.** This tourist office is close to the city docks in the Stikine Inn. ⊠ *107 Stikine Ave.,* ☎ *907/874–3901 or 800/367–9745,* 🆇 *907/874–3905,* 🌐 *www.wrangell.com/chamber.* ☉ *Weekdays 10–4 and when cruise ships are in port.*

OFF THE
BEATEN PATH

ANAN CREEK WILDLIFE OBSERVATORY – About 30 mi southeast of Wrangell in the Tongass National Forest, Anan is one of Alaska's premier black- and brown-bear viewing areas. Each summer, from early July to mid-August, as many as 30–40 black bears gather at this Southeast stream to feed on pink salmon. On an average visit of about two hours, you might spot two to four bears. Forest Service interpreters are on hand to answer questions from July through September. The site is accessible only by boat or floatplane.

Lodging

$$–$$$$ 🏨 **Harding's Old Sourdough Lodge.** This lodge made of hand-milled cedar sits on the docks in a beautifully converted construction camp. The Harding family welcomes you with home-baked sourdough breads and local seafood in the big, open dining–living room. Guest rooms have modest country-style furnishings, and a private suite (large enough for six people) has a luxuriously large bathroom with a heated floor and a hot tub. Meals ($16 for dinner) are also available for guests. ✉ *1104 Peninsula St., Box 1062, 99929,* ☎ *907/874–3613 or 800/874–3613,* FAX *907/874–3455,* WEB *www.akgetaway.com. 16 rooms. Dining room, sauna, steam room, boating, meeting room, travel services, airport shuttle. AE, D, DC, MC, V.*

$$–$$$ 🏨 **Stikine Inn.** On the dock in the main part of town, this inn has great views of Wrangell's harbor. Rooms are simply decorated with older furnishings. Large windows in the Waterfront Grill overlook the harbor. Staples include burgers, cross-cut waffle fries, pasta, and homemade pizzas. ✉ *2 blocks from ferry terminal, 107 Stikine Ave., Box 990, 99929,* ☎ *907/874–3388 or 888/874–3388,* FAX *907/874–3923,* WEB *www.stikine.com. 33 rooms. Restaurant. AE, D, MC, V.*

$$ 🏨 **Grand View Bed & Breakfast.** Two miles from town, this contemporary hillside home provides spectacular views across Zimovia Strait. Rooms, some with antiques and some decorated Alaskan style, have private baths and entrances, along with TVs and phones. The friendly owners, John and Judy Baker, prepare delectable breakfast specials, including freshly baked rolls. ✉ *Box 927, 99929,* ☎ FAX *907/874–3225,* WEB *www.grandviewbnb.com. 4 rooms. No credit cards.*

$$ 🏨 **Roadhouse Lodge.** This homestead-style waterfront lodge 4½ mi from downtown has a collection of relics from all over the state, giving it an early Alaska museum feel. Locals and visitors alike hang out in the lodge's restaurant, where its kitchen serves wholesome, tasty, and ample meals. (Dinners are open to the public, but breakfast and lunch are only for lodge guests.) Specialties include steaks, fresh halibut, local prawns (sautéed, deep-fried, or boiled in the shell), and Indian fry bread. The guest rooms have dark wood paneling and eclectic furnishings. ✉ *Mile 4, Zimovia Hwy., Box 1199, 99929,* ☎ *907/874–2335,* FAX *907/874–3104. 10 rooms. Restaurant, bar, travel services, airport shuttle. MC, V.*

$$ 🏨 **Rooney's Roost Bed & Breakfast.** This century-old home just a block from downtown has been lovingly remodelled and filled with modern collectibles. Four guest rooms are available, three of which have private baths. Friendly owners, a large-screen television, and a filling gourmet breakfast add to its homey appeal. ✉ *206 McKinnon St., 99929,* ☎ *907/874–2026,* WEB *www.rooneysroost.com. 4 rooms. Airport shuttle. MC, V.*

$ 🏨 **Shakes Slough Cabins.** If you're a hot-springs or hot-tub enthusiast, these Forest Service cabins on the Stikine River, accessible from Wrangell, are worth checking out. Shakes Slough Hot Springs are a short boat ride away from the cabins. Here you can soak in both an open-air hot tub and an enclosed version. Reservations are required for the cabins; request details from the **Forest Service office** in Wrangell or make reservations by calling **ReserveUSA** at ☎ 877/444–6777. *Forest Service:* ✉ *525 Bennett St., Wrangell 99929,* ☎ *907/874–2323,* FAX *907/874–7595. 2 cabins. Hot springs. AE, D, MC, V.*

Guided Tours

Alaska Tugboat Tours (☎ 907/874–3101 or 888/488–4386, WEB www.
alaskatugtours.com) takes groups of four–six guests through the Inside Passage aboard a vintage 1967 tugboat that's been transformed
into a comfortable floating resort. Cruises may be a single day or several days in length and include whale-watching, mountain biking, and
sightseeing. **Rain Walker Expeditions** leads excellent bus tours of the
Wrangell area. **Sunrise Aviation** (☎ 907/874–2319 or 800/874–2311,
FAX 907/874–2546) is a charter-only air carrier that offers trips to the
Anan Creek Wildlife Observatory, LeConte Glacier, or Forest Service
cabins. **Breakaway Adventures** (☎ 907/874–3455 or 888/385–2488,
WEB www.breakawayadventures.com) leads day trips up the majestic
Stikine River by jet boat, including a visit to beautiful Chief Shakes
Glacier, along with time to take a dip at Chief Shakes Hot Springs.

Outdoor Activities and Sports

Fishing

Numerous companies schedule salmon and trout fishing excursions ranging in length from an afternoon to a week. Contact the **Wrangell Visitor Center** for information on guide services and locations.

Golf

Muskeg Meadows Golf Course (☎ 907/874–3443, FAX 907/874–7100),
in a wooded area ½ mi from town, is a well-maintained 9-hole course
with a driving range. Golf clubs and pull carts can be rented.

Hiking

Rain Walker Expeditions (☎ 907/874–2549, WEB www.rainwalker-
expeditions.com) leads two-hour, half-day, or full-day guided natural
history, botany, wildlife, and bird-watching tours of wild places near
Wrangell.

Shopping

You'll find vendors selling local crafts, including children selling gar-
nets from a nearby quarry, at covered shelters near the Wrangell city
dock. **River's Edge Fine Arts and Gifts** (✉ 107 Stikine Ave., ☎ 907/
874–3593), just off the lobby of the Stikine Inn, carries a selection of
prints, hand-sewn clothing, carved wooden bowls, furniture, jewelry,
and pottery. A local marine artist, Brenda Schwartz, often works in
her studio inside this shop.

PETERSBURG

Getting to Petersburg is an experience, whether you take the "high road"
by air or the "low road" by sea. Alaska Airlines claims the shortest jet
flight in the world, from takeoff at Wrangell to landing at Petersburg.
The schedule calls for 20 minutes of flying, but it's usually more like
15. At sea level only ferries and smaller cruisers can squeak through
Wrangell Narrows with the aid of more than 50 buoys and range
markers along the 22-mi crossing. The inaccessibility of Petersburg is
part of its off-the-beaten-path charm. Unlike in several other Southeast communities, you'll never be overwhelmed here by hordes of
cruise passengers; only the smaller ships can reach the town.

At first sight Petersburg may make you think you're in the old country, with tidy white homes and storefronts lining the streets. Bright-color
swirls of leaf and flower designs (called rosemaling) decorate a few older
homes, and row upon row of sturdy fishing vessels pack the harbor, in-

voking the spirit of Norway. No wonder—this prosperous fishing community was founded by Norwegian Peter Buschmann in 1897.

The Scandinavian heritage is gradually being submerged by the larger American culture, but you may still occasionally hear Norwegian spoken, especially during the Little Norway Festival held here each year on the weekend closest to May 17. If you're in town during the festival, be sure to partake in one of the fish feeds that highlight the Norwegian Independence Day celebration. You won't find better folk dancing and beer-batter halibut outside Norway.

One of the most pleasant things to do in Petersburg is to roam among the fishing vessels tied up at dockside in the town's expanding harbor. This is one of Alaska's busiest, most prosperous fishing communities, and the variety of seacraft is enormous. You'll see small trollers, big halibut vessels, and sleek pleasure craft. Wander, too, around the fish-processing structures (though be prepared for the pungent aroma). By watching shrimp, salmon, or halibut catches being brought ashore, you can get a real appreciation for this industry and the people who engage in it.

Exploring Petersburg

Although Petersburg is a pretty enough town to explore, here the workaday world of commercial fishing is more important than rolling out the red carpet for tourists. The main attractions are the town's Norwegian heritage and its magnificent mountain-backed setting. The country around Petersburg offers a plethora of off-the-beaten-path outdoor fun, from whale-watching and glacier-gazing to brown-bear viewing, hiking, and fishing.

A Good Walk

The **Petersburg Visitor Information Center** ㉚ at 1st and Fram streets is a logical spot to begin any walking (or biking) tour of Petersburg. Just a block up the hill, the **Clausen Memorial Museum** ㉛ is a testimony to life in Petersburg. From here, head back downhill to Nordic Drive (Main Street), turning left and then right onto historic Sing Lee Alley. Follow it to the **Sons of Norway Hall** ㉜ along scenic **Hammer Slough** ㉝. Walk back through the center of town on Nordic Drive. On the north side of downtown, steps lead down to the water at scenic **Eagle's Roost Park** ㉞.

TIMING

Petersburg is small enough to walk around in an hour, but you may want to spend more time biking around the back roads farther from town.

Sights to See

㉛ **Clausen Memorial Museum.** The museum interprets commercial fishing and the cannery industry, the era of fish traps, the social life of Petersburg, and Tlingit culture. Don't miss the 126½-pound king salmon, the largest ever caught, as well as the Tlingit dugout canoe; two fish-trap anchors; the Cape Decision lighthouse station lens; and *Earth, Sea and Sky*, a 3-D sculpted wall mural outside. ⊠ *203 Fram St., 99833,* ☎ *907/772–3598.* ⌑ *$2.* ☉ *May–mid-Sept., Mon.–Sat. 9:30–4:30, Sun. 12:30–4:30; mid-Sept.–Apr., call for hrs.*

㉞ **Eagle's Roost Park.** Just north of the Petersburg Fisheries cannery, this park is a great place to spot eagles, especially at low tide. On a clear day you will also discover dramatic views of the sharp-edged Coast Range, including the 9,077-ft summit of Devils Thumb.

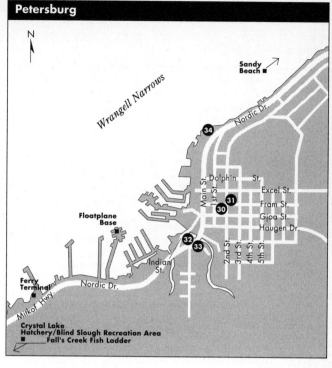

Petersburg

33 Hammer Slough. Stop along this pool for a vision of houses and buildings on high stilts reflected perfectly in still waters; it's best seen at high tide.

30 Petersburg Visitor Information Center. This office is a good source for local information. ✉ *1st and Fram Sts., Box 810,* ☎ *907/772–4636,* FAX *907/772–3646,* WEB *www.petersburg.org.* ◷ *May–Sept., Mon.–Sat. 9–5, Sun. noon–4; Oct.–Apr., weekdays 10–2.*

32 Sons of Norway Hall. The large, white barnlike structure that stands just south of the Hammer Slough is the headquarters of an organization devoted to keeping alive the traditions and culture of the old country. ✉ *Sing Lee Alley,* ☎ *907/772–4575.*

OFF THE
BEATEN PATH

FALLS CREEK FISH LADDER – Coho and pink salmon migrate upstream in late summer and fall at this fish ladder. ✉ *Mile 10.8, Mitkof Hwy.*

BLIND SLOUGH RECREATION AREA – This recreation area includes a number of sites scattered along the Mitkof Highway 15–20 mi south of Petersburg. **Blind River Rapids Trail** is a handicapped-accessible 1-mi path that leads to a three-side shelter overlooking the river before it loops back through the muskeg. Not far away is a bird-viewing area where several dozen trumpeter swans overwinter. In the summer you're likely to see many ducks and other waterfowl here. At Mile 18, the state-run **Crystal Lake Hatchery** releases thousands of king and coho salmon each year. The kings return in June and July, and the coho in August and September. Nearby is a popular picnic area. Four miles south of the hatchery is a Forest Service campground.

LECONTE GLACIER – Petersburg's biggest draw lies about 25 mi east of town and is accessible only by water or air. LeConte Glacier is the continent's southernmost tidewater glacier and one of its most active, often calving off so many icebergs that the tidewater bay at its face is car-

peted shore to shore with floating bergs. Ferries and cruise ships pass it
at a distance.

Dining and Lodging

$–$$ ✕ **Alaskafe Coffeehouse and Bistro.** This comfortable coffeehouse
and lunch spot in downtown Petersburg, above Coastal Cold Storage,
serves vegetarian soups, colorful salads, pastries, and filling Italian-style
panini sandwiches grilled to order. You can browse through a selection of books and magazines, or even rent their computer for Internet
access while you're waiting for your meal. ⊠ *306B Nordic Dr.,* ☎ *907/
772–5282. No credit cards.*

$–$$ ✕ **Pellerito's Pizza.** Although it has a few tables, this always-crowded
pizza joint primarily specializes in take-out pizzas, pizza by the slice,
wraps, and giant calzones. You'll also find ice cream, muffins, and
espresso. ⊠ *1105 S. Nordic Dr., across from ferry terminal,* ☎ *907/
772–3727. MC, V.*

$ ✕ **Coastal Cold Storage.** This busy little shop in the heart of Peters-
burg serves daily lunch seafood specials including fish chowders, beer-
batter halibut, and halibut enchiladas. Fresh seafood and cooked crabs
are also available for takeout. ⊠ *Excel and N. Nordic Dr.,* ☎ *907/
772–4171,* WEB *www.crabbroker.com. AE, MC, V. Closed Sun.*

$$$–$$$$ 🏨 **Scandia House.** Exuding an old-country, Norwegian atmosphere,
this hotel on Petersburg's main street, a fixture since 1910, was rebuilt
following a 1995 fire. Rosemaling designs adorn the exterior. The in-
terior is squeaky clean, with contemporary oak furniture, and some
rooms have kitchenettes, king-size beds, or in-room hot tubs and a view
of the harbor. A Continental breakfast of homemade muffins and cof-
fee warms the small but relaxing lobby in the morning. ⊠ *110 Nordic
Dr., Box 689, 99833,* ☎ *907/772–4281 or 800/722–5006,* FAX *907/772–
4301. 30 rooms, 3 suites. Kitchenettes, minibars, boating, bicycles, car
rental. AE, D, DC, MC, V. CP.*

$$ 🏨 **Tides Inn.** This is the largest hotel in town, a block uphill from Petersburg's main thoroughfare. Rooms have comfortable furnishings,
and some kitchens. Rooms in the newer wing have views of the boat
harbor. The coffee is always on in the small lobby, and in the morning you're welcome to complimentary juices, muffins, and pastries. ⊠
307 N. 1st St., Box 1048, 99833, ☎ *907/772–4288 or 800/665–8433,*
FAX *907/772–4286. 48 rooms. Car rental. AE, D, DC, MC, V. CP.*

$$ 🏨 **Water's Edge Bed & Breakfast.** Along the shore of Frederick Sound
1½ mi north of Petersburg, this family-run B&B offers either a creek-
side or waterside room. Seals, eagles, and whales are often seen just
outside the door. A deluxe Continental breakfast is served, and the li-
brary is stocked with books on Alaska and natural history. Take ad-
vantage of the owners' Kaleidoscope Cruises or borrow the bikes or
canoe to explore on your own. Lodging-cruise packages are offered.
⊠ *705 Sandy Beach Rd., Box 1201, 99833,* ☎ *907/772–3736 or 800/
868–4373,* WEB *www.alaska.net/~bbsea. 2 rooms. Boating, bicycles, li-
brary, airport shuttle. No credit cards. CP.*

Guided Tours

Stop by the visitor center for a complete listing of local tour compa-
nies. **Kaleidoscope Cruises** (☎ 907/772–3736 or 800/868–4373, WEB
www.alaska.net/~bbsea) conducts whale-watching and glacier ecology
boat tours led by professional biologists and naturalists. **Pacific Wing**
(⊠ Airport on Hagen Dr., ☎ 907/772–9258) is an air-taxi operator
that gets high marks from locals for its flightseeing tours over the Stikine
River and LeConte Glacier. **Tongass Kayak Adventures** (☎ 907/772–
4600, WEB www.tongasskayak.com) leads half-day sea kayak trips from

Petersburg, along with longer trips to LeConte Bay and elsewhere in the area. **Viking Travel** (⊠ 101 Nordic Dr., ☎ 907/772–3818, FAX 907/772–3940) books whale-watching, glacier, sea kayaking, and other charters with local operators.

Nightlife and the Arts

Bars and Nightclubs

The **Harbor Bar** (⊠ Nordic Dr., ☎ 907/772–4526), with ship's wheels, ship pictures, and a mounted red snapper, is true to the town's seafaring spirit. Sample the brew and blasting sounds at the smoky **Kito's Kave** (⊠ Sing Lee Alley, ☎ 907/772–3207) and examine the outrageous wall decor—a Mexican painting on black velvet, a mounted Alaska king salmon, and two stuffed sailfish from a tropical fishing expedition.

Outdoor Activities and Sports

Bicycling

Because of its small size, most of Petersburg can be covered by bicycle. A good route to ride is along the coast on Nordic Drive past the lovely homes and to Sandy Beach. Coming back to town, take the interior route (Haugen Drive) and you'll pass the airport, "Tent City" (housing for cannery workers), and some pretty churches before returning to the waterfront. **Petersburg Bicycle Rentals** (⊠ 1216 S. Nordic Dr., ☎ 907/772–3829) rents bikes to explore the area.

Diving

If you're feeling adventurous, spend an afternoon with **Southeast Diving** (⊠ 208 Haugen Dr., ☎ 907/772–2446). Some of the best marine life can be found under the waters of Frederick Sound.

Shopping

Seafood

At **Tonka Seafoods,** across the street from the Sons of Norway Hall, you can tour the plant and sample smoked or canned halibut and salmon. ⊠ *Sing Lee Alley,* ☎ *907/772–3662 or 888/560–3662,* WEB *www. tonkaseafoods.com.* ⊙ *Weekdays 8–5.*

Art Galleries

A stroll down Sing Lee Alley at the south end of Nordic Drive will take you past several stores and galleries selling local artists' work. **Raven's Nest Gallery** (☎ 907/772–4004) sells handcrafted items and artwork. The appropriately named **Cubbyhole** (☎ 907/772–2717) sells Norwegian-style handicrafts.

Bookstore

Set back off the alley in a beautiful big white house that served as a boardinghouse to fishermen and schoolteachers is **Sing Lee Alley Book Store** (⊠ Sing Lee Alley, ☎ 907/772–4440), which stocks books on Alaska, best-sellers, cards, and gifts.

SITKA

Sitka was the home to Tlingit people for centuries prior to the 18th-century arrival of the Russians. In canoes up to 60 ft long, the Tlingits fished and traded throughout the Alaskan Panhandle and even as far south as California. Unfortunately for them, Russian territorial governor Alexander Baranof coveted the Sitka site for its beauty, mild climate, and economic potential. In the island's massive timber forests he saw raw materials for shipbuilding. Its location offered trading routes as far west as Asia and as far south as California and Hawaii. In 1799

Baranof negotiated with the local chief to build a wooden fort and trading post some 6 mi north of the present town. He called the outpost St. Michael Archangel and moved a large number of his Russian and Aleut fur hunters there from their former base on Kodiak Island.

The Tlingits soon took exception to the ambitions of their new neighbors. Reluctant to pledge allegiance to the czar and provide free labor, in 1802 they attacked Baranof's people and burned his buildings. Baranof, however, was away on Kodiak at the time. He returned in 1804 with a formidable force, including shipboard cannons. He attacked the Tlingits at their fort near Indian River, site of the present-day 105-acre Sitka National Historical Park, and forced them to flee north to Chichagof Island.

In 1821 the Tlingits returned to Sitka to trade with the Russians, who were happy to benefit from the tribe's hunting skills. Under Baranof and succeeding managers, the Russian-American Company and the town prospered, becoming known as "the Paris of the Pacific." Besides the fur trade, the community built a major shipbuilding and repair facility, sawmills, and forges and even initiated an ice industry. The Russians shipped blocks of ice from nearby Swan Lake to the booming San Francisco market. In 1800 Baranof shifted the capital of Russian America to Sitka from Kodiak.

The town declined after its 1867 transfer from Russia to the United States but became prosperous again during World War II, when it served as a base for the U.S. effort to drive the Japanese from the Aleutian Islands. Today its most important industries are fishing, government, and tourism.

Exploring Sitka

It is hard not to like Sitka, with its eclectic blending of Native, Russian, and American history and a setting that is both dramatic and beautiful. This is one of the best Inside Passage towns to explore on foot, with such sights as St. Michael's Cathedral, Sheldon Jackson Museum, Sitka National Historical Park, and the Alaska Raptor Rehabilitation Center topping the town's must-see list.

A Good Walk

A good place to begin a tour of Sitka is the distinctive onion-dome **St. Michael's Cathedral** ㉟, right in town center. Next, head to **Harrigan Centennial Hall** ㊱, a block behind the cathedral along Harbor Drive. Inside are the interesting Isabel Miller Museum and an information desk that opens when cruise ships are in port. From Harrigan Centennial Hall, turn right on Lincoln Street and continue a block to the **Russian Bishop's House** ㊲, one of the symbols of Russian rule, dating from 1842. Continue out Lincoln Street along the harbor to Sheldon Jackson College, where the **Sheldon Jackson Museum** ㊳ is packed with Native cultural artifacts. Another ½ mi up is the **Sitka National Historical Park** ㊴, where you can watch Native artisans craft carvings and silver jewelry. Behind the main building, paths take you through the rain forest past tall totem poles and to the site of a Tlingit fort from the battle of 1804. A signed trail crosses the Indian River (watch for spawning salmon in late summer) and heads to the **Alaska Raptor Center** ㊵, for an up-close look at bald eagles.

Return to town along Sawmill Creek Road to the small Sitka National Cemetery, where you turn left on Jeff Davis Street. Continue downhill to Lincoln Street and turn right, following it back to Harrigan Centennial Hall. From here, walk along Harbor Drive for two blocks and take the path to the summit of **Castle Hill** ㊶, where Russia transferred

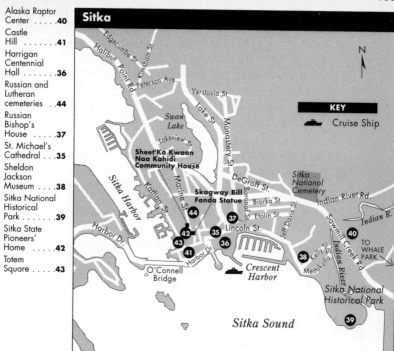

Alaska to American hands. Follow the path down the other side of the hill to view the impressive **Sitka State Pioneers' Home** ㊷, with the statue of pioneer "Skagway Bill" Fonda. Across the street is **Totem Square** ㊸, with its tall totem pole and three ancient anchors. Adjacent to the Pioneers' Home is the **Sheet'ka Kwaan Naa Kahidi Community House** cultural center. Native dances take place here in the summer. Turn right at the center and pass the reconstructed Russian blockhouse that tops a nearby hill. End your walk at the **Russian and Lutheran cemeteries** ㊹, along Marine Street a block from the blockhouse. The grave of Princess Maksoutoff, a member of the Russian royal family, is here.

TIMING

Sitka has many attractions, and you can easily spend a full day exploring this culturally rich area. You can accomplish the walk in two to three hours if you do not spend much time at each stop.

Sights to See

🖐 ㊵ **Alaska Raptor Center.** You have the unique experience of viewing American bald eagles and other wild Alaskan birds up close at this center set on a beautiful tract of land crisscrossed by hiking trails. This nonprofit organization rescues dozens of birds a year and houses those unable to return to the wild. Informative tours and a video are offered. ☎ 907/747–8662. 💲 $10 mid-May–Sept., free (but no formal tours) Oct.–mid-May. ☉ Mid-May–Sept., when cruise ships are in port; Oct.–mid-May, hrs vary.

㊶ **Castle Hill.** On this hill Alaska was formally handed over to the United States on October 18, 1867, and the first 49-star U.S. flag was flown on January 3, 1959, signifying Alaska's statehood. To reach the hill and get one of Sitka's best views, take the first right off Harbor Drive just before the O'Connell Bridge; then go into the **Baranof Castle Hill State Historic Site** entrance. A paved path takes you to the top of the hill, overlooking Crescent Harbor. Several Russian residences on the hill, including Baranof's castle, burned down in 1894.

㊱ Harrigan Centennial Hall. Out front of this contemporary brick building a block from St. Michael's Cathedral sits a replica of a Tlingit war canoe. Inside you'll find a volunteer-staffed information desk provided by the Sitka Convention & Visitors Bureau; the **Isabel Miller Museum,** with its collection of Russian and American historical artifacts; and an auditorium for New Archangel Dancers performances. ⊠ *Harbor Dr.,* ☎ *907/747–6455 museum; 907/747–5940 Visitors Bureau.* ☉ *Museum May–Sept., daily 8–5; Oct.–Apr., Tues.–Sat. 10–4. Information Desk May–Sept., daily 8–5.*

㊹ Russian and Lutheran cemeteries. Most of Sitka's Russian dignitaries are buried in these sites off Marine Street. The most distinctive grave belongs to Princess Maksoutoff (died 1862), wife of the last Russian governor and one of the most illustrious members of the Russian royal family to be buried on Alaskan soil.

㊲ Russian Bishop's House. Now a registered historic landmark, this house facing the harbor was constructed by the Russian-American Company for Bishop Innocent Veniaminov in 1842. Inside the house, one of the few remaining Russian-built log structures in Alaska, are exhibits on the history of Russian America, including a room where a portion of the house's structure is peeled away to expose Russian building techniques. ⊠ *501 Lincoln St.,* ☎ *907/747–6281.* ☜ *$3.* ☉ *May–Sept., daily 9–1 and 2–5; Oct.–Apr. by appointment.*

★ **㊟ St. Michael's Cathedral.** One of Southeast Alaska's best-known national landmarks had its origins in a log structure erected between 1844 and 1848. In 1966 the church was destroyed in a fire that swept through the downtown business district. As the fire engulfed the building, townspeople risked their lives and rushed inside to rescue the cathedral's precious icons, religious objects, vestments, and other treasures brought to the church from Russia. Using original measurements and blueprints, an almost exact replica of onion-domed St. Michael's was built and dedicated in 1976. Today, visitors can see what could possibly be the largest collection of Russian icons in the United States, among them the much-prized *Our Lady of Sitka* (also known as the *Sitka Madonna*) and the *Christ Pantocrator* (*Christ the Judge*) on either side of the doors of the interior altar screen. Other objects include ornate Gospel books, chalices, crucifixes, much-used silver-gilt wedding crowns dating to 1866, and an altar cloth made by Princess Maksoutoff. ⊠ *Lincoln St.,* ☎ *907/747–8120.* ☜ *$2 donation requested.* ☉ *May–Sept., daily 7:30–5:30 when cruise ships are in port; Oct.–Apr., variable hrs.*

★ **㊳ Sheldon Jackson Museum.** At **Sheldon Jackson College,** this octagonal museum, which dates from 1895, contains priceless Indian, Aleut, and Eskimo items collected by Dr. Sheldon Jackson (1834–1909), who traveled the remote regions of Alaska as an educator and missionary. Carved masks, Chilkat blankets, dogsleds, kayaks—even the impressive helmet worn by Chief Katlean during the 1804 battle against the Russians—are displayed. ⊠ *801 Lincoln St.,* ☎ *907/747–8981.* ☜ *$4.* ☉ *Mid-May–mid-Sept., daily 8–5; mid-Sept.–mid-May, Tues.–Sat. 10–4.*

★ **㊴ Sitka National Historical Park.** The main building at this park has a small museum with historical exhibits and artifacts and shows a video about 19th-century conflicts between Tlingits and Russians. Also here is the **Southeast Alaska Indian Cultural Center,** where Native artists and artisans demonstrate silversmithing, weaving, wood carving, and basketry. Behind the center, a wide 1-mi path takes you through the forest and along the shore of Sitka Sound. Scattered along the way are some of the most skillfully Native-carved totem poles in Alaska, including several from the 1904 St. Louis World's Fair. Others are more recent creations. The trail passes a grassy meadow that once contained a sturdy Tlingit fort; the 1804 battle between the Russians and Tlingits was fought here. Keep going on the trail to see spawning salmon from the footbridge over Indian River. ⊠ *106 Metlakatla St.,* ☎ *907/747–6281,* WEB *www.nps.gov/sitk.* ⛅ *Free.* ☉ *Mid-May–Sept., daily 8–5; Oct.–mid-May, weekdays 8–5.*

㊷ Sitka State Pioneers' Home. The large, four-level, red-roof structure with the imposing 14-ft statue in front is the first of several state-run retirement homes for Alaska's senior citizens. The statue, symbolizing Alaska's frontier sourdough spirit, was modeled by an authentic pioneer, William "Skagway Bill" Fonda. It portrays a determined prospector with pack, pick, rifle, and supplies on his back heading for the gold country. Adjacent to the Pioneers' Home is **Sheet'ka Kwaan Naa Kahidi Community House,** where you can watch Native dance performances throughout the summer. A re-created Russian blockhouse caps the small hill directly behind the community center. ⊠ *Lincoln and Katlian Sts.*

㊸ Totem Square. On this square directly across the street from the Pioneers' Home are three anchors discovered in local waters believed to be of 19th-century British origin. Look for the double-headed eagle of czarist Russia carved into the cedar of the totem pole in the park.

Dining and Lodging

$$–$$$$ ✕ **Channel Club.** Once you've surveyed the dozens of salads arrayed on the salad bar, you might not even make it to the steak and seafood for which this restaurant, festooned with fishnet, floats, and whalebone carvings, is known. A courtesy van provides door-to-door service if you're without transportation. ⊠ *Mile 3.5, 2906 Halibut Point Rd.,* ☎ *907/747–9916. AE, DC, MC, V.*

$$$$ 🏨 **Rockwell Lighthouse.** On an island ¾ mi from town, Burgess Bauder (a local veterinarian) rents out his 1,600-square-ft, four-story lighthouse, hand-built in the 1980s with coastal woods and brass lights. The light at the top is built to Coast Guard specifications. Accommodations for four couples include a modern kitchen. A curving staircase wraps up the inside of the lighthouse, amid its nautical decor. The price includes transportation to and from the lighthouse, $35 extra for use of the hot tub. In summer, you can use a small motorboat, but when it's stormy the owner shuttles visitors. ⊠ *Box 277, 99835,* ☎ FAX *907/747–3056. 4 rooms. Dining room, hot tub, boating. No credit cards.*

$$$$ 🏨 **Westmark Shee Atika.** Conveniently in the heart of town, Sitka's nicest hotel has large rooms and a lobby decorated with Tlingit Native art. Many rooms overlook Crescent Harbor; nicest rooms are the corner suites. Downstairs, the Raven Dining Room serves seafood, pasta, and steak as well as such specials as beer-batter halibut or a homemade bread bowl with clam chowder. Top it off with a slice of ultra-rich Mississippi mud pie. ⊠ *330 Seward St., 99835,* ☎ *907/747–6241; 800/544–0970 in the U.S.; 800/999–2570 in Canada;* FAX *907/747–5486,* WEB *www.westmarkhotels.com. 98 rooms, 3 suites. Restaurant, bar, room service. AE, D, DC, MC, V.*

$$$–$$$$ 🏨 **Cascade Inn.** A few miles out of town, this motel is conveniently attached to a grocery, video, and liquor store. The large rooms have simple furnishings and balconies that face the water and Mt. Edgecumbe volcano. Some include kitchenettes. A deck with a hot tub and a barbecue pit sits just above the water. ⊠ *2035 Halibut Point Rd., 99835,* ☎ *907/747–6804 or 800/532–0908,* FAX *907/747–6572,* WEB *www.travelsitka.*

com/cascade. 10 rooms. Grocery, kitchenettes, hot tub, bicycles, laundry service, travel services. D, MC, V.

$$ 🖭 **Sitka Hotel.** Built in 1939, this friendly, old-fashioned hotel with a Victorian-style lobby is right downtown. The rooms mix Victorian-style brass beds and wallpaper with contemporary furniture. A cozy no-smoking lounge provides a comfy place to relax, and convenient off-street parking is available. ⊠ *118 Lincoln St., 99835,* ☎ *907/747–3288,* ℻ *907/747–8499,* 🕸 *www.sitkahotel.com. 57 rooms. MC, V.*

$ 🖭 **White Sulphur Springs Cabin.** This Tongass National Forest public-use cabin 65 mi outside Sitka has nearby hot springs. Like many other Forest Service cabins, this cabin sleeps four (bring your own sleeping bags) and has bunk beds, a woodstove, table, and outhouse. No mattresses, cooking utensils, or any services are provided, so you must bring all of your supplies. The cabin faces the Pacific Ocean and has a nearby hot springs bathhouse. Access is by boat (you'll need to walk in from a nearby cove) or helicopter. ☎ *907/747–6671 information; 877/444–6777 reservations,* 🕸 *www.reserveusa.com. 1 cabin. AE, D, MC, V.*

Guided Tours

Sitka Tours (☎ 907/747–8443, ℻ 907/747–7510) meets ferries and cruise ships, and leads both bus tours and historical walks. In addition, they transport ferry passengers into Sitka. **Tribal Tours** (☎ 907/747–7290 or 888/270–8687, ℻ 907/747–3770, 🕸 www.sitkatribal.com) emphasizes Sitka's rich Native culture, with bus or walking tours and with dance performances at the Tribal Community House.

Allen Marine Tours (☎ 907/747–8100 or 888/747–8101, 🕸 www. allenmarine.com) leads boat-based wildlife tours three times a week in the summer. These typically include a visit to a seabird colony, and the chance to see humpback whales and other marine mammals.

Nightlife and the Arts

Bars

As far as the locals are concerned, a spot in one of the green-and-white vinyl booths at **Pioneer Bar** (⊠ 212 Katlian St., ☎ 907/747–3456), across from the harbor, is a destination unto itself. It's vintage Alaska, with hundreds of pictures of local fishing boats, occasional live music, and pickup pool games.

Dance

The **New Archangel Dancers of Sitka** perform authentic Russian Cossack–type dances whenever cruise ships are in port. This all-female troupe tours extensively, with a mix of traditional dance styles. Tickets are sold a half hour before performances; a recorded message (☎ 907/747–5516) gives the schedule a week in advance. Performances take place in Harrigan Centennial Hall. **Sheet'ka Kwaan Naa Kahidi Dancers** (☎ 907/747–7290 or 888/270–8687, 🕸 www.sitkatribal.com) perform Tlingit dances in full Native regalia at the Sheet'ka Kwaan Naa Kahidi Community House on Katlian Street. The dance schedule is listed on the board at Harrigan Centennial Hall.

Festivals

Southeast Alaska's major classical chamber-music festival is the annual **Sitka Summer Music Festival** (⊠ Box 3333, 99835, ☎ 907/747–6774, 🕸 www.sitkamusicfestival.org), a three-week June celebration of concerts and special events held in Harrigan Centennial Hall. The **Sitka WhaleFest** (⊠ Box 1226, 99835, ☎ 907/747–5940, ℻ 907/747–3739) is held around town the first weekend of November when the whales are plentiful (as many as 80) and tourists are not.

Outdoor Activities and Sports

Bird-Watching and Hiking

Seven miles north of Sitka along Halibut Point Road are two bird-watching and hiking trails. The **Starrigavan Estuary Life Interpretive Trail** provides views of spawning salmon and waterfowl and has a platform for bird-watchers. The **Starrigavan Forest & Muskeg Interpretive Trail** has great views of the valley along Starrigavan Creek.

Canoeing and Kayaking

Above Old Harbor Books, **Baidarka Boats** (☎ 907/747–8996, FAX 907/747–4801, WEB www.kayaksite.com) guides excellent half-day sea kayaking trips in the Sitka area, and also rents kayaks for those who want to head out on their own. Instruction is provided and no experience is necessary. **Alaska Travel Adventures** (☎ 907/789–0052 or 800/478–0052, WEB www.alaskaadventures.com) offers a three-hour kayaking tour in protected waters south of Sitka, and has a remote cabin on the water.

Shopping

Art Galleries

Fairweather Prints (✉ 209 Lincoln St., ☎ 907/747–8677, WEB www.fairweatherprints.com) consists of "wearable art," with handprinted Alaskan designs on shirts, dresses, and other clothing. **Impressions** (✉ 239 Lincoln St., ☎ 907/747–5502 or 888/747–5502) is a fine downtown gallery with art prints and limited editions from Southeast Alaskan artists, including Evon Zerbetz and Rie Muñoz. Housed within an 1895 home next to the Bishop's House, **Sitka Rose Gallery** (✉ 419 Lincoln St., ☎ 907/747–3030) has two small galleries comprising Alaskan paintings, sculptures, Native art, and jewelry.

Bookstore

Old Harbor Books (✉ 201 Lincoln St., ☎ 907/747–8808) has an impressive collection of Alaskan titles, along with a knowledgeable staff. It's a book lovers' bookstore. Directly behind the bookstore is the ever-popular **Backdoor Cafe** (☎ 907/747–8856), with espresso and pastries.

JUNEAU

Juneau, Alaska's capital and third-largest city, is on the North American mainland but can't be reached by road. The city owes its origins to two colorful sourdoughs, Joe Juneau and Dick Harris, and to a Tlingit chief named Kowee. The chief led the two men to rich reserves of gold in the outwash of the stream that now runs through the middle of town and in quartz rock formations back in the gulches and valleys. That was in 1880, and shortly after the discovery a modest stampede resulted in the formation of first a camp, then a town, then finally the Alaska district government capital in 1906.

For 60 years or so after Juneau's founding, gold was the mainstay of the economy. In its heyday the AJ (for Alaska Juneau) gold mine was the biggest low-grade ore mine in the world. It was not until World War II, when the government decided it needed Juneau's manpower for the war effort, that the AJ and other mines in the area ceased operations. After the war, mining failed to start up again, and government became the city's principal employer.

Juneau is full of contrasts. The historic downtown buildings and dramatic hillside position provide a frontier feeling, but the city's cosmopolitan nature comes through in fine museums, noteworthy restaurants, and a literate and outdoorsy populace. In addition to enjoying the city itself, you will discover a tramway to alpine trails atop Mt. Roberts, densely forested wilderness areas, quiet bays for sea kayaking, and even a famous drive-up glacier. Surrounded by beautiful wilderness and glaciers in its backyard, Juneau is the cultural center of Alaska.

Exploring Juneau

Juneau is an obligatory stop on the Inside Passage cruise and ferry circuit and enjoys an overabundance of tourists in midsummer. Downtown Juneau is compact enough so that most of its main attractions are within walking distance of one another. Note, however, that the city is very hilly, so your legs will get a real workout. Along with the Alaska State Museum and Mt. Roberts Tramway, be sure to make time for a tour to Mendenhall Glacier and the Gastineau Salmon Hatchery.

A Good Walk

A good starting point is **Marine Park** ㊺, right along the cruise-ship dock. For an introduction to public lands in the area, walk up Marine Way and turn right on Whittier Street to reach the engaging **Alaska State Museum** ㊻, filled with artifacts and art from around the state. From here, circle back along Willoughby Avenue to the **State Office Building** ㊼. Catch the elevator to the eighth-floor atrium and head out onto the observation deck for vistas across Gastineau Channel. Then continue out the east side of the building onto 4th Street. The small but informative **Juneau-Douglas City Museum** ㊽ sits a short distance away at 4th and Calhoun streets. The unimpressive banklike building across the street is the **Alaska State Capitol** ㊾. Next stop is the **Governor's Mansion** ㊿, a few minutes uphill on Calhoun Street. If you have the time and energy, you may want to continue along Calhoun, across the Gold Creek Bridge, and then down along 12th Street to the quiet **Evergreen Cemetery** (51), where town fathers Joe Juneau and Dick Harris are buried.

Backtrack to the Governor's Mansion and retrace your steps down Calhoun Street to the overpass. Climb the steps and cross the footbridge to 5th Street, then turn left up Main Street, followed by a right on 7th Street. Next stop is the artifact-filled old home of Judge Wickersham, the **House of Wickersham** (52) on 7th and Seward streets. From here on, you will be working your way back downhill, so the walking gets easier. The **St. Nicholas Russian Orthodox Church** (53) occupies the corner of 5th and Gold streets, and the **Log Cabin Visitor Center** (54) is just a couple of blocks away at 3rd and Seward streets. By now you probably have a good taste of Juneau; step inside for the complete details.

Now it's time to explore the historic buildings and busy shops of downtown Juneau, particularly those along **South Franklin Street** (55). Check out the Alaskan Hotel, the Alaska Steam Laundry Building, and the Senate Building before dipping inside the always crowded **Red Dog Saloon** (56) at the intersection of South Franklin Street aand Admiral Way. A few more minutes' walking will take you to the **Mt. Roberts Tramway** (57), a great way to reach alpine country for a hike overlooking Juneau and Gastineau Channel.

TIMING

To cover downtown Juneau's many interesting sights, you should allow at least three or four hours for exploring. Add more time to ride the Mt. Roberts Tramway or for the side trip to Evergreen Cemetery.

Sights to See

㊾ **Alaska State Capitol.** Built in 1930, this building with southeastern Alaskan marble pillars houses the governor's office and hosts state legis-

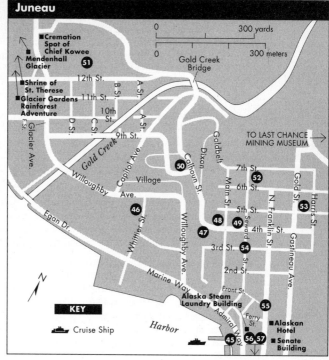

lature meetings during the winter months. Historic photos line the up-stairs walls. You can pick up a self-guided tour brochure as you enter. ⊠ *Corner of Seward and 4th Sts.,* ☎ *907/465–2479.* ⊘ *Weekdays 8–5.*

46 Alaska State Museum. Alaska's finest museum appeals to all tastes. Native Alaskan buffs will enjoy examining the 38-ft walrus-hide umiak built by Eskimos and a re-created interior of a Tlingit tribal house. Natural-history exhibits include stuffed brown bears and a two-story-high eagle nesting tree. Mining displays and contemporary art complete the collection. ⊠ *395 Whittier St.,* ☎ *907/465–2901.* ⊠ *$5.* ⊘ *Mid-May–mid-Sept., weekdays 9–6, weekends 10–6; mid-Sept.–mid-May, Tues.–Sat. 10–4.*

51 Evergreen Cemetery. Many Juneau pioneers, including Joe Juneau and Dick Harris, are buried here. A meandering gravel path leads through the graveyard, and at the end of it is the monument commemorating the cremation spot of Chief Kowee.

50 Governor's Mansion. The three-level colonial-style home was completed in 1912. Tours of the residence are, unfortunately, not permitted. ⊠ *716 Calhoun Ave.*

52 House of Wickersham. At the top of the hill behind the Capitol stands the former residence of James Wickersham, pioneer judge and delegate to Congress. The home, constructed in 1898, contains memorabilia from the judge's travels throughout Alaska—from rare Native basketry and ivory carvings to historic photos and a Chickering grand piano that came " 'round the Horn" to Alaska in the 1870s. The tour provides a glimpse into the life of this dynamic man and also includes tea and sourdough cookies. ⊠ *213 7th St.,* ☎ *907/586–9001,* WEB *www.dnr.state.ak.us/parks.* ⊠ *$2 requested donation.* ⊘ *Mid-May–Sept., Thurs.–Tues. 10–noon and 1–5 (closed Wed., additional hrs when cruise ships are in port); Oct.–Apr., by appointment.*

🐾 **48** **Juneau-Douglas City Museum.** Among the exhibits interpreting local mining and Tlingit history are old mining equipment, historic photos, and pioneer artifacts, including a century-old store and kitchen. Also of interest are a Juneau time line, exhibits on commercial fishing and steamships, historic paintings, a hands-on area for children, and a half-hour video of Juneau's history. ⊠ *114 4th St.,* ☎ *907/586–3572.* 🎫 *$3.* ⊙ *May–Sept., weekdays 9–5, weekends 10–5; Oct.–Apr., Fri.– Sat. noon–4 or by appointment.*

54 **Log Cabin Visitor Center.** Modeled after a 19th-century structure, this building served first as a Presbyterian church, then as a brewery. Stop in for a walking-tour map and information on all the tours in Juneau and the surrounding areas. ⊠ *134 3rd St., at Seward St.,* ☎ *907/586– 2201 or 888/581–2201.* ⊙ *May–Sept., weekdays 8:30–5, weekends 9– 5; Oct.–Apr., weekdays 9–5.*

45 **Marine Park.** On the dock where the cruise ships tie up is a little urban oasis with benches, shade trees, and shelter. It's a great place to enjoy an outdoor meal purchased from one of Juneau's many street vendors. A visitor kiosk is staffed according to cruise-ship schedules.

57 **Mt. Roberts Tramway.** The tram whisks you from the cruise terminal 1,800 ft up the side of Mt. Roberts. After the six-minute ride, passengers can take in a film on the history and legends of the Tlingits, visit the nature center, go for an alpine walk on hiking trails, purchase Native crafts, or experience fine mountain-view dining from the decks. The smoke-free bar serves locally brewed beers. ☎ *907/463–3412 or 888/ 461–8726,* 🌐 *www.goldbelttours.com.* 🎫 *$19.75.* ⊙ *May–Sept., daily 9–9.*

★ **56** **Red Dog Saloon.** The frontierish quarters of the Red Dog have housed an infamous Juneau watering hole since 1890. Every conceivable surface in this two-story bar is cluttered with life preservers, business cards, and college banners; and when tourist season hits, a little atmospheric sawdust covers the floor as well. Bands pump out dance tunes when cruise ships are docked. ⊠ *278 S. Franklin St.,* ☎ *907/463–9954.*

53 **St. Nicholas Russian Orthodox Church.** Quaint, onion-domed, and built in 1894, St. Nicholas is the oldest Russian church building in Southeast Alaska. A small gift shop is adjacent. ⊠ *326 5th St.,* ☎ *907/780– 6320.* 🎫 *$2 requested donation.* ⊙ *Tours mid-May–Sept., weekdays 8–5 and most Sat.*

55 **South Franklin Street.** The buildings on South Franklin Street (and Front as well), among the oldest and most interesting structures in the city, house curio and crafts shops, snack shops, and two salmon shops. Many reflect the architecture of the 1920s and '30s, and some are even older. The small **Alaskan Hotel** opened in 1913 and retains its period trappings. The barroom's massive, mirrored oak back bar is accented by Tiffany lights and panels. The 1901 **Alaska Steam Laundry Building,** with a windowed turret, now houses a coffeehouse and other stores. The **Senate Building** is across the street.

47 **State Office Building.** At this government building you can have a picnic lunch with the state workers on the eighth-floor patio. On most Fridays at noon, you can stop by for concerts played inside the four-story atrium on a grand old theater pipe organ, a veteran of the silent-movie era. ⊠ *4th St. and Calhoun Sts.*

....

OFF THE   **LAST CHANCE MINING MUSEUM** – A 1½-mi hike or taxi ride behind town,
BEATEN PATH   this small museum is housed in one of the buildings from Juneau's his-
               toric AJ Gold Mine. The collection includes old mining tools and equip-

ment, minerals, and a 3-L
907/586–5338. ☎ $3. ☉
3:30–6:30.

GASTINEAU SALMON HATCHERY
as salmon fight their way up a fi
Inside the hatchery you will learn (
of salmon. A retail shop sells gifts a
nel Dr., ☎ 907/463–4810. ☎ $3 (
days 10–6, weekends 10–5; Oct.–Ap.

GLACIER GARDENS RAINFOREST ADVENTU
rain forest 8 mi north of Juneau are ponds,
large atrium, and gardens with cascades of
usual tree formations. Guided tours (on cover
along the 4 mi of paved paths, and a 580-ft-high overlook provides dramatic views across Mendenhall Glacier. ☒ 7600 Glacier Hwy., ☎ 907/
790–3377. ☎ $15.50 including guided tour. ☉ May–Sept., daily 9–6.

★ **MENDENHALL GLACIER** – Juneau's famous drive-up glacier, 13 mi north of
downtown, spans 12 mi and is fed by the massive Juneau Icefield. Like
many other Alaskan glaciers, it is slowly retreating up the valley, losing
100 ft a year as massive chunks of ice calve into the small lake separating Mendenhall from the **Mendenhall Visitor Center.** The center houses
exhibits on the glacier, a theater and bookstore, educational exhibits,
and panoramic views. Nature trails lead along Mendenhall Lake and
into the mountains overlooking Mendenhall Glacier. Several companies
lead bus tours to the glacier. ☒ End of Glacier Spur Rd., off Mendenhall
Loop Rd., ☎ 907/789–0097. ☉ May–Sept., daily 8–6; Oct.–Apr.,
Thurs.–Fri. 10–4, weekends 9–4.

SHRINE OF ST. THERESE – A self-guided pilgrimage to the shrine is well
worth the 23-mi journey from downtown Juneau (a taxi should cost at
least $45). Built in the 1930s, this stone church and its 14 stations of
the cross are the only inhabitants of a serene tiny island that is accessible via a 400-ft-long pedestrian causeway. Sunday services are held at
1 PM June through August. The "honesty-box" gift shop sells crucifixes,
books, T-shirts, and souvenirs. ☒ 5933 Lund St., ☎ 907/780–6112.
☉ Daily.

NATIVE VILLAGES – If you're interested in knowing how the Native
Alaskan village peoples of Southeast Alaska live today, you can fly or
take the state ferry LeConte to Kake, Angoon, or Hoonah. You won't
find much organized touring in any of these communities, but you will
find hotels (advance reservations are strongly suggested), and guided
fishing, natural-history, and wildlife-watching trips can be arranged by
asking around. In Kake, contact the **Waterfront Lodge** (☒ Box 222,
Kake 99830, ☎ 907/785–3472). In Angoon, try the **Whalers' Cove
Lodge** (☒ Box 101, Angoon 99820, ☎ 907/788–3123 or 800/423–
3123, WEB www.whalerscovelodge.com). In Hoonah is the **Keex' Kwaan
Lodge** (☒ Box 320, Hoonah 99829, ☎ 907/945–3434).

Dining and Lodging

$$$$ ✕ **Gold Creek Salmon Bake.** Trees, mountains, and the rushing water
★ of Salmon Creek surround the comfortable, canopy-covered benches
and tables at this salmon bake. Fresh-caught salmon is cooked over an
alder fire and served with a simple but succulent sauce of brown sugar,
margarine, and lemon juice. For $24 you are served salmon, pork
spareribs, and chicken along with hot baked beans, rice pilaf, salad, corn
bread, and blueberry cake. Wine and local Alaskan Amber beer are extra.

...an pan for gold in the stream or wander up the hill
...remains of the Wagner Gold Mine. A free round-trip bus
...downtown hotels is included. ⌧ *1061 Salmon Lane Rd.,* ☎
...789–0052 or 800/323–5757, WEB *www.alaskaadventures.com. MC,*
V. Closed Oct.–Apr.

$$$ ✕ **Thane Ore House Salmon Bake.** Four miles south of town, Thane
 ★ Ore House has a waterside setting and indoor dining. Food served in-
cludes salmon, halibut, barbecued beef ribs, salad, baked beans, and
corn bread. The Gold Nuggett Revue, an enjoyable musical comedy with
cancan dancing by a local group, complements your dinner. A free
round-trip bus ride from downtown hotels is included. ⌧ *4400 Thane
Rd., 4 mi south of Juneau,* ☎ *907/586–3442. MC, V. Closed Oct.–Apr.*

$$$ ✕ **Mike's Place.** Well off the beaten tourist path—it's across the bridge
from Juneau in the community of Douglas—Mike's has been serving
up seafood, steak, pasta, and salads for decades. Locals come for the
finest steaks in the area, but Mike's treatment of tiny Petersburg
shrimp—fried and sautéed—is also noteworthy. The salad bar offers
a light alternative, and lunch specials are reasonably priced. It's a romantic spot, with white linens on the tables and live jazz on summer
weekends. ⌧ *1102 2nd St., Douglas,* ☎ *907/364–3271. AE, D, DC,
MC, V. Closed Mon. No lunch weekends.*

$$$ ✕🏨 **Summit Restaurant.** Built in 1889, this building served as a brothel
 ★ until 1958 and now operates as an upscale restaurant with old-fash-
ioned lodging. The restaurant, an intimate candlelit place with a cop-
per-top bar, serves such specialties as pan-seared razor clams, rack of
lamb, and big porterhouse steaks. Upstairs, the **Inn at the Waterfront**
offers reasonably priced lodging ($$–$$$), but the furnishings are
from an earlier era, with baths down the hall. ⌧ *455 S. Franklin St.,
99801,* ☎ *907/586–2050,* FAX *907/586–2999. Reservations essential,
dinner only. AE, D, DC, MC, V. Closed for lunch in winter.*

$$–$$$ ✕ **The Fiddlehead.** Less than a half mile from the center of town,
 ★ Juneau's favorite restaurant is actually two restaurants in one, both
smoke free. Downstairs you can get a casual breakfast, lunch, or din-
ner in a bright room accented by stained glass and modern art. The
menu includes plenty of vegetarian items and an eclectic assortment
of entrées ranging from justifiably famous smoked halibut chowder to
Black Angus meat loaf. Homemade bread and cookies from the restau-
rant's bakery are always a hit. Di Sopra, upstairs, has a more formal
atmosphere with a full bar, piano jazz on summer weekends, and a
heartier menu. Here you can sample braised lamb shank, duck confit
with oyster mushrooms, marinated medallions of venison, or fresh
seafood while rubbing elbows with the legislative elite. ⌧ *429
Willoughby Ave.,* ☎ *907/586–3150,* WEB *www.alaska.net/~fiddle. AE,
D, DC, MC, V.*

$$–$$$ ✕ **Hangar on the Wharf.** Crowded with both locals and travelers, the
Hangar is housed in the building where Alaska Airlines started busi-
ness. The whitewashed wood, stainless-steel accents, and vintage air-
plane parts and photos create a casual dining experience. Expansive
views of Gastineau Channel and Douglas Island can be enjoyed from
the bar and restaurant. A wide selection of entrées, including locally
caught halibut and salmon, jambalaya, filet mignon, and great burg-
ers, make this a Juneau hot spot. You'll also find one of the largest se-
lections of draught beers anywhere in Southeast Alaska, with two
dozen brews available. ⌧ *2 Marine Way, Merchants Wharf Mall,* ☎
907/586–5018. AE, D, MC, V.

$$$$ 🏨 **Baranof Hotel.** The Baranof has long been Juneau's most prestigious
 ★ address. The tasteful woods and period lamps in the dark art deco lobby
and most rooms create an atmosphere reminiscent of 1939, when the

hotel first opened. Downstairs dining is available in a casual restaurant as well as in the luxurious Gold Room, which serves some of the finest meals in Juneau. Twenty rooms have either a kitchenette (typically booked during the winter legislative session) or exercise equipment. Rooms on the front side have the best views, but street noises may keep you awake at the lower levels. Nicest are spacious corner suites on the seventh to ninth floors, where you can look across Juneau's busy harbor to the densely forested mountains of Douglas Island. ⊠ *127 N. Franklin St., 99801,* ☎ *907/586–2660; 800/544–0970 for reservations;* FAX *907/586–8315,* WEB *www.westmarkhotels. com. 179 rooms, 17 suites. Restaurant, coffee shop, lobby lounge, hair salon, meeting room, travel services. AE, D, DC, MC, V.*

$$$$ ⛱ **Frontier Suites Airport Hotel.** Near the airport in Mendenhall Valley, 9 mi from Juneau, this hotel is a great option for families. All rooms have modern, functional furniture and full kitchens with a stove, refrigerator, microwave, dishes, silverware, and pans. Suites have separate bedrooms and living rooms (with sleeper sofas) and two televisions. Two bunk rooms include a miniloft for older children. Downstairs, **J.R.'s Cafe** serves a varied menu, including fresh Alaskan seafood and prime rib. ⊠ *9400 Glacier Hwy., 99801,* ☎ *907/790–6600 or 800/544–2250,* FAX *907/790–6612,* WEB *www.frontiersuites.com. 104 rooms, 40 suites. Restaurant, bar, kitchenettes. AE, D, DC, MC, V.*

$$$$ ⛱ **Garside House B&B.** Opened in 2001, this grand Victorian home sits atop a downtown Juneau hill, with exquisite views of the surrounding country. Originally built in 1903, the house has been completely renovated in a lavish blend of old and new including antique furnishings, a marble-floor billiard room, a lap pool, wine cellar, garden waterfall, and Internet access. Gourmet breakfasts are served downstairs each morning. ⊠ *224 4th St., 99801,* ☎ *907/586–6382,* FAX *907/586–3284,* WEB *www.garsidehouse.com. 5 rooms, 3 suites. Lap pool, billiards. AE, D, DC, MC, V.*

$$$$ ⛱ **Goldbelt Hotel Juneau.** A high-rise by Juneau standards, the seven-
★ story Goldbelt is one of Juneau's finest lodging places, with well-appointed rooms (including such touches as speaker phones, hair dryers, and irons) and a free airport shuttle. Waterside rooms on the upper level offer views across Gastineau Channel. Deluxe suites have king-size beds, and 15 are equipped with treadmills or stationary bikes. A Chilkat blanket and other artifacts are displayed in the lobby, and the adjacent Chinook's restaurant serves three meals a day. ⊠ *51 W. Egan Dr., 99801,* ☎ *907/586–6900 or 888/478–6909,* FAX *907/463–3567,* WEB *www.goldbelt.com. 104 rooms, 1 suite. Restaurant, lobby lounge, room service, meeting room, airport shuttle. AE, D, DC, MC, V.*

$$$$ ⛱ **Grandma's Feather Bed.** Walking into the warm and inviting atmosphere of this small Victorian-style hotel feels as if you're visiting someone's home. Cheerful colors brighten each of the spacious rooms, which come with jetted bathtubs and feather comforters; some have fireplaces and kitchen nooks. The complimentary breakfast buffet includes all-you-can-eat pancakes, omelets, and French toast. ⊠ *2348 Mendenhall Loop Rd., 99801,* ☎ *907/789–5566,* FAX *907/789–2818. 14 rooms. Restaurant, airport shuttle. AE, D, DC, MC, V.*

$$$$ ⛱ **Guesthouse Inn & Suites.** At this all-suites inn, within walking distance of the airport and 9 mi from downtown, rooms include kitchenettes and king-size beds; some have hot tubs. Perfect for business travelers and families, this inn is also one of the only Juneau lodging places with a full-size swimming pool. ⊠ *1800 Shell Simmons Dr., 99801,* ☎ *907/790–6435 or 888/559–9846,* FAX *907/790–6621,* WEB *www.guesthousealaska.com. 94 rooms. Kitchenettes, indoor pool, hot tub, gym, airport shuttle. AE, D, MC, V.*

$$$$ 🏠 **Pearson's Pond Luxury Inn and Garden Spa.** Guests at this luxurious private retreat can enjoy an amazing view of the great blue Mendenhall Glacier. Built on a small lake, the large home has a three-tier deck with two hot tubs, a fitness center, and campfire area. The rooms range in size: ask for one of the two large ones with water views, cathedral ceilings, and small lofts. All rooms are private and include either jetted tubs or fireplaces, plus efficiency kitchens stocked with essentials for a make-it-yourself breakfast. Activities include yoga on the deck each morning, hiking or cross-country skiing, relaxing in the hot tub, and evening wine and cheese. You can also bob around the lake in the rowboat, paddleboat, or kayak. The owners also have two modern condos nearby, which comfortably sleep four people. ⊠ *4541 Sawa Circle, 99801,* ☎ *907/789–3772 or 888/658–6328,* 📠 *907/789–6722,* 🌐 *www.juneau.com/pearsons.pond. 3 suites. In-room data ports, kitchenettes, massage (extra charge), boating, fishing, bicycles, laundry service. AE, D, DC, MC, V.*

$$$–$$$$ 🏨 **The Prospector.** A short walk west of downtown and next door to the State Museum, this small but modern hotel is frequented by business travelers and legislators. Rooms are spacious, with most containing kitchenettes. **T. K. McGuire's** dining room and lounge serves prime rib, steaks, and seafood. ⊠ *375 Whittier St., 99801,* ☎ *907/586–3737; 800/ 331–2711 outside Alaska; 800/478–5866 in Alaska;* 📠 *907/586– 1204,* 🌐 *www.prospectorhotel.com. 14 rooms, 44 suites. Restaurant, lobby lounge. AE, D, DC, MC, V.*

$$$ 🏠 **Sentinel Island Lighthouse.** A few miles north of Juneau and adjacent to a rock where Steller's sea lions haul out, this operating lighthouse provides a spectacular setting to watch whales and eagles. Guests have the entire 6-acre island to roam around on. Simple accommodations include bunks in the lighthouse and in an adjacent building; you can also pitch a tent on a platform facing the water. Water and cooking facilities are provided for all accommodations. The lighthouse is managed by Gastineau Channel Historical Society, and access is by charter boat or helicopter (around $650 round-trip for up to six people). You can also paddle to the island by sea kayak. ⊠ *Box 21264, Juneau 99802,* ☎ *907/586–5338. 6 bunks in two buildings. No credit cards.*

$$ 🏨 **Alaskan Hotel.** This historic 1913 hotel in the heart of downtown
★ Juneau sits over the popular bar of the same name; rooms can be a bit noisy when bands are playing. The older but well-maintained guest rooms are on three floors and have antiques and iron beds. The flocked wallpaper, floral carpets, and Tiffany windows are reminiscent of the hotel's original gold rush–era opulence. The least-expensive rooms do not have televisions and share a bath down the hall. ⊠ *167 S. Franklin St., 99801,* ☎ *907/586–1000 or 800/327–9347,* 📠 *907/463–3775,* 🌐 *www.ptialaska.net/~akhotel. 42 rooms, 22 with bath. Bar. D, DC, MC, V.*

$ 🏠 **U.S. Forest Service Cabins.** Scattered throughout Tongass National For-
★ est, these rustic cabins offer a charming and cheap escape for just $25– $45 per cabin. Most are fly-in units, accessible by floatplanes from virtually any community in the Southeast. These public-use cabins have bunks for six to eight occupants, tables, stoves, and outdoor privies, but no electricity or running water. You provide your own sleeping bag, food, and cooking utensils. Bedside reading in most cabins includes a diary kept by visitors—add your own adventure. ⊠ *Juneau Ranger District, 8465 Old Dairy Rd., Juneau 99801,* ☎ *907/586–8800; 877/444–6777 for reservations,* 🌐 *www.reserveusa.com. 150 cabins. AE, D, MC, V.*

$ ⛺ **U.S. Forest Service Campgrounds.** Eight Forest Service–maintained campgrounds are scattered around Tongass National Forest and are accessible from the communities of Juneau, Sitka, Ketchikan, Petersburg, and Thorne Bay. All have pit toilets and sites for RVs and tents, but not all provide drinking water. Reservations are possible for some of these campgrounds, but space is generally available without a reservation. ⊠ *Juneau Ranger District, 8465 Old Dairy Rd., Juneau 99801,* ☎ *907/586–8800; 877/444–6777 for reservations,* WEB *www.reserveusa. com. D, MC, V.*

Guided Tours

Boating and Kayaking

The Native-owned **Auk Ta Shaa Discovery** (☎ 907/586–8687 or 800/ 820–2628, WEB www.goldbelttours.com) leads sea kayak excursions to islands north of Juneau, along with rafting trips down the Mendenhall River. **Alaska Travel Adventures** (☎ 907/789–0052, WEB www. alaskaadventures.com) leads Mendenhall River floats.

Auk Nu Tours (☎ 907/586–8687 or 800/820–2628, WEB www. auknutours.com) has all-day catamaran tours to the beautiful glaciers of Tracy Arm Fjord and operates a passenger ferry between Juneau and Gustavus (near Glacier Bay National Park). **Fjord Express** (☎ 907/766– 3395 or 800/320–0146, WEB www.alaskafjordlines.com) provides passenger ferry service connecting Juneau with Haines and Skagway on a daily basis in the summer.

Helicopter Flightseeing

Several local companies offer helicopter flightseeing trips that take you to the spectacular glaciers flowing from Juneau Icefield. Most have booths along the downtown cruise-ship dock. All include a touchdown on a glacier, with a chance to romp on these rivers of ice. Some also offer trips that include a dogsled ride on the glacier. Prior to taking a helicopter flight from any of these companies, ask about their safety record. A number of accidents have occurred in recent years, including some with fatalities. Flightseeing is quite controversial in Juneau, where locals are concerned over noise from the almost-constant din of helicopter activity throughout the summer. **Coastal Helicopters** (☎ 907/789–5600, WEB www.coastalhelicopters.com) lands on Herbert or Taku Glacier. **ERA Helicopters** (☎ 907/586–2030 or 800/843–1947, WEB www.eraaviation. com) has a one-hour trip that includes landing on Norris Glacier. **Temsco Helicopters** (☎ 907/789–9501, WEB www.temscoair.com) lands on Mendenhall Glacier. **Northstar Trekking** (☎ 907/790–4530, WEB www. glaciertrekking.com) leads an excellent two-hour glacier hike.

Sightseeing

Juneau Trolley Car Company (☎ 907/586–7433, WEB www.juneautrolley. com) conducts narrated tours, stopping at a dozen or so of Juneau's historic and shopping attractions. **Mendenhall Glacier Tours** (☎ 907/ 789–5460) leads guided bus tours that include a visit to Mendenhall Glacier. Contact the **Juneau Convention and Visitors Bureau** (☎ 907/ 586–2201 or 888/581–2201) for other companies that provide tours to Mendenhall Glacier.

Former hardrock miners lead three-hour tours of the historic **AJ Mine** (☎ 907/463–5017) south of Juneau. A gold-panning demonstration is included, and approximately 45 minutes of the tour takes place inside the old tunnels that lace the mountains. Mine tours depart from downtown by bus.

Taku Glacier Lodge (☎ 907/586–8258, FAX 907/789–2021, WEB www. takuglacierlodge.com) is a remote and historic lodge south of Juneau along Taku Inlet. Hole-in-the-Wall Glacier is directly across the inlet from the lodge, and nature trails wind through the surrounding coun-

try, where black bears and bald eagles are frequently sighted. Floatplanes take guests from Juneau on a scenic trip to the lodge, where they
are served a delicious lunch or dinner, and then flown back three hours
later. No overnight stays are available.

Nightlife and the Arts

Bars

The **Alaskan Hotel** bar (⊠ 167 S. Franklin St., ☎ 907/586–1000) is about
as funky a place as you'll find in Juneau: flocked-velvet walls, antique
chandeliers above the bar, and vintage Alaskan frontier brothel decor.
Sit back and enjoy the live music or take turns with the locals at the
open mike. When the ships are in, the music at **Red Dog Saloon** (⊠ 278
S. Franklin St., ☎ 907/463–9954) is live and the crowd gets livelier.

Alaskan Brewing Company. If you're a beer fan, look for this local brewery's Alaskan Amber, Pale Ale, Frontier, and Smoked Porter beer,
brewed and bottled in Juneau. You can also visit the microbrewery and
sample various brews while touring the bottling operation. ⊠ 5429
Shaune Dr., ☎ 907/780–5866. ☉ May–Sept., Mon.–Sat. 11–4:30,
with tours every half hour. Oct.–Apr., Thurs.–Sat. 11–4:30.

Music Festivals

The annual weeklong **Alaska Folk Festival** (⊠ Box 21748, 99802, ☎
907/463–3316, WEB www.juneau.com/aff) is staged each April in Juneau,
drawing singers, banjo masters, fiddlers, and even cloggers from all over
the state. During the last week of May, Juneau is the scene of **Juneau
Jazz 'n Classics** (⊠ Box 22152, 99802, ☎ 907/463–3378, WEB www.
juneau.com/music), which celebrates music from Bach to Brubeck.

Theater

Southeast Alaska's only professional theater company, **Perseverance
Theater** (⊠ 914 3rd St., Douglas, ☎ 907/364–2421) presents everything from Broadway and Shakespeare to locally written plays.

Outdoor Activities and Sports

Cross-Country Skiing

During the winter, the **Parks and Recreation Department** (☎ 907/586–
5226) sponsors a group ski and snowshoe outing each Wednesday and
Saturday morning when there's sufficient snow. You can rent skis and
get advice about touring the trails and ridges around town from **Foggy
Mountain Shop** (⊠ 134 N. Franklin St., ☎ 907/586–6780).

Downhill Skiing

The only downhill area in the Southeast, **Eaglecrest** (⊠ 155 S. Seward
St., Juneau 99801, ☎ 907/790–2000; 907/586–5330 for recorded ski
information), on Douglas Island, just 30 minutes from downtown
Juneau, offers late November to mid-April skiing and snowboarding
on a well-groomed mountain with two double chairlifts, cross-country trails, a beginner's platter pull, ski school, ski-rental shop, cafeteria, and tri-level day lodge. Enjoy the northern lights while you night
ski from January through mid-March.

Fitness Clubs

The **Juneau Racquet Club** (⊠ 2841 Riverside Dr., ☎ 907/789–2181),
about 10 mi north of downtown, adjacent to Mendenhall Mall, will
accommodate visitors at its first-class indoor tennis and racquetball
courts. Facilities include sauna, hot tub, exercise equipment, massage
tables, sports shop, and snack bar. **JRC Downtown** (⊠ W. Willoughby

Ave., ☎ 907/586–5773) is a smaller version of the club. Both charge $13 per day for nonmembers.

Gold Panning

Gold panning is fun, especially for children, and Juneau is one of the Southeast's best-known gold-panning towns. Sometimes you actually uncover a few flecks of the precious metal in the bottom of your pan. You can buy a pan at almost any Alaska hardware or sporting-goods store. **Alaska Travel Adventures** (☎ 907/789–0052, WEB www.alaskaadventures. com) has gold-panning tours near the famous Alaska-Juneau Mine.

Golf

Juneau's par-three, 9-hole **Mendenhall Golf Course** (✉ 2101 Industrial Blvd., ☎ 907/789–1221) is pretty modest, but does rent clubs and has spectacular vistas.

Hiking

The **Parks and Recreation Department** (☎ 907/586–5226) in Juneau sponsors a group hike each Wednesday morning and on Saturday in summer. Hikers can contact the **U.S. Forest Service** (☎ 907/586–8790) for trail books and maps.

Sea Kayaking

Auk Ta Shaa Discovery (☎ 907/586–8687 or 800/820–2628, WEB www. goldbelttours.com) operates sea kayaking trips in the Juneau area. **Alaska Travel Adventures** (☎ 907/789–0052) conducts sea kayaking trips to Mendenhall Glacier. Experienced kayakers can rent boats and equipment from **Juneau Outdoor Center** (☎ 907/586–8220) in Douglas. **Adventure Sports** (☎ 907/789–5696) rents kayaks in Mendenhall Valley and at Auke Bay.

Shopping

Art Galleries

Rie Muñoz, of the **Rie Muñoz Gallery** (✉ 2101 Jordan Ave., ☎ 907/789–7411, WEB www.riemunoz.com) in Mendenhall Valley, is one of Alaska's best-known artists, creator of a stylized, simple, and colorful design technique that is much copied but rarely equaled. Other artists' work is also on sale at the Muñoz Gallery, including woodblock prints by nationally recognized artist Dale DeArmond. Various books illustrated by Rie Muñoz and written by Alaskan children's author Jean Rogers are for sale. In downtown Juneau, see Rie Muñoz's paintings and tapestries at **Decker Gallery** (✉ 233 S. Franklin St., ☎ 907/463–5536 or 800/463–5536).

Clothing

Kodiak Coat (✉ 174 S. Franklin St., Suite 108, ☎ 907/463–4986, WEB www.kodiakcoat.com) occupies a small shop inside the Emporium Mall. The owner designs and sews waterproof and breathable coats, hats, and mittens, all made to withstand Alaska's rugged climate.

Seafood

Taku Smokeries (✉ 550 S. Franklin St., ☎ 907/463–5033 or 800/582–5122, WEB www.takusmokeries.com), at the south end of town near the cruise-ship docks, processes nearly 6 million pounds of fish, mostly salmon, a year. You can view the smoking procedure through large windows and then purchase the packaged fish in the deli-style gift shop or have some shipped back home.

ADMIRALTY ISLAND AND GLACIER BAY NATIONAL PARK AND PRESERVE

Admiralty Island

58 *10 mi west of Juneau.*

The island is famous for its lush rain forests and abundant wildlife, including one of the largest concentrations of brown bears anywhere on the planet. The island's Tlingit inhabitants called it Kootznoowoo, meaning "fortress of the bears." Ninety-six miles long, with 678 mi of coastline, Admiralty—the second-largest island in the Southeast—is home to an estimated 1,500 bears, or almost one per square mile. **Admiralty Island National Monument** has a system of public-use cabins, a canoe route that crosses the island via a chain of lakes and trails, the world's highest density of nesting bald eagles, large concentrations of humpback whales, and some of the region's best sea kayaking and sportfishing. ⊠ *8461 Old Dairy Rd., Juneau 99801,* ☎ *907/586–8790.*

More than 90% of Admiralty Island is preserved within the Kootznoowoo Wilderness. Its chief attraction is **Pack Creek,** where you can watch brown bears feeding on salmon. One of Alaska's premier bear-viewing sites, Pack Creek is co-managed by the U.S. Forest Service and the Alaska Department of Fish and Game. Permits are required during the main viewing season, from June 1 through September 10, and only 24 people per day are allowed to visit Pack Creek from July 5 through August 25. Reservations can be mailed to the Forest Service beginning February 20. ⊠ *8461 Old Dairy Rd., Juneau 99801,* ☎ *907/ 586–8800,* WEB *www.fs.fed.us/r10/chatham/anm.* ☞ *$50.*

Lodging

$$$$ ▥ **Thayer Lake Lodge.** One of Southeast Alaska's oldest lodges, Thayer
★   Lake is on land within the Admiralty Island National Monument. Bob and Edith Nelson built this small, rustic lodge-and-cabins operation, which houses up to 10 people (5 in each cabin), after World War II. They built it mostly with their own labor and used local timber. Today it is run by their son Eric and his family. Lake fishing is unsurpassed for cutthroat and Dolly Varden trout (though they're not overly large). You can take a canoe or motorboat on the 9-mi-long lake that laps the sandy beach fronting the lodge. Simple family-style meals are served in the lodge. Many visitors opt for a complete package that includes a floatplane flight from Juneau, lodging, and meals, plus a guided trip to Pack Creek. These all-inclusive trips start at $1,090 per person for two nights and three days. ⊠ *Box 8897, Ketchikan 99901,* ☎ *907/ 789–5646 in summer; 907/225–3343 in winter,* FAX *907/247–7053,* WEB *www.alaskabearviewing.com. 2 cabins. Dining room, kitchenettes, hiking, boating, fishing. MC, V. Closed mid-Sept.–late May.*

Guided Tours

Alaska Discovery (⊠ 5449 Shaune Dr., Suite 4, Juneau, ☎ 907/780–6226 or 800/586–1911, FAX 907/780–4220, FAX www.akdiscovery.com) leads single and multiday trips to Pack Creek that include a floatplane trip, sea kayaking, and guided bear viewing. **Alaska Coastal Airlines** (☎ 907/789–7818, WEB www.alaskacoastal.com) offers flightseeing to many areas around Juneau. **Ward Air** (☎ 907/789–9150, WEB www.wardair.com) is a long-established company with flightseeing trips to Glacier Bay and the Juneau Icefield.

Glacier Bay National Park and Preserve

★ ㉙ *60 mi northwest of Juneau.*

Near the northern end of the Inside Passage, Glacier Bay National Park and Preserve is one of the jewels of the entire national park system. Visiting Glacier Bay is like stepping back into the Little Ice Age—it's one of the few places in the world where you can approach massive tidewater glaciers. With a noise that sounds like cannons firing, bergs the size of 10-story office buildings sometimes come crashing from the "snout" of a glacier. The crash sends tons of water and spray skyward, and it propels mini–tidal waves outward from the point of impact. **Johns Hopkins Glacier** calves so often and with such volume that the large cruise ships can seldom come within 2 mi of its face.

Glacier Bay is a recently formed (and still forming) body of water fed by the runoff of the ice fields, glaciers, and mountains that surround it. Captain James Cook and then Captain George Vancouver sailed by Glacier Bay and didn't even know it. At the time of Vancouver's sailing in 1794, the bay was hidden behind and beneath a vast glacial wall of ice. The glacier face was more than 20 mi across and in places more than 4,000 ft in depth. It extended more than 100 mi to its origins in the St. Elias Mountain Range. Since then, due to warming weather and other factors not fully understood, the face of the glacial ice has melted and retreated with amazing speed, exposing 65 mi of fjords, islands, and inlets.

It was Vancouver who named the magnificent snow-clad **Mt. Fairweather,** which towers over the head of the bay. Legend has it that Vancouver named Fairweather on one of the Southeast's most beautiful blue days—and the mountain was not seen again during the following century. An exaggeration, to be sure, but overcast, rainy weather is certainly the norm here.

In 1879, about a century after Vancouver's sail-by, one of the earliest white visitors to what is now Glacier Bay National Park and Preserve came calling. Naturalist John Muir was drawn by the flora and fauna that had followed in the wake of glacial withdrawals and fascinated by the vast ice rivers that descended from the mountains to tidewater. Today, the naturalist's namesake glacier, like others in the park, continues to retreat dramatically. Its terminus is now scores of miles farther up the bay from the small cabin he built at its face during his time there.

Glacier Bay is a marvelous laboratory for naturalists of all persuasions. Glaciologists, of course, can have a field day. Animal lovers can hope to see the rare glacial "blue" bears of the area, a variation of the black bear, which is here along with the brown bear; whales feasting on krill; mountain goats in late spring and early summer; and seals on floating icebergs. Birders can look for the more than 200 species that have already been spotted in the park, and if you're lucky, you may witness two bald eagles engaging in aerobatics.

A remarkable panorama of plants unfolds from the head of the bay, which is just emerging from the ice, to the mouth, which has been ice-free for more than 200 years. In between, the primitive plants—algae, lichens, and mosses—that are the first to take hold of the bare, wet ground give way to more complex species: flowering plants such as the magenta dwarf fireweed and the creamy dryas, which in turn merge with willows, alders, and cottonwood. As the living plants mature and die, they enrich the soil and prepare it for new species to follow. The climax of the plant community is the lush spruce-and-hemlock rain forest, rich in life and blanketing the land around **Bartlett Cove.** ✉ *Box 140, Gustavus 99826,* ☎ *907/697–2230,* 🆆🅴🅱 *www.nps.gov/glba.*

Glacier Bay National Park and Preserve

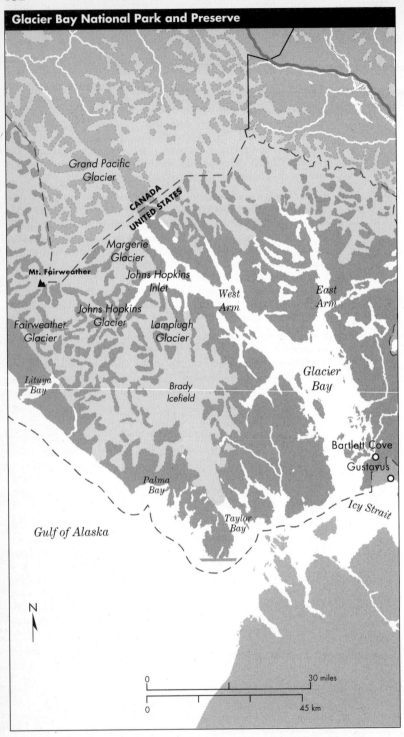

Grand Pacific
Glacier

CANADA
UNITED STATES

Margerie
Glacier

Johns Hopkins
Inlet

West
Arm

East
Arm

Mt. Fairweather

Johns Hopkins
Glacier

Lamplugh
Glacier

Fairweather
Glacier

Glacier
Bay

Lituya
Bay

Brady
Icefield

Bartlett Cove

Gustavus

Palma
Bay

Icy Strait

Gulf of Alaska

Taylor
Bay

N

0   30 miles

0   45 km

Gustavus

60 *50 mi west of Juneau, 75 mi south of Skagway.*

For airborne visitors, Gustavus is the gateway to Glacier Bay National Park. The long, paved jet airport, built as a refueling strip during World War II, is one of the best and longest in Southeast Alaska, all the more impressive because of its limited facilities at the field. Alaska Airlines, which serves Gustavus daily in the summer, has a large, rustic terminal at the site, and from a free telephone on the front porch of the terminal you can call any of the local hostelries for a courtesy pickup. Smaller light-aircraft companies that serve the community out of Juneau also have on-site shelters.

Gustavus has no downtown. In fact, Gustavus is not a town at all. The 150 or so year-round residents are most emphatic on this point; they regularly vote down incorporation. Instead, Gustavus is a scattering of homes, farmsteads, arts-and-crafts studios, fishing and guiding charters, and other tiny enterprises peopled by hospitable individualists. It is, in many ways, a contemporary example of the frontier spirit in Alaska.

Dining and Lodging

$–$$ ✕ **Strawberry Point Cafe.** There's nothing fancy here, just wholesome cooking that stars locally caught seafood (from Dungeness crab to king salmon and shrimp), along with burgers, pasta, and sandwiches. This small and homey establishment buzzes with activity most summer evenings. Friday night is pizza night. ⊠ *On the dock road,* ☎ *907/ 697–2227. AE, D, DC, MC, V. Closed Oct.–Apr.*

$$$$ 🏨 **Bear Track Inn.** Built of handcrafted spruce logs, this family-owned inn sits on a 57-acre property facing majestic Icy Strait. Soaring 30-ft ceilings open up the lobby, where a central fireplace, comfortable over-stuffed couches, rustic wooden tables, and moose-antler chandeliers invite warmth and relaxation. The inn's spacious guest rooms are luxuriously furnished. In addition to such local specialties as Dungeness crab, Alaskan spotted prawns, or salmon in parchment, the full-service restaurant serves steak, halibut, salmon, crab, caribou, and even musk ox. The knowledgeable staff will help you design your own customized itinerary of outdoor activities from a long list of options. The room rate (packages range from one to seven nights) includes air or ferry transportation from Juneau, ground transportation, and meals. ⊠ *255 Rink Creek Rd., 99826,* ☎ *907/697–3017 or 888/697–2284,* FAX *907/697–2284,* WEB *www.beartrackinn.com. 14 rooms. Restaurant, hiking, boating, fishing, travel services, airport shuttle. AE, D, MC, V. Closed Oct.–Jan.*

$$$$ 🏨 **Glacier Bay Country Inn.** Bears and moose might peek into this ram-
★   bling log structure with marvelous cupolas, dormers, gables, and porches, which was built from local hand-logged timbers yet has modern amenities. Some cabins include antiques and open log-beam ceilings. Innkeepers Ponch and Sandi Marchbanks charter two boats, each of which sleeps four to six. Gourmet meals are included in the room rate. Among the guests' favorites: steamed Dungeness crab, homemade fettuccine, and rhubarb custard pie. ⊠ *Halfway between airport and Bartlett Cove, Box 5, 99826,* ☎ *907/697–2288 or 800/ 628–0912,* FAX *907/697–2289,* WEB *www.glacierbayalaska.com. 6 rooms, 5 cabins. Restaurant, boating, fishing. AE, D, MC, V. Closed Oct.– mid-May.*

$$$$ 🏨 **Glacier Bay Lodge.** This lodge within the national park is constructed of massive timbers and blends well into the thick rain forest surrounding it on three sides. The modern yet rustic rooms are accessible by boardwalks. If it swims or crawls in the sea hereabouts, you'll find it on the menu in the rustic dining room. A guest favorite is the halibut baked *aleyeska*, a fillet baked in a rich sauce of sour cream, cheese, and onions. Activities include whale-watching, kayaking, and naturalist-led hikes. ⊠ *Box 266, Gustavus 99826 (226 2nd Ave. W, Seattle, WA 98119),* ☎ *907/697–2226 in summer; 800/451–5952;* 𝔽𝔸𝕏 *206/623–7809,* 𝕎𝔼𝔹 *www.glacierbaytours.com. 56 rooms. Restaurant, boating, bicycles. AE, D, DC, MC, V. Closed mid-Sept.–mid-May.*

$$$$ ▦ **Gustavus Inn.** Built in 1928 and established in 1965, this inn con-
★   tinues a tradition of gracious Alaska rural living. In the remodeled original homestead building, rooms are decorated in New England–
farmhouse style. Here you can indulge in Glacier Bay sightseeing trips,
fishing expeditions, bicycle rides around the community, and berry picking in season. Hosts David and Jo Ann Lesh heap bountiful servings
of seafood and fresh vegetables on the plates of overnight guests and
others who reserve for family-style meals in the cozy farmhouse-style
dining room in advance ($25). Dinnertime is 6:30 sharp. ⊠ *Mile 1,
Gustavus Rd., Box 60, 99826,* ☎ *907/697–2254 or 800/649–5220,*
𝔽𝔸𝕏 *907/697–2255; 913/649–5220 in winter,* 𝕎𝔼𝔹 *www.gustavusinn.com.
13 rooms, 11 with bath. Restaurant, fishing, travel services, airport
shuttle. AE, MC, V. Closed mid-Sept.–mid-May.*

$$$$ ▦ **Meadow's Glacier Bay Guest House.** This stunning modern home
★   is an idyllic lodging option for couples and families. Large windows
face Icy Strait, home to summertime populations of humpback whales.
Some rooms have private patio entrances, and all have their own
baths. Each morning owner Meadow Brook, a chef and cookbook author, creates a memorable gourmet breakfast. Groups can rent the entire home for functions. ⊠ *Box 93, 99826,* ☎ *907/697–2348 or 877/
766–2348,* 𝔽𝔸𝕏 *907/697–2348,* 𝕎𝔼𝔹 *www.glacier-bay-alaska.com. 4
rooms. Boating, fishing, airport shuttle. AE, MC, V.*

$$–$$$$ ▦ **A Puffin's Bed & Breakfast.** Alaskan crafts adorn these five attractive
cabins amid a wooded homestead. The main lodge has a social area and
kitchen for the guests, and a full breakfast is included. The owners also
operate Puffin Travel for fishing, kayaking, sightseeing charters, and Glacier
Bay cruises. A two-bedroom house is available to rent, but it's not part
of the B&B. ⊠ *¼ mi off Wilson Rd., Box 3, 99826,* ☎ *907/697–2260
or 800/478–2258,* 𝔽𝔸𝕏 *907/697–2258,* 𝕎𝔼𝔹 *www.puffintravel.com. 6 cab-
ins, 4 with attached bath. Breakfast room, boating, fishing, travel ser-
vices, airport shuttle. No credit cards. Cabins closed mid-Sept.–mid-May;
house available year-round.*

Guided Tours

Glacier Bay is best experienced from the water, whether from the deck
of a cruise ship, on a tour boat, or from the level of a sea kayak. Na-
tional Park Service naturalists come aboard to explain the great glaciers,
to point out features of the forests, islands, and mountains, and to help
spot black bears, brown bears, mountain goats, whales, porpoises, and
birds.

Air Excursions (☎ 907/697–2375 or 800/354–2479) operates Glacier
Bay flightseeing tours from Gustavus, plus flights to Juneau several times
a day in the summer. The boat *Spirit of Adventure* (☎ 907/697–2226
in summer; 800/451–5952 year-round, 𝕎𝔼𝔹 www.glacierbaytours.com),
which departs daily from the dock at Bartlett Cove, near Glacier Bay
Lodge, hosts all-day tours of Glacier Bay with Park Service naturalists
aboard. A separate boat, the *Crystal Fjord*, provides camper and sea
kayaker drop-offs up the bay.

Outdoor Activities and Sports

SEA KAYAKING

The most adventurous way to explore Glacier Bay is by paddling your
own kayak through the bay's icy waters and inlets. But unless you're

an expert, you're better off signing on with the guided tours. You can book one of **Alaska Discovery**'s (✉ 5310 Glacier Hwy., Juneau 99801, ☎ 907/780–6226 or 800/586–1911, WEB www.akdiscovery.com) five- or eight-day guided expeditions. Alaska Discovery provides safe, seaworthy kayaks and tents, gear, and food. Its guides are tough, knowledgeable Alaskans, and they've spent enough time in Glacier Bay's wild country to know what's safe and what's not. You can also take a guided one-day kayak trip from Bartlett Cove if you're just looking for a chance to explore the area. **Spirit Walker Expeditions** (✉ Box 240, 99826, ☎ 907/697–2266 or 800/529–2537, FAX 907/697–2701, WEB www.seakayakalaska.com) leads one- to eight-day sea kayaking trips to various parts of Icy Strait (but not within Glacier Bay itself).

Kayak rentals for unescorted Glacier Bay exploring and camping can be arranged through **Glacier Bay Sea Kayaks** (✉ Bartlett Cove, Box 26, 99826, ☎ 907/697–2257, WEB www.glacierbayseakayaks.com). Prior to going out, you will be given instructions on handling the craft plus camping and routing suggestions. **Sea Otter Kayak** (✉ Box 228, 99826, ☎ 907/697–3007, FAX 907/697–2338, WEB www.he.net/~seaotter) rents kayaks, gives instructions on their use, and supplies the essentials.

HAINES

The town of Haines encompasses an area that has been occupied by Tlingit peoples for centuries. Missionary S. Hall Young and famed naturalist John Muir were intent on establishing a Presbyterian mission in the area, and with the blessing of local chiefs, they chose the site that later became Haines. It's hard to imagine a more beautiful setting— a heavily wooded peninsula with magnificent views of Portage Cove and the snowy Coast Range. Unlike most other cities in Southeast Alaska, Haines, 80 mi northwest of Juneau, can be reached by the 152-mi Haines Highway, which connects at Haines Junction with the Alaska Highway. It's also accessible by the state ferry and by scheduled plane service from Juneau. The Haines ferry terminal is 4½ mi northwest of downtown, and the airport is 4 mi west.

The town has two distinct personalities. On the northern side of the Haines Highway is the portion of Haines that grew up around the Presbyterian mission. In the 1890s, Jack Dalton maintained a toll route from the settlement of Haines into the Yukon, charging $1 for foot passengers and $2.50 per horse. His Dalton Trail later provided access for miners during the 1897 gold rush to the Klondike. The following year, when gold was discovered on the nearby Porcupine River, Haines became a supply center and jumping-off place for those goldfields as well.

South of the highway the town looks like a military post, which is what it was for nearly half a century. In 1903 the U.S. Army established a post—Ft. William Henry Seward—at Portage Cove just south of town. For 17 years (1923–39) the post, renamed Chilkoot Barracks in commemoration of the gold-rush route, was the only military base in the territory. That changed with World War II. Following the war, the post closed down and the buildings were sold to private individuals. They are now part of a National Historic Landmark.

The Haines–Fort Seward community today is recognized for the Native dance and art center at Fort Seward, as well as for the superb fishing, camping, and outdoor recreation to be found at Chilkoot Lake, Portage Cove, Mosquito Lake, and Chilkat State Park on the shores of Chilkat Inlet. Northwest of the city is the Alaska Chilkat Bald Eagle Preserve. Thousands of eagles come here each winter to feed on a late run of chum salmon, making it one of Alaska's premier bird-watching sites.

Exploring Haines

Haines is a delightful place to explore on foot. Local weather is drier than in much of Southeast Alaska, and the town exudes a down-home friendliness. Perhaps this is because Haines sees fewer cruise ships, or maybe it's the grand landscape and ease of access to the mountains and sea.

A Good Walk

Start your walking tour of Haines downtown at the helpful **Haines Convention and Visitors Bureau** ⑥ on 2nd and Willard streets, where you can pick up a walking tour brochure. Walk two blocks up 2nd Avenue and turn right on Main Street; the **Sheldon Museum and Cultural Center** ⑥ is just a block away. Step inside for an introduction to the area and its history. From here, head a block downhill to the busy small boat harbor, filled with commercial-fishing boats and pleasure craft. Turn right on Front Street and follow the shoreline ¼ mi to Lookout Park, a fine place to take in the view on a sunny day. Turn uphill here on steps next to a small cemetery with graves dating from the 1880s. The steps emerge on Mission Street; follow it to 2nd Avenue and turn left for one block to the **American Bald Eagle Foundation** ⑥, a museum and research center for these majestic birds. Continue out 2nd Avenue another ⅓ mi to the most interesting sight in Haines, **Fort William H. Seward National Historic Landmark** ⑥. Turn right as you enter the grounds past **Halsingland Hotel** ⑥, originally the commanding officer's quarters. Circle the parade ground, passing the majestic line of officers' homes along the top, and then back down to **Alaska Indian Arts** ⑥, housed within the old fort hospital. The Chilkat Center for the Arts is just behind, and the central parade ground contains a tribal house and trapper's cabin.

TIMING

Plan to take two hours for this ramble around Haines, and longer if you want to explore the various sights in depth. Local companies offer bus tours that include all these sights plus the "Dalton City" buildings at the fairgrounds and the Alaska Chilkat Bald Eagle Preserve (get information at the visitors bureau).

Sights to See

🄲 ⑥ **Alaska Indian Arts.** A workshop for the craftspeople of a nonprofit organization dedicated to the revival of Tlingit art is set up in the former fort hospital, between the parade ground and the Chilkat Center for the Arts. You can watch Natives carving totem poles, metalsmiths working in silver, and other artists doing silk-screen printing. ⊠ *Fort Seward,* ☎ *907/766–2160.* ⊙ *Weekdays 9–noon and 1–5 and some evenings when cruise ships are in port.*

🄲 ⑥ **American Bald Eagle Foundation.** The main focuses here are bald eagles and the Chilkat Preserve, explored in lectures, displays, and videos. A diorama also shows examples of local animals. The gift shop sells natural-history items. The foundation also sponsors bald eagle research cooperatively with the University of Alaska. ⊠ *2nd Ave. at Haines Hwy., Box 49, 99827,* ☎ *907/766–3094,* FAX *907/766–3095,* WEB *www.baldeagles.org.* ⊡ *$2.50.* ⊙ *Mid-May–mid-Sept., Mon.–Thurs. 9 AM–10 PM, Fri. 9–5, Sat. 1–4, Sun. 1–5; mid-Sept.–mid-May, Mon., Wed., Fri. 1–4.*

⑥ **Fort William H. Seward National Historic Landmark.** Circle the sloping parade ground of Alaska's first army post, where clapboard struc-

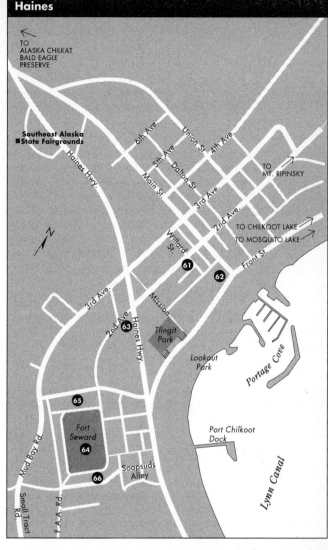

tures stand against a mountain backdrop. The Haines Convention and Visitors Bureau provides walking tour brochure of the fort.

61 **Haines Convention and Visitors Bureau.** At this helpful tourist office you can pick up walking tours of both Haines and Fort Seward, learn about lodging and attractions, check out menus from local restaurants, or pick up a hiking brochure. ⊠ *2nd Ave. near Willard St., Box 530, 99827,* ☎ *907/766–2234 or 800/458–3579,* WEB *www.haines.ak.us.* ☉ *Mid-May–mid-Sept., daily 9–8; always open when cruise ships are in port; mid-Sept.–mid-May, weekdays 8–5.*

65 **Halsingland Hotel.** In Fort Seward, wander past the huge, stately, white-column former commanding officer's home, now a part of the hotel on Officer's Row.

62 **Sheldon Museum and Cultural Center.** Steve Sheldon began assembling Native artifacts, Russian items, and gold-rush memorabilia, such as Jack Dalton's sawed-off shotgun, in the 1880s and started an exhibit of his finds in 1925. The core of what's here is this Alaskan family's personal collection. Particularly noteworthy are the Chilkat Native artifacts, including an 18th-century carved ceremonial hat from the Murrelet Clan, Chilkat blankets, and a model of a Tlingit tribal house. The impressive lens came from Eldred Rock Lighthouse, just south along Lynn Canal. ⊠ *11 Main St., Box 269,* ☎ *907/766–2366,* FAX *907/766–2368.* ▣ *$3.* ☉ *Mid-May–mid-Sept., daily 10–5; mid-Sept.–mid-May, weekdays 10–5.*

OFF THE
BEATEN PATH

HAINES HIGHWAY – Whether you plan to travel its full length or not, you should spend at least a bit of time on this scenic highway, which is paved on both sides of the border. It starts at Mile 0 in Haines and continues 152 mi to Haines Junction, where it joins the Alaska Highway in the Canadian Yukon. At about Mile 6 there's a delightful picnic spot near the Chilkat River. At Mile 9.5 the view of Cathedral Peaks, part of the Chilkat Range, is magnificent. From Mile 19 to Mile 21 you can see the Alaska Chilkat Bald Eagle Preserve. At Mile 33 is a roadside restaurant called, aptly, **Mile 33,** where you can refill your gas tank and coffee mug, grab a burger, and stock up on home-baked goods. The United States–Canada border lies at Mile 42; stop at Canadian customs and be sure to set your clock ahead one hour.

★ **ALASKA CHILKAT BALD EAGLE PRESERVE –** In winter, the preserve is home to the largest concentration of bald eagles in the world. Thousands come to feast on the late run of salmon in the clear, ice-free waters of the Chilkat River, heated by underground warm springs. November and December are the best months for viewing. ⊠ *Mile 19–Mile 21.*

CHILKAT STATE PARK – This park on the Chilkat Inlet has beautiful and accessible viewing of both the Davidson and Rainbow glaciers along with public campgrounds. ⊠ *Box 430, Haines 99827,* ☎ *907/766–2292.*

DALTON CITY – An 1890s gold-rush town was re-created as a set for the movie *White Fang* and moved to the **Southeast Alaska State Fairgrounds** (☎ *907/766–2476*), less than a mile from downtown. The movie set buildings now house local businesses, including the **Klondike Restaurant and Saloon,** with good Tex-Mex, an old-fashioned bar, microbrewery, and live music on Friday night. The five-day-long **Southeast Alaska State Fair,** held the second week of August, is one of several official regional blowouts, and in its homegrown, homespun way it's a real winner. In addition to the usual collection of barnyard animals, the fair has live music, rides on a vintage 1920 Herschal-Spillman carousel, local culinary arts, and Native dances, totemic crafts, and fine art and photography. ▣ *$7.*

Dining and Lodging

$$–$$$ ✕ **Bamboo Room.** Pop culture meets greasy spoon in this unassuming coffee shop with red vinyl booths. The menu includes sandwiches, burgers, fried chicken, and halibut fish-and-chips, but the place really is at its best for an all-American breakfast. The bar has pool, darts, a big-screen TV, and a jukebox. ⊠ *2nd Ave. near Main St.,* ☎ *907/766–2800,* FAX *907/766–3374. AE, D, DC, MC, V.*

$$–$$$ ✕ **The Wild Strawberry.** Just a few doors down from the visitor center, this café provides a bright escape from a rainy day. Owned by a family of commercial fishermen, the restaurant specializes in fresh salmon and halibut caught on their own boats. Popular menu items include smoked salmon chowder, crab and artichoke three-cheese melt (with fresh Dungeness crab), panini sandwiches, and salads. Everything is homemade, and some of the produce is locally grown. Open for breakfast and lunch, the restaurant also offers a children's menu. ⊠ *138 2nd Ave.,* ☎ *907/766–3608. MC, V. Closed Jan.–Mar.*

$ ✕ **Mountain Market.** Meet the locals over coffee (including espresso in all its variations) and a fresh-baked pastry at this busy corner natural-foods store and deli. Mountain Market is also great for lunchtime sandwiches, wraps, soups, and salads. ⊠ *3rd Ave. and Haines Hwy.,* ☎ *907/766–3340,* 🆑 *907/766–3339. MC, V.*

$$$$ ▦ **Weeping Trout Sports Resort.** Enjoy wilderness with style at this small resort on Chilkat Lake—reachable only by boat or plane—where you can golf on a 9-hole course, fish, relax, and refresh, and *not* be bothered by telephones (the lodge does have one for emergencies). The two cabins are clean but basic. One sleeps up to eight and has a toilet. The other has an outhouse and sleeps six in a sleeping loft with three beds. You'll find showers in the nearby main lodge. The restaurant, open to the public Saturday night, serves set four-course, family-style meals ($72 per person including round-trip transportation), which typically include beef, pork, or seafood. ⊠ *Box 129, 99827,* ☎ *907/766–2827,* 🆑 *907/ 766–2824,* 🆆 *www.weepingtrout.com. 2 cabins. Restaurant, 9-hole golf course, fishing. MC, V. Closed mid-Oct.–mid-May.*

$$$–$$$$ ▦ **Captain's Choice Motel.** In the summer, overflowing flower boxes surround the perimeter of this contemporary motel in downtown Haines. Rooms are standard, but those on the second floor open onto a deck with tables and chairs. A patio down below serves as a nightly meeting place where guests enjoy libations and conversation. All rooms include small refrigerators, and the honeymoon suite has a Jacuzzi tub. ⊠ *108 2nd Ave. N, Box 392, 99827,* ☎ *907/766–3111 or 800/478– 2345;* 🆑 *907/766–3332,* 🆆 *www.capchoice.com. 40 rooms, 3 suites. Refrigerator, travel services, car rental. AE, D, DC, MC, V.*

$$–$$$ ▦ **Ft. Seward Lodge.** This lodge, restaurant, and saloon has, over time, served as the fort's PX, soda fountain, bowling alley, and gymnasium. The raw-wood decor and sparse interior brings the pioneering spirit of Alaska to life. The dining room even comes with a mechanical red-velvet swing left over from wilder times. All-you-can-eat Dungeness crab dinners are $22, or choose beef, chicken, or pasta from the menu. Save room for their "ice screaming" pie. The lodge's rooms are clean, but not at all fancy; the least expensive share a bath and lack televisions or phones, and two have well-equipped kitchenettes and ocean views. ⊠ *39 Mud Bay Rd.,* ☎ *907/766–2009 or 800/478– 7772,* 🆑 *907/766–2006,* 🆆 *www.ftsewardlodge.com. 10 rooms. Restaurant, bar, airport shuttle. DC, MC, V.*

$$–$$$ ▦ **Halsingland Hotel.** Fort Seward's commanding officers once lived in the big white Victorian building that today houses this hotel. Many rooms have original claw-foot bathtubs and nonworking cast-iron fireplaces; all are carpeted and have wildlife and historic photos on the walls. The **Commander's Room Restaurant and Lounge** prides itself on its seafood and steaks, but burgers and fish-and-chips are also on the menu. In summer, at the Tlingit tribal house nearby, the Halsingland prepares an all-you-can-eat salmon bake ($23) five nights a week. ⊠ *Fort Seward, Box 1589, 99827,* ☎ *907/766–2000; 800/542–6363 in the U.S.; 800/478–2525 in Yukon Territory and British Columbia;* 🆑 *907/766–2445,* 🆆 *www.haines.ak.us/halsingland. 58 rooms, 52 with bath. Restaurant, bar, travel services. AE, D, DC, MC, V.*

Guided Tours

Adventure

Alaska Nature Tours and Backcountry Outfitters (☎ 907/766–2876, 🆑 907/766–2844) conducts bird-watching and natural-history tours through the Alaska Chilkat Bald Eagle Preserve and leads hiking treks in summer and ski tours in winter. A full-service kayak outfitter in Haines, **Deishu Expeditions** (☎ 907/766–2427 or 800/552–9257, 🆆 www.

seakayaks.com) leads guided trips for a day or a week. They also rent kayaks for do-it-yourselfers.

Boating and Fishing

Alaska Cross-Country Guiding and Rafting (☏ FAX 907/767–5522) conducts cabin-based fly-in, raft-out trips down the Tsirku River through the Alaska Chilkat Bald Eagle Preserve; photo trips to the eagle preserve for small groups only; and wilderness backpacking, glacier hiking, and fly-in trips to remote cabins.

Chilkat Cruises (☏ 907/766–2100, WEB www.chilkatcruises.com) provides a ferry service primarily oriented to cruise-ship visitors who land in Skagway and come to Haines for the day. Boats cross the waterway several times a day in the summer, but they don't stop en route. **Haines-Skagway Water Taxi** (☏ 907/766–3395 or 888/766–3395, WEB www.alaskafjordlines.com) operates a fast catamaran between Haines and Skagway twice a day in the summer, stopping to look for whales and other wildlife along the way. They also offer a day trip from Haines to Juneau and back.

For information on numerous sportfishing charter boats in Haines, contact the **Haines Convention and Visitors Bureau** (☏ 907/766–2234 or 800/458–3579).

Flightseeing

Housed a few doors up the street from the visitor center, **Mountain Flying Service** (☏ 907/766–3007 or 800/766–4007, WEB www.flyglacierbay.com) leads flightseeing trips to nearby Glacier Bay National Park. **Wings of Alaska** (☏ 907/789–0790, WEB www.wingsofalaska.com) flies to Juneau and Skagway.

Nightlife and the Arts

Bars

Locals might rule the pool tables at **Fogcutter Bar** (✉ 122 Main St., ☏ 907/766–2555), but the jukebox is often up for grabs at this lively spot. **Haines Brewing Company** (✉ 108 Whitefang Way, ☏ 907/766–3823) is a microbrewery in the Dalton City buildings at the fairgrounds. Commercial fisherfolk gather nightly at **Harbor Bar** (✉ Front St. at the Harbor, ☏ 907/766–2444), a bar and restaurant dating from 1907. You might catch some live music here in summer. Inside one of the oldest buildings in town (it was once a brothel), the **Pioneer Bar** (✉ 2nd Ave. near Main St., ☏ 907/766–3443) has historical photographs on the walls and a large-screen television for sports.

Dance

The **Chilkat Indian Dancers** (☏ 907/766–2160) perform at the Tribal House on the fort's parade grounds. This multicultural performance includes traditional Tlingit dances using ceremonial rattles, masks, and the famed Chilkat blankets. Performances cost $10 and are held one night a week (typically when a cruise ship is in port) June–August.

Outdoor Activities and Sports

Bicycling

Sockeye Cycle Company (✉ 24 Portage St., Box 829, 99827, ☏ 907/766–2869, WEB www.cyclealaska.com) specializes in guided mountain tours in and around the backcountry of Haines; they also rent, service, and sell bikes.

Hiking

Battery Point Trail is a fairly level path that hugs the shoreline for 2 mi, providing fine views across Lynn Canal. The trail begins a mile east of town, and a campsite can be found at Kelgaya Point near the end. For other hikes, pick up a copy of "Haines Is for Hikers" at the Haines Convention and Visitors Bureau.

Shopping

Art Galleries

A surprising number of artists live in the Haines area, and you will find their works in several local galleries. **Form and Function Art Gallery** (⊠ 211 Willard St., ☎ 907/766–2539) has an impressive collection of handcrafted, Native artwork.

One of the nicest galleries in Haines, **Wild Iris Gallery** (⊠ Portage St. just up from the cruise-ship dock, ☎ 907/766–2300) display attractive jewelry, prints, and fashion wear created by owners Madeleine and Fred Shields.

SKAGWAY

Skagway is a short hop (14 mi) north of Haines if you take the Alaska Marine Highway ferry. If you go by road, the distance is 359 mi, as you have to take the Haines Highway up to Haines Junction, Yukon, then take the Alaska Highway 100 mi south to Whitehorse, and then drive a final 100 mi south on the Klondike Highway to Skagway. North-country folk call this well-traveled sightseeing route the Golden Horseshoe or Golden Circle tour, because it takes in a lot of gold-rush country in addition to lake, forest, and mountain scenery.

However you get to Skagway, you'll find the town an amazingly preserved artifact from one of North America's biggest, most storied gold rushes. Most of the downtown district forms part of the Klondike Gold Rush National Historical Park, a unit of the national park system dedicated to commemorating and interpreting the frenzied stampede that extended to Dawson City in Canada's Yukon. Old false-front stores, saloons, and brothels—built to separate gold-rush prospectors from their grubstakes going north or their gold pokes heading south—have been restored, repainted, and refurnished by the federal government and Skagway's citizens. Although it feels a little like a Disney theme park in spots, when you walk down Broadway today, the scene is not appreciably different from what the prospectors saw in the days of 1898, except the street is now paved to make your exploring easier.

Skagway had only a single cabin still standing when the Yukon gold rush began. At first, the argonauts, as they liked to be called, swarmed to Dyea and the Chilkoot Trail, 9 mi west of Skagway. Skagway and its White Pass Trail didn't seem as attractive until a dock was built in town. Then it mushroomed overnight into the major gateway to the Klondike, supporting a wild mixture of legitimate businesspeople, con artists (among the most cunning was Jefferson "Soapy" Smith), stampeders, and curiosity seekers.

Three months after the first boat landed in July 1897, Skagway numbered perhaps 20,000 persons and had well-laid-out streets, hotels, stores, saloons, gambling houses, and dance halls. By the spring of 1898, the superintendent of the Northwest Royal Mounted Police in neighboring Canada would label the town "little better than a hell on earth."

A lot of the "hell" ended with a shoot-out one pleasant July evening in 1898. Good guy Frank Reid (the surveyor who laid out Skagway's streets so wide and well) faced down bad guy Soapy Smith on a dock downtown near the present ferry terminal. After a classic exchange of gunfire, Smith lay dead and Reid lay dying. The town built a substantial

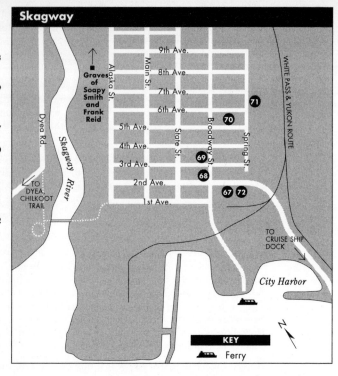

Skagway

City Harbor

KEY

⛴ Ferry

monument at Reid's grave. You can see it in Gold Rush Cemetery and read the current inscription on it: "He gave his life for the honor of Skagway." For Smith, whose tombstone was continually chiseled and stolen by vandals and souvenir seekers, today's grave marker is a simple wooden plank.

When the gold rush played out after a few years, the town of 20,000 dwindled to 700. The White Pass & Yukon Railroad kept the town alive until 1982, when it began to run in summers only. By this time, however, tourism revenue was sufficient to compensate for any economic loss suffered as a result of the railroad's more limited schedule.

Exploring Skagway

Skagway's compact downtown makes it ideal to explore by foot. Nearly all the historic sights are within a few blocks of the cruise-ship and ferry dock, so you can take all the time you want. Skagway runs on tourism, as you will discover the minute you step from a ferry or cruise ship. Unless you're willing to hike into the backcountry on the Chilkoot Trail, you aren't likely to find a quiet Alaskan experience around Skagway.

A Good Walk

A good starting point is the corner of 1st Avenue and Main Street, where a marker notes the infamous 1898 gun battle between Soapy Smith and Frank Reid. Head two blocks east along 1st Avenue and turn left on Broadway Street into the heart of the town. Be sure to stop by the old White Pass & Yukon Railroad Depot at 2nd Avenue and Broadway, which now houses the **Klondike Gold Rush National Historical Park** ⑥⑦ visitor center. Check out the exhibits and films, or join a ranger-led tour to learn more about Skagway's fascinating history. Next door is the White Pass & Yukon Route Depot, a modern structure that blends well with the town's many Victorian-era buildings. The next block up

Broadway contains several of the town's best-known buildings. The two-centuries-old Red Onion Saloon remains a favorite place to imbibe under the watchful eyes of "working girl" mannequins. Next door is the **Arctic Brotherhood Hall** ⑥⑧, with its driftwood-stick false front. Inside you will find the helpful **Skagway Convention and Visitors Bureau** for local information. Next up the street is the **Golden North Hotel** ⑥⑨, filled with gold rush–era furnishings, plus a restaurant and brewery. Across the street sits the old Mascot Saloon, which now houses Park Service historical exhibits and public rest rooms. Back on Broadway, continue two more blocks before turning right on 5th Avenue to the Park Service's **Moore Cabin** ⑦⓪, Skagway's oldest structure. The beautifully restored Skagway City Hall sits directly in front of the new **Trail of '98 Museum** ⑦①. Return to Broadway and follow it to 6th Avenue, where historic Eagles Hall is home to *The Days of '98 with Soapy Smith* show.

If you are up for a longer walk continue 2 mi out of town along Alaska Street to the **Gold Rush Cemetery,** where you'll find the graves of combatants Soapy Smith and Frank Reid. (A city bus takes you most of the way to the cemetery for $2 each direction.) No tour of Skagway is complete without a train ride on the famed **White Pass & Yukon Route Depot.** Trains depart from the corner of 1st Avenue and Broadway several times a day in the summer.

TIMING

The six blocks that compose the heart of downtown Skagway can be explored in a half hour, but you will almost certainly want to spend more time learning about the gold rush in the Park Service's historical buildings and the Trail of '98 Museum. (If you include the 4-mi round-trip walk to the Gold Rush Cemetery, plan on three to four hours.) Most visitors also enjoy exploring Skagway's many shops, restaurants, and other attractions.

Sights to See

★ ⑥⑧ **Arctic Brotherhood Hall.** The Arctic Brotherhood was a fraternal organization of Alaskan and Yukon pioneers. To decorate the exterior false front of their Skagway lodge building, local members created a mosaic out of 20,000 pieces of driftwood and flotsam gathered from local beaches. The AB Hall now houses the **Skagway Convention and Visitors Bureau,** along with public rest rooms. ✉ *Box 1025, Broadway, 99840,* ☎ *907/983–2854; 888/762–1898, message only,* WEB *www.skagway. org.* ☉ *May–Sept., daily 8–6; Oct.–Apr., weekdays 8–5.*

⑥⑨ **Golden North Hotel.** Alaska's oldest hotel was built in 1898 and retains its gold rush–era appearance. The upstairs rooms are furnished with period pieces, and downstairs is a fine restaurant and bar.

★ ⑥⑦ **Klondike Gold Rush National Historical Park.** In what was once the White Pass & Yukon Route rail depot, this park contains exhibits, photos, and artifacts from the White Pass and Chilkoot trails and is of special interest if you plan to take a White Pass train ride, drive the nearby Klondike Highway, or hike the Chilkoot "Trail of '98." Films, ranger talks, and walking tours are offered. Special free Robert Service poetry performances take place two evenings a week at the visitor center. ✉ *2nd Ave. at Broadway,* ☎ *907/983–2921,* WEB *www.nps.gov/klgo.* ☉ *June–Aug., daily 8–8; May and Sept., daily 8–6; Oct.–Apr., weekdays 8–5.*

⑦⓪ **Moore Cabin.** Built in 1887 by Capt. William Moore, the tiny cabin marks the birthplace of Skagway. An early homesteader, Moore prospered from the flood of miners, constructing a dock, warehouse, and sawmill to supply them, and selling land for other ventures. Its interior walls are covered with turn-of-the-20th-century newspapers. Next door, the larger **Moore House** (1897–98) contains interesting exhibits on the Moore family. Both structures are maintained by the Park Service, and the main house is open daily in the summer. ⊠ *Off 5th Ave.*

★ ⑦ **Trail of '98 Museum.** At this museum, directly behind Skagway City Hall, you'll find gambling paraphernalia from the old Board of Trade Saloon on display along with a 19th-century Tlingit canoe (one of the only two like it on the West Coast), historic photos, gold scales, a red-and-black sleigh, and a Salvation Army organ. ⊠ *700 Spring St.,* ☎ *907/983–2420.* ⊡ *$2.* ⊙ *May–Sept., daily 9–5; Oct.–Apr., hrs vary.*

OFF THE
BEATEN PATH

KLONDIKE HIGHWAY – The highway, which starts at the foot of State Street, often parallels the older White Pass railway route as it travels northwest to Carcross and Whitehorse in the Canadian Yukon. It meets the Alaska Highway, which you follow northwest into Whitehorse, and then heads on its own again to terminate at Dawson City, on the shores of the Klondike River. From start to finish, it covers 435 mi. Along the way the road climbs steeply through forested coastal mountains with jagged, snow-covered peaks. It passes by deep, fish-filled lakes and streams in the Canadian high country, where you might spot a mountain goat, moose, black bear, or grizzly. If you're driving the Klondike Highway north from Skagway, you must stop at Canadian customs, Mile 22. If you're traveling south to Skagway, check in at U.S. customs, Mile 6. And remember that when it's 1 PM in Canada at the border, it's noon in Skagway.

★ **WHITE PASS & YUKON ROUTE** – Visitors to Skagway can travel at least part of the way along the gold-rush route aboard the White Pass & Yukon Route (WP & YR) narrow-gauge railroad. The historic (started in 1898) gold-rush railroad's diesel locomotives tow vintage viewing cars up the steep inclines of the route, hugging the walls of precipitous cliff sides and providing views of craggy peaks, plummeting waterfalls, lakes, and forests. It's open mid-May to late September only, and reservations are highly recommended.

Several options are available. Twice daily (three times on Tuesday and Wednesday) the WP & YR leaves Skagway for a three-hour round-trip excursion to the White Pass summit. Sights along the way include Bridal Veil Falls, Inspiration Point, and Dead Horse Gulch. The fare is $78. Through service to Whitehorse, Yukon, is offered daily as well—in the form of a train trip to Fraser, where bus connections are possible on to Whitehorse. The one-way fare to Whitehorse is $95. Special steam excursions (Saturday for $156) and a Chilkoot Trail hikers' service ($25 to Fraser from Lake Bennett) are also offered. Call or visit their Web site for information (☎ 907/983–2217; 800/343–7373 in the U.S. and Canada, WEB www.whitepassrailroad.com).

CHILKOOT TRAIL – If you're a strong and experienced backpacker who likes a challenge, you might want to hike the highly scenic, historic Chilkoot Trail, route of the 1897–98 gold-rush sourdoughs, from Skagway into Canada. Most hikers will need four to five days for the 33-mi hike. Expect steep slopes and wet weather, along with exhilarating vistas at the summit across the much drier Canadian landscape. Deep snow often covers the pass until late summer. The trail stretches from Dyea (9 mi out a dirt road from Skagway) to Lake Bennett and includes a climb up Chilkoot Pass at the United States–Canada border. The National Park Service maintains the American side of the pass as part of **Klondike Gold Rush National Historical Park;** the Canadian side is part of the **Chilkoot Trail National Historic Park.** A backcountry permit is required.

The trail is generally in good condition (particularly in the lower stretches); the forest, mountain, and lake country is both scenic and richly historic, and primitive campsites are strategically located along the way. The Chilkoot is not, however, an easy walk: you'll encounter lots of ups and downs before you cross the pass and reach the Canadian high country, and rain is likely. To return to Skagway, hikers usually catch the White Pass & Yukon Route train from Lake Bennett. The fare is $65, and these trains run daily.

For details, maps, and backcountry permits (C$35), contact the Park Service's summer-only Chilkoot Trail Center (⊠ 1st Ave. and Broadway, ☎ 907/983–2921, 867/667–3910, or 800/661–0486, WEB www.nps.gov/klgo) in the historic Martin Itgen House. Trail permits are also available through Parks Canada (☎ 907/983–2921, 867/667–3910, or 800/661–0486).

Dining and Lodging

$$–$$$ ✕ **Skagway Fish Company.** This small seasonal eatery serves a variety of fresh fish, including salmon, oysters, clams, halibut, and prawns for lunch and dinner. Most popular is the halibut fish-and-chips, served with a side of homemade coleslaw for $11. Tables overlooking the harbor surround the central bar. Baby-back ribs, pork chops, and steaks, along with a New York–style cheesecake topped with strawberries fill out the menu. ⊠ *On the waterfront,* ☎ *907/983-3474. MC, V. Closed Oct.–Apr.*

$$–$$$ ✕ **Stowaway Cafe.** Always crowded, this noisy little harborside café
★ is just a few steps from the cruise-ship dock. Not surprisingly, seafood is the attraction—including prawns Gorgonzola, seafood lasagna, and a hot scallop and bacon salad—but you also can choose tasty steaks, chicken, or smoked ribs. The café is only open daily 4–10, but the owners also run Go-Away Cafe, a tiny lunchtime take-out place in the same building. ⊠ *Congress Way,* ☎ *907/983-3463. Reservations essential. AE, MC, V. Closed Oct.–Apr. No lunch.*

$$$–$$$$ 🏨 **Skagway Inn Bed & Breakfast.** Each room in this downtown Vic-
★ torian inn is named after a different gold-rush gal. The building, one of Skagway's oldest, was built in 1897. Rooms share a Victorian motif, with antiques and cast-iron beds; some have mountain views. The bathrooms are shared, one to every two rooms. Olivia's Restaurant serves up a mean homemade potpie filled with seafood, chicken, or beef every lunch hour and freshly caught seafood every night. ⊠ *655 Broadway, Box 500, 99840,* ☎ *907/983-2289 or 888/752-4929,* FAX *907/983-2713,* WEB *www.skagwayinn.com. 12 rooms share 6 baths. Restaurant, airport shuttle. AE, D, MC, V. Closed Oct.–Apr.*

$$$ 🏨 **Mile Zero Bed & Breakfast.** In a quiet residential area a few blocks from downtown, this modern and comfortable B&B contains spacious and well-insulated guest rooms, all with private entrances, phones, and baths. A Continental breakfast is served each morning. Mile Zero is primarily for adults, though well-behaved children are allowed. ⊠ *9th Ave. and Main St., 99840,* ☎ *907/983-3045,* FAX *907/983-3046,* WEB *www.mile-zero.com. 5 rooms. AE, MC, V.*

$$$ 🏨 **The White House.** Just about two blocks from downtown Skagway, this B&B is a welcome addition to the roster of housing choices in Skagway. Built in 1902 by Lee Guthrie, a gambler and owner of one of the town's most profitable gold-rush saloons, the white clapboard, two-story house is furnished with original Skagway antiques and handmade quilts. The warm dining room and sitting room invite conversation while hearty homemade breakfasts are served up, and later in the day you can unwind with a cup of tea and a movie on the communal VCR. ⊠ *8th Ave. and Main St., Box 41, 99840,* ☎ *907/983-9000,* FAX *907/983-*

9010, WEB *www.skagway.com/whitehouse. 10 rooms. Laundry service, airport shuttle. AE, MC, V.*

$$-$$$ ⊡ **Golden North Hotel.** No question about it, this is Alaska's most his-
★   toric hotel, built in 1898 in the heyday of the gold rush—golden dome
and all. Pioneer Skagway families have contributed period furnishings
to each of the hotel's rooms, and the stories of those families are posted
on the walls of each unit. Claw-foot tubs, brass beds, and Victorian-style
wallpaper and carpets add to the allure of this classy old three-story hotel.
Downstairs, century-old beer recipes from the original Skagway Brewing Company have been put back to good use in a microbrewery inside
the Golden North Restaurant, where 13 brews are on draught. The restaurant specializes in charbroiled steaks and king crab, but also has a sushi
bar and Chinese specialties. Tables out front provide great places to
soak up the sun on a summer day. ⊠ *3rd Ave. and Broadway, Box 343,
99840,* ☎ *907/983–2451 or 888/222–1898,* FAX *907/983–2755,* WEB
*www.goldennorthhotel.com. 31 rooms, 27 with bath. Restaurant, bar,
sushi bar. AE, D, DC, MC, V. Closed Oct.–Mar.*

$$ ⊡ **Wind Valley Lodge.** A long walk or a short drive from downtown,
this lodge provides simple yet modern accommodations. The crackle
of a fire warms the lobby on cool days, and a free shuttle will take you
downtown. ⊠ *22nd Ave. and State St., Box 354, 99840,* ☎ *907/983–
2236,* FAX *907/983–2957,* WEB *www.alaskan.com/windvalleylodge. 29
rooms. Airport shuttle. AE, D, MC, V. Closed Oct.–Mar.*

Guided Tours

Alaska Sled Dog Adventures (☎ 907/983–3990, FAX 907/983–3392, WEB
www.alaskasleddog.com) leads a 2½-hr wheeled (no snow) sled-dog
tour that ends at historic Dyea.

Haines-Skagway Water Taxi (☎ 907/766–3395 or 888/766–3395,
WEB www.alaskafjordlines.com) operates a high-speed boat between
Haines and Skagway twice daily in the summer, stopping to look for
whales and other wildlife along the way. They also lead day trips from
Skagway to Juneau and back.

Jewell Garden Tours (☎ 907/983–2111, WEB www.jewellgardens.com)
conducts three-hour tours that include time in these colorful and his-
toric gardens, a cooking demonstration, and a lunch with fresh gar-
den produce.

Packer Expeditions (☎ 907/983–2544, WEB www.packerexpeditions.com)
guides day trips that include a helicopter flight from Skagway, a 5-mi
hike to Laughton Glacier, and a train ride back to town.

Skagway Street Car Co. (☎ 907/983–2908, FAX 907/983–3908, WEB www.
skagwaystreetcar.com) revisits the gold-rush days in the original 1937 White
Motor Company streetcars. These popular tours are sold aboard the cruise
ships; advance reservations are recommended for nonpassengers. Call one
to two weeks ahead in peak season to be sure of a space.

Nightlife and the Arts

Bars

Imbibe with the locals at **Moe's Frontier Bar** (⊠ Broadway between
4th and 5th Aves., ☎ 907/983–2238), a longtime fixture on the Skag-
★   way scene. At **Red Onion Saloon** (⊠ Broadway at 2nd Ave., ☎ 907/
983–2222), where upstairs was once a gold-rush brothel, you'll find
a convivial crowd of Skagway locals and visitors. An impromptu jam
with cruise-ship musicians gets under way almost every afternoon. Thurs-
day night is when local musicians strut their stuff. The saloon closes
up shop for winter.

Theater

Since 1927, locals have performed a show called **The Days of '98 with Soapy Smith** at Eagles Hall. You'll see cancan dancers, learn a little local history, and watch desperado Soapy Smith being sent to his reward. If you stop in for the evening show, you can enjoy a few warm-up rounds of mock gambling with Soapy's money. Performances of Robert Service poetry start a half hour before each show time. ✉ *Broadway and 6th Ave., 96726 (Box 695, Honaunau, HI 96726 in winter),* ☎ *907/983–2545 in summer; 808/328–9132 in winter,* WEB *www.alaskan.com/daysof98.* ✄ *$14.* ☉ *Daily 10:30, 2:30, and 8.*

SOUTHEAST ALASKA A TO Z

To research prices, get advice from other travelers, and book travel arrangements, visit www.fodors.com.

AIR TRAVEL

Alaska Airlines operates several flights daily from Seattle and other Pacific Coast and southwestern cities to Ketchikan, Wrangell, Petersburg, Sitka, Glacier Bay, and Juneau (☞ Smart Travel Tips A to Z for airline numbers). The carrier connects Juneau to the northern Alaskan cities of Yakutat, Cordova, Anchorage, Fairbanks, Nome, Kotzebue, and Prudhoe Bay. Wings of Alaska can connect you from Juneau to several towns, including Haines and Skagway.

Every large community in Southeast Alaska, and many smaller ones, has air-taxi services that fly you from town to town and, if you're seeking backcountry adventures, into remote wilderness cabins. Local chambers of commerce can provide lists of Bush-plane services.

➤ AIRLINES AND CONTACTS: **Wings of Alaska** (☎ 907/789–0790, WEB www.wingsofalaska.com).

BOAT AND FERRY TRAVEL

From the south, the Alaska Marine Highway operates stateroom-equipped vehicle and passenger ferries from Bellingham, Washington, and from Prince Rupert, British Columbia. The vessels call at Ketchikan, Wrangell, Petersburg, Sitka, Juneau, Haines, and Skagway, and they connect with smaller vessels serving Bush communities; in all, a dozen Southeast towns are served by state ferries. In the summer, staterooms on the ferries are always sold out before sailing time; reserve months in advance. If you are planning to take a car on the ferry, early reservations for vehicle space are also highly recommended. This is particularly true for recreational vehicles. B.C. Ferries operates similar passenger and vehicle ferries from Vancouver Island, British Columbia, to Prince Rupert. From here, travelers can connect with the Alaska Marine Highway System.

➤ BOAT AND FERRY INFORMATION: **Alaska Marine Highway** (✉ Box 25535, Juneau 99802-5535, ☎ 907/465–3941 or 800/642–0066, WEB www.dot.state.ak.us/ferry). **B.C. Ferries** (✉ 1112 Fort St., Victoria, B.C., Canada V8V 4V2, ☎ 250/386–3431, WEB www.bcferries.bc.ca).

BUS TRAVEL

Year-round service between Anchorage and Skagway is available from Alaska Direct Bus Lines. Alaskon Express provides summertime connections between Whitehorse, Anchorage, Fairbanks, Haines, and Skagway, with other stops en route. Though it's a long ride, you can travel Greyhound Lines of Canada from Vancouver or Edmonton to Whitehorse and make connections there with Alaska Direct or Alaskon buses to Skagway or Haines.

➤ BUS INFORMATION: **Alaska Direct Bus Lines** (✉ Box 501, Anchorage 99510, ☎ 907/277–6652 or 800/770–6652). **Alaskon Express** (Gray

Line, ☎ 907/277–5581 or 800/544–2206, WEB www.graylineofalaska.
com). **Greyhound Lines** (☎ 604/662–3222 or 800/661–8747, WEB www.
greyhound.ca).

CAR TRAVEL

Only Skagway and Haines, in the northern Panhandle, and tiny Hyder,
just across the border from Stewart, British Columbia, are accessible
by conventional highway. To reach Skagway or Haines, take the Alaska
Highway to the Canadian Yukon's Whitehorse or Haines Junction, respectively, and then drive the Klondike Highway or Haines Highway
southwest to the Alaska Panhandle. You can reach Hyder on British
Columbia's Cassiar Highway, which can be reached, in turn, from Highway 16 just north of Prince Rupert.

EMERGENCIES

➤ EMERGENCY SERVICES: **Police, fire, ambulance** (☎ 911).

HOSPITALS

➤ CONTACTS: **Bartlett Memorial Hospital** (✉ 3260 Hospital Dr.,
Juneau, ☎ 907/586–2611). **Haines Medical Clinic** (✉ next to the Visitor Information Center, ☎ 907/766–2521). **Ketchikan General Hospital** (✉ 3011 Tongass Ave., ☎ 907/225–5171). **Petersburg Medical
Center** (✉ 103 Fram St., ☎ 907/772–4291). **Sitka Community Hospital** (✉ 209 Moller Dr., ☎ 907/747–3241). **Skagway Medical Clinic**
(✉ 310 11th Ave., between State St. and Broadway, ☎ 907/983–
2255; 907/983–2418 after hours and for emergencies). **Wrangell General Hospital** (✉ 310 Bennett St., ☎ 907/874–7000).

PHARMACIES

➤ JUNEAU: **Juneau Drug Co.** (✉ 202 Front St., ☎ 907/586–1233). **Ron's
Apothecary Shoppe** (✉ 9101 Mendenhall Mall Rd., about 10 mi north
of downtown in Mendenhall Valley, next to the Super Bear market, ☎
907/789–0458; 907/789–9522 after-hours number for prescription
emergencies).

➤ KETCHIKAN: **Downtown Drugstore** (✉ 300 Front St., ☎ 907/225–
3144). **Race Avenue Drugs** (✉ 2300 Tongass Ave., across from the Plaza
shopping mall, ☎ 907/225–4151). After hours, call **Ketchikan General Hospital** (☎ 907/225–5171).

➤ PETERSBURG: **Rexall Drugs** (✉ 215 N. Nordic Dr., ☎ 907/772–
3265). After hours, call **Petersburg Medical Center** (☎ 907/772–4291).

➤ SITKA: **Harry Race Pharmacy** (✉ 106 Lincoln St., ☎ 907/747–
8006). **White's Pharmacy** (✉ 705 Halibut Point Rd., ☎ 907/747–5755).
Sitka Community Hospital (✉ 209 Moller Dr., ☎ 907/747–3241 after
hours).

➤ WRANGELL: **Stikine Drugs** (✉ 202 Front St., ☎ 907/874–3422).
Wrangell General Hospital (✉ 310 Bennett St., ☎ 907/874–7000
after hours).

LODGING

B&B RESERVATION SERVICE

The Alaska Bed & Breakfast Association Inside Passage Chapter books
B&B accommodations in most Southeast communities.

➤ LOCAL AGENTS: **Alaska Bed & Breakfast Association Inside Passage
Chapter** (✉ Box 22800, Juneau 99802, ☎ 907/789–8822, FAX 907/780–
4673, WEB www.accommodations-alaska.com).

TOURS

ADVENTURE

➤ CONTACTS: **Alaska Discovery** (✉ 5310 Glacier Hwy., Juneau, ☎ 907/
780–6226 or 800/586–1911, FAX 907/780–4220, WEB www.akdiscovery.
com). **Alaska Tugboat Tours** (☎ 907/874–3101 or 888/488–4386, WEB

www.alaskatugtours.com). **Cape Fox Tours** (☎ 907/225–4846, FAX 907/225–3137, WEB www.capefoxtours.com). **Tongass Kayak Adventures** (☎ 907/772–4600, WEB www.tongasskayak.com).

AIR CHARTERS AND FLIGHTSEEING

➤ CONTACTS: **Air Excursions** (☎ 907/697–2375 or 800/354–2479), in Gustavus. **Mountain Flying Service** (☎ 907/766–3007 or 800/766–4007, WEB www.flyglacierbay.com), in Haines. **Pacific Airways** (☎ 907/225–3500 or 877/360–3500, WEB www.flypacificairways.com), in Ketchikan. **Pacific Wing** (☎ 907/772–9258), in Petersburg. **ProMech Air** (☎ 907/225–3845, WEB www.promechair.com), in Ketchikan. **Sunrise Aviation** (☎ 907/874–2319 or 800/874–2311, FAX 907/874–2546, WEB www.pnw.com/sunrise), in Wrangell. **Wings of Alaska** (☎ 907/789–0790, WEB www.wingsofalaska.com), in Juneau.

BICYCLING

➤ CONTACTS: **Cycle Alaska** (✉ Box 240711, Douglas, ☎ 907/780–2253). **Petersburg Bicycle Rentals** (✉ 1216 S. Nordic Dr., Petersburg, ☎ 907/772–3829). **Sockeye Cycle Company** (✉ 24 Portage St., Box 829, Skagway 99827, ☎ 907/766–2869, WEB www.cyclealaska.com).

BOATING

➤ CONTACTS: **Alaska Cross-Country Guiding and Rafting** (☎ FAX 907/767–5522). **Alaska Travel Adventures** (☎ 907/789–0052, WEB www.alaskaadventures.com). **Auk Nu Tours** (☎ 907/586–8687 or 800/820–2628, WEB www.auknutours.com). **Auk Ta Shaa Discovery** (☎ 907/586–8687 or 800/820–2628, WEB www.goldbelttours.com). **Spirit Walker Expeditions, Inc.** (✉ Box 240, Gustavus 99826, ☎ 907/697–2266 or 800/529–2537, FAX 907/697–2701, WEB www.seakayakalaska.com).

HELICOPTER FLIGHTSEEING

All of the following operators fly from Juneau.
➤ CONTACTS: **Coastal Helicopters** (☎ 907/789–5600, WEB www.coastal-helicopters.com). **ERA Helicopters** (☎ 907/586–2030 or 800/843–1947, WEB www.eraaviation.com). **Northstar Trekking** (☎ 907/790–4530, WEB www.glaciertrekking.com). **Temsco Helicopters** (☎ 907/789–9501, WEB www.temscoair.com).

NATURE

Alaska Nature Tours and Backcountry Outfitters runs bird-watching and nature trips, plus hiking and skiing trips, from Haines. Kaleidoscope Cruises runs whale-watching and glacier ecology boat tours from Petersburg.
➤ CONTACTS: **Alaska Nature Tours and Backcountry Outfitters** (☎ 907/766–2876, FAX 907/766–2844). **Kaleidoscope Cruises** (☎ 907/772–3736 or 800/868–4373, WEB www.alaska.net/~bbsea).

SIGHTSEEING

Alaska Cruises has catamaran cruises from Ketchikan to Misty Fiords National Monument. Juneau Trolley Car Company makes stops at a dozen or so of Juneau's sights. Metlakatla Tours conducts a variety of tours from Metlakatla. Seaport Limousine leads guided tours of the Hyder area. Sitka Tours runs sightseeing, historical, and raptor tours in Sitka. Skagway Street Car Co. lets you revisit Skagway's gold-rush days in the original 1937 White Motor Company streetcars while showing you the sights.
➤ CONTACTS: **Alaska Cruises** (☎ 907/225–6044 or 800/228–1905, FAX 907/225–8636, WEB www.goldbelttours.com). **Juneau Trolley Car Company** (☎ 907/586–7433, WEB www.juneautrolley.com). **Metlakatla Tours** (☎ 907/886–4441 or 877/886–8687). **Seaport Limousine** (☎ 250/636–2622). **Sitka Tours** (☎ 907/747–8443, FAX 907/747–7510).

Skagway Street Car Co. (☎ 907/983–2908, FAX 907/983–3908, WEB www.skagwaystreetcar.com).

TRAIN TRAVEL

Southeast Alaska's only railroad, the White Pass & Yukon Route, operates between Skagway and Fraser, British Columbia. The tracks follow the historic path over the White Pass summit—a mountain-climbing, cliff-hanging route of 28 mi each way. Bus connections are available at Fraser to Whitehorse, Yukon.

➤ CONTACTS: **White Pass & Yukon Route** (WP & YR, ☎ 800/343–7373, WEB www.whitepassrailroad.com).

VISITOR INFORMATION

Hours of operation of the following visitor information centers are generally mid-May through August, daily 8–5 and additional hours when cruise ships are in port; September–mid-May, weekdays 8–5.

➤ TOURIST INFORMATION: **Alaska Department of Fish and Game** (⌂ Box 25526, Juneau 99802-5526, ☎ 907/465–4112; 907/465–4180 for sportfishing seasons and regulations; 907/465–2376 for license information). **Alaska Division of Parks** (⌂ 400 Willoughby Ave., Suite 400, Juneau 99801, ☎ 907/465–4563). **Haines Convention and Visitors Bureau** (⌂ 2nd Ave. near Willard St., Box 530, Haines 99827, ☎ 907/766–2234 or 800/458–3579, WEB www.haines.ak.us). **Juneau Convention and Visitors Bureau** (⌂ 134 3rd St., Juneau, ☎ 907/586–2201 or 888/581–2201, WEB www.traveljuneau.com). **Ketchikan Visitors Bureau** (⌂ 131 Front St., Ketchikan 99901, ☎ 907/225–6166 or 800/770–3300, WEB www.visit-ketchikan.com). **Klondike Gold Rush National Historical Park** (⌂ visitor center, 2nd Ave. and Broadway, Box 517, Skagway 99840, ☎ 907/983–2921, WEB www.nps.gov/klgo). **Petersburg Visitor Information Center** (⌂ 1st and Fram Sts., Box 649, Petersburg 99833, ☎ 907/772–4636, WEB www.petersburg.org). **Prince of Wales Chamber of Commerce** (⌂ Box 497, Craig 99921, ☎ 907/826–3870, WEB www.princeofwalescoc.org). **Sitka Convention and Visitors Bureau** (⌂ 303 Lincoln St., Box 1226, Sitka 99835, ☎ 907/747–5940, WEB www.sitka.org). **Skagway Convention and Visitors Bureau** (⌂ 525 5th Ave., Box 415, Skagway 99840, ☎ 907/983–2854 or 888/762–1898, WEB www.skagway.org). **Southeast Alaska Tourism Council** (⌂ Box 20710, Juneau 99802, ☎ 907/586–4777 or 800/423–0568; for a Southeast Alaska travel planner, WEB www.alaskainfo.org). **Stewart-Hyder Chamber of Commerce** (⌂ Box 306, Stewart, B.C., Canada V0T 1W0, ☎ 250/636–9224, FAX 250/636–2199, WEB www.stewartbchyderak.homestead.com). **U.S. Forest Service** (⌂ Juneau Ranger District 8465 Old Dairy Rd., Juneau 99801, ☎ 907/586–8800, WEB www.fs.fed.us/r10/tongass). **Wrangell Visitor Center** (⌂ 107 Stikine Ave., Box 49, Wrangell 99929, ☎ 907/874–3901 or 800/367–9745, WEB www.wrangell.com).

SOUTH CENTRAL ALASKA

INCLUDING PRINCE WILLIAM SOUND, HOMER, AND THE KENAI PENINSULA

Stretching from Prince William Sound
to the Alaska Peninsula, from Kodiak Island
and the Kenai Peninsula to the edges of
the vast Alaskan Interior, South Central is
an outdoor playground for fishing, hiking,
wildlife-watching, and rafting. The truly
adventurous can ski in Valdez. Kodiak,
just offshore in the Gulf of Alaska, is
known as the Emerald Island and the
home of the famous Kodiak brown bear.

By Robin
Mackey Hill
and Kent
Sturgis

Updated by
Tom Reale

A NCHORAGE MAY DOMINATE THE REGION IN SIZE, recognition, and political clout, but don't let that mislead you into thinking Anchorage *is* South Central Alaska. The city is actually an anomaly—a modern, urban environment amid historic ports, wilderness outposts, and fishing towns. It also functions as the gateway to some of Alaska's most spectacular parks and wilderness areas, most of which are accessible by floatplane, the Alaska Railroad, or car.

The city lies near the convergence of two of Alaska's most magnificent mountain systems. To the east of the city and sweeping on to the southwest are the Chugach Mountains, a young, active, and impressively rugged range notable for its high coastal relief. Near-mile-high valley walls and peaks rise almost directly from the sea. Across Cook Inlet to the southwest march the high volcanic peaks of the Alaska Range, part of the Pacific Ocean's great Ring of Fire, but snowcapped nonetheless. Farther north in the Alaska Range, and visible from Anchorage on clear days, shimmers Mt. McKinley, with Mt. Foraker at its shoulder—the towering granite giants of the North American continent. Also visible from town are the Talkeetna Range, to the northeast, and the Kenai Range, just across Turnagain Arm and forming the spine of Anchorage's playground, the Kenai Peninsula.

South Central starts with the port towns on the Gulf of Alaska, Prince William Sound, and Cook Inlet—Cordova, Valdez, Whittier, Seward, Seldovia, Kodiak, Homer, Kenai—with their harbors, ferries, glaciers, and ocean life. Unlike the towns and cities of Interior Alaska, where the common theme of gold-rush history links most of the communities, South Central towns and cities have very different personalities. Kodiak, for example, is a busy commercial-fishing port, whereas Homer is a funky tourist town and artists colony on beautiful Kachemak Bay. Then come those mountains, curled like an arm embracing the region. Talkeetna, at the western limits of South Central, is where mountaineers gather to launch their assaults on towering Mt. McKinley. On the eastern border, the defunct copper mine outside McCarthy lies at the foot of the Wrangell Mountains.

Nature lovers can rejoice at the meeting of these mountain ranges, for they bring together a wide sampling of Alaska's flora and fauna. Dall sheep and mountain goats dance their way around the heights of the Chugach and Kenai mountains. Tree species mingle here, too, including three different varieties of spruce—Sitka, black, and white. You'll see larch, birch, cottonwood, and aspen turn golden in the crisp days of late summer and early autumn. South Central is also Alaska's farm country. In the Matanuska-Susitna Valley, under an ever-present summertime sun, 75-pound cabbages are a common occurrence.

Pleasures and Pastimes

Boating
You'll find abundant opportunities for boating on lakes, rivers, and the ocean in South Central. Boaters should exercise caution, however, because local waters are icy cold and can be deadly. Even a life jacket will not save you if hypothermia sets in. Ask locals about conditions before setting out on any but the smallest, most placid lakes. Also, beware of the exposed land on the mudflats of Turnagain Arm between Anchorage and Portage—the huge expanse of seemingly dry ground can quickly turn into a muddy morass when the incoming tide comes roaring in. Keep off, no matter how safe it appears to be.

Canoe and kayak parties in the South Central utilize Prince William Sound, Kachemak Bay, and the Tangle Lakes region. Access is off the Denali Highway, 20 mi west of Paxson. This mountainous country on the southern flank of the Alaska Range forms the headwaters of the Delta River. You can spend a few lazy hours paddling near the road or take an extended trip requiring overnight camping and portages.

Fishing

South Central has Alaska's most accessible fishing. Thousands of tourists flock to the Kenai River and its tributaries for trophy king salmon, which can reach nearly 100 pounds. Saltwater fishing yields huge halibut, cod, and shellfish. Drift boats are a good means of access to the fishing holes. Boat rentals and guide services are available all along the South Central coastline. Fishing licenses are required for all fresh- and saltwater fishing, including gathering clams and shellfish. Licenses are available at sporting-goods, grocery, and drug stores statewide. Nonresident licenses can be purchased for 1-, 3-, 7-, or 14-day periods, or for an entire calendar year. King salmon stamps are also required if you intend to pursue kings. Call the **Alaska Department of Fish and Game** (☎ 907/267–2218) for information.

Exploring South Central

South Central Alaska can be broken down into three general subregions—communities south of Anchorage along the Kenai Peninsula, communities north of Anchorage in the Matanuska-Susitna (Mat-Su) Valley and beyond, and the towns and bays of Prince William Sound. The region is ideal for exploring by boat, train, car, RV, or plane. All but a couple of the coastal communities are on the road system. For the most part, roads have two lanes and are paved. Traffic, especially on the Kenai Peninsula, can be bumper to bumper on summer weekends, so give yourself plenty of time; better yet, try to travel midweek. Long summer days give you plenty of daylight for exploring.

Numbers in the text correspond to numbers in the margin and on the South Central Alaska map.

Great Itineraries

IF YOU HAVE 3 DAYS

Spend them on the Kenai Peninsula. Head south out of Anchorage along the Seward Highway and Turnagain Arm and stop in the ski town of Girdwood for a light lunch and a stroll before continuing southeast to **Portage Glacier** ③ and the Begich-Boggs Visitor Center in the **Chugach National Forest** ②. Take a day hike out of **Hope** ⑥ or a boat trip into **Kenai Fjords National Park** ⑧ out of 🏕 **Seward** ⑦. After spending the night in Seward, work your way down to 🏕 **Homer** ⑪. There's plenty to see and do along Kachemak Bay, including taking a dinner cruise over to Halibut Cove or trying your luck at landing a huge halibut. On your way back up to Anchorage, stop for a bite to eat in **Kenai/Soldotna** ⑩ and make any other stops you missed during the trip down.

IF YOU HAVE 5 DAYS

Follow the three-day itinerary above, return to Anchorage, and head north out of town the next day along the Glenn Highway. Wander the back roads between **Palmer** ⑯ and **Wasilla** ⑰, continuing up to Hatcher Pass and the Independence Mine. Visit a couple of area attractions, such as the Musk Ox Farm or the Iditarod Trail Headquarters, before working your way up to 🏕 **Talkeetna** ⑱ for the night. The other option for day and night three is a backpacking trip into 🏕 **Denali State Park** ⑲. On your way back to Anchorage, stop along the roadside for a short hike or a picnic.

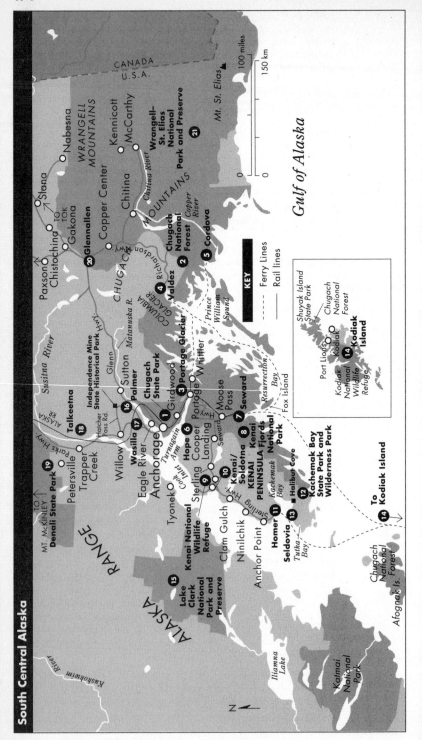

South Central Alaska

CANADA
U.S.A.

100 miles
150 km

Nabesna

WRANGELL
MOUNTAINS

Kennicott
McCarthy

Wrangell-
St. Elias
National
Park and Preserve

Stana
Chistochina
Gakona
TO TOK

Paxson

Copper Center

Chitina

Chitina River

Mt. St. Elias

21

Glennallen   20

Richardson Hwy.

CHUGACH

Copper
River

MOUNTAINS

Chugach
National
Forest

2

Cordova

5

Valdez

4

Gulf of Alaska

Susitna River

Matanuska R.

Glenn Hwy.

COLUMBIA
GLACIER

Independence Mine
State Historical Park

Sutton

Palmer

Chugach
State Park

16

Portage Glacier

3

Girdwood

Whittier

Prince
William
Sound

Shuyak Island
State Park

Chugach
National
Forest

Port Lions

Kodiak

Kodiak
Island

14

Talkeetna   18

ALASKA RR

Hatcher Pass Rd.

Wasilla

17

Willow

Eagle River

Anchorage

Turnagain Arm

1

Portage

Moose
Pass

Seward

7

Resurrection
Bay

Fox Island

Kodiak
National
Wildlife
Refuge

Parks Hwy.

Trapper
Creek

Petersville

Denali State Park   19

TO MT. McKINLEY

Hope   6

Cooper
Landing

Sterling

Kenai/
Soldotna

10

9

KENAI
PENINSULA

Seward Hwy.

Kenai
Fjords
National
Park

8

Kachemak Bay
State Park and
Wilderness Park

Halibut Cove

12

Tyonek

Cook Inlet

Kenai National
Wildlife Refuge

Sterling Hwy.

Clam Gulch

Ninilchik

Anchor Point

Homer

11

Seldovia   13

Tutka
Bay

Kachemak
Bay

To
Kodiak Island

14   To Kodiak Island

ALASKA   RANGE

Lake Clark
National
Park and
Preserve

15

Iliamna
Lake

Kuskokwim River

Katmai
National
Park

Chugach
National
Forest

Afognak Is.

N

KEY

Ferry Lines
Rail lines

Follow the five-day itinerary before cutting over to 🔂 **Valdez** ④, which you should use as a base. Take a day trip past Columbia Glacier; see the sights, including the Alyeska Pipeline Terminal; or take a hike in the surrounding Chugach Mountains. Consider flying across the sound to **Cordova** ⑤, or into McCarthy and the nearby Kennicott Mine in **Wrangell–St. Elias National Park and Preserve** ㉑. Adventurers may consider an excursion to 🔂 **Kodiak Island** ⑭ to watch for Kodiak brown bears and to explore the island's Russian origins. If hiking is your passion, you can spend the entire seven days on a guided backcountry trip through the park or venture farther afield to the pristine 🔂 **Lake Clark National Park and Preserve** ⑮. If exploring Prince William Sound is more to your liking, arrange for a kayak trip out of Valdez or Cordova.

When to Tour South Central Alaska

The region is most alive with visitors and recreational activities between Memorial Day and Labor Day, which is also when it is the most crowded with people enjoying the spectacular fishing and boating, hiking and backpacking, and wildlife spotting and flightseeing. Fall comes early—in mid- to late August—to South Central but can be a gorgeous time to travel. Trees are painted gold and orange, and mountaintops are dusted with snow. Dining and lodging options outside Anchorage may be limited in winter, as many businesses close during the off-season.

Fodor's Choice

No two people will agree on what makes a perfect vacation, but here are some of our South Central favorites for starters. Each of these is detailed later in this chapter.

Uniquely Alaska

★ **Exit Glacier.** Even longtime Alaskans are wowed by the opportunity to come nearly face to face with this ancient river of ice just outside Seward.

★ **Halibut Cove.** It's Alaska just as you would imagine it: houses built on stilts huddled against snowy mountains, reachable only by water.

★ **Kenai Fjords and Resurrection Bay cruise.** Cruises depart Seward daily for scenic tours of the surrounding waters. Spot migrating whales (mid-April), sea lions, sea otters, an array of seabirds, and calving glaciers.

★ **Kennicott Mine and McCarthy.** Take the extra time to plan a detour to the historic town of McCarthy and the Kennicott Mine, surrounded by the Wrangell–St. Elias Mountains, for local color, unforgettable views, and the fascinating history of the once thriving copper-mining town.

★ **Resurrection Pass Trail.** Colorful wildflowers and wildlife draw hikers from around the world to this accessible 38-mi wilderness trail through the Kenai Mountains, perfect for a short day hike or a weeklong backpacking expedition.

Taste Treats

★ **Blue-ribbon pies.** The pies at the Colony Inn in Palmer are consistent winners at the Alaska State Fair. Try the banana-cream strawberry or the fresh fruit pies.

★ **Kahiltna Birch Syrup.** Alaska is one of the few places on the planet where birch syrup is commercially produced, and several companies sell the syrup in gift shops and craft fairs around the state. One of the best is Kahiltna Birch Works, a family operation based in the wilderness west of Talkeetna.

Dining

★ **Homestead Restaurant.** Built from logs, this former roadhouse outside Homer specializes in steaks, seasonal seafood, and spectacular views of the mountains and hanging glaciers across Kachemak Bay. *$$$–$$$$*

★ **Ray's Waterfront.** Reserve a harborside seat at this fine Seward restaurant, where the service is attentive and the halibut and salmon are grilled to perfection. The seafood chowder is excellent, too. *$$–$$$*

Lodging

★ **Talkeetna Alaskan Lodge.** With great food, a cozy ambiance, and panoramic views of the Alaska Range and Mt. McKinley, this lodge offers luxury amid a wilderness setting.

★ **Teddy's Inn the Woods.** This impeccably furnished bed-and-breakfast near Seward is the ideal resting spot for the harried traveler.

★ **U.S. Forest Service Cabins.** Reserve one of these simple, rustic retreats and let the wilderness surround you.

After Hours

★ **Fairview Inn.** Local bands entertain an eclectic crowd at this Talkeetna mountaineering landmark.

★ **Salty Dawg Saloon.** Near the end of the Homer Spit, this low-hung bar with sawdust floors is a favorite of those who like to carve their names on the tables and shoot pool in the back.

PRINCE WILLIAM SOUND

The sound covers some 15,000 square mi—15 times the size of San Francisco Bay. It receives an average of 150 inches of rain a year and is home to more than 150 glaciers, 20 of them reaching tidewater. Along its shoreline are quiet bays, trickling waterfalls, and hidden coves perfect for camping. In addition to hosting brown bears, gray wolves, and marten, the sound thrives with a variety of birds and all manner of marine life, including salmon, halibut, humpback and killer whales, sea otters, sea lions, and porpoises. Bald eagles often soar overhead or perch in tall trees. The sound was heavily damaged by the *Exxon Valdez* oil spill in 1989. The oil has sunk into the beaches below the surface and is sometimes uncovered after storms and high tides. What lasting effect this lurking oil will have on the area is still being studied and remains the topic of much debate.

Chugach State Park

❶ *Bordering Anchorage to the east.*

Chugach State Park is Alaska's most accessible wilderness. Nearly half a million acres in size, the park rises from the coast to more than 8,000 ft, with mountains bearing such colorful names as Williwaw Peak, Temptation Peak, Mt. Magnificent, and Mt. Rumble. The park has nearly 30 trails—from 2 mi to 30 mi long—totaling more than 150 mi, suitable for shorter hikes, weeklong backpacking, and mountain biking. Easy-to-follow cross-country routes extend from one park entrance to another, allowing multiday excursions and a variety of loop trips. This is not your typical urban park—it's real wilderness, home to Dall sheep, mountain goats, brown bears, and several packs of wolves who reside on the edge of town. Many of the trails were blazed by early miners who usually sought the easiest passes. There are also some comfortable roadside campgrounds for people traveling by car or bicycle. Trailheads are scattered around the park's perimeter from Eklutna Lake, 30 mi north of Anchorage, to the trailhead for the Crow Pass Trail near

Girdwood, 37 mi to the south. Some of the more popular trailheads charge a daily parking fee of $5. The Eagle River Nature Center or the park headquarters near Potter Marsh 12 mi south of town has park information. ⊠ *Headquarters, Mile 115, Seward Hwy., HC 52, Box 8999, Indian 99540,* ☎ *907/345–5014.*

The views from high perches in this park are heady. You can look down on the city of Anchorage, observe the great tides in Cook Inlet, gaze north toward Mt. McKinley, or delineate the grand procession of snowy peaks across the inlet, marching down the Alaska Peninsula. The most frequently climbed alpine perch in Alaska is **Flattop Mountain,** on Chugach Park's western edge, ascended by hikers of all abilities. The trailhead is at the Glen Alps parking lot on the hillside above town.

Eagle River Road leads 12 mi into the mountains from the bedroom community of Eagle River. The **Eagle River Nature Center,** at the end of Eagle River Road, has wildlife displays, telescopes for wildlife spotting, and volunteers to answer questions, lead hikes, and host naturalist programs throughout the year. A cabin that sleeps eight and a pair of yurts (insulated tents) that sleep four and six are available for rental. Cost is $55 per night for nonmembers of the nature center, and a walk-in of about 1½ mi is required. Amenities include woodstoves, firewood, and outdoor latrines. ⊠ *Eagle River Rd.,* ☎ *907/694–2108.* ☉ *May 1–Memorial Day, Tues.–Sun. 10–5; Memorial Day–Labor Day, Sun.–Thurs. 10–5, Fri.–Sat. 10–7; Labor Day–late Sept., Tues.–Sun. 10–5; Oct.–Apr., Fri.–Sun. 10–5.* 🚗 *Parking $5.*

Camping

$ ⚠ **Alaska State Park Campgrounds.** You'll find three road-accessible campgrounds in Chugach Park, at Eklutna Lake, Bird Creek, and Eagle River. All are within a short drive from Anchorage. The sites have picnic tables, fire pits, water, and latrines and are available on a first-come, first-served basis. ⊠ *Alaska State Parks, HC52, Box 8999, Indian 99540,* ☎ *907/345–5014. 3 campsites. No credit cards. Closed roughly Oct.–Apr.*

Outdoor Activities and Sports

Main trailheads in the park are at the top of O'Malley, Huffman, and DeArmoun roads; south of Anchorage at Potter Valley, McHugh Creek, and Bird Ridge on the Seward Highway; and to the north of town at Arctic Valley Road (6 mi out) and Eagle River Road (13 mi out). The **Little Rodak Trail** is less than 1 mi long and has a viewing platform that overlooks the Eagle River valley. **Albert Loop Trail** behind the nature center has markers that coordinate with a self-guided hike along its 3-mi route; pick up a brochure at the Eagle River Nature Center.

Chugach National Forest

❷ *40 mi east of Anchorage.*

Sprawling east of Chugach State Park, Chugach National Forest encompasses nearly 6 million acres to embrace a major part of the Kenai Peninsula as well as parts of Prince William Sound. It's the second-largest national forest in the United States, exceeded in size only by the Tongass in Southeast Alaska.

Recreational opportunities here include hiking; camping; backpacking; fishing; boating; mountain biking; horseback riding; hunting; rock climbing; flightseeing; and in the winter, snowshoeing, cross-country skiing, ice climbing, snowmobiling, and dog mushing. Hiking trails offer easy access into the heart of the forest. You can go for a short walk in the woods, pack a lunch and go for a hike looking for birds and wildlife, or embark on a multiday backpacking excursion. You can also take the opportunity to fish a backcountry lake or just indulge yourself in a part of Alaska that's seldom seen by visitors. At all but the most popular trailheads, a five-minute stroll down a wooded trail leads you to the sights, smells, and tranquility of backcountry Alaska.

The Seward Highway between Anchorage and Seward has a number of trail access points. (Check the highway for mile markers, with the distance measured from Seward.) At Mile 63.7 south of Turnagain Pass is the turnoff to the Johnson Pass Trail, a relatively flat trail to walk. Seven miles farther south, take the Hope Highway 18 mi to its end and find the Porcupine Campground. From there, the Gull Rock Trail follows the shore of Turnagain Arm for 5 mi, offering scenic views across the Arm and the chance to spot beluga whales as they forage for salmon. Farther south on the Seward Highway at Mile 23.1, the Ptarmigan Creek trail starts at the campground and climbs into the mountains, ending next to a placid lake surrounded by snowy peaks.

Be prepared to be self-sufficient when entering Chugach Forest. Trailheads typically offer nothing more than a place to park and perhaps an outhouse. Running water, trail maps, and other amenities that you may have come to expect when visiting national forests in the Lower 48 are not available here. Also, be "bear aware" whenever you travel in bear country, and all of Alaska is bear country (☞ Bear Facts box *in* Chapter 2). Be aware of your surroundings, and make noise when traveling, especially in areas of reduced visibility. Bears will most likely make themselves scarce as long as they've got some advance warning of your arrival.

For information on recreational opportunities in the forest, call forest headquarters in Anchorage (☎ 907/271–2500) or the Alaska Public Lands Information Center (☎ 907/271–2737, WEB www.fs.fed.us/r10/chugach).

Outdoor Activities and Sports

★ **Resurrection Pass Trail,** a 38-mi-long backpacking trail through the Chugach National Forest, draws hikers and backpackers from around the world for its colorful wildflowers in spring and summer and the chance to spot wildlife. Moose, caribou, Dall sheep, mountain goats, black and brown bears, wolves, coyotes, and lynx all traverse the forest. Carry binoculars for the best viewing opportunities. Scan every place for movement or anything that doesn't look like a rock, a bush, or a tree, especially whenever you see an open area.

The northern end of the trail starts south of the town of Hope, following an old mining trail through the Kenai Mountains to its end near the town of Cooper Landing. Side trails lead to trailheads along the Seward Highway at Summit Creek and Devil's Pass Creek. The well-maintained trail offers easy access to open country above tree line. Besides U.S. Forest Service Cabins, the Forest Service has provided several "official" campsites along the trail where you'll find a cleared patch of ground and a fire ring; however, you're free to pitch your tent wherever you like.

Lodging

$ ▣ **U.S. Forest Service Cabins.** Along trails, near wilderness alpine
★ lakes, in coastal forests, and on saltwater beaches, these rustic cabins offer retreats for the solo hiker or a group of friends. Some cabins are built of logs, and some are A-frames. Most have tables, chairs, wood-burning stoves, and bunks, but no electricity, running water, or bedding. Many require a fly-in or boat ride, although some can be reached

by car and then foot. ☎ 877/444–6777 *for reservations,* WEB *www. ReserveUSA.com/static/ak2.html. 41 cabins. D, MC, V.*

$ 🏕 **U.S. Forest Service Campgrounds.** The Forest Service maintains 18 campgrounds, 14 of them road-accessible, within Chugach National Forest. All of the road-accessible campgrounds have toilet facilities, usually outhouses, and drinking water available from hand pumps. The Russian River Campground has a three-day limit during salmon-fishing season in June and July. Most have sites suitable for RVs as well as tents. Reservations (for a fee) are accepted at only a limited number of sites. ☎ 877/444–6777 *reservations,* WEB *www.ReserveUSA.com/ static/ak1.html. 18 campgrounds. D, MC, V.*

Portage Glacier

★ ❸ *54 mi southeast of Anchorage.*

Portage Glacier is one of Alaska's most frequently visited tourist destinations. A 6-mi side road off the Seward Highway leads to the **Begich-Boggs Visitor Center** (☎ 907/783–2326), on the shore of Portage Lake and named after two U.S. congressmen who disappeared on a small-plane journey out of Anchorage in 1972. Unfortunately, the glacier is receding rapidly, so the view across the lake is not as good as it used to be.

The mountains surrounding Portage Glacier are covered with smaller glaciers. A 1-mi hike west brings you to the **Byron Glacier** overlook. The glacier is notable for its accessibility—it's one of the few places where you can hike onto a glacier from the road system. In summer, naturalists lead free weekly treks in search of microscopic ice worms. Several hiking trails are accessible from the Seward Highway, including the Old Johnson Trail and the path up Bird Ridge. Both offer spectacular views of **Turnagain Arm,** where explorer Captain Cook searched for the Northwest Passage. Local lore has it that the arm is so named because Cook entered it repeatedly, only to be forced to turn back by the huge tide. The tide is so powerful it sometimes rushes up the arm as a tidal bore—a wall of water that goes up an inlet. Keep an eye out for black bears in all the Portage side valleys in the summer.

🐾 **Big Game Alaska** is a 45-acre drive-through wildlife center just before the Portage Glacier turnoff. Moose, bison, elk, caribou, Sitka black-tailed deer, musk ox, great horned owls, a black bear, and a bald eagle, many of them orphaned in the wild, now live in the park. There are also snack and gift shops. ✉ *Mile 79, Seward Hwy.,* ☎ *907/783–2025,* FAX *907/783–2370.* 💲 *$5.* ☉ *May–Sept., daily 9–7; Oct.–Apr., daily 10–dusk.*

Little remains of the community of **Portage** as a result of the 1964 earthquake. The ghost forest of dead spruce in the area was created when the land subsided by 6 ft–10 ft after the quake, and saltwater penetrated inland from Turnagain Arm, killing the trees. A tumbledown building or two still stand along the highway, and a café stands at the turnoff to Portage Glacier.

En Route Through no fault of its own, **Whittier,** a former army supply port, has become little more than a launching site for those traveling by boat into Prince William Sound. Apart from two inns and a handful of restaurants and small shops, you will probably find little reason to linger here—other towns are more picturesque and entertaining, but on a clear day the sound and surrounding snowcapped mountains make for fabulous views. Until June 2000, Whittier was linked to the road system by ferry and by a rail shuttle service from Portage. The new road through the railroad tunnels has opened up the town to more car traffic. Tolls for this road are $15 for passenger vehicles, $40 for RVs and cars pulling trailers.

Guided Tours

Gray Line of Alaska (☎ 907/277–5581 or 800/478–6388) leads summer boat tours (from mid-May to mid-September) along the face of Portage Glacier aboard the 200-passenger *Ptarmigan* for $25.

Shopping

On your way to Portage, look for **Indian Valley Meats** (✉ Huot Circle, 23 mi south of Anchorage on the Seward Hwy., ☎ 907/653–7511), where workers sell the smoked salmon and musk ox, reindeer, and buffalo sausage made on the premises. They'll also smoke, can, and package the fish you've caught and arrange for shipping anywhere in the world.

Valdez

❹ *6 hrs northeast of Portage by water, 304 mi east of Anchorage.*

Valdez (pronounced val-*deez*) is the largest of the Prince William Sound communities. This year-round ice-free port was originally the entry point for people and goods going to the Interior during the gold rush. Today that flow has been reversed, with Valdez harbor being the southern terminus of the trans-Alaska pipeline, which carries crude oil from Prudhoe Bay and surrounding oil fields nearly 800 mi to the north. This region, with its dependence on commercial fishing, is still feeling the aftereffects of 1989's massive oil spill. Much of Valdez looks new because the business area was relocated and rebuilt after its destruction by the 1964 Good Friday earthquake.

Many Alaskan communities have summer fishing derbies, but Valdez may hold the record for the number of such contests, stretching from late May into September for halibut and various runs of salmon. If you go fishing, by all means enter the appropriate derby. Every summer the newspapers run sob stories about tourists who landed possible prizewinners but couldn't share in the glory because they hadn't forked over the five bucks to officially enter the contest. The **Valdez Silver Salmon Derby** is held the entire month of August. Fishing charters abound in this area of Prince William Sound, and for good reason: these fertile waters provide some of the best saltwater sportfishing in all of Alaska.

A pleasant attraction on a rainy day, if you ever tire of gazing at the 5,000-ft mountain peaks surrounding Valdez, is the **Valdez Museum.** It explores the lives, livelihoods, and events significant to Valdez and surrounding regions. Exhibits include a restored 1880s Gleason & Baily hand-pumped fire engine, a 1907 Ahrens steam fire engine, a 19th-century saloon, a saltwater aquarium, and an exhibit on the 1989 oil spill and the changes it has brought to the area. At a separate site, (✉ 436 Hazlet Ave., ☜ $1.50), a 35-ft by 40-ft model of **Historical Old Town Valdez,** depicts the original town that was wiped out by the 1964 earthquake. ✉ 217 Egan Dr., ☎ 907/835–2764, WEB *www.alaska.net/~vldzmuse/index.html.* ☜ $3. ☉ June–Aug., daily 9–6; Sept.–May, weekdays 11–5, Sat. noon–4.

★ A visit to **Columbia Glacier,** which flows from the surrounding Chugach Mountains, certainly should be on the agenda. Its deep aquamarine face is 5 mi across, and it calves new icebergs with resounding cannonades. This glacier is one of the largest and most readily accessible of Alaska's coastal glaciers. The state ferry travels past the face of the glacier, and scheduled tours of the glaciers and the rest of the sound are available by boat and aircraft from Valdez and Whittier.

To visit the **Alyeska Pipeline Terminal,** the end of the 800-mi-long pipe that starts on the North Slope of the Brooks Range, call Valdez Tours (☏ 907/835–2686). The two-hour tours outline all the operations from pumping the oil out of the ground above the Arctic Circle to loading it onto the tankers in Valdez and shipping it out to the refineries. The tour costs $17.50 and is offered at 10, 1, and 7:30 daily.

Dining and Lodging

$–$$$ ✕ **Mike's Palace.** This busy restaurant with typical Italian-diner decor is a favorite of locals. The menu includes veal, terrific pizza, beer-batter halibut, steaks, and Greek specialties, gyros included. ✉ *On the harbor, 201 N. Harbor Dr.,* ☏ *907/835–2365. MC, V.*

$ ✕ **Gold Rush Café.** This café serves fresh homemade pastries and espresso in the morning, sandwiches and burritos, and a full slate of breakfast menu items. The main event here, though, is lunch, with pasta; homemade soups; gourmet sandwiches; vegetarian entrées; and, in summer, local seafood. Soups range from salmon chowder in summer to curry vegetable. There is no smoking in the café. ✉ *310 Egan Dr.,* ☏ *907/835–5455. MC, V. Closed Sun. No dinner.*

$$$–$$$$ 🏨 **Guesthouse Inn.** This comfortable chain hotel, formerly the Village Inn, has an impressive list of standard amenties, including 25-inch TVs with VCRs in every room, data ports and voice mail, refrigerators, coffeemakers, and microwaves. Room rate includes a deluxe complimentary Continental breakfast. ✉ *100 Meals Ave., 99686,* ☏ *907/835–4445 or 800/478–4445,* ℻ *907/835-2437,* 🕸 *www.guesthousealaska. com. 78 rooms. In-room data ports, refrigerators, gym, laundry facilities. AE, D, DC, MC, V.*

Guided Tours

Numerous charter operators, including **Alaskan Wilderness Sailing & Kayaking** (✉ Box 1313, Valdez 99686, ☏ 907/835–5175, ℻ 907/835–3765), lead tours of this portion of Prince William Sound aboard a 40-ft sailboat, as well as overnight kayaking trips to and from a camp set up on Growler Island. **Alpine Aviation Adventures** (☏ 907/835–4304; 800/478–4304 in Alaska; ℻ 907/835–2523), based in Valdez, gives aerial tours of Columbia Glacier, Prince William Sound, and the Wrangell Mountains.

Valdez-based **Columbia Glacier Wildlife Cruises/Lu-Lu Belle** (☏ 907/835–5141 or 800/411–0090; ℻ 907/835–5899 in summer; ☏ ℻ 800/411–0090 off-season) leads small-group wildlife viewing and cruise tours to Columbia Glacier. **Gray Line of Alaska** (☏ 907/277–5581 or 800/478–6388) conducts tours of the pipeline terminal May–September, departing from the Guesthouse Inn. Price for the pipeline terminal tour is $23.

Keystone Raft & Kayak Adventures (☏ 907/835–2606 or 800/328–8460, ℻ 907/835–4638) provides all gear for guided raft and kayak tours on rivers rated up to Class V in the Valdez and Copper River Valley areas. **Prince William Sound Cruises and Tours** (☏ 907/835–4731 or 800/992–1297, ℻ 907/835–3765), based in Valdez, leads Prince William Sound glacier cruises, island cookouts, overnight trips, and wilderness camps.

Cordova

❺ *6 hrs southeast of Valdez by water, 150 mi east of Anchorage by air.*

Perched on Orca Inlet in eastern Prince William Sound, Cordova began life early in the 20th century as the port city for the Copper River–Northwestern Railway, which was built to serve the Kennicott copper mines 191 mi away in the Wrangell Mountains. With the mines and the railroad shut down since 1938, Cordova's economy now depends heavily on fishing. Attempts to develop a road along the abandoned railroad line connecting to the state highway system were dashed by the 1964 earthquake, so Cordova remains isolated. Access to the community is limited to airplane or ferry. A small town with the spectacular backdrop of snowy Mt. Eccles, Cordova is the gateway to the Copper River delta—one of the great birding areas of North America.

The **Cordova Historical Museum** emphasizes Native artifacts as well as pioneer, mining, and fishing history. Displays include an 1840s handcrafted lighthouse lens and a stuffed 800-pound leatherback turtle. Afternoon video programs and an informative brochure outline a self-guided walking tour of the town's historical buildings. The gift shop sells masks, pottery, and children's books. ⊠ *622 1st St.,* ☎ *907/424–6665.* ▨ *$1.* ☽ *Memorial Day–Labor Day, Mon.–Sat. 10–6, Sun. 2–4; Labor Day–Memorial Day, Tues.–Fri. 1–5, Sat. 2–4.*

Drive out of town along the Copper River Highway and visit the **Million Dollar Bridge,** at Mile 48, where you can view the **Childs Glacier.** Although there is no visitor center, a covered viewing area right next to the bridge enables you to watch the face of the glacier and read the informational plaques while you wait for a huge chunk of ice to topple into the river. The waves produced by falling ice frequently wash migrating salmon onto the riverbank, and the local brown bears have been known to patrol the river's edge looking for an easy meal, so keep your eyes wide open.

Dining and Lodging

$$$ ✕ **Powder House Bar & Restaurant.** On clear summer evenings you can relax on the deck overlooking Eyak Lake at this roadside bar and enjoy whatever the cook's in the mood to fix: homemade soups, sandwiches, sushi, and seasonal seafood are all possibilities. If you're lucky or skillful in your fishing endeavors, the kitchen staff will cook your catch. On Friday and Saturday, shrimp and steak are added to the menu. ⊠ *Mile 2.1, Copper River Hwy.,* ☎ *907/424–3529. AE, MC, V.*

$–$$$ ✕ **Ambrosia.** Pastas, hamburgers, and steaks are served behind the generic storefront, but it's the pizzas, basic and hearty, that have earned this place its reputation among locals. ⊠ *410 1st St.,* ☎ *907/424–7175. AE, MC, V.*

$ ✕ **Killer Whale Café.** Have a breakfast of espresso and baked goods or an omelet at this bookstore café. For lunch you can choose from a deli menu of soups, salads, and sandwiches, followed by a fresh, homemade dessert. On the back balcony, tables overlook the harbor. ⊠ *507 1st St.,* ☎ *907/424–7733. No credit cards. Closed Sun. No dinner.*

$$$ ▤ **Reluctant Fisherman Inn.** This waterfront restaurant with its collection of Native art and artifacts is a good place to watch the commercial-fishing fleet and sample local halibut or salmon. The inn caters to tourists, sportfishermen, and businesspeople. Many of the comfortable, nautical-theme rooms overlook the harbor. The restaurant serves local seafood, including a king salmon chili, as well as pastas and espresso. ⊠ *407 Railroad Ave., 99574,* ☎ *907/424–3272 or 800/770–3272,* ᶠᴬˣ *907/424–7465,* ᵂᴱᴮ *www.cordovaak.com. 41 rooms. Restaurant, bar, in-room data ports, coin laundry, travel services, airport shuttle, car rental. AE, D, DC, MC, V.*

$$ ▤ **Northern Nights Inn B&B.** Commanding a dramatic view of Orca Inlet just a couple of blocks above downtown Cordova, this B&B has rooms furnished with turn-of-the-20th-century antiques. If owner Becky Chapek doesn't have room for you, she'll serve as a valuable source of information on other B&Bs in town. She also operates van tours around town and to the Million Dollar Bridge, and she can

transport you to and from the airport as well. ⊠ *500 3rd St., Box 1564, 99574,* ☎ *907/424–5356,* WEB *www.northernnightsinn.com. 4 rooms. AE, D, MC, V.*

Guided Tours

Cordova Air Service (☎ 907/424–3289; 800/424–7608 in Alaska; FAX 907/ 424–3495) leads aerial tours of Prince William Sound on planes with wheels or floats. **Prince William Sound Adventures** (☎ 907/424–5474) conducts flightseeing as well as sportfishing and other air charters.

Outdoor Activities

BIRD-WATCHING

Spring migration to the **Copper River delta** provides some of the finest avian spectacles in the world. Species—including the Western sandpiper, American dipper, orange-crowned warbler, and short-billed dowitcher—number 14 million. Trumpeter swans and dusky Canada geese can also be seen. The **Copper River Delta Shorebird Festival** (☎ 907/ 424–7212), held the first week of May, includes five days of workshops and guided field trips.

Shopping

Orca Book & Sound Co. (⊠ 507 1st St., ☎ 907/424–5305), closed Sunday, is much more than a bookstore. In addition to books, it sells music, art supplies, children's toys, and locally produced art. The walls often double as a gallery for local works or traveling exhibits, and they specialize in old, rare, out of print, and first edition books, especially Alaskana. In the back is the Killer Whale Café.

KENAI PENINSULA

The Kenai Peninsula, thrusting into the Gulf of Alaska south of Anchorage, is South Central's playground, offering salmon and halibut fishing, spectacular scenery, and wildlife viewing. Commercial fishing is important to the area's economy; five species of Pacific salmon run up the aqua-color Kenai River every summer. Campgrounds and trailheads for backwoods hiking are strung along the roads. Along the way, you can explore three major federal holdings on the peninsula—the western end of the sprawling Chugach National Forest, Kenai National Wildlife Refuge, and Kenai Fjords National Park.

Hope

❻ *39 mi west of Portage, 87 mi south of Anchorage.*

The little gold-mining community of Hope is 87 mi south of Anchorage by road, but just across Turnagain Arm. To visit, however, you must drive all the way around, as no ferry service exists. Hope was founded by miners in 1896 but now consists mainly of retirement homes for former Anchorage residents. The old log cabins and weathered frame buildings in the town center are favorite photography subjects. You'll find lots of gold panning, fishing, and hiking opportunities here, and the northern trailhead for the 38-mi-long Resurrection Pass Trail is nearby. Contact the U.S. Forest Service for information on campgrounds, cabin rentals, and hikes in this area.

Lodging

$$ 🏠 **Bear Creek Lodge.** Of the six cabins here, four are around a pond and two are down by the creek. Each is carpeted and has both a woodstove and an electric heater. The cabins vary in size, with the largest sleeping up to six. A central bathhouse has hot showers and toilets. The lodge café serves breakfast, lunch, and dinner year-round. Try the stir fry, pork chops, or pasta with meat sauce. ⊠ *Mile 15.9, Hope Hwy.*

(Box 140, Hope 99605), ☎ *907/782–3141. 6 cabins without bath. Café. MC, V.*

Seward

❼ *74 mi south of Hope, 127 mi south of Anchorage.*

Seward, at the head of Resurrection Bay, was founded in 1903 when survey crews arrived at this ice-free port to begin planning for a railroad to the Interior. Since then the town has relied heavily on tourism and commercial fishing, and its harbor is important for loading coal bound for Asia. One of the peninsula's major communities, it lies at the south end of the Seward Highway, which connects with Anchorage and is the southern terminus of the Alaska Railroad. Seward also is the launching point for excursions into Kenai Fjords National Park, where you can spy calving glaciers, sea lions, whales, and otters.

Seward, like Valdez, was badly damaged by the 1964 earthquake. A movie illustrating the upheaval caused by the disaster is shown from June 1 until Labor Day, Monday through Saturday at 2 PM in the **Seward Community Library.** Russian icons and paintings by prominent Alaskan artists are on exhibit. ⊠ *5th Ave. and Adams St.,* ☎ *907/224–3646.* ▣ *Movie $3.* ⊙ *Weekdays noon–8, Sat. noon–6.*

The **Seward Museum** displays photographs of the quake's damage, model rooms and artifacts from the early pioneers, and historical up to current information on the Seward area. ⊠ *336 3rd Ave., at Jefferson St.,* ☎ *907/224–3902.* ▣ *$3.* ⊙ *Mid-May–Sept., daily 9–5; Oct.–mid-May, weekends noon–4. Hours may vary seasonally: call the museum for recorded information.*

The first mile of the historic original **Iditarod Trail** runs along the beach and makes for a nice, easy stroll, as does the city's printed walking tour—available at the visitors bureau, the converted railcar at the corner of 3rd Avenue and Jefferson Street, or the Seward Chamber of Commerce Visitor Center at Mile 2 on the Seward Highway. For a different view of the town, drive out **Nash Road,** around Resurrection Bay, and see Seward as it appears nestled at the base of the surrounding mountains.

★ ℭ The **Alaska SeaLife Center,** which opened in May 1998, is a world-class research and visitor facility complete with massive cold-water tanks and outdoor viewing decks. Filled with Alaska's abundant marine life, including harbor seals and sea lions, as well as films, hands-on activities, and a gift shop, the center was partially funded with reparations money from the *Exxon Valdez* oil spill. The center performs cold-water research on fish, seabirds, and marine mammals; provides educational experiences for the general public and school groups; and rehabilitates injured marine wildlife. ⊠ *301 Railway Ave.,* ☎ *907/224–6300 or 800/224–2525,* FAX *907/224–6320,* WEB *www.alaskasealife.org.* ▣ *$12.50.* ⊙ *Mid-May–Sept., daily 8–8; Oct.–mid-May, daily 10–5.*

A short walk from the parking lot along a paved path will bring you
★ face to face with **Exit Glacier** (☞ Kenai Fjords National Park), just outside Seward. Look for the marked turnoff at Mile 3.7 as you enter town or ask locals for directions.

Dining and Lodging

$$–$$$$ ✕ **Harbor Dinner Club & Lounge.** Local seafood is the best choice in this comfy, family-run restaurant. Try a halibut burger and fries for lunch, prime rib or lobster for dinner. There's also dancing in the lounge. ⊠ *220 5th Ave.,* ☎ *907/224–3012. AE, D, DC, MC, V.*

$$–$$$$ ✕ **Ray's Waterfront.** True to its name, this dining spot has views of the
★ bay and a small-boat harbor. Sea otters and sea lions have occasionally
been known to swim right past the large picture windows. Seafood is
the specialty here; the seafood chowder is a must-try. ✉ *Small-boat harbor,* ☎ *907/224–5606. AE, D, DC, MC, V. Closed Nov.–Mar. 20.*

$$$$ 🏨 **Best Western Hotel Seward.** Decorated in resplendent gold-rush style,
this downtown hotel is convenient to restaurants, shopping, and the
Alaska SeaLife Center. In each of its elegant rooms, you'll find a VCR,
king- or queen-size bed, and a phone in the bathroom as well as the
bedroom; some rooms have bay views. The hotel runs a shuttle to
the harbor and is close to the ferry. ✉ *221 5th Ave. (Box 670, 99664),*
☎ *907/224–2378 or 800/528–1234,* 𝖥𝖠𝖷 *907/224–3112,* 𝖶𝖤𝖡 *www.
bestwesternseward.com. 38 rooms. Refrigerators, outdoor hot tub. AE,
D, DC, MC, V.*

$$$$ 🏨 **Breeze Inn.** This big, modern hotel is convenient to the harbor. The
rooms are bright and airy, with custom-made wooden furnishings.
Alaskan wildlife photos adorn the walls. The annex building is all no-
smoking, and the preferred rooms overlook the harbor. ✉ *Box 2147,
99664,* ☎ *907/224–5237 or 888/224–5237,* 𝖥𝖠𝖷 *907/224–7024,* 𝖶𝖤𝖡
*www.sewardalaskamotel.com. 86 rooms. Restaurant, no-smoking
rooms, refrigerators. AE, MC, V.*

$$$$ 🏨 **Great Alaska Adventure Lodge.** You don't need to be a fisherman
★ to appreciate the hospitality of the Great Alaska Adventure Lodge, mid-
way between Seward and Homer. Daily activities are individually
scheduled. Mornings begin with coffee delivered to your room. Af-
ternoons culminate in a complimentary happy hour. Activities include
a range of natural history and soft adventure options, and there is a
remote bear-viewing camp. And if you do fish, this is definitely the place
to be: the guides are top-notch, and seven world records have been set
from the camp's riverbanks. Rates include lodging, meals, and most
activities, and the basic fishing package—two days and one night, all
expenses covered, including a fishing guide—runs $950 per person. Guest
rooms are in the main lodge or in riverside cabins. ✉ *Mile 82.5, Ster-
ling Hwy. (3381 Sterling Hwy., Sterling 99672; in winter: Box 2670,
Poulsbo, WA 98370),* ☎ *907/262–4515 or 800/544–2261; 360/697–
6454 in winter,* 𝖥𝖠𝖷 *907/262–8797; 360/697–7850 in winter,* 𝖶𝖤𝖡 *www.
greatalaska.com. 20 rooms. Dining room, hiking, boating, fishing.
AE, MC, V. Closed Oct.–mid-May.*

$$$$ 🏨 **Kenai Fjords Wilderness Lodge.** An hour's boat ride from Seward,
this wilderness lodge sits within a quiet, forest-lined cove on Fox Is-
land in Resurrection Bay. Visitors stay in cabins tucked inside the
spruce forest. Each cabin has expansive views of the bay and sur-
rounding mountains, as well as private baths with shower, two beds,
and woodstoves. Lodging rates include meals, boat transportation to
the island, and a cruise of Kenai Fjords National Park. Meals are
served family style in the main lodge. Hiking trails make it possible to
explore the island. Guided kayak trips and coastal wildlife tours can
also be arranged. ✉ *Box 1889, Seward 99664,* ☎ *907/224–8068 or
800/478–8068,* 𝖥𝖠𝖷 *907/224–8934,* 𝖶𝖤𝖡 *www.kenaifjords.com. 8 cab-
ins. Dining room, hiking, travel services. AE, D, MC, V. Closed Oct.–
mid-May.*

$$$$ 🏨 **Kenai Princess Wilderness Lodge.** Elegantly rustic might best describe
★ this sprawling complex approximately 45 mi from Seward on a bluff
overlooking the famed Kenai River. Paths lead from the main lodge to
charming bungalows, each containing four spacious units. Buildings
higher on the bluff house eight units. Rooms have a king or two dou-
ble beds, TV, a wood-burning fireplace, comfortable sitting areas, and
porches. There's also a nature trail. Staff can arrange for fishing, flight-
seeing, horseback riding, and river rafting. The Eagle's Crest Restau-

rant serves a variety of Alaska fare including local seafood and rein-deer. ⊠ *Mile 47.7, Sterling Hwy. (Box 676, Cooper Landing 99572),* ☎ *907/595–1425 or 800/426–0500,* FAX *907/595–1424,* WEB *www.princess.com/dest/we_kenai.html. 86 rooms. Restaurant, bar, 3 outdoor hot tubs, gym, camping, shop. AE, DC, MC, V.*

$$$$ 🏠 **Seward Windsong Lodge.** Opened in 1997 as part of a statewide chain of lodges, the Seward Windsong rests in a forested setting near the banks of the Resurrection River. Rooms are decorated in warm plaids, pine furniture, and Alaskan prints, and include coffeemakers, data ports, and TVs. The lodge is just down the road from Exit Glacier. A full-service restaurant is on the premises. ⊠ *Mile 0.6, exit Glacier Rd., about 2 mi north of Seward (2525 C St., Anchorage 99503),* ☎ *907/265–4501 or 888/959–9590,* FAX *907/263–5559,* WEB *www.sewardwindsong.com. 98 rooms, 10 suites. Restaurant, bar, shop, meeting rooms. AE, D, MC, V.*

$$$ 🏠 **Teddy's Inn the Woods.** Set back from the road in a forest of spruce
★   trees in parklike surroundings, this B&B has room for up to six in an outbuilding. The furnishings are impeccable, and the two decks are prime sun-lounging spots. Two cubbyhole bunks are especially child-friendly, and the breakfast of fresh homemade pastries just might be comple-mented with freshly smoked salmon. ⊠ *Mile 23, Seward Hwy. in Moose Pass (29792 Seward Hwy., Seward 99664),* ☎ *907/288–3126. 1 room. MC, V.*

$$–$$$ 🏠 **Alaska's Treehouse B&B.** Enjoy spectacular views of the Chugach
★   Mountains from the solarium and from the hot tub on the tiered deck in this quiet rustic retreat. The hand-built wood-fired sauna is perfect for relaxing in after a hike or ski along nearby trails. Breakfast, included in the room rate, includes sourdough pancakes with homemade wild-berry sauces. A two-bedroom suite sleeps five comfortably. ⊠ *½ mi off Seward Hwy. at Mile 7 (Box 861, 99664),* ☎ *907/224–3867,* FAX *907/224–3978,* WEB *www.seward.net/treehouse. 1 room, 1 suite. Dining room, outdoor hot tub, sauna. No credit cards.*

Guided Tours

Alaska Heritage Tours (☎ 907/265–4500 or 877/258–6877, FAX 907/263–5559) conducts a variety of tours that cover itineraries from Se-ward to Anchorage, Talkeetna, Denali, Prince William Sound, and Valdez. **Alaska Wildland Adventures** (☎ 907/783–2928 or 800/478–4100) in Cooper Landing operates a tidy, pleasant resort and outdoor adventure center on the Kenai River at Mile 50.1 of the Sterling High-way. **Fish House** (⊠ small-boat harbor, ☎ 907/224–3674 or 800/257–7760) is Seward's oldest booking agency for deep-sea fishing.

Outdoor Activities and Sports

RUNNING

The footrace best known among Alaskans is Seward's annual **Mt. Marathon Race,** run on the 4th of July since 1915. It doesn't take the winners very long—44 minutes or so—but the route is straight up the mountain (3,022 ft) and back down to the center of town. The field is limited, past participants have priority, and early registration is re-quired—applications go out February 1. For more info contact the **Se-ward Chamber of Commerce** (⊠ Box 749, Seward 99664, ☎ 907/224–8051, FAX 907/224–5353).

Shopping

Bardarson Studio (⊠ Across from the small-boat harbor, ☎ 907/224–5448), selling everything from prints and watercolors to sculpture and beaded earrings, is a browser's dream. There's a kiddie cave for children and a video-viewing area for nonshoppers. At **I.R.B.I. Custom Alaska Knives** (⊠ Mile 20, Seward Hwy., ☎ 907/288–3616) father and son craftsmen

Irvin and Virgil Campbell handcraft beautiful, functional knives and *ulus* (Alaska Native "women's knives"), with local and exotic antler ivory and horn for handles. **The Ranting Raven** (✉ 224 Fourth Ave., ☎ 907/ 224–2228) is a combination gift shop, bakery, and lunch spot. You can indulge in fresh baked goods, espresso drinks, and daily lunch specials such as quiche, focaccia, and homemade soups while perusing the packed shelves of Russian handicrafts and artwork, Native crafts, and jewelry.

Kenai Fjords National Park

★ **8** *125 mi south of Anchorage.*

Photogenic Seward is the gateway to the 670,000-acre Kenai Fjords National Park. This is spectacular coastal parkland incised with sheer, dark slate cliffs rising from the sea, ribboned with white waterfalls, and tufted with deep-green spruce. Kenai Fjords presents a rare opportunity for an up-close view of blue tidewater glaciers as well as some remarkable ocean wildlife. If you take a day trip on a tour boat out of Seward, you can be pretty sure of seeing sea otters, crowds of Steller's sea lions lazing on the rocky shelves along the shore, a porpoise or two, bald eagles soaring overhead, and tens of thousands of seabirds. Humpback whales and orcas are also sighted occasionally. Tours range in length from 4 hours to 10 hours. The park's coastal fjords are also a favorite of sea kayakers, who can camp or stay in public-use cabins reserved through headquarters. Backcountry travelers should be aware, however, that much of the park's coastline has been claimed by local Native organizations and is now private property. Be sure to check with park headquarters to avoid trespassing.

One of the park's chief attractions is **Exit Glacier,** which can be reached by the one road that passes into Kenai Fjords. Trails inside the park lead to an overlook of the vast **Harding Icefield.** ✉ *Box 1727, Seward 99664,* ☎ *907/224–3175,* 🌐 *www.nps.gov/kefj.*

Guided Tours

Kenai Coastal Tours (☎ 907/277–2131 or 800/478–8068) leads day trips into Kenai Fjords National Park. It also conducts combination train–cruise–motor-coach trips from Anchorage. **Kenai Fjords Tours** (☎ 907/276–6249; 800/478–8068; 907/224–8068 in Seward; ℻ 907/ 276–1064) is the oldest and largest company running tours through the park. **Mariah Tours** (☎ 907/224–8068 or 800/270–1238, ℻ 907/ 224–8625) operates smaller boats through the park and into the Chiswell Islands with a maximum of 16 passengers per boat mid-May through mid-September.

Lodging

$ 🏕 **National Park Service Cabins.** The Kenai Fjords National Park manages four cabins including three along the coast, favored by sea kayakers and for summer use only. Accessible only by boat or floatplane, they must be reserved in advance. The cabins cost $35 per night: three have a three-night limit, and the North Arm cabin can be reserved for up to nine nights since it's considerably farther out than the others. The park's lone winter cabin is at Exit Glacier and is a stopping place for many skiers, mushers, and snow machiners (the local name for snowmobilers). ✉ *1212 4th Ave., Box 1727, Seward 99664,* ☎ *907/224–3175 to reserve the winter cabin; 907/271–2737 in Anchorage for the summer rentals. 4 cabins. MC, V.*

Kenai National Wildlife Refuge

9 *95 mi northwest of Kenai Fjords National Park, 150 mi southwest of Anchorage.*

The U.S. Fish and Wildlife Service administers nearly 2 million acres on the Kenai Peninsula in one of its prime wildlife refuges. The **Kenai National Wildlife Refuge** takes in a portion of the Harding Icefield as well as two large and scenic lakes, Skilak and Tustumena. The refuge is not only the finest moose habitat in the region, but its waterways are great for canoeing and kayaking. The U.S. Fish and Wildlife Service maintains a canoe system, campgrounds, and four free cabin shelters, available on a first-come, first-served basis. Two of the cabin shelters are fly-ins; you can hike or canoe to the other two. For information (including canoe rentals), contact the Alaska Public Lands Information Center in Anchorage.

Camping

$ ⚠ **Kenai National Wildlife Refuge Campgrounds.** The U.S. Fish and Wildlife Service maintains 14 road-accessible campgrounds in the Kenai refuge, with a total of 130 sites, 110 of which are suitable for RVs, though there are no hookups. Only two of the campgrounds (Hidden Lake and Upper Skilak Lake) charge fees for camping. All have toilet facilities, and all but three have drinking water. The campgrounds also have picnic tables, fire pits, nearby hiking trails, and fishing. The maximum length of stay is 14 consecutive days. ⊠ *Kenai National Wildlife Refuge, Box 2139, Soldotna 99669-2139,* ☎ *907/262–7021,* WEB *kenai.fws.gov. 14 campgrounds. Reservations not accepted. No credit cards.*

Kenai/Soldotna

➓ *116 mi northwest of Seward, 148 mi southwest of Anchorage.*

The towns of Kenai and Soldotna are often mentioned almost interchangeably due to their physical proximity. Soldotna, with its strategic location on the peninsula's northwest coast, takes its name from a nearby stream; it's a corruption of the Russian word for "soldier," although some say the name came from a Native American word meaning "stream fork." Today, this city of 3,900 residents is the commercial and sportfishing hub of the Kenai Peninsula. Along with its sister city of Kenai, whose onion-domed Holy Assumption Russian Orthodox Church highlights the city's old town, it is home to Cook Inlet oil-field workers and their families. Soldotna's commercial center stretches along the Sterling Highway, making this a stopping point for those traveling up and down the peninsula. The town of Kenai lies near the end of the road that branches off the Sterling Highway in Soldotna. Near Kenai is Captain Cook State Park, one of the least-visited state parks on the road system. This portion of the peninsula is level and forested, with numerous lakes and streams pocking and crisscrossing the area. Trumpeter swans return here in the spring and sightings of moose and caribou are common.

In addition to fishing, clam digging is also popular at **Clam Gulch,** 24 mi south of Soldotna on the Sterling Highway. This is a favorite of local children, who love any excuse to dig in the muddy, sloppy goo. Ask locals on the beach how to find the giant razor clams (recognized by their dimples in the sand). The clam digging is best when tides are minus 4 or 5 ft. A sportfishing license, available at grocery, sporting-goods, and drug stores, is required.

Dining and Lodging

$-$$$ ✕ **The Duck Inn.** The Duck Inn serves Italian and Mexican dishes, as
★ well as pizzas, chicken, steaks, and seafood. Portions are generous, and the variety of items on the menu guarantees something for everyone. Locally caught halibut is a specialty, prepared in enough different ways to stave off feelings of halibut overload. ⊠ *43187 Kalifornsky Beach Rd., 99669,* ☎ *907/262–1849. AE, MC, V.*

$–$$$ ✕ **Sackett's Kenai Grill.** At a wide spot in the road on the shore of Kenai
★   Lake, the Kenai Grill offers fine dining amid a scenic setting. Although
the place doesn't impress from the outside or inside, the food clearly
makes up for any aesthetic shortcomings and the view of the lake and
the surrounding Kenai Mountains combine to make for a memorable
dining experience. Try the specialty of the house, the smoked prime
rib, or one of the fresh seafood or creative pasta dishes. ✉ *Mile 47.4
Sterling Highway, Cooper Landing, 99572,* ☎ *907/595–1827.AE,
MC, V.*

$$$$ 🏨 **Best Western King Salmon Motel.** This clean, comfortable member
of the reliable Best Western franchise has large, airy rooms including
some with kitchenettes. If you're traveling by RV, you'll find a park
complete with full hookups available for $20 per night. ✉ *35546
Kenai Spur Rd., 99669,* ☎ *907/262–5857, 888/262–5857,* ℻ *907/262–
9441. 49 rooms. Restaurant, in-room data ports, kitchenettes (some),
coin laundry. AE, D, DC, MC, V.*

Outdoor Activities and Sports

FISHING

Anglers from around the world come for the salmon-choked streams
and rivers, most notably the **Kenai River** and its companion, the **Rus-
sian River.** Deep-sea fishing for salmon and halibut out of **Deep Creek**
is challenging Homer's position as the preeminent fishing destination
on the southern Kenai Peninsula. This fishery is unusual in that trac-
tors launch boats off the beach and into the Cook Inlet surf. The local
campground and RV lot is packed on summer weekends.

Area phone books list some 300 fishing charters and guides, all of whom
stay busy during the hectic summer fishing season. Try **Hi Lo Charters**
(☎ 907/283–9691 or 800/757–9333) for salmon fishing trips on the
world-famous Kenai River. The **Sports Den** (☎ 907/262–7491) can ar-
range fishing trips on the river, the saltwater, or a remote fly-in loca-
tion for salmon, trout, or halibut.

Homer

★ ⑪ *77 mi south of Soldotna, 226 mi south of Anchorage.*

At the southern end of the Sterling Highway lies the city of Homer, on
the head of a narrow spit that juts into beautiful Kachemak Bay.
Founded just before the turn of the 20th century as a gold-prospect-
ing camp, this community was later used as a coal-mining headquar-
ters. Today the town of Homer is an eclectic community filled with
tacky tourist paraphernalia, commercial-fishing facilities—including
boats, canneries, and repair yards—and a thriving group of local
artists, sculptors, actors, and writers. An annual influx of college kids
referred to locally as "spit rats" works the slime lines in the process-
ing factories while living in tents on the spit. They mix freely with for-
eign tourists and Alaskans who make annual pilgrimages to the Halibut
Capital of the World. The variety of local architecture includes every-
thing from homes that are little more than assemblages of driftwood,
flotsam, and jetsam to featureless steel commercial buildings and mag-
nificent homes on the hillside overlooking the surrounding bay, moun-
tains, forests, and glaciers. In addition to highway and air access,
Homer also has regular ferry service to Seldovia.

★ ☾ The **Pratt Museum** has a saltwater aquarium; an exhibit on the 1989 Prince
William Sound oil spill; a wildflower garden; a gift shop; and pioneer,
Russian, and Alaska Native displays. You can spy on wildlife with
robotic video cameras set up on a seabird rookery and at the McNeil
River bear sanctuary. There's also a refurbished homestead cabin and

outdoor summer exhibits along the trail out back. ⊠ *Bartlett St. off Pioneer Ave.,* ☎ *907/235–8635,* WEB *www.prattmuseum.org.* ⊡ *$6.* ☉ *May–Sept., daily 10–6; Oct.–Dec. and Feb.–Apr., Tues.–Sun. noon–5.*

Kachemak Bay abounds in wildlife, including a large population of puffins and eagles. Tour operators take you past bird rookeries or across the bay to gravel beaches for clam digging. Most fishing charters include an opportunity to view whales, seals, porpoises, and birds close up. At the end of the day, walk along the docks on Homer Spit and watch commercial-fishing boats and charter boats unload their catch.

★ Directly across from the end of the Homer Spit is **Halibut Cove,** a small community of people who make their living on the bay or by selling handicrafts. Spend a relaxing afternoon or evening meandering along the boardwalk and visiting galleries. The cove itself is lovely, especially during salmon runs, when fish leap and splash in the clear water. You'll find several lodges on this side of the bay, on pristine coves away from summer crowds. The *Danny J* ferries people across from Homer Spit, with a stop at the rookery at Gull Island and two or three hours to walk around Halibut Cove, for $42. The ferry makes two trips daily: the first leaves Homer at noon and returns at 5 PM, the second leaves at 5 PM and returns at 10 PM. Central Charters handles all booking.

Dining and Lodging

$$$–$$$$ ✕ **Homestead Restaurant.** This former log roadhouse 8 mi from town
★ is a favorite of locals who appreciate artfully presented food served amid contemporary art. The Homestead specializes in steak and prime rib, and seasonal fish and shellfish prepared with garlic, citrus fruits, or spicy ethnic sauces. Epic views of the bay, mountains, and hanging glaciers are yours for the looking. A full wine list and bar are available. ⊠ *Mile 8.2, East End Rd.,* ☎ *907/235–8723. AE, MC, V. Closed Jan.–Mar.*

$$–$$$$ ✕ **Café Cups.** It's hard to miss this place as you drive down Pioneer Avenue—look for the huge namesake cups on the building's facade. One of Homer's oldest restaurants, this café serves lunch and dinners that make the most of the locally abundant seafood, complemented by a terrific wine list. It's one of the few small restaurants in Alaska where the menu includes a variety of vegetarian dishes. ⊠ *162 W. Pioneer Ave.,* ☎ *907/235–8330. MC, V.*

$$–$$$ ✕ **Saltry in Halibut Cove.** This restaurant serves local seafood as sushi
★ or prepares it with curries and pastas. For libations, you can choose from a wide selection of imported beers. The deck overlooks the boat dock and the cove. Dinner seatings are at 6 and 7:30; before or after dinner, you can stroll around the boardwalks at Halibut Cove and visit the art shops and soak up the view. Reservations are essential for the ferry (at a reduced $22 round-trip), which leaves Homer Spit at 5 PM. A noon ferry ($44) will take you to Halibut Cove for lunch, ($5–$17), stopping along the way for wildlife viewing. ⊠ *Halibut Cove (contact Central Charters,* ☎ *907/235–7847 or 800/478–7847). Reservations essential. AE, D, MC, V. Closed early Sept.–late May.*

$$$–$$$$ ✕🖾 **Land's End.** This sprawling blue-and-white complex at the very end of the spit has wide-open views of the bay. Most of the rooms face the bay and have telephones and TVs but otherwise vary widely. The decor in some is nautical, in others floral. Some are perfect for a couple, some big enough for a family—five large rooms have lofts. As might be expected, the restaurant ($$–$$$$) specializes in seafood, including halibut, scallops, oysters, and clams; burgers and steak are also served. ⊠ *4786 Homer Spit Rd., 99603,* ☎ *907/235–0400; 800/478–0400 in Alaska;* FAX *907/235–0420,* WEB *www.lands-end-resort.com. 80 rooms. Restaurant, bar, spa, gym. AE, D, DC, MC, V.*

$$–$$$$ ⊞ **Driftwood Inn.** Rooms in this cozy, friendly inn are bright and come
★ in various configurations, including those perfect for families (small pets
are okay). Downstairs has a comfortable sitting room with fireplace,
TV, books, and videos. A small eating area has serve-yourself coffee,
tea, pastries, and hot and cold cereal. A microwave, refrigerator, bar-
becue, and fish-cooking and -cleaning area are also available. Visitors
using the on-site camping area and full-hookup RV park have full ac-
cess to the inn's facilities. ⊠ *135 W. Bunnell St., 99603,* ☎ *907/235–
8019 or 800/478–8019,* ⅎⅩ *907/235–8019,* ⒲ⒺⒷ *www.thedriftwoodinn.
com. 20 rooms, 11 with bath. Dining room, camping. D, DC, MC, V.*

Guided Tours

Central Charters (⊠ 4241 Homer Spit Rd., 99603, ☎ 907/235–7847
or 800/478–7847) arranges fishing and ferry trips to Halibut Cove,
around Kachemak Bay, and across to Seldovia. **Homer Ocean Charters**
(☎ 907/235–6212 or 800/426–6212) on the Spit offers fishing, hunt-
ing, and sightseeing trips, as well as ocean kayaking and water-taxi ser-
vices and remote cabin rentals. They also lead cruises to The Rookery
Restaurant—$50–$69 includes the round-trip passage with narration
by a naturalist and a three-course meal.

Nightlife and the Arts

Dance to lively bands at **Alice's** (⊠ 195 E. Pioneer Ave., ☎ 907/235–
★ 7650). The Spit's **Salty Dawg Saloon** (☎ 907/235–9990) is a tumble-
down lighthouse, sure to be frequented by a carousing fisherman or
two.

Shopping

ART AND GIFTS

A variety of art by the town's residents can be found in the galleries
on and around Pioneer Avenue. The gift shop at the **Pratt Museum** stocks
natural-history books, locally crafted or inspired jewelry, note cards,
and gifts for children. The **Bunnell Street Gallery** (⊠ corner of Main
and Bunnell Sts., ☎ 907/235–2662) displays innovative contemporary
art primarily produced in Alaska. The gallery, which occupies the first
floor of a historic trading post, also hosts workshops, lectures, musi-
cal performances, and other community events.

FOODSTUFFS

Alaska Wild Berry Products (⊠ 528 E. Pioneer Ave., ☎ 907/235–
8858) sells chocolate-covered candies, jams, jellies, sauces, and syrups
made from wild berries handpicked on the Kenai Peninsula, as well as
an extensive variety of Alaskan-theme gifts and clothing. Although once
produced here, most items are now made at the company's Anchor-
age location. Sharing the front porch with the Bunnell Street Gallery,
Two Sisters Bakery (⊠ 106 W. Bunnell St., ☎ 907/235–2280) serves
fresh bread baked on the premises, coffee, muffins, soup, and pizza,
and offers daily lunch specials.

Kachemak Bay State Park and Wilderness Park

⓬ *10 mi southeast of Homer.*

Kachemak Bay State Park and Wilderness Park, accessible by boat or
Bush plane, protects more than 350,000 acres of coast, mountains,
glaciers, forests, and wildlife on the lower Kenai Peninsula. Recreational
opportunities include boating, sea kayaking, fishing, hiking, and beach-
combing. Facilities are minimal but include 20 primitive campsites, five
public-use cabins, and a system of trails accessible from Kachemak Bay.
⊠ *Kenai State Parks Office, Box 1247, Soldotna 99669,* ☎ *907/262–
5581 or 907/235–7024.*

Lodging

$$$$ ▣ **Kachemak Bay Wilderness Lodge.** Across Kachemak Bay from
★ Homer, this luxurious lodge offers wildlife-viewing opportunities and
panoramic mountain, glacier, and bay vistas in an intimate setting for
up to 12 guests. The main log building has a piano and a big stone
fireplace to warm you after a day of hiking, fishing, kayaking, or touring in one of the lodge's five guided boats (some of the guided fly-out
trips may cost extra). Scattered throughout the woods, the rustic cabins are decorated with antiques. Dinners spotlight seafood—clams, mussels, crab, and fish—caught in the bay. The price is per person for a
five-day, four-night all-inclusive package. ⊠ *Box 956, Homer 99603*,
☎ *907/235–8910*, FAX *907/235–8911*, WEB *www.alaskawildernesslodge.
com. 4 cabins, 1 room in the lodge. Dining room, hot tub, sauna, hiking, boating, fishing. No credit cards. Closed Oct.–Apr.*

$–$$ ▣ **Alaska State Parks Cabins.** Three public-use cabins are within
Kachemak Bay's Halibut Cove Lagoon area, another is near Tutka Bay
Lagoon, and a fifth is at China Poot Lake. All but the lakeside cabin
are accessible by boat; China Poot can be reached only by foot from
the boat landing on the beach or by floatplane to the lake. The cabins
have wood bunks, table, and chairs, but no running water or electricity. Four of the five cabins sleep up to six people (the other, the Overlook cabin at Halibut Cove, sleeps eight) and all must be reserved up
to six months in advance. ⊠ *Alaska State Parks Information Center,
550 W. 7th Ave., Suite 1260, Anchorage 99501-3557*, ☎ *907/269–8400.
5 cabins. No credit cards.*

$ ⚠ **Alaska State Parks Campsites.** Twenty primitive, free campsites with
pit toilets and fire rings are scattered along the shores of Kachemak
Bay across from Homer and are accessible by boat (water taxis operate here daily in summer). The sites are available on a first-come, first-
served basis, and camping is allowed nearly everywhere in the park,
not restricted to developed sites. ⊠ *Alaska State Parks, Kenai Area Office, Box 1247, Soldotna 99669*, ☎ *907/235–7024 or 907/262–5581*,
WEB *www.dnr.state.ak.us/parks/units/kbay/kbay.htm. 6 campgrounds.
Reservations not accepted. No credit cards.*

Seldovia

⑬ *16 mi south of Homer.*

Seldovia, isolated across the bay from Homer, retains the charm of an
earlier Alaska. The town's Russian bloodline shows in its onion-dome
church and its name, meaning "herring bay." Those who fish use
plenty of herring for bait, catching record-size salmon, halibut, and king
or Dungeness crab. You'll find excellent fishing whether you drop
your line into the deep waters of Kachemak Bay or cast into the surf
for silver salmon on the shore of Outside Beach, near town. Stroll through
town and along the slough, where frame houses rest on pilings.

Dining and Lodging

$ ✕ **The Buzz.** This coffee shop sells espresso, monster-size baked goods,
breakfast burritos, quiche, and homemade granola. For lunch, try
pasta, chili, or soup with homemade bread. ⊠ *231 Main St., next to
the harbormaster's office*, ☎ *907/234–7479. MC, V. Closed Oct.–Feb.*

$$$–$$$$ ▣ **Across the Bay Tent & Breakfast Adventure Co.** A step up the com-
★ fort ladder from camping, this beachfront compound is reachable by
water taxi from Homer. You stay in sturdy canvas-floor tents with twin
beds, and a large common room has hardwood floors and a piano. Prices
vary depending on whether you do your own cooking or eat meals pre-
pared by the staff. A propane stove and grill, as well as pots, pans, and
picnic tables, are provided. Otherwise, host-prepared meals are hearty

and served family style. A beach is great for walking and clamming; escorted kayak trips and mountain bikes are available for an extra charge. ⊠ *Mile 8, Jakalof Bay Rd., 8 mi from Seldovia (Box 81, Seldovia 99663 in summer; Box 112054, Anchorage 99511 in winter),* ☎ *907/235–3633 in summer; 907/345–2571 in winter,* WEB *www.tentandbreakfastalaska. com. 5 tents. Dining room, sauna, boating, bicycles. MC, V. Closed late Sept.–early May.*

$$–$$$ 🏨 **Seldovia Boardwalk Hotel.** This hotel with a fabulous view of the harbor has immaculate modern rooms, half of which face the water. A large, sunlit parlor downstairs has a woodstove and coffee service. Many guests stay at this no-smoking hotel as part of a tour from Homer that includes a narrated wildlife cruise and a 30-minute flightseeing trip back to Homer. The proprietors can also arrange charter-fishing or sea kayaking trips. ⊠ *Box 72, 99663,* ☎ *907/234–7816 or 800/238–7862,* WEB *www.alaskaone.com/boardwalk. 14 rooms. No-smoking room. D, MC, V.*

Kodiak Island

⑭ *248 mi southwest from Anchorage by air.*

Alaska's largest island is accessible only by air from Anchorage and by ferry from Homer and Seward. Russian explorers discovered the island in 1763, and Kodiak served as Alaska's first capital until 1804, when the government was moved to Sitka. Situated as it is in the northwestern Gulf of Alaska, Kodiak has been subjected to several natural disasters. In 1912 a volcanic eruption on the nearby Alaska Peninsula covered the town site in knee-deep drifts of ash and pumice. A tidal wave resulting from the 1964 earthquake destroyed the island's large fishing fleet and smashed Kodiak's low-lying downtown area.

Today, commercial fishing is king in Kodiak. Despite its small population—about 15,000 people scattered among the several islands in the Kodiak group—the city is among the busiest fishing ports in the United States. The harbor is also an important supply point for small communities on the Aleutian Islands and the Alaska Peninsula.

Floatplane and boat charters are available from Kodiak to numerous remote attractions not served by roads. Chief among these areas is the 1.6-million-acre **Kodiak National Wildlife Refuge,** lying partly on Kodiak Island and partly on Afognak Island to the north, where spotting the enormous Kodiak brown bears is the main goal of a trip. Seeing the Kodiak brown bears, which weigh a pound at birth but up to 1,500 pounds when full grown, is worth the trip to this rugged country. The bears are spotted easily in July and August, feeding along salmon-spawning streams. Charter flightseeing trips are available to the area, and exaggerated tales of encounters with these impressive beasts are frequently heard. ⊠ *1390 Buskin Rd., Kodiak 99615,* ☎ *907/487–2600.*

As part of America's North Pacific defense in World War II, Kodiak was the site of an important naval station, now occupied by the Coast Guard fleet that patrols the surrounding fishing grounds. Part of the old military installation has been incorporated into **Abercrombie State Park and Campground,** 3½ mi north of Kodiak on Rezanof Drive. Self-guided tours take you past concrete bunkers and gun emplacements.

The **Baranov Museum** presents artifacts from the area's Russian origins. On the National Register of Historic Places, the building was built in 1808 by Alexander Baranov to warehouse precious sea-otter pelts. W. J. Erskine made it his home in 1911. On display are samovars, Russian Easter eggs, Native baskets, and other relics from the early Native Koniags and the later Russian settlers. A collection of 40 albums of archive photography portrays various aspects of the island's history. ⊠ *101 Marine Way,* ☎ *907/486–5920,* FAX *907/486–3166.* ⊡ *$2.* ⊙ *May–Sept., daily 10–4; Oct.–Apr., Mon.–Wed. and Fri.–Sat. 10–3.*

The ornate **Holy Resurrection Russian Orthodox Church** is a visual feast, both inside and out. The cross-shape building is topped by two onion-shape blue domes, and the interior contains brass candle stands, distinctive chandeliers, and numerous icons representing Orthodox saints. Three different churches have stood on this site since 1794. Built in 1945, the present structure is on the National Register of Historic Places. ⊠ *Corner of Mission Rd. and Kashevaroff Rd.,* ☎ *907/486–3854 (parish priest).* ⊙ *By appointment.* ⊡ *Donations accepted, but not required.*

★ The **Alutiiq Museum and Archaeological Repository** is home to one of the largest collections of Eskimo materials in the world and contains archaeological and ethnographic items dating back 7,500 years. The museum displays only a fraction of its more than 100,000 artifacts, including harpoons, masks, dolls, stone tools, seal-gut parkas, grass baskets, and pottery fragments. The museum store sells Native arts and educational materials. ⊠ *215 Mission Rd., Suite 101,* ☎ *907/486–7004,* WEB *www.alutiiqmuseum.com.* ⊡ *$2 donation requested.* ⊙ *Memorial Day–Labor Day, weekdays 9–5, Sat. 10–5; Labor Day–Memorial Day, Tues.–Fri. 9–5, Sat. 10:30–4:30.*

Dining and Lodging

$$$–$$$$ ✕ **Road's End.** You know a place is good if locals are willing to drive 42 mi each way to eat—30 of those miles along a gravel road. Such is the case at this lunch and dinner place out the Chiniak Road from Kodiak. Steaks, hamburgers, homemade pies, and a seafood platter that includes halibut, shrimp, and scallops are popular fare. What better reason to get out and explore a bit? ⊠ *Mile 42, Chiniak Rd.,* ☎ *907/486–2885. No credit cards. Closed Mon. and Feb.–Apr.*

$ ✕ **Beryl's.** Kodiak's only sweetshop serves espresso, ice cream, and baked goods as well as breakfast and lunch (hamburgers, sandwiches, and salads). In addition, the gift shop sells imported Russian and European items, as well as "the finest candy in Kodiak," according to the owner. ⊠ *202 Center Ave.,* ☎ *907/486–3323. MC, V. No dinner.*

$$$$ ⊞ **Best Western Kodiak Inn.** Rooms here have soothing floral decor and some overlook the harbor. However, the rooms with harbor views are on the street, so if a quiet room is a priority, take one in the back. The Chartroom Restaurant has harbor views and serves local seafood and standard American fare, including steak and pasta. The bar has live music on Friday. ⊠ *236 Rezanof St. W, 99615,* ☎ *907/486–5712 or 888/563–4254,* FAX *907/486–3430,* WEB *www.ptialaska.net/kodiakinn. 81 rooms. Restaurant, bar, refrigerators, hot tub. AE, D, DC, MC, V.*

$$$$ ✕⊞ **Kodiak Buskin River Inn.** This modern lodge is a five-minute walk
★ from the main terminal at the airport, about 4½ mi from downtown. Rooms are large and well kept (all have voice mail and some have data ports), and service is friendly. Guests can fish for salmon in the river out back. The Eagle's Nest ($$–$$$$) serves local seafood, including king crab, scallops, and a chilled seafood sampler. They also serve Cajun prawns, tempura vegetables, pasta, and a variety of steaks. The atmosphere is semiformal, with candlelike lamps on each table. ⊠ *1395 Airport Way, 99615,* ☎ *907/487–2700 or 800/544–2202,* FAX *907/487–4447,* WEB *www.kodiakadventure.com. 50 rooms. Restaurant, bar, fishing, airport shuttle. AE, D, DC, MC, V.*

Guided Tours

Dig Afognak (⊠ Box 1277, Kodiak 99615, ☎ 907/486–6357 or 800/770–6014, FAX 907/486–6529) gives would-be archaeologists a chance to work alongside professionals during a seven-day dig and to learn about the island's natural history. **Kodiak Island Charters** (☎ FAX 907/ 486–5380 or 800/575–5380) operates boat tours for fishing, hunting, and sightseeing aboard the 43-ft *U-Rascal*. They'll take you on a combined halibut and salmon trip, with sightseeing and whale-watching thrown in as well.

MATANUSKA-SUSITNA VALLEY AND BEYOND

Giant homegrown vegetables and the headquarters of the best-known dogsled race in the world are among the most prominent attractions of the Matanuska-Susitna (Mat-Su) Valley. The valley, lying an hour north of Anchorage by road, draws its name from its two largest rivers, the Matanuska and the Susitna, and is bisected by the Parks and Glenn highways. Major cities are Wasilla on the Parks Highway and Palmer on the Glenn Highway. To the east, the Glenn Highway connects to the Richardson Highway by way of several high mountain passes sandwiched between the Chugach Mountains to the south and the Talkeetnas to the north. At Mile 103 of the Glenn Highway, the massive Matanuska Glacier comes almost to the road.

Lake Clark National Park and Preserve

⑮ *100 mi west of Anchorage by air.*

When the weather is good, an idyllic choice beyond the Mat-Su Valley is the 3.4-million-acre Lake Clark National Park and Preserve, on the Alaska Peninsula and a short flight from Anchorage. The parklands stretch from the coast to the heights of two grand volcanoes: **Mt. Iliamna** and **Mt. Redoubt,** both topping out above 10,000 ft. The country in between holds glaciers, waterfalls, and turquoise-tint lakes. The 50-mi-long **Lake Clark,** filled by runoff waters from the mountains that surround it, is an important spawning ground for thousands of red, or sockeye, salmon.

The river running is superb in this park. You can make your way through dark forests of spruce and balsam poplars or you can hike over the high, easy-to-travel tundra. The animal life is profuse: look for bears, moose, Dall sheep, wolves, wolverines, foxes, beavers, and minks on land; seals, sea otters, and white (or beluga) whales offshore. Wildflowers embroider the meadows and tundra in spring, and wild roses bloom in the shadows of the forests. Plan your trip to Lake Clark for the end of June or early July, when the insects may be less plentiful. Or consider late August or early September, when the tundra glows with fall colors. ⊠ *4230 University Dr., Suite 311, Anchorage 99508,* ☎ *907/ 271–3751.*

Lodging

$$$$ 🏠 **Farm Lodge.** Near park headquarters in Port Alsworth, the farm was built as a homestead back in the 1940s and has been a lodge since 1977. Two modern duplexes house as many as 20 guests in private rooms that have either bunk or double beds. A large, manicured, and fenced lawn with flower and vegetable gardens surrounds the main lodge, where home-cooked meals including fresh vegetables, salmon, wild game, and domestic meats are served. The lodge also provides flight services and guided trips. ⊠ *Box 1, Port Alsworth 99653,* ☎ *907/781–2208 or 888/ 440–2281,* FAX *907/781–2215,* WEB *www.lakeclarkair.com. 5 rooms. Dining room, fishing. AE, D, MC, V.*

Palmer

⑯ *40 mi north of Anchorage.*

In 1935 the federal government relocated about 200 farm families from the Depression-ridden Midwest to the Mat-Su Valley, and some elements of these early farms remain around Palmer. The valley has developed into the state's major agricultural region. Good growing conditions result in some outsize vegetables—such as 100-pound cabbages.

★ ⏱ You'll find a variety of outsize vegetables at the **Alaska State Fair,** which runs 11 days, ending on Labor Day (it will be held August 23–September 2, 2002). Locals whoop it up with midway rides, livestock and 4-H shows, bake-offs, home-preserved produce contests, food, and live music. ⊠ *Alaska State Fairgrounds, Mile 40.2, Glenn Hwy. (2075 Glenn Hwy.), Palmer 99645,* ☎ *907/745–4827 or 800/850–3247,* FAX *907/746–2699,* WEB *www.alaskastatefair.org.* ⊡ *$8.*

On a sunny day the town of Palmer looks like a Swiss calendar photo, with its old barns and log houses silhouetted against craggy Pioneer Peak. On nearby farms (on the Bodenburg Loop off the old Palmer Highway) you can pay to pick your own raspberries and other fruits ⏱ and vegetables. At **Pyrah's Pioneer Peak Farm** (⊠ Mile 2.8, Bodenburg Loop, ☎ 907/745–4511), which cultivates 35 kinds of fruits and vegetables and begins harvesting in mid-June, the peak picking time occurs around mid-July.

⏱ The **Musk Ox Farm** conducts 30-minute guided tours from May to September. In addition to the 40-some animals roaming outside, there's a hands-on museum and a gift shop. ⊠ *Mile 50.1, Glenn Hwy.,* ☎ *907/745–4151.* ⊡ *$8.50.* ⊙ *May–Sept., daily 10–6; Oct.–Apr., by appointment.*

Gold mining was an early mainstay of the Mat-Su Valley's economy. ★ You can tour the long-dormant **Independence Mine** on the Hatcher Pass Road, a loop that in summer connects to the Parks Highway just north of Willow to the Glenn Highway near Palmer. (The gravel roads leading to the gold mine are rough and full of potholes, even under the best of conditions.) In the 1940s as many as 200 workers were employed by the mine. Today it is a 271-acre state park and a cross-country ski area in winter. Only the wooden buildings remain, one of them a red-roof mine now used as a visitor center. ⊠ *Independence Mine State Historical Park, 19 mi from Glenn Hwy. on Hatcher Pass Rd.,* ☎ *907/745–3975,* WEB *www.dnr.state.ak.us/parks/units/indmine.htm.* ⊡ *$5 per vehicle, tours $3.* ⊙ *Visitor center June 5–Labor Day, daily 11–7; grounds year-round.*

Dining and Lodging

$$ ✕▦ **Colony Inn.** All guest rooms in this lovingly restored historic ★ building are tastefully decorated with antiques and quilts. The building was used as a women's dormitory during the farm colonization of the 1930s. The small café ($$) serves light breakfasts, lunches, and Friday-night dinners. The homemade pie recipes have won blue ribbons at the Alaska State Fair. Inn reservations and check-in are handled at the Valley Hotel. Smoking is not allowed anywhere in the inn. ⊠ *325 E. Elmwood St., 99645,* ☎ *907/745–3330; 800/478–7666 in Alaska,* FAX *907/746–3330,* WEB *www.colonyinnalaska.com. 12 rooms. Restaurant, no-smoking rooms. AE, D, MC, V.*

$$–$$$ ▦ **Hatcher Pass Lodge.** This lodge has spectacular views and can serve as base camp for hiking, berry picking, and—in fall and winter—ski-

ing. Most rooms and cabins have queen-size beds. The cabins have chemical toilets and water coolers; guests shower in the lodge. The restaurant's Continental menu ($$–$$$) includes fondues, halibut, and gourmet pizzas. The bar serves up cappuccinos and hot buttered rum for chilly nights. ✉ *Box 763, 99645,* ☎ *907/745–5897,* FAX *907/745–1200,* WEB *www.hatcherpasslodge.com. 3 rooms, 9 cabins without shower. Restaurant, bar, sauna. AE, D, MC, V.*

$$ 🏨 **Valley Hotel.** Built in 1948, this three-story budget hotel has clean rooms with quilts and carpets. The building also houses a 24-hour, no-smoking coffee shop, hair salon, lounge, and massage therapist. Both smoking and no-smoking rooms are available. ✉ *606 S. Alaska St., 99645,* ☎ *907/745–3330; 800/478–7666 in Alaska,* FAX *907/746–3330,* WEB *www.valleyhotelalaska.com. 33 rooms. Bar, coffee shop, no-smoking rooms, hair salon. AE, D, MC, V.*

Wasilla

⑰ *42 mi north of Anchorage, 10 mi west of Palmer.*

Wasilla is one of the valley's original pioneer communities and over time has served as a supply center for farmers, gold miners, and mushers. Today, fast-food restaurants and strip malls line the Parks Highway. Rolling hills and more scenic vistas can be found by wandering the area's back roads.

The **Museum of Alaska Transportation and Industry,** on a 15-acre site, exhibits some of the machines that helped develop Alaska, from dogsleds to jet aircraft, and everything in between. The Don Sheldon Building houses aviation artifacts as well as antique autos and photographic displays. A snow machine exhibit also is on display. ✉ *Take Parks Hwy., turn south at Neuser Rd. at Mile 47, follow the road ¾ mi to the end,* ☎ *907/376–1211,* FAX *907/376–3082.* 💰 *$5.* ☼ *May–Sept., daily 9–6.*

Wasilla is the headquarters and official starting point for the Iditarod Trail Sled Dog Race, run each March from here to Nome, more than 1,000 mi to the northwest. A ceremonial start is held on Anchorage's 4th Avenue the first Saturday in March, then continues from Wasilla the following day. The **Iditarod Trail Headquarters** displays dogsleds, mushers' clothing, and trail gear, and you can catch video highlights of past races. The gift shop sells Iditarod items. During the summer, dogsled rides on wheels are available for $5. ✉ *Mile 2.2, Knik Rd.,* ☎ *907/376–5155,* WEB *www.iditarod.com.* 💰 *Free.* ☼ *Memorial Day–mid-Sept., daily 8–7; mid-Sept.–Memorial Day, weekdays 8–5.*

Dining and Lodging

$$–$$$$ ✕ **Evangelo's Trattoria.** The food is good and the servings ample at this spacious local favorite on the Parks Highway at the north end of town. Try the garlic-sautéed shrimp in a white-wine butter sauce or a mammoth calzone. The pizzas are loaded with goodies and a salad bar offers a fresh selection. ✉ *Frontier Mall, Mile 42.5, Parks Hwy.,* ☎ *907/376–1212. AE, MC, V.*

$$–$$$ ✕ **Cadillac Café.** Hearty fare fills the menu at this diner-style café, including homemade pies; big, hand-pressed burgers; exotic pizzas turned out of a stone, wood-fired oven; and southwestern-style Mexican food. The decor is described by the owner as "Alaska minimalist," but the booths are plush and comfortable, and hand-rubbed wood is much in evidence. Light breakfasts are served during the week but weekend breakfasts are hearty. ✉ *Mile 49 at Pittman St., Parks Hwy.,* ☎ *907/357–5533. AE, D, MC, V.*

$$$–$$$$ ⊡ **Best Western Lake Lucille Inn.** This well-maintained resort on Lake Lucille (at Mile 43.5 on the Parks Highway) provides easy access to several recreational activities, including boating in summer and ice-skating and snowmobiling in winter. Half of the inn's bright and cheery rooms have private balconies overlooking the lake. All rooms have voice mail and data ports. ⊠ *1300 W. Lake Lucille Dr., 99654, ☎ 907/373–1776 or 800/528–1234, FAX 907/376–6199, WEB www.bestwestern.com/ lakelucilleinn. 50 rooms, 4 suites. Restaurant, lobby lounge, hot tub, sauna, health club, boating, meeting room. AE, D, DC, MC, V.*

$$$–$$$$ ⊡ **Yukon Don's B&B.** Each of the spacious, immaculate, log-parti-
   ★   tioned rooms in this converted barn is decorated according to a theme. The Denali Room has posters of the mountain, snowshoes, crampons, and other climbing gear. A dogsled and other race paraphernalia mark the Iditarod Room. A rooftop room offers a spectacular, 360-degree panorama of the mountains and river valleys. A bear coat that you are welcome to try on and mounted grizzlies and sheep are in the large natural-history room. ⊠ *2221 Yukon Circle (1830 E. Parks Hwy., Suite 386, 99654), ☎ 907/376–7472 or 800/478–7472, FAX 907/376–7470, WEB www.yukondon.com. 4 rooms share 2 baths, 3 suites, 1 cabin. Sauna, gym. MC, V.*

Talkeetna

❽ *56 mi north of Wasilla, 112 mi north of Anchorage.*

Talkeetna lies at the end of a spur road near Mile 99 of the Parks Highway. Mountaineers congregate here to begin their assaults on Mt. McKinley in Denali National Park. The Denali mountain rangers have their climbing headquarters here, as do most glacier pilots who fly climbing parties to the mountain. The **Talkeetna Historical Society Museum,** across from the Fairview Inn, explores the history of Mt. McKinley climbs. A carved pole at the town cemetery honors deceased mountaineers.

Dining and Lodging

$$–$$$$ ✕⊡ **Talkeetna Roadhouse.** This log roadhouse has a common sitting area and plain rooms in a variety of sizes, including a bunk room with four beds. Sizable breakfasts are the orders of the day at the restaurant ($–$$), along with soup-and-salad combos, sandwiches, desserts, and pies, all made from scratch and using local produce and fresh berries whenever possible. It's a popular place with locals and with climbers who use Talkeetna's air taxis to reach nearby Mt. McKinley. The hotel operates as a B&B in winter. ⊠ *Main St. (Box 604, 99676), ☎ 907/ 733–1351, FAX 907/733–1353, WEB www.talkeetnaroadhouse.com. 8 rooms share 3 baths. Restaurant. MC, V. No dinner. Restaurant closed Oct.–Nov. and weekdays Dec.–mid-Apr.*

$$$–$$$$ ⊡ **Talkeetna Alaskan Lodge.** Opened in May 1999, this luxury hotel
   ★   has excellent views of Mt. McKinley, nature trails, and a full-service dining room and bar. Rooms are modern, in the style of an Alaska hunting lodge. The Great Room has comfortable seating, a huge stone fireplace in the center of the room, and an espresso bar. The tour desk can arrange flightseeing, river trips, or any other Alaska adventure you can imagine. ⊠ *2525 C St., Suite 405, Anchorage 99503, ☎ 907/265–4501 or 888/959–9590, FAX 907/263–5559, WEB www.talkeetnalodge.com. 200 rooms. Restaurant, bar, meeting room. AE, D, MC, V.*

$$$ ⊡ **Swiss-Alaska Inn.** Family-run since 1976, this rustic-style property is well known among those who come to fish in the Talkeetna, Susitna, and Chulitna rivers. Floral decor embellishes the bright rooms, all of which are nonsmoking. Menu selections at the restaurant ($$) include halibut, salmon, buffalo burgers, and the owner's secret-recipe Swiss-style French toast. ⊠ *East Talkeetna, by the boat launch (Box 565,*

A PRIVILEGED COMMUNION

BETWEEN 1903 AND 1912, eight expeditions walked the slopes of 20,320-ft Mt. McKinley. But none had reached the absolute top of North America's highest peak (also commonly known by the Native name Denali, meaning "the High One"). Among those who failed were some of North America's premier explorers and climbers. Thus the stage was set for Hudson Stuck, a self-described American amateur mountaineer who had previously climbed in Great Britain, the western United States, and Canada.

Stuck came to Alaska in 1904, drawn not by mountains but by a missionary calling. As the Episcopal Church's archdeacon for the Yukon River region, he visited Native villages year-round. His passion for climbing was unexpectedly rekindled in 1906, when he saw from afar the "glorious, broad, massive uplift" of McKinley, the "father of mountains." Five years after that wondrous view, Stuck pledged to reach McKinley's summit—or at least try. For his climbing party he picked three Alaskans experienced in snow and ice travel, though not in mountaineering: Harry Karstens, a well-known explorer and backcountry guide who would later become the first superintendent of Mt. McKinley National Park; Robert Tatum, Stuck's missionary assistant; and Walter Harper, part Native, who served as Stuck's interpreter and dog-team driver.

Assisted by two sled-dog teams, the group began its expedition on St. Patrick's Day, 1913, at Nenana, a village 90 mi northeast of McKinley. A month later, they began their actual ascent of the great peak's northern side, via the Muldrow Glacier. The glacier's surface proved to be a maze of crevasses, some of them wide chasms with no apparent bottom. Care-

fully working their way up-glacier, the climbers established a camp at 11,500 ft. From there they had to ascend a steep and jumbled ridgeline. Moving slowly, the team chopped a staircase up several miles—and 3,000 vertical ft—of rock, snow, and ice. Their progress was delayed several times by high winds, heavy snow, and near-zero visibility.

By May 30, the climbers had reached the top of the ridge (later named in Karstens' honor) and moved into a high glacial basin. Despite subzero temperatures to 21°F, they kept warm at night by sleeping on sheep and caribou skins and covering themselves with down quilts, camel's-hair blankets, and a wolf robe.

On June 6, the team established its high camp at 18,000 ft. The following morning was bright, cloudless, and windy. Three of the climbers suffered headaches and stomach pains, but given the clear weather everyone agreed to make an attempt. They left camp at 5 AM and by 1:30 PM stood within a few yards of McKinley's summit. Harper, who had been leading all day, was the first to reach the top, soon followed by the others. After catching their breath, the teammates shook hands, said a prayer of thanks, made some scientific measurements, and reveled in their magnificent surroundings. In his classic book *The Ascent of Denali*, Hudson Stuck later reflected, "There was no pride of conquest, no trace of that exultation of victory some enjoy upon the first ascent of a lofty peak, no gloating over good fortune that had hoisted us a few hundred feet higher than others who had struggled and been discomfited. Rather, was the feeling that a privileged communion with the high places of the earth had been granted."

99676), ☎ 907/733–2424, FAX 907/733–2425, WEB *www.swissalaska. com*. 20 rooms. Restaurant, no-smoking rooms. AE, D, MC, V.

$$ ⊡ **Fairview Inn.** Built in 1923, the Fairview is truly a historic spot—
★ it's listed in the National Register of Historic Places. It oozes local color, from the bear rug nailed to the ceiling over the bar to photographs of local characters and former owners on the wall. You're likely to meet members of Mt. McKinley climbing expeditions if you visit during the early-summer climbing season. You'll also hear lots of good, local music but be forewarned: you'll hear it even if you don't want to, so if a good night's sleep is important, check first to see if the band will be playing. The inn is open year-round, but food is served only from Memorial Day to Labor Day in the outdoor beer garden. ⊠ *101 Main St. (Box 1109, Talkeetna 99676)*, ☎ 907/733–2423, FAX 907/733– 1067, WEB *www.denali-fairview.com*. 6 rooms, shared baths. Restaurant, bar. AE, MC, V.

Guided Tours

Hudson Air Service (☎ 907/733–2321 or 800/478–2321, FAX 907/733– 2333) has a fleet of four airplanes to take you on flightseeing trips, glacier landings, and remote drop-offs. **K2 Aviation** (☎ 907/733–2291 or 800/764–2291, FAX 907/733–1221) lands you on a glacier and also leads overnight trips to Denali National Park. **Talkeetna Air Taxi** (☎ 907/733–2218 or 800/533–2219, FAX 907/733–1434) conducts a breathtaking exploration flight close to massive Mt. McKinley, as well as fly-in hiking trips and glacier landings.

Mahay's Riverboat Service (☎ 907/733–2223 or 800/736–2210) conducts guided jet-boat tours, scenic cruises, and fishing on the Susitna and Talkeetna rivers. **Denali Floats** (☎ 907/733–2384 or 800/651–5221) leads scenic raft trips on the Susitna River, complete with shore lunch and occasional musical accompaniment, and can arrange wilderness expeditions to suit your schedule. **Tri-River Charters** (⊠ Box 312, Talkeetna 99676, ☎ 907/733–2400) operates fishing trips out of Talkeetna and on the nearby Deshka River, and can provide all the necessary tackle and gear.

Denali State Park

⑲ *34 mi north of Talkeetna, 132 mi north of Anchorage.*

Overshadowed by the larger and more charismatic Denali National Park and Preserve in the Interior, "Little Denali" offers excellent access (it's bisected by the Parks Highway), beautiful views of Mt. McKinley, scenic campgrounds, and prime wilderness hiking and backpacking opportunities within a few miles of the road system. Between the Talkeetna Mountains and the Alaska Range, Denali State Park combines wooded lowlands and forested foothills topped by alpine tundra. ⊠ *Alaska State Parks, Mat-Su Area Office, HC 32, Box 6706, Wasilla 99687*, ☎ 907/745–3975.

The park's chief attraction, other than McKinley views, is the 35-mi-long **Curry-Kesugi Ridge,** which forms a rugged spine through the heart of the park that is ideal backpacking terrain. Another destination favored by backcountry travelers is the **Peters Hills,** accessible from Petersville Road in Trapper Creek.

Lodging and Camping

$$$$ ⊡ **Mount McKinley Princess Wilderness Lodge.** When the sky is clear and Mt. McKinley is visible in the Alaska sky, this lodge has excellent views of North America's highest peak, especially from the lobby with its large stone fireplace. On private land inside Denali State Park, this hillside lodge is surrounded by forest and overlooks the Chulitna River. You stay in bungalow-style guest rooms and the tour desk can arrange

horseback rides, river-rafting trips, naturalist walks, flightseeing, fishing, mountain bikes, and alpine hikes. ⊠ *Mile 133, Parks Hwy.,* ☎ *907/733–2900 or 800/426–0500,* FAX *907/733–2922,* WEB *www. princess.com/dest/we_mckinley.html. 238 rooms, 4 suites. Restaurant, café, hot tubs. AE, D, DC, MC, V. Closed mid-Sept.–mid-May.*

$ ⊞ **Alaska State Parks Cabins.** Two public-use cabins are in Denali State Park, along the shores of Byers Lake. Both are equipped with bunks, wood-burning stove, table, and benches, but they have no running water or electricity. ⊠ *Alaska State Parks Public Information Center, 3601 C St., Suite 200, Box 107001, Anchorage 99510–7001,* ☎ *907/269– 8400. 2 cabins without bath. No credit cards. Closed in winter.*

$ ⚠ **Alaska State Parks Campgrounds.** Three roadside campgrounds are within Denali State Park, at Byers Lake, Lower Troublesome Creek, and Denali View North. All are easily accessible from the Parks Highway and have picnic tables, fire pits, drinking water, and latrines. The Byers Lake campground also has a boat launch and nearby hiking trails. Sites are available on a first-come, first-served basis. ⊠ *Alaska State Parks, HC 32, Box 6706, Wasilla 99654,* ☎ *907/745–3975,* WEB *www.dnr. state.ak.us/parks/units/denali2.htm. No credit cards. Closed Oct.–Mar.*

Glennallen

⟨20⟩ *187 mi northeast of Anchorage.*

This community of 900 residents is the gateway to Wrangell–St. Elias National Park and Preserve. It's 124 mi from Glennallen to McCarthy, the last 58 mi on unpaved gravel. This town is also the service center for the Copper River basin and is a fly-in base for several wilderness outfitters.

Dining and Lodging

$–$$$ ✕ **Caribou Restaurant.** This friendly place serves such typical roadside fare as burgers, hot sandwiches, meat loaf, pancakes, and charbroiled steak. Sweet rolls, pies, and other treats are baked fresh daily. ⊠ *Downtown Glennallen, Mile 187, Glenn Hwy.,* ☎ *907/822–4222. AE, D, MC, V.*

$$$$ ⊞ **Caribou Hotel.** This modern hotel is clean and comfortable, with rooms decorated in mauve and sea green. Unless you're on a strict budget, be sure to ask for a room in the main building and not in the trailerlike annex out front, where rooms are spartan and share a bath. Several rooms in the main building have hot tubs. Three suites have kitchens. The owners operate a nearby B&B and a property with three two-bedroom apartments and a one-bedroom apartment. ⊠ *Box 329, 99588,* ☎ *907/822–3302; 800/478–3302 in Alaska;* FAX *907/822–3711,* WEB *www.alaskan.com/caribouhotel. 83 rooms, 63 with bath, 3 suites. Kitchenettes (some). AE, D, DC, MC, V.*

Wrangell–St. Elias National Park and Preserve

⟨21⟩ *77 mi southeast of Glennallen, 264 mi east of Anchorage.*

In a land of many grand and spectacularly beautiful mountains, those in the 9.2-million-acre Wrangell–St. Elias National Park and Preserve have been singled out by many Alaskans as the finest of them all. This extraordinarily compact cluster of immense peaks toward the southeastern part of Alaska belongs to four different mountain ranges. ⊠ *Mile 105.5, Old Richardson Hwy., Box 439, Copper Center 99573,* ☎ *907/822–5234.*

Covering an area some 100 mi by 70 mi, the **Wrangells** tower above the 2,500-ft-high Copper River Plateau, and the peaks of Mts. Jarvis, Drum, Blackburn, Sanford, and Wrangell rise 15,000 ft–16,000 ft from sea level.

The white-iced spire of **Mt. St. Elias,** in the St. Elias Range, reaches more than 18,000 ft. It's the fourth-tallest mountain on the North American continent and the crown of the planet's highest coastal range.

The park's coastal mountains are frequently wreathed in snow-filled clouds, their massive height making a giant wall that contains the great storms brewed in the Gulf of Alaska. As a consequence, they bear some of the continent's largest ice fields, with more than 100 glaciers radiating from them. One of these, the **Malaspina Glacier,** is 1,500 square mi—larger than the state of Rhode Island. This tidewater glacier has an incredible pattern of black-and-white stripes made by the other glaciers that coalesced to form it. Look for it on the coast north of Yakutat if you fly between Juneau and Anchorage.

Rising through many life zones, the Wrangell–St. Elias Park and Preserve is largely undeveloped wilderness parkland on a grand scale. The area is perfect mountain biking and hiking terrain, and the rivers invite rafting for those with expedition experience. The mountains attract climbers from around the world; most of them fly in from ★ Glennallen or Yakutat. The nearby abandoned **Kennicott Mine** is one of the park's main visitor attractions. Limited services are available in ★ the end-of-the-road town of **McCarthy.** Facilities include guest lodges, a B&B, and a restaurant. There's no gas station or post office.

The park is accessible from Alaska's highway system, via one of two gravel roads. The unpaved **Nabesna Road** leaves the Glenn Highway–Tok Cutoff at the village of Slana and takes you 45 mi into the park's northern foothills. The better-known route is the **McCarthy Road,** which stretches 60 mi as it follows an old railroad bed from Chitina to the Kennicott River. At the end of the road you must park and cross the river via a footbridge.

Before setting out make sure both you and your car are prepared. Your car should be equipped with a working jack and a properly inflated spare tire, or else potholes, old railroad ties, and occasional railroad spikes may leave you stranded.

Lodging

$$$$ 🛏 **Kennicott Glacier Lodge.** This cozy, modern wooden lodge in the ghost ★ town of Kennicott has small but clean and nicely furnished rooms. Historical photos of the former copper mine line the walls. Dinner is a "wilderness gourmet" of soups, pastries, breads, and desserts served family style. Breakfast and lunch are served restaurant style, but the same exceptional attention to detail and freshness is evident. Afterward, relax in the spacious living room or on the front porch. The front desk can arrange glacier trekking, flightseeing, rafting, and alpine hiking for additional fees, and an evening tour of Kennicott is included in the room rate. A vacation package is offered that includes room and all meals. ✉ *Box 103940, Anchorage 99510,* ☎ *907/258–2350 or 800/582–5128,* FAX *907/248–7975,* WEB *www.kennicottlodge.com. 25 rooms. Dining room, hiking, meeting room. AE, D, MC, V. Closed mid-Sept.–mid-May.*

$$$$ 🛏 **Ultima Thule Outfitters.** This remote fly-in-only lodge on the Chitina River in Wrangell–St. Elias National Park and Preserve offers a wonderful chance to experience an "air-safari adventure." The cost is $990 per person per day, with a four-day minimum. Included in your stay are breathtaking flightseeing, rafting, climbing, hiking, fishing, mushing, and skiing excursions, among others. The family-style meals include local foods such as fish, game, and vegetables from the garden, and homemade bread, pies, and cakes. Oak floors, wallpaper, wood-burning stoves, and brass beds provide the comforts of home Bavarian style. ✉ *1015 H St., Anchorage 99501,* ☎ FAX *907/258–0636,* ☎ *800/653–8934 satellite phone,*

WEB *www.alaskan.com/ultimathule. 6 cabins. Dining room, sauna, hiking, boating, fishing, cross-country skiing. No credit cards.*

$ ⚑ **Alaska State Parks Campgrounds.** The state maintains 23 campgrounds in the Matanuska-Susitna–Copper River region. Most can accommodate RVs up to 35 ft long, though electrical hookups are not available. Length of stay varies from 4 days to 15 days. All have toilet facilities, and most have drinking water, picnic sites, fire pits, fishing, and nearby hiking trails. ✉ *Alaska State Parks, Mat-Su Area Office, HC 32, Box 6706, Wasilla 99654,* ☎ *907/745–3975. Reservations not accepted. 23 campgrounds. No credit cards. Closed Oct.–May.*

Outdoor Activities and Sports

St. Elias Alpine Guides (☎ 907/345–9048 or 888/933–5427) gives introductory mountaineering lessons, leads excursions ranging from half-day glacier walks to monthlong backpacking trips, and conducts guided tours of historic Kennicott buildings and day raft trips from Kennicott. This service, which is owned by experienced mountaineer Bob Jacobs, has been in business more than 20 years.

SOUTH CENTRAL ALASKA A TO Z

To research prices, get advice from other travelers, and book travel arrangements, visit www.fodors.com.

AIR TRAVEL

Anchorage is the air hub of the South Central region, served by major national and international airlines and well stocked with smaller carriers and local air-taxi operators. ERA Aviation flies to Homer, Kenai, Valdez, Cordova, and Kodiak. Reservations are handled by Alaska Airlines. For flights to the Alaska Peninsula, the Aleutians, and western Alaska Bush villages, call PenAir.

➤ CONTACTS: **ERA Aviation** (☎ 907/243–3300 or 800/866–8394). **PenAir** (☎ 907/243–2323 or 800/448–4226).

BOAT AND FERRY TRAVEL

Ferries are a great way to explore the South Central coast, with its glaciers, mountains, fjords, and sea mammals. The ferries between Valdez and Whittier run by way of Columbia Glacier in summer, where it is not unusual to witness giant fragments of ice calving from the face of the glacier into Prince William Sound.

The Alaska Marine Highway, the state-run ferry operator, has scheduled service to Valdez, Cordova, Whittier, Seward, Homer, and Seldovia on the mainland; to Kodiak and Port Lions on Kodiak Island; and to the port of Dutch Harbor in the Aleutian Islands. The same agency runs the ferries that operate in Southeast Alaska, but the two systems connect only on once-a-month sailings. The system operates on two schedules; summer (May–September) sailings are considerably more frequent than fall and winter service. Check your schedules carefully: ferries do not stop at all ports every day. Reservations are required on all routes; they should be made as far in advance as possible, particularly in summer.

➤ BOAT AND FERRY INFORMATION: The **Alaska Marine Highway** (✉ Box 25535, Juneau 99802-5535, ☎ 907/465–3941 or 800/642–0066, FAX 907/277–4829).

BUS TRAVEL

Year-round service runs between Fairbanks and Anchorage by way of Denali National Park and also down to Homer, at the very tip of the Kenai Peninsula. Alaska Direct Bus Lines provides service between Anchorage and Fairbanks and also to Whitehorse and Skagway. The Park Connection has regularly scheduled shuttle service between Seward, Anchorage, and Denali National Park mid-May to mid-September. Seward Bus Line serves Anchorage, Portage, and Seward. A subsidiary offers service between Anchorage and Homer. The Alaskon Express is operated by Gray Line of Alaska and provides scheduled service between Whitehorse, Fairbanks, Valdez, Skagway, Denali National Park, Anchorage, and other communities en route. Haines is easily accessible from Skagway via water taxi.

➤ Bus Information: **Alaska Direct Bus Lines** (☎ 907/277–6652 or 800/770–6652, ℻ 907/338–1951). **Alaskon Express** (☎ 907/277–5581 or 800/478–6388). **Park Connection** (☎ 800/208–0200; 907/224–7116 for Seward same-day bookings; 907/683–1240 for Denali same-day bookings). **Seward Bus Line** (☎ 907/563–0800 or 907/224–3608, ℻ 907/224–7237).

CAR TRAVEL

Keep in mind that all but a few miles of the road system consist of two-lane highways, not all of which are paved. Two highway routes offer a choice for travel by car between Fairbanks and Anchorage. Heading north from Anchorage, the Parks Highway (turn left off Glenn Highway near Palmer) passes through Wasilla, up the Susitna River drainage area and through a low pass in the Alaska Range, then down into the Tanana Valley and Fairbanks. This route passes the entrance to Denali National Park and roughly parallels the Alaska Railroad. A longer route (436 mi) follows the Glenn Highway to the Richardson Highway, then heads north to Fairbanks through the Copper River valley. This route makes possible a side trip to Valdez, and it's the most direct connection to the Alaska Highway, joining it at Tok.

You can also link the two routes by using the Denali Highway, which, despite its name, doesn't run through Denali National Park. Rather, it connects the Richardson Highway with the Parks Highway between the towns of Paxson and Cantwell. You can make a huge figure eight by using the Denali, but be advised that this 135-mi-long road isn't paved except for relatively short sections at either end, and services are limited. Don't start the trip without a full tank of gas and at least one real spare tire, just to be on the safe side.

➤ Contacts: **State Department of Transportation** (☎ 907/243–7675) in Anchorage for hot-line reports on highways during snow season.

EMERGENCIES

➤ Emergency Services: **Police, ambulance, emergency** (☎ 911). **Alaska State Troopers** (☎ 907/269–5722 Anchorage; 907/822–3263 Glennallen; 907/235–8239 Homer; 907/486–4121 Kodiak; 907/745–2131 Palmer; 907/224–3346 Seward; 907/262–4052 Soldotna; 907/835–4359 Valdez).
➤ Hospitals: Cordova: **Cordova Medical Center** (✉ 602 Chase Ave., ☎ 907/424–8000). Glennallen: **Crossroads Medical Center** (✉ Mile 187.5, Glenn Hwy., ☎ 907/822–3203). Homer: **South Peninsula Hospital** (✉ 4300 Bartlett St., ☎ 907/235–8101). Kodiak: **Providence Kodiak Island Medical Center** (✉ 1915 E. Rezanof Dr., ☎ 907/486–3281). Palmer: **Valley Hospital** (✉ 515 E. Dahlia St., ☎ 907/746–8600). Seldovia: **Seldovia Medical Clinic** (✉ 252 Seldovia St., ☎ 907/234–7825). Seward: **Providence Seward Medical Center** (✉ 417 1st Ave., ☎ 907/224–5205). Soldotna: **Central Peninsula General Hospital** (✉ 250 Hospital Pl., ☎ 907/262–4404). Valdez: **Community Hospital** (✉ 911 Meals St., ☎ 907/835–2249).

LODGING
B&BS
➤ Local Agents: **Accommodations on the Kenai** (✉ Box 2956-F, Soldotna 99669, ☎ 907/262–2139, 𝖶𝖤𝖡 www.aokreservations.com). **Alaska**

Private Lodgings/Stay with a Friend (⊠ 704 W. 2nd Ave., Anchorage 99501, ☎ 907/258–1717, FAX 907/258–6613, WEB www.alaskabandb. com).

TOURS

ARCHAEOLOGY

➤ TOUR OPERATORS: **Dig Afognak** (⊠ Box 1277, Kodiak 99615, ☎ 907/486–6014 or 800/770–6014, FAX 907/486–2514).

BOATING AND GLACIERS

➤ TOUR OPERATORS: **Alaskan Wilderness Sailing & Kayaking** (⊠ Box 1313, Valdez 99686, ☎ 907/835–5175, FAX 907/835–3765). **Columbia Glacier Wildlife Cruises/Lu-Lu Belle** (☎ 907/835–5141 or 800/411– 0090, FAX 907/835–5899 in summer, ☎ FAX 800/411–0090 off-season). **Homer Ocean Charters** (☎ 907/235–6212 or 800/426–6212). **Kenai Coastal Tours** (☎ 907/277–2131 or 800/770–9119). **Kenai Fjords Tours** (☎ 907/224–8068 in Seward; 907/276–6249; 800/478–8068; FAX 907/276–1064). **Keystone Raft & Kayak Adventures, Inc.** (☎ 907/ 835–2606 or 800/328–8460, FAX 907/835–4638). **Kodiak Island Char- ters** (☎ FAX 907/486–5380 or 800/575–5380). **Mariah Tours** (☎ 907/ 224–8623 or 800/270–1238, FAX 907/224–8625). **Prince William Sound Cruises and Tours** (☎ 907/835–4731 or 800/992–1297, FAX 907/835– 3765). **26 Glacier Cruise** (Phillips' Cruises & Tours, ⊠ 519 W. 4th Ave., Suite 100, Anchorage 99510).

FISHING

➤ TOUR OPERATORS: **Central Charters** (⊠ 4241 Homer Spit Rd., Homer 99603, ☎ 907/235–7847 or 800/478–7847). **Fish House** (⊠ Small-boat harbor, Seward, ☎ 907/224–3674 or 800/257–7760). **U-Rascal** (☎ 907/486–5380).

FLIGHTSEEING

➤ TOUR OPERATORS: **Alpine Aviation Adventures** (⊠ Valdez, ☎ 907/ 835–4304; 800/478–4304 in Alaska; FAX 907/835–2523). **Cordova Air Service** (☎ 907/424–3289; 800/424–7608 in Alaska; FAX 907/424– 3495). **Ketchum Air Service Prince William Sound Adventures** (☎ 907/424–3350).

GENERAL INTEREST

➤ TOUR OPERATORS: **Alaska Heritage Tours** (☎ 907/265–4500 or 877/258–6877, FAX 907/263–5559). **Alaska Wildland Adventures** (☎ 907/783–2928 or 800/334–8730). **Gray Line of Alaska** (☎ 907/277– 5581 or 800/478–6388).

HIKING

Information on locations and difficulty of trails is available at the Alaska Public Lands Information Center at 4th and F streets in An- chorage. Another good resource is *55 Ways to the Wilderness in South Central Alaska,* published by the Mountaineers and available at most local bookstores.

TRAIN TRAVEL

The Alaska Railroad Corporation operates the Alaska Railroad, which is said to be the last railroad in North America that still makes flag stops to accommodate the homesteaders, hikers, fishing parties, and other travelers who get on and off in remote places. The 470-mi main line runs up Alaska's rail belt between Seward and Fairbanks via An- chorage. There's daily service between Anchorage and Fairbanks in sum- mer, and in winter one round-trip per week (Anchorage to Fairbanks on Saturday, Fairbanks to Anchorage on Sunday). Service to Seward from Anchorage runs mid-May to September 1 only. Adults are allowed two pieces of luggage to a maximum of 50 pounds. There's a $20 charge for bicycles; camping equipment is allowed on a space-available basis.

For information on the luxury-class Ultradome service between Anchorage and Fairbanks, contact Princess Tours about its *Midnight Sun Express.* Westours/Gray Line of Alaska operates the *McKinley Explorer* on Alaska Railroad trains as well.

➤ TRAIN INFORMATION: **Alaska Railroad Corporation** (✉ Box 107500, Anchorage 99510, ☎ 907/265–2494 or 800/544–0552, FAX 907/265–2323). **Princess Tours** (☎ 206/728–4202 or 800/835–8907). **Westours/ Gray Line of Alaska** (☎ 907/277–5581 or 800/478–6388).

TRANSPORTATION AROUND SOUTH CENTRAL ALASKA

Anchorage is the central hub, connected by rail and road to Seward and Whittier. Valdez can be reached by a rather indirect but interesting road route (the Glenn Highway to the Richardson Highway) out of Anchorage. The Seward and Sterling highways connect to most of the places you'll want to see on the Kenai Peninsula, including the small towns of Hope, Soldotna, and Homer. South Central's other "highway," the ferry-driven Marine Highway, connects with Kodiak, Whittier, Seward, Valdez, Dutch Harbor, Homer, Seldovia, and Cordova via the gulf. Air taxis are also a viable means of transportation around South Central.

VISITOR INFORMATION

➤ CONTACTS: **Alaska Public Lands Information Center** (✉ 605 W. 4th Ave., Anchorage 99501, ☎ 907/271–2737). **Bureau of Land Management** (✉ Box 147, Glennallen 99588, ☎ 907/822–3217). **Cordova Chamber of Commerce** (✉ Box 99, Cordova 99574, ☎ 907/424–7260). **Homer Chamber of Commerce** (✉ 135 Sterling Hwy., Box 541, Homer 99603, ☎ 907/235–5300). **Kenai Peninsula Visitor Information Center** (✉ 44790 Sterling Hwy., Soldotna 99669, ☎ 907/262–1337). **Kodiak Island Convention and Visitors Bureau** (✉ 100 Marine Way, Kodiak 99615, ☎ 907/486–4782). **Palmer Chamber of Commerce** (✉ Box 45, Palmer 99645, ☎ 907/745–2880). **Seward Visitors Bureau** (✉ Mile 2, Seward Hwy., Box 749, Seward 99664, ☎ 907/224–8051). **U.S. Fish and Wildlife Service** (✉ Alaska Regional Office, 1011 E. Tudor Rd., Anchorage 99503, ☎ 907/786–3487). **U.S. Forest Service** (✉ 3301 C St., Room 300, Anchorage 99503, ☎ 907/271–2500). **Valdez Convention and Visitors Bureau** (✉ 200 Chenega St., Box 1603, Valdez 99686, ☎ 907/835–2984). **Wasilla Chamber of Commerce** (✉ 1830 E. Parks Hwy., A-116, Wasilla 99654, ☎ 907/376–1299).

7 THE INTERIOR

INCLUDING FAIRBANKS, THE DALTON HIGHWAY, AND THE YUKON

Bounded by the Brooks Range to the north and the Alaska Range to the south, the Interior is home to Mt. McKinley and Denali National Park. Fairbanks, founded in 1901 by a merchant and a prospector who struck it rich, is the gateway to the Far North— the Arctic and the Bering Coast—and to Canada's Yukon Territory, whose gold-rush history is preserved in towns such as Dawson City and Whitehorse.

By Kent Sturgis

Updated by
Tom Reale

T HE IMAGE OF 1890 ALASKA, with its heady gold rushes set to the jangling sounds of countless honky-tonk saloons, has its roots in the Interior. Gold fever struck in Circle and Eagle in the 1890s, spread into Canada's Yukon Territory in the big Klondike gold rush of 1898, then came back to Alaska's Interior when Fairbanks hit pay dirt in the 1900s. The broad, swift Yukon River was the rush's main highway. Flowing almost 2,300 mi from Canada to the Bering Sea, just below the Arctic Circle, it carried prospectors across the border in search of instant fortune.

Although Fairbanks has grown up into a small city, many towns and communities in the Interior seem little changed. Soaking in the water of the Chena Hot Springs Resort, you can almost hear the whispers of the gold seekers exaggerating their finds and claims, ever alert for the newest strike. Early missionaries set up schools in the Bush, and the nomadic Alaskan Native peoples were herded to these regional centers for schooling and "salvation." Interior Alaska is still flecked with Indian villages. Fort Yukon, on the Arctic Circle, is the largest Athabascan village in the state.

Alaska's most recent gold rush—the pipeline carrying black gold from the oil fields in Prudhoe Bay south to the port of Valdez—snakes its way through the heart of the Interior. The pipeline itself is something of an enigma: it's a symbol of commercial interests against the environment yet also a monumental construction that hugs the land as a giant necklace. The Richardson Highway, which got its start as a gold stampeders' trail, parallels the trans-Alaska pipeline on its route south of Fairbanks.

Gold itself is glittering anew in the Interior. Fairbanks, the site of the largest gold production in Alaska in pre–World War II days, is the location of the Fort Knox Gold Mine, which is expected to double Alaska's gold production. The start-up of the mine is occurring more than a century after the discovery of gold in the Klondike in 1896 and the massive stampede of prospectors to Dawson City in 1898.

The Alaska Range—the "great wall" dividing the Interior from the South Central region—rises more than 20,000 ft. Its grandest member, Mt. McKinley (known among Athabascan-speaking Native people as *Denali,* or "the High One"), rises 18,000 sky-filling ft from base to peak (one of the highest uplifts in the world); and at 20,320 ft above sea level, it is the highest peak in North America. (Although Mt. Everest reaches more than 29,000 ft above sea level, it rises only 11,000 ft above the Tibetan Plateau.)

This tumultuous landscape was formed by the head-on collision of two tectonic plates. Between them, in the Denali fault system, lies the largest crack in the earth's crust on the North American continent. As high as it is, this barrier between South Central and the Interior Plateau gathers colder weather and bears a fine glacial system. These ice-capped mountains resemble the way a large part of the continent looked during the Ice Age. Flying in a small plane over the black-striped glaciers of the Alaska Range can be a dazzling experience.

Pleasures and Pastimes

Climate
The Interior experiences wild climate fluctuations. During the summer months, with the sun shining nearly 24 hours a day, heat piles up and lies thick on the land—you may want to go sleeveless at 11 PM. Thun-

derstorms trailing gauzy streamers of rain move across the landscape. In the winter it gets so cold (−50°F or below) that a glass of boiling water flung out a window will explode. Parking meters in Fairbanks routinely have electrical outlets for heaters to keep cars from freezing solid. Dry snow glitters in the air. Smog freezes in the Fairbanks bowl.

Dogsledding

Alaska is to dog mushing what Kentucky is to horse racing, and the Interior is arguably the prime mushing spot in Alaska. A host of dog-mushing races are held here, including everything from short sprint races with small teams to the Yukon Quest International, the second-longest sled-dog race in the world next to the Iditarod. But mushing isn't a sport solely for racers. Many people live in the Interior just so they can spend their free time in winter mushing their dogs. Skijoring—being pulled on skis by dogs—is also a pastime here. A web of trails surrounds many communities. Find out more information at the Alaska Public Lands Information Center.

Flora and Fauna

This part of Alaska has, through many millennia, escaped glaciation and thus formed a refuge for the Ice Age flora and fauna that were crowded out of other areas by ice and intense cold. Many species of plants and animals survived only in this refugium. Notably, certain species of birds continue to follow age-old patterns of migration and spend summers in the Interior's vast, prodigiously rich wetlands.

Below the tundra of the Alaska Range, the trees of the taiga take over: dark spiky spruce; paper birch; aspen; and, in the wetter places, cottonwood. The soft green leaves of the deciduous trees shine golden in the autumn. Among and around the trees, fireweed paints the landscape soft magenta. The meadows are blue with lupine in the spring, summer brings succulent berries, and fall splashes the berry leaves with crimson. Winter turns this world frigid, white, and crisp with ice.

Stretching farther to the north, the Interior puts the near-vertical terrain of the Alaska Range behind it and assumes a more horizontal character, with low, rounded hills. Tundra and taiga persist, with soft greens spiked by dark spruce trees, and deep green-gold mossy muskegs squish like soggy trampolines underfoot. Lakes gleam like black mirrors.

Hiking

Below the high, snowy reaches of the Alaska Range, the lower foothills are often stained with color, evidence of their ancient, restless past. Polychrome Pass in Denali National Park is aptly named: it commands a vista of rose-, orange-, gray-, and soft brown–shaded slopes fingered by swards of green alpine tundra. This high tundra is fine hiking country, but in other areas, the ground is tufted with slippery tussocks, and even the most nimble-footed will be forced into balancing acts.

Several developed trails offer hikers everything from an afternoon outing to an expedition of several days. Water is often scarce along the trails, so make sure you pack enough. Those adventuresome souls interested in following their own paths off the developed trails will find lots of space to go exploring. However, be well informed before you start. Although still beautiful and mostly wild, Alaska has many dangers for the unsuspecting, and private property needs to be respected here as it is elsewhere. A necessary stop for hikers is at the Alaska Public Lands Information Center in Fairbanks. The staff there is helpful and knowledgeable and in many cases can tell you about areas from personal experience.

Hot Springs Retreats

Forty below zero isn't a temperature that inspires thoughts of swimming, but that's what visitors have done for many years at the three hot-springs resorts in the Interior. The discovery by early miners of natural hot springs in the frozen wilderness just north of Fairbanks sent them scrambling to build communities around this heaven-sent phenomenon. The areas around the hot springs also make excellent bases for fishing, hiking, snowshoeing, or cross-country skiing. Each of the resorts is accessible by road and air from Fairbanks.

Wild and Scenic Rivers

Great rivers travel through this landscape: the Tanana, the Nenana, the Kuskokwim, and one of the world's most powerful—the mighty Yukon. (Only four rivers in the Americas have a greater capacity of water than the Yukon: the Amazon, the St. Lawrence, the Mississippi, and the Missouri.) Twenty miles wide in places, the Yukon travels for 2,300 mi, from Canada to the Bering Sea, and runs through some of the most beautiful country of the Interior Plateau. The Yukon River has a firm place in history because it served as a pathway for countless people as they moved through the North American continent (many people still travel the river by boat in the summer and by snowmobile across its frozen surface in the winter).

The Bureau of Land Management is in charge of three Wild and Scenic Rivers, each of which has a special draw. Beaver Creek, which threads through the White Mountain National Recreation Area north to the Yukon, offers good fishing—arctic grayling, northern pike, and burbot—and spectacular vistas. Along the rapid-ripped Birch Creek, moose, caribou, and birds are easily spotted. The beautiful Fortymile River offers a range of canoeing terrain, from Class I to IV rapids.

Exploring the Interior

Interior Alaska is neatly sandwiched between two monumental mountain ranges—the Brooks Range to the north and the Alaska Range to the south. Important cities and towns are spread along two major transportation routes. The Yukon River flows east–west in the northern half of the region. Interior Alaskans often define their area by the road system. A few highways cut through this great land, and only one connects Alaska to the rest of the world. The Alaska Highway, still often referred to as the Alcan, enters Alaska by way of Yukon Territory, Canada.

On the eastern edge of the state lies Fortymile Country and, just across the border, the Yukon Territory. In Alaska the Taylor Highway cuts through Fortymile Country, connecting Eagle, a gold-rush town, to the Alaska Highway. A cutoff connects the Taylor to the Top of the World Highway, which runs through Dawson City, a town that's a celebration of mining history. Both highways are gravel. The Alaska Highway officially ends in Delta Junction, where the Richardson Highway leads to Fairbanks. The highways run through fairly flat land, by Alaska standards, though they do get close to some mountains. The George Parks Highway connects Fairbanks to Anchorage and, passing right by Denali National Park, it is naturally flanked by sensational scenery.

North of Fairbanks are three highways, one of which stretches into the Arctic. All three wind through wild, wooded country. The Steese Highway heads northeast through alpine country and dead-ends in Circle at the Yukon River. Before reaching Circle, a cutoff heads to Arctic Circle Hot Springs. The Elliott Highway takes you northwest to the beginning of the Dalton Highway and then to a dead end at Manley Hot Springs on the Tanana River. The final main highway in the Interior

211

Interior and the Yukon

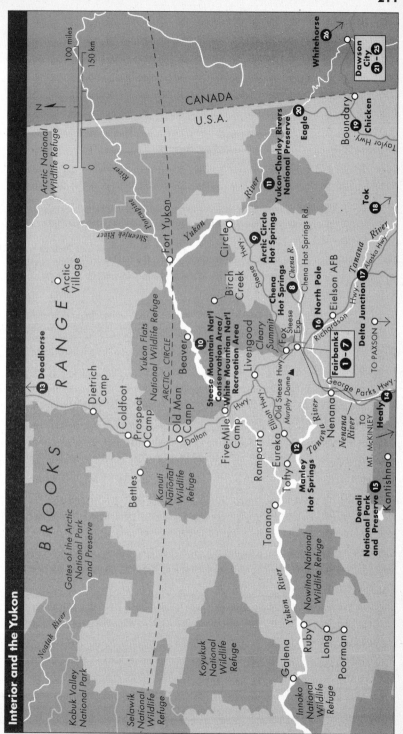

CANADA

U.S.A.

Arctic National
Wildlife Refuge

100 miles

150 km

N

Porcupine River

Sheenjek River

Fort Yukon

Arctic Village

B R O O K S   R A N G E

Gates of the Arctic
National Park
and Preserve

Noatak River

Kobuk Valley
National Park

Selawik
National
Wildlife
Refuge

Innoko
National
Wildlife
Refuge

Kanuti
National
Wildlife
Refuge

Bettles

Dietrich
Camp

Coldfoot

Prospect
Camp

Old Man
Camp

Dalton

Deadhorse 13

Beaver

Yukon Flats
National Wildlife Refuge

ARCTIC CIRCLE

Dalton Hwy.

Five-Mile
Camp

Steese Mountain Nat'l
Conservation Area/
White Mountain Nat'l
Recreation Area

Birch
Creek

Circle

Arctic Circle
Hot Springs 9

Yukon-Charley Rivers
National Preserve

Eagle 20

Boundary 19

Chicken 19

Taylor Hwy.

Tok 18

Dawson City 21 - 25

Whitehorse 26

Yukon River

Yukon River

10

Livengood

Cleary
Summit

Murphy Dome

Eureka

Elliott Hwy.

Rampart

Tanana

Ruby

Long

Poorman

Galena

Koyukuk
National
Wildlife
Refuge

Nowitna National
Wildlife Refuge

Manley
Hot Springs

Minto

Tofty 12

Fox

Steese
Exp.

Steese Hwy.

Old Steese Hwy.

Chena
Hot Springs 8

Chena R.

Chena Hot Springs Rd.

North Pole 16

Eielson AFB

Richardson Hwy.

Fairbanks 1 - 7

Nenana

Tanana River

Nenana
River

George Parks Hwy.

Healy 14

TO
MT. McKINLEY

Denali
National Park
and Preserve 15

Kantishna

Delta Junction 17

TO PAXSON

Tanana River

Alaska Hwy.

is the Dalton, which goes to the north coast of Alaska. The highway cuts through the Brooks Range, an imposing collection of rocky Arctic peaks, and spills out onto the tundra of the North Slope.

The Denali Highway, oddly enough, isn't in Denali National Park. It connects the towns of Paxson and Cantwell, running for 135 mi through tundra and spruce forests. Most of the road is unpaved, and services are few and far between, so make sure you've got a full tank of gas and at least one real spare tire.

Numbers in the text correspond to numbers in the margin and on the Interior and the Yukon, Fairbanks, Denali National Park and Preserve, and Dawson City maps.

Great Itineraries

IF YOU HAVE 3 DAYS

Spend a day in 🏨 **Fairbanks** ①–⑦, taking in the trans-Alaska pipeline, University of Alaska Museum, and the Riverboat Discovery tour. Try to end your day at Alaskaland so that you can have dinner at the Alaska Salmon Bake. The next day head to 🏨 **Denali National Park and Preserve** ⑮ and do some hiking or take a white-water rafting trip down the nearby Nenana River. Spend the night in the park area, but be sure to call ahead for room or campsite reservations, and for seats on the bus—the park area is very crowded in the summer. The next morning get up early to take a shuttle bus to Eielson Visitor Center at the park entrance, and start the third day exploring the national park. Stay in Fairbanks the last night, catching dinner and a show at the Ester Gold Camp.

IF YOU HAVE 5 DAYS

Follow the three-day itinerary; then spend the fourth day in 🏨 **Fairbanks** ①–⑦, taking the tour of El Dorado Gold Mine, where you can pan for gold, and visiting the **Fairbanks Ice Museum** ② if you missed it earlier. That afternoon head out to the scenic Chena Hot Springs Road for some delicious homemade pie at Tack's General Store and a relaxing soak at Chena Hot Springs Resort in 🏨 **Chena Hot Springs** ⑧. Spend the night at the resort or head back to town and consider stopping for dinner at Two Rivers Lodge.

IF YOU HAVE 10 DAYS

Follow the five-day itinerary; then head east to the Fortymile and Klondike gold-rush areas, visiting some of the unique attractions along the Richardson and Alaska highways, such as the Santa Claus House in **North Pole** ⑯, the Knotty Shop just south of North Pole, and Rika's Roadhouse in **Delta Junction** ⑰. Spend the night in 🏨 **Tok** ⑱. The next day take the gravel Taylor Highway up to 🏨 **Eagle** ⑳ and the Yukon River. Take the walking tour of Eagle in the morning, and then drive to 🏨 **Dawson City** ㉑–㉕, spending a day or two there. From Dawson you can go back to Fairbanks the way you came, or—if you're up for the 337-mi drive—you can continue on to **Whitehorse** ㉖, on the Alaska Highway. If a long drive doesn't suit you, on day six hop a flight to Dawson, spend a couple of days there, and then return for more Fairbanks attractions.

When to Tour the Interior

The Interior is characterized by bitter cold in winter with temperatures as low as –80°F. But summers are among the warmest in Alaska, with a few days each month from May to August enjoying temperatures in the high 80s or 90s. From the first week of May to the middle of August, it's bright enough at midnight to read a newspaper outdoors. Sunny days or partly cloudy ones, sometimes punctuated with afternoon cloudbursts, are the norm.

Tourism is big business in Alaska, but many of the attractions shut down after tourist season, which generally runs from Memorial Day to Labor Day. Consider coming early or late in the season to avoid the rush. Higher elevations and northern areas could have snow as early as mid-August. It's been known to snow in Fairbanks in May. Mid- to late August brings fall colors, ripening berries, and active wildlife, but it also brings more chance of rain. If you are a sports enthusiast, come to Interior Alaska in the winter, March especially, when the dark days of winter are over, lots of snow blankets the ground, and there's lots of radiant sun.

Fodor's Choice

No two people will agree on what makes a perfect vacation, but here are some of our Interior favorites for starters. Each of these is detailed later in this chapter.

Uniquely Alaska

★ **Mt. McKinley.** "The Great One," when not shrouded in mist, is a sight to behold and one of Alaska's premier attractions.

★ **Northern Lights.** Winter visitors to Alaska often experience nature's spectacular northern lights. Watch them at Chena Hot Springs near Fairbanks. The Hot Springs resort offers year-round activities from dogsled riding and snowmobiling in the winter to swimming and camping in the summer (☞ Celestial Rays of Light box, *below*).

Taste Treats

★ **Pike's Landing.** A Sunday in Fairbanks is not complete without brunch at Pike's, where you can take in the river view as you decide where to spend the rest of your day.

★ **Salmon Bake.** The salmon bake, an Alaskan tradition, is available at Alaskaland in Fairbanks, at McKinley/Denali Salmon Bake near the entrance to Denali National Park, and in Tok.

Lodging

★ **Chena Hot Springs Resort.** After indulging in this resort's year-round recreation opportunities, ranging from dog mushing and sleigh rides in the winter to camping and hiking in the summer, spend a day soaking in its hot springs–warmed hot tubs or swimming pool. $$$$

★ **Fairbanks Princess Riverside Lodge.** Relax and watch water-skiers and floatplanes on the river at this luxury hotel on the Chena River, with its expansive deck and manicured lawns. $$$$

★ **Pike's Waterfront Lodge.** Next door to the Princess, this rustic Fairbanks lodge offers spectacular views of the Chena River. $$$$

Dining

★ **Gambardella's Pasta Bella.** This family-run eatery serves up "the mother of all lasagnas" at a cozy location at the edge of downtown Fairbanks.

★ **Pump House Restaurant.** A longtime Fairbanks institution, this is where locals take their out-of-town guests when they want to impress them with the best dining experience the town has to offer.

After Hours

★ **The Blue Loon.** At this convivial saloon outside Fairbanks, you can watch second-run movies or play volleyball while eating a tasty meal washed down with a fresh local brew.

★ **Midnight Mine.** Have a beer and a game of darts with Fairbanks locals and make friends with Sam the dog.

FAIRBANKS

Its nickname, the Golden Heart, reflects Fairbanks's economic history as well as its geographical location. Surrounded by wilderness, it lies between the rugged Alaska and Brooks mountain ranges and serves as the hub of the Interior. Here the Parks and Richardson highways end and several Bush commuter air services base their operations. But Fairbanks got its start as a gold-mining town in 1901, and this has been cause for celebration by its residents since then. Many of the old homes and commercial buildings trace their history to the early days of the city, especially in the downtown area, with its narrow, winding streets following the contours of the Chena River.

Exploring Fairbanks

The best way to see the sights of Fairbanks is to combine a walking tour with some driving. You can get a taste for the best there is to see, and make plans to come back and revisit those spots that encourage more extensive and detailed examination.

A Good Tour

Start downtown by parking in the two-hour lot on Cushman Street between 1st and 2nd avenues. Stop at the **Fairbanks Convention and Visitors Bureau** ①, in the log cabin on 1st Avenue, for information and brochures from the helpful local staff. Turn right on 1st Avenue, and then take another right to cross the Cushman Street Bridge. Try to visualize all of downtown under 8 ft of water as it was in 1967. The Chena River flood control project was initiated shortly thereafter, making future recurrences highly unlikely. Stroll across the bridge to the river overlook on the right.

Recross the bridge and head south on Cushman Street, then left on 2nd Avenue, and walk for a block to the Lacey Street Theater, home of the **Fairbanks Ice Museum** ②. Cool off and take in the artfully carved ice sculptures. Turn north (left) on Lacey Street, left again on 1st Avenue, and stop at the Golden Heart Plaza, on the far side of 1st Avenue, with beautiful floral displays in summer and the *Unknown First Family* statue dedicated to Interior Alaska families. Retrace your steps to pick up your car. Turn right on Cushman Street, take a left on 1st Avenue, and drive parallel to the river to Cowles Street, the third left. Follow Cowles Street to Airport Way, and turn right, then right again on Peger Road. Take an immediate right into the **Alaskaland** ③ parking lot.

Take the Avenue of the Flags exit, turn right onto Wilbur Street, and right again on Airport Way. Take Airport Way to University Avenue and take a right. Cross the Chena River and stay on University Avenue until you get to Taku Drive. Turn left onto the **University of Alaska Fairbanks** ④ campus. Take the first right on Tanana Drive, then left at the stop sign at Yukon Drive. Take Yukon Drive for ½ mi to the **Alaska Range overlook** ⑤. If it's a clear day, and it usually is, you can see the Alaska Range and Mt. McKinley far to the south. Continue on Yukon Drive to Sheenjek Street and the **University of Alaska Museum** ⑥ on the right. No trip to Fairbanks is complete without a visit to this museum. A fascinating series of informative displays presents Alaska history, anthropology, natural history, and geography. When you leave the museum, continue on Yukon Drive to Kantishna Drive and turn right, then left on Sheep Creek Road to the Georgeson Botanical Garden, where researchers study the unique growing environment of the Far North. Continue on Sheep Creek Road for 1 mi and turn right on Miller Hill Road, then right again on Yankovich Road for just under

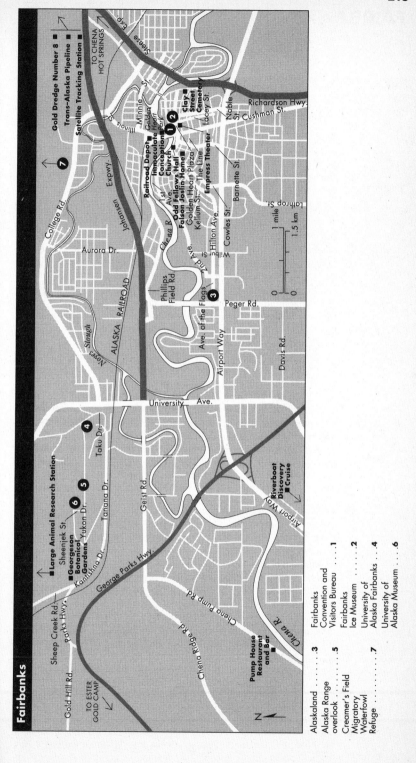

Fairbanks

Alaskaland 3
Alaska Range
overlook 5
Creamer's Field
Migratory
Waterfowl
Refuge 7

Fairbanks
Convention and
Visitors Bureau 1
Fairbanks
Ice Museum 2
University of
Alaska Fairbanks . . .4
University of
Alaska Museum 6

½ mi to the Large Animal Research Station, where scientists study the habits of musk ox, caribou, and reindeer.

Retrace your route back to Sheep Creek Road, and follow it past the intersection with Kantishna Drive, where the road turns into Tanana Drive. After the sharp left curve, turn right on Taku Drive, right again on Farmer's Loop Road, then left on College Road. Turn left on Danby and follow the road straight ahead to the bird-watching area at **Creamer's Field Migratory Waterfowl Refuge** ⑦.

TIMING

The walking and driving parts of the tour can be done in an hour to an hour and a half, but you can extend that time considerably by exploring the various spots. Taking the time to study the exhibits at the University Museum alone can extend the tour to nearly an entire day. Let your interests and the weather determine your schedule, and make the most of your visit to Alaska's Golden Heart city.

Sights to See

★ ☾ ❸ **Alaskaland.** The 44-acre park set along the Chena River near downtown Fairbanks has several museums, an art gallery, theater, civic center, Native village, large children's playground, miniature golf course, antique merry-go-round, restaurants, and a gold-rush town consisting of historic buildings saved from urban renewal. The complex has log-cabin gift shops and **Mining Valley,** an outdoor museum of mining artifacts surrounding an indoor-outdoor Alaska Salmon Bake restaurant. President Warren Harding traveled in the plush *Denali* railcar when he came north in 1923 to hammer the golden spike on the Alaska Railroad. The 227-ft stern-wheeler *Nenana* is the second-largest wooden vessel in existence. A national historic landmark, the *Nenana* was built by the railroad in 1933 to serve the rivers of Interior Alaska. Inside is a diorama of the course the riverboat took on the Yukon and Tanana rivers around the turn of the 20th century. The **Crooked Creek and Whiskey Island Railroad,** a small-gauge train, circles the park. No-frills RV camping is available for $10 a night in the west end of the large parking lot on Airport Way. ⊠ *Alaskaland Park, Airport Way and Peger Rd.,* ☎ *907/459–1087,* ℻ *907/459–1199.* 🎫 *Free.* ☯ *Daily 11–9.*

❺ **Alaska Range overlook.** The entire north side of the Alaska Range is visible at this overlook, a favorite spot for time-lapse photography of the midwinter sun just peeking over the southern horizon on a low arc. Nearly always distinguishable on a clear day are three major peaks, called the Three Sisters because they appear quite similar to one another. From your left are **Mt. Hayes,** 13,832 ft; **Mt. Hess,** 11,940 ft; and **Mt. Deborah,** 12,339 ft. Much farther to the right, toward the southwest, hulks **Mt. McKinley,** the highest peak in North America. On some seemingly clear days it's not visible at all. At other times the base is easy to see but the peak is lost in cloud cover. Often when Mt. McKinley is entirely visible, **Mt. Foraker,** the second-highest peak in the Alaska Range, also can be seen. It appears as a small pyramid just to the right of the base of Mt. McKinley. It seems small because it is 75 mi farther away than Mt. McKinley. ⊠ *West Ridge, University of Alaska Fairbanks campus, Yukon Dr.; look for the parking area just east of the University of Alaska Museum.*

❼ **Creamer's Field Migratory Waterfowl Refuge.** This is a great place to view historic farm buildings, waterfowl, cranes, songbirds, and moose and to learn about the history of Fairbanks. Three pleasant nature trails offer walking tours through the historic buildings and through fields, forest, and wetlands. **Creamer's Dairy,** from 1910 to 1966 the farthest-north dairy in North America and now on the National Register of Historic Places, is also here. The barns and buildings are still standing and the farmhouse is now a nature and visitor center. ⊠ *1300 College Rd.,* ☎ *907/459–7307 or 907/459–7301,* WEB *www.creamersfield.org.*

❶ Fairbanks Convention and Visitors Bureau. At this visitor center on the river at the Cushman Street Bridge you can pick up a map for a self-guided 1½-hour walking tour through the historic downtown area. The bureau also has maps for a two-hour do-it-yourself driving tour. Points of interest on the tours include **Golden Heart Park,** home of the *Unknown First Family* statue; the **Clay Street Cemetery,** with its marked and unmarked graves of early pioneers; the **Empress Theater,** the first concrete structure in Interior Alaska; the stately **Falcon Joslin Home,** the oldest frame house in Fairbanks still at its original location; the **Line,** home of the red-light district until the mid-1950s; **Odd Fellows Hall,** a bathhouse for gold miners until the pipes froze in the winter of 1910–11; and the historic **Immaculate Conception Church,** which was raised off its foundation in 1911 and rolled across the frozen Chena River on logs pulled by horses. ⊠ *550 1st Ave.,* ☎ *907/456–5774; 800/ 327–5774 recording;* FAX *907/452–2867,* WEB *www.explorefairbanks.com.*

❷ Fairbanks Ice Museum. The ice carvings showcased around Fairbanks in winter, especially the Ice Art competition held in March, are on display. The Ice Showcase, a large glass-wall display, is kept at 20°F. The chilly environment allows ice sculptors to demonstrate their skills and sculptures throughout the summer. "Freeze Frame" is a large-screen film demonstrating the techniques of ice sculpture. The museum is in the historic Lacey Street Theater, on the corner of 2nd Avenue and Lacey Street. ⊠ *500 2nd Ave.,* ☎ *907/451–8222,* FAX *907/456–1951.* 🎫 *$6.* ☉ *Late May–mid-Oct., daily 10–9.*

❹ University of Alaska Fairbanks. The university has earned an international reputation for its Arctic research, including a study of the aurora borealis, or northern lights. A free two-hour student-guided campus walking tour is offered weekdays throughout the summer. Tours of the following campus facilities are also offered from June 1 to August 31 (hours vary): the **Large Animal Research Station** (⊠ Yankovich Rd. off Ballaine Rd. behind the university, 🎫 $5; ☉ June–Aug., Tues., Thurs., and Sat. 11 and 1:30; Sept., Sat. 1:30), which houses caribou, musk ox, and reindeer; the **Arctic Region Supercomputing Center** (⊠ Butrovitch Bldg.), where researchers use high-performance supercomputers to solve problems in science and engineering for the high latitudes and the Arctic; the **Geophysical Institute** (⊠ West Ridge, about 1 mi from the campus center), a center of atmospheric and earthquake research; the **Poker Flat Research Range** (⊠ Steese Hwy., 33 mi northeast of Fairbanks), where the university launches rockets studying the aurora borealis; and the **Georgeson Botanical Garden of the Agricultural and Forestry Experiment Station Farm** (⊠ west end of campus; ☉ daily 8–8, tours Fri. at 2), where researchers study Interior Alaska's unique, short, but intense midnight-sun growing season. ⊠ *University of Alaska, Office of University Relations, 202 Eielson Bldg.,* ☎ *907/474–7581,* WEB *www.uaf.edu.* ☉ *Tour schedule varies; call for details or inquire at the Fairbanks Convention and Visitors Bureau.*

★ ❻ University of Alaska Museum. A stuffed grizzly bear—8 ft, 9 inches tall—guards the entrance to the ethnographic, historic, and fine arts collection divided into five Alaska regions: Southeast, Interior, South Central, Southwest, and the western Arctic coast. Blue Babe, a mummified steppe bison that lived 38,000 years ago during the Pleistocene epoch, was preserved in permafrost (permanently frozen ground), complete with claw marks indicating attack by a saber-toothed tiger. The bison's remains were found by gold miners in 1979. Besides the usual "don't touch" exhibits, the museum has several "please touch" items, including the molars of a mammoth and a mastodon, a gray whale skull, and a 5,495-pound copper nugget. Audio guides are available for an additional $3. ⊠ *907 Yukon Dr., West Ridge, University of Alaska campus,* ☎ *907/474-7505,* FAX *907/474-5469,* WEB *www.uaf.edu/ museum.* ⊠ *$5.* ☉ *June–Aug., daily 9–7; May and Sept., daily 9–5; Oct.–Apr., weekdays 9–5, weekends noon–5.*

OFF THE
BEATEN PATH

GOLD DREDGE NUMBER 8 – Imagine a giant gold dredge making its own waterway as it chews through the gold pay dirt, crawling along at a snail's pace and processing tons of rock and gravel. Built by Bethlehem Shipbuilders in 1928, the dredge was operated by the Fairbanks Exploration Company until its retirement in 1959. The five-deck ship is more than 250 ft long and took millions of dollars' worth of gold out of the Goldstream and Engineer creeks north of Fairbanks. *Gold Dredge Number 8* has been declared a National Historic District by the National Park Service, one of the few privately owned districts in the nation. This mining vessel came to rest at Mile 9, Old Steese Highway. Since 1997, Holland America/Westours has been refurbishing and expanding the museums and exhibits on the grounds. The price of admission entitles you to the necessary tools, some gold-panning instructions, and a chance to find "colors" at the sluice or to seek gold independently in old tailings from the mining days. A sit-down, family-style miner's pot-roast stew is served from 11 AM to 3 PM for an additional $8.50. The dredge (and the miner's stew) is a featured stop on Gray Line of Alaska's tours. ⊠ *1755 Old Steese Hwy. N, Fairbanks 99712,* ☎ *907/457-6058.* ⊠ *$21.* ☉ *Mid-May–mid-Sept., daily 9–5.*

TRANS-ALASKA PIPELINE – Just north of Fairbanks you can see and touch the famous trans-Alaska pipeline. The parking lot, just off the Steese Highway, has a sign loaded with information. Informative guides staff a small visitor center, and a small gift shop carries pipeline company memorabilia. ⊠ *Mile 7.5, Steese Hwy.,* ☎ *907/456-9391,* FAX *907/456-9392.* ⊠ *Free.* ☉ *Visitor center mid-May–Sept., daily 8–5.*

SATELLITE TRACKING STATION – Weather and technology buffs of all ages can get an inside view of the National Oceanic and Atmospheric Administration Satellite Tracking Station, on the Steese Highway north of Fairbanks. The facility has a dozen satellite dishes (including two enormous dishes 85 ft in diameter) that receive information from satellites orbiting hundreds of miles above the earth. Equipment at the station relays the electronic information to processing centers that convert the data into images of the earth's surface. You can see high-resolution images taken from the station's 10 polar-orbiting satellites, and tour the computer room and the grounds. ⊠ *Mile 13.5, Steese Hwy., 1300 Eisele Rd.,* ☎ *907/ 451-1200,* FAX *907/451-1209.* ⊠ *Free.* ☉ *May–Sept., weekdays 8–4:30, Sat. 9–3.*

Dining and Lodging

$$$–$$$$
★

✕ **Pike's Landing.** Enjoy lunch on a huge outside deck (it seats 420) overlooking the Chena River, or dine inside in the elegant dining room of an extended log cabin. The meals range in price up to $38 for steak and lobster and rank with the best in the Interior. For a less-expensive dinner, something in the $10 range, relax in the sports bar and catch a view of the river. The palate-pleasing Sunday brunch offers a huge array of tempting dishes and an irresistible dessert table. ⊠ *4438 Airport Way,* ☎ *907/479-7113. AE, D, DC, MC, V.*

$$–$$$$ ✕ **Pump House Restaurant.** This mining pump station turned restau-
★ rant built alongside the Chena River serves American and specifically
Alaskan seafood dishes. You can't go wrong with its house specialties
of seafood chowder and Alaskan reindeer stew. The furnishings and
floor are of rich, polished wood. An Alaskan grizzly bear in a glass
case is on sentry next to the hostess station. Bill and Vivian Bubbel,
who in the late 1970s made the restaurant a Fairbanks favorite, pur-
chased the Pump House in January 1996 and kept the restaurant an
Interior top choice. Wednesday night is karaoke night in the bar. ⊠
Mile 2.0, Chena Pump Rd., ☎ *907/479–8452. AE, D, MC, V. No lunch
Sept. 15–May 15.*

$$$ ✕ **Alaska Salmon Bake.** This indoor-outdoor restaurant in Alaskaland's
★ Mining Valley serves mouthwatering salmon cooked over an open fire
with a special lemon and brown-sugar sauce. Also available at the all-
you-can-eat dinner are halibut, barbecued beef ribs, 19-ounce porter-
house steaks, a salad bar, and homemade blueberry cake. ⊠ *Airport
Way and Peger Rd.,* ☎ *907/452–7274 or 800/354–7274. MC, V.
Closed mid-Sept.–mid-May. No lunch.*

$$–$$$ ✕ **Gambardella's Pasta Bella.** Known simply as Gambardella's, this
★ family-run Italian restaurant at the edge of downtown is a favorite among
locals. The place is small but cozy, with covered outside seating in the
summer. The menu includes salads, pasta, pizza, vegetarian entrées, and
submarine sandwiches on homemade bread. Its specialties, however,
are lasagna, which the *Seattle Times* described as "the mother of all
lasagnas"; the seafood fra diavolo; and the clam pizza. ⊠ *706 2nd Ave.,*
☎ *907/456–3417,* ℻ *907/456–3425. AE, MC, V. No lunch Sun.*

$$–$$$ ✕ **Ivory Jack's.** Jack "Ivory" O'Brien used to deal in Alaskan ivory
★ and whalebone out of this small restaurant tucked into the gold-rich
hills of the Goldstream Valley on the outskirts of Fairbanks. New
York Yankees, Elvis, Dartmouth University, and dog mushing paraphernalia adorn the large, open and airy bar/restaurant. The menu lists
no fewer than 15 choices of appetizers as well as burgers, pizza, and
fine-dining dishes. For a $6 cover charge, you can catch some live local
music on weekends. ⊠ *2581 Goldstream Rd.,* ☎ *907/455–6666. AE,
D, DC, MC, V.*

$$$$ 🏨 **Fairbanks Princess Riverside Lodge.** This luxury lodge sits on the
★ banks of the Chena River just off the road to Fairbanks International
Airport. Gold, russet, green, and burgundy accents warm the rustic decor.
Its Edgewater Restaurant welcomes diners in suits and evening gowns
or duct tape–patched Carhartts work clothes, and its Sunday brunch
is not to be missed. The expansive wooden deck, which faces a scenic
section of the Chena River, draws a crowd in summer. ⊠ *4477 Pikes
Landing Rd., 99709,* ☎ *907/455–4477 or 800/426–0500,* ℻ *907/455–
4476. 325 rooms. 2 restaurants, bar, steam room, health club, coin laundry, meeting rooms, airport shuttle. AE, DC, MC, V.*

$$$$ 🏨 **Pike's Waterfront Lodge.** This hotel and conference center on the
★ banks of the Chena River opened in May of 2000. Rustic elegance dominates the decor including a high-ceiling lobby with log supporting
columns and log overhead beams, two scenic Alaskan murals, and ubiq-
uitous taxidermy pieces. The rooms have either a king or two queen
beds, desk and armoire, coffeemakers, phones with data ports, and cable
and pay-per-view TV. Rooms with a river view are worth the extra $10
per night. The restaurant serves a buffet breakfast in the summer,
lunch, and a casual dinner. For a more formal dining experience, walk
across the parking lot to Pike's Landing restaurant. ⊠ *1850 Hoselton
Rd., 99709,* ☎ *877/774–2400 or 907/456–4500,* ℻ *907/456–4515,*
🖳 *www.pikeslodge.com. 182 rooms. Sauna, spa, gym, airport shuttle. AE, D, MC, V.*

$$$$ ⚐ **Sophie Station Hotel.** This spacious hotel near the airport is one of the better hotels in Fairbanks, thanks to its quiet location, helpful staff, and pleasantly warm decor. All rooms are suites with kitchens that include a full-size range and refrigerator. Comfy furniture, rich upholstery, and Alaskan artwork enhance its decor. The restaurant, Zach's, serves breakfast, lunch, and dinner, with such specialties as buffalo burgers. ⊠ *1717 University Ave., 99709,* ☎ *907/479–3650 or 800/528–4916,* ℻ *907/479–7951,* ⓦⓔⓑ *www.fountainheadhotels.com. 147 suites. Restaurant, bar, kitchenettes, airport shuttle. AE, D, DC, MC, V.*

$$$$ ⚐ **Westmark Fairbanks Hotel and Conference Center.** This snazzy, full-service hotel, close to downtown, is built around a courtyard on a quiet street. All rooms have a rose-and-burgundy motif and a writing desk; some have a StairMaster or stationary bike. A conference center, 24-hour business services center, and personal voice mail make it a good choice for business travelers. The Bear 'n Seal serves up steaks and seafood. ⊠ *813 Noble St., 99701,* ☎ *907/456–7722 or 800/544–0970,* ℻ *907/451–7478,* ⓦⓔⓑ *www.westmarkhotels.com. 244 rooms. Restaurant, bar, laundry service, business services, meeting room, airport shuttle. AE, D, DC, MC, V.*

$$$–$$$$ ⚐ **The Villages.** Though close to downtown, this establishment is tucked away in a wooded area. Two studios and one-, two-, and three-bedroom suites are available. Dining tables in the full kitchens seat four, and the sitting rooms have living room–size sofas, comfortable easy chairs, and 25-inch stereo TVs. The contrast of off-white wallpaper and dark burgundy carpeting provides a pleasant warmth to some of the rooms. The bedrooms in the suites all come with 19-inch portable television sets equipped with VCRs and cable. ⊠ *205 Palace Circle, 99701,* ☎ *907/456–7612 or 800/770–7612,* ℻ *907/456–8358. 32 suites. Kitchenettes, laundry service. AE, D, DC, MC, V.*

$$–$$$$ ⚐ **Comfort Inn–Chena River.** Perched on a wooded bank of the Chena River directly across the water from Alaskaland, this Comfort Inn has a full-length, glass-enclosed indoor pool and hot tub. The rooms have TVs with satellite access and some rooms have small refrigerators and microwaves; 60% are smoke free. The room rate includes Continental breakfast. ⊠ *1908 Chena Landings Loop, 99701,* ☎ *907/479–8080 or 800/228–5150,* ℻ *907/479–8063,* ⓦⓔⓑ *www.choicehotels.com. 74 rooms. No-smoking rooms, refrigerators, indoor pool, hot tub, airport shuttle. AE, D, DC, MC, V.*

$$–$$$$ ⚐ **Cranberry Ridge B&B.** The proprietors, Mike and Floss Caskey, a fifth-generation Alaskan family, designed and built this small B&B, north of Fairbanks off Farmers Loop Road. The contemporary house's position affords magnificent views of the Alaska Range. The two guest rooms share a bath and a large sitting and family area and can be taken together as a suite. Each morning you can expect fresh-baked pastries (possibly peach cobbler), a full breakfast with smoked salmon quiche, a large fruit tray, and coffee. Mike Caskey leads Arctic Circle and Mt. McKinley flightseeing tours in his Cessna 185 for up to three passengers for $230 an hour. ⊠ *705 Cranberry Ridge Dr., 99712,* ☎ *907/457–4424 or 888/326–4424,* ⓦⓔⓑ *www.AlaskaFlyingTours.com. 2 rooms share bath. AE, D, DC, MC, V.*

$$–$$$ ⚐ **Crestmont Manor B&B.** This elegant colonial-style B&B is tastefully appointed with handmade quilts and furnishings and antique fixtures. The rooms offer privacy, and comfort for the guests is a top priority of the house. You can relax on the deck while contemplating the sweeping view of the Chena River valley and the Alaska Range. Breakfast, with quiche, fresh pastries, juice, and coffee, is a pleasant affair. The property is smoke free. ⊠ *510 Crestmont Dr., 99709,* ☎ *907/456–3831,* ℻ *907/456–3841,* ⓦⓔⓑ *www.mosquitonet.com/~crestmnt. 5 rooms. No-smoking rooms, laundry service, business services. AE, MC, V.*

Guided Tours

Adventure
Northern Alaska Tour Company (✉ Box 82991, Fairbanks 99708, ☎ 907/474–8600, 𝔽𝔸𝕏 907/474–4767, 𝕎𝔼𝔹 www.northernalaska.com) leads half- and full-day excursions to the Arctic Circle and Yukon River and two- and three-day fly-drive tours to Prudhoe Bay, Barrow, and the Brooks Range.

Cruising and Canoeing
The excitement and color of the city's riverboat history and the Interior's cultural heritage are relived each summer aboard the **Riverboat Discovery** cruise (✉ Alaska Riverways, Dale Rd. Landing, near Fairbanks International Airport, ☎ 907/479–6673), a four-hour narrated trip by stern-wheeler along the Chena and Tanana rivers to a rustic Native village setting on the Tanana River. The cruise provides a glimpse of the lifestyle of the dog mushers, subsistence fishermen, traders, and Native Alaskans who populate the Yukon River drainage. Sights along the way include operating fish wheels, a Bush airfield, float-planes, a smokehouse and cache, log cabins, and Iditarod champion Susan Butcher's dog kennels. Captain Jim Binkley, his wife, Mary, and their children have operated the Discovery cruises for more than 50 years. Their family, with its four generations of river pilots, has run great rivers of the north for more than 100 years. The cruise costs $39.95, and two cruises run daily (8:45 and 2) mid-May to mid-September.

Sightseeing
Gray Line of Alaska (☎ 800/478–6388, 𝕎𝔼𝔹 www.graylinealaska.com) runs a four-hour sightseeing tour of the city that includes the *Gold Dredge Number 8* and a lunch of miner's stew for $60.

Nightlife and the Arts

Fairbanks supports a year-round arts program that rivals many larger communities. Summer visitors to Fairbanks will find that the lack of a true "night"—thanks to the midnight sun—doesn't seem to hinder nightlife at all. Check the Kaleidoscope section in the Thursday *Fairbanks Daily News–Miner* for current nightspots, plays, concerts, and art shows.

The Arts
FESTIVALS
The **Fairbanks Summer Arts Festival** (✉ Box 80845, Fairbanks 99708, ☎ 907/474–8869, 𝔽𝔸𝕏 907/479–4329, 𝕎𝔼𝔹 www.fsaf.org) has grown from a small jazz festival for adults to a major University of Alaska Fairbanks–affiliated annual event attracting students worldwide. Spread over two weeks in late July and early August, the festival presents music, dance, theater, opera, ice-skating, and visual-arts instruction.

Every July Fairbanks hosts the **World Eskimo-Indian Olympics,** when northern peoples from Alaska and Canada gather to compete in traditional Native athletic competitions and dances. Every March, Fairbanks is the site of the **World Ice Art Championships,** a carving competition that draws ice artists from around the world. The annual **Winter Carnival,** held in mid-March, hosts dog-mushing and skijoring competitions, basketball tournaments, a craft fair, fur auctions, and various winter events in Fairbanks and in outlying areas.

Nightlife
CABARET THEATER
For an evening of varied and high-quality entertainment head to **Ester Gold Camp** (✉ 3175 College Rd., No. 1, Ester 99709-3703, ☎ 907/479–

2500 or 800/676–6925, FAX 907/474–1780), a former gold-mining town about 5 mi west of Fairbanks on the Parks Highway. Its 11 historical structures date to the early 1900s and include the rustic Malemute Saloon, which is open daily from 2 PM to midnight. The camp, which is on the National Register of Historic Places, comes alive at night with a show in the saloon ($14) featuring gold rush–era songs, stories, and Robert Service poetry; a beautiful northern lights photography show ($8) in the Firehouse Theatre; and a dinner buffet ($25.95) serving crab, halibut, and reindeer stew in yet another building. Plan your evening to catch dinner and all the shows. The camp has a hotel with semiprivate bathrooms, RV parking, a gift shop, and complimentary evening bus service to and from Fairbanks. The camp is open late May to early September.

The **Palace Theatre and Saloon** (☎ 907/456–5960 or 800/354–7274) at Alaskaland is one of the livelier summer spots. The Palace's *Golden Heart Revue* ($14), a musical-comedy show about the founding and building of Fairbanks, begins at 8:15 nightly. A later, slightly more risqué performance ($14), *The Late Show,* which pokes fun at the Alaskan lifestyle, starts at 10 PM on Friday and Saturday nights from mid-May to mid-September.

SALOONS

A favorite watering hole among miners, truckers, university students, homesteaders, ex-hippies, and the younger set is the **Howling Dog Saloon** (✉ 2160 Old Steese Hwy., ☎ 907/457–8780), in Fox, 11 mi north of Fairbanks. Be ready for a big crowd and loud, authentic rock and roll. All-night volleyball games out back are part of the ambience of
★ the Dog, which also serves up pizza. The **Blue Loon Saloon** (☎ 907/457–5666), at Mile 353.5, Parks Highway, between Ester and Fairbanks, presents year-round rock and roll and folk music and sells a variety of microbrews to complement its full-service menu. The head chef formerly worked at the Chena Pump House, and the menu is steps above standard bar fare. There's a volleyball court, a campfire area, RV parking, and movies every evening at 7 (except Monday).

The **Senator's Saloon** (☎ 907/479–8452) at the Pump House Restaurant is the place to hear easy-listening music alongside the Chena River on a warm summer evening. Don't be alarmed by the exterior appearance
★ of the **Midnight Mine** (☎ 907/456–5348), within walking distance of downtown at 308 Wendell Street. It's a very friendly neighborhood bar with a *Cheers* ambiance with darts, Foosball, pool, and a big-screen TV. Sam the dog is likely to greet you as you come in.

SQUARE DANCING

There are square-dancing clubs in Fairbanks, North Pole, Delta Junction, and Tok. The groups are affiliated with the **Alaskaland Dance Center** (☎ 907/452–5699), which holds frequent dances where visitors are welcome.

Outdoor Activities and Sports

Participant Sports

BICYCLING

Bicyclists in Fairbanks use the paved paths from the University of Alaska campus around Farmers Loop to the Steese Highway. Another path follows Geist and Chena Pump roads into downtown Fairbanks. A shorter, less strenuous route is the bike path between downtown and Alaskaland along the south side of the Chena River. Maps showing all the bike paths are available at the **Fairbanks Convention and Visitors Bureau** (☞ Exploring Fairbanks). Mountain bikers can test their skills during the summer on the ski trails of the University of Alaska Fairbanks and the Birch Hill Recreation Area, or on many of the trails and dirt roads around Fairbanks. Stop by the **Alaska Public Lands Information Center** for mountain biking information.

BOATING

For relaxing boating in or near Fairbanks, use Chena River access points at Nordale Road east of the city, the Cushman and Wendell Street bridges near downtown, Alaskaland park above the Peger River Bridge, the state campground, and the University Avenue Bridge.

The Tanana is riverboat country. On this river and others in the Yukon River drainage, Alaskans use long, wide, flat-bottom boats powered by one or two large outboard engines. The boats include a lift to raise the engine a few inches, allowing passage through the shallows, and some of the engines come equipped with a jet unit instead of a propeller to allow more bottom clearance. Arrangements for riverboat charters can be made in almost any river community. Ask at the **Fairbanks Convention and Visitors Bureau** (☞ Exploring Fairbanks).

DOGSLEDDING

At **Tivi Haus** (⊠ Mile 2, Kallenberg Rd., off Cripple Creek Rd. at Mile 349, Parks Hwy.; call first for directions, ☎ 907/474–8702, FAX 907/479–7601) learn about the official state sport from a family of dog mushers who offer dinner and then a ride with the dogs. In summer (mid-June–Labor Day), ride on the dog-powered Arfmobile. In winter (December–March), take a dogsled ride and possibly see the northern lights. Overnight lodging and cross-country skiing are available.

FISHING

Although a few fish can be caught right in town from the Chena River, avid fishermen can find outstanding angling by hopping a plane or riverboat. Fishing trips include air charters to **Lake Minchumina** (an hour's flight from Fairbanks), known for good pike fishing and a rare view of the north sides of Mt. McKinley and Mt. Foraker. Another charter trip by riverboat or floatplane will take you pike fishing in the **Minto Flats,** west of Fairbanks off the Tanana River, where the mouth of the Chatanika River spreads through miles of marsh and sloughs.

Salmon run up the **Tanana River** most of the summer, but they're not usually caught on hook-and-line gear. Residents take them from the river with gill nets and fish wheels, using special commercial and subsistence permits. Check the Outdoors section in the Friday *Fairbanks Daily News–Miner* newspaper for weekly updates on fishing in the Interior.

GOLD PANNING

You can pan for gold in several places without fear of jumping a claim. **Alaskan Prospectors** (⊠ 504 College Rd., ☎ 907/452–7398) is the oldest mining and prospecting supply store in the state. In addition to maintaining a rocks and minerals museum, it sells gold pans and books and videos on mining. The employees can offer lots of valuable advice for the neophyte gold bug, so don't be put off by the store's outward appearance—once you get inside, you'll find enough interesting material to keep you occupied for hours. **El Dorado Gold Mine** (⊠ 1975 Discovery Dr., ☎ 907/479–7613) conducts two-hour tours of a seasonal mining operation that include a ride on a narrow-gauge railroad. The tours cost $27.95. **Chatanika Gold Camp** (⊠ Mile 27.9, Steese Hwy., ☎ 907/389–2414) provides a water trough for panners at an authentic gold camp.

GOLF

Chena Bend (☎ 907/353–6223), a beautifully maintained army course open to civilians, is an 18-hole spread on nearby Ft. Wainwright. The 9-hole course at the **Fairbanks Golf and Country Club** (☎ 907/479–

6555) straddles Farmers Loop just north of the university. The 18-hole course at the **North Star Golf Club** (✉ 330 Golf Club Dr., ☎ 907/457–4653; 907/455–8362 in winter, FAX 907/457–3945) is on the Old Steese Highway, ⁷⁄₁₀ mi past Chena Hot Springs Road.

HIKING
On the edge of Fairbanks is the 1,800-acre **Creamer's Field Migratory Waterfowl Refuge** (☞ Exploring Fairbanks), which has three nature trails. The longest trail is 2 mi, and one is accessible to people who use wheelchairs.

RUNNING
Two of Fairbanks's best runs are the **Midnight Sun Run** each June on the weekend nearest the summer solstice and the September **Equinox Marathon,** a tough run up and down the large Ester Dome, northwest of the city. Check with local sporting-goods stores for race schedules.

SKIING
The Interior has some of the best weather and terrain in the nation for cross-country skiing, especially during the late fall and early spring. Among the developed trails in the Fairbanks area, the ones at the **Birch Hill Recreation Area,** on the city's north side, and the **University of Alaska Fairbanks** are lighted to extend their use into the winter nights. Cross-country ski racing is a staple at several courses on winter weekends. The season stretches from October to late March or early April. Other developed trails can be found at **Chena Hot Springs Resort, White Mountain National Recreation Area,** the **Chena Lakes Recreation Area,** and the **Two Rivers Recreation Area.** For more information check with the **Alaska Public Lands Information Center.**

For downhill skiing, **Mt. Aurora/Skiland** (☎ 907/456–7669 or 907/389–2314), on the Steese Highway about 20 mi from Fairbanks at Cleary Summit, has a chairlift, 20+ runs ranked intermediate to expert, and a 1,100-ft vertical drop. There's lodging in an old gold-camp bunkhouse, dog mushing, snowmobile rides, and aurora viewing. It's open weekends from December to mid-April. **Moose Mountain** (☎ 907/479–8362), off Murphy Dome Road, has beginner, intermediate, and a few advanced slopes; it's open November–April, Thursday–Sunday. **Birch Hill** (☎ 907/353–7053), in Ft. Wainwright, has a chairlift and beginner and intermediate runs; it's open November–April, Thursday–Sunday.

Spectator Sports
BASEBALL
Scores of baseball players, including Tom Seaver, Dave Winfield, and Jason Giambi, have passed through Fairbanks on their way to the major leagues. The Interior city is home to the **Alaska Goldpanners** (☎ 907/451–0095, WEB www.goldpanners.com), a member of the Alaska Baseball League, a string of amateur baseball organizations throughout the state. Players are recruited from college teams nationwide, and the summer season (mid-June–early August) generates top-caliber competition. Home games are played at Growden Field, along Lower 2nd Avenue at Wilbur Street, not far from Alaskaland. The baseball park hosts the **Midnight Sun Baseball Game,** a Fairbanks tradition in which the Goldpanners play baseball at midnight of the summer solstice without benefit of artificial lights. This is thrilling (and possibly chilly) to watch on a clear, sunny night when the daylight never ends.

CURLING
Hundreds of Fairbanksans participate each year in curling, a game in which people with brooms play a giant version of shuffleboard on ice. Curlers have an almost fanatical devotion to their sport, and they're eager to explain its finer points to the uninitiated. This ancient Scot-

CELESTIAL RAYS OF LIGHT

THE LIGHT SHOW OFTEN begins simply, as a pale yellow-green luminous band that arches across Alaska's night sky. Sometimes the band will quickly fade and disappear. Other nights, however, it may begin to waver, flicker, and pulsate. Or the quiescent band may suddenly explode and fill the sky with curtains of celestial light that ripple wildly above the northern landscape. Growing more intense, these dancing lights take on other colors: pink, red, blue, or purple. At times they appear to be heavenly flames, leaping across the sky. Or perhaps they're exploding fireworks, or cannon fire.

Known to scientists as the aurora borealis, the luminous nighttime bands and ribbons that appear in Alaska's skies are also commonly called the northern lights. Watching them, it is sometimes possible to see a rhythm in their movements. Or at least imagine one. It's also easy to imagine why many northern cultures, including those of Alaska's Native peoples, have created myths to explain auroral displays. If you watch closely, what started out as patches, arcs, or bands can be magically transformed into vaporous, humanlike figures. Some of Alaska's Native groups have traditionally believed the lights to be spirits of their ancestors. According to one belief, the spirits are celebrating with dance and drumming; another says they're playing games. There's also a tradition that says the lights are torches, carried by spirits who lead the souls of recently deceased people to life in the "afterworld."

Non-Natives, too, have occasionally created stories around the brightly flashing lights. During Alaska's gold-rush era, for instance, some stampeders supposed the aurora to be reflections of ore deposits. Even renowned wilderness explorer John Muir allowed the northern lights to spark his imagination. Once while traveling through Southeast Alaska in 1890, Muir stayed up all night to watch a gigantic, glowing auroral bridge and bands of "restless electric auroral fairies" who danced to music "too fine for mortal ears."

Scientists have a more technical explanation for these heavenly apparitions. They tell us that the aurora borealis is an atmospheric phenomenon that's tied to explosive events on the sun's surface, known as solar flares. Those flares produce a stream of charged particles, the "solar wind," which goes shooting off into space. When such a wind intersects our planet's magnetic field, most of the particles are deflected; some, however, are deflected into the earth's upper atmosphere, where they collide with gas molecules such as nitrogen and oxygen. The resulting reactions produce glowing colors. The aurora is most commonly a pale yellowish green, but its borders are sometimes tinged with pink, purple, or blue. Especially rare is the all-red aurora, which appears when charged solar particles collide with oxygen molecules up to 150 mi high.

Although the science may seem complex and difficult to comprehend, the results are pure beauty. Alaska has some of the world's brightest auroras, with the best light shows occurring in a band that stretches from the Alaska Range into the Arctic. In Fairbanks, northern lights may appear more than 200 nights per year (they're much less common in Anchorage, partly because of urban glare). Alaska's long hours of daylight hide the aurora in summer, so the best viewing is from September through April. **Chena Hot Springs Resort** (✉ Chena Hot Springs, ☎ 907/452–7867) has a glassed-in and heated hut set up on a hillside for gazing at the northern lights. **North Star Tours** (✉ Box 71677, Fairbanks, ☎ 907/451–1125) runs aurora tours to Mt. Aurora/Skiland from December into April. They'll arrange pickup and delivery to your hotel, supply warm clothes if needed, and offer an "aurora insurance" plan if you're the gambling type.

tish game was brought to Alaska and the Yukon during the Klondike gold rush. The **Fairbanks Curling Club** (✉ 1962 2nd Ave., 99701, ☎ 907/452–2875) hosts an annual international bonspiel (match) on the first weekend of April. The club season runs from early October through the middle of April.

SLED-DOG RACES

From November to March, a constant string of sled-dog races is held throughout the region, culminating in the **North American Open Sled-Dog Championship,** which attracts international competition to Fairbanks. Throughout Alaska, sprint races, freight hauling, and long-distance endurance runs are held in late February and March, during the Alaska season when longer days afford enjoyment of the remaining winter snow. Men and women often compete in the same classes in the major races. For children, various racing classes are based on age, starting with the one-dog category for the youngest.

In Fairbanks many of the sprint races are organized by the **Alaska Dog Mushers Association** (☎ 907/457–6874), one of the oldest organizations of its kind in Alaska, and held at its Jeff Studdert Sled Dog Racegrounds at Mile 4, Farmers Loop. Held in February, the **Yukon Quest International Sled-Dog Race** (☎ 907/452–7954) is an endurance race covering more than 1,000 mi between Fairbanks and Whitehorse, Yukon Territory, via Dawson and the Yukon River. You can get more details from the visitor center in either city or by calling the Yukon Quest office in Fairbanks.

HOCKEY

At the nearby University of Alaska Fairbanks, the **Nanooks** (☎ 907/474–6868) play NCAA Division I hockey.

RIVERBOAT RACING

Another summer highlight is riverboat racing sanctioned by the **Fairbanks Outboard Association.** These specially built 22-ft racing boats are powered by 60-horsepower engines and reach speeds of 70 mi per hour. Weekend races throughout the summer and fall begin and end either at the Pump House Restaurant or at Pike's Landing, just off Airport Way near Fairbanks International Airport. The season's big event in late June is the **Yukon 800 Marathon,** a two-day, 800-mi race between Fairbanks and Galena by way of the Chena, Tanana, and Yukon rivers. The **Roland Lord Memorial Race,** from Fairbanks to Nenana and back, is held in early August.

Shopping

Crafts

The **Arctic Travelers Gift Shop** (✉ 201 Cushman St., ☎ 907/456–7080) has a wide selection of Athabascan beadwork. **Beads and Things** (✉ 537 2nd Ave., ☎ 907/456–2323) sells Native handicrafts from around the state. The **Great Alaskan Bowl Company** (✉ 4630 Old Airport Rd., ☎ 907/474–9663) sells lathe-turned bowls made out of Alaskan birch.

Jewelry

In her small, eponymous shop, **Judie Gumm Designs** (✉ 3600 Main St., Ester 99725, ☎ 907/479–4568), Ms. Gumm fashions stunning silver and gold designs best described as sculptural interpretations of northern images. Moderately priced and easy to pack, her jewelry makes a nice memento of your trip north. Ester is 5 mi west of Fairbanks off the George Parks Highway—follow the signs.

Outerwear and Outdoor Gear

Simon Rakower, the owner of the Far North bike shop **All Weather Sports** (⊠ 4001 Geist Rd., No. 12, ☎ 907/474–8184, WEB www.allweathersports.com), invented the double-wide mountain bike rim—the Snow-Cat—so that competitors in IditaSport, a mountain bike, snowshoe, and ski version of the Iditarod Trail Sled Dog Race, would be able to pedal their bikes on snow-packed trails. His shop carries a full line of extra-wide rim wheels, studded bicycle tires, and other items hard to find anywhere else. He sells and rents bikes, and the shop specializes in repairs of bikes damaged in transit to Alaska.

Apocalypse Design (⊠ 101 College Rd., ☎ 907/451–7555) makes its own specialized cold-weather clothing for dog mushers and winter adventurers. Travelers from colder sections of the Lower 48 will appreciate the double-layer fleece mittens, among other items.

AROUND FAIRBANKS

The three roads north of Fairbanks head straight out of civilization. They all dead-end at water—two at rivers and one on the Arctic Ocean. This is the direction in which to head if you want to see untamed Alaska and cross paths with some rugged, independent people.

Chena Hot Springs

★ ❽ *62 mi northeast of Fairbanks.*

The 57-mi, paved Chena Hot Springs Road, which starts 5 mi outside Fairbanks, leads to Chena Hot Springs, a favorite playground of many Fairbanks residents. Several attractions lie along the road, including Tack's General Store and Greenhouse Café, Chena River State Recreation Area, and Chena Hot Springs Resort.

Dining and Lodging

$$$–$$$$ ✕ **Two Rivers Lodge.** Fairbanksans are known to make the 40-mi round-trip for the delicious dinners at this restaurant, which serves up fine beef and Alaskan seafood dishes and often offers crab specials. Specialties include hand-cut, aged filet mignon steaks and prime rib. Don't be discouraged by the outward appearance of the building. Its rustic log decor belies the elegance of the menu. For a study in contrasts, Alaskan style, stop in the saloon first for a predinner refreshment. ⊠ *Mile 16, Chena Hot Springs Rd.,* ☎ *907/488–6815,* FAX *907/488–9761. AE, D, MC, V. No lunch.*

$–$$ ✕ **Tack's General Store and Greenhouse Café.** Tack's, an almost essential pit stop, serves up homemade pies (fruit, berry, and cream) that draw locals back again and again. Many people plan a hard day of play in the nearby Chena River State Recreation Area, with a stop at Tack's on the way back. The café is open for breakfast, lunch, and dinner from 8 to 8. The main building is an old-fashioned post office, gas station, and general store that carries everything from dog food and office supplies to baskets, fabrics, hardware, gardening supplies, and the ever-popular "notions." During the summer, the owners operate a greenhouse next door. ⊠ *Mile 23.5, Chena Hot Springs Rd.,* ☎ *907/488–3242,* FAX *907/488–9010. MC, V.*

$$$$ ▥ ⚠ **Chena Hot Springs Resort.** Fairbanksans come in droves, especially in winter, to this resort at the end of Chena Hot Springs Road for a day of soaks in the hot springs–warmed hot tubs or swimming pool and various outdoor sports. Summer activities include fishing, horseback riding, gold panning, camping, flightseeing, canoeing, and mountain biking. In winter you can go cross-country skiing, snowmobiling,

dogsledding, sleigh riding, and Snow-Cat touring. ATV tours are given year-round. The Aurorarium is a large, glassed-in room for viewing the northern lights. The dining room serves three meals a day. There are sports-equipment rentals, camping sites, and heated cabins without running water. ⊠ *Box 73440, Fairbanks 99707,* ☎ *907/452–7867 or 800/478–4681,* FAX *907/456–3122,* WEB *www.chenahotsprings.com. 80 rooms, 10 cabins. Restaurant, bar, massage, horseback riding, camping, fishing, mountain bikes, cross-country skiing, sleigh rides, snowmobiling, coin laundry, meeting room. AE, D, DC, MC, V.*

Outdoor Activities and Sports

BOATING

The **Chena River State Recreation Area,** along Chena Hot Springs Road from Mile 26 to Mile 51, has numerous well-marked river-access points. The lower sections of the river area are placid, but the area above the third bridge, at Mile 44.1, can be hazardous for inexperienced boaters.

HIKING

The **Chena River State Recreation Area,** which straddles Chena Hot Springs Road from Mile 26 to Mile 51, has a few hiking trails. The Granite Tors Trail, a 15-mi loop, can be done in a day and offers a view of the upper Chena Valley. Carry plenty of drinking water on this trip because of limited water sources. A shorter hike is the 3½-mi Angel Rocks Trail, near the eastern boundary of the area. This area is managed by the Alaska Division of Parks (☎ 907/451–2695), which also maintains five area public-use cabins, although only one is reachable by car.

Steese Highway

From Fairbanks: 128 mi northeast to Central, 136 mi to Circle Hot Springs, 162 mi to Circle.

The Steese Highway follows the Chatanika River and several other creeks along the southern part of the White Mountains. It eventually climbs into weatherworn alpine mountains, peaking at Eagle Summit (3,624 ft), about 100 mi from Fairbanks, and drops back down into forested creek beds en route to Central. At Central you can drive the 30-plus mi on a winding gravel road to Circle, a small town on the Yukon River, or you can take the 8-mi road south to **Arctic Circle Hot Springs,** with soothing hot springs and outdoor adventures close at hand. The highway is paved to Mile 44 and usually in good shape. A possible exception is during winter, when Eagle Summit is sometimes closed due to drifting snow.

Lodging

$–$$$ 🏨 ⛰ **Arctic Circle Hot Springs.** A three-hour drive from Fairbanks, Arctic Circle Hot Springs has a hotel dating from 1930, with hostel-style rooms, suites, cabins, and a small campground (with pads and electrical hookups). The hot springs feed an Olympic-size outdoor pool, and snowmobiling, cross-country skiing, and hiking trails are nearby; dogsled rides are available in the winter. The resort is at the end of an 8-mi spur road that begins at Central on the Steese Highway. You can fly from Fairbanks to the small airstrip nearby. ⊠ *Mile 8.3, Circle Hot Springs Rd., Box 30069, Central 99730,* ☎ *907/520–5113,* FAX *907/ 520–5116. 25 rooms, 4 suites, 15 cabins. Restaurant, bar, pool, massage, gym, library, meeting room. MC, V.*

$$ 🏨 ⛰ **Historic Chatanika Gold Camp.** Formerly known as the Old F. E. Gold Camp, this lodge was the bunkhouse for the miners working the dredges for the F. E. Gold Co. in the early 1900s. The 55-acre site

is on the National Register of Historic Places. The dining room has the world's largest coal cookstove still in operation. The rooms in the hotel share bathrooms. Additionally, there are two four-room log cabins, each with two shared bathrooms and jet tubs. The area is a wonderland for local winter-sports enthusiasts, summertime hikers, and aurora viewers. ⊠ *Mile 27.9, Steese Hwy., 5550 Steese Hwy., Fairbanks 99712,* ☎ *907/389–2414,* FAX *907/389–2797. 26 rooms, 6 shared baths; 2 cabins, 4 units in each cabin, sharing 2 baths. Restaurant, bar, meeting room. AE, MC, V.*

$$ 🏨 **Chatanika Lodge.** This cedar lodge is a gathering spot for rocket scientists from the nearby Poker Flat Research Range and for mushers (guests can take dogsled rides), snowmobilers, and local families. The eclecticism of the clientele is matched by that of the furnishings: diamond willow lamps and a variety of wild animal trophy heads and skins, including bear, lynx, and wolf. The rooms generally have a double and single bed, sink, and TV. The bathrooms and showers are down the hall. ⊠ *Mile 28.6, Steese Hwy., 5760 Steese Hwy., Fairbanks 99712,* ☎ *907/389–2164,* FAX *907/389–2166. 10 rooms share 4 baths. Restaurant, bar, snowmobiling. MC, V.*

Outdoor Activities and Sports

BOATING

The **Chatanika River,** a choice spot for canoeists and kayakers, has a wilderness feel to it yet is fairly close to Fairbanks. The most northerly access point is at Cripple Creek campground, near Mile 60 of the Steese Highway. Other commonly used access points are at Long Creek (Mile 45, Steese Highway), at the state campground where the Chatanika River crosses the Steese Highway at Mile 39, and at the state's Whitefish Campground, where the river crosses the Elliott Highway at Mile 11. Below this point, the stream flows into the Minto Flats, and access is more difficult.

Water in the Chatanika River may or may not be clear, depending on mining activities along its upper tributaries. In times of very low water, the upper Chatanika River is shallow and difficult to navigate. Avoid the river in times of high water, especially after heavy rains, because of the danger of sweepers, floating debris, and hidden gravel bars. Contact the Alaska Public Lands Information Center to find out the status of the river.

Steese Mountain National Conservation Area and White Mountain National Recreation Area

⑩ *About 31 mi northeast of Fairbanks.*

The **Bureau of Land Management** (⊠ BLM Headquarters, 1150 University Ave., Fairbanks 99709, ☎ 907/474–2200) administers the Steese Mountain National Conservation Area and the White Mountain National Recreation Area. Both preserves are accessible by car. The White Mountain Recreation Area has limited camping facilities from June to November. The BLM also has three campsites on the Taylor Highway between Tok and Eagle at Miles 48.5, 82, and 160.

In the Steese National Conservation Area you can take a four- to five-day float trip on the lively, clear-water **Birch Creek,** a challenge with its several rapids along its 126 mi. Moose, caribou, and birds are easily spotted. Access is at Mile 94 of the Steese Highway. This stream winds its way north through the historic mining country of the Circle District. The takeout point is at the Steese Highway Bridge, 15 mi from Circle. From there Birch Creek meanders on to the Yukon River well below the town.

Rising out of the White Mountain National Recreation Area, **Beaver Creek** makes its easy way north. If you have enough time, it's possible to run its entire 268-mi length to the Yukon (if you make a shorter run, you will have to go out by small plane).

Lodging

$ 🛏 **BLM Public-Use Cabins.** The BLM manages 11 public-use cabins in the White Mountain NRA, with 300 mi of interconnecting trails. Designed primarily for winter use by dog mushers, snow machiners (snowmobilers), and cross-country skiers, cabins provide shelter for summer backpackers although summer access is limited by mountainous and boggy terrain. The cabins have bunk beds, woodstoves, tables, and chairs. Permits are required and available up to 30 days in advance. ✉ *BLM Headquarters, 1150 University Ave., Fairbanks 99709, ☎ 907/474–2200 or 800/437–7021. 11 cabins. MC, V.*

$ ⚠ **BLM Campgrounds.** The BLM manages three road-accessible campgrounds in the Steese Highway area and another along the Dalton Highway. They all have picnic tables, fire pits, latrines, and well water. They're available on a first-come, first-served basis. In addition, you'll find several undeveloped campsites along the Dalton—old gravel pits with no facilities, available free of charge. ✉ *BLM Headquarters, 1150 University Ave., Fairbanks 99709, ☎ 907/474–2200. 4 campsites. No credit cards.*

Outdoor Activities and Sports

HIKING

The BLM maintains the moderately difficult 20-mi **Summit Trail,** from the Elliott Highway, near Wickersham Dome, north into the White Mountain National Recreation Area. This hiking trail can be done as a day hike or overnight backpacking trip. It quickly rises into alpine country with 360-degree vistas that include lots of wildland, the trans-Alaska pipeline, and a pipeline pump station. You can see many wildflowers in early summer. Look for the parking lot at Mile 28.

Yukon–Charley Rivers National Preserve

⓫ *20 mi north of Eagle, 100 mi east of Fairbanks.*

The 126-mi stretch of the Yukon River running between the small towns of Eagle and Circle—former gold-rush metropolises—is protected in the 2.5-million-acre Yukon–Charley Rivers National Preserve (✉ National Park Service, 201 1st Ave., Doyon Bldg., Fairbanks 99701, ☎ 907/456–0281). As its name suggests, this parkland also covers the pristine watershed of the Charley River, a crystalline white-water stream flowing out of the Yukon-Tanana uplands. This waterway provides fine river running. You can put in a raft or a kayak (with a small plane) at the headwaters of the Charley River and travel 88 mi down this joyful, bouncing waterway.

In great contrast to the Charley River, the Yukon River is an inexorably powerful stream, dark with mud and glacial silt. The only bridge built across it holds the trans-Alaska pipeline, north of Fairbanks. The river surges deep, and to travel on it in a small boat is a humbling, if magnificent, experience. You can drive from Fairbanks to Eagle (via the Taylor Highway off the Alaska Highway) and to Circle (via the Steese Highway) and from either of these arrange for a ground-transportation shuttle back to your starting city at the end of your Yukon River trip. Weeklong float trips down the river from Eagle to Circle, 150 mi away, are possible. For information, contact the **National Park Service** (☎ 907/547–2233) in Eagle. If planning a trip here, you should note that no developed campgrounds or other visitor facilities exist within the preserve itself, though low-impact backcountry camping is permitted.

Outdoor Activities and Sports

CROSS-COUNTRY SKIING, SNOWMOBILING, AND SNOWSHOEING

Once past Mile 20 of the Steese Highway, even though you're only an hour from downtown Fairbanks, you enter a countryside that seems to have changed little in 100 years. Mountains loom in the distance, and in winter, a solid snowpack of 4–5 ft makes the area great for snowshoeing, backcountry skiing, and riding snowmobiles—Alaskans refer to them as snow machines, and calling them snowmobiles automatically brands you as someone from "outside."

Arctic Cat snowmobiles can be rented at **Snow-RV** (⊠ 5760 Old Steese Hwy., off Steese Hwy. at Mile 28.5, at Chatanika Lodge [Box 10804, Fairbanks 99710], ☎ 907/389–7669, FAX 907/389–5665). Rentals are available by the hour or for several days. Guided rides are required for those from out of state.

HIKING

The BLM maintains the **Pinnell Mountain National Recreation Trail,** connecting Twelve-Mile Summit and Eagle Summit on the Steese Highway. This 27-mi-long trail passes through alpine meadows and along mountain ridges, all above the tree line. It has two emergency shelters. No dependable water supply is available in the immediate vicinity. Most hikers spend three days making the trip. The **Alaska Public Lands Information Center** has information on the trail.

The **Circle-Fairbanks Historic Trail** stretches 58 mi from the vicinity of Cleary Summit to Twelve-Mile Summit. This route, which is not for novices, follows the old summer trail used by gold miners; in winter they generally used the frozen Chatanika River to make this journey. The trail has been roughly marked and cleared, but there are no facilities and water is scarce along much of it. Most of the trail is on state land, but it does cross valid mining claims, which must be respected. Although you'll find rock cairns and mileposts along the trail, no well-defined tread exists, so it's easy to become disoriented. The State Department of Natural Resources strongly recommends that backpackers on this trail equip themselves with the following USGS topographical maps: Livengood (A-1), Circle (A-6), Circle (A-5), and Circle (B-4). The Alaska Public Lands Information Center has detailed information about the trail.

Elliott Highway

From Fairbanks: 28 mi north to Wickersham Dome, north 73 mi to Dalton Hwy. junction, 152 mi northwest to Manley.

⑫ The Elliott Highway, which starts in Fox, takes you to the Tanana River and the small community of **Manley Hot Springs.** A colorful, close-knit "end-of-the-road" place, this town originally was a trading center for placer miners who worked the nearby creeks. Residents maintain a small public campground, across from Manley Roadhouse. Northern pike are caught in the nearby slough, and a dirt road leads to the Tanana River with its summer runs of salmon. The Manley Hot Springs Resort has closed, but the hot springs are only a short walk from the campground. The highway is paved for 28 mi outside Fairbanks.

Lodging

$$ 🏠 **Manley Roadhouse.** Built in 1906 in the midst of the gold rush into the Interior, this roadhouse is among the oldest in Alaska. Today it caters to a diverse crowd of vacationers, miners, and road maintenance crews.

The restaurant serves breakfast, lunch, and dinner. Rather than being known for the food or the rooms, which occupy the original roadhouse and several cabins, the bar earns bragging rights for its 250 brands of liquor and 20 varieties of beer. ⊠ *Mile 152, Elliott Hwy., Manley Hot Springs (Box 1, Manley Hot Springs 99756),* ☎ *907/672–3161. 14 rooms, 6 with bath; 3 cabins. Restaurant, bar. AE, MC, V.*

Outdoor Activities and Sports

HIKING

The BLM maintains the 22-mi **Summit Trail** from the Elliott Highway, near Wickersham Dome, north into the White Mountain National Recreation Area.

Dalton Highway

From Fairbanks: 140 mi north to the Yukon River, 199 mi to the Arctic Circle, 259 mi to Coldfoot, 329 mi to Atigun Pass, 499 mi to Deadhorse.

The Dalton Highway is a road of "onlys." It's the only road that goes to the Beaufort Sea, it's the only Alaskan road to cross the Arctic Circle, and it has the state's only bridge across the Yukon River. The 414-mi gravel road starts 84 mi from Fairbanks on the Elliott Highway and runs northwest of Fairbanks to the North Slope oil fields at Prudhoe Bay. It was built in 1974 and 1975 to open a truck route necessary to build the facilities at Prudhoe and the northern half of the trans-Alaska pipeline. For a few months a ferry was used to carry loads across the Yukon River, until the present bridge was completed late in 1975.

The road is named for James Dalton, a pioneer Alaskan engineer who recognized early the potential of oil on the North Slope. If you are planning to drive the Dalton Highway, remember these tips: slow down and move to the side of the road for trucks; leave your headlights on at all times; yield on one-lane bridges; pull to the side of the road when stopping for pictures or the view; carry at least one spare tire; and consider bringing extra gas and purchasing a citizen's band radio. Remember there are no services between Coldfoot and Prudhoe Bay, a distance of nearly 250 mi.

The Dalton Highway has two **visitor centers** open in the summer. One is just north of the Yukon River bridge and has no phone. The other is in Coldfoot (☎ 907/678–5209). The centers are operated by the Fish and Wildlife Service, the National Park Service, and the BLM. A picnic area and a large, colorful sign mark the spot where the road crosses the Arctic Circle.

The **Wiseman Trading Co.,** a museum and general store 12 mi north of Coldfoot, is run by Coldfoot Services–Slate Creek Inn.

⑬ Today the road is still used to carry oil-field supplies and is now open all the way to **Deadhorse,** just shy of the Arctic coast. This town exists mainly to service the oil fields of Prudhoe Bay. Scenery isn't in great supply, but it does have important facilities for travelers, including fuel, vehicle maintenance, a general store, an airport, a post office, hotels, and restaurants. Oil-field tours and shuttles to the Arctic Ocean leave daily from the three hotels in Deadhorse. The two tours offered are a one-hour tour to the ocean for $25, and a 2½-hour tour and video screening ($50) that also take in Mile 0 of the trans-Alaska pipeline. For tour reservations call the **Arctic Caribou Inn** (☎ 907/659–2368) or the ☞ **Prudhoe Bay Hotel.**

Lodging

Five camping areas plus many scenic turnouts are along the road. Only one of the camping areas (Marion Creek, at Mile 180) is developed. Most of the rest are gravel pads, sometimes with outhouses. Call the **Alaska Public Lands Information Center** for more information.

$$$$ **Prudhoe Bay Hotel.** This hotel is in the community of Deadhorse, and like much of the town it was built mainly to house pipeline workers. The result is spartan but comfortable guest rooms. There is a TV room with a big-screen TV. The restaurant (all meals are included in the room rate) serves gourmet pizza and American fare in an all-you-can-eat buffet. ✉ *Airport Rd., across from the airport (Pouch 340004, Prudhoe Bay 99734),* ☎ *907/659–2449,* FAX *907/659–2752,* WEB *www.prudhoebayhotel.com. 180 rooms, 15 with bath. Restaurant, gym. MC, V.*

$$$ **Arctic Caribou Inn.** This hotel is made of trailer-type units, with basic rooms. The restaurant serves American fare in an all-you-can-eat buffet. ✉ *Airport Rd. (Box 340111, Deadhorse 99734),* ☎ *907/659–2368 or 877/659–2368,* FAX *907/659–2692,* WEB *www.arcticcaribouinn.com. 45 rooms. Restaurant. MC, V. Closed Labor Day–Memorial Day.*

$$$ **Yukon Ventures Alaska.** On the Yukon River, this property has a motel; a tire repair shop; and gasoline, diesel fuel, and propane. The motel is basic and clean, built from surplus pipeline-worker housing. None of the rooms have private baths, but two (one for men, one for women) have showers and are centrally located. The restaurant serves large portions of diner fare. ✉ *Mile 56, Dalton Hwy., Box 60947, Fairbanks 99706,* ☎ *907/655–9001. 40 rooms share 3 baths. Restaurant. MC, V.*

$–$$$$ **Coldfoot Camp.** Fuel, tire repairs, and towing are available here in Coldfoot. Basic and clean rooms are built from surplus pipeline-worker housing. The 24-hour restaurant serves generous portions of truck-stop fare. The complex has a 20-space RV hookup and post office. Although the place looks more than a little offbeat, bear in mind that it's the only facility of any sort within a hundred miles or more, so you'll have to adjust your standards accordingly. ✉ *Mile 175, Dalton Hwy., Box 9041, Coldfoot 99701,* ☎ *907/474–3400,* FAX *907/474–4767. 81 rooms, 52 with bath. Restaurant, shop. MC, V.*

Guided Tours

Princess Tours (☎ 907/479–9660 or 800/426–0442) runs tour buses on the Dalton from Fairbanks all the way to Prudhoe Bay, with a variety of services, including an overnight at Coldfoot, a tour of the oil field, and air service from Prudhoe Bay back to Fairbanks or Anchorage. Tours operate once a week from June through August. **Northern Alaska Tour Company** (☎ 907/474–8600) conducts van tours and boat tours of the Yukon River with Yukon River Tours. **Trans Arctic Circle Treks** (☎ 907/479–5451 or 800/336–8735, FAX 800/479–8908) has an extensive menu of guided trips ranging in duration from 1 day to 11 days, covering areas from Anchorage and Southwest Alaska to Barrow and Prudhoe Bay. It is the only tour company with a winter "Adventures to the North Slope" trip.

Outdoor Activities and Sports

FISHING

Although this is not a prime fishing area, fish, mostly grayling, populate the streams along the Dalton. You'll do better if you are willing to hike more than ¼ mi from the road, where fishing pressure is the heaviest. Lakes along the road have grayling, and some have lake trout and arctic char. The Alaska Department of Fish and Game puts out a pamphlet titled "Sport Fishing Along the Dalton Highway," which is also available at the **Alaska Public Lands Information Center.**

HIKING

No trails have been officially established along the road, but hikers willing to pick their own route can explore much of the area. The road passes near the **Yukon Flats National Wildlife Refuge,** the **Kanuti National Wildlife Refuge,** the **Arctic National Wildlife Refuge,** and just east of **Gates of the Arctic National Park and Preserve.** Check with the **Alaska Public Lands Information Center.** Chances of seeing wildlife are fairly good, as this is grizzly bear and caribou habitat.

Healy

⑭ *11 mi north of Denali National Park, 109 mi south of Fairbanks, 248 mi north of Anchorage.*

Coal mining fuels the economy of Healy, which is home to the **Usibelli Coal Mine,** the largest mine of its kind in the state and Alaska's only commercially viable coal mining operation. Each summer overflow crowds from Denali National Park and Preserve stream into this small community of 500 people on the George Parks Highway, north of the entrance, to park. However, more and more frequently, Fairbanks-area residents and visitors from the Lower 48 and other countries are seeking out Healy's year-round lodging and the magnificent views.

Healy is close to the **Stampede Trail,** which offers those interested in snowmobiling, mushing, cross-country skiing, and mountain biking a way to enter the northern expanse of Denali National Park and Preserve. This wide, well-traveled path begins where Stampede Road ends and leads to the former gold-rush boomtown of Kantishna, 90 mi inside the park. Take the George Parks Highway 2 mi north of Healy to Mile 251.1, where Stampede Road intersects the highway. Eight miles west on Stampede Road is a parking lot and the start of the Stampede Trail.

Dining and Lodging

$–$$$ ✕ **Totem Inn.** For standard American fare at reasonable prices, this restau-
★ rant draws a crowd from travelers along the George Parks Highway and visitors to Healy and Denali National Park. Pizzas, steaks, sandwiches, and a Sunday lunch buffet are served all year-round. The kitchen is open daily 7 AM–11 PM. ⊠ *Mile 248.7, George Parks Hwy.,* ☎ *907/683–2420. D, MC, V.*

$$$$ 🏨 **Denali Wilderness Lodge.** This backcountry, fly-in-only lodge sits on the Wood River in a vast wilderness expanse adjacent to Denali National Park. Guests stay in cozy private cabins, complete with electricity and running water, a rarity in such remote circumstances. The room price includes all meals, which are served family style in a large, airy dining room. Fresh ingredients are flown in daily, and most food is homegrown or homemade. Activities include hiking, either on your own or accompanied by a staff naturalist, horseback riding, canoeing, gold panning, and evening nature programs; you can also sit back and relax in Alaska's quiet and solitude. Flightseeing trips are available for an additional fee. ⊠ *Winter (Sept. 12–May 30) Box 120, Trout Lake, WA 98650; Summer (May 31–Sept. 11) Box 50, Denali, AK 99755,* ☎ *800/ 541–9779,* WEB *www.denaliwildernesslodge.com. 22 rooms. Restaurant, bar, hiking, horseback riding, boating, private airstrip. MC, V.*

$$$–$$$$ 🏨 **Motel Nord Haven.** This motel, with wood trim throughout, has rooms with one or two queen-size beds, a telephone, television, and a private bath. It's set on 5 wooded acres and protected from the road. As a result it offers a secluded feeling other lodgings along the George Parks Highway lack. Rooms with two queen beds can accommodate up to five people at no additional charge. A Continental breakfast is served and pack box lunches will be prepared for clients to carry along on

their explorations. ⊠ *Mile 249.5, George Parks Hwy., Box 458, 99743,* ☎ *907/683–4500 or 800/683–4501,* FAX *907/683–4503,* WEB *www.motelnordhaven.com. 28 rooms, 4 with kitchenettes. Meeting room. AE, MC, V.*

$$$ 🏠 **Denali Dome Home.** This all-year B&B is housed in a huge, 7,200-square-ft, modified geodesic dome. Each guest room has a private bath, TV, VCR, and phone; one has a sauna and one a jetted tub. A common room has a TV, fireplace, and Alaska-related books and videos. The fireplace fits 5-ft-long logs and the high ceiling is enhanced by tall windows that provide spectacular views of nearby mountains. ⊠ *137 Healy Spur Rd., Box 262, 99743,* ☎ *907/683–1239,* FAX *907/683–2322,* WEB *www.denalidomehome.com. 7 rooms. Breakfast room, in-room VCRs. AE, D, MC, V.*

$$ 🏠 **Stampede Lodge.** The current owners have toned down the appearance of the former Healy Hotel, which had been a bright blue. Now the modern Alaskan structure is gray with dark green trim. All the rooms have private baths and phones. Breakfast, lunch, and dinner are served at the lodge's restaurant, the Bushmaster Grill. ⊠ *Mile 248.8, George Parks Hwy., Box 380, 99743,* ☎ *907/683–2242 or 800/472–2370,* FAX *907/683–2243,* WEB *www.alaskaone.com/stampede/index.htm. 29 rooms. Restaurant. AE, D, MC, V.*

DENALI NATIONAL PARK AND PRESERVE

⑮ *11 mi south of Healy, 120 mi south of Fairbanks, 240 mi north of Anchorage.*

The most accessible of Alaska's national parks and one of only three connected to the state's highway system, 6-million-acre Denali National Park and Preserve is one of North America's finest and easiest places to see wildlife in its natural environment. Nowhere in the world is there more spectacular background scenery to these wildlife riches, with 20,320-ft Mt. McKinley looming above forested valleys, tundra-topped hills, and the glacier-covered peaks of the Alaska Range.

Also commonly known by its Athabascan Indian name *Denali*, "the High One," North America's highest mountain is also the world's tallest when measured from base to top: the great mountain rises more than 18,000 ft above surrounding lowlands. Unfortunately for visitors with little time to spend in the area, McKinley is wreathed in clouds on average two days of every three during the summer. However, if you plan ahead and venture far enough into the park, you'll have a better chance of seeing the mountain in all its glacier-capped magnificence.

Although most Denali visitors are content to watch Mt. McKinley from afar, more than 1,000 adventurers walk the mountain's slopes each summer. About half of them succeed in "summiting" the peak during the May to July climbing season. The great majority of McKinley mountaineers fly to the mountain's base camp on the Kahiltna Glacier at 7,200 ft, then follow the West Buttress Route, generally considered the safest and easiest path to the top. Whatever route they take, climbers must deal with avalanches, glacial crevasses, high altitude, and extreme cold. Even in summer, temperatures high on McKinley can fall to −30°F or −40°F. The mountain is so large it creates its own weather, and storms frequently batter its upper slopes with winds of 100 mph or more. If you feel you must attempt the peak, talk to the park service people about procuring a guide. The hazards of climbing Denali are frequently underestimated, and prospective adventurers must be aware of the dangers. Fatalities are unfortunately an occasional occurrence.

You need not climb Mt. McKinley to appreciate Denali; the park is both a hiker's and wildlife-watcher's paradise. The one 88-mi road into the heart of the park is unpaved after the first 14.8 mi, and in summer you can travel on shuttle buses, from which you can see grizzly bears, wolves, caribou, and moose. The bulk of the parkland, however, is accessible only on foot in summer or by dog team or cross-country skis in winter.

For all the challenges of access and planning, those who explore Denali are certain to reap many rewards: wilderness solitude, a sense of discovery, wildlife encounters, and a greater appreciation of the landscape's immensity and the rigors of the sub-Arctic climate.

Geology and Terrain

Several of Denali's most spectacular landforms are deep in the park. The multicolor volcanic rocks at Cathedral Mountain and Polychrome Pass remind many travelers of the vivid hues of the desert Southwest. The braided channels of glacially fed streams such as the Teklanika, Toklat, and McKinley rivers serve as "highway routes" for both animals and hikers. The debris- and tundra-covered ice of the Muldrow Glacier, one of the largest glaciers to flow out of Denali National Park's high mountains, is visible from Eielson Visitor Center, at Mile 66 of the park road. Wonder Lake, a dark and narrow "kettle pond" that's a remnant from Alaska's Ice Ages, lies at the end of the park road near Kantishna.

The most prominent geological feature of the park is the Alaska Range, a 600-mi-long crescent of summits that separates South Central Alaska from the Interior. These peaks are all immense, but the truly towering ones are Mt. Hunter (14,573 ft), Mt. Foraker (17,400 ft), and Mt. McKinley (20,320 ft). Mt. McKinley's granite heart is covered with glacial ice, which is hundreds of feet thick in places. Glaciers, in fact, are abundant along the entire Alaska Range, and a few are visible from the park road. Muldrow Glacier is only 5 mi from the road, near Mile 67.

Flora

Vegetation in the park consists largely of taiga and tundra. Taiga is coniferous forest that exists in moist areas below tree line of 2,000 feet, consisting mainly of spruce trees. These trees have very shallow root systems due to the layer of permafrost that lies just under the surface of the land, and they are subject to the vagaries of wind and land movements. A turnoff and informational sign on the road near the park entrance points out an area of "drunken forest," where the uppermost layer of soil has shifted on the permafrost, moving the trees around and leaving them in a disheveled state that suggests some sort of arboreal inebriation. Ground cover in the taiga forest includes such shrubs as dwarf birch, blueberry, and willows. From the road, the taiga looks open, with wide views and very few trees, but the dense bushes make it difficult for inexperienced travelers.

The rest of the land mass that isn't permanently covered by ice and snow is overlaid by tundra, which consists of a variety of plant types including lichens, berries, and woody plants—all in miniature. This complex carpet of low-lying vegetation generates brilliant color, especially in August, when the subtle variations of green begin to turn into the colors similar to those sought out by "leaf peepers" in the Lower 48. By the time the autumn colors max out in September, the tundra is ablaze with brilliant swaths of deep red among more restrained hues of yellows and greens. Most tundra areas enable easy hiking, but there are exceptions. After a while, you may learn to evaluate tundra "walkability" from a distance, distinguishing by color and texture which areas are like a springy carpet and a delight to walk on and which are too moist for comfort and can turn an enjoyable hike into a boot-sucking slog.

Wildlife

Nearly every wild creature that walks or flies in South Central and Interior Alaska inhabits the park. Thirty-eight species of mammals reside here, from wolves and bears to little brown bats and pygmy shrews that weigh a fraction of an ounce. The park also has a surprisingly large avian population in the summer, when some 160 species have been identified. Most of the birds migrate in fall, leaving only two dozen year-round resident species, including ravens, boreal chickadees, and hawk owls. Some of the summer birds travel thousands of miles to nest and breed in sub-Arctic valleys, hills, and ponds. The northern wheatear comes here from southern Asia, warblers fly here from Central and South America, and the arctic tern annually travels 24,000 mi while seasonally commuting between Denali and Antarctica.

The most sought-after species among visitors are the large mammals: grizzlies, wolves, Dall sheep, moose, and caribou. All inhabit the forest or tundra landscape that surrounds Denali Park Road. While traveling the park road you can expect to see Dall sheep finding their way across high meadows, grizzlies and caribou frequenting stream bottoms and tundra, moose in the forested areas both near the park entrance and deep in the park, and the occasional wolf or fox that may dart across the road. Keep in mind that, as one park lover put it, "this ain't no zoo." You might hit an off day and have few viewings—enjoy the surroundings anyway. Under no circumstances should you feed the animals or birds (a mew gull or ground squirrel may try to share your lunch).

Exploring Denali

To spend a full day in Denali, plan to stay in or near the park entrance the night before and the night of your bus trip. This way you can get an early start on a morning bus, get far enough into the interior to increase your wildlife-viewing opportunities, and maybe catch a glimpse of Mt. McKinley. The animals are most active early in the morning and in the evening. If you're willing to catch one of the first buses out before 6 AM, you'll have less competition for seats.

The real wilderness experience in Danali is reserved for those who get off the buses and walk. There are excellent day hikes near the entrance, and overnight options are unlimited, since there are no formal trails. Many hikers follow riverbeds or ridges. To avoid potentially dangerous encounters with wildlife, follow the advice of park rangers about routes and safety.

The **visitor center** near the park's entrance (at Milepost 237.3 of the Parks Highway) can fill all your information needs, from campground registration to bus reservations, backcountry permits, and daily schedules for naturalist presentations and sled-dog demonstrations by the park ranger. A video kiosk provides park information including flora, fauna, and bear avoidance. A bookstore stocks titles on Denali's animals, wildflowers, and geology. The Backcountry Reservations desk has hiking information including current data on animal sightings, river crossing conditions, weather, and closed areas. ⊠ *Box 9, Denali National Park, 99755,* ☎ *907/683–2294 year-round; 907/683–1266 in summer.* ⊠ *$5, $10 family. Shuttle buses:* ☎ *800/622–7275; 907/272–7275 in Alaska;* FAX *907/264–4684,* WEB *www.nps.gov/dena.* ⊠ *$12–$30, plus $4 reservation fee.*

238

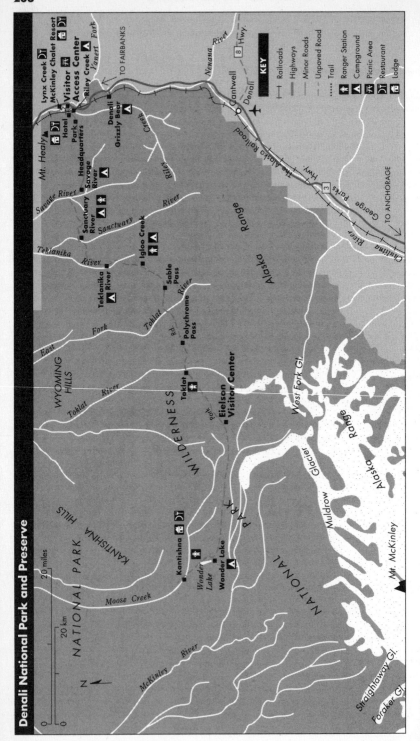

Denali National Park and Preserve

You can reach the park by bus or by car along the George Parks Highway. The Alaska Railroad line runs through Denali and stops at the park on its runs between Anchorage and Fairbanks. When you arrive at the park entrance, stop at the visitor center to pick up your camping permit and your bus passes. Only one road penetrates Denali's expansive wilderness: the 90-mi Denali Park Road, which winds from the park entrance to Wonder Lake and Kantishna, the historic mining community in the heart of the park. The first 14 mi of the road are open to all vehicles, but beyond the checkpoint at the Savage River only tour and shuttle buses and vehicles with permits are allowed to travel. Bicycles are currently allowed on the park road. The road, however, is suitable only for mountain bikes.

Shuttle buses travel as far as Wonder Lake, nearly 90 mi from the park entrance; seats can be reserved in advance, with reservations accepted beginning in late February. Making the entire trip to Wonder Lake and back will take 10 hours or more, but you can get off along the route and catch another bus in either direction.

The shuttle bus system is designed to minimize disturbances to the park's wildlife. Large, potentially dangerous animals roam the park at will, and the park's primary mission is to protect the animals that live here and to keep conflicts between humans and animals at a minimum. It's quite common to see large sections of the park declared off-limits to visitors, including sensitive denning or nesting areas important to wildlife.

Seeing the park at its best requires time. The road is unpaved beyond the 14-mi checkpoint, and the speed limit is 35 mph. Add in frequent stops to view wildlife, rest stops, and the time it takes to negotiate the hills and turns. The general rule, however, is the farther in you go, the better the views of McKinley and the more likely you are to see wildlife.

Nature Trails and Short Walks

Both day hiking and backpacking can be supreme in Denali. The park's entrance area has a system of forest and tundra trails. These range from easy to challenging and are therefore suitable for visitors of all ages and hiking abilities. Along these paths you may see beavers working on their lodges in Horseshoe Lake; red squirrels chattering in trees; red foxes hunting squirrels and other rodents; sheep grazing on tundra plants; golden eagles soaring above high alpine ridges; and moose feeding on willow, one of their favorite foods. You should be cautious around moose and enjoy them from a distance; weighing 1,000 pounds or more, they can cause severe injuries despite their harmless appearance. If you encounter a moose at close range acting aggressively, run from it immediately to leave its "personal space." Just the opposite is true for Denali's grizzlies. Most important, **never** run from a bear. You may trigger its predatory chase instincts and have the bear respond to you as prey (☞ Bear Facts box *in* Chapter 2). A little caution and a large dose of common sense will assure you a safe trip in the park. A summary of bear-safety tips is available at the visitor center.

Longer Hikes

The only relatively long, marked trail for hiking in the park, Mt. Healy Overlook Trail gains 1,700 ft in 2.5 mi and takes about four hours round-trip, with outstanding views of the Nenana River below and the Alaska range above. It's also a great starting point for backcountry hiking. You'll find few trails in the backcountry, however. In tundra areas, you set your own routes, and in forested and brushy areas, you have to bushwhack. The one exception is to find game trails through thick brush, but be advised that these trails were pioneered by bears, moose, and caribou. Whenever you're in an area of restricted visibility, make plenty of noise to announce your presence, and allow the resident critters to move away ahead of you. Because this is bear country, the park service provides backpackers with bearproof food containers. Use of these containers is mandatory. You can plan your itinerary with park rangers and use the shuttle bus for transportation to and from your starting point. No firearms are permitted.

Scenic Drives and Views
You can disembark at any point along the road in the park for hiking and sightseeing, then catch the next bus in either direction to continue your trip. Buses run continuously, and you'll seldom have to wait more than a half hour to catch a ride. Polychrome Pass, at Mile 46 of the park road, is a popular place to disembark, walk around, and take in the wide views of the stream valleys and tundra below. Many visitors turn around at Eielson Visitor Center, at Mile 66 of the park road. But on blue-sky days you might wish to go the distance to Wonder Lake, which has one of the grandest views of Denali. The Eielson-to–Wonder Lake stretch is particularly beautiful from mid-August to early September, when the tundra is ablaze with autumn's yellows, reds, and oranges. If you can't get a spot on one of the buses into the park, you can drive to the parking lot next to the Savage River at Mile 14. From there you can hike on nearby trails, climb the rock that gives the river its name, or head up onto one of the nearby ridge tops.

When to Go
Summer is the prime visiting time for Denali—the area is loosed from winter's icy grip and the animals are awake, active, and cruising for food and/or companionship. Most of the park lies above the tree line and gets 16 to 20 hours of daylight—which means you'll have plenty of time to enjoy the expansive view of unspoiled landscape and catch a few glimpses of Alaskan wildlife in the open spaces. However, late spring and early autumn also provide opportunities to see the area when visitor traffic is lessened, but be advised that the onset of winter and the appearance of spring are far different from the Lower 48, and even from the seasonal changes in Anchorage. In early summer, trails may be muddy and all the trees won't be fully leafed out, but young animals may be more readily visible. The park is open all winter, although services are curtailed and the road into the park is blocked by snow. Intrepid travelers can visit the park on dogsleds, snowshoes, or cross-country skis and get a glimpse of Denali that's seldom seen by outsiders.

What to Pack
Whether hiking in the high mountains or driving the park road, you should always come prepared for the park's highly variable summer weather. At lower elevations the weather can vary from hot and sunny to near freezing and drizzly, and those changes can sometimes occur within a few hours, so you'll want to bring along appropriate clothing and gear. Dress in layers. If you'll be hiking, carry polypropylene long underwear followed by layers of wool or synthetic materials such as fleece. Even if you're not planning on taking a long hike, you should carry durable rain gear, preferably made of a breathable material. In theFar North, cotton is not your friend—once it gets wet, it stays wet for too long, drawing warmth away from your body. Remember to bring binoculars and a camera, as Denali is one of the country's premiere outdoor photography locations.

Dining

$$$–$$$$ ✕ **Tamarack Inn.** Dine on American cuisine by the light of a fireplace at this inn, which houses one of the best-known restaurants on the road from Anchorage to Fairbanks. It serves breakfast, lunch, and dinner in summer, and dinner only in winter. ⊠ *Mile 298, Parks Hwy., 6 mi south of Nenana,* ☎ *907/832–5455. AE, MC, V. Closed Mon.–Tues. in Jan.*

$$–$$$$ ✕ **The Perch.** This fine-dining restaurant sits atop a forested hillside, and its bay windows present a panoramic view of the surrounding Alaska Range foothills. The Perch serves breakfast, lunch, and dinner, offering home-baked breads and desserts along with steak and seafood. Cabin rentals are available year-round for $95 with a private bath, $65 shared. ⊠ *Mile 224, Parks Hwy., Denali National Park,* ☎ *907/683–2523 or 888/322–2523,* WEB *www.alaskaone.com/perchrest. AE, D, MC, V.*

$–$$$ ✕ **Lynx Creek Pizza.** This casual restaurant 1 mi north of the park entrance is a local hangout, good for pizza, sandwiches, salads, ice cream, and some Mexican entrées. You order at the front and grab a seat at picnic-table benches. ⊠ *Mile 238.6, Parks Hwy.,* ☎ *907/683–2547. AE, D, DC, MC, V. Closed in winter.*

$–$$$ ✕ **McKinley/Denali Salmon Bake.** This rustic building 1 mi north of the park entrance serves breakfast, lunch, and dinner and looks as if it might blow away in a stiff wind. Baked fresh salmon tops the menu; steaks, burgers, and chicken are also available. Shuttle service is provided to area hotels. ⊠ *Mile 238.5, Parks Hwy.,* ☎ *907/683–2733 in summer. AE, D, DC, MC, V. Closed Oct.–Apr.*

Lodging

No hotel rooms are available inside the park. However, hotels, motels, RV parks, B&Bs, and campgrounds are clustered along the highway near the park entrance and in the town of Healy, 10 mi north.

$$$$ 🏠 **Camp Denali.** Camp Denali is a group of log cabins in the heart of ★ the park near the end of the park road. The cabins at the camp are comfortable and rustic, and the nearby communal buildings have electricity, running water, and showers. Many consider it the best place to stay in the park because of its charm and delicious home cooking (for guests only), and it's the only facility within the park that has a view of Mt. McKinley. The owners also run Northface Lodge, just 1 mi from Camp Denali. Knowledgeable staffs at both places acquaint you with the surrounding wilderness and lead evening natural-history programs and guided outings. The price listed is per cabin per night, and packages include stays of either three or four nights. Transportation to the lodge is by van over the 85-mi-long road from the park entrance, and the trip for pickups and deliveries of guests is made twice a week. ⊠ *Box 67, Denali National Park, 99755,* ☎ *907/683–2290,* FAX *907/683–1568,* WEB *www.campdenali.com. 17 cabins. Dining room, hiking, boating, fishing, mountain bikes. No credit cards. Closed mid-Sept.–early June.*

$$$$ 🏠 **Denali Backcountry Lodge.** In the community of Kantishna at the ★ end of the park road, these cabins offer private baths and individual climate controls, a rarity in such remote parts. Activities include naturalist programs; hiking; fishing; gold panning; mountain biking; and, for an extra fee, flightseeing when weather permits. Family-style meals emphasizing Alaskan fare are included in the room rate. Access to the lodge by van along the park road is the same system used by Camp Denali, and it takes a good part of a day to travel either way, so staying for at least two nights is necessary if you want to participate in any activities. ✉ *Box 810, Girdwood 99587,* ☎ *907/783–1342 or 800/ 841–0692,* 𝔽𝔸𝕏 *907/783–1308,* 𝕎𝔼𝔹 *www.denalilodge.com. 30 cabins. Restaurant, bar, hiking, fishing, mountain bikes. MC, V. Closed mid-Sept.–early June.*

$$$$ 🏠 **Denali Crow's Nest Log Cabins.** These spartan, cantilevered log cabins 1 mi north of the park entrance are on a forested hillside with river and mountain views. Each has its own bath. ✉ *Mile 238.5, Parks Hwy., Box 70, Denali National Park, 99755,* ☎ *907/683–2723 or 888/ 917–8130,* 𝔽𝔸𝕏 *907/683–2323,* 𝕎𝔼𝔹 *www.denalicrowsnest.com. 39 rooms. Restaurant, bar, hot tub. MC, V. Closed Oct.–mid-May.*

$$$$ 🏠 **Denali Princess Wilderness Lodge.** This hotel overlooking the Nenana River has large rooms decorated in rich forest colors. Complimentary shuttle service is provided to the park and railroad station. The large Summit Dining Room offers an estimable view and fine dining. Burgers and more casual fare are available at the Cruiser's Café, which can also supply picnic lunches. ✉ *Mile 238.5, Parks Hwy., 1 mi north of the park entrance, Box 110, Denali National Park, 99755,* ☎ *907/683–2282; 800/426–0500 for reservations;* 𝔽𝔸𝕏 *907/683–2545. 353 rooms. Restaurant, bar, café, outdoor hot tub. AE, DC, MC, V. Closed mid-Sept.–mid-May.*

$$$$ 🏠 **Denali River Cabins.** This cluster of riverside cabins next to McKinley Village Lodge and 6 mi south of the park entrance provides cozy comfort along the Nenana River. A boardwalk connects the cedar-sided cabins, all with double beds, to the river. The management operates park excursions and a courtesy shuttle service to and from the train depot. ✉ *Mile 231, Parks Hwy., Box 210, Denali National Park, 99755,* ☎ *907/683–2500 or 800/230–7275,* 𝔽𝔸𝕏 *907/683–2502,* 𝕎𝔼𝔹 *www.denalirivercabins.com. 48 rooms, 54 cabins. Restaurant, hot tub, sauna. AE, D, MC, V. Closed in winter.*

$$$$ 🏠 **Denali River View Inn.** This hotel sits atop a bluff overlooking the Nenana River, just north of the park entrance. Modern rooms—with a blue-and-beige color scheme, private baths, and a no-smoking policy—set above the highway rather than along it, offer a quiet experience. ✉ *Mile 238.4 Parks Highway, Box 49, Denali National Park, 99755,* ☎ *907/683–2663,* 𝔽𝔸𝕏 *907/683–7433,* 𝕎𝔼𝔹 *www.alaskan.com/ denaliriverview. 12 rooms. No-smoking rooms. D, MC, V. Closed mid-Sept.–mid-May.*

$$$–$$$$ 🏠 **Denali Cabins.** This cabin complex near the highway and 8 mi south of the park entrance has hot tubs and barbecue grills. All units have private baths. Complimentary shuttle service to the park visitor center is provided. The restaurant on site, the Loose Moose, is open from 6 AM to 10 PM. ✉ *Mile 229, Parks Hwy., Box 229, Denali National Park, 99755,* ☎ *907/683–2643 in summer; 888/560–2489 year-round; 907/258–0134 off-season;* 𝔽𝔸𝕏 *907/683–2595; 907/243–2062 off-season,* 𝕎𝔼𝔹 *www.alaskan.com/denalicabins. 43 cabins. MC, V. Closed mid-Sept.–mid-May.*

Camping

If you want to camp in the park, either in a tent or an RV, seven campgrounds are available with varying levels of access and facilities. Three of the campgrounds—Riley Creek (near the park entrance), Savage River (Mile 12.8), and Teklanika (Mile 29)—have spaces that accommodate tents, RVs, and campers. Morino is restricted to tent campers who arrive without a motor vehicle, and Sanctuary River (Mile 22), Igloo Creek (Mile 34), and Wonder Lake (Mile 85) have tent spaces only. Access to these three camping areas is by shuttle bus only. The bus service runs special camper buses with extra storage space for campers with gear.

If you're camping overnight in Denali's wilderness, you must obtain a special permit (free of charge) from rangers at the visitor center. You must also choose an area to camp. Denali's backcountry is divided into 43 units and only a limited number of campers are allowed each night in most units. The most desirable units are near the middle of the park, in areas with open tundra and wide-open vistas. These fill up faster than the low-lying areas, many of which are moist and have high mosquito populations. The best strategy for securing good backpacking areas is to arrive a couple of days early, stay at one of the facilities near the park entrance, and check in at the backcountry desk early each morning until you can get the unit you desire.

$ ⚠ **McKinley RV Park and Campground.** This campground is about 10 mi outside the park. It has a variety of RV sites, from "basic" to those with full electricity, water, and sewer. Two-person tent sites are also available, as are a dump station, public showers, laundry facilities, deli, espresso bar, ice, and propane. ⊠ *Mile 248.5, Parks Hwy., Healy 99743,* ☎ *907/683–2379 or 800/478–2562.*

$ ⚠ **National Park Service Campgrounds.** There are seven campgrounds inside the park: three are open to private vehicles for tent and RV camping, three are reached by shuttle bus only and are restricted to tent camping, and one is for backpacking only. All have toilet facilities, most have drinking water, and a couple have nearby hiking trails. All are open from late May to September, depending on snow conditions, and one is open year-round. They cost $12 a night plus a onetime $4 reservation fee. You can apply for a site at the visitor center, but it's wise to reserve in advance. ⊠ *Denali National Park Headquarters, Box 9, Denali National Park, 99755,* ☎ *907/683–2294 for information; 907/ 272–7275; 800/622–7275 for reservations. AE, D, MC, V. All but Riley Creek (no visitor facilities) closed Oct.–late May.*

Guided Tours

Privately operated bus trips with boxed snacks are available through **Denali Park Resorts** (☎ 907/276–7234 or 800/276–7234). The Tundra Wildlife Tour costs $71, and the shorter Natural History Tour costs $37. **Alaska-Denali Guiding** (☎ 907/733–2649, WEB www.denaliexpeditions./ com) leads backpacking trips in Denali National Park and elsewhere in the state, including the Brooks Range. They also conduct mountaineering expeditions to Denali and other peaks in the Alaska Range, and lead mountaineering seminars and climbs for all levels of climbing expertise. **Mountain Trip** (☎ 907/345–6499) guides climbing expeditions on Mt. McKinley and other Alaska Range peaks (experience required).

Besides exploring the park on your own, you can take free ranger-guided "discovery hikes" and learn more about the park's natural and human history. Rangers lead daily hikes throughout the summer. Ask about them at the visitor center.

Outdoor Activities and Sports

Kayaking and Rafting

Several privately owned raft and tour companies operate along the Parks Highway near the entrance to Denali, and they schedule daily rafting, both in the fairly placid areas on the Nenana and through the 10-mi-long Nenana River canyon, which contains some of the roughest white water in North America.

Denali Outdoor Center (⊠ Box 170, Denali Park, 99755, Mile 238.5, Parks Hwy., ☎ 907/683–1925 or 888/303–1925, WEB www.

denalioutdoorcenter.com) takes adventuresome people on guided trips down the Nenana River rapids in inflatable kayaks. No river experience is necessary. The kayaks, called Duckies, are easy to get out of, stable, and self-bailing. The company leads a variety of rafting trips and teaches white-water kayaking. All gear, including full dry suits, is provided. Mountain bike tours and rentals are also available.

Denali Raft Adventures (☎ 907/683–2234 or 888/683–2234, FAX 907/683–1281, WEB www.denaliraft.com) launches its rafts several times daily on two- or four-hour, all-day, and overnight scenic and white-water raft trips on the Nenana River. Courtesy pickup at hotels and the train depot is available.

Alaska Raft Adventures books white-water and scenic raft trips along Nenana River through Denali Park Resorts (☎ 907/276–7234 or 800/276–7234, FAX 907/258–3668). **Nenana Raft Adventures** (☎ 907/683–7238 or 800/789–7238, FAX 907/683–1618) runs four- and six-hour rafting trips along Nenana River and puts all its rafters in dry suits.

Mountain Biking

Mountain biking is allowed on the park's dirt road, and no permit is required for day trips. The first 14 mi of the road is paved. Beyond the Savage River checkpoint the road is dirt and gravel and during the day is traversed by the park buses, which can make for a very dust-intensive experience. Late night, when the midnight sun is shining and after the buses have ceased shuttling passengers for the day, can be a rewarding time to bike and view the park's wildlife.

RICHARDSON HIGHWAY

The Richardson Highway stretches 364 mi, from Fairbanks to the all-year, ice-free port of Valdez. The Richardson takes travelers the final 98 mi from the official end of the Alaska Highway in Delta Junction to Fairbanks, but it is not a mere connecting route. The first road built in Alaska, the Richardson offers fantastic mountain views while also providing excellent river and lake fishing. Named after Gen. Wilds P. Richardson, first president of the Alaska Road Commission, the highway evolved from a pack train trail and dogsled route that mail carriers and gold seekers followed in the early 1900s to a two-lane asphalt highway in 1957. It's a four-lane, divided highway from Fairbanks to North Pole, home of the Santa Claus House gift shop, with its towering Santa silhouette, and the North Pole Coffee Roasting Company, which provides many Fairbanks-area restaurants with fresh-roasted coffee. The Richardson also links Fairbanks with Delta's farm country and the winter and summer recreation areas near Summit Lake in the Alaska Range. At Paxson, the Richardson takes travelers to the Denali Highway, a gravel road leading west through the Alaska Range to campgrounds and fishing in the Tangle Lakes area and, later, to Denali National Park and Preserve. Fifty-six miles south of the Denali Highway, the Richardson borders Wrangell–St. Elias National Park, the largest U.S. national park.

North Pole

🔟 *15 mi southeast of Fairbanks, 85 mi northwest of Delta Junction.*

Christmas lives in North Pole all year long. Many of the street names maintain the theme, including Santa Claus Lane and St. Nicholas Drive. The prime attraction here is the **Santa Claus House,** a must-see if you have young children. Also a favorite of locals is the Chena Lakes Recreation Area.

Off the Richardson Highway just south of North Pole, **Chena Lakes Recreation Area** offers hiking, swimming, boating, camping, picnicking, dog mushing, and cross-country skiing. Created by the Army Corps of Engineers as part of the Chena River Flood-Control Project, it is now operated by the local government, the **Fairbanks North Star Borough** (Parks and Recreation Dept., ☎ 907/488–1655).

Outdoor Activities and Sports

FISHING

Rainbow trout are not native to the Interior, but they are stocked in some lakes. **Birch Lake** (✉ Mile 303.5), **Harding Lake** (✉ Mile 321.4), and **Quartz Lake** (✉ Mile 277.8), easily accessible from the Richardson Highway between Fairbanks and Delta Junction, are good trout-fishing spots. All have campgrounds and boat-launching areas. The **Salcha River,** 40 mi below Fairbanks on the Richardson Highway, is a spot for catching migrating salmon in the fall.

Shopping

The **Knotty Shop** (✉ Mile 332, 32 mi south of Fairbanks, ☎ 907/488–3014) has a large selection of Alaskan handicrafts, as well as a mounted wildlife display and a yard full of spruce burl sculptures, including a 6-ft mosquito. It also serves soft drinks and ice cream over a counter carved from spruce burl.

The **Santa Claus House Gift Shop** (✉ Mile 349, 101 St. Nicholas Dr., 14 mi south of Fairbanks, ☎ 907/488–2200) is hard to miss. Look for the giant Santa statue and the Christmas mural on the side of the building. The store has a variety of toys, gifts, and Alaskan handicrafts. Santa is often on duty to talk to children, and two reindeer are kept in a pen outside the store.

Delta Junction

⑰ *100 mi southeast of Fairbanks, 106 mi northwest of Tok, 266 mi north of Valdez.*

As the hub of the state Delta Agricultural Project, Delta Junction has the manner of a small farming town. Although the project has had many difficulties, grain and dairy farms still define the area. In summer Delta becomes a bustling rest stop for road-weary tourists traveling the Alaska and Richardson highways. Delta is also known for its access to good fishing and its proximity to the Delta Bison Range. However, don't expect to see the elusive bison, as they roam free and generally avoid people.

Dining and Lodging

$$–$$$ ✕ **Pizza Bella.** This restaurant serves up delicious pizzas and other Italian and American entrées. The decor is a slice of Italy. ✉ *Mile 265,* ☎ *907/895–4841 or 907/895–4524. MC, V.*

$–$$ ✕ **Rika's Roadhouse.** This historic landmark, part of Big Delta State Historical Park, is well worth a detour if you're nearby. The restaurant serves breakfast and lunches, featuring delectable home-baked goods. The beautifully restored grounds, gardens, and historic buildings are meticulously maintained, and free tours are given. ✉ *Mile 275,* ☎ *907/895–4201,* ☒ *907/895–4787. AE, D, MC, V. No dinner. Closed mid-Sept.–mid-May.*

$$–$$$$ ☷ **Tangle Lakes Lodge.** This newly constructed lodge, rebuilt from the ground up after a fire in the winter of 1998, is 22 mi west of Paxson and consists of a main lodge building housing the restaurant ($$–$$$) and bar and 10 log cabins set on the shores of the lake. (One of the cabins is large enough to sleep 10–12 and rents for $175 a night.) The cozy cabins are heated by wood or propane stoves, and the lights are propane. The main building has running water, showers, and two bathrooms. Here you're surrounded by rolling tundra—home to moose, caribou, grizzly bears, and wolves—and the fishing for grayling, salmon, rainbow, and lake trout is exceptional. The lodge owner is well known as the best source of accurate and up-to-date birding information in the area. ⊠ *Mile 22, Denali Hwy., Box 670386, Chugiak 99567,* ☎ *907/688–9173,* 𝔽𝔸𝕏 *907/688–9174,* 𝕎𝔼𝔹 *www.alaskan.com/tanglelakes. 10 cabins. Restaurant, bar, boating, fishing. MC, V.*

$$ 🏨 **Alaska 7 Motel.** Cheap and clean accommodations right off the highway are what you get here—small refrigerators and color televisions with satellite service in each room. Some units have kitchenettes, and some have phones. ⊠ *Mile 270.3, Box 1115, 99737,* ☎ *907/895–4848,* 𝕎𝔼𝔹 *www.alaskan.com/ak7motel. 16 rooms. Refrigerators, kitchenettes (some). AE, D, DC, MC, V.*

$$ 🏨 **Black Spruce Lodge.** This comfortable, rustic lodge with 10 cabins is a 10-minute pontoon-boat shuttle ride from the parking area at a nearby campground. The lodge sits on the shore of Quartz Lake, rife with rainbow trout, arctic char, and landlocked silver salmon. Winter visitors can rent ice houses as shelter when fishing through the ice. ⊠ *10 mi northwest of Delta Junction (Box 265, 99737),* ☎ *907/388–2409. 10 cabins. Bar, boating, fishing. MC, V. Closed Oct.–Nov. and Apr.*

$$ 🏨 **Kelly's Country Inn Motel.** Delta residents most often put visitors up at this downtown motel. It has clean, modern rooms, including some with kitchenettes, decorated in neutral colors. ⊠ *Mile 266.5, Box 849, 99737,* ☎ *907/895–4667,* 𝔽𝔸𝕏 *907/895–4481,* 𝕎𝔼𝔹 *www.kellysalaskacountryinn. com. 21 rooms. Kitchenettes (some). AE, MC, V.*

FORTYMILE COUNTRY

A trip through the Fortymile Country up the Taylor Highway will take you back in time more than a century—when gold was the lure that drew hardy travelers to Interior Alaska. It's still one of the few places to see active mining without leaving the road system.

The 160-mi Taylor Highway runs north from the Alaska Highway at Tetlin Junction, 12½ mi south of Delta Junction. It's a narrow rough-gravel road that winds along mountain ridges and through valleys of the Fortymile River. The road passes the tiny community of Chicken and ends in Eagle at the Yukon River. This is one of only three places in Alaska where the river can be reached by road. A cutoff just south of Eagle connects to the Canadian Top of the World Highway leading to Dawson City in the Yukon Territory. This is the route many Alaskans take to Dawson City. The highway is not plowed in winter, so it is snowed shut from fall to spring. Watch for road reconstruction.

Tok

⓲ *12 mi west of Tetlin Junction, 175 mi southwest of Dawson City.*

At the junction of the Glenn Highway and the Alaska Highway, Tok is a main supply center for the loggers, miners, and hunting guides who live and work along the surrounding streams or in the millions of acres of spruce forest nearby. Each summer Tok, with a resident population of less than 1,500, becomes temporary home to thousands of travelers, including those traveling up the Alaska Highway from the Lower 48.

If you can't travel into the Fortymile Country itself, you can catch the flavor of the region at the **Tok Main Street Visitors Center** (⊠ Mile 1314, Alaska Hwy., 99780, ☎ 907/883–5775).

Dining and Lodging

$$–$$$ ✕ **Fast Eddy's Restaurant.** It's much better than the name would in-
dicate: the chef makes his own noodles for chicken noodle soup, and
the homemade hoagies and pizza are a welcome relief from the roadhouse hamburgers served by most Alaska Highway restaurants. It's open
6 AM–midnight (but no soup after 5). ⊠ *Mile 1313.3, Alaska Hwy.,*
☎ *907/883–4411. AE, D, MC, V.*

$$$$ 🏨 **Westmark Tok.** This hotel, part of a chain, is reliable, comfortable,
and well appointed. The spacious dining room is a welcome respite when
traveling the long stretches between civilization outposts along the Alaska
Highway. ⊠ *Box 130, junction of Alaska and Glenn Hwys., 99780,*
☎ *907/883–5174 or 800/544–0970,* FAX *907/883–5178,* WEB *www.*
westmarkhotels.com. 92 rooms. Restaurant, bar, shop. AE, D, DC, MC,
V. Closed Oct.–May.

Shopping

The **Burnt Paw** (⊠ intersection of Alaska and Glenn Hwys., ☎ 907/
883–4121, FAX 907/883–5680, WEB www.sketers.com/burntpaw) sells
jade and ivory, Alaskan ceramics, crafts, paintings, smoked salmon—
even sled-dog puppies. It also rents cozy cabins ($99 for two, includ-
ing a Continental breakfast) and has sled-dog demonstrations at 7:30
every night except Sunday from June through August. In Northway,
south of Tok, **Naabia Niign** (⊠ Mile 1264, Alaska Hwy., ☎ 907/778–
2298, FAX 907/778–2366) is a Native-owned crafts gallery with an excellent selection of locally made birch baskets, beadwork items, and
fur moccasins and gloves.

Chicken

19 *78 mi north of Tok, 109 mi west of Dawson City.*

Chicken was once in the heart of major gold-mining operations, and
the remains of many of these works are visible along the highway. Here
you'll find a country store, bar, liquor store, café, and gas station. Ask
about tours of the old mining operations ($5) at the café, which hosts
a salmon barbecue every afternoon from 4 PM to 8 PM. Be careful not
to trespass on private property. Miners rarely have a sense of humor
about trespassing.

Outdoor Activities and Sports

CANOEING

The beautiful **Fortymile River** offers everything from a 38-mi run to a
lengthy journey to the Yukon and then down to Eagle. Its waters range
from easy Class I to serious Class IV (possibly Class V) stretches. Only
experienced canoeists should attempt boating on these rivers, and
rapids should be scouted beforehand. Several access points can be
found off the Taylor Highway.

CanoeAlaska (⊠ Box 735, Tok 99780, ☎ 907/883–2628) has been
conducting guided canoe and raft trips on Interior Alaska rivers for
25 years. Trips begin in mid-May and continue through Labor Day and
range from two to eight days on rivers that vary in difficulty and re-
moteness. They also lead multiday Voyager trips—16 people in a 34-
ft Voyager canoe—and offer weekend canoe instructional programs by
ACA-certified instructors.

Eagle

20 *95 mi north of Chicken, 144 mi northwest of Dawson City.*

Eagle was once a seat of government and commerce for the Interior.
An army post (Ft. Egbert) operated here until 1911, and territorial judge

James Wickersham had his headquarters in Eagle until Fairbanks began to grow from its gold strike. The population peaked at 1,700 in 1898. Today it is fewer than 200.

The **Eagle Historical Society** (☎ 907/547–2325) has a two-hour walking tour ($5 fee) that visits six museum buildings while regaling participants with tales of the famous people who have passed through this historic Yukon River border town. Tours begin at the courthouse at 9 each morning, from Memorial Day to mid-September.

YUKON TERRITORY

Gold! That's what called Canada's Yukon Territory to the world's attention with the Klondike gold rush of 1897–98. Although Yukon gold mining today is mainly in the hands of a few large companies that go almost unnoticed by the visitor, the territory's history is alive and thriving.

Though the international border divides Alaska from Yukon Territory, the Yukon River tends to unify the region. Early prospectors, miners, traders, and camp followers moved readily up and down the river with little regard to national boundaries. An earlier Alaska strike preceded the Klondike find by years, yet Circle was all but abandoned in the stampede to the creeks around Dawson City. Later gold discoveries in the Alaskan Fortymile Country, Nome, and Fairbanks reversed that flow across the border into Alaska.

Dawson City

109 mi east of Chicken.

Dawson City today forms the heart of the Yukon's gold-rush remembrances. Since the first swell of the gold rush more than 100 years ago, many of the original buildings are gone, victims of fire, flood, and weathering. But enough of them have been preserved and restored to give more than a glimpse of the city's onetime grandeur. In a period of three years up to the turn of the 20th century, Dawson was transformed into the largest, most refined city north of San Francisco and west of Winnipeg. It had grand new buildings with running water, telephones, and electricity. The city's population, only about 1,500 now, numbered almost 30,000 in 1899.

Regular air service to Dawson is available from Fairbanks. You can also drive the Taylor Highway route, leaving the Alaska Highway at Tetlin Junction and winding through the Fortymile Country past the little communities of Chicken and Jack Wade Camp into Canada. The border is open 8 AM to 8 PM in summer. The Canadian section of the Taylor Highway is called Top of the World Highway. Broad views of range after range of tundra-covered mountains stretch in every direction. Travelers heading north on the Alaska Highway can turn north at Whitehorse to Dawson City, then rejoin the Alaska Highway by taking the Taylor Highway south. This adds about 100 mi to the trip.

Today you can recapture some of Dawson City's former magnificence
㉑ at the reconstructed **Palace Grand Revue** (⊠ King St. between 2nd and 3rd Aves., ☎ 867/993–6217). Every night from late May to mid-September performances of the Gaslight Follies are staged. Admission
㉒ is $15 or $17, depending on where you choose to sit. **Diamond Tooth Gertie's Gambling Hall** (⊠ Arctic Brotherhood Hall, Queen St., ☎ 867/993–5525), for adults 19 and over only, presents live entertainment and three different cancan shows three times a night, seven days a week. It is the only authentic, legal gambling establishment operating in all

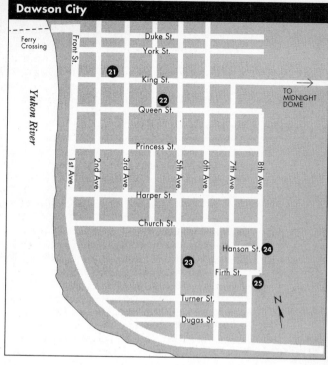

of the North. Yes, there really was a Diamond Tooth Gertie—Gertie Lovejoy, a prominent dance-hall queen who had a diamond between her two front teeth.

23 The **Dawson City Museum** has a variety of gold-rush exhibits. You'll also find numerous relics next door, including trains from the Klondike Road Railroad that operated along the gold creeks. ⊠ *Territorial Administration Bldg., 5th Ave.,* ☎ *867/993–5291.* ☞ *$5.* ☉ *Mid-May–Labor Day, daily 10–6.*

Tours visit the old "diggings." A highlight is a visit to **Bonanza Creek and *Dredge Number 4,*** a wooden-hull gold dredge about 10 minutes outside town.

Scholars still argue the precise details of the tenure of writers Robert Service and Jack London in Dawson City, but no dispute exists that between Service's poems and London's short stories, the two did more

24 than anyone else to popularize and romanticize the Yukon. **Robert Service's cabin** (⊠ 8th Ave. and Hanson St., ☎ 867/993–5566) has been restored, and his poetry is read daily at 10 and 3 for a $6 admission

25 charge. **Jack London's cabin** (⊠ 8th Ave. and Firth St., ☎ 867/993–6317) is literally a stone's throw from the Service cabin. It's open daily from 10 to 1 and 2 to 6, with half-hour talks at 11:30 and 2:30 for a $3 admission. The small museum contains photos, documents, and letters from London's life and the gold-rush era.

Dining and Lodging

$$$–$$$$ ✕ **Marina's.** At this eatery, the menu includes fresh whole-wheat thin-crust pizzas, salads, and classic southern Italian dishes modified in some instances to include local salmon and Alaskan halibut. Elegant and subdued decor, with a tin-embossed ceiling and dark wood antique furnishings surrounds the dining area. ⊠ *5th Ave. across from the Westmark,* ☎ *867/993–6800. AE, DC, MC, V.*

$$$$ ⊡ **Downtown Hotel.** A large collection of artwork, including mushing scenes, from area artists accents the early 1900s decor of this hotel. The Jack London Grill is a best bet: go for the Canadian and American regional specialties including daily appetizer, pasta, and prime rib specials. The restaurant serves three meals a day and has an outside deck for summer dining. ⊠ *2nd Ave. and Queen St., Box 780, Y0B 1G0,* ☎ *867/993–5346; 800/661–0514 for reservations;* FAX *867/993–5076,* WEB *www.downtown.yk.net. 59 rooms. Restaurant, bar, hot tub, meeting room, airport shuttle. AE, D, DC, MC, V.*

$$$$ ⊡ **Eldorado Hotel.** The lobby of this hotel has gold rush–era decor. During the summer tourist season, the staff dresses up in 1898-era garb. However, the modern rooms, some with kitchenettes, are outfitted with decidedly non-1898 amenities such as cable TV and remote controls. ⊠ *3rd Ave. and Princess St., Box 338, Y0B 1G0,* ☎ *867/993–5451; 800/764–3536 from Alaska; 800/661–0518 from B.C. and the Yukon;* FAX *867/993–5256. 52 rooms. Dining room, bar, kitchenettes (some), laundry service, airport shuttle. AE, D, DC, MC, V.*

$$$$ ⊡ **Westmark Dawson City.** This downtown two-story hotel is built around a central courtyard and is convenient to the sights. With its flocked wallpaper and lace curtains, the lobby recalls the days of the gold rush. Rooms are decorated in soft blues and greens. ⊠ *5th Ave. and Harper St., Box 420, Y0B 1G0,* ☎ *867/993–5542 or 800/544–0970,* FAX *867/993–5623,* WEB *www.westmarkhotels.com. 131 rooms. Dining room, bar. AE, D, DC, MC, V. Closed Sept. 10–May 14.*

$$$ ⊡ **Triple "J" Hotel.** This clean, quiet compound of log cabins is next to Diamond Tooth Gertie's. There is a central hotel, a detached motel-like addition, and log cabins with kitchenettes. All rooms have TVs, coffeemakers, phones, and private baths. ⊠ *5th Ave. and Queen St., Box 359, Y0B 1G0,* ☎ *867/993–5323 or 800/764–3555,* FAX *867/993–5030,* WEB *www.triplejhotel.com. 29 rooms, 18 cabins. Restaurant, bar, kitchenettes (some), meeting room, airport shuttle. AE, DC, MC, V.*

Whitehorse

❷⑥ *337 mi southeast of Dawson City, 600 mi southeast of Fairbanks.*

Whitehorse began as an encampment near the White Horse Rapids of the Yukon River. It was a logical layover point for gold rushers—most coming north along the Chilkoot Trail from Alaska—in the late 1890s who headed north toward Dawson to seek their fortune. The next great population boom came during World War II with the building of the Alcan—the Alaska-Canada Highway. Today, this city of more than 22,000 residents is Yukon's center of commerce, communication, and transportation and the seat of the territorial government.

Besides being a great starting point for explorations of other areas of the Yukon, the town itself has plenty of diversions and recreational opportunities. You can easily spend a day exploring its array of museums and cultural displays—research the Yukon's mining and development history, look into the backgrounds of the town's founders, learn about its indigenous First Nations people, and gain an appreciation of the Yukon territory from prehistoric times up to the present. You can obtain a free three-day parking permit at **City Hall** (⊠ 2121 2nd Ave., ☎ 867/668–8687).

The logical place to start touring Whitehorse is the **Yukon Visitor Reception Centre,** which is housed in the block-long, pine-sided headquarters for Yukon Tourism. Anything to do with the Yukon can be found in the reception center. ⊠ *100 Hanson St.,* ☎ *867/667–3084,* FAX *867/ 667–3546,* WEB *www.touryukon.com.* ☉ *May–Sept., daily 8–8; Oct.–Apr., weekdays 9–noon and 1–4:30.*

Near the Whitehorse Visitor Reception Centre is the Yukon Territorial Government Building. It is worth a visit to see the **Yukon Permanent Art Collection,** a display of works by Yukon artists depicting northern people and their culture. In addition to the collection on the premises, a brochure available at the visitor center leads you on a neighborhood art walk, giving locations of galleries and art shops. ⊠ *2nd Ave. and Hanson St.,* ☎ *867/667–5811.* ⚑ *Free.* ☼ *Weekdays 8:30–5.*

The **MacBride Museum** is your best general introduction to the spirit and heritage of the Yukon. More than 5,000 square ft of exhibits display natural history, geology, archaeology, First Nations, Mounties in the North, the gold rush, and the city of Whitehorse. Outdoor artifacts include Sam McGee's cabin—the same Sam McGee immortalized in Robert Service's famous poem "The Cremation of Sam McGee"— the Whitehorse telegraph office, as well as various transportation vehicles. ⊠ *1st Ave. and Wood St.,* ☎ *867/667–2709,* FAX *867/633– 6607,* WEB *www.macbridemuseum.com.* ⚑ *$5.* ☼ *Mid-May–Labor Day, daily 10–6; Labor Day–mid-May, Thurs.–Sat. noon–4.*

The **Waterfront Walkway** along the Yukon River will take you past a few stops of interest. Your walk starts on the path along the river just east of the MacBride Museum entrance on 1st Avenue. Traveling upstream (south), you'll go by the old White Pass & Yukon Route Building, on Main Street.

The former Yukon Visitor Reception Centre at the Whitehorse Airport is the home of the **Yukon Beringia Interpretive Centre,** which presents the story of the Yukon during the Ice Age. Beringia is the name given to the large subcontinental landmass of eastern Siberia and Interior Alaska and the Yukon, which were linked by the Bering Land Bridge during the Ice Age. The center unfolds extensive information on the area's prehistoric origins, and pays tribute to the First Nations people and the miners who have contributed information and exhibits to the museum. The center displays large dioramas depicting the lives of animals in Ice Age Beringia and replicas of skeletons of the animals who lived there. *Mile 914, Alaska Hwy.,* ☎ *867/667–8855,* WEB *www. beringia.com.* ⚑ *$6.* ☼ *May–Sept., daily 8–6.*

★ The **SS Klondike,** a national historic site, is dry-docked in Rotary Park. The 210-ft stern-wheeler was built in 1929, sank in 1936, and was rebuilt in 1937. In the days when the Yukon River was the transportation link between Whitehorse and Dawson City, the *Klondike* was the largest boat plying the river. ⊠ *S. Access Rd. and 2nd Ave.,* ☎ *867/ 667–4511.* ⚑ *$3.* ☼ *May–Sept., daily 9–6:30.*

If you're in Whitehorse during late summer, it's possible to see the chinook (king) salmon that hold one of nature's great endurance records: longest fish migration in the world. The **Whitehorse Rapids Dam and Fish Ladder** has interpretive exhibits, display tanks of freshwater fish, and a platform for viewing the fish ladder. The best time to visit is August, when between 150 and 2,100 salmon (average count is 800) use the ladder to bypass the dam. ⊠ *End of Nisutlin Dr.,* ☎ *867/633–5965.* ⚑ *Free.* ☼ *June–Labor Day, daily; hrs vary, so call ahead.*

Miles Canyon, a 10-minute drive south of Whitehorse, is both scenic and historic. Although the dam below it makes the canyon seem relatively tame, it was this perilous stretch of the Yukon River that determined the location of Whitehorse as the starting point for river travel north. In 1897 Jack London won the admiration—and cash—of fellow stampeders headed north to the Klondike goldfields because of his steady hand as pilot of hand-hewn wooden boats here. You can hike on trails along the canyon or take a two-hour cruise aboard the M. V. *Schwatka* and experience the canyon from the waters of Lake Schwatka, which obliterated the Whitehorse Rapids when the dam creating the lake was built in 1959. ⊠ *Miles Canyon Rd., 2 mi south of Whitehorse (Box 4001, Whitehorse, Yukon Territory Y1A 3S9),* ☎ *867/668–4716,* FAX *867/633–5574.* ⊡ *$18.* ☉ *Cruises early–mid-June and mid-Aug.–early Sept., daily at 2; mid-June–mid-Aug., daily at 2 and 7.*

At **Takhini Hot Springs,** off the Klondike Highway, there's swimming in the spring-warmed water (suits and towels are available for rent), horseback riding, areas for camping and picnicking, a convenience store, and a "licensed" (beer and wine) restaurant. ⊠ *Kilometer 10, Takhini Hot Springs Rd., 17 mi north of Whitehorse,* ☎ *867/633–2706.* ⊡ *$5; RV campsites with power $17.50, without $15, tent sites $12.50.* ☉ *May–Sept., daily 7 AM–10 PM; Oct.–Apr., Thurs.–Sun. 10–10.*

The **Canyon City Archaeological Dig** offers a glimpse into the past of the local First Nations people. Long before the area was developed by Western civilizations, the First Nations people used the Miles Canyon area as a seasonal fish camp. An archaeological dig was completed in the 1990s, and the site is open to the public. The Yukon Conservation Society conducts free tours of the area twice a day in summer; they also lead walks and hikes from short, child-friendly tours to challenging five–six hour scrambles on the nearby mountains. All the hikes are free, and provide a great way to see the surrounding countryside with local naturalists. The society office houses a bookstore on Yukon history and wilderness, and sells souvenirs, maps, and posters. ⊠ *302 Hawkins St.,* ☎ *867/668–5678.* ⊡ *Free.* ☉ *Tours July–Aug., Mon.–Fri. 10 and 2.*

The **Yukon Wildlife Preserve** provides a fail-safe way of photographing rarely spotted animals in a natural setting. Animals roaming freely here include elk, caribou, mountain goats, musk ox, bison, mule deer, and Dall and Stone sheep. Two-hour tours can be arranged through Gray Line Yukon. ⊠ *Gray Line Yukon, 208G Steele St.,* ☎ *867/668–3225,* FAX *867/667–4494.* ⊡ *$19.* ☉ *Tours mid-May–mid-Sept., daily.*

Dining and Lodging

$–$$ ✕ **The Chocolate Claim.** This charming little deli serves fresh-baked breads ★   and pastries, homemade soups and sandwiches, salads, and quiches. Artwork—ranging from paintings and pottery to rugs and quilts by local artists and artisans—are on display and for sale. There's outdoor seating complemented by flower boxes available for sunny days. ⊠ *305 Strickland St.,* ☎ *867/667–2202. MC, V. Closed Sun.*

$$$$ ✕▥ **Westmark Whitehorse Hotel and Conference Center.** In the heart of downtown, this full-service hotel provides comfortable accommodations. The carpeted lobby has low tables and plush chairs, an espresso bar, and a beautiful model of the Klondike riverboat. A nightly Klondike vaudeville show, the Frantic Follies, is performed in summer. The restaurant serves pork chops, filet mignon, salmon, and low-calorie selections. ⊠ *2nd Ave. and Wood St., Box 4250, Y1A 3T3,* ☎ *867/393–9700 or 800/544–0970,* FAX *867/668–2789,* WEB *www.westmarkhotels. com. 176 rooms, 5 suites. Restaurant, bar, barbershop, shop, meeting rooms, travel services. AE, MC, V.*

$$$–$$$$ ▥ **High Country Inn.** At this mountainside inn, you'll find tastefully appointed modern rooms. Deluxe suites come with kitchenettes. Public areas are cozy, and the location is close to the SS *Klondike* and the public swimming pool. ⊠ *4051 4th Ave., Y1A 1H1,* ☎ *867/667–4471 or 800/554–4471,* FAX *867/667–6457,* WEB *www.highcountryinn.com. 95 rooms, 5 suites. Restaurant, bar, kitchenettes (some). AE, DC, MC, V.*

Outdoor Activities and Sports

SLED-DOG RACE

Whitehorse and Fairbanks organize the **Yukon Quest International Sled-Dog Race** (☎ 867/668–4711) in February. The race's starting line alternates yearly between the two cities, and in 2002 it will be in Fairbanks. This is one of the longest and toughest races in the North.

HIKING

The **Kluane National Park and Reserve,** west of Whitehorse, has millions of acres for hiking. The **Yukon Conservation Society** (☎ 867/668–5678) leads hiking expeditions of varying lengths and degrees of difficulty.

INTERIOR A TO Z

To research prices, get advice from other travelers, and book travel arrangements, visit www.fodors.com.

AIR TRAVEL

Alaska Airlines and Delta Airlines fly the Anchorage–Fairbanks route. Both have connecting routes to the Lower 48 states (☞ Air Travel *in* Smart Travel Tips A to Z for airline numbers). Air North, based in Whitehorse, has direct, scheduled air service between Alaska and Canada, flying regular runs from Fairbanks and Juneau to the Yukon Territory towns of Dawson City and Whitehorse.

In much of the Bush, federally subsidized mail runs make regular air schedules possible. From Fairbanks, you can easily catch a ride on the mail run to small, predominantly Native villages along the Yukon River or to Eskimo settlements on the Arctic coast. Frontier Flying Service has an extensive roster of scheduled flights that includes Anchorage, as well as many of the Bush villages in northwest Alaska, the Interior, and the North Slope of the Brooks Range. Larry's Flying Service has scheduled flights to more than a dozen Bush villages as well as charter service and flightseeing tours. Tanana Air Service flies freight and passengers to almost 30 villages along the Yukon and in the Interior and western Alaska. Wright Air Service flies from their Fairbanks base to Interior and Brooks Range villages. For commuter flights out of Anchorage, ERA Aviation flies to Cordova, Whitehorse, Homer, Iliamna, Kenai, Kodiak, and Valdez. Peninsula Airways serves the Aleutian and Pribilof Island groups and communities in Southwest Alaska from their base in Anchorage.

➤ AIRLINES AND CONTACTS: **Air North** (☎ 867/668–2228 or 800/764–0407). **ERA Aviation** (☎ 907/243–6633 or 800/866–8394, ⓦⒺⒷ www.era-aviation.com). **Frontier Flying Service** (☎ 907/474–0014; 800/478–6779 in Alaska, ⓦⒺⒷ www.frontierflying.com). **Larry's Flying Service** (☎ 907/474–9169, ⓦⒺⒷ www.larrysflying.com). **Peninsula Airways** (☎ 907/243–2323 or 800/448–4226, ⓦⒺⒷ www.penair.com). **Tanana Air Service** (☎ 907/474–0301). **Wright Air Service** (☎ 907/474–0502; 800/478–0502 in Alaska).

BUS TRAVEL

The most common run is between Fairbanks and Anchorage by way of Denali National Park and Preserve. However, you can take side trips by bus or van to such places as Circle Hot Springs, on the Steese Highway north of Fairbanks, and into the Yukon Territory. For more information about bus service throughout the Interior, contact Princess Tours. Alaska Direct Bus Lines has year-round service. The Alaskon Express provides scheduled service between Whitehorse, Fairbanks,

Valdez, Skagway, Denali National Park, Anchorage, and other communities en route. Haines is accessible from Skagway via water taxi.

The Park Connection provides regularly scheduled shuttle service between Seward, Anchorage, and Denali National Park mid-May to mid-September. Denali Overland Transportation serves Anchorage, Talkeetna, and Denali National Park with charter bus and van service. Fairbanks has a city bus system. For information about schedules ask at the **Fairbanks Convention and Visitors Bureau** (☞ Visitor Information).

➤ Bus Information: **Alaska Direct Bus Lines** (☎ 907/277–6652 or 800/770–6652) has year-round service. **Alaskon Express** (☎ 907/277–5581 or 800/478–6388, WEB www.graylineofalaska.com). **Denali Overland Transportation** (☎ 907/733–2384, FAX 907/733–2385). **Park Connection** (☎ 907/245–0200 or 800/208–0200, WEB www.alaska-tour.com). **Princess Tours** (☎ 800/426–0442).

CAR RENTAL
People flying into Anchorage and renting a car can reach the Interior on the Parks Highway or the Glenn and Richardson highways. All are paved, in good condition, and offer spectacular views. The Parks Highway route is shorter by a few miles and passes by Denali National Park and Preserve, but traffic is busier.

➤ Local Agencies: **Avis** (☎ 907/474–0900; 800/478–2847 in Alaska; 800/331–1212 worldwide). **Budget Car and Truck Rental** (☎ 907/474–0855; 800/248–0150 in Alaska). **Hertz** (☎ 907/452–4444, 907/456–4004, or 800/654–3131). **Payless Car Rental** (☎ 907/474–0177).

CAR TRAVEL
In the Interior your choices of side trips by road from Fairbanks include the Steese Highway to historic Circle on the Yukon River, with its legacy of gold mining; the Dalton Highway, across the Yukon River and along the trans-Alaska pipeline; and the Taylor Highway (closed in winter), connecting the Alaska Highway near Tok with the historic towns of Eagle on the Alaska side of the border and Dawson City, Yukon Territory, in Canada. These are mainly well-maintained gravel roads. However, summer rain can make them slick and dangerous.

Only one road connects Alaska to the Outside—the Alaska Highway. The highway starts in Dawson Creek, British Columbia, in Canada. It is paved but long, almost 1,500 mi to Fairbanks. Lots of people make this trek in the summer, so there are ample restaurants and motels along the way. Winter driving takes more planning, as many businesses and service stations shut down for the season. An alternative route through part of Canada is the Cassiar Highway, which leaves the Yellowhead Highway several miles northwest of Prince Rupert and connects to the Alaska Highway just outside Watson Lake. The Cassiar is a more scenic drive but may have long sections of gravel road. Summer road construction somewhere along the Alaska Highway is a given.

For road reports in Alaska call the State Department of Transportation in Fairbanks. For conditions in the Yukon Territory, call the Department of Community and Transportation Services.

➤ Contacts: **State Department of Transportation** (☎ 907/456–7623) in Fairbanks. **Department of Community and Transportation Services** (☎ 867/667–8215).

EMERGENCIES
➤ Doctors and Dentists: Dawson City (Yukon Territory): **Dawson City Nursing Station** (☎ 867/993–4444). Fairbanks: **Bassett Army Hos-**

pital (☎ 907/353–5172 or 800/478–5172); **Fairbanks Memorial Hospital** (☎ 907/452–8181); **Medical Dental Arts Building** (☎ 907/452–1866 or 907/452–7007). Tok: **Public Health Clinic** (☎ 907/883–4101). Whitehorse (Yukon Territory): **General Hospital** (☎ 867/668–9444).
➤ EMERGENCY SERVICES: **Police, emergency assistance** (☎ 911). **Alaska State Troopers: Delta Junction** (☎ 907/895–4344), **Fairbanks** (☎ 907/451–5100), **Nenana** (☎ 907/832–5554), **Tok** (☎ 907/883–5111). **Royal Canadian Mounted Police: Dawson Creek** (☎ 250/782–5211), **Whitehorse** (☎ 867/667–5555).

TOURS

ADVENTURE TOURS
➤ TOUR OPERATORS: **Northern Alaska Tour Company** (⊠ Box 82991, Fairbanks 99708, ☎ 907/474–8600, ℻ 907/474–4767).

CANOEING
➤ TOUR OPERATORS: **CanoeAlaska** (⊠ Box 735, Tok 99780, ☎ 907/883–2628).

CLIMBING
➤ TOUR OPERATORS: **Alaska-Denali Guiding** (⊠ ☎ 907/733–2649). **Mountain Trip** (☎ 907/345–6499).

CRUISING
➤ TOUR OPERATORS: **Riverboat Discovery** (⊠ Alaska Riverways, Dale Rd. Landing, near Fairbanks International Airport, ☎ 907/479–6673). **Yukon River Tours** (⊠ 214 2nd Ave., Fairbanks 99701-4811, ☎ 907/452–7162, ℻ 907/452–5063).

SIGHTSEEING
➤ TOUR OPERATORS: **Denali Park Resorts** (☎ 907/276–7234; 800/276–7234 for information). **Gray Line of Alaska** ☎ 800/478–6388). **Northern Alaska Tour Company** (☎ 907/474–8600). **Princess Tours** (☎ 907/479–9660 or 800/426–0442). **Trans Arctic Circle Treks** (☎ 907/479–5451). **Westours** (☎ 907/456–7741 or 800/478–6388).

TRAIN TRAVEL
Between late May and early September, daily passenger service is offered between Anchorage and Fairbanks by way of Talkeetna and Denali National Park and Preserve. You can choose more conventional and considerably less expensive seating in reconditioned coach cars with access to dining, lounge, and dome cars, operated by the Alaska Railroad. Because of the scenery, there is no such thing as a poor seat. Beyond your window, a panorama will unfold, with scenes of alpine meadows and snowcapped peaks and the muddy rivers and taiga forests of the Interior. If you're looking for a bit more luxury in your rail experience, passengers may ride in one of the window-dome cars with luxury seating, an outdoor viewing platform, and gourmet dining operated by Princess Tours. Holland America/Westours also offers rail trips in special cars that cater to their clients with a bit more personal attention and a more sumptuous menu than you'll find on the Alaska Railroad cars. However, all the Princess and Holland America cars are part of the same train and are pulled by the same engines as the "standard" AKRR cars.
➤ TRAIN INFORMATION: **Alaska Railroad** (☎ 907/456–4155 or 800/544–0552). **Holland America/Westours** (☎ 907/456–7741 or 800/478–6388). **Princess Tours** (☎ 206/336–6000 or 800/426–0442).

VISITOR INFORMATION
➤ TOURIST INFORMATION: **Alaska Public Lands Information Center** (⊠ 250 Cushman St., Suite 1A, Fairbanks 99701, ☎ 907/456–0527; ℻

907/456–0514). **Alaska Department of Fish and Game** (⊠ 1300 College Rd., Fairbanks 99701, ☎ 907/459–7207). **Delta Chamber of Commerce** (⊠ Mile 1422, Alaska Hwy., 99737, ☎ 907/895–5068). **Fairbanks Convention and Visitors Bureau** (⊠ 550 1st Ave., 99701, ☎ 907/456–5774 or 800/327–5774, FAX 907/452–4190). **Klondike Visitors Association** (⊠ Front and King Sts., Box 389F, Dawson City, Yukon Territory, Canada Y0B 1G0, ☎ 867/993–5575). **Nenana Visitor Center** (⊠ A and 4th Sts., 99760, ☎ 907/832–9953). **Tok Main Street Visitors Center** (⊠ Mile 1314, Alaska Hwy., 99780, ☎ 907/883–5775). **Whitehorse Visitor Reception Centre** (⊠ 100 Hanson St., Box 2703, Whitehorse, Yukon Territory, Canada Y1A 2C6, ☎ 867/667–3084).

8 THE BUSH

INCLUDING NOME,
BARROW, PRUDHOE BAY,
AND THE ALEUTIAN ISLANDS

The Bush, more a spirit than a place, is the last frontier of the Last Frontier. In the Southwest are coastal lands and waters rich in wildlife. Farther north, from Nome to Barrow, much of the ground is permanently frozen, and for months at a time the sun never sets—or never rises. In the Arctic are the Eskimo, the Prudhoe Bay oil fields, huge caribou herds, and Barrow, America's northernmost community.

A LASKANS CALL IT THE BUSH—those wild and lonely bands of
territory beyond cities, towns, highways, and railroad corridors
stretching from the Kodiak Archipelago, Alaska Peninsula,
and Aleutian Islands in the south through the Yukon-Kuskokwim
Delta and into the northern High Arctic. It is a land where caribou roam
and, in its northern regions, the sun really does shine at midnight. It
is a land that knows the soft footsteps of the Eskimos and the Aleuts,
the scratchings of those who search for oil and gold, and the ghosts of
almost-forgotten battlefields of World War II.

By Stanton H.
Patty

Updated by
Bill Sherwonit

It is a vast, misunderstood wonderland—bleak yet beautiful, harsh yet
bountiful. A look across the Arctic tundra in summer yields the mira-
cle of bright wildflowers growing from a sponge of permafrost ice water.
In the long, dark Arctic winter, a painter's-blue kind of twilight rises
from the ice and snowscapes at midday. Spring and fall are fleeting moments when the tundra awakens from its winter slumber or turns
briefly brilliant with autumn colors.

The Arctic is separated by the Brooks Range from the rest of the state,
and the Brooks Range itself is so grand that it contains several mountain systems. Each has its own particular character, ranging from pale,
softly rounded limestone mountains in the east and west to the towering granite spires and faces of the Arrigetch Peaks in the heart of the
range. Large portions of the Brooks Range's middle and western sections are preserved within Gates of the Arctic National Park and neighboring Noatak National Preserve.

North of the Brooks Range, a great apron of land called the North Slope
tilts gently until it slides under the Beaufort Sea and the Arctic Ocean.
The vast sweep of this frozen tundra brightens each summer with yellow Arctic poppies and dozens of other wildflower species that seem
to stretch into infinite distances. Permafrost has worked over this land
for centuries and fragmented it into giant polygons that make a fascinating pattern when viewed from the sky.

Great herds of caribou—hundreds of thousands of them—move in slow
waves across the tundra, feeding and fattening for the next winter and
attempting to stay clear of wolves and grizzlies. And out on the Arctic Ocean's Beaufort Sea, polar bears, stained a light gold from the oil
of seals they have killed, pose like monarchs on ice floes, swinging their
heads as if warning humans to keep their distance. One of Alaska's
premier wildlands, the Arctic National Wildlife Refuge, protects mountain and tundra landscape important to caribou, polar bears, grizzlies,
wolves, musk ox, and other Arctic wildlife.

The rivers that drain the Brooks Range have names such as Kongakut,
Kobuk, and Sheenjek. These speak of the Native peoples who have lived
here for thousands of years. The great Noatak River defies the Arctic's northerly drainage pattern and runs east–west, making a right-
angle turn before emptying into Kotzebue (*kots*-eh-bew) Sound.

The colorful Eskimo town of Kotzebue is the jumping-off point to much
of this area; it is the largest Native village in the state. Eskimo ceremonial dances are demonstrated at Kotzebue's Living Museum of the
Arctic, as is the Eskimo blanket toss, a sport dating to ancient times,
when Eskimo hunters were bounced high in the air so they could see
across ice ridges in their search for seals and other wildlife.

The Bush

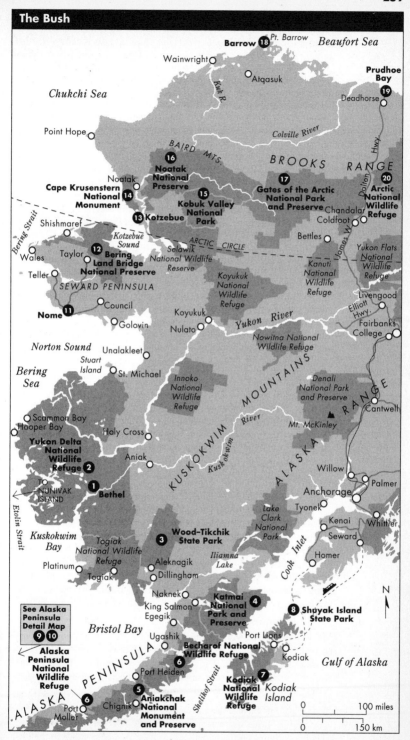

Barrow 18 · Pt. Barrow · *Beaufort Sea*

Wainwright

Atqasuk

Chukchi Sea

Prudhoe Bay 19

Deadhorse

Point Hope

Kuk R.

Colville River

BAIRD MTS.

16 Noatak National Preserve

B R O O K S   R A N G E

Noatak

Cape Krusenstern National Monument 14

15 Kobuk Valley National Park

17 Gates of the Arctic National Park and Preserve

Chandalar

Coldfoot

20 Arctic National Wildlife Refuge

Dalton Hwy.

13 Kotzebue

Kotzebue Sound

ARCTIC CIRCLE

Bettles

James W.

Shishmaref

Bering Strait

Selawik National Wildlife Reserve

Yukon Flats National Wildlife Refuge

12 Bering Land Bridge National Preserve

Taylor

Wales

Teller

SEWARD PENINSULA

Koyukuk National Wildlife Refuge

Kanuti National Wildlife Refuge

Livengood

Elliott Hwy.

Nome 11

Council

Golovin

Koyukuk

Nulato

Yukon River

Fairbanks

College

Norton Sound

Unalakleet

Stuart Island

St. Michael

Nowitna National Wildlife Refuge

Bering Sea

Scammon Bay

Hooper Bay

Holy Cross

Aniak

Innoko National Wildlife Refuge

K U S K O K W I M   M O U N T A I N S

Kuskokwim River

Denali National Park and Preserve

Mt. McKinley

A L A S K A   R A N G E

Cantwell

Yukon Delta National Wildlife Refuge 2

1 Bethel

TO NUNIVAK ISLAND

Etolin Strait

Willow

Palmer

Anchorage

Tyonek

Kenai

Whittier

Seward

Kuskokwim Bay

Togiak National Wildlife Refuge

3 Wood-Tikchik State Park

Lake Clark National Park

Iliamna Lake

Aleknagik

Dillingham

Platinum

Togiak

Cook Inlet

Homer

Naknek

King Salmon

Egegik

Katmai National Park and Preserve 4

8 Shuyak Island State Park

See Alaska Peninsula Detail Map 9 10

Alaska Peninsula National Wildlife Refuge

Bristol Bay

Ugashik

Becharof National Wildlife Refuge

Port Lions

Kodiak

Gulf of Alaska

A L A S K A   **6**   P E N I N S U L A

Port Moller

Chignik

6 Port Heiden

5 Aniakchak National Monument and Preserve

Shelikof Strait

7 Kodiak National Wildlife Refuge

Kodiak Island

N

0   100 miles

0   150 km

Another coastal community, this one first settled by prospectors, is the former gold-rush boomtown of Nome, where you can still pan for gold. In the spring, the going gets wild when Nome hosts a zany golf tournament with "greens" painted on the ice of the Bering Sea coast. Nome also serves as the end of the 1,049-mi Iditarod Trail Sled Dog Race, which begins in Anchorage the first Saturday in March.

Within Southwest Alaska are the highly productive wetlands of the Yukon-Kuskokwim Delta. Sloughs, ponds, marshes, mud, streams, and puddles in these flat regions near sea level can slow water travel to a standstill. Birds thrive here, and the waters teem with life. Farther south, Bristol Bay is the site of the largest salmon runs in the world. Nearby Wood-Tikchik encompasses huge lake systems within the nation's largest state park. And on the upper Alaska Peninsula, the brown bears of Katmai rule a vast national park, sharing salmon and trout streams with wary sportfishermen and always receiving the right-of-way. Also in the Southwest, the lower Alaska Peninsula and the Aleutian Islands reach well into the Pacific Ocean toward Alaska's closest point to Japan. This chain beckoned Russian explorers to Alaska in the 18th century. Along the islands, weathered onion-dome Russian Orthodox churches in Aleut villages brace against the fierce Pacific winds.

Dutch Harbor, in the Aleutians, a former U.S. Navy base pounded by Japanese bombs in 1942, is one of America's busiest commercial-fishing ports. Deep-sea trawlers and factory ships venture from here into the stormy north Pacific Ocean and the Bering Sea for harvests of bottom fish, crab, and other catches. Unalaska, an ancient Aleut village, is Dutch Harbor's across-the-bay neighbor and home to one of the oldest Russian Orthodox churches in Alaska. North of the Aleutian chain in the Bering Sea, the remote volcanic islands called the Pribilofs support immense populations of birds and sea mammals as well as two small Aleut communities, St. George and St. Paul.

The Bush also is where America's largest oil field, Prudhoe Bay, was discovered in 1968. At its peak, more than 2 million barrels a day of North Slope crude from Prudhoe and neighboring lesser basins flowed southward via the 800-mi pipeline to the port of Valdez, on Prince William Sound in South Central Alaska, to help fuel the Lower 48 states. Now the flow has diminished to about 1 million barrels per day.

As roads in the Bush are few, airplanes—from jetliners to small Bush planes—are the lifelines. Visitors throughout Alaska hear about the legendary pilots of the Far North—Noel and Sig Wien, Bob Reeve, Ben Eielson, Harold Gillam, Joe Crosson, Jack Jefford, and the others—who won their wings in the early years. They are Alaska's counterparts to the cowboy heroes of the Wild West. The Bush is where America's favorite humorist, Will Rogers, died in a crash with famed aviator Wiley Post in 1935.

Visitors should be aware that many of the Bush communities have voted to be dry areas in order to fight alcohol-abuse problems affecting Alaska's Native people. The sale and possession of alcohol is prohibited. Enforcement is strict, and bootlegging is a felony. Nome, of course, remains wet, with numerous lively saloons.

Bush Alaskans have a deep affection for their often-raw land, which is difficult to explain to strangers. They talk of living "close to nature," a cliché, perhaps, until you realize that these Alaskans reside in the Bush all year long, adapting to brutal winter weather and isolation. They have accepted the Bush for what it is: dramatic and unforgiving.

Pleasures and Pastimes

Fishing

Alaska's Bush regions offer some of the state's premier sportfishing. Southwest Alaska is especially well known around the world for its remarkable salmon migrations and healthy populations of native rainbow trout. The easiest way to find the fish is to arrange for a guided trip—many sportfishing guides combine fishing and river-floating adventures—or visit a lodge. The Alaska Department of Fish and Game, National Park Service, and U.S. Fish and Wildlife Service can provide lists of guides and outfitters who operate in the region's parks and refuges.

Native Culture

More and more, Native communities throughout Alaska are reconnecting with and celebrating their cultural traditions. Nowhere is this movement stronger than in the Bush. At the same time, many rural communities are recognizing the value of tourism to local economies, and a growing number of cultural tours and activities are being offered in rural villages—from drumming and dancing to arts-and-crafts exhibits and potlatches, which are traditional Native gatherings with songs, food, and gift-giving.

Shopping

Alaska's Arctic is known for Eskimo arts, ranging from wildlife figures carved from walrus ivory to bracelets and other jewelry fashioned from ivory, gold, Alaska jade, and other local materials. The Marine Mammals Protection Act permits the purchase of walrus-ivory goods from Native Alaskans. Nome, Kotzebue, and Barrow all have reputable gift shops. Prices range from about $10 for tiny earrings to hundreds of dollars for ceremonial masks and other major pieces.

Wildlife Viewing

From the brown bears of Katmai National Park to the seals and seabirds of the Pribilofs and the caribou herds and wolf packs of the Arctic, the Bush in spring and summer is a place of great activity. The Alaska Peninsula has Alaska's—and the world's—largest gathering of brown bears, which congregate at clear-water streams to feed on the huge runs of salmon that return each summer. Millions of sea- and shorebirds breed in the Aleutian and Pribilof islands annually, and all sorts of marine mammals—sea lions, seals, sea otters, porpoises, and whales—inhabit coastal waters. Two of the continent's largest caribou herds, the Western Arctic and Porcupine, roam across the Arctic's mountains, valleys, and coastal plains. By far the easiest way for most travelers to see wildlife is to participate in guided tours, though independent travelers can also expect to see abundant animals if they do their homework before visiting Alaska and plan trips well in advance.

Exploring the Bush

Philosophically speaking, the Bush is more of a lifestyle than a location. Technically, it's a place in Alaska that can't be reached by road. Beginning in the southwestern part of the state, a tour of the Bush can begin in Bethel, an important Bush outpost on the Yukon-Kuskokwim Delta, surrounded by the Yukon Delta National Wildlife Refuge; off the mainland coast is the undeveloped wilderness of Nunivak Island. Next is the Alaska Peninsula, which juts out between the Pacific Ocean and the Bering Sea; here is Katmai National Park, Aniakchak National Monument and Preserve, and the Becharof and Alaska Peninsula National Wildlife Refuges. To the south of the Alaska Peninsula is the Kodiak Archipelago, where you'll find the Kodiak National Wildlife Refuge and Shuyak Island State Park, while the Aleutian Islands start where the peninsula ends and sweep southwest toward Japan.

The Pribilof Islands lie north of the Aleutians, 200 mi off Alaska's coast. Head north along the Bering Sea coast and you come to Nome, just below the Arctic Circle. North of Nome is the Bering Land Bridge National Preserve. Kotzebue, just above the circle, is a coastal Eskimo town surrounded by sea and tundra and a jumping-off place for several parklands: Kobuk Valley, Noatak, Cape Krusenstern, and Gates of the Arctic (though the latter is more easily reached from the town of Bettles). Barrow, another Eskimo community, sits at the very top of the state, the northernmost town in the United States. Follow the Arctic coastline eastward and you reach Deadhorse, on Prudhoe Bay, the custodian to the region's important oil and gas reserves. And east of Prudhoe Bay is the Arctic National Wildlife Refuge.

Numbers in the text correspond to numbers in the margin and on the Bush and Alaska Peninsula, Aleutians, and Pribilof Islands maps.

Great Itineraries

Because of its immense size—the Bush encompasses a third of the state—and the expense of transportation, it's best to give yourself at least a week and preferably more when exploring Alaska's rural regions. But even with a week or two, you'll see no more than a small slice of Alaska's wildest and most remote parts. The easiest way to go, of course, is through a package tour. For those with shorter amounts of time, many companies offer one-, two-, or three-day tours to Arctic communities.

IF YOU HAVE 3 DAYS

Visit ⛰ **Katmai National Park and Preserve**'s ④ Brooks Falls and Camp, where brown bears can be seen fishing for salmon, and take the bus tour to the Valley of Ten Thousand Smokes, formed in 1912 by a giant volcanic eruption. Or visit ⛰ **Dutch Harbor** ⑨ and Unalaska in the Aleutian Islands, where guided fishing and wildlife-watching trips can be arranged. If you're visiting in winter, consider ⛰ **Bethel** ①, which hosts one of the state's premier dogsled races, the Kuskokwim 300, each January and the Camai Dance Festival in late March.

IF YOU HAVE 5 DAYS

On guided wildlife tours, visit ⛰ **St. Paul Island** ⑩, one of the Pribilof Islands in the Bering Sea. Or if fishing is your thing, stay at one of the region's many lodges; you'll find several in and around ⛰ **Katmai National Park and Preserve** ④ and **Wood-Tikchik State Park** ③.

IF YOU HAVE 7 DAYS OR MORE

Take a kayaking trip on ⛰ **Shuyak Island State Park** ⑧ while staying in comfortable public-use cabins; or go with guides on a river-floating trip through the **Arctic National Wildlife Refuge** ⑳, where you're likely to see caribou, grizzlies, lots of birds, and perhaps even musk ox or wolves. In winter, consider a mushing expedition through ⛰ **Gates of the Arctic National Park and Preserve** ⑰, but be prepared for harsh weather and rustic tent camping.

When to Tour the Bush

The best time to visit is from June through August, when the weather is mildest (though you should still anticipate cool, wet, and sometimes stormy weather), daylight hours are longest, and the wildlife is most abundant.

Fodor's Choice

Uniquely Alaska

★ **Iditarod Trail Sled Dog Race.** The "Last Great Race on Earth" begins the first Saturday of March in Anchorage and ends, more than 1,049 mi later, on Front Street in Nome.

★ **Katmai National Park and Preserve.** Each summer, brown bears gather here to feed on salmon at Brooks Falls—and thousands of people from around the world watch the bears fish from viewing platforms along the Brooks River.

★ **McNeil River bears.** As many as 100 or more brown bears, the coastal subspecies of grizzlies, come to this Alaska Peninsula stream each summer to feed on salmon, making this the largest gathering of brown bears in Alaska—and the world.

★ **St. Paul Island.** Visitors to this remote Bering Sea island in the Pribilof Archipelago can watch members of the world's largest fur seal herd and also see dozens of bird species.

Lodging

★ **Brooks Lodge.** Within walking distance of Katmai's Brooks River and Falls, the lodge provides easy access to bear-viewing platforms and world-class fly-fishing for salmon and rainbow trout, in the midst of the Alaskan wilderness. $$$$

★ **Grand Aleutian Hotel.** This spacious hotel sits in the unlikeliest of places, the rough-edged and remote fishing town of Unalaska/Dutch Harbor. The hotel's Chart Room Restaurant offers fine dining. $$$$

★ **Top of the World Hotel.** This hotel in Barrow, on the beach facing the Arctic Ocean, has seafront rooms with views of Arctic pack ice even in the middle of summer. $$$$

Dining

★ **Pepe's North of the Border.** With its extensive selection of Mexican dishes and warm hospitality, dining at this local favorite will make you forget you're in the nation's northernmost community. $–$$$$

SOUTHWEST

The Southwest region encompasses some of Alaska's most remote, inaccessible, and rugged land- and seascapes. Ranging from the Alaska Peninsula down through the Aleutian chain, it also includes many islands within the Bering Sea, among them the Pribilof Islands, as well as the Bristol Bay watershed, the Kodiak Archipelago, and the Yukon-Kuskokwim Delta. A place of enormous biologic richness, it is the seasonal home to many of North America's largest breeding populations of seabirds and waterfowl and also supports the world's densest population of brown bears and the world's greatest salmon runs. Given all this richness, it's no surprise to learn that Southwest Alaska boasts some of Alaska's premier parklands and refuges, from Katmai National Park to Aniakchak National Monument and the Kodiak National

Wildlife Refuge. Here, too, are dozens of rural communities, most of them small, remote Native villages whose residents continue to lead subsistence-gathering lifestyles.

Bethel

❶ *400 mi west of Anchorage.*

Spread out on the tundra along the Kuskokwim River, Bethel is a frontier town with 6,000 or so residents, originally established by Moravian missionaries in the late 1800s. One of rural Alaska's most important trading centers, it is a hub for more than 50 Native villages in a region roughly the size of the state of Oregon. The surrounding lowland tundra is a rich green in summer and turns fiery shades of red, orange, and yellow in autumn, when plants burst with blueberries, cranberries, blackberries, and salmonberries. Salmon, arctic grayling, and Dolly Varden trout fill the area's many lakes, ponds, and streams, providing excellent fishing just a few miles outside town. The wetlands are also important breeding grounds for many varieties of birds.

The town is also the northernmost freshwater port for oceangoing vessels. Among its businesses are radio and television stations, a theater, hotel, two banks, a credit union, newspaper, two colleges (including a newly founded tribal college), and the largest Alaska Native Health Service field hospital in the state, which is contracted to the tribally owned Yukon-Kuskokwim Health Corporation.

Each year, on the last weekend in March, Bethel hosts a regional celebration called the Camai Dance Festival (in Yup'ik, *camai* means "hello"). Held in the high school gym, which is filled to capacity for the three-day event, this festival draws dance groups from dozens of villages.

Opened in 1995, the **Yupiit Piciryarait Cultural Center** showcases artifacts and artwork of three Native cultures: Athabascan, Cup'ik and Yup'ik. In its three galleries you'll find historic and prehistoric treasures: masks, statues, and carvings in ivory, baleen, and whalebone. Two permanent collections include numerous implements and tools used in traditional subsistence lifestyles. A small gift shop has locally made artwork for sale, including water-grass baskets, wooden spirit masks, ivory-handle knives, grass and reindeer-beard dance fans, yo-yos, dolls, and seal-gut raincoats. ⊠ *Cultural Center,* ☎ *907/543–1819,* WEB *www.avcp.org.* ⊠ *Free (donations requested).* ☉ *Tues.–Sat. noon–5.*

Dining and Lodging

$–$$$ ✕ **Alice's Kitchen.** This rural café-style downtown restaurant specializes in Chinese food, with daily lunch and dinner specials. It also serves American-style steaks and seafood dishes. ⊠ *473 Ridgecrest St.,* ☎ *907/543–2272. No credit cards.*

$$$–$$$$ ⌂ **Bentley's Porter House B&B.** This large two-story inn sits on Front Street, along the banks of the Kuskokwim River in downtown Bethel, and prides itself on Alaska-style hospitality. Built in the mid-1980s, its lower floor once housed a newspaper operation but has since been remodeled. Rooms are decorated according to theme, including an African Room, a Southwestern U.S. Room, and an English Countryside Room. All rooms have cable TV; several overlook the Kuskokwim River. Besides the main inn, rooms are available in a nearby duplex and cottage. The price includes a full breakfast. ⊠ *624 Front St., Box 529, 99559,* ☎ *907/543–3552,* FAX *907/543–3230. 30 rooms share 14 baths. AE, D, DC, MC, V.*

$$$–$$$$ ▣ **Pacifica Guest House.** This inn, which actually consists of three de-
tached buildings, provides a quiet stay and insightful tips from the Bush-
savvy owners. All of the clean, Alaskan crafts and artwork adorn the
modern rooms, some of which share a bath. Just next door in a so-
larium setting, Diane's Café serves gourmet meals, by Bush or any stan-
dards. You can sample Alaska salmon or halibut, steaks or roasts, or
go with the vegetarian and heart-healthy meals. ⌧ *1220 Hoffman Hwy.,
Box 1208, 99559,* ☎ *907/543–4305,* 🖷 *907/543–3403 or 907/543–
5715. 30 rooms, 14 with bath. Restaurant, library, meeting room. AE,
D, DC, MC, V.*

Shopping
BOOKSTORE

The **Moravian Bookstore** (⌧ 301 3rd Ave., ☎ 907/543–2474) stocks
a variety of arts and crafts as well as books about religion and Eskimo
culture. It is open Monday–Saturday 11–5:30.

OFF THE   **NUNIVAK ISLAND –** Due west of Bethel, and separated from the Yukon-
BEATEN PATH Kuskokwim Delta by Etolin Strait, Nunivak Island is an important wildlife
             refuge. Part of the **Yukon Delta National Wildlife Refuge,** this site is
             noted for its large herd of reindeer, a transplanted herd of musk ox,
             and the Eskimo settlement of Mekoryuk.

             For information on the island, contact the **U.S. Fish and Wildlife Service**
             (☎ 907/543–3151, WEB www.r7.fws.gov) in Bethel. Visitors, lured by fine
             ivory carvings, masks, and items knit from qiviut (musk ox) wool, should
             check with **ERA Aviation** (☎ 800/866–8394, WEB www.eraaviation.com)
             about accommodations, which are limited and far from deluxe.

Yukon Delta National Wildlife Refuge

❷ *Surrounds Bethel.*

At 20 million acres, Yukon Delta is the nation's largest wildlife refuge;
nearly one-third of that acreage is water, in the form of lakes, sloughs,
bogs, creeks, and rivers. The two most significant of these waters are
the **Yukon and Kuskokwim Rivers,** Alaska's two largest rivers. As they
flow toward the Bering Sea, these rivers carry huge amounts of sedi-
ment; over the millennia, these sediments have formed an immense delta
that serves as critical breeding and rearing grounds for an estimated
100 million shorebirds and waterfowl. More than 50 species of birds
nest here, traveling from nearly every state and province in North Amer-
ica and from all of the continents that border the Pacific Ocean. All
of North America's cackling Canada geese and more than half the con-
tinent's population of black brant are born here. Other birds making
the annual pilgrimage to the Yukon Delta refuge include emperor
geese, tundra swans, gulls, jaegers, cranes, loons, snipe, sandpipers, and
the rare bristle-thighed curlew.

Not all of the refuge is flat wetlands. North of the Yukon River are
the Nulato Hills, site of the 1.3-million-acre **Andreafsky Wilderness
area,** which includes both forks of the Andreafsky River, one of
Alaska's specially designated Wild Rivers. Rainbow trout, arctic char,
and grayling flourish in upland rivers and creeks; pike, sheefish, and
burbot thrive in lowland waters. These abundant waters are also
spawning grounds to five species of Pacific salmon. Several species of
mammals, ranging from black and grizzly bears to moose, beaver,

mink, and arctic foxes inhabit the refuge's lands. Occasionally, wolves venture into the delta's flats from neighboring uplands.

Given the abundance of fish and wildlife, it's not surprising that the delta holds special importance to residents of Bethel and other villages in the region. Yup'ik Eskimos have lived here for thousands of years; despite modern encroachment, the Eskimos continue their centuries-old subsistence lifestyle.

Recreational use of the refuge includes wildlife observation, hiking, boating, and fishing. Access is by boat or aircraft only and, as in most of Alaska's remote wildlands, visitor facilities are minimal. Refuge staff can provide tips on recreational opportunities and guides and outfitters who operate in the refuge. ✉ *Box 346, Bethel 99559*, ☎ *907/543–3151*, WEB *www.r7.fws.gov*.

Wood-Tikchik State Park

❸ *150 mi southeast of Bethel, 300 mi southwest of Anchorage.*

In the Bristol Bay region, Wood-Tikchik State Park—the nation's largest state park—is a water-based wildland despite its inland setting. Two separate groups of large, idyllic, interconnected lakes, as much as 45 mi long, dominate the park. Besides the many large lakes and clear-water streams that fill its 1.55 million acres, its landscape includes rugged, snowcapped mountains, forested foothills, and vast expanses of lowland tundra. Everything from grizzlies and caribou to porcupines, eagles, and loons inhabit the park's forests and tundra, but Wood-Tikchik is best known for its fish. Its lakes and streams are critical spawning habitat for five species of Pacific salmon; they also support healthy populations of rainbow trout, arctic char, arctic grayling, and northern pike. The abundance of fish attracts anglers from around the world. Boaters, including rafters and kayakers, also come to explore its expansive and pristine waterways.

Managed as a wild area, Wood-Tikchik has no maintained trails and few other visitor amenities. Most of its campsites are primitive and those who plan to explore the park should be experienced in backcountry travel and camping. Access is by either boat or air. *Mid-May–Sept.:* ✉ *Box 3022, Dillingham 99576*, ☎ *907/842–2375; Oct.–mid-May:* ✉ *550 W. 7th Ave., Suite 1380, Anchorage 99501*, ☎ *907/269–8698.*

You can also travel from **Dillingham,** the town closest to Wood-Tikchik, by boat or by air to view the walruses offshore on **Round Island** within **Walrus Islands State Game Sanctuary.**

Katmai National Park and Preserve

★ ❹ *100 mi southeast of Wood-Tikchik, 290 mi southwest of Anchorage.*

For an extraordinary perspective on the awesome power of volcanoes, visit the 4-million-acre Katmai National Park and Preserve. In this wild, remote landscape at the northern end of the Alaska Peninsula, moose and almost 30 other species of mammals, including foxes, lynx, and wolves, share the scene with bears fishing for salmon from stream banks or in the water. At the immensely popular **Brooks Falls and Camp,** you can be sure of seeing brown bears when the salmon are running in July. No special permits are required here, though there is a $10 day-use fee at Brooks. Ducks are common along the park's rivers, lakes, and outer coast; so are whistling swans, loons, grebes, gulls, and shorebirds.

Bald eagles perch on rocky pinnacles by the sea. More than 40 species of songbirds alone can be seen during the short spring and summer season. Marine life abounds in the coastal area, with Steller's sea lions and hair seals often observed on rock outcroppings.

Compared with roads and facilities at Denali National Park, those at Katmai are quite primitive, but therein lies part of the park's charm. The first visitors to the Katmai area arrived more than 4,000 years ago. Some evidence exists, in fact, that Native Alaskan people inhabited Katmai's eastern edge for at least 6,000 years. On the morning of June 1, 1912, a 2,700-ft mountain called **Novarupta** erupted. The earth shook in violent tremors for five straight days. When the quakes subsided, rivers of white-hot ash poured into the valley. A foot of ash fell on Kodiak Island, 100 mi away. Winds carried the ash to eastern Canada and as far as Texas. While Novarupta was belching pumice and scorching ash, another explosion occurred 6 mi east. The mountaintop peak of **Mt. Katmai** collapsed, creating a chasm almost 3 mi long and 2 mi wide. The molten andesite that held up Mt. Katmai had rushed through newly created fissures to Novarupta and was spewed out. Sixty hours after the first thunderous blast, more than 7 cubic mi of volcanic material had been ejected, and the green valley lay under 700 ft of ash. Everyone fled from Katmai and other villages; no one was killed.

By 1916 things had cooled off. A National Geographic expedition led by Dr. Robert F. Griggs reached the valley and found it full of steaming fumaroles, creating a moonlike landscape. The report on what Griggs dubbed the **Valley of Ten Thousand Smokes** inspired Congress in 1918 to set it and the surrounding wilderness aside as a national monument. Steam spouted in thousands of fountains from the smothered streams and springs beneath the ash and gave the valley its name. Although the steam has virtually stopped, an eerie sense of earth forces at work remains, and several nearby volcanoes still smolder.

The Native peoples never returned to their traditional village sites, but many now live in other nearby communities. They are joined by sightseers, anglers, hikers, and other outdoor enthusiasts who migrate to the Katmai region each summer. Fish and wildlife are still plentiful, and a few "smokes" still drift through the volcano-sculpted valley.

No roads lead to the national park, at the base of the Alaska Peninsula. Planes wing from Anchorage along Cook Inlet, rimmed by the lofty, snowy peaks of the Alaska Range. They land at **King Salmon,** near fish-famous Bristol Bay, where passengers transfer to smaller floatplanes for the 20-minute hop to **Naknek Lake** and Brooks Camp. Travel to Brooks from King Salmon is also possible by boat. All visitors are required to check into the park ranger station, next to Brooks Lodge, for a mandatory bear talk.

From Brooks Lodge, a daily tour bus with a naturalist aboard makes the 23-mi trip through the park to the **Valley Overlook.** Hikers can walk the 1½-mi trail for a closer look at the pumice-covered valley floor. (Some consider the return climb strenuous.)

The Katmai area is one of Alaska's premier sportfishing regions. It's possible to fish for rainbow trout and salmon at the **Brooks River,** though seasonal closures have been put in place to prevent conflicts with bears, and only fly-fishing is permitted. For those who would like to venture farther into the park, seek out the two other backcountry lodges, Grosvenor and Kulik, set in prime sportfishing territory, or contact fishing guide services based in King Salmon. A short walk up the

Brooks River brings you to Brooks Falls, where salmon can be seen from a viewing platform (on a trail separated from the river to avoid confrontations with bears) as they leap a 6-ft barrier. ✉ *National Park Service, Box 7, King Salmon 99613,* ☎ *907/246–3305,* WEB *www.nps. gov/katm.*

★ At the northern end of the Alaska Peninsula, 200 mi southwest of Anchorage, **McNeil River State Game Sanctuary** was established in 1967 to protect the world's largest gathering of brown bears. The main focus is **McNeil Falls,** where bears come to feed on chum salmon returning to spawn. During the peak of the chum run (July to mid-August) dozens of brown bears congregate at the falls. As many as 30–70 bears, including cubs, have been observed along the river in a single day. No more than 10 people a day, always accompanied by one or two state biologists, are allowed to visit bear-viewing sites from June 7 through August 25. Because demand is so high, an annual drawing is held in mid-March to determine permit winners. Applications must be received by March 1 to be eligible. Nearly all visitors fly into McNeil sanctuary on floatplanes. Most arrange for air-taxi flights out of Homer, on the Kenai Peninsula. Once you are in the sanctuary, all travel is on foot. ✉ *Alaska Department of Fish and Game, Division of Wildlife Conservation, 333 Raspberry Rd., Anchorage 99518–1599,* ☎ *907/267–2182,* WEB *www.state.ak.us/adfg.*

Lodging and Camping

All of the four lodges below are on inholdings within Katmai National Park. Three are inland, and Katmai Wilderness Lodge is on the remote outer coast.

$$$$ 🏨 **Brooks Lodge.** All the attractions of Katmai National Park are at
★ this lodge's doorstep: world-class fly-fishing for rainbow trout, lake trout, arctic grayling, and salmon; brown-bear viewing; and tours to the Valley of Ten Thousand Smokes. Accommodations are in detached modern cabins complete with showers, private toilet facilities, heat, and electricity; they accommodate two to four people. The cabins surround the main lodge, which boasts a spectacular view of aquamarine Naknek Lake; it has a circular stone fireplace and dining area where buffet-style meals are served three times daily. ✉ *Katmailand, 4125 Aircraft Dr., Anchorage 99502,* ☎ *907/243–5448 or 800/544–0551,* FAX *907/243–0649,* WEB *www.bearviewing.net. 16 cabins. Bar, dining room, hiking, fishing. MC, V. Closed mid-Sept.–May.*

$$$$ 🏨 **Grosvenor Lodge.** Once you've arrived at this remote Katmai National Park lodge, reachable only by floatplane, you have access by motorboat to numerous rivers and streams filled with sport fish. The lodge can accommodate six people in three cabins with heat and electricity and a shared separate bathhouse. The main lodge houses a kitchen, dining room, lounging area, and bar and has an excellent view of Grosvenor Lake. Three-, four-, and seven-night price packages include airfare from Anchorage, meals, lodging, and guiding. ✉ *Katmailand, 4125 Aircraft Dr., Anchorage 99502,* ☎ *907/243–5448 or 800/544–0551,* FAX *907/243–0649,* WEB *www.katmailand.com. 3 cabins with shared bath. Bar, dining room, fishing. MC, V. Closed Oct.–May.*

$$$$ 🏨 **Katmai Wilderness Lodge.** Built on land owned by the Russian Orthodox Church, this rustic lodge straddles the rugged outer coast of Katmai National Park, along the shores of Kukak Bay. Mountains, coastal flats, and the waters of Shelikof Strait surround the log cabin–style lodge. The primary recreational activities include bear viewing, sea kayaking, and fishing for halibut and salmon. Visitors may stay from one night to a week or more. Price includes a round-trip flight from Kodiak, meals, lodging, and guide services. ⊠ *Box 4332, Kodiak 99615,* ☎ *800/488–8767,* FAX *907/486–6798,* WEB *www.katmai-wilderness.com. 7 rooms. Dining room. No credit cards. Closed Oct.–mid-May.*

$$$$ 🏨 **Kulik Lodge.** Positioned along the gin-clear Kulik River, between Nonvianuk and Kulik lakes, this remote wilderness lodge is also reachable only by floatplane. It accommodates up to 28 anglers and is popular as a base for fly-out fishing to hot spots in the surrounding Katmai wilderness. Guests stay in two- or four-person cabins with electricity and private baths. In the evening, when fishing's done for the day, guests gather in the spruce lodge, which has a large stone fireplace, dining area, and bar. Three-, four-, or seven-night packages include airfare from Anchorage, meals, lodging, and guiding. ⊠ *Katmailand, 4125 Aircraft Dr., Anchorage 99502,* ☎ *907/243–5448 or 800/544–0551,* FAX *907/243–0649,* WEB *www.katmailand.com. 12 cabins. Bar, dining room, fishing. MC, V. Closed Oct.–May.*

$ 🏕 **Brooks Campground.** This National Park Service campground is near Brooks Lodge, where campers can pay to eat and shower. There are designated cooking and eating shelters, latrines, well water, and a storage cache to protect food from the ever-present brown bears. Reservations are required. ⊠ *Katmai National Park, Box 7, King Salmon 99613,* ☎ *907/246–3305; 800/365–2267 for reservations,* WEB *www.nps.gov/katm. D, MC, V. Closed mid-Sept.–May.*

Guided Tours

Katmai Air Services (☎ 907/246–3079 in King Salmon summer only; 800/544–0551 in Anchorage, WEB www.katmailand.com) can arrange flightseeing tours of the park. **Katmailand** (⊠ 4125 Aircraft Dr., Anchorage 99502, ☎ 907/243–5448 or 800/544–0551, FAX 907/243–0649, WEB www.katmailand.com) assembles packages to Katmai National Park.

Aniakchak National Monument and Preserve

❺ *100 mi southwest of Katmai National Park.*

Aniakchak, an extraordinary living volcano, rises to the south of Katmai. It has one of the largest calderas in the world, with a diameter averaging 6 mi across and the small **Surprise Lake** within it. Although Aniakchak erupted as recently as 1931, the explosion that formed the enormous crater occurred before history was written. Because the area is not glaciated, geologists place the blowup after the last Ice Age. It was literally a world-shaking event. Marking the volcano's significance, Congress in 1980 established the 586,000-acre Aniakchak National Monument and Preserve.

This is wild and forbidding country, with a climate that brews mist, clouds, and winds of great force much of the year. Although the **Aniakchak River** (which drains Surprise Lake) is floatable, it has stretches of Class III and IV white water navigable only by expert river runners, and you must travel through open ocean waters to reach the nearest community, Chignik Bay (or get picked up by plane, along the coast); this makes the run an ambitious undertaking. An alternative way to enjoy Aniakchak is to wait for a clear day and fly to it in a small plane able to land you on the caldera floor or on Surprise Lake. However you choose to see it, it's an unforgettable experience. But be aware that there are no trails, campgrounds, ranger stations, or other visitor facilities here; you must be prepared to be self-sufficient.

Aniakchak is both remote and expensive to reach. The only easy access is by air, usually from the town of King Salmon. Thus few people visit this spectacular place—and those who do are likely to have the caldera all to themselves. ⊠ *Aniakchak National Monument and Preserve, Box 7, King Salmon 99613,* ☎ *907/246–3305,* W̅E̅B̅ *www. nps.gov/ania.*

Becharof and Alaska Peninsula National Wildlife Refuges

❻ *Adjacent to Aniakchak National Monument and Preserve, 250 to 450 mi southwest of Anchorage.*

Stretching along the southern edge of the Alaska Peninsula, these two refuges encompass nearly 6 million acres of towering mountains, glacial lakes, broad tundra valleys, and coastal fjords. Volcanoes dominate the landscape—14 in all, including 9 considered active. **Mount Veniaminov** last erupted in 1993. Other glimpses of volcanic activity include **Gas Rocks,** where gases continually seep through cracks in granitic rocks, and **Ukrinek Marrs,** a crater that bears the marks of a violent eruption in 1977.

Besides its rugged volcanic landscape, these two refuges are best known for their abundant wildlife. More than 220 species of resident and migratory wildlife seasonally inhabit the region, including 30 land and 11 marine mammals, nearly 150 varieties of birds, and 35 species of fish. Caribou, wolves, and moose roam the region's tundra; sea lions, seals, seabirds, and waterfowl thrive along the rocky shores; and bald eagles and falcons nest on craggy cliffs above the coast. You'll find brown bears nearly everywhere, from coastal lowlands to high mountain ridges.

Becharof Lake, at 35 mi long and up to 15 mi wide, is the second-largest lake in Alaska (behind Lake Iliamna). Fed by 2 rivers and 14 major creeks, it serves as a nursery to the world's second-biggest run of salmon. **Ugashik Lakes** are known for their salmon and trophy grayling. The world record grayling, nearly 5 pounds (most grayling weigh a pound or less) was caught at Ugashik Narrows in 1981.

Remote and rugged, with weather that is frequently stormy, the Becharof and Alaska Peninsula refuges draw mostly anglers and hunters; however, backpackers, river runners, and mountain climbers also occasionally visit. No visitor facilities are available here and the only access is by boat or plane. Most visitors begin their trips in King Salmon and use guides or outfitters. ⊠ *Box 277, King Salmon 99613,* ☎ *907/246–3339,* W̅E̅B̅ *www.r7.fws.gov.*

Kodiak National Wildlife Refuge

❼ *50 mi south of Katmai National Park, 300 mi southwest of Anchorage.*

The 1.9-million-acre Kodiak National Wildlife Refuge lies mostly on Kodiak Island and partly on neighboring Afognak and Uganik Islands, in the Gulf of Alaska. All are part of the Kodiak Archipelago, separated from Alaska's mainland by the often stormy Shelikof Strait. Within the refuge are rugged mountains, tundra meadows and lowlands, thickly forested hills, lakes, marshes, and hundreds of miles of pristine coastline. No place in the refuge is more than 15 mi from the ocean. The weather here is generally wet and cool, and storms born in the North Pacific often bring heavy rains.

Dozens of species of birds inhabit the refuge each spring and summer, including Aleutian terns, horned puffins, black oystercatchers, ravens, ptarmigan, and chickadees. At least 200 pairs of bald eagles live on the islands year-round, nesting on shoreline cliffs and in tall trees. Seeing the Kodiak brown bears—the world's largest carnivores, along with polar bears—weighing only a pound at birth but up to 1,500 pounds when full grown, is worth the trip to this rugged country. When they emerge from their dens in spring, the bears feed on sedges and grasses, but become fish eaters when salmon return in early summer. In fall, the bears depend heavily on Kodiak's berries. Kodiak's brown bears share the refuge with only a few other land mammals native to the archipelago: red fox, river otter, short-tailed weasel, little brown, and tundra vole.

Kodiak's waters are valuable spawning grounds for five species of Pacific salmon, which return to the refuge in a series of runs that begin in May and last into October. Other resident species include rainbow trout, steelhead, Dolly Varden, and arctic char. The abundance of fish—and bears—makes the refuge popular with anglers, hunters, and wildlife watchers. The only access here is by boat or plane. Refuge staff will provide lists of guides, outfitters, and air taxis. ⊠ *1390 Buskin River Rd., Kodiak 99615,* ☎ *907/487–2600,* WEB *www.r7.fws.gov.*

Lodging

$ ⌂ **Kodiak Refuge Public-Use Cabins.** It's possible to rent one of seven recreation cabins (accessible by floatplane or boat) within the refuge for up to seven days (longer in the off-season). Set along the coast and on inland lakes, the cabins include bunks with mattresses, kerosene heaters, tables, and benches. Reservations are awarded through quarterly lotteries, held on the first of January, April, July, and October. ⊠ *1390 Buskin River Rd., Kodiak 99615,* ☎ *907/487–2600,* WEB *www. r7.fws.gov. 7 cabins. Reservations essential. No credit cards. Cabins on inland lakes are usually not accessible in winter.*

Shuyak Island State Park

❽ *50 mi north of Kodiak Island.*

The 46,000-acre Shuyak Island State Park is one of the newest—and most overlooked—units in the state parks system. At the northern end of the Kodiak Archipelago, it's accessible only by plane or boat. Its rugged outer coastline is balanced by a more protected system of interconnected bays, channels, and passages that make the park a favorite with sea kayakers. It also offers excellent wildlife viewing, especially for seabirds and sea mammals, and top-notch sportfishing for salmon. Wildlife ranges from Sitka black-tailed deer and brown bears to sea otters, sea lions, bald eagles, puffins, and whales. The park has four public-use cabins but no developed campgrounds; limited hiking trails pass through old-growth coastal rain forest. ⊠ *Alaska State Parks, Kodiak District Office, HCR 3800, Kodiak 99615,* ☎ *907/486–6339,* WEB *www.dnr.state.ak.us.*

Lodging and Camping

$$ ⌂ **Alaska State Parks Cabins.** Alaska State Parks maintains four recreational public-use cabins on Shuyak Island. All are accessible by boat or plane only. The cabins may be rented for up to seven days. Each has a woodstove, propane lights, hot plate, four bunks, outside shower and wash area, cooking utensils, and pit toilets. You can make reservations up to six months in advance. ⊠ *Alaska State Parks, Kodiak District Office, HRC 3800, Kodiak 99615, or DNR Public Information Center, 550 W. 7th Ave., Suite 1260, Anchorage 99501,* ☎ *907/ 486–6339 or 907/269–8400,* FAX *907/486–3320,* WEB *www.dnr.state.ak. us. 4 cabins. MC, V.*

$ ⚠ **Alaska State Parks Campgrounds.** The state has three road-accessible campgrounds (Ft. Abercrombie, Buskin River, and Pasagshak) on Kodiak Island, with a total of 35 tent sites. All have toilets, drinking water, and fishing, and two have nearby hiking trails. Camping at Pasagshak is free; the campgrounds at Ft. Abercrombie and Buskin River charge $10 a night. ⊠ *Alaska State Parks, Kodiak District Office, HCR 3800, Kodiak 99615,* ☏ *907/486–6339,* FAX *907/486–3320,* WEB *www. dnr.state.ak.us. Reservations not accepted. No credit cards. Closed about mid-Oct.–mid-May.*

Outdoor Activities and Sports

KAYAKING

Contact Alaska State Parks in Kodiak for the names of companies offering guided trips in Shuyak State Park.

Aleutian Islands

The Aleutians begin 540 mi southwest of Anchorage and stretch more than 1,000 mi.

Separating the North Pacific Ocean from the Bering Sea, the Aleutian Islands (also called the Chain) stretch from the Alaska Peninsula in a southwesterly arc toward Japan. The distance from the point nearest the Alaska mainland, Unimak Island, to the most distant island, Attu, is more than 1,000 mi. This volcanic, treeless archipelago consists of about 20 large islands and several hundred smaller ones. The Aleutian Islands and surrounding coastal waters make up one of the most biologically rich areas in Alaska, with abundant seabird, marine mammal, and fish populations.

Before the Russians came, the islands were dotted with Aleut villages. Today's communities include **Nikolski,** on Umnak Island; **Unalaska,** on Unalaska Island; **Atka,** on Atka Island; and **Cold Bay,** at the peninsula's tip. The hardy Aleuts work at commercial fishing or in canneries and as expert guides for those who hunt and fish. The settlements are quite small, and accommodations are scarce.

Visitors are not allowed to visit Shemya Island, which has a remote U.S. Air Force base, without special permission. Because of downsizing, the military has closed its Adak operation and the base's infrastructure has been used to start a new town and commercial-fishing port.

❾ Dutch Harbor, on Unalaska Island, is by far the most populous destination in the Aleutian Islands and in recent years has served as its tourism center. The Japanese bombed Dutch Harbor during World War II, and you can still see concrete bunkers, gun batteries, and a partially sunken ship left over from the war. In addition to military history, you'll find a hotel and restaurants that rival those on Alaska's mainland, and a variety of guided adventure tours.

Dining and Lodging

$–$$$$ ✕ **Stormy's Restaurant.** This family-style restaurant serves a variety of American and ethnic foods, including Chinese and Japanese (there's even a sushi bar). Dishes include pizza, fried chicken, and seafoods. Less than 1 mi across the bridge from downtown Dutch Harbor, this is Unalaska's oldest eatery. ⊠ *2nd Ave. and Broadway, Unalaska village,* ☏ *907/581–1565. MC, V.*

$$$$ ✕🖼 **Grand Aleutian Hotel.** This hotel won an architectural award for
★   its chalet-inspired design, which includes a stone fireplace in its three-story atrium lobby. Guest rooms have views of Margaret Bay or Unalaska Bay. In-room amenities include hair dryer, clock radio, and

Alaska Peninsula, Aleutians, and Pribilofs

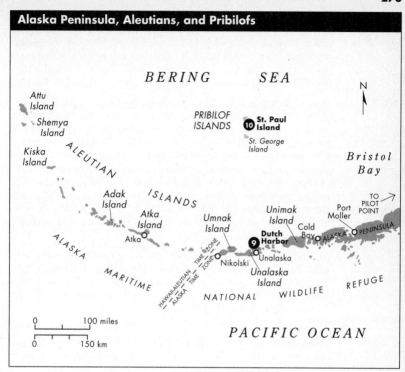

cable TV; some suites have a whirlpool tub. The Chart Room Restaurant and Lounge ($$–$$$$) offers fine dining and specializes in Pacific Rim cuisine with locally caught seafood. Guided activities include bird-watching as well as halibut and salmon fishing. ⊠ *498 Salmon Way, Box 921169, Dutch Harbor 99692-1169,* ☎ *907/581–3844 or 800/891–1194,* FAX *907/581–7150,* WEB *www.grandaleutian.com. 112 rooms, 6 suites. 2 restaurants, 2 bars, fishing, meeting room, travel services, airport shuttle. AE, D, DC, MC, V.*

$$$ 🏨 **Unisea Inn.** This hotel on the water offers clean, comfortable rooms with cable TV and telephones. Try to book a room with a view of the small-boat harbor. Mexican fare, burgers, and sandwiches are served in the Unisea Inn Sports Bar and Grill ($$–$$$). Sit back and watch satellite broadcasts of spectator sports or try your hand at darts, pool, or video games. Live bands play Top 40 or country music six nights a week. ⊠ *185 Gilman Rd., Box 921169, Dutch Harbor 99692,* ☎ *907/581–1325; 800/891–1194 for reservations;* FAX *907/581–1633. 25 rooms. Restaurant, sports bar, hair salon, airport shuttle. AE, D, DC, MC, V.*

Pribilof Islands

200 mi north of the Aleutian Islands, 800 mi southwest of Anchorage.

The Pribilof Islands are misty, fogbound breeding grounds of seabirds and northern fur seals. Five islets make up the Pribilof group—a tiny, green, treeless oasis, with rippling belts of lush grass contrasting with red volcanic soil. In early summer seals come home from far Pacific waters to mate, and the larger islands, St. Paul and St. George, are overwhelmed with scenes of frenzied activity. Their sounds can roll out several miles to sea.

The islands are a 1,600-mi round-trip from Anchorage, over the massive snowy peaks of the Alaska Peninsula and past the rocky islands of the Aleutian chain. This was the supply route for U.S. forces during World War II, when Japan invaded Attu and Kiska islands toward the tip of the chain. During the Bering Sea leg, a playful pod of whales may be lurking below.

Wildlife watching is what brings nearly all visitors to the Pribilof Islands. Together, St. Paul and St. George islands are seasonal homes to nearly 1 million fur seals (about 80% of them on St. Paul) and 200 species of birds. Some birds migrate here from as far away as Argentina, whereas others are year-round residents. Of special interest to birders are the rare Asian vagrants sometimes blown here by strong western winds. Most spectacular of all is the islands' seabird population: each summer more than 2 million seabirds gather at traditional Pribilof nesting grounds; about 90% of them breed on St. George. The Pribilofs are also home to foxes, and sea lions and whales are occasionally spotted off their shores.

For most travelers, it is much easier and more cost-efficient to participate in package tours that arrange air travel from Anchorage, lodging, ground transportation on the islands, and guided activities. Visitors planning to come here on their own should be aware that guest accommodations in the Pribilofs are very limited.

★ ⑩ At **St. Paul Island,** nature lovers can watch members of the largest northern fur seal herd in the world and more than 180 varieties of birds. In town, you can visit with local residents; about 500 descendants of Aleut-Russians live here now, in the shadow of the old Russian Orthodox church and the vestiges of Aleut culture. **St. George Island** is home to nearly to 2 million nesting seabirds, but it is much less frequently visited because no organized tours go there and accommodations are limited.

Dining and Lodging

$$$ ✕ **Trident Sea Foods.** This cafeteria-style eatery—the island's only restaurant—serves fish processors as well as visitors to St. Paul Island. Plan your day carefully because meals are served according to a strict schedule: breakfast 7–8, lunch noon–1, and dinner 5–6. ⊠ *Downtown St. Paul, 2 blocks from the King Eider Hotel,* ☎ *907/546–2377. No credit cards.*

$$$$ 🏨 **King Eider Hotel.** More functional than luxurious, this rustic three-story clapboard hotel is filled in summer by tour groups. The original part of this historic landmark dates to the late 1800s; it's been expanded four times since. The hotel has simply furnished rooms, a TV room, reading lounge, and gift shop. If you are traveling on your own, make reservations months in advance. ⊠ *523 Tolstoi St., Box 88, St. Paul 99660,* ☎ *907/546–2477 or 907/278–2312,* ℻ *907/546–5026,* 🕸 *www.alaskabirding.com. 25 rooms, 5 shared baths. Travel services. AE, MC, V.*

$$$$ 🏨 **St. George Tanaq Hotel.** A national historic landmark, St. George Island's only hotel is a small, rustic building with dark wood interior and a mix of modern and vintage furniture. Rooms are sparsely furnished with shared baths. Its shared kitchen and dining area, with stove, refrigerator, and cooking utensils, is important on an island with no restaurant. ⊠ *Downtown, Box 939, St. George 99591,* ☎ *907/272–9886 or 907/859–2255,* ℻ *907/859–2230,* 🕸 *www.stgeorgetanaq.com. 10 rooms, 4 shared baths. MC, V.*

Guided Tours

Contact **Tanadgusix Village Corporation of St. Paul Island** (✉ 1500 W. 33rd Ave., Suite 220, Anchorage 99503, ☎ 907/278–2312 or 877/424–5637, WEB www.alaskabirding.com) for St. Paul Island tour information.

NORTHWEST AND THE ARCTIC

This is a largely roadless region of long, dark, sunless winters and short, bright summers, when the sun remains in the sky around the clock for nearly three months. It's the land of Eskimos and huge caribou herds and polar bears, a place where people still lead subsistence lifestyles and where traditional Native culture is making a strong comeback. It's also a place of gold rushes and America's largest oil field as well as being a region with many of Alaska's wildest and most remote parklands and one of the country's premier refuges, the Arctic National Wildlife Refuge.

Nome

⑪ *540 mi northwest of Anchorage.*

More than a century has passed since a great stampede for gold put a speck of wilderness called Nome on the Alaska map, but gold mining and noisy saloons are still mainstays in this frontier community on the icy Bering Sea. Mainly a collection of ramshackle houses and low-slung commercial buildings, Nome looks like a vintage gold-mining camp or the neglected set of a western movie—rawboned, rugged, and somewhat shabby. What the town lacks in appearance is made up for with a cheerful hospitality and colorful history.

Only 165 mi from the coast of Siberia, Nome is considerably closer to Russia than either Anchorage or Fairbanks. And though you'll find a local road system, to get to Nome you must either fly or mush a team of sled dogs.

Nome's golden years began in 1898, when three prospectors—known as the "Lucky Swedes"—struck rich deposits on Anvil Creek, about 4 mi from what became Nome. The news spread quickly. When the Bering Sea ice parted the next spring, ships from Puget Sound, down by Seattle, arrived in Nome with eager stampeders. An estimated 15,000 people landed in Nome between June and October of 1900. Among the gold-rush luminaries were Wyatt Earp, the old gunfighter from the O.K. Corral, who mined the gold of Nome by opening a posh saloon; Tex Rickard, the boxing promoter, who operated another Nome saloon; and Rex Beach, the novelist.

Nome is also proud to be the hometown of General James H. Doolittle, the Tokyo raider of World War II. When Doolittle's bombers hit Japan in a daring raid in 1942, the headline in the *Nome Nugget* proudly announced: "NOME TOWN BOY MAKES GOOD!"

A network of 250 mi or so of gravel roads around the town lead to creeks and rivers for gold panning or fishing for trout, salmon, and arctic grayling. You can also see reindeer, bears, foxes, and moose in the wild on the back roads that once connected early mining camps and hamlets. Independent travelers with hardy vehicles should go exploring. **Alaska Cab Garage** (☎ 907/443–2939) rents jeeps, pickup trucks, or vans, both two- and four-wheel drive. **Stampede Car Rentals** (☎ 907/443–5598) rents pickup trucks, jeeps, or vans for those who would like to explore Nome and its outskirts. Because the sun stays up late in the summer months, drive to the top of **Anvil Mountain,** near Nome, for a panoramic view of the old gold town and the Bering Sea. Be sure to carry mosquito repellent.

For exploring downtown, stop at the **Nome Convention and Visitors Bureau** (✉ Front St., ☎ 907/443–6624; 800/478–1901 in Alaska only, FAX 907/443–5832, WEB www.nomealaska.org) for a historic-walking-tour map, a city map, and information on local activities from flight-seeing to bird-watching.

Dining, Lodging, and Camping

$$–$$$$ ✕ **Fort Davis Roadhouse.** The Roadhouse, which specializes in prime rib and seafood, is where locals go for a night out. Friday and Saturday are buffet nights, and on Sunday the roadhouse serves brunch, which includes Belgian waffles, crepes, and eggs Benedict. Above the dining area is a lounge with live music and room for dancing. Some visitors fall for the Bering Ball, a infamously potent cocktail that most locals seem to avoid. Taxis serve the area. ✉ *Nome–Council Rd., 1½ mi east of town,* ☎ *907/443–2660. MC, V. Closed Mon.–Tues. No lunch except for Sun. brunch.*

$–$$$ ✕ **Fat Freddie's.** This popular café-style eatery overlooking the Bering Sea serves New York steak and prime rib, plus its notable burgers and seafood. Guests at the Nome Nugget Inn can enter directly from the hotel. ✉ *50 Front St.,* ☎ *907/443–5899. AE, MC, V.*

$–$$$ ✕ **Polar Cub.** Standard American diner food, from omelets to steak, fills the menu here. Locals like to linger over coffee, making it a good place to eavesdrop on area issues or just gaze out at the Bering Sea. With its sea views, good prices, and friendly service, the Cub is a great place for early-morning breakfast. ✉ *Next to the seawall, off Front St., downtown,* ☎ *907/443–5191. AE, D, MC, V.*

$$$$ ⊞ **Camp Bendeleben.** This lodge is in Council, an early 1900s gold-mining camp, about 75 mi northeast of Nome, along the clear-water Niukluk River. You can fish for arctic char, grayling, and four species of salmon; other outdoor activities include bird-watching and wildlife photography. Packages include all meals and transportation between the lodge and Nome. Prices vary considerably, depending on whether you stay at the lodge or remote tent camps and whether or not you choose to be guided when fishing. There is a three-night minimum. *In summer:* ✉ *Box 1045, Nome 99762; in winter: 2320 Colony Loop, Anchorage 99507,* ☎ FAX *907/522–6663,* WEB *www.campbendeleben.com. 3 rooms. Dining room, fishing. No credit cards. Closed Oct.–May.*

$$$ ⊞ **Nome Nugget Inn.** The architecture and decor of the Nugget Inn combine every cliché of the Victorian gold-rush era. Authentic it's not, but fun it is. Outside, a signpost marks the mileage to various points, serious and silly, around the globe. Inside, frontier memorabilia abounds in the lobby and lounge. Rooms are small and clean but not nearly as atmospheric. Arctic tour groups stay here. ✉ *Box 1470, Front St., 99762,* ☎ *907/443–2323 or 877/443–2323,* FAX *907/443–5966,* WEB *www. nomenuggetinn.com. 47 rooms. Restaurant, bar. AE, DC, MC, V.*

$ ⚠ **Bureau of Land Management Campground.** BLM manages a free campground at Mile 40 of the Nome-Taylor Highway. The campground has six tent sites, toilet facilities, and nearby fishing. The maximum length of stay is 14 days. The campground has a pit toilet and fire rings for cooking, but the only water is in nearby Salmon Lake and Pilgrim River; it must be boiled or otherwise treated. ✉ *Bureau of Land Management, Nome Field Office, Box 925, 99762,* ☎ *907/443–2177 in Nome; 907/474–2231 in Fairbanks; 800/437–7021,* WEB *aurora.*

ak.blm.gov. 6 tent sites. Fishing. Reservations not accepted. No credit cards. Closed Oct.–Apr.

Outdoor Activities and Sports

★ The famed 1,049-mi **Iditarod Trail Sled Dog Race**—the Olympics of sled-dog racing—reaches its culmination in Nome in mid-March. Racers start in Anchorage for a trip of nine days to two weeks. The arrival of the mushers heralds a winter carnival. For dates, starting times, and other information, contact the Iditarod Trail Committee (⊠ Box 870800, Wasilla 99687, ☎ 907/376–5155, WEB www.iditarod.com).

Shopping

Nome is one of the best places to buy ivory, because many of the Eskimo carvers from outlying villages come to Nome first to offer their wares to dealers. The **Arctic Trading Post** (⊠ Bering and Front Sts., ☎ 907/443–2686) has an extensive stock of authentic Eskimo ivory carvings and other Alaskan artwork, jewelry, and books. The **Board of Trade Ivory Shop** (☎ 907/443–2335) on Front Street specializes in ivory carvings but also sells Native Alaskan artwork and handicrafts. **Chukotka-Alaska** (⊠ 514 Lomen, ☎ 907/443–4128) sells both Native Alaskan and Russian artwork and handicrafts as well as books and furs.

Bering Land Bridge National Preserve

12 *100 mi north of Nome.*

The frozen ash and lava of the 2.8-million-acre Bering Land Bridge National Preserve lie between Nome and Kotzebue immediately south of the Arctic Circle. The Imuruk lava flow is the northernmost flow of major size in the United States, and the paired *maars* (clear volcanic lakes) are a geological rarity.

Of equal interest are the paleontological features of this preserve. Sealed into the permafrost are flora and fauna—bits of twigs and leaves, tiny insects, small mammals, even remnants of woolly mammoths—that flourished here when the Bering Land Bridge linked North America to what is now Russia. Early peoples wandered through this treeless landscape, perhaps following the musk ox, whose descendants still occupy this terrain. A remarkable 250 species of flowering plants thrive in this seemingly barren region, and tens of thousands of migrating birds. More than 100 species, including ducks, geese, swans, sandhill cranes, and various shorebirds and songbirds, come here from around the world each spring. You may hear the haunting call of loons on the many clear lakes and lagoons.

The Bering Land Bridge National Preserve has no trails, campgrounds, or other visitor facilities. Access is largely by air taxi, although there is a road north of Nome that passes within walking distance. ⊠ *National Park Service, Box 220, Nome 99762, ☎ 907/443–2522, or Box 1029, Kotzebue 99752, ☎ 907/442–3890, WEB www.nps.gov/bela.*

Kotzebue

13 *170 mi northeast of Nome.*

Kotzebue, Alaska's largest Eskimo community, is home to around 3,500 residents. It lies 26 mi above the Arctic Circle, on Alaska's northwestern coast. "We have four seasons—June, July, August, and winter," a tour guide jests. But don't worry about the sometimes-chilly weather—the local sightseeing company has snug, bright loaner parkas for visitors on package tours.

Strung out in clusters of weather-bleached little houses and a few public buildings on the gravelly shore of Kotzebue Sound, Kotzebue provides visitors with a glimpse of the way Alaska's Eskimos live today. It was an ancient Eskimo trading center; now it is an example of the new spirit nudging Alaska's Natives into the state's mainstream culture without leaving their traditions behind.

The **NANA** (Northwest Alaska Native Association, ☎ 907/442–3301 or 800/478–3301, 🕸 www.nana.com) Regional Corporation, one of the 13 Native corporations formed when Congress settled the Alaskan Natives' aboriginal land claims in 1971, has its headquarters in Kotzebue. It was NANA that built the **Living Museum of the Arctic** (☎ 907/265–4100 or 907/442–3301, www.nana.com) in 1977 and turned it into one of Alaska's top-rated museums. Bleachers face a stage where stories are told, and after the storytelling, a cultural slide show relates the wisdom of the elders, followed by traditional Eskimo singing and dancing and a blanket toss in which audience members are invited to participate. It may look like a game, but it was serious business in the early days, when Eskimo hunters were launched high in the air from blankets of walrus or seal hide to scan the seas for game. You may even be urged to take a turn on the bouncing blanket. The museum is open when tour groups are in town or by special arrangement. Admission to the museum is free, but a fee is charged to attend cultural programs. After attending programs at the museum, many visitors stop at the **Inu-Craft Gift Shop** (☎ 907/442–3331, 🕸 www.nana.com) in the Nullagvik Hotel. It stocks a good selection of Native arts and crafts as well as T-shirts, sweatshirts, and postcards.

Tours of the museum can be arranged through NANA's **Tour Arctic** program (☎ 907/265–4100 or 907/442–3301, 🕸 www.nana.com), in which visitors may participate in a guided "Kotzebue Tour" or a "Native Village Excursion." Prices vary, depending on the tour.

Visitors hiking the wildflower-carpeted tundra around Kotzebue enter a "living museum" dedicated to **permafrost,** the permanently frozen ground that lies just a few inches below the spongy tundra. Even Kotzebue's 6,000-ft airport runway is built on permafrost—with a 6-inch insulating layer between the frozen ground and the airfield surface to ensure that landings are smooth, not slippery.

Kotzebue serves as a gateway for three exceptional national **wilderness areas:** Cape Krusenstern National Monument, Kobuk Valley National Park, and Noatak National Preserve. North and east of Kotzebue is the **Brooks Range,** one of Alaska's great mountain ranges. Stretching across the state, much of the range is protected by Gates of the Arctic National Park and Preserve and the Arctic National Wildlife Refuge.

Dining and Lodging

$–$$$$ ✕ **Kotzebue Pizza House.** Although this cozy pizza parlor serves pizza and Chinese food, locals especially tout the burgers here, which are among the best in the state. ⊠ *2nd Ave. and Bison St., downtown,* ☎ *907/442–3432. No credit cards.*

$$$$ ⊡ **Nullagvik Hotel.** This downtown hotel overlooking Kotzebue Sound is built on pilings driven into the ground because the heat of the building would melt the underlying permafrost and cause the hotel to sink. The modern rooms, decorated with images of Eskimo life, have sitting areas and cable TV. Public sitting areas on each floor offer picture-window views of the bay. Insist on a ground-floor room; there's no elevator to the second or third floor, and rooms there can get unbearably

hot. The hotel's coffee shop–restaurant ($$–$$$$) serves standard American fare in addition to a few local specialties, such as reindeer and fresh Arctic fish. Meals are sometimes served buffet style when big tour groups are in the hotel. ⊠ *308 Shore Ave., Box 336, 99752,* ☎ *907/442–3331,* FAX *907/442–3340. 74 rooms. Restaurant, travel services. AE, D, DC, MC, V.*

Cape Krusenstern National Monument

⓮   *10 mi north of Kotzebue.*

Just north of Kotzebue, the 560,000-acre Cape Krusenstern National Monument has important cultural and archaeological value. This is a coastal parkland, with an extraordinary series of beach ridges built up by storms over a period of at least 5,000 years. Almost every ridge—more than 100 in all—contains artifacts of different human occupants, representing every known Arctic Eskimo culture in North America. The present Eskimo occupants, whose culture dates back some 1,400 years, use the fish, seals, caribou, and birds of this region for food and raw materials much as their ancestors did. They are also closely involved in the archaeological digs in the park that are unearthing part of their own history.

Cape Krusenstern is a starkly beautiful Arctic land shaped by ice, wind, and sea. Its low, rolling gray-white hills scalloped with light-green tundra attract hikers and backpackers, and kayakers sometimes paddle its coastline. The monument is valuable also for human and historical reasons, and it should be experienced as something like a marvelous living museum. It's possible to camp in the park, but be mindful, as are the Native people when they rig their big white canvas tents for summer fishing, that any tent pitched along the shore is subject to fierce winds.

Check with the National Park Service in Kotzebue about hiring a local guide to interpret this unusual scene. The monument, which has no visitor facilities, is accessible by air taxi and by boat from Kotzebue. ⊠ *National Park Service, Box 1029, Kotzebue 99752,* ☎ *907/442–3890,* WEB *www.nps.gov/cakr.*

Kobuk Valley National Park

⓯   *65 mi east of Kotzebue.*

Kobuk Valley National Park lies entirely north of the Arctic Circle, along the southern edge of the Brooks Range. Its 1.14 million acres contain remarkable inland deserts and the **Great Kobuk Sand Dunes,** and are home to interesting relict (or remnants of otherwise extinct) flora. In addition to the **Kobuk River,** this park contains two smaller rivers that provide delightful salmon running. These brilliantly clear streams are accessible by wheeled plane, and each offers a good week's worth of pleasure (if the weather cooperates).

Another place of special interest is the **Onion Portage.** Human occupation here dates back 12,500 years; herds of caribou that once fed the Woodland Eskimo centuries ago are still hunted at Onion Portage by present-day Eskimo residents of the region.

Kobuk Valley National Park is, like most other Alaska parks, undeveloped wilderness with no visitor facilities. It's a good place for backpacking and river trips. In nearby Kotzebue, the National Park Service has a visitor center where staff can provide tips for travel into the park.

The villages of Kobuk and Kiana both provide immediate takeoff points and have air service. ✉ *National Park Service, Box 1029, Kotzebue 99752,* ☎ *907/442–3890,* WEB *www.nps.gov/kova.*

Noatak National Preserve

🔟 *20 mi northeast of Kotzebue.*

Adjacent to Gates of the Arctic National Park and Preserve, the 6.5-million-acre Noatak National Preserve takes in much of the basin of the **Noatak River.** This is the largest mountain-ringed river basin in the United States that is still relatively wild (part of it is designated a Wild and Scenic River). Along its 425-mi course, this river carves out the "Grand Canyon of the Noatak," which serves as a migration route between Arctic and sub-Arctic ecosystems. Its importance to wildlife and plants has resulted in this parkland's designation as an International Biosphere Reserve.

The Noatak River also serves as a natural highway for humans and offers particular pleasures to river runners, with inviting tundra to camp on and the Poktovik Mountains and the Igichuk Hills nearby for good hiking. Birding can be exceptional: horned grebes, gyrfalcons, golden eagles, parasitic jaegers, owls, terns, and loons are among the species you may see. Visitors may also observe grizzly bears, Dall sheep, wolves, caribou, or lynx. As with other parks and preserves in this northwest corner of Alaska, no facilities are available and visitors are expected to be self-sufficient. ✉ *National Park Service, Box 1029, Kotzebue 99752,* ☎ *907/442–3890,* WEB *www.nps.gov/noat.*

Gates of the Arctic National Park and Preserve

🔟 *180 mi east of Kotzebue.*

The Gates of the Arctic National Park and Preserve is entirely north of the Arctic Circle, in the center of the Brooks Range; at 8.2 million acres, it's the size of four Yellowstones. This is parkland on a scale suitable to the country. It includes the **Endicott Mountains** to the east and the **Schwatka Mountains** to the southwest, with the **Arrigetch Peaks** in between. *Arrigetch* is an Eskimo word meaning "fingers of a hand outstretched," which aptly describes the immensely steep and smooth granite peaks that have attracted many mountaineers and backcountry explorers, past and present. To the north lies a sampling of the Arctic foothills, with their colorful tilted sediments and pale green tundra. Lovely lakes are cupped in the mountains and in the tundra.

The ultimate wilderness, this landscape captured the heart of Arctic explorer and conservationist Robert Marshall in the 1930s. Accompanied by local residents, Marshall explored much of the region now included within Gates and named many of its features, including Frigid Crag and Boreal Mountain, two peaks on either side of the North Fork Koyukuk River. These were the original "gates" for which the park is named.

Wildlife known to inhabit the park include barren-ground caribou, grizzlies, wolves, moose, Dall sheep, wolverines, and a wide variety of smaller mammals and birds. The village of Bettles is a dropping-off point for the Gates of the Arctic, which has no developed trails, campgrounds, or other visitor facilities (though there is a wilderness lodge on private land within the park). You can fly in commercially and charter an air taxi into the park. ✉ *National Park Service, 201 1st Ave., Fairbanks 99701,* ☎ *907/456–0281,* WEB *www.nps.gov/gaar.*

Lodging

$$$$ 🏠 **Peace of Selby Wilderness.** Because of its location along Selby/Nar-
vak Lake within Gates of the Arctic National Park, Peace of Selby allows you to explore one of the world's last great wilderness areas, the
Brooks Range. Crafted from white spruce, the main lodge includes a
dining area, kitchen, small library, bathroom, and loft for lounging and
sleeping. Beds have linens, comforters, and homemade quilts, and
meals are cooked with fresh vegetables, fruits, and meats that arrive
on the charter plane with guests. If you want to rough it, you can stay
in sleeping bags and cook your own meals in a rustic log cabin or a
large canvas "wall" tent. Cabins and wall tents are also available at
two remote lake sites and along the Kobuk River. Peace of Selby specializes in wilderness expeditions that may include hiking, wildlife
photography, river floating, and fishing. Late winter and early spring
activities include guided dog-mushing expeditions and Nordic skiing.
⊠ *Box 86, Manley Hot Springs 99756,* ☎ FAX *907/672–3206,* WEB
*www.alaskawilderness.net. 1 room in lodge, 4 cabins, wall tents. Din-
ing room, hiking, boating, fishing, cross-country skiing, library. No credit
cards. Closed mid-Sept.–mid-June, except for specially arranged expeditions in Mar. and Apr.*

Outdoor Activities and Sports

Contact **Sourdough Outfitters** (⊠ Box 66, Bettles 99726, ☎ 907/692–
5252, FAX 907/692–5557, WEB www.sourdoughoutfitters.com) for summer backpacking and river trips (from family float trips to wild-rapid
running and fishing expeditions) and winter dogsled trips in the Brooks
Range.

Barrow

⓲ *330 mi northeast of Kotzebue.*

The northernmost community in the United States, Barrow sits just 1,300
mi from the North Pole on the Beaufort Sea. For 82 days, from May
to August, the sun stays above the horizon. It is the best place in
Alaska to catch the legendary midnight sun. An umiak (Eskimo skin
boat); a fish-drying rack; and drifting Arctic pack ice, often close to
shore, complete the scene. Barrow's 4,000 residents, many of them Natives (only Kotzebue has a larger Eskimo population), live in a modern village but maintain traditional Eskimo activities such as whale
hunting. The Barrow airport is the site of the **Will Rogers and Wiley
Post Monument,** commemorating the 1935 crash of the American humorist and the pilot 15 mi south of town.

Visitors arriving in Barrow usually come on a one- or two-day tour
from Alaska Airlines. Packages include a bus tour of the town's dusty
roads and major sights. A highlight is **Mound 44,** where the frozen body
of a 500-year-old Eskimo was discovered. Scientists have been studying her remains to learn more about pre-Outside-contact Eskimo life
and culture. An **early warning radar installation** once watched for incoming Soviet missiles. The air force has since mothballed its big
dishes, but Barrow duty must have given special meaning to the term
"cold war." Without a doubt, the best part about visiting the top of
the world is walking along the sandy beach and seeing the pack ice
stretching across the horizon, even in the middle of summer.

Dining and Lodging

$$–$$$$ ✗ **Ken's Restaurant.** Basic burgers, steaks, and Chinese food are the
staples at this simply furnished family restaurant with good daily spe-

THE PIPELINE HIGHWAY

STRETCHING 800 MI across the 49th state, the trans-Alaska pipeline is both an engineering marvel and a reminder of Alaska's economic dependence on oil and gas production. It begins at Prudhoe Bay, along the Arctic Ocean, and snakes its way south to the port town of Valdez, on the shores of Prince William Sound. Along the way, the pipeline carries crude oil across three mountain ranges, 34 major rivers—including the mighty Yukon—and hundreds of smaller creeks. Though much of it is buried, more than half of the pipeline runs above ground where it is held aloft by 78,000 vertical supports. Visitors can see sections of it along some of Alaska's major roadways, most notably the Dalton Highway.

Alaska's northernmost highway, the Dalton parallels the pipeline for more than 400 mi while connecting Interior Alaska to North Slope oil fields. It was built so that trucks could haul supplies to Prudhoe Bay and pipeline construction camps in Alaska's northern reaches. Hence its other name: the Haul Road.

Thousands of 18-wheeler rigs continue to drive the Dalton Highway each year, but since 1995 they've had to share the 414-mi route with recreational travelers. This doesn't mean the Dalton has become an easy drive. It's narrow as highways go, often winding, has several steep grades, and sections may be heavily potholed or washboarded. Besides being tough on vehicles, the road has few visitor facilities. Public access ends at Deadhorse, the support town for Prudhoe Bay's industrial operations; the only way to visit the oil fields or reach the ocean is by group tour (scheduled daily in summer).

The origins of the Haul Road and trans-Alaska pipeline can be traced to 1968, when oil companies announced the discovery of a major field at Prudhoe Bay. A lawsuit by environmental groups temporarily halted work on the proposed pipeline across Alaska, but Congressional legislation authorizing its construction was signed into law in November 1973. Things moved quickly after that. Work on the Haul Road began the following April and was finished in five months. Forty-eight inches wide and up to 60 ft long, the first pipes were installed in March 1975; 27 months later, oil began moving down the pipeline and reached Valdez on July 28, 1977. Four days later, the *ARCO Juneau* headed south with the first tanker load of Prudhoe Bay crude. Total cost of the trans-Alaska pipeline project: $8 billion.

By the start of 2001, the pipeline had transported more than 13 billion barrels (or 545 billion gallons) of oil across Alaska. At its peak in 1988, 2.14 million barrels of oil flowed through the pipeline in a day's time. By early 2001, the daily flow had dropped to 1 million barrels.

The trans-Alaska pipeline was designed and built and continues to be operated by the Alyeska Pipeline Service Company, a consortium of seven oil companies. Concerns about spills and corrosion led in 1990 to the formation of a Joint Pipeline Office, composed of nine state and federal regulatory agencies. There have been a number of temporary shutdowns and spills over the pipeline's 30-plus years, but as of early 2001, the only catastrophic event connected to the trans-Alaska pipeline project was the 1989 *Exxon Valdez* oil spill, in which 270,000 barrels of oil oozed from the damaged tanker into Prince William Sound.

cials and the best prices in town. ⊠ *Above the airport terminal building,* ☎ *907/852–8888. No credit cards.*

$–$$$$ ✕ **Pepe's North of the Border.** The warmth of Pepe's will make you
★ forget that you're in the middle of the Arctic tundra. Murals depicting Mexican village scenes highlight the Mission-style decor, and an extensive selection of Mexican dishes makes this restaurant a favorite of locals and visitors alike. Dinner at Pepe's is surprisingly refined for being on the very fringe of civilization. ⊠ *Next to the Top of the World Hotel,* ☎ *907/852–8200. DC, MC, V.*

$$$$ 🏨 **Top of the World Hotel.** Frontier touches at this popular hotel on the
★ shore of the Arctic Ocean include one complete stuffed polar bear and the mounted head of another. All rooms have cable TV, a telephone, and a private bath. Guests can mingle in the lobby, at the coffee bar, or in front of the community television. Ask for a room with an ocean view. ⊠ *1200 Agviq St., Box 189, 99723,* ☎ *907/852–3900 or 800/882–8478; 800/478–8520 in Alaska;* 𝖥𝖠𝖷 *907/852–6752,* 🌐 *www.asrc.com/ topworld.htm. 50 rooms. Coffee shop. AE, D, DC, MC, V.*

$$$ 🏨 **Barrow Airport Inn.** As the name says, this modern and well-appointed property is convenient to the airport. Standard rooms come with cable TV and telephones; nine rooms have full kitchenettes and the others have a microwave and refrigerator. A complimentary Continental breakfast is served daily. ⊠ *1815 Momegana St., Box 933, 99723,* ☎ *907/ 852–2525,* 𝖥𝖠𝖷 *907/852–2528. 16 rooms. Travel services. D, MC, V.*

Shopping

The AC Value Center or, as it's known locally, **Stuaqpak** (the "Big Store"; ⊠ 4725 Ahkovak St., ☎ 907/852–6711, 🌐 www.alaskacommercial. com) is the largest store in town. Though it mainly sells groceries, the store also stocks Eskimo crafts made by locals, including furs, parkas, mukluks, and ceremonial masks. Be sure to visit the **Arctic Development Council Building** (⊠ 1250A Agvik St., ☎ 907/852–4146), which sells Eskimo arts and crafts from villages along the North Slope, including baleen baskets and artwork, sealskin bags, and ivory carvings. Money from sales goes directly to the artisans. Credit cards (MC, V) are accepted for certain items only.

Prudhoe Bay

⑲ *250 mi southeast of Barrow.*

Most towns have museums that chronicle local history and achievements. Deadhorse is the town anchoring life along Prudhoe Bay, but it could also serve as a museum dedicated to humankind's hunt for energy and our ability to adapt to harsh conditions.

The costly, much-publicized Arctic oil and gas project is complex and varied. One-day tours explore the tundra terrain from oil pipes to sandpipers. Along with spotting caribou, wildflowers, and an unusual stand of willow trees at the edge of the Arctic Ocean, the field tour surveys oil wells, stations, and oil-company residential complexes—small cities themselves. Your guide will discuss the multimillion-dollar research programs aimed at preserving the region's ecology and point out special tundra vehicles known as Rollagons, whose great weight is distributed to diminish their impact on delicate terrain.

In the past, individual travelers rarely turned up in Deadhorse and Prudhoe Bay. But now that the Dalton Highway has been opened as far north as Deadhorse, adventurous independent travelers are finding their way north. Still, most people traveling to Deadhorse either work here or come on a tour with one of Alaska's airlines or motor-coach operators. And even those who travel here on their own must join a guided tour (arranged through the Arctic Caribou Inn) if they wish to cross the oil fields to get to the Arctic Ocean. Visitors traveling on their own should also be aware that there are no restaurants here, though meals can sometimes be arranged through the hotel.

Arctic National Wildlife Refuge

20 *70 mi southeast of Prudhoe Bay.*

The 18-million-acre Arctic National Wildlife Refuge, lying wholly above the Arctic Circle, is administered by the U.S. Fish and Wildlife Service and contains the only protected Arctic coastal lands in the United States (and some of the very few protected in the world), as well as millions of acres of mountains and alpine tundra, in the easternmost portion of the Brooks Range.

This is the home of one of the greatest remaining groups of caribou in the world, the **Porcupine Caribou Herd.** The herd, numbering around 150,000, is unmindful of international boundaries and migrates back and forth across Arctic lands into Canada, flowing like a wide river across the expansive coastal plain, through U-shape valleys and alpine meadows, and over high mountain passes. The refuge's coastal areas also serve as critical denning grounds for polar bears, which spend most of their year on the Arctic Ocean's pack ice. Other residents here are grizzly bears, Dall sheep, wolves, musk ox, and dozens of varieties of birds, from snowy owls to geese and tiny songbirds. The refuge's northern areas host legions of breeding waterfowl and shorebirds each summer.

As in many of Alaska's more remote parks and refuges, there are no roads here, no developed trails, campgrounds, or other visitor facilities. This is a place to experience true wilderness—and to walk with care, for the plants are fragile and the ground can be soft and wet in summer. You can expect snow to sift over the land in almost any season and should anticipate subfreezing temperatures even in summer, particularly in the mountains. Many of the refuge's clear-flowing rivers are runnable, and tundra lakes are suitable for base camps (a Kaktovik or Fort Yukon air taxi can drop you off and pick you up). The hiking, too, can be invigorating. It can also be extremely challenging for those not used to crossing wet, tussocky tundra or slippery scree deposits of rocks. But the effort is worth it; upon scrambling up a ridge, you'll look out upon wave after wave of mountains, in a wilderness that seems to stretch forever. For refuge information, contact the Fairbanks office of the Public Lands Information Center.

THE BUSH A TO Z

To research prices, get advice from other travelers, and book travel arrangements, visit www.fodors.com.

AIR TRAVEL

Alaska Airlines is among the major carriers serving Alaska from Seattle, and it flies within Alaska to most major communities (☞ Smart Travel Tips A to Z for airline numbers). Peninsula Airways serves the communities on the Alaskan Peninsula, the Aleutian and Pribilof islands, and parts of the Interior and Northwest.

Many Anchorage and Fairbanks air taxis serve the Bush in addition to Bush-based carriers such as Bering Air, which also offers local flight-seeing tours and, weather and politics permitting, flights to Provideniya, on the Siberian coast across the Bering Strait. Cape Smythe Air Service serves the communities of the North Slope plus Kotzebue. Frontier Flying Service serves the Interior and the Bering and Arctic coasts. Wright Air Service flies throughout the Interior and Arctic Alaska.

Besides flights on those carriers, information about certified air-taxi operations is available from the Federal Aviation Administration. Individual parks and Alaska Public Lands Information Centers also can supply lists of reputable air-taxi services. Make your reservations in advance, and plan for the unexpected; weather can delay a scheduled pickup for days.

➤ AIRLINES AND CONTACTS: **Alaska Airlines** (☎ 800/426–0333, WEB www. alaskaair.com). **Alaska Public Lands Information Center** (✉ 250 Cushman St., Suite 1A, Fairbanks 99701, ☎ 907/456–0527, WEB www.nps. gov.aplic). **Bering Air** (✉ Box 1650, Nome 99762, ☎ 907/443–5464; 800/478–5422 in Alaska; 907/443–5620 Russian desk; FAX 907/443–5919, WEB www.beringair.com). **Cape Smythe Air Service** (✉ 1707 Ahkovak St., Box 549, Barrow 99723, ☎ 907/852–8333, FAX 907/852–2509, WEB www.capesmythe.com). **Federal Aviation Administration** (✉ Flight Standards District Office, 4510 W. International Airport Rd., Anchorage 99502-1088, ☎ 907/271–2000, FAX 907/271–4777, WEB www.faa.gov). **Frontier Flying Service** (✉ 5245 Airport Industrial Way, Fairbanks 99709, ☎ 907/474–0014; 800/478–6779 in Alaska, FAX 907/474–0774, WEB www.frontierflying.com). **Peninsula Airways** (✉ 6100 Boeing Ave., Anchorage 99502, ☎ 907/243–2323 or 800/448–4226, FAX 907/243–6848, WEB www.penair.com). **Wright Air Service** (✉ 3842 University Ave., Box 60142, Fairbanks 99706, ☎ 907/474–0502; 800/478–0502 in Alaska; FAX 907/474–0375).

BOAT AND FERRY TRAVEL
The Alaska state ferry makes monthly trips April through October to Kodiak, Dutch Harbor/Unalaska, and several other Bush communities in southwestern Alaska.

➤ BOAT AND FERRY INFORMATION: **Alaska State Ferry** (Alaska Marine Highway System; ✉ 1591 Glacier Ave., Juneau 99801, ☎ 800/382–9229 or 800/642–0066, FAX 907/465–2476, WEB www.state.ak.us/ferry).

CAR TRAVEL
The James W. Dalton Highway—formerly the construction road for the trans-Alaska pipeline—is Alaska's only highway to the High Arctic. Popularly known as the Haul Road, this 414-mi, all-gravel road begins about 73 mi north of Fairbanks, connecting with the Steese and Elliott highways to points south. Private vehicles may travel the entire length of the highway to Deadhorse. However, access to oil company facilities and the shore of the Arctic Ocean is limited to commercial operators.

Vehicle services are limited along the highway. There are plans to add new facilities, but currently fuel, repairs, food, and lodging are available at only three places: the Yukon River crossing (Mile 56), Coldfoot (Mile 175), and Deadhorse (Mile 414). Motorists are cautioned not to expect assistance from truckers shuttling between Prudhoe Bay and Fairbanks. For Dalton Highway information, contact the Fairbanks office of the Alaska Public Lands Information Center.

Neither the Arctic and near-Arctic communities of Nome, Kotzebue, and Barrow nor Bethel, the Aleutian chain, or the Pribilof Islands have highway connections to the rest of Alaska.

➤ CONTACTS: **Alaska Public Lands Information Center** (✉ 250 Cushman St., Suite 1A, Fairbanks 99701, ☎ 907/456–0527, WEB www.nps.gov.aplic).

EMERGENCIES
DOCTORS AND DENTISTS
A statewide air-ambulance service operates through Alaska Regional Lifeflight in Anchorage.

➤ CONTACTS: **Alaska Regional Lifeflight** (☎ 800/478–9111). **Maniilaq Health Center** (✉ Kotzebue, ☎ 907/442–3321, WEB www.maniilaq.org).

EMERGENCY SERVICES
➤ CONTACTS: **Police** (☎ 907/852–6111 in Barrow; 907/442–3351 in Kotzebue; 907/443–5262 in Nome, WEB www.eskimo.com/~nsbpd.com in Barrow, www.kotzebuepolice.com in Kotzebue). **State Troopers** (☎ 907/852–3783 in Barrow; 907/442–3222 or 800/789–3222 in Kotzebue; 907/443–5525 in Nome, WEB www.state.ak.us).

HOSPITALS
➤ CONTACTS: **Norton Sound Regional Hospital** (✉ Nome, ☎ 907/443–3311). **Samuel Simmonds Memorial Hospital** (✉ Barrow, ☎ 907/852–4611).

OUTDOORS AND SPORTS
For information about camping, hiking, and fishing, contact the following:

➤ CONTACTS: **Alaska Department of Fish and Game** (✉ Box 25526, Juneau 99802-5526, ☎ 907/465–4100 for general information about fish and wildlife; 907/465–4180 for sportfishing seasons and regulations; 907/465–2376 for licenses, WEB www.state.ak.us). **Alaska State Parks Information** (✉ 550 W. 7th Ave., Suite 1260, Anchorage 99501, ☎ 907/269–8400, FAX 907/269–8401, WEB www.dnr.state.ak.us). **Anchorage Alaska Public Lands Information Center** (✉ 605 W. 4th Ave., Suite 105, Anchorage 99501, ☎ 907/271–2737, FAX 907/271–2744, WEB www.nps.gov/aplic). **Fairbanks Alaska Public Lands Information Center** (✉ 250 Cushman St., Suite 1A, Fairbanks 99701, ☎ 907/456–0527, FAX 907/456–0514, WEB www.nps.gov/aplic). **National Park Service Alaska Regional Office** (✉ 2525 Gambell St., Anchorage 99503, ☎ 907/257–2696, WEB www.nps.gov/parks.html). **U.S. Fish and Wildlife Service** (✉ 1011 E. Tudor Rd., Anchorage 99503, ☎ 907/786–3309, FAX 907/786–3495, WEB www.r7.fws.gov).

TOURS
Package tours are the most common way of traveling to Bush communities, where making your flight connections and having a room to sleep in at the end of the line are no small feats. Guided trips, or stays in wilderness lodges, can be arranged in many of the Bush's remote parklands and wildlife refuges. Independent travel, particularly for campers and hikers, can be highly rewarding, but it takes careful planning. During peak season—late May through Labor Day—planes, state ferries, hotels, and sportfishing lodges are likely to be crowded with travelers on organized tours. Booking well ahead is recommended; many Alaska travelers make their reservations a year in advance.

The type of tour you choose will determine how you get there. On air tours—which include travel to most Bush communities—you will fly to and from your destination. On motor-coach tours to Deadhorse and

Prudhoe Bay, you will travel at least one way by coach. Each type of tour has its own advantages: air travel is faster and gives you an aerial perspective of the Arctic; motor-coach tours travel at a more leisurely pace and give you a ground-level view of sweeping tundra vistas. However, most Bush locales can be reached only by plane.

Most tours to Arctic towns and villages are short—one, two, or three days. These often can be combined with visits to other regions of the state. Packages may include stays at wilderness lodges.

The Bush is home to many Native Alaskan groups, many of which are active in tourism. Often, local Native corporations act as your hosts—running the tours, hotels, and attractions. Nome Tour and Marketing in Nome (book through Alaska Airlines Vacations), provides ground transportation, accommodations, and other services for visitors. The NANA Development Corporation provides ground transportation and accommodations in Kotzebue as well as at Prudhoe Bay in conjunction with motor-coach tours. If you visit Barrow and stay at the Top of the World Hotel, Tundra Tours (book through Alaska Airlines Vacations), another Native operation, will be your host. On Gambell Island (book through Alaska Village Tours), local residents also run all the ground operations.

➤ CONTACTS: **Alaska Airlines Vacations** (✉ Box 68900, SEARV, Seattle, WA 98168, ☎ 800/468–2248, WEB alaskaair.com). **NANA Development Corporation** (☎ 800/478–3301, WEB www.nana.com), or book through Princess Tours or Gray Line of Alaska.

BUS

In the summer tourist season, tour operators run trips up the Dalton Highway out of Fairbanks and Anchorage. Travelers go one way by air, the other by motor coach. The route crosses the rugged Brooks Range, the Arctic Circle, and the Yukon River. It also brushes the edges of the Gates of the Arctic National Park and the Arctic National Wildlife Refuge. Gray Line of Alaska operates package tours that travel the Dalton Highway to Deadhorse. Princess Tours runs tours along the Dalton Highway.

The Northern Alaska Tour Company conducts ecotours to the Arctic Circle and Prudhoe Bay that emphasize natural and cultural history, wildlife, and geology. Groups are limited to 25 people on Arctic day tours and to 10 on Prudhoe Bay overnight trips. Some tours are completely ground-based; others include a mix of ground and air travel.

➤ CONTACTS: **Gray Line of Alaska** (✉ 1980 S. Cushman, Fairbanks 99701, ☎ 907/451–6835; 800/887–7741 in Alaska). **Northern Alaska Tour Company** (✉ Box 82991, Fairbanks 99708, ☎ 907/474–8600, FAX 907/474–4767, WEB www.northernalaska.com). **Princess Tours** (✉ 2815 2nd Ave., Suite 400, Seattle, WA 98121, ☎ 206/336–6000 in Seattle; 907/479–9660 in Fairbanks; 800/835–8907 for reservations, WEB www.princess.com).

PLANE

Alaska Airlines Vacations packages air tours to Barrow, Nome, and Kotzebue. Local arrangements are taken care of by Native ground operators. These trips are especially good for travelers who would otherwise move about independently. The Alaska Travel Industry Association can give tips on air travel and flightseeing opportunities throughout the Bush.

➤ CONTACTS: **Alaska Airlines Vacations** (✉ Box 68900, SEARV, Seattle, WA 98168, ☎ 800/468–2248, WEB alaskaair.com). The **Alaska Travel Industry Association** (✉ 2600 Cordova St., Suite 201, An-

chorage 99501, ☎ 907/929–2842 or 800/667–8489, FAX 907/561–
5727, WEB wwwtravelalaska.com).

VISITOR INFORMATION

➤ CONTACTS: **Alaska Travel Industry Association** (✉ 2600 Cordova
St., Suite 201, Anchorage 99501, ☎ 907/929–2842 or 800/667–8489
for a vacation planner, FAX 907/561–5727, WEB wwwtravelalaska.com).
Bethel Chamber of Commerce (✉ Box 329, Bethel 99559, ☎ 907/543–
2911, FAX 907/543–2255, WEB home.gci/~chamber1/bethel.htm). **Nome
Convention and Visitors Bureau** (✉ Box 240, Nome 99762, ☎ 907/
443–5535 or 800/478–1901 in Alaska, FAX 907/443–5832, WEB www.
nomealaska.org). **Southwest Alaska Municipal Conference** (✉ 3300
Arctic Blvd., Suite 203, Anchorage 99503, ☎ 907/562–7380, FAX 907/
562–0438, WEB www.southwestalAska.com). **Unalaska-Dutch Harbor
Convention and Visitors Bureau** (✉ Box 545, Unalaska 99685, ☎ 907/
581–2612 or 877/581–2612, FAX 907/581–2613, WEB www.arcticnet).

9 PORTRAITS OF ALASKA

Native Alaskans

Alaska: A Geological Story

Books and Videos

NATIVE ALASKANS

The history of Alaska's Native peoples—Eskimos, Indians, and Aleuts—is not unlike that of aboriginal people throughout Central and North America. After they had held domain over their land for thousands of years, their elaborate societies were besieged by a rapid onslaught of white settlers. Unable to stem the tide, they were forced into retreat.

The first European to visit Alaska—in 1728—was Vitus Bering, a Dane serving in the Russian navy. Bering died on his journey home, but survivors returned to Russia with a rich booty of sea-otter furs, sparking a stampede that would crush the traditional lifestyles of Alaska's Native peoples. The way was open for eager Russian fur traders who plundered Aleut territory along the Aleutian Islands.

Records indicate that the Native population of the Aleutian chain dropped from perhaps 20,000 to about 2,500 in the first 50 years of Russian rule. Diseases took a heavy toll, but the more ruthless among the Russian frontiersmen were also responsible—killing Aleut leaders to discourage uprisings. Stories of brutality are common. One trader, Feodor Solovief, reportedly tied together 12 Aleuts and fired a musket ball through them to see how far it would penetrate. It stopped in the body of the ninth man.

In 1867, when the United States purchased Alaska, the Natives were classified in the Treaty of Cession as "uncivilized tribes." To early tourists, they were little more than "those charming folk you take pictures of in their quaint villages."

Early missionaries and government teachers in Southeast Alaska ordered Indian totem poles destroyed, mistakenly believing them to be pagan symbols. Important works of art were lost. The totem poles of the Tlingit and Haida Indians were—and still are—simply the decorative record of outstanding events in the life of a family or clan.

The plight of the Natives improved little as Alaska grew more prosperous by exploiting its great natural resources. A painful split between traditional and modern living developed—public health experts call it "a syndrome of grief." Under increasing pressure from this clash of cultures, alcoholism grew to epidemic levels, and the suicide rate of Alaskan Natives climbed to twice that of Native Americans living on reservations in the continental United States. Still, by the 1960s, Native groups were making major strides toward claiming overdue political clout. In 1966, Native leaders from across the state gathered and organized the present Alaska Foundation of Natives. It was a fragile coalition of differing cultures, but the meeting was a significant move. With 16% of the state's population, a unified Native voice was suddenly a political force to be reckoned with.

At the same time, Eskimo leaders founded the *Tundra Times* and selected Howard Rock, a quiet, articulate man from Point Hope village, as its editor. Rock, whose background was in art rather than journalism, quickly prodded Natives to press their aboriginal land claims.

"The natives are reticent by nature, and time was passing them by," the Eskimo editor said. "At first, it was kind of discouraging. Nothing happened. And then, one by one, the Native leaders started speaking up."

The *Tundra Times* helped file the first suit for Native land claims. More lawsuits followed, and soon the whole state was tied up in litigation. Oil companies, hungry to build a pipeline from the newly discovered giant oil field at Prudhoe Bay to Valdez, on Alaska's southern coast, soon realized they could not get federal construction permits until the Native land claims were settled.

In 1971 the Natives won a spectacular settlement in Congress: 40 million acres of land and almost $1 billion in cash. The settlement has not been a cure-all for the many problems of Alaska's Natives. Poverty is still widespread, as little of the land-claims money (allocated mostly to 13 regional, for-profit Native corporations by Congress) has trickled down to the village level. But the settlement has given many a sense of dignity and purpose. Several villages in the Arctic have voted themselves "dry" (prohibiting alcohol) to combat drinking problems. A new cadre of Native leaders is taking charge to help its people.

Today, the fundamental issue is whether the Natives will be allowed by the larger Alaskan society to pursue their own future, says Byron Mallott, former chief operating officer of Sealaska Corp., the regional Native corporation for Southeast Alaska.

"In one way, Alaska is truly the last frontier," Mallott says. "Will the final chapter of the total and unremitting decimation of our nation's Native American people be written in Alaska—or will, with the benefit of the lesson of history, Alaska be the place where Native peoples finally are able to become a part of the overall society with their pride, strength, and ethnicity intact?" There are, he adds, few guideposts to suggest the answer.

Most of Alaska's Natives still reside in widely scattered communities spread across the half-million square mi of Alaska. Unlike the Native Americans of the Lower 48 states, the Alaskan Natives have never been restricted to reservations. Many villages remain isolated, the preference of traditional villagers; others have plunged into modern life with mixed results. Recently, Alaska's Native peoples have become more enterprising in the tourist business. No longer content to let out-of-state tour operators have all the business, they are now starting to take charge of tours in their communities.

The various Native peoples tend to group in well-defined regions. Here is a brief look at the different Native cultures and their locations.

Eskimos. Most of Alaska's more than 40,000 Eskimos are found in scattered settlements along the Bering Sea and Arctic Ocean coasts, the deltas of the lower Yukon and Kuskokwim rivers in western Alaska, and on remote islands in the Bering Sea such as St. Lawrence, Nunivak, and Little Diomede. The principal Arctic and sub-Arctic Eskimo communities include Barrow, Kotzebue, Nome, Gambell, Savoonga, Point Hope, Wainwright, and Shishmaref.

The Eskimos are divided into two linguistic groups: the Inupiat of the Far North and the Yup'ik, who reside mostly along the coastal regions of the west. The Yup'ik share the same dialect as the Eskimos of Siberia. Both groups are famed for their hunting and fishing skills. They are also noted craftspeople, carving animals and creating jewelry from Native materials.

Indians. Alaska has four major Indian cultures: Tlingit, Haida, Athabascan, and Tsimshian.

Once among North America's most powerful tribes, the **Tlingits** (pronounced *klink*-its) are found mostly throughout coastal Southeast Alaska. They number about 13,000 and are found in cities such as Juneau, Ketchikan, and Sitka, and in villages from Hoonah, near Juneau, to Klukwan, near Haines.

The Tlingits developed a highly sophisticated culture and fought hard against Russian incursions. Social status among early Tlingits depended on elaborate feasts called potlatches. Heads of families and clans vied in giving away vast quantities of valuable goods, their generosity so extravagant at times that the hosts fell into a form of ancient bankruptcy. There are still potlatches for important occasions, such as funerals, but they are greatly scaled down from earlier times.

Haidas are also found mainly in Southeast Alaska, as well as in British Columbia. They number only about 1,000 in Alaska. Their principal community is Hydaburg on Prince of Wales Island, near Ketchikan. The Queen Charlotte Islands of British Columbia are another Haida center. Historically, the Haidas were far-ranging voyagers and traders. Some historians credit the artistic Haidas with originating totem carving among Alaska's Natives.

Most of Alaska's 7,000 or so **Athabascan** Indians are found in the villages of Alaska's vast Interior, including Ft. Yukon, Stevens Village, Beaver, Chalkyitsik, and Minto, near Fairbanks. Other Athabascans are scattered from the Kenai Peninsula–Cook Inlet area, near Anchorage, to the Copper River area near Cordova. Linguistically, the Athabascans are related to the Navajos and Apaches of the American Southwest. They were driven out of Canada by Cree tribes more than 700 years ago.

The ancestral home of the **Tsimshian** (pronounced *simp*-shee-ann) Indians was British Columbia, but Tsimshian historians say their forebears roamed through much of southeastern Alaska fishing, hunting, and trading long before the arrival of the white man. The 1,000 or so Tsimshians of Alaska settled in 1887 on Annette Island, near Ketchikan, when a dissident Church of England lay missionary, William Duncan, led them out of British Columbia to escape religious persecution. The town of Metlakatla on Annette Island is their principal community. Their artwork includes a variety of wood carvings, from totem poles to ceremonial masks.

Aleuts. With their villages on the Aleutian Islands, curving between Siberia and Alaska like broken beads, the Aleuts (pronounced al-ee-*oots*) were first in the path of early explorers and ruthless fur traders. There are about 7,000 Aleuts in Alaska today, their principal communities being Dutch Harbor/Unalaska, Akutan, Nikolski, and Atka in the Aleutians and St. Paul and St. George in the Pribilof Islands. Grass basketry, classed by museums as some of the best in the world, is the principal art of the Aleuts. Finely woven baskets from Attu, at the tip of the Aleutian chain—where villages were destroyed in American-Japanese combat during World War II and never rebuilt—are difficult-to-obtain treasures.

— Stanton H. Patty

ALASKA:
A GEOLOGICAL STORY

Most people know about Alaska's oil and gold. But did you know that the state has a desert? That camels once roamed here? That there's a fault line nearly twice as long as the San Andreas Fault? That the largest earthquake ever to hit North America struck Alaska in 1964 and affected the entire planet? That the state has 80 potentially active volcanoes and approximately 100,000 glaciers?

All these physical wonders are geological in origin and are in addition to a North Slope oil supply that accounts for 25% of U.S. production and more than 10% of U.S. consumption, and caches of gold that fueled more than 20 rushes.

Nearly all visitors will have at least one encounter with a glacier (with 29,000 square mi of them, they're hard to miss). Courtesy of the Pleistocene Ice Ages, high latitude location, and abundant moisture from the North Pacific, Alaska is home to approximately 100,000 of these large sheets of ice. The vast majority are in the southern and southeastern parts of the state, as these are the areas with the most moisture. How much moisture? Portions of the Chugach Mountains can gather 600 inches of snow each year, an amount that is comparable, in rain, to the annual precipitation in Seattle. In north-central Alaska, the Brooks Range contains a glacial field of approximately 280 square mi. Although small by Alaskan standards, it is larger than all the glacial fields in the rest of the United States combined, which comprise approximately 230 square mi.

There are alpine or valley glaciers, those that form high in mountain valleys and travel to lower elevations. Alaska is home to several of the great alpine glaciers in the world, found in the high country of the Alaska Range, the Talkeetna, Wrangell, Chugach,

St. Elias, and Coast mountains. Some, such as the Bering Glacier, come tantalizingly close to the water. At more than 100 mi in length, and with an area of more than 2,250 square mi, the Bering is the longest and largest Alaskan glacier, its seclusion guarded by Cape St. Elias and the stormy waters of the Gulf of Alaska. Also impressive are the Hubbard, its imposing terminus dominating the head of isolated Yakutat Bay; and the Columbia, foreboding and threatening, calving icebergs that tack in line like Nelson's fleet across the mouth of Valdez Arm.

The Malaspina Glacier is an unusual piedmont glacier. Formed by the coalescence of several glaciers, this 850-square-mi mass is lobate, or fan-shape, and occupies a benchland on the northwest side of Yakutat Bay. So much of the Alaska Range, Wrangell, Chugach, St. Elias, and Coast mountains are covered by glacial ice that it is often more appropriate to talk about ice fields than individual glaciers.

Then there are the great tidewater glaciers of Prince William Sound and southeastern Alaska. Alpine glaciers that come right to the water's edge, they creak, moan, thunder, and calve off great bergs and little bergeys. The world's longest is the previously mentioned Hubbard Glacier, which, because it stretches over 70 mi from its head in Canada to its terminus in Yakutat Bay, is both an alpine and a tidewater glacier. Sixteen tidewater glaciers can be found in Glacier Bay National Park, 20 in Prince William Sound. Some are advancing, some retreating. Hubbard has not only advanced in recent years, but has surged. In 1986, a surge by Hubbard blocked the Russell Fjord at the upper end of Yakutat Bay, turning it into Russell Lake. Later that year, the portion of the glacier acting as a dam in front of

Russell Lake gave way, violently releasing the backed-up water to an elevation of 83 ft above sea level. Pretty impressive when you stop to think that the Russell Fjord is normally at sea level. Surging glaciers can move downhill hundreds of feet per day. The Hubbard's greatest surge was in September 1899, when it advanced ½ mi into the bay in just five minutes, courtesy of an earthquake.

Glaciologists are interested in knowing more about how glaciers, especially tidewater glaciers, advance and retreat. The Columbia Glacier, both an alpine and a tidewater glacier like the Hubbard, in Prince William Sound is approximately 40 mi long, covers more than 400 square mi, and flows to sea level from 10,000- to 12,000-ft peaks in the Chugach Range. Its width at the terminus can be as much as 4 mi; its ice thickness can reach 900 ft (on average 300 ft above the water and 600 ft below). It is also only 8 mi from the shipping lanes traveled by oil tankers leaving the Alaska pipeline terminal at Valdez. Columbia has been receding since the early 1980s, sending berg after berg into Prince William Sound and into the shipping lanes to Valdez, and now that it's receding, it has the potential to calve even more bergs. Although a shallow sill, or shoal, of underwater glacial deposits keeps icebergs more than 100 ft thick from entering Prince William Sound, some big bergs still make it to the shipping lanes. Columbia's calving took its toll just after midnight on March 29, 1989, when Captain Hazlewood of the *Exxon Valdez* steered too far east while trying to avoid bergs in Valdez Arm and ran aground on Bligh Reef.

You can see many glaciers from the Alaska Marine Highway. The tidewater glaciers of Glacier Bay and the Malaspina and Hubbard glaciers in Yakutat Bay are best seen by boat or ship. Sailing into Valdez Arm, you may see more of the Columbia Glacier than you want—it's often coming to see you in the form of scores of bergs and bergeys—often forcing you east toward Bligh Reef. Once you are safely ashore in Valdez it's time to look at valley glaciers. You can access either the Valdez or Worthington glacier by road. If in the Matanuska Valley, go see the Matanuska Glacier. If on the Kenai Peninsula, try either the Exit or Portage glacier. If you are visiting Juneau, the Mendenhall Glacier is on the outskirts of town.

More than 80 volcanoes in Alaska are potentially active. Novarupta, Pavlof, Augustine, Redoubt, and Spurr are Alaskan volcanoes that are part of the "Ring of Fire," the volcanic rim of the Pacific. From Mt. Wrangell at 144 degrees west longitude in Southeast Alaska to Cape Wrangell at 173 degrees east longitude at the tip of the Aleutian archipelago, southern Alaska exists, to paraphrase historian Will Durant, by volcanic decree . . . subject to change.

Anchorage (and the greater Cook Inlet area) is a great place to watch volcanoes erupt. Augustine, Redoubt, and Spurr volcanoes have put on shows up and down the Cook Inlet in recent years; the Mt. Spurr eruption of August 1992 temporarily stopped air travel in and out of Anchorage. The most violent Alaskan eruption? The 2½-day eruption of Novarupta in 1912 in what is now Katmai National Park. The 2½ cubic mi of ash deposited there has left an Alaskan legacy: the surreal Valley of Ten Thousand Smokes.

The length of a fault system and whether or not the fault is straight over great distances are of interest to geologists. Fault length is related to earthquake magnitude. Generally speaking, the longer a fault, the greater the potential magnitude. Impressed by the 600-mi length of California's San Andreas? The onshore portion of the Denali Fault System is more than 1,000 mi long. Numerous long faults around the world move horizontally. This produces some interesting results if the fault trace is not straight. A fault system such as the Denali has a large component of horizontal movement (called strike-slip motion): crustal blocks on either side move past each other, rather than up or down. If a strike-slip fault bends, one of two situations results: a gap or hole in the crust (usually filled by volcanic outbreaks and/or sediments sloughing into the hole), or a compression of the bend, resulting in vertical uplift (mountains). Which condition occurs is a function of fault motion, whether into or out of the bend. South of Fairbanks, the Denali Fault System changes trend, from northwest–southeast to northeast–southwest. The sense of horizontal motion is into the bend, resulting in vertical uplift. What mountain just happens to be in the vicinity? Mt. McKinley, at 20,320 ft, the tallest mountain in North America. Moreover, its relief (difference in elevation between the base and top of the mountain), at 18,000 ft, is unsurpassed. Mt. Everest is more than 29,000 ft, but "only" 11,000 ft above the Tibetan Plateau that forms its base.

With such big faults, it's no wonder geologists look at Alaska as big earthquake country. Seward, Valdez, Whittier, and Anchorage are just some of the more prominent names associated with the Good Friday Earthquake of 1964. Upgraded in 1977 to magnitude 9.2, the Good Friday quake is the largest on record for North America. Fifteen to thirty seconds is not unusual for ground motion in a big, destructive earthquake; Alaskans shook for three to four minutes during the Good Friday quake. The epicenter was about 6 mi east of College Fjord in Prince William Sound, some 70 mi east of Anchorage. Vertical deformation (uplift or down-dropping of the land) affected an area of 100,000 square mi. By the time the shaking had stopped, the area of Latouche Island had moved 60 ft to the southeast and portions of the Montague Island area were uplifted by as much as 30 ft. The area of Portage was down-dropped by approximately 10 ft. The largest tsunami (often misnamed as a tidal wave) that hit Hilo, Hawaii, checked in at 12½ ft; the largest at Crescent City, California was 13 ft; and in Chenega, Alaska, Native residents were never sure what rose from the sea to smite them . . . just that it was 90 ft tall. The entire planet was affected: the area in which the quake was felt by people

is estimated at 500,000 square mi— South Africa checked in to report that groundwater was sloshing around in wells.

Geologists generally describe tsunamis with respect to displacement on a fault underwater. They use the more general term "seismic sea wave" when other things, such as submarine landslides, cause enormous waves. The 90-ft seismic sea wave that hit Chenega was topped by the 220-ft wave reported from the Valdez Arm area. But a few years earlier in southeastern Alaska, on the evening of July 9, 1958, an earthquake in the Yakutat area dumped an enormous landslide into the head of Lituya Bay. The result was a seiche, or splash wave, which traveled 1,740 ft up the opposite mountainside.

Impressed yet? In the last century the average recurrence interval for Alaskan earthquakes in excess of 8.0 on the Richter Scale is 10 years. The recurrence interval for earthquakes over 7.0 is just over a year. Never mind California—Alaska is the most seismically active state in the Union. Volcanic hazard? Well, Pavlof has averaged an eruption every 6 years over the last 240.

Earthquakes, volcanoes—it's not called the "Ring of Fire" for nothing. The North American and Pacific tectonic plates are battling all the way from California to Japan. The two battle awfully hard in Alaska.

And now about that desert. The North Slope of Alaska is 80,000 square mi of frozen, windswept desert where Inupiat Eskimos live. It's a desert from the climatological perspective that the North Slope receives less than 10 inches of precipitation each year. If you go around the west end of the Brooks Range you can even find sand dunes—Great Kobuk, Little Kobuk, and Hunt River sand dune fields. Temperatures during the short, cool summers are usually between 30°F and 40°F. Temperatures during the winter can average –20°F. In winter, the Arctic Ocean moderates temperatures on the North Slope . . . but there is nothing to moderate the wind.

The first people to "come into the country" came across the Bering Land Bridge from Asia, between 10,000 and 40,000 years ago. The Bering Land Bridge was a product of the Pleistocene epoch—the "Great Ice Age"—that lowered sea level enough for the bridge to form. At the start of the Mesozoic era (beginning about 245 million years before the present), sandstones and conglomerates deposited in a warm, shallow sea marked the beginning of Prudhoe Bay. That abundant organic matter is now abundant oil under the North Slope. Also during the Mesozoic era, oil-bearing shales were deposited in the Cook Inlet, home of Alaska's first oil boom; copper and silver deposits were formed in what is now the Copper River country; Cretaceous swamps in South Central Alaska became the Matanuska coalfield; and gold was emplaced around present-day Fairbanks and near Nome on the Seward Peninsula.

The oldest rocks in Alaska are of Precambrian age (the "Time Before Life") and are in southwestern Alaska. They have been dated at 2 billion years of age, nearly half the age of the earth. Rocks 1 billion years old have been identified in the area of the Brooks Range south to the Yukon River. Interestingly, the 1-billion-year-old rocks are native; the 2-billion-year-old rocks are expatriates. In fact, southern and southeastern Alaska are composed of a mosaic or quilt of microplates, all much smaller than continent size. Some terranes (blocks or fragments of the earth's crust that may vary in age, geologic character, or site of origin) arrived in Alaska from as far south as the equator.

Certain Alaskan rocks tell a tale of warm climates and seas. Evidence? Hike the Holitna River basin in Southwest Alaska and look for fossil remains of the many trilobites (those now-extinct three-lobed marine arthropods that scavenged the bottoms of warm, shallow, Cambrian seas—parents, if you don't know what they look like, ask your children). The central interior of Alaska evidently was never covered by ice but was instead a cool steppe land roamed by mammoths, bison, horses, saber-toothed cats, and camels. Yes, camels.

Alaska's stunning expanse incorporates fire and ice, wind and rain, volcano, glacier, windswept tundra, towering rain forest, and mist-shrouded island. Its geologic story covers a great deal of time and distance and has produced (and is producing) some of the most exquisite land anywhere. In the north, the rocks tell a story of relative stability—geological homebodies born and raised. In the south, the patchwork terranes tell a tale of far-traveled immigrants coming into the country. Geological processes that have produced, and are still producing, both homebodies and expatriates create a land in constant flux. But the majesty of the land . . . that is the unchanging legacy of Alaska.

— Dr. Charles Lane

1

Books and Videos

297

BOOKS AND VIDEOS

Books

Alaska has long been a setting for tales of heroes, great journeys, and people's epic struggle with nature. Novels with rich descriptions of the state's people, wildlife, and landscapes include Jack London's classic *Call of the Wild* (Tor Books), in which a dog named Buck returns to his canine roots in the Arctic wilderness; Ivan Doig's *The Sea Runners* (Penguin), an adventure set in 1853, when Alaska still belonged to Russia; *Athabasca* (out of print), an Alistair MacLean thriller set around the trans-Alaska pipeline; and *Sitka* (Signet), by the popular chronicler of the American frontier, Louis L'Amour. *Alaska* (Random House), by James Michener, is a weighty historical novel about the state from prehistoric to modern times.

Alaskan authors have written a number of mystery novels about their state. Among the best are Sue Henry's *Murder on the Iditarod Trail* (Avon); John Straley's *The Woman Who Married a Bear* (Signet), about the adventures of private eye Cecil Younger; and Dana Stabenow's *A Cold-Blooded Business* (Berkley Publishing Group), whose hero is Aleut private investigator Kate Shugak.

Alaska has produced an even more significant collection of high-quality nonfiction literature. John McPhee's *Coming into the Country* (Noonday Press) is considered by some to be the most insightful book ever written about Alaska. Joe McGinniss, in *Going to Extremes* (Plume), presents a provocative "outsider's" portrait of Alaska's varied communities, people, and landscapes. Winner of the John Burroughs Medal for nature writing, Richard Nelson's *The Island Within* (Vintage Books) explores his intimate relationship with wilderness and wildlife near his Southeast Alaska

home. Velma Wallis's best-selling *Two Old Women: An Alaska Legend of Betrayal, Courage and Survival* recounts a traditional Native Alaskan story.

For lovers of adventure, Art Davidson's *Minus 148: First Winter Ascent of Mt. McKinley* (Cloudcap Press) describes the harrowing survival story of mountaineers caught in a ferocious storm on North America's highest peak. Jon Krakauer's *Into the Wild* wonderfully reconstructs the life and death of a young man who died in the Alaskan wilderness while on a personal vision quest. *Fish Camp: Life on an Alaskan Shore* (Island Press), by Nancy Lord, describes the natural and cultural history of the place where she and her partner have fished for salmon the past two decades. Former Alaska poet laureate John Haines has written several books of poetry and essays. Among his best is the memoir *The Stars, the Snow, the Fire* (Graywolf Press), which recounts 25 years in Alaska's wilderness. Another compelling collection of essays, with natural-history themes, is Sherry Simpson's *The Way Winter Comes* (Sasquatch Books). One anthology of special note is Wayne Mergler's *The Last New Land: Stories of Alaska Past and Present* (Alaska Northwest Books), a wide-ranging collection of poems, short stories, and essays about Alaska; another is Bill Sherwonit's *Denali: A Literary Anthology* (The Mountaineers Books), which presents a century's worth of published stories about Alaska's "High One" and the surrounding wilderness.

Videos

The Last Frontier has also inspired a number of filmmakers. *White Fang* (1991), based on the Jack London novel, is a Walt Disney production about the life of a wild wolf dog and the hardships prospectors faced during the Klondike gold rush. The movie set is now a tourist destination in Haines. Another dog story is told in the animated family film *Balto* (1995), one of the canine heroes in Alaska's 1925 Great Race of Mercy, in which mushers and dog teams carried diphtheria serum to Nome to stop an outbreak of the deadly disease.

A number of action-adventure pictures have also taken place in Alaska. Filmed south of Anchorage, *Runaway Train* (1985) is a thriller starring Jon Voight; the scenery and ending are equally dramatic. *On Deadly Ground* (1994) stars Steven Seagal as an oil-company troubleshooter who rebels after discovering his employers are exploiting the land and Native peoples. A portion of *Star Trek VI* (1991) was filmed on the Knik Glacier, northeast of Anchorage. *Limbo* (1999), set in Southeast Alaska, is a frontier drama that centers on a commercial fisherman who's grown afraid of the sea.

INDEX

NOTES

NOTES

NOTES

NOTES

NOTES

NOTES

NOTES

NOTES